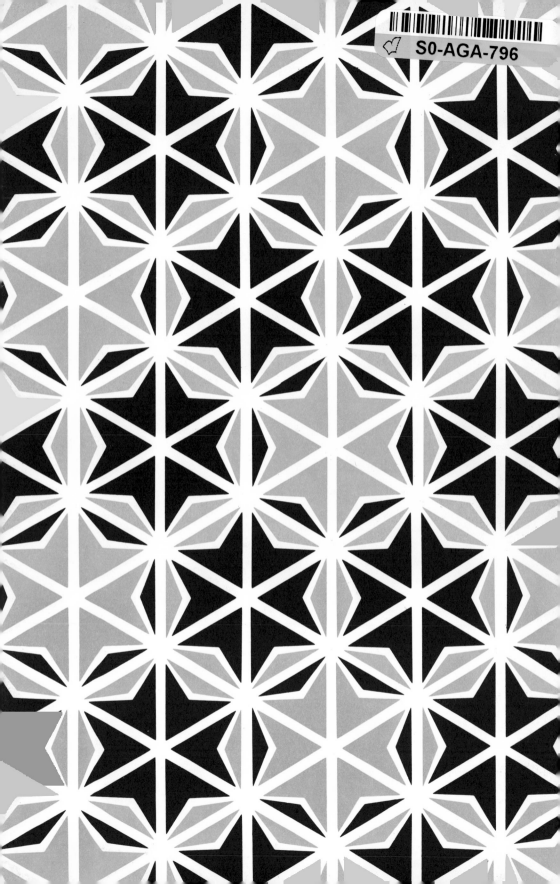

Delta

frontispiece: Portrait of C. E. Woolman by Houston artist Anthony Wills, presented to Woolman by Delta pilots in 1964.

DELTA

THE HISTORY
OF AN AIRLINE

W. David Lewis
and
Wesley Phillips Newton

THE
UNIVERSITY OF GEORGIA PRESS
ATHENS

Set in 10 on 12 point Trump Medieval type
Printed in the United States of America

Library of Congress Cataloging in Publication Data

Lewis, Walter David, 1931–
  Delta.
  Bibliography.
  Includes index.
    1. Delta Air Lines, inc.—History.   I. Newton, Wes-
ley Phillips, joint author.   II. Title
HE9803.D44L48   387.7'06'575   78-11259
          ISBN 0-8203-0465-4

Photo Credits

Appreciation is extended to the Delta Public Relations
Department (photos from Delta, C&S, and Northeast)
and to all interested individuals who contributed illustrations for this book.

To
RICHARD S. MAURER
and
HAROLD F. WILLIAMSON

Contents

Preface

SO FAR AS we are aware, this is the first history of an American commercial airline to be written by professional historians having full access to the business records, correspondence, and personnel of the corporation involved. In 1972 we approached Delta Air Lines about the possibility of writing such a history, under conditions that would insure its scholarly integrity. The company, already considering various ways of observing its fiftieth anniversary as a passenger carrier in 1979, was receptive to our ideas. A series of discussions involving ourselves, Delta executives, academic officials, and professional advisers resulted in a decision to proceed under funding granted to Auburn University by the Delta Air Lines Foundation. A plan was worked out under which large quantities of Delta records were deposited temporarily in the Auburn University Archives, where much of the research took place, and the book was written entirely at Auburn during such time as we could spare from our normal academic duties. The funds granted by the foundation were used strictly for the expenses incurred in carrying out the project, under university supervision.

From the outset we recognized Delta's desire for a book that could be read with interest and pleasure by a nonacademic audience, without impairing its scholarly value. We therefore committed ourselves to a narrative style consistent with this aim. We also decided to undertake a large number of personal interviews with active and retired Delta employees who had figured significantly in the development of the firm, and Delta cooperated fully in facilitating these. All matters of fact and interpretation rested in our hands, with the company reserving the right to ask that we substantiate any statements whose accuracy it might question. In the final chapter, dealing with current developments some of which involved ongoing litigation or unfinished regulatory proceedings, we limited ourselves mainly to printed materials, public documents, and interviews with officers of the corporation. Otherwise, we ranged as widely as possible in our quest for historical evidence. Throughout the project Delta respected our scholarly status, enabling the study to be researched and written in a manner consistent with our professional obligations.

Inevitably, in dealing with a vast array of source materials covering the development of so large and complex an organization over a timespan exceeding half a century, we were unable—even in a book as long as this one turned out to be—to explore in depth every aspect of Delta's operations. Our commitment to a lively narrative style also precluded a heavy use of quantitative data or a theoretical emphasis. Our study focuses upon major milestones in the emergence and growth of the enterprise, the personalities who contributed to its evolving strategy and style, the steady expansion of its route system, the ever-changing composition of its fleet, and the nature of its relationships with federal regulatory agencies. While we have tried to convey a sense of the broad historical backdrop against which the development of Delta unfolded, we have concentrated upon the company itself, tracing its rise from humble beginnings to the status of one of the five largest domestic airlines in the United States.

Above all we have tried to account for those characteristics that have made Delta unique in the airline industry and to underscore the growth of the tightly knit "family feeling" that has consistently been Delta's greatest single asset. Our efforts to understand this phenomenon have led us to attempt to see the company's evolution as it might have looked from inside as well as outside the organization and to try to capture something of the spirit that contributed so importantly to the success of the firm. Because that spirit owes so much to the enduring influence of Delta's founding father, Collett Everman Woolman, and to the paternalistic approach that he followed throughout his extraordinary career, we have stressed his personal role in the development of the enterprise with which his name became synonymous and the human characteristics which he stamped so indelibly upon its corporate image. Our desire to explain how this southern-born and southern-based company retained the characteristics of an extended family for so many years despite its constantly increasing size also accounts in part for our occasional use of anecdotal or semi-anecdotal materials as a means of attempting to penetrate the ethos of this intensely people-oriented airline.

Delta's imposing stature in commercial aviation today owes much to the fact that during the course of its development the company absorbed two other carriers in mergers: Chicago and Southern (C&S) in 1953 and Northeast Airlines nearly two decades later. Accordingly, we have devoted considerable space to the early history of those firms. Partly because of the immense impact that its acquisition had upon Delta's subsequent evolution, and partly because no full-scale history of C&S had appeared in print, we have devoted two complete chapters to its emergence and growth. Because of the comparatively recent nature of the Northeast merger and the fact that an extended history of that New-England–based company had already been published, we did not give an equal amount of space to its development up to the time it was absorbed by Delta in 1972. Northeast's highly colorful beginnings and valiant struggle for survival are, however, summarized at some length in two separate sections of the book.

During the course of our research we have incurred debts of gratitude to a large number of persons without whose cooperation and support this project could not possibly have been completed. Among the many active and retired members of the Delta organization to whom we are particularly obligated are Ronald W. Allen, T. P. Ball, W. T. Beebe, Bernard Biedenharn, James W. Callison, Joseph A. Cooper, Charles H. Dolson, Hoyt Fincher, Arthur C. Ford, Richard W. Freeman, Sr., David C. Garrett, Jr., Debra B. Griffeth, Hollis L. Harris, Ike Lasseter, T. M. Miller, Robert Oppenlander, Carleton Putnam, Frank F. Rox, Linda S. Sherman, George Snellings, Paul T. Talbott, and Juanita Burnett Whiddon. Special thanks are due to veteran Delta employees Marjorie C. Langford, who contributed in literally thousands of ways to the success of the project; Harriette S. Parker, who supported our efforts from the beginning and was particularly helpful in the selection of photographs; and Frances Conner, who provided valuable assistance in preparing route maps and statistical appendixes. We extend our gratitude to all those persons who consented to grant us oral history interviews. Unfortunately time and the press of getting on with the task precluded our interviewing but a fraction of those thousands who have made or are making the history of Delta.

Among Auburn University officials, students, and staff, we are indebted to Stephanie Bond, Chester C. Carroll, J. Wayne Flynt, Dorothy Ghent, William C. Highfill and the staff of Ralph Brown Draughon Library, Edward H. Hobbs, Gerald W. Johnson, Allen W. Jones and the staff of the Auburn University Archives, Malcolm C.

McMillan, and Felix Pretsch. We also acknowledge with deep thanks the immense contributions made to our venture by the superb typing skills of Sharon Harper, the copy-editing expertise of Estelle Whelan, and the indexing abilities of Mary Fortenberry.

Malcolm M. MacDonald provided early encouragement in our search for a suitable publisher and played a key role in our decision to submit our manuscript to the University of Georgia Press. We are grateful to him as well as to Paul Zimmer and Karen Orchard for their cooperation and assistance throughout the publication process.

The distinguished business historian Harold F. Williamson of Northwestern University played an indispensable role in our project by advising us from the start, criticizing successive drafts of the manuscript, and giving us the inestimable benefit of his wisdom and encouragement. We owe him far more than these few words of thanks can possibly express. We also appreciate the interest taken in our venture by Albro Martin, editor of the *Business History Review*, and Paul Uselding, editor of the *Proceedings of the Business History Conference*, who accepted two brief extracts from our work for separate publication in their respective journals. Other historians who provided valuable criticism and advice included Richard Barsness, Roger E. Bilstein, Thomas Crouch, Nick A. Komons, William M. Leary, Jr., and Merritt Roe Smith.

Eddie Holland of the Division of Aeronautics of the State of Arkansas was particularly helpful in supplying information about Delta's first airline flight. Travis Oliver III provided photographs and documents. We are also grateful to Sidney A. Stewart for reading three chapters dealing with events in which he had played a significant part.

Auburn University supported our early researches with a grant for which we here express our appreciation.

Richard S. Maurer, vice-chairman of the board and corporate secretary of Delta Air Lines, played a crucial role throughout in making this study possible. His careful reading of the manuscript, much of which deals with developments in which he was an active participant, spared us more errors than we care to contemplate, and his sensitivity to our professional needs was of utmost importance in enabling us to carry out our work in accordance with the canons of professional accountability.

While gratefully acknowledging the help and advice of all the foregoing persons, we willingly exonerate them from blame for such errors, omissions, or shortcomings as may remain, accepting these as our own responsibility. And, of course, we cannot close without expressing our deepest thanks to our wives, Carolyn and Merlin, and to our families generally, for encouraging us to persevere throughout an extremely long and arduous project and enduring the many frustrations and inconveniences that are inevitably a part of the creative process. They, too, can claim much of the credit for whatever success we have achieved, in this as in so many other ventures.

W. DAVID LEWIS
WESLEY PHILLIPS NEWTON

CHAPTER 1

Takeoff

S UNLIGHT FILTERS THROUGH the early morning haze as the members of several flight crews arrive at Delta's vast employee parking lot: pilots in traditional black with gold trim, flight attendants in sky blue, orange, and tan. The air is still damp from an all-night rain. A company bus bearing Delta's distinctive slanting red, white, and blue triangles picks them up, and steam rises from moist pavements as they pass the sprawling jet base where during the night a Lockheed L-1011 TriStar has been checked and serviced for transcontinental flight to the West Coast. On the web of interstate highways and access roads girdling the airport complex, a steadily mounting volume of traffic converges on the terminal, dominated by the familiar green tower proclaiming boldly on its façade the name of the metropolis that it serves: Atlanta.[1]

The bus arrives at the crew scheduling center. The three members of the cockpit crew who will fly the L-1011 to California disembark, led by a senior captain with more than thirty-five years of seniority with Delta; he learned his job flying a Douglas DC-3, still remembered with affection as ship 40, the first airliner of its type ever acquired by the company. The first and second officers are considerably younger than the captain and, like many commercial airline pilots, have recent military backgrounds.

Among the other passengers disembarking from the bus are several of the L-1011 flight attendants. The senior member has been with Delta since 1956, when it first won access to Washington, D.C., and New York City. She first flew in a Douglas DC-7, the piston-driven ship that was then queen of the Delta fleet. The other attendants look like college coeds, but altogether they have logged thousands of hours in the air.

The cockpit crew goes to the operations office to study a computerized flight plan prepared by company meteorologists and dispatchers; it is plotted to ensure the passengers a comfortable ride, avoiding turbulence wherever possible. After consulting a series of maps of wind currents and weather movements aloft, the captain checks with the meteorology department about some choppy air that is expected as a weak front moves across New Mexico. Meanwhile, using his own calculations, the first officer works up a flight plan to verify the computerized version. After a brief conversation the three men agree that the best possible course is the one that the computer has charted. Before leaving they check their mailboxes for messages or recent additions to *Jeppesen's Airway Manual*, the industry-wide "pilot's bible," which contains route charts, information about airports, and other navigational aids. At the same time, the flight attendants have checked their own mailboxes for messages relating data that might affect the performance of their duties on the upcoming trip.

The pilots and attendants proceed through the main passenger terminal; the entrance lobby is teeming with activity despite the early hour. Behind a long row of counters, Delta agents are making out tickets for customers and punching out coded queries on computer-connected modules that return answers about hotel and motel reservations, surface transportation, entertainment, and sightseeing attractions in the ninety-three cities on the company's route system. Baggage is tagged and disappears on conveyor belts to be loaded onto motorized carts for transfer to the appropriate gate areas. Overhead electronic scanners flash information about incoming and outgoing flights, constantly changing as arrivals and departures occur.

Two of the concourses that radiate from the entrance lobby of Hartsfield International Airport serve Delta traffic exclusively. At the gatehouse selected for the TriStar flight, passengers are already being checked in by blue-coated agents, who ask about seating preferences and issue boarding passes. A senior passenger-service agent in a red blazer assists people who have to make tight connections on the West Coast or have physical handicaps requiring special seating arrangements. In accordance with long-standing company policy, ground employees are shifted to different positions from time to time so that they may become familiar with various responsibilities. All promotions to higher posts, including executive ones, must come from within the organization, which strengthens incentive and enhances morale.

The captain and first officer board the Delta TriStar, which is docked outside the gatehouse; its white fuselage, with the familiar red and blue markings, gleams in the sunlight. The second officer, meanwhile, walks slowly around the giant ship, carefully studying every exterior detail in order to detect any irregularity that might impair its airworthiness. Earlier, a mechanic of the line maintenance crew conducted this same "walkaround" and inspected log books on board for records of previous performance of cockpit equipment, engines, and cabin safety apparatus. But the second officer makes his own supplemental examination in order to be sure that no defect has gone unnoticed. Where safety is concerned, nothing is taken for granted.

The tempo of activity in and around the TriStar intensifies. Trucks carrying catered meals and beverages arrive and are unloaded by means of a conveyor belt. At the same time the plane's enormous Rolls Royce engines receive their own nourishment: thousands of gallons of kerosene pumped into the fuel tanks. Tugs scurry around the ship, towing carts laden with containerized baggage capsules and mail sacks; two containers at a time are deposited mechanically in cavernous storage bins on the lower deck and are locked into place. A ramp agent supervises the process in accordance with instructions from a load planner who sits in a nearby enclosure, consulting an assortment of charts and tables on which the weight of the materials being stowed, the amount of fuel required for the trip, and the number of passengers expected are recorded. Standard formulas are used to calculate the approximate weight of the passengers, which varies from season to season because of differences in the clothes that they wear. It is particularly important to determine where the plane's center of gravity will be when the craft is fully loaded, because its position affects critical computations involving flight performance.

In the cockpit the captain sees a light glow on his console, heralding a radio message from the flight-dispatch office: the weather front across the Southwest is intensifying, but turbulence in the area should not be unduly severe; everything points to an uneventful trip. The captain briefs the senior flight attendant on general weather conditions, and she in turn gives the captain the names of the cabin crew and their stations.

Meanwhile, the other flight attendants are preparing for passengers to come aboard. Many of the travelers will look upon the flight attendants chiefly as servers of food and beverages or as pretty or handsome faces to enliven the tedium of the nonstop flight, but the attendants, now busily deploying buffet equipment, trays, and serving carts, are also skilled professionals, concerned as much about the passengers' safety as they are about their comfort. They have been thoroughly drilled in procedures that will go into effect should any unexpected contingencies occur.

The gatehouse is now jammed with passengers; the company's vast but coordinated network of travel agents, ticket offices, and reservations personnel has filled every one of the huge ship's seats for the westward flight. The gatehouse agent signals the cabin crew, who emerge to receive the boarding public. The physically disabled and those with children in arms head the stream pouring through the telescoping passageway that connects the gatehouse to the plane. Just inside, a flight attendant removes the top portion of each boarding pass in order to obtain a final accurate count of the passengers. While the wide-bodied craft gradually fills up, other attendants help to stow personal belongings in overhead compartments, to locate assigned seats, and to distribute stereo headphones to travelers who want to listen to music during the trip.

Back in the cockpit, surrounded by myriad dials, instruments, and switches, the crew is carefully completing a long checklist: the second officer reads each item aloud, and at each step the captain and first officer confirm that the pertinent equipment is ready. Some instrument settings, like those involving radio, must be checked in operation; others are merely noted visually. All the items are checked off orally, and the entire procedure is taped into the flight recorder as required by federal regulations.

Clearance forms giving the final weights and measurements are brought aboard, and all doors and hatches are secured. Using data from these forms and charts on his work table, the second officer computes the power setting needed for takeoff and the "V speeds" that the ship must attain at critical points as it accelerates down the runway and takes to the air. This information, along with the points at which the aircraft can safely be stopped on the runway, is given to the captain on "takeoff data" cards.

Below, on the ground, a mechanic signals that the plane is cleared to start its engines, and the TriStar begins to pulsate with energy. It is pushed backward by a tug until it clears the ships parked on either side; then, under the supervision of Delta ground personnel, it taxis down the finger leading to an exit lane. At this point Federal Aviation Administration (FAA) ground control takes over and assigns an access route to the predetermined runway. As the plane taxis toward the runway with a rhythmic sway, the flight attendants inside are explaining the emergency oxygen system, making sure that seat belts are tightened, and tending to other last-minute details. Then, throbbing with controlled power, the TriStar moves into place at the head of the takeoff runway, where guidance passes to the FAA tower control.

The captain signals the senior flight attendant with two chimes on the intercom that all preparations for takeoff have been completed in the cockpit; she gives the same signal in response to indicate that the cabin is also ready. The ship is cleared for takeoff, and the whine of the engines rises to a full-throated roar as the TriStar starts its rush down the long runway, gaining momentum as it reaches one "V speed," then another. Suddenly the ground falls away, and the L-1011 climbs into the Georgia sky.

Such takeoffs occur so often that the average passenger takes them for granted, rarely stopping to reflect that commercial aviation, despite its enormous scope and the sophistication of the equipment involved, is barely half a century old. There are many people still living who were born before the Wright brothers made the world's first successful flights at Kitty Hawk, North Carolina, in 1903; it is conceivable that someone aboard our 264-passenger L-1011 could have flown one of Delta's first passenger flights, in a tiny six-place Travel Air during the late 1920s and, farfetched as it may seem, been acquainted with the young aviation enthusiast who built the company into the great airline it ultimately became. In his well-known essay, *Self-Reliance*, Emerson declared that "an institution is the lengthened shadow of one man."[2] Surely few business enterprises have ever owed more to a single personality than Delta Air Lines owes to Collett Everman Woolman.

Woolman was born in Indiana in 1889 and grew up around Champaign-Urbana, Illinois, where his father taught physics at the University of Illinois. C.E.'s interest in aviation emerged early; on one occasion during his childhood he and some friends tried to build a giant passenger kite, commandeering most of the clothesline available in the neighborhood to control it. Fortunately, it was wrecked before anybody attempted to fly in it.

In his sophomore year in college, Woolman learned that the first world aviation meet was to be held in 1909 at Rheims, France. During his summer vacation he "played chambermaid" to more than eight hundred traveling calves in order to get there. On the return trip he helped pioneer aviator Claude Grahame-White overhaul a rotary engine in the ship's hold in preparation for an air show to be held in Boston. He had already had experience on airplane engine repairs in Urbana, when a crude plane had had to make a forced landing right on the university campus.[3]

Woolman, a tall blue-eyed youth, was graduated from the University of Illinois in 1912 with a bachelor's degree in agriculture. There was as yet no hint that he was destined for a phenomenal career in commercial aviation. In fact, apart from racing and stunt-flying exhibitions by such daredevils as Arch Hoxsey and Ralph Johnstone, both of whom had crashed to their deaths not long after Woolman's boat trip to France, this field of business enterprise could scarcely be said to exist in the United States.

Woolman was graduated less than a decade after December 17, 1903, the date on which the Wright brothers had made the world's first successful flights in a powered heavier-than-air machine from windswept Kill Devil Hill at Kitty Hawk. Far from appreciating the significance of this accomplishment, the American public was scarcely awakened to the fact that the air age was underway until about 1908, by which time hundreds of flights had been made by the Wrights and other aviation pioneers. During the next few years the exploits of such daring pilots as the ill-fated Hoxsey and Johnstone, known as the Gold Dust Twins, and the luckier Bert Acosta, who somehow managed to survive despite a penchant for flying under bridges, attracted crowds of spectators at air shows throughout the country. Many Americans, including a fiercely grinning Theodore Roosevelt, also experienced the thrill of their first plane rides, but there was as yet little to suggest the likelihood of dependable passenger service by air. As the deaths of many intrepid "birdmen" attested, the flimsy aircraft of the day, built of bicycle parts, piano wire, and other rudimentary components, were notoriously dangerous to operate, and their tiny engines were incapable of putting anything but small payloads aloft. In addition, their airspeeds of forty to fifty miles per hour were decidedly inferior to the performance of locomotives, which could travel at least twice as fast; even an automobile, given a good road, could make better time. Under such circumstances, airplanes were mainly objects of public curiosity, and their business potential for anything except stunting, racing, and joyriding seemed minimal.[4]

So in 1912 Woolman journeyed southward and began farming in Mississippi, becoming manager of a 7,000-acre plantation in the Red River country of northern Louisiana. In 1913 he joined the extension department of Louisiana State University at Baton Rouge and, following the passage of the Smith-Lever Act in 1914, became one of the first county agents in Louisiana, serving Ouachita Parish from a headquarters in its chief city, Monroe, which was to become the birthplace of Delta Air Lines. By 1916 C.E. was back in Baton Rouge after having been promoted to district supervisor of the agricultural extension service in northwestern and north-central Louisiana. In that same year, he returned briefly to Champaign to marry home economics teacher Helen Fairfield.[5]

The Woolmans began married life at Baton Rouge, where C.E. continued his work with the agricultural extension service. As he traveled throughout the northern parts of Louisiana, consulting with planters and representatives of financial institutions that depended heavily upon the marketing of agricultural commodities, he became increasingly concerned about the relentless foraging of the boll weevil, which in the early twentieth century annually destroyed an alarming percentage of the southern cotton crop. Although he did not know it at the time, this concern would ultimately lead him into his life work in commercial aviation.

In the world at large, these years marked the end of aviation's brief infancy. During World War I the airplane was streamlined to some degree, and its speed was significantly increased. More powerful engines, among them the famous twelve-cylinder American Liberty design, were developed, permitting larger payloads and reasonably dependable operation over fairly long distances. Experienced pilots, rare and short-lived before the war, had become more numerous, as had trained aviation mechanics. Airports multiplied under the spur of wartime needs, and navigational techniques were improved. Perhaps most important of all for the future of American aviation, prominent businessmen first became involved in the promotion of flying after tasting the profits gleaned from wartime contracts with such federal agencies as the Aircraft Production Board. Airplane manufacturing, formerly infinitesimal in scope and dollar value, became, at least temporarily, a large-scale industry. Such firms as the Wright-Martin Aircraft Company emerged; one of its backers, Wall Street financier Richard F. Hoyt, was to figure prominently in the early history of the crop-dusting venture out of which Delta Air Lines was born.[6]

The period of World War I was also crucial for the development of American commercial aviation, witnessing the beginnings of effective airmail service in the United States. As Delta's own experience later proved, participation in such service was an indispensable basis for the establishment of profitable passenger-carrying airlines. Although sacks of mail had been carried on earlier occasions by both balloons and airplanes, organized airmail delivery did not begin in America until May 1918, when a route from Washington, D.C., to New York was initiated through the cooperation of the Post Office Department and the United States Army. Periodic accidents claimed the lives of pilots flying open-cockpit planes without modern instruments in all sorts of weather over such dangerous routes as the notorious "hell stretch" across the Allegheny Mountains, but the service prevailed and was extended to Chicago in 1919. In the following year, it reached San Francisco.[7]

Thanks to the able leadership of Assistant Postmaster General Paul D. Henderson, who spearheaded the building of a transcontinental system of beacon lights and other navigational aids, by the mid-1920s the United States possessed the largest and most dependable airmail service in the world. In 1925 Congress passed the Kelly Act, under which the operation of airmail routes was turned over to private business interests through a system of competitive bids—a step of the greatest significance for the development of Delta and other commercial airlines. The following year, the Air Commerce Act laid what has been called "the legislative cornerstone for the development of commercial aviation in America," granting authority for the supervision of civil aviation to the Department of Commerce. Under the newly founded Aeronautics Branch, an elaborate program of government inspection, safety regulation, licensing, mapping, weather reporting, and research was created, and a system of airways and ground-based navigation aids was established. American commercial aviation had begun to spread its wings.[8]

Conditions were still not ripe, however, for effective competition between airborne passenger operations and the nation's flourishing network of railroads. The few American airlines that had already emerged—the first being the St. Petersburg–Tampa Airboat Line, which had enjoyed a brief existence shuttling passengers across Tampa Bay in 1914—had operated primarily over bodies of water, where they were free of competition from the locomotive. Although the business firms that were awarded airmail contracts under the Kelly Act did carry occasional passengers, the airways were still used primarily for the transport of mail rather than people. A few companies that had failed to win airmail contracts did, however, experience fleeting success with passenger operations, and in 1927 Western Air Express, which flew a mail route between Los Angeles and Salt Lake City, launched a passenger service under a grant from the Daniel Guggenheim Fund; within two years the company repaid an equipment loan from the profits.

Meanwhile, Congress acted further to stimulate the development of airmail service by amending the Kelly Act to cut red tape and reduce the cost of postage. Encouraged by the dependability of service rendered by private contractors, the Post Office Department opened bidding in 1927 for the so-called Columbia Line, the main artery spanning the continent from San Francisco to New York, which had continued to be operated by army pilots while the results of free enterprise were tested on feeder routes. Believing that no single firm was capable of providing coast-to-coast service, the government split the giant route into two sections, with Chicago as the midpoint. The eastern segment was won by National Air Transport (NAT), which was already flying the mail run between Dallas–Fort Worth and Chicago. The western branch was awarded to Boeing Air Transport, organized by the Seattle aircraft manufacturer William E. Boeing.

Responding to the growing scope and profitability of airmail, and also to the public reaction to Charles Lindbergh's spectacular flight from New York to Paris in April 1927, major financial interests began to invest more and more heavily in aviation securities. Small-time operators were squeezed out, and a wave of mergers took place in 1928 and 1929, the very period in which tiny Delta first tried to soar as a passenger carrier. One of the giant combines which emerged at that time was the North American Aviation Company, financed in part by General Motors; it absorbed Eastern Air Transport, which operated between New York and Florida and would one day become Delta's most bitter competitor. Another fledgling, Transcontinental Air Transport (TAT), launched an ambitious but unprofitable passenger service between New York and Los Angeles, using both airplanes and Pullman cars to negotiate the 48-hour run. Later, after merging with Western Air Express and being rebaptized as TWA, it too would figure at various points in Delta's history.

During this same period one of the greatest of all American aviation enterprises, United Air Lines, emerged out of a combination of firms including NAT and Boeing Air Transport. It was in turn associated with United Aircraft and Transport Corporation, a large manufacturing concern which included such notable subsidiaries as Pratt and Whitney, developer of the famous Wasp engine, and the Hamilton Aircraft Company. Finally, out of a welter of smaller firms whose operations sprawled from New York to the Mexican border and on to the Pacific, a vast holding company called the Aviation Corporation (AVCO) took shape, which spawned what ultimately became known as American Airlines. Among its many components was the Southern Air Transport System, which in turn included an airline once known as the St. Tammany–Gulf Coast, flying between New Orleans and Atlanta by way of Mobile and Birmingham. Partly because of its acquisition of such enterprises, AVCO was to play a crucial role in frustrating Delta's first attempts to win an airmail contract.

Meanwhile, in the South, the struggle against the boll weevil was entering its climactic phase. Shortly after World War I, a potent dry insecticide, calcium arsenate, had been developed to deal with this menace, but applying it on the ground was both cumbersome and expensive.[9] Brief experiments with aerial crop dusting seem to have begun as early as 1918, with little or no success.[10] Significant progress first occurred in Ohio, where in 1921 cooperation between state and municipal officials and the United States Army led to an experiment in which a military aircraft from McCook Field in Dayton sprayed poison with considerable success on a grove of catalpa trees infested with defoliating worms. Similar efforts continued in Ohio and elsewhere, but the focus of commercial development soon began to center on Louisiana, where Dr. Bert R. Coad, an entomologist at the United States Department of Agriculture's Delta Laboratory at Tallulah, had received a small government grant to conduct tests on attacking cotton pests from the air.

Apart from the problems he encountered in securing sufficient financial support, Coad's main difficulties arose from inadequate airplanes, for he had to rely on the army for obsolete wartime models that had never been intended for agricultural use. The immediate postwar years saw the design and production of better models, but primarily for military or sporting purposes; even the burgeoning airmail system relied mainly on de Havilland biplanes left over from the European conflict. Under these circumstances it was only natural that a manufacturing enterprise launched in Ogdensburg, New York, in 1920 concentrated first on designing a military trainer. The enterprise was the Huff Daland Company, founded by Thomas H. Huff and Elliot Daland, and it was destined to play a special role in the development of Delta Air Lines. Having achieved only limited success in the sale of military aircraft, the company's officers began to look for other opportunities in the restricted market of the early 1920s. They ultimately found them in aerial crop dusting.[11]

While Huff Daland struggled through its infancy, in 1922 Coad—with the aid of two Curtiss Jennies on loan from the army—began a series of experiments that resulted in an improved insecticide mixture and better means of storing and releasing it. Woolman, whose extension work brought him into frequent contact with Coad, was an observer of these experiments.[12] Encouraged by the general results, Coad fought for more federal support and better equipment but had made only modest headway when in 1923 George B. Post, a Huff Daland vice-president, happened to land at Tallulah on his way to demonstrate a biplane trainer to the military in Texas. This accidental meeting between Coad and Post led ultimately to the rise of a major commercial airline.[13]

Intrigued by the sales possibilities in aerial crop dusting if it ever became commercialized, Post persuaded the Huff Daland Company to cooperate with Coad and other specialists employed by the federal government in designing a special aircraft for this type of work. When no other private enterprise showed enough interest in the resulting plan to take the first plunge, the Ogdensburg firm itself decided to do so, and in 1924 it created a separate crop-spraying division, Huff Daland Dusters, Inc. For a short time Post directed this unit, but it soon passed to other administrators, one of whom, the well-known army pilot Captain Harold R. Harris, was persuaded by Huff and Post to secure temporary leave from military service. In 1925 he took charge of flying activities for the new firm, and the next year he resigned permanently from the army.

Another early addition to the staff was even more decisive in shaping the company's future: C. E. Woolman also joined the dusting division in 1925. Many years later Harris recalled that Woolman had first been introduced to Post by Coad, who was attracted by Woolman's ingratiating personality and agricultural expertise and who saw that the dusting division "was unable to sell its services with the personnel it had." As Harris succinctly put it: "Coad was right. C.E.W. was a great salesman." Coad himself remained with the Department of Agriculture until 1931, when he became a prominent staff member of the Delta organization.[14]

The headquarters of Huff Daland Dusters was first established at Macon, Georgia. There were probably two reasons: the Macon city government had offered an adequate airfield in a day when such facilities were rare, and spraying was extensively conducted over Georgia peach orchards, as well as the cotton fields in this and neighboring southeastern states. Servicing a variety of agricultural operations gave the Dusters longer employment in what was basically seasonal work. In addition to demonstrating aerial dusting techniques at various southeastern locations, Harris recruited a suitable force of maintenance personnel and pilots. Not surprisingly, many of them came from the best source then available: the military. Using the 200 h.p. Wright Whirlwind J-4 engine in the Huff Daland Puffer, as the duster came to be known, the company conducted operations in units of two or more planes, each unit staffed by two pilots, a mechanic, and an entomologist. Woolman was soon able to work out a set of guidelines and procedures for negotiating contracts with customers, arranging terms of payment, calculating costs, keeping track of physical assets, and evaluating the performance of employees.[15]

In 1925 Huff Daland Dusters took the critical step of shifting its base from Macon to Monroe, Louisiana. Woolman and Coad were probably responsible for this move; Woolman already knew the city well from having served as county agent there, and Coad's Delta Laboratory at Tallulah was only a short distance to the east. In addition, certain influential Monroe area businessmen were enthusiastic about aviation and convinced of its commercial potential. As a result of negotiations between Huff Daland and local leaders, the municipalities of Monroe and West Monroe agreed to provide a public airfield with a hangar 160 feet long and 60 feet wide; Huff Daland consented to occupy the field for three years and to make Monroe headquarters for all its operations. Actually this association was the beginning of a much longer marriage between the company (and its successor, Delta Air Lines) and the northeastern Louisiana city. An old landing ground known as Smoot Field was the initial base; in 1927 flooding led to the choice of a better site, Selman Field. Selman remained headquarters for dusting and subsequent airline operations until Delta moved its base to Atlanta in 1941.

Monroe was a good location for the fledgling company in the 1920s. It was then the center of natural-gas production in the United States and was also strategically located for crop dusting. Nearby were the vast cotton fields of the Mississippi Delta country, which beckoned the Puffers to come skimming in, while the dew was still on the ground or after a rain shower, to release their streams of deadly calcium arsenate on the hungry weevils. Although these operations were focused mainly on cotton, Huff Daland also experimented with dusting sugarcane and continued to spray peach orchards. In time its aerial services were applied to an even broader variety of crops.

The scope of operations was soon extended northward to North Carolina; by 1927 it included Arkansas, Texas, and California, where cantaloupes were sprayed in the Imperial Valley. Huff Daland Dusters did not long remain the sole aerial spraying firm in the United States, but it was by all odds the best known; within a few years the company was operating more than twenty aircraft, one of the largest private aerial fleets in the world. Its volume of business increased markedly in 1925 and 1926, the first two full years of operations, and its efficiency also improved notably over the same period. In 1925 its planes applied insecticides to a total of 52,599 acres; the figure rose to 87,684 acres in 1926, an increase of 66.6 percent. But the actual total flying days for all aircraft decreased from 710 in 1925 to 384 in 1926, clearly reflecting more efficient use of equipment.[16]

In 1925 the parent Huff Daland manufacturing company shifted its base from upstate New York to Bristol, Pennsylvania, where it had access to better plant and transportation facilities. In 1926, reflecting this move, the firm changed its name to Keystone Aircraft Corporation. The agricultural spraying division, however, continued to do business as Huff Daland Dusters. Beginning in 1925 the subsidiary extended its dusting operations to Mexico, and in 1926 Woolman went to South America to head an initial investigation of sales possibilities on the cotton-growing estates of the Peruvian coastal valleys.[17] Harris himself came to Peru to set up flying operations during the first half of 1927. In that South American country the cotton season comes several months before it begins in the United States, which enabled the dusting division to spread its activities over much of the year. In Peru such veteran pilots as Dan Tobin assisted their superiors in obtaining signatures on a special Spanish-language version of the Huff Daland contract, flew photographic missions, and released clouds of dust over countless rows of plants. It was hard but gratifying work. "The results I got on my first day's dusting have been simply splendid and everybody is just tickled to death," Tobin reported to Woolman in the spring of 1928 after Woolman had returned from a trip home. "Old ship is running like a top," Tobin continued. "Am expecting a big gang here on Monday to see the thing . . . this dusting business is the rage . . . here right now."

The rage spread as planters in more and more valleys signed their names to contracts.[18]

Huff Daland's Peruvian operations quickly took on another dimension, which was connected with a significant diplomatic offensive that the United States government had launched in 1927. American officials feared that the Latin American airline activities of certain European countries—particularly France and Germany—might expose the Panama Canal to the danger of aerial destruction. An opportunity to dominate the air routes of Latin America appeared when a small United States line, Pan American Airways, began to operate between Cuba and Florida in 1927. By extending unprecedented diplomatic assistance and a lucrative airmail subsidy, Washington encouraged Pan American to expand its operations throughout Latin America. Powerful Wall Street interests also became involved, and these same financiers gained control of both Keystone and its subsidiary, Huff Daland Dusters. The presence of Huff Daland in Peru was fortunate for the American cause, because the crop-dusting firm could serve as a stalking-horse for Pan American's ultimate entry into that country. Equally important was the presence of Harold B. Grow, a veteran flyer in the United States Navy, who in 1928 contracted with the Peruvian government to direct all aviation in that country. Woolman, on orders from his superiors—which had been formulated in discussions among financial moguls and government officials in New York, Pennsylvania, and Washington, D.C.—placed a bid in Huff Daland's name for a Peruvian airline concession and airmail contract, potentially lucrative plums that German interests were also seeking. Grow's influence in the Peruvian government was crucial in the success of this bid.[19]

Woolman also proved to be an able diplomat. On June 5, 1928, he sent a jubilant note to Harris, who had since returned to Louisiana: "Last week we got the permit signed. . . . Phone just rang . . . the [mail] contract . . . has been signed . . . the permit merely gave us the right to fly . . . [the contract] gives us . . . exclusive mail rights in Peru." Harris relayed word of this success to the financial overlords in New York.[20] Thanks to the work of Grow, Harris, and Woolman, the stage was set for the penetration of United States airline operations into the Andean region—operations with obvious strategic implications. In addition, the concession they had won led ultimately to the establishment of a new international air carrier:

Panagra, organized as a joint venture by Pan American Airways and the Grace steamship interests in 1929.[21]

Since leaving Illinois in 1912 to seek his fortune in the South, Woolman had gained experience that would be of much benefit in his subsequent career. Thorough familiarity with the problems of farmers, a down-to-earth ability to communicate with customers, and an infectious enthusiasm for aviation as an aid to the development of agriculture had won for him an important place in a growing new industry. By the late 1920s he was already beginning to sense wider horizons into which his developing interests might lead him. Soon he would return to the United States from South America and begin the transformation of a crop-dusting subsidiary into something much more significant.

CHAPTER 2

The Emergence of Delta:
Birth, Trauma, and Survival

URING THE LATE 1920s Woolman encountered a series of challenges and opportunities which led him more and more decisively into aspects of commercial aviation transcending the aerial spraying of crops. In the process, the dusting aspect was separated from the parent Keystone Corporation and a passenger line was begun under a name which, in slightly altered form, would one day become world famous. It was no easy matter, however, for a small company to survive in an industry that was already experiencing formidable pressures toward consolidation, and Woolman's fledgling venture nearly died in infancy.

Before returning to the United States from Peru in the fall of 1928, Woolman busied himself in preparations for the commencement of service under the aerial permit he had helped to win for the Keystone overlords. In July he and several associates traveled in an open-cockpit plane from Lima to Guayaquil, Ecuador, in an effort to win a similar concession from the government of that country. One of his companions, R. S. Webber, who later became a Delta employee, wrote a colorful letter to his wife describing the flight. On one of several hops, he noted, they encountered "quite a bit of fog which forced us down near the water and for fifteen minutes we would have been up against it in case of a forced landing." On another leg, pilot Dan Tobin "followed the beach line about 30 feet above the surf and that is quite an experience at 100 miles per hour." The travelers were received with much enthusiasm in Guayaquil, and both the Ecuadorian and Peruvian presses devoted considerable space to the event. C. W. Berl, a Huff Daland entomologist who was then stationed in Peru, observed that it was "the first time that a passenger and mail have been carried by airplane between the two countries," and pointed out that the entire trip had taken only eight and a half hours as opposed to five days required for a similar journey by coastwise vessels.[1]

But even Woolman's considerable powers of salesmanship could not win airline rights from the Ecuadorian administration, which was at that time receiving belated recognition from Washington and had already been successfully courted by German airline interests operating out of Colombia. Woolman also took the first steps toward securing airline rights in Chile, but negotiations with that country were still dragging after his departure from South America.[2]

Early in September, Woolman saw to the chartering of a Pan American subsidiary in Peru, Peruvian Airways Incorporated, which ultimately received the Huff Daland contract and concession. Within a matter of days, Harris shipped Woolman a six-passenger enclosed-cabin Fairchild for the new airline. Following an elaborate ceremony on September 13 at the Lima airport, attended by Woolman, Grow, President Augusto Leguía (the air-minded dictator of Peru), and other dignitaries, the plane flew from the capital to Paita and Talara with Tobin at the controls.[3] Thus commercial air service fostered by a strategic imperative was inaugurated. For Woolman it marked the first time he had ever become involved in the actual operation of an airline, and the experience whetted his appetite for further such opportunities—which, as it turned out, were already in the offing.

These opportunities were taking shape back in the United States, in what may aptly be termed an atmosphere of entrepreneurial "wheeling and dealing." Financier Richard F. Hoyt, representing the controlling Wall Street interests, decided to liquidate the dusting operations of Keystone's Huff Daland subsidiary and to sell the assets involved. So far as Hoyt and his colleagues were concerned, Huff Daland Dusters had served its main purpose by helping to secure an airline foothold in Peru. This advantage was to be exploited by the chosen instrument of American aviation diplomacy, which the financiers had helped to design—Pan American Airways. On the other hand, the absentee owners were not indifferent to the aspirations of the personnel who were actually running Huff Daland Dusters. In the summer of 1928, the field managerial staff (or operating group, as it was called) of the Dusters consisted of Woolman and Harris, both of whom were vice-presidents; Irwin E. Auerbach, comptroller; and a secretary named Catherine FitzGerald, who had come to Monroe in 1926 from Keystone headquarters and who was destined to become one of the first women ever elected to the board of directors of an American airline. As an indication of the regard of the overlords for the operating group, the three men were each presented with 330 shares of Huff Daland common stock in July 1928; FitzGerald received 10 shares.[4]

The operating group apparently had a contingency plan for acquiring the assets of Huff Daland Dusters if an opportunity ever arose. Now, it seemed clear, that opportunity had arisen. On August 24 Harris arrived in New York City, having previously learned of the financiers' intention to dispose of the dusting assets. He wrote Auerbach the next day that Hoyt had informed Keystone and Huff Daland representatives of his desire "to close out the dusters to the pilots on any terms (or to anybody else, as far as that goes) . . . that he would sell out for forty thousand dollars, and all notes if necessary. . . . It looks like a golden opportunity for us to do some good for ourselves." Harris also informed Auerbach that he was sending a copy of the same letter to Woolman so that the latter "will have some idea of what is going on."[5]

As Harris soon discovered, a great deal was "going on" in New York. Financier Edgar N. Gott, chief executive of the Keystone organization, was locking horns with Juan Trippe, the dynamic young leader of Pan American. Trippe was angling for greater control over the joint enterprises in which Keystone and Pan American were engaged, while Gott was trying to secure adequate reimbursement to Keystone and its Huff Daland subsidiary for their recent efforts on behalf of Trippe's firm in South America, including payment for the vital Peruvian concession. Harris, moving adroitly, was instrumental in working out a monetary settlement. At the same time, in a move that probably fitted in with the operating group's strategy for acquiring the dusting assets in both North and South America, he accepted an offer from Pan American to go to Peru. While there, he would administer dusting operations, supervise the transfer of Huff Daland's nondusting equipment to the fledgling Peruvian Airways, and direct Pan American's activities in the Andean area for a six-month period.[6]

Harris left for South America late in September; soon after his arrival Woolman returned home. The next step in the strategy worked out by the operating group seems to have consisted of a move by Auerbach to secure from the Keystone overlords options to purchase, in separate lots, Huff Daland's American assets for $40,000 and its Peruvian assets for $15,000. He was to raise $20,000 in cash locally as down payment on the former assets, with the additional $20,000 to be pledged in notes. Woolman, Auerbach, and Harris were then to organize and manage a new dusting company, with operations in the United States and perhaps in Peru. Just how the Peruvian assets were to be acquired is not clear, but the idea of ultimately unloading this part of the operation to other investors was evidently being entertained.[7] Auerbach obtained the options from Gott; these instruments were worded so vaguely as to make it unclear which persons were to receive them. This fact apparently gave Auerbach the idea to sell both the American and Peruvian assets for his own aggrandizement.[8]

Woolman returned to Baton Rouge, where he still maintained his residence. To get there he had to travel by boat and train; considering that he had just helped establish a pioneer airline in South America, this may have stimulated him to think about the need for similar ventures closer to home. After a brief visit with his wife and family he proceeded to the Huff Daland headquarters in Monroe, where a crisis awaited him. As he informed Harris in an agitated letter, "Auerbach seemed shot to pieces . . . and spent a lot of time trying to sell me . . . that you had let us down and that the only thing was for us to take things over and do the best we could with them." Woolman refused to believe Auerbach and pointed out that in Peru "the last thing before [Harris] left the boat . . . we had shaken hands and said 'It's the three of us . . . now for our wives and babies.'" Woolman also discovered that local aviation enthusiasts Prentiss M. Atkins, a Monroe hardware dealer, and Travis Oliver, a prominent Monroe banker, had declined to enter the proposed new dusting venture, despite Harris's previous assurances that they would invest. The more he consulted with Auerbach, the more evasive and irritable the latter became. At one point he accused both Woolman and Harris of failing to cooperate, but, when pressed, he refused to elaborate. Writing to Harris late in October, Woolman concluded, "Harry, it seems to read that he thinks he can put the whole thing over by himself . . . and is cutting our throats at the first chance he has." A day later, emphasizing the increasing seriousness of the situation, Woolman sent Harris a wire voicing the same sentiments.[9]

These suspicions were well justified. On October 24, at about the time Woolman arrived from Peru, Auerbach had prepared a number of identical proposals for sale of the United States assets for $40,000, naming himself, as representative of Huff Daland Dusters, sole agent. One such proposal was sent to Woolman in Baton Rouge.[10] This move seems not to have been a blunder on Auerbach's part but rather a calculated effort to make it appear to outsiders that no mutual arrangement had ever existed and that Woolman was simply another possibly interested buyer for the assets. Auerbach's ploy and Woolman's continued probing reveal clearly what had happened, but despite his outrage Woolman did not lose his head. Instead, he quickly communicated his findings to Gott at Keystone headquarters in Pennsylvania. The latter, shocked, dispatched an emissary named John S. Woodbridge, who arrived in Monroe by train about November 1. Auerbach met him and, as Woolman informed Harris a few days later, "gave you and me HELL for about half an hour [and] intermittently for a couple of hours more, even bringing Mrs. Woolman into the picture. I didn't know this until later or I'd have changed his map." By contrast, Woolman found Woodbridge to be "a fine fellow and a square shooter."

Assisted by other Huff Daland employees in Monroe, along with Coad at Tallulah, Woolman and Woodbridge undertook to see what could be salvaged from a badly deteriorated situation. Woodbridge found that various Huff Daland pilots and ground personnel had become disgruntled with Auerbach. When it became plain that the potential investors in the Monroe area would not negotiate further so long as the comptroller remained involved, Auerbach's association with Huff Daland came to an abrupt end. Woodbridge wrote to Gott that Auerbach's sealed proposals had done much harm, spawning rumors "among planters that the Company is going out of business. . . . Little barnstorming companies are springing up like mushrooms." Woodbridge recommended that Woolman be allowed to proceed with operations, regardless of whether the company remained connected with Keystone or was purchased by local interests. The Monroe group, Woodbridge speculated, would eventually invest, but its members had been on a duck hunt and were now wrapped up in the absorbing presidential race of 1928, which was about to reach its climax. Besides, they would have to consult with Coad, "who is their adviser." Woodbridge praised Woolman for his "inexhaustible efforts" and steady optimism that, once the new American dusting company was launched, he and Harris could earn enough profit on the sale of the dusting assets in Peru "to meet notes on this local sale."[11]

Woolman's tenacity, fueled by anger at Auerbach's betrayal, and his natural gifts for salesmanship came to the fore during those hectic days of late October and early November. What he accomplished, with the aid of Woodbridge, was the birth of Delta Air Lines. It was a time of high stakes and high drama. Both Woolman and

Woodbridge telegraphed appeals for investment funds to key figures in the Keystone and Huff Daland organizations, including Huff and Daland themselves; Daland contributed a crucial $5,000. Woolman persuaded Travis Oliver, a leading banker in Monroe, to invest personally and to use his influence on other area businessmen to follow suit. It was not only Woolman's skill at salesmanship that prevailed in the emergency but also his good name in the Monroe area, established since his early days as county agent. By November 8, $12,000 of the requisite $20,000 down payment had been subscribed by local investors, as Oliver wired to Gott, who was handling the transaction for the New York financiers. "Local people," the Monroe banker assured Gott, "pledge cooperation to Woolman and Harris." [12]

On November 12 Woolman signed an agreement with Keystone–Huff Daland, in which he, acting for himself and his associates, purchased the American dusting assets for $20,000 in cash and $20,000 in notes. On November 18 Woolman, Oliver, and D. Y. Smith, a wealthy local planter, appeared before a notary public in Monroe to begin the process of incorporating a new company, Delta Air Service, Inc., whose name had been suggested by Catherine FitzGerald after the lush Mississippi Delta region in which the enterprise was based. The company received its charter at the Ouachita Parish Courthouse on December 3; initially the board consisted of Smith as president, Woolman as first vice-president, Harris as second vice-president, and Oliver as treasurer. The initial capital stock was fixed at 800 shares, worth $100 each. [13]

Although Woolman wrote to Harris that they seemed to be "started well over the hill and going strong," there were still problems. It was unclear just how much profit Huff Daland Dusters had reaped in its approximately four years of operations, for the financial records were in disarray. In addition, the equipment was not in the best condition, and Woolman and Harris were yet uncertain how long they wanted to keep operating in Peru. But crops still required dusting, and enthusiasm for aviation remained alive in the Monroe area. Although many communities the size of Monroe were interested in aviation, few had an organizer of Woolman's talents and so enthusiastic and influential a business leader as Oliver, who for years had been insisting on the potential of aerial transport. Interest in aviation was also stimulated by an airmail survey flight that touched down in June of the same year, periodic visits by Army planes and several modern civilian transport types, and newspaper

accounts of Huff Daland's efforts in South America, including the
July flight to Guayaquil and the September launching of service by
Peruvian Airways. Then, too, it was the magic age of Lindbergh,
who had just completed his tour of the country to publicize aviation
in general and air transport in particular. Fortunately perhaps for
what Woolman, Oliver, and other aviation enthusiasts in Monroe
were attempting to accomplish, the Lone Eagle had come to Louisiana in October, stopping over in New Orleans for two days amid
great fanfare.[14]

At Delta there was plenty of work to be done: signing planters to
dusting contracts, repairing and refurbishing equipment, and continuing a flying school that Huff Daland Dusters had operated. An
immediate prospect for new activity also presented itself in the
latter part of 1928, in the form of a federal advertisement for bids on
a Mississippi River project that would require a float plane to fly up
and down the river to inspect the levee system during the flood
season. Delta won the contract, let by the Army Corps of Engineers,
and the company soon sent pilot Don Dice, in a Travel Air open-
cockpit plane with pontoons, to inspect the powerful "Ole Man,"
whose ragings had produced the great flood of 1927.[15]

Before long, Woolman began to plan a much more significant type
of operation. The idea had undoubtedly been germinating for some
time. Among the personal papers inherited by Delta after his death
is a copy of a federal airmail survey made in June 1928, while he
was still in South America. Undoubtedly he had pondered the data
on a proposed route linking such cities as Shreveport, Monroe, Jackson, Meridian, Tuscaloosa, and Birmingham. The report had actually noted that Monroe possessed an air service that would be a likely
candidate for a mail contract; now that speculation seemed destined
to become a reality. But Woolman was not thinking primarily in
terms of airmail at that time; his thoughts were centered on creating
a passenger carrier. Early in 1929 he sought counsel from an airline
based in Minnesota which conducted the type of regional service
that he was contemplating. The reply provided helpful advice on
logistics, the demographic aspects of such service, and other operational problems.[16]

Obviously one could not establish passenger operations without
a plane capable of serving as an airliner. It probably would have been
impossible for the struggling Delta enterprise, still encumbered
with debt from the circumstances of its founding, to afford even the
relatively small aircraft that Woolman had used to inaugurate the

Andean service, not to mention the big craft of that day—the Ford and Fokker trimotors. At this point, however, a fortunate opportunity presented itself. Not far from Monroe, in the small Louisiana town of Bastrop, lived John S. Fox, a businessman and investor, son of a wealthy pioneer pulp- and paper-mill owner in Kansas City, Missouri. The younger Fox had learned to fly in 1926. At about the same time he had met John Howe, an aviator from Arkansas, who, as sales agent for the Travel Air Company of Kansas, sold Fox an open-cockpit single-engine Command Aire biplane in 1928. Howe also sold Fox on the idea of starting an air service at Bastrop; it was to concentrate mainly on taking local people for joyrides, but both men had notions of starting an airline. With this thought in mind, Fox added another plane: a high-wing, single-engine, six-passenger, enclosed-cabin Travel Air.

Fox and Woolman met early in 1929, and soon thereafter Delta purchased the assets of the Fox Flying Service. Woolman thus had his airliner, plus Fox's option on another second-hand six-passenger Travel Air. In return, Fox received $20,000 in Delta stock. He was also allowed to purchase an additional $35,000 worth of shares, making him the largest Delta stockholder by far. Appointed an officer of the company, the debonair Fox and his vivacious wife, Irene, moved, as the Woolmans had also done by that time, to Monroe. John Howe, by then a Delta employee, was at the controls of the Travel Air that took off on June 17, 1929, for the company's first passenger flight from Dallas, Texas, to Monroe, Louisiana.[17]

One of the Delta passengers to fly later that summer from Birmingham, Alabama, Delta's eastern terminus, was Herbert Hahn, representing the Birmingham Junior Chamber of Commerce. Chief pilot Pat Higgins was at the controls of the Travel Air which taxied across the bumpy turf of Roberts Field to the runway and stirred up a cloud of summer dust as it gathered momentum for the takeoff. Looking back many years later when he was seventy-three years old, Hahn recalled that the weather was "nice and the flight was perfect." There were stops in Tuscaloosa, Monroe, and Shreveport. The final destination was the western terminus at Dallas, "where a dinner was given by Delta for aviation people," climaxing a public-relations flight with trimmings that set the trend for similar promotions in the future. Before the summer was over, Fort Worth, Texas, and Meridian, Mississippi, were added to Delta's schedule.[18]

Meanwhile, dusting operations were resumed in South America to meet a deadline imposed by Peruvian authorities as a condition for permission to continue the service. In 1929 Harris and Woolman exercised their option to purchase Huff Daland's assets in Peru, but they subsequently liquidated the investment on terms that appear to have yielded them some profit. Even before the sale was completed in 1931, Harris had become more deeply involved in the operations of Panagra, the airline venture that had emerged from Pan American's liaison with the Grace Steamship Company; he was correspondingly less interested in his connections with the Delta organization, and he ultimately severed all ties with Delta to become a Panagra vice-president.[19]

In the fall of 1929 twenty-seven individuals, estates, and other institutions held 1,225 shares of stock in Delta's Louisiana-based operation. The shares were valued at $100 each. The two largest shareholders were Woolman with 150 and Fox with 570 shares. The Keystone–New York interests held 148.5 and Oliver 22.5 shares. The rest were held primarily by individuals and estates in the Monroe area. In early 1930 an audit of Delta's books showed that the dusting operation earned a profit of $20,121.85 for the period from November 12, 1928, to December 31, 1929. The same audit, however, revealed an ominous loss of $32,603.37 for the airline operation.[20] Obviously, the company could not long survive such substantial deficits; nevertheless, it continued to forge ahead, and actually expanded its services in the hope of attracting increased patronage.

At the beginning of 1930 the Delta Travel Airs were providing twice-a-day schedules between Dallas and Monroe; by May of that year they were affording such service all the way from Fort Worth to Birmingham. On June 12, 1930, flights were also begun in and out of Atlanta, the firm's future official home.[21] But the mounting debts that accompanied expansion of operations made it imperative that Delta secure an airmail contract from the federal government or drop the passenger business entirely. In April 1930 Woolman wrote Harris that Delta had made "a pretty fair profit on dusting and sales operations but, of course, a loss on the air passenger line . . . with the Watres Bill now before Congress we have great hopes of coming in . . . for air mail over the run."[22] This letter underscores the urgency with which C. E. Woolman and other Delta officials pursued such a contract in 1930.

The legislation to which Woolman was referring was the McNary–Watres Act, passed in the spring of 1930, which laid the foundations for the establishment of most of the major airlines that still dominate American commercial aviation today. The bill encouraged the use of larger transport planes by prescribing payment to carriers based on the amount of space made available for mail, rather than on a pound rate. Under this law Postmaster General Walter F. Brown received broad powers to award airmail contracts, which he ultimately used to favor certain big airlines at the expense of others and to bring about a series of mergers that have had permanent effects on the industry.[23]

As the pioneer in providing passenger service over its route, Delta believed that it had a good claim to an airmail contract under the new law, and the firm promptly set about the task of enlisting public support in its behalf. In May 1930 representatives from twelve southeastern cities, most of which were served by Delta, gathered in Jackson, Mississippi, to prepare a set of resolutions petitioning federal officials to award Delta an airmail subsidy. The result was a letter to the Post Office Department underlining the quality of service rendered by the airline, pointing to the company's accident-free record, praising the caliber of its management, and urging the postmaster general to give Delta "every consideration possible" for an airmail contract over the route it had developed.[24]

Postmaster General Brown, however, desired above all else to replace the tangled web of airways existing at the end of the 1920s with a soundly financed, well-organized, and effectively managed system of transcontinental lines intersected at various points by feeder routes. He believed that this goal could best be achieved by awarding airmail contracts to heavily capitalized carriers, and he was willing to use heavy-handed methods to achieve his aims if need be. Although he had toyed with the idea of giving some subsidies to smaller "independents" on a trial basis to see whether they could establish profitable operations over important routes, he dropped this approach when he failed to secure adoption of a clause in the McNary–Watres Act that would have given him authority to award contracts on a noncompetitive basis for short periods of time. Instead, the act required competitive bidding for all new airmail routes. It also provided that only an existing mail contractor with a successful record of not less than two years' service could be granted a route certificate, the duration of which was not to exceed ten years from the original date on which service commenced. Such carriers could also be awarded extensions to their original routes at the postmaster general's discretion.[25]

Brown's lack of enthusiasm for the smaller independents dimmed

Delta's hopes of winning any sort of airmail subsidy. After the passage of the McNary–Watres Act a group of airline representatives were invited by Brown to meet in Washington to map plans for dividing up the airmail contracts authorized by the new legislation—a somewhat dubious procedure in view of the act's manifest endorsement of competitive bidding but very much in line with Brown's desire for order and stability. Unable to agree among themselves and harboring considerable mutual distrust, the interested parties turned to Brown as an "umpire" who could work out "voluntary rearrangements." By then the postmaster general had abandoned all idea of working with the smaller independents and did not even invite Woolman to the meeting, though Woolman received a phone tip from a friend and came anyway, arriving late. He quickly sized up what was going on and began a campaign to salvage what he could from a bad situation, with the aid of Senator Edwin S. Broussard of Louisiana and E. V. Moore, a Washington attorney representing Delta in the national capital.[26]

According to the testimony that Woolman gave four years later to a Senate committee chaired by Hugo Black of Alabama, which was investigating irregularities in the awarding of airmail contracts under Brown's leadership, the postmaster general had privately conceded the merit of Delta's claim to having established "legitimate pioneer operations over an important route" and had promised that the firm "would certainly be taken care of." With Brown's tacit encouragement, Delta tried to work out an arrangement with Eastern Air Transport, which expected to win an airmail contract between Atlanta and New Orleans. Woolman had hopes of inducing Eastern to sublet this contract to Delta, but he failed—partly, he believed, because Eastern thought it was going to receive the contract anyway and was not interested in making concessions to Delta. In this regard, however, Eastern was mistaken. According to information that reached Woolman through Moore, the postmaster general did not appreciate Eastern's stubborn attitude toward Delta and even threatened to deny renewal of that firm's existing airmail contracts, let alone extend them. As a result of his annoyance, Brown decided upon another approach, which left Eastern out of the running for a route west of Atlanta.[27]

Brown, however, was no more willing than before to give Woolman's line an airmail contract on its own account. Instead, he shifted his favor from Eastern to Aviation Corporation, which had grown from small beginnings in 1927 into what historian Henry

Ladd Smith has justly called a "super holding company." Here the importance of AVCO's recent acquisition of Southern Air Transport, which in turn had bought out St. Tammany–Gulf Coast Airways, became apparent. St. Tammany–Gulf Coast had flown the Birmingham-to-Atlanta run well before Delta had provided service between those two cities. Brown therefore decided to recognize AVCO as the pioneer operator on that segment and to throw in the remainder of the route from Birmingham to Fort Worth under the so-called extension principle, with some compensation to Delta for the loss of its pioneering stake in the route.

Powerless to alter the course that Brown had settled upon, Woolman and his associates soon began negotiating with AVCO, at the suggestion of Hainer Hinshaw, an aviation promoter who had powerful political connections in Washington and was then an officer of American Airways, which had been organized in January 1930 as AVCO's main operating subsidiary. In New York, Woolman and Moore parleyed with Frederic G. Coburn and Graham B. Grosvenor, the president and former president of AVCO. The initial understanding was that AVCO would buy a controlling interest in Delta, which would then continue to operate the route from Atlanta to Fort Worth as a junior partner of the giant combine. This agreement, however, was never put in writing, and Grosvenor subsequently informed Woolman that the situation had "considerably changed."[28] The reason for the about-face was undoubtedly the decision by Comptroller General John R. McCarl, announced July 24, 1930, that the clause of the McNary–Watres Act granting to the postmaster general authority to extend existing routes and award them to favored companies could not be construed as empowering him to grant to an airline an extension longer than the route that it had flown under previous airmail legislation. This ruling ended AVCO's hopes of an "extension contract" and forced American Airways to seek the route through a competitive bid. It also forced Brown to seek another means of eliminating unwelcome applicants. He thereupon demanded that all bidders must have conducted night-flying operations over a route at least 250 miles long for not less than six months in order to qualify for an airmail contract. Considering that no such stipulation appeared in the McNary–Watres Act, this maneuver was high-handed indeed.[29]

Delta's hopes of winning an airmail contract on its own were thus worse than ever. Brown and his advisers, determined to limit the number of lines entering the competitive bidding that was now in-

escapable in view of the McCarl ruling, arbitrarily decided to dis-
qualify any contender that did not have the degree of night-flying
experience stipulated by Brown. Delta had no such experience, and
its leaders seem to have decided at this point that their best course
of action was to sell out to AVCO under the most favorable terms
they could obtain. A sheaf of telegrams in Woolman's records shows
that he and his associates kept constant political pressure on Brown,
largely through Senator Broussard, to require AVCO to give fair
reimbursement to Delta for the losses incurred in developing the
route from Atlanta to Fort Worth. In later testimony before the
Black committee, Hinshaw confirmed that Delta had put up a persistent fight for a proper settlement. Delta planes kept operating
over the Atlanta-to-Texas route until AVCO actually secured the
coveted contract from the Post Office Department and began to provide service on October 1, 1930, after which further competition
was hopeless. In the end AVCO paid Delta a settlement, which
Hinshaw testified was somewhere between $102,000 and $107,000.
According to Woolman this sum represented about fifty cents for
every dollar that Delta had spent in developing the route. In the
1934 investigation Senator Black posed the question "You sold because you had to, did you not, Mr. Woolman?" Woolman's laconic
reply: "Well, it was that or else."[30]

Although Delta theoretically sold its entire operation to AVCO,
Woolman and his associates had no idea of leaving aviation. In an
agreement dated November 3, 1930, Southern Air Fast Express, an
AVCO subsidiary, conveyed to Travis Oliver, acting as trustee for
an unspecified group of associates, an assortment of planes, motors,
office equipment, tools, calcium arsenate, and other supplies corresponding closely to previous inventories of Delta and Huff Daland
assets, for a consideration of $12,500. A handwritten appendix also
specified that Oliver and his colleagues could continue to use the
name Delta Air Service, Inc. for any type of operation except conducting a scheduled airline. With this document, which was witnessed by D. Y. Smith and John S. Fox, Delta reacquired the assets
necessary to carry on its crop-dusting operations.[31]

Oliver continued to hold the firm's assets for almost two months
after they were reacquired from AVCO, waiting until the enterprise
had been rechartered by the state of Louisiana under a new name,
Delta Air Corporation. The new charter was extremely broad: it
authorized Delta to "manufacture, buy, sell, hire, lease, import, ex-
port, deal in, deal with, operate or otherwise use at any place within

or without the United States, airplanes, aircraft, airships, mono-
planes, biplanes, hydro-airplanes, machines, flying apparatus or
other mechanical contrivances or devices for aerial operation or
navigation, of any and every kind and description, and any future
improvements or developments of the same." As if this wording
were not sufficiently explicit, subsequent language granted authority "to use machines and motors previously described . . . for the
carrying and transporting of passengers, goods, wares, merchandise,
mail, express and freight, for all kinds of commercial purposes, including agricultural and forestry, such as dusting, seeding and plowing, planting and fertilizing, forestry patrol and survey," along with
a variety of other potential operations, including flying schools.[32]
On December 31, 1930, when the new charter went into effect,
Oliver conveyed to Delta Air Corporation the property that he had
acquired as a trustee in early November.[33]

In effect, Delta was reverting to its former status as a crop-dusting
firm, but it would stay out of other types of commercial operations,
including the transport of passengers, only so long as it had to. Although it was barred from conducting scheduled passenger flights
under its old name because of the agreement with AVCO, there
was no reason why it could not provide such service, or do anything
else that required wings, under its new name and charter whenever
conditions seemed encouraging. Delta was thus like a climbing aircraft struck by lightning. It had been forced to level off and switch
to an alternate system, but it managed to stay in flight as the dark
storm of the Great Depression boiled around it. As for Woolman,
though not named in the agreement with AVCO, he remained the
vice-president and chief nerve center of the enterprise. Indeed, as the
events of the next few years would show, he, more than any other
person, would keep the company alive during its darkest hours.

CHAPTER 3

Doldrums

THE ESSENTIAL FACT regarding the development of Delta in the early 1930s can be expressed very simply: the company survived. That it was able to do so during an era in which the United States experienced the greatest economic disaster in its history, the Great Depression, was attributable chiefly to the human resources with which Delta confronted, and endured, the bleakest period in its own corporate epic. One factor was particularly crucial: the leadership of C. E. Woolman. In the end, hardship had a positive side: out of this trying era came enduring characteristics and traditions that were to play a vital role in the firm's subsequent progress, many of them shaped by Woolman's evolving managerial style. Nevertheless, it was a time of formidable discouragements, climaxed by the withdrawal from the venture of one of its most important financial backers. Then, in 1934, the sky brightened as Congress launched an investigation of alleged favoritism in the awarding of airmail contracts under the Hoover administration. As a result of disclosures elicited from a parade of witnesses, existing contracts were canceled and companies that had lost out in the 1930 scramble for route awards were permitted to resubmit bids to the Post Office Department. Suddenly the way was open for Delta, armed with an indispensable federal subsidy, to resume operations as a mail and passenger carrier.

As the decade of the thirties began, Delta's exclusion from an airmail contract for the southeastern route it had established from Fort Worth to Atlanta left it no alternative but to return mainly to crop-dusting to eke out what proved to be a precarious livelihood. Unfortunately, most of Delta's business records and correspondence for the depression years have disappeared, but the few that remain indicate that the going was extremely difficult. Writing to Harris in South America in April of that year, Woolman was gloomy about the prospects of making money from spraying crops. "Dusting this year does not look too promising," he confided to his business associate. Unseasonably cold weather throughout much of the Cotton

Belt had "virtually eliminated" the weevil menace for the time being, and a new competitor, Curtis Flying Service, operating out of
Houston, was offering to dust crops at the pathetically low figure of
thirty-five cents an acre. "On top of this," Woolman moaned, "with
the low cotton prices the farmers are completely 'broke.'"

Casting about for some ray of hope, Woolman mentioned that
Delta had acquired from the Curtiss-Wright Company a franchise to
sell its products in Louisiana and Mississippi, "for the most complete plane franchise in the United States." Surviving records, however, give no account of precisely what the franchise involved and
what profit, if any, accrued. Woolman also found some grounds for
optimism in the condition of the facilities at Selman Field. In addition to the original large brick hangar with which Harris was familiar, there was a tile-roofed "very fine administration building (put up
by Standard Oil) and a small storage hangar 40 × 60, for dead storage,
and the Parish is promising a 110 by 120 steel hangar at an early
date."[1]

The construction of the new hangar was deferred when the mail
contract went by the boards, but the dusting business did improve
as Woolman, following a strategy that had paid off in the past, journeyed south of the Rio Grande in search of additional revenue.
Returning to Monroe in December 1930 with a Mexican dusting
contract, he assumed a bold stance and expressed stubborn faith
when he told the local press that he had "every confidence that . . .
Delta . . . will be able to operate along the lines for which it was established, that of scientific control of those pests which are a menace
to agriculture." Woolman emphasized both his hopes for the future
and the accomplishments of the immediate past. He spoke glowing-
ly of the praise given to Delta Air Service by government officials
and AVCO representatives during the recent negotiations in Washington. Delta's safety record as a passenger carrier had never been
blemished by a major accident, and only twice had its Travel Airs
been obliged to land for minor adjustments. Looking to the future,
Woolman pointed not only to the Mexican contract but also to in-
quiries about the Delta dusting technique which were coming in
from England, Germany, and other European countries. To be sure,
these queries produced no additional business for the new Delta Air
Corporation, but they did indicate its spreading fame.[2]

Woolman also informed the press that the same basic managerial
staff would lead Delta under its new corporate form and name.[3]
Smith was to continue as president, Woolman as vice-president, and

Oliver as treasurer. Oliver's former duties as secretary were assigned to Catherine FitzGerald. The board of directors was to be composed of these same four plus Malcolm S. Biedenharn and Prentiss M. Atkins. Biedenharn was an early investor in Delta and a son of the first man in the United States to bottle Coca-Cola. Atkins was, like Oliver, an original investor in Delta and a longtime aviation enthusiast. For reasons that were not immediately apparent, John Fox was absent from the board of the reconstituted enterprise, but he did continue as general manager.[4]

The newspapermen who took down Woolman's hopeful statements about Delta could scarcely have been awed by its capital structure. Under the new corporate arrangement, the total authorized number of shares of common stock was only 5,000, of which few apparently were actually issued. The amount of paid-in capital had also been greatly reduced—to $10,000. Woolman held 140 of the outstanding shares; Biedenharn 100; Smith, Oliver, and Atkins 75 each; and FitzGerald 25.[5] The new Delta was a severely trimmed-down version of the enterprise that had once enjoyed connections with powerful Wall Street interests.

But the firm's human assets in the early 1930s remained essentially unimpaired. Of the small cadre whose dedication kept Delta alive throughout this time of trial, Woolman was by far the most important. In general, the directors took little part in the conduct of day-to-day operations and seem to have met as a group only on rare occasions. Despite his status as general manager, Fox had no experience in agriculture or crop dusting, and his enthusiasm seems to have waned following the failure to win an airmail contract. Among the officers, therefore, it was Woolman, thoroughly familiar with every aspect of the company's business and deeply committed to its survival, who "ran the show." Increasingly his personality and that of Delta became inseparable, each mirroring the other; likewise, the policies that he established grew into enduring corporate traditions. In every way, he was the heart of the enterprise.

Photographs of Woolman taken then and later show a big raw-boned individual, six feet one inch tall and weighing slightly in excess of two hundred pounds. His broad face and somewhat folksy style exuded good nature; as one account put it, "There is in his speech and manner a suggestion of the warmth and homespun qualities of Will Rogers, to whom he is sometimes likened." An acquaintance of the early period at Monroe recalled him speaking with a loud voice that sometimes became almost bombastic, and a newspaper writer later reported that he had the "handshake of a lumberjack." Other descriptions that appeared throughout his career, however, characterized him as quiet, unassuming, humble, even shy. Clearly he was a complex man. Wayne Parrish, editor of *American Aviation* and a longtime friend, may have captured his inner essence most accurately by stating that Woolman was a loner who, despite having many acquaintances and admirers, was lonely deep down. If so, however, this did not prevent him from projecting a public image that was hearty, outgoing, and gracious. However they may disagree, the impressions of most associates who knew him well confirm that Woolman was a highly charismatic human being, a man of great personal charm. As the years went by and his stature as the father of the company grew, he came to be regarded by Delta employees with a mixture of awe and veneration. In a paternalistic tradition already well established in the South, Delta became not simply a business corporation but something of an extended family as well.[6]

Though raised in a midwestern academic environment, Woolman had come to reflect the attitudes of most white southerners through his experience in working with them as county agent, salesman, and business executive. He was fond of assuming what Parrish described as the guise of "the innocent, gullible country boy," and some competitors, particularly in the early years, seem to have made the mistake of looking upon him as something of a "rube." Behind the homespun appearance, however, was a shrewd mind and an inexhaustible ambition. Woolman clearly recognized the practical value of cultivating the "common touch." As he later recalled, he had been the first county agent in Louisiana to hold a college degree. Sensing that this was as much a potential stigma as an asset, he had used the geniality that came so naturally to him to establish rapport with a wide variety of clients ranging from simple tenant farmers to self-made businessmen and landed aristocrats. Subsequently, the same approach stood him in good stead with Huff Daland and Delta. C. B. McMahan of Monroe, who was an early pilot with American Airways before establishing an aerial pipeline survey company, compared him to a successful down-to-earth farmer, while Elmer Culpepper, who was employed at the parish prison farm at the northeast corner of Selman Field and became well acquainted with the Delta staff, likened Woolman's manner to that of a friendly politician. A newspaper vignette published after Woolman became well known as an airline executive depicted him on an earlier occasion squatting along a dirt road with a denim-clad farmer who had been resisting the sale of part of his land to permit the expansion of an airport. Both men were chewing tobacco—though Woolman did not ordinarily indulge in this habit—and talking as if they had known one another for years. In the end, according to the account, the farmer relented. The story may be apocryphal, but it is nonetheless indicative of the skill in human relations which Woolman possessed and which must have contributed heavily to Delta's survival in the depression years.[7]

Another Woolman trait, already in evidence during the same period, was a deep concern, characteristic of a paternalistic style of management, for the welfare of employees who worked loyally and faithfully under him. In one respect this was his feeling for his own wife and children written large; earlier in the creation of Delta, he had pledged to work for wife and babies and to resort, if necessary, to fisticuffs to defend his wife's honor. Carleton Putnam, an airline pioneer whose fortunes later became intertwined with those of the Delta patriarch, once observed that when Woolman talked about the people who worked under him, "there was a special light in his eyes." In the early 1930s and later, he tried diligently to maintain a personal relationship with the family he headed. It was fairly easy, of course, to know by name every employee of the tiny dusting organization, and to be able to converse with each of them familiarly as occasion arose, but the degree to which Woolman was committed to such contact as a matter of policy would be revealed in the future when it became a Delta tradition despite the increasing size of the company. Even when his prodigious memory failed and he could not remember the name or special interests of an employee, he did his best, like a seasoned politician, to create the impression that he had full command of such details. There was no question of insincerity here; viewing himself as a father, he did everything possible to fulfill the role.

Yet another policy, recalled by longtime Delta employee Esther Tarver, was Woolman's commitment to emphasizing the value he placed upon the contributions made to the firm's welfare by employees holding the lowest positions within the organization as well as by those exercising higher responsibilities. No facet of the dusting operation was too small to escape his attention; any evidence of special initiative or diligence on the part of a staff member was quickly noticed and encouraged. Again, as Tarver pointed out, this was not merely true in Monroe when the small scale of Delta's operations facilitated it; intimate familiarity with the functions performed by every employee remained a hallmark of Woolman's managerial style. After airline service was resumed in 1934, he made frequent tours around the system to keep abreast of special needs and problems as they arose. On such trips he always sought out "ramp personnel" with whom to discuss such matters before he moved on to those of higher rank.[8]

Fitting a common American business stereotype, Woolman was a "workaholic" who found little time to play with his children or enjoy social activities unless they were related to company affairs. He drove himself harder than his employees; in later years he would chide Delta executives who found it necessary to work on weekends, saying that he was the only person in the organization who had so much to do that he had to spend Saturdays and Sundays catching up. He was also tightfisted; the desperately straitened circumstances facing the firm in the early 1930s intensified a passion on his part for efficiency and thrift which became proverbial throughout the Delta organization. On the personal level, he and his family had to live a Spartan existence, occupying a small house rented for a modest $40 per month, and he ran the company with the same concern for careful husbanding of resources. Monroe businessman Bernard Biedenharn, brother of Malcolm and himself destined to become a director of the firm, rented hangar space at Selman and frequently observed Woolman walking around scavenging rubber bands, paper clips, and other seemingly inconsequential items that employees had discarded. Similarly, Elmer Culpepper recalled seeing Woolman picking up old rags around the hangar and having them laundered for reuse. Woolman's purpose was probably in part symbolic and dramatic; what better way could he have found to impress personnel with the need to conserve Delta's slender resources? Such tactics, however, continued long after the company moved its headquarters away from Monroe. Veteran executive Richard S. Maurer later recalled a service award banquet during the 1950s in which Woolman jokingly reminded a mechanic—there to receive a coveted service pin before an audience of several hundred people— about some long-forgotten occasion on which he had thrown a small piece of safety wire on a hangar floor only to have the eagle-eyed patriarch retrieve it and hand it back to him with the comment, "Here's something you probably didn't know you dropped." The mechanic, catching the spirit of the occasion, acted properly abashed while members of the audience exchanged knowing remarks about

Woolman's hatred of waste. As W. L. Alexander, an early Delta investor from the Monroe area, once expressed it, Woolman had a knack for making himself "firmly but gently understood." [9]

Woolman, of course, was not the only paternalistic figure in the aviation industry during its formative years; it was a common managerial style, practiced by such powerful men as Juan Trippe of Pan American and war hero Eddie Rickenbacker of Eastern. Such personalities were typical, and probably essential, at this stage of the industry's development. But Woolman played the role with his own characteristic nuances; even after Delta spread its wings in later years and began to soar, he cultivated an image of simplicity, homely wisdom, fatherly kindness, and living by the Golden Rule. His style was summed up by one discerning observer who called him a "gentle autocrat." [10]

During the bleak years administering a shrunken enterprise in Monroe, therefore, Woolman was laying the foundations of a managerial role he would someday play upon a much larger stage. His leadership won him the loyalty and steadfast cooperation of a small group of employees and business associates, most of whom would remain members of the Delta family for the rest of their lives. One of these was chief pilot Pat Higgins, an ex-Marine flyer whose career would be cut tragically short by cancer. Another was mechanic Gene Berry, a farm boy from Ouachita Parish who was hired in June 1931 after Woolman had noticed how he constantly followed maintenance chief Doug Culver around the hangar, learning by observation how the firm's aircraft were serviced. Ultimately Berry would outlive Woolman and supervise the restoration of a dusting plane for presentation to the Smithsonian Institution in the patriarch's honor. Still another early employee was Leo Hartman, a local teacher who worked with Delta as an entomologist during the summer months. Nor should one neglect to mention the Monroe area businessmen who continued to support the enterprise despite its failure to secure an airmail contract and the scanty nature of the revenues that dribbled in during the depression years. Probably the most important of these was Travis Oliver, the aviation enthusiast and community booster who had risen from extreme poverty to a position of power as the city's leading banker and who made a lifelong practice of aiding young men who seemed to him to show promise of significant achievements. Without his financial backing and that of the Central Savings Bank, which he headed, Delta could not possibly have stayed in business. [11]

There was also the ever-capable and devotedly loyal secretary, Catherine FitzGerald, who at first had not wanted to move south from her native Ogdensburg, New York, but who finally came to enjoy living in the region. From the beginning, her role went beyond that of typing letters and keeping track of records; as one of the company's officers and directors, she was consulted on policy matters as well. Mrs. Leo Hartman, for example, later claimed that "Miss Fitz" had influenced her superiors not to permit the wives of dusting personnel to accompany their husbands on trips away from Monroe to other agricultural locations, apparently because she thought that the men would be distracted from their work. Over the years FitzGerald would become an institution in herself and remain in active service with the company until after Woolman's death.[12]

At some point in 1931 the staff received a particularly valuable addition when Dr. Bert R. Coad left the United States Department of Agriculture and joined Delta as chief entomologist. As perhaps the most significant pioneer in the development of aerial crop dusting, he brought enormous expertise to the organization and was to remain with it for thirty-five years, running the dusting division while the main focus of its activities became increasingly concentrated upon airline operations. His many contacts were undoubtedly instrumental in helping the firm survive the early years of the depression, and he played a significant role in the development of business strategy. In 1933, for example, Delta moved into Florida at his initiative in order to extend the spraying season. The company's main base in that state was Homestead, a truck-farming center. Mrs. Hartman later recalled the dust and heat of southern Florida and the sometimes grubby accommodations there, once wives were finally allowed to accompany their husbands into the field. She also remembered, with a shudder, a thriving species of reptile life that company entomologists often encountered in the fields while planning dusting operations—the rattlesnake.[13]

Monroe itself played an indispensable role in keeping Delta alive; though it would eventually prove unsatisfactory as the headquarters of a growing airline, it could and did nurture the firm through the difficult depression era. With a population of about thirty-two thousand in 1931, it was the largest and most important city in northeastern Louisiana, the hub of the various rural parishes surrounding it. When the weather was suitable for dusting, Monroe reflected the type of climate typical of the area—damp and verdant. The Great Depression hit Monroe hard, and both Oliver's Central Savings Bank

and the Ouachita National Bank had to struggle to survive. They—
and Delta—made it through the period because of the area's natural
assets, including its lush agricultural lands, natural gas from a field
encompassing four hundred square miles, and strategic commercial
location. Most importantly, the municipality and the parish in
which it was located continued to lease Delta the facilities of Selman Field, which were improved in 1931 when a graveled runway
was constructed, which Mrs. Hartman remembered years later as
the "cinder path." The chief reason for this improvement was probably the desire of Oliver and other local leaders to retain the airmail
and passenger services rendered by American Airways, the corporation that had been organized by AVCO to absorb and control its
sprawling network of subsidiaries. Such services into Monroe had
been temporarily discontinued after Delta had lost out in the scramble for a government mail subsidy in 1930, and the new runway may
have helped to get them back. Nonetheless, Delta also benefited
from the addition, and from the opportunity to service American's
planes.[14]

Delta's own physical assets were meager; as of 1931 it possessed
twelve planes. Seven of these were Huff Daland Petrels, or Puffers,
worth about $2,500 each; three Travel Airs were valued at slightly
less. A Travel Air and a Command Aire, valued at $750 each, were
used in a flying school maintained by the company; they also saw
service in taxi flights and in that lingering phenomenon of early
aviation, barnstorming. Keeping the dusters airworthy involved long
hours of work for Culver, Berry, and other members of the maintenance staff; in later years such local residents as Bernard Biedenharn
and C. B. McMahan retained vivid memories of the rebuilding, can-
nibalization, and repair of the little craft, often performed late into
the night. McMahan recalled particularly the durability of the
planes; on one occasion he had watched anxiously while one approached Selman with half a lower wing gone after having hit a telephone wire. Miraculously the pilot still managed to make a safe
landing. Swooping down out of the sky and climbing upward again
after releasing dense clouds of spray, the Puffers ranged far afield to
garner revenue for the firm. Mrs. Hartman remembered some operations as far away as the Midwest for wheat and Kentucky for "spotty
cotton."[15]

Running any sort of business during the depression was a challenge; surviving file cards on prospects contacted in 1931 indicate
how hard it was to find customers. In Curtis, Louisiana, planter

George Murray was "broke and will do his [own] dusting this season." Judge J. G. Palmer, a landowning agriculturist from Shreveport, was "not interested and said not to bother him about dusting." Yet another Shreveport area planter, J. H. Fillilove, told the Delta agent that he was "cutting down acreage." There was also plenty of competition. J. Earl Porter of Caldwell, Texas, informed Delta that he had used an outfit called Quick Dusters and intended to patronize them again. George Chance of Bryan, Texas, was "waiting on Curtis," the Houston-based firm about which Woolman had complained to Harris in 1930. The blighting impact of the depression was often apparent; for example, R. J. Irvin of Yazoo City, Mississippi, told a Delta representative that he had "lost his place." But the situation was not completely negative. After a first contact, W. B. de Yampert of Wilmot, Arkansas, was reported as a "good prospect." Less than a month later he had signed a letter committing himself to Delta. Fortunately a number of other cards from the 1931 file told the same story. Much of Delta's dusting business in these years, however, came from a very few sources, such as the English-owned Delta and Pine Land Company of Scott, Mississippi, the spraying of whose cotton acreage for August 1931 alone yielded the firm a gross income of more than $9,000 at seven cents per pound of calcium arsenate. The same corporation paid Delta more than $11,000 for the month of August 1933, at a price reduced to six cents per pound of the dusting poison.[16]

Even during these years of hard scrabble and watchful waiting, Delta did not depend exclusively upon dusting; indeed, without supplementary income from other sources, it might not have been able to stay in business. As the agency managing Selman Field, it could sell a number of services. Visiting planes were rented hangar space, serviced, protected by night watchmen, repaired when necessary, and given mandatory periodic inspections. Surviving invoices offer glimpses of the way in which Delta eked out its precarious existence. On February 3, 1931, United States Department of Commerce Stinson monoplane NC-8438, piloted by John M. Armstrong, received thirty-five gallons of aviation gasoline at twenty-six cents a gallon, for a total of $9.10. On February 24, 1931, Sikorsky aircraft NC-51V, piloted by Harry Howze, received four quarts of aviation oil for a total of $1.60, and the owner, Standard Oil Company of Louisiana, was billed $2.00 for "1 night's storage." Military planes sometimes stopped at Selman and contributed to Delta's meager income. On the nights of June 13 and 14, 1932, for example, Lieutenant John D. Williamson of the Army Air Corps interrupted a cross-country flight and stored his aircraft in a Selman hangar, for which his branch of the armed forces was assessed $2.00. On July 14, 1932, Delta mechanics performed a standard "50 hour" check on a Department of Commerce plane and a "20 hour" check on its engine; when a one-night storage fee was added to the bill, it totaled $17.63. One can almost see Woolman poring over his books and muttering, "Every little bit counts."

American Airways was a frequent recipient of Delta's attention in this period, maintaining office space at Selman for which it was charged rent that rose from a modest $10.00 a month in 1931 to $15.00 in 1933. On January 26 Ray Fortner, pilot of American's Fokker trimotor 804-E, made two long-distance calls, one to Shreveport and the other to Dallas, to check ahead on some aspects of his run, for which American was billed a total of $1.40. In August 1931 the same pilot had to have eight quarts of no. 120 aviation oil, totaling $3.20, and a half-hour's labor to repair a broken exhaust pipe that cost his company $1.25. Other services included changing batteries, cleaning or replacing spark plugs, and checking primary and ground wires. On February 16, 1933, a Delta mechanic spent two and a half hours removing a propeller, exhaust ring, shutters, cylinders, and piston to locate the source of engine trouble in one of American's Stinson trimotors and putting it back together, for a total charge to the passenger firm of $5.00.[17]

Several local aviation enthusiasts kept their planes at Selman, further augmenting Delta's meager revenues. Bernard Biedenharn, for example, owned a four-place Curtiss Robin; both it and his British de Havilland Gypsy Moth were serviced by Delta personnel. Biedenharn had become intrigued by airplanes in 1930 while flying to Shreveport in a Delta Travel Air to see an exhibition of the latest outboard motors. The Delta pilot had shown him how to work the controls, and by the time they landed in Shreveport, Biedenharn was no longer much interested in outboard motors; with characteristic enthusiasm and energy, he plunged into the sport of aviation. His planes, along with such other craft as a Stinson monoplane owned by H. C. Miller of the Monroe Sand and Gravel Company and a Travel Air open-cockpit type belonging to C. Faser, Jr., president of a Monroe drug concern, were often seen in and around Selman. Travelers on adjacent roads and people working in nearby fields would watch as they soared off the ground, grew small in the distant sky,

A Huff Daland Duster in action in Louisiana.

In 1924, in Macon, Georgia, Delta Air Lines first took to the air as Huff Daland Dusters.

Huff Daland Dusters' fleet at one time was the largest privately owned aircraft fleet in the world. Woolman is at extreme left.

Huff Daland Dusters became Delta Air Service in 1928, and on June 17, 1929, the company inaugurated passenger service with the single-engine Travel Air S-6000-B, which carried six passengers and cruised at ninety miles per hour.

Delta became Delta Air Corporation in 1930 with General Offices in Monroe, Louisiana, where the company had established dusting headquarters in 1925.

In Peru, Woolman secured airmail rights enabling Huff Daland to become the first American airline operating south of the equator in the western hemisphere, inaugurating service in 1927. Woolman *(fourth from left)* is greeted at the Peruvian airport by an official delegation including Peru's President Leguia *(center, with hands folded)*.

Woolman (*second from left*) poses with other Delta personnel in front of the Travel Air.

Laigh Parker joined Delta in 1934 as general traffic manager and headed the company's traffic and marketing functions for twenty-five years.

Catherine FitzGerald, early corporate officer and long-time secretary to C. E. Woolman.

Pat Higgins and Laigh Parker beside the Stinson-T, Model SM-6000-B.

A 1929 ad depicts Delta's route system and the Travel Air. Originally stretching from Dallas to Jackson, the route was extended to Birmingham on September 1, 1929, and to Atlanta on June 12, 1930.

and later glided in to land. Biedenharn received a special discount from Delta, storing his Robin for $25.00 a month; he sometimes also rented the four-passenger plane to the company. Miller was charged $30.00 a month to keep his Stinson at the field. Smaller planes, such as Faser's Travel Air, rated lower fees.[18] These planes sometimes required expensive maintenance; sports flying then as now was a costly hobby. Given the time put in by Delta mechanics, however, the bills were not unreasonable. For more than ninety hours' work on the Gypsy Moth on one occasion in 1933, for example, Biedenharn was billed only $77.83.[19]

Now and then people came in for flying lessons. In 1931 F. P. Robinson of Bastrop received ten and three-quarters hours of instruction in a Delta aircraft, followed by a quarter hour in his own plane. This training, which also included pilot Pat Higgins's time, cost Robinson $146.78. After receiving flying lessons at Selman, H. C. Miller, accompanied by a Delta pilot, made a two-day flying trip to St. Louis. The fee for the pilot was $11.80 a day, and his incidental traveling expenses came to $53.81. Occasionally, Delta planes and pilots were called upon for photographic work. In 1932, for example, a Delta pilot flew two members of the Louisiana Highway Commission on a twenty-five-minute flight to photograph and inspect high-water conditions at the main bridge across the Ouachita River. The fee was $14.58.[20]

Delta thus managed to stay alive as the money trickled in, but there were many discouragements. At some point during this period of doldrums, Woolman and Delta sustained a particularly heavy blow when John Fox announced that he wanted to pull out. His widow Irene recalled later that he did so in 1931 or 1932, but, as Fox's name does not appear as one of the directors in the reorganized Delta Air Corporation in December 1930, it is possible that he had decided to cash in his stock even earlier. According to Mrs. Fox, Delta's failure to win an airmail contract in 1930 was the major factor in her husband's decision; apparently he lost faith in the future of the air-transport business, at least so far as Delta was concerned, and was not willing to continue his involvement in a firm seemingly destined to remain limited to crop dusting. Woolman, Mrs. Fox recalled, was appalled to see his major investor bow out, but there was nothing he could do. It took some time and negotiation before a settlement was made, but Fox was ultimately paid off at fifty cents on the dollar.[21] Like Woolman he had followed a beacon, but unlike

Woolman he had lost it in the gloom. All in all, it was probably the most discouraging development to occur to the company in a period full of hardship and anxiety.

Fox was soon to regret his decision, however, for events in the nation's capital suddenly opened a way for Delta to get back into the business of carrying airmail and passengers. Ever since 1930, when Postmaster General Brown had interpreted the McNary–Watres Act in such a way as to grant lucrative airmail contracts to large carriers and to squeeze out smaller operators, pressure had been building for an investigation of alleged improprieties. Shortly after Franklin D. Roosevelt was inaugurated in 1933, a full-scale probe was launched by Senator Hugo Black of Alabama. On January 11, 1934, Woolman appeared in Washington, D.C., as a witness before the committee, which was seeking to uncover the circumstances that had led him to sell Delta's airline operations to AVCO after having been shut out of the bidding on an airmail contract. At one point chairman Black asked, "Did the company who got the line have any experience of any kind or character on your line?" Woolman answered, "No one had flown that line but ourselves." A moment later Black asked, "Did you sell out because you wanted to sell out?" Woolman replied, "We sold out because it seemed the expedient thing to do." "Why?" Black asked. "Because," Woolman said, "it would be impossible to compete with a line carrying airmail and it was impossible and has proven repeatedly, to make money in carrying passengers alone." The testimony offered by Woolman and others who had lost out in Brown's apportionment of airmail routes, combined with disclosures by those who had profited from his favoritism, soon led to a reshuffling of the deck. All existing airmail contracts, except those held by Pan American (the only international airmail carrier supported by the federal government at that time), were canceled in February.[22]

By executive order Franklin D. Roosevelt directed the Army Air Corps to fly the mails on an emergency basis, and military pilots commenced operations on February 19. Inexperienced in this type of flying, the army was at first not up to the task, and a number of crashes and several deaths soon resulted. On March 10, responding to a crescendo of national protest, Roosevelt called a temporary halt to the experiment, but soon ordered its resumption pending completion of a plan to return to the use of private contractors. While the air corps suffered more crashes and more casualties (twelve deaths in all during the course of the operations, five of which took place in actual mail flights and the other seven in training and ferrying missions), its general operational efficiency improved as time went on; this, however, did nothing to appease such prominent critics as Charles A. Lindbergh, who continued to mount a clamorous assault on the president. Furthermore, the costs of the army service far exceeded previous outlays, making private contractors seem much less mercenary than some had been depicted in the Black committee hearings. In April, Postmaster General James A. Farley, who by virtue of his position played a key role in these dramatic and controversial events, called for bids on the various routes. He insisted, however, that no company represented at the "spoils conference" held by Brown, at which Eastern, American, and other lines had received valuable route concessions, could be eligible for a new award unless reorganized and "cleansed" of executives who had attended in 1930. Various companies were given three-month contracts in lieu of more permanent arrangements; some began operations as soon as the army finally terminated its airmail service in May.[23]

Woolman saw in these swiftly moving events an opportunity to reenter the airline business. Although he was slightly affected by the shadow of Farley's ban on those who had attended the "spoils conference," at which he had been an uninvited and unwelcome intruder, he was not deterred from proposing to the directors that Delta bid on what was basically its old route, won by AVCO in 1930. Delta did not have to reorganize under the Farley scheme, for in 1934 it was operating under a different charter from that which had existed at the time of the "spoils conference." On May 22 the board agreed to attempt a return to airline operations, and Malcolm Biedenharn was dispatched to Washington with Delta's bid on route 24, running from Charleston, South Carolina, to Fort Worth, Texas, via Columbia, Augusta, Atlanta, Birmingham, Meridian, Jackson, Monroe, Shreveport, and Dallas. Eastern and American, purged of executives who had taken part in the "spoils conference" and with slightly altered corporate identities to satisfy Farley, bid 41 cents and 43.5 cents a pound respectively; Delta's bid was 24.8 cents. It thus appeared that fate might be going to smile on Woolman and his associates at last. Despite being the lowest bidder, however, the Louisiana firm had to endure a frustrating delay; May ended and the first week of June passed with no postal decision on route 24. Then, after what must have been an agonizing wait, Delta was finally awarded the coveted prize on June 8.[24]

Looking back upon the past few years, Woolman and his associates could appreciate what Thomas Paine had meant by writing about "the times that try men's souls." It had been a period of great stringency, reaching its nadir when Fox had decided to pull out of the enterprise. Now, however, the ordeal was about to end. For Delta, the way was clear to resume a climb to cruising altitude.

CHAPTER 4

The Return of the Airliner

FEDERAL APPROVAL of Delta's bid for an airmail contract on route 24 set off a burst of activity leading within two short months to the establishment of both mail and passenger operations. During the mid-1930s the company expanded its payroll, improved its flight equipment with the purchase of new aircraft, endured the trauma of a plane crash, and worked hard to develop a growing clientele. Although crop dusting continued throughout the southeastern states and parts of Mexico under Coad's direction, it was no longer the main focus of the company's activities and will figure only incidentally in the remainder of this study. From 1934 on, Delta's destiny lay with the growth and development of the airline division.

Delta's return to the status of a commercial airline was fraught with irony. In 1930 it had sold its passenger ships to AVCO; in 1934 American, AVCO's creation, in turn had to sell planes to Delta— five high-wing fabric-covered Stinson trimotors, Stinson-Ts as they were called, that it had been operating over the route from Dallas–Fort Worth to Charleston. Delta purchased these planes simply because they were immediately available and relatively cheap. Priced when new at about $22,500, they were sold to Delta for about $5,400 each.

Rather than attempting to retrain dusting personnel on any extensive scale to fly these planes, Delta began to hire new pilots from various sources. American itself was the source of several veteran flyers, one of whom, Charles H. Dolson, was gradually to rise from the rank of pilot to that of Delta's highest executive, a rare accomplishment in the airline industry. Many years later Dolson recalled that he and another pilot, Lee McBride, had been put on temporary furlough by American because of the 1934 mail cancellation. They were soon recalled, but it was too late; they had already secured free plane rides to Washington and had attended the opening of bids on some of the routes being reawarded by the Post Office Department. Standing directly behind Postmaster General Farley as the bids were announced, they copied down the names of the firms offering their services for the lowest amounts. Among these companies was Delta, competing for route 24.

Dolson and McBride went back to their hotel in Washington and wrote letters to all the low bidders, Delta included. After the company's bid had been finally accepted by the Post Office Department in early June, Delta offered them jobs. Dolson recalled that Don Dice, another former pilot in the American organization, probably had helped out by recommending them; he had once been employed by Standard Oil and in that capacity had taken part in business dealings with the dusting firm. Dice went to work for Delta on June 15, 1934; two days later, Dolson and McBride joined him on the company payroll.[1]

For Woolman and his associates, however, starting up as a commercial airline again was not merely a matter of purchasing planes and recruiting pilots. New facilities and corporate changes were also necessary. On May 22, 1934, even before a bid on the route between Fort Worth and Charleston had been submitted, the company's board had met at the Central Savings Bank and Trust Company in Monroe. According to the recollections of such stockholders as H. L. Rosenhein, the members had met only on a few occasions since the company had been reconstituted in 1930. Certainly the scope of operations did not require intensive supervision; the only summary business statements that have survived show tangible assets totaling scarcely $50,000 during the early years of the decade. Tax records indicate that Delta was still pitifully small in the spring of 1934: for the preceding year its total state tax had been a minuscule $25.59 and its parish tax even less, $17.80.[2]

In the wake of recent developments in Washington, however, change and anticipation were in the air as the meeting of May 22 came to order. The first item of business was the resignation of Woolman as an officer and director of the company; this move undoubtedly reflected the fact of his attendance at the infamous "spoils conference" in 1930. His presence there, though unsolicited by Postmaster General Brown, raised the possibility that he might be technically ineligible to hold an executive position under the new guidelines for airmail awards set forth by James A. Farley and soon to be formalized in section 7(d) of the federal Air-Mail Act of 1934. Woolman, however, did assume the title of general manager; despite its executive overtones, nobody seems to have objected, either in Monroe or in Washington. To succeed Woolman as a member of the board, the directors made a significant choice: Clarence E. Faulk, a Louisiana entrepreneur with newspaper-publishing and other financial interests in the mid-South and Texas; he was a potential replacement for Fox as a source of capital.[3]

At Travis Oliver's behest, the board passed resolutions authorizing an increase in stock from 5,000 to 8,000 shares at five dollars per share, to be sold for cash, contingent upon the company's obtaining the contract for route 24. Two thousand shares at five dollars each were set aside to be offered on option to "any person or persons who will assist the corporation in the matter of executing as sureties or indemnitors the necessary bid bond and indemnity bond" stipulated by federal regulations; Joseph H. Biedenharn and Carl H. McHenry agreed to perform this role with backing from Woolman, who pledged some personal stock that he owned in other enterprises as collateral for the risk they were assuming. Once again local capitalists had stepped into the breach when various surety companies had refused to execute the bonds. To provide further protection for the sureties and Woolman, a $10,000 mortgage was executed against Delta's total assets, with the Central Savings Bank and Trust Company serving as trustee.[4]

Shortly thereafter Catherine FitzGerald resigned as secretary and member of the board. She was asked to step down from her lofty but largely titular positions to make way for McHenry, who took over both roles; like the devoted company servant that she was, she loyally complied. Obviously not a militant feminist, she seems to have been contented with her subsequent appointment as assistant treasurer and her duties as Woolman's private secretary.[5]

On June 11 Malcolm Biedenharn read a letter from the Post Office Department announcing that Delta had been selected to carry airmail over route 24 and presenting the contract to be ratified. After explaining the provisions of this instrument, he was empowered to sign it for Delta and to execute a mandatory $1,000 contractor's bond with the federal government. The board then authorized the officers of the firm to borrow up to $25,000 on Delta's behalf in order to meet the new needs resulting from reentry into the airline business. The company's financial structure was further strengthened at a meeting on the next day, when its charter was amended to increase the capital shares of common stock to 50,000. In a related move, the board voted to increase the number of directors from six to nine.[6]

Although Faulk would play a much more active role in company affairs as president than his predecessor, D. Y. Smith, had done, Woolman continued to run Delta's day-to-day operations as general manager with the same zeal and determination that had seen the firm through the dark era just ended. No move of any importance was made without his personal involvement, and the organization continued to bear the stamp of his personality. One of his first tasks was to set up an administrative hierarchy corresponding to the company's altered functions now that the commencement of airmail and passenger service was in prospect. Pat Higgins, formerly chief dusting pilot, became operations manager for the airline, charged with overseeing the flying and maintenance of the newly acquired Stinson Ts. A traffic department was established to attract patronage and look after the needs of the traveling public; to head it, Woolman tapped Laigh C. Parker, who had just come to Delta in May from a position as district traffic manager for American in charge of the territory comprising Monroe, Jackson, and Meridian. To supervise financial procedures Woolman selected as his chief accountant L. B. Judd, a local resident who had joined the firm in 1928 as an entomologist but had quickly demonstrated a keen grasp of business affairs. It was a compact managerial team that rubbed shoulders in the small office at Selman, but one that was adequate to the needs of the fledgling airline while Coad looked after the dusting division.[7]

The flying staff assembled under Higgins continued to increase as other pilots joined Dolson, McBride, and Dice; they included such seasoned personnel as Tip Schier, who had served with a Pan American Airways subsidiary based in Cuba; Dick Conover, formerly of Transcontinental and Western Air; and Andrew (Andy) Dixon, also from TWA.[8] It was not long before these veteran flyers were taking to the air for their new employers. On June 19 Dolson and another recent recruit made a trip to familiarize themselves with the terrain between Monroe and Dallas, using Bernard Biedenharn's Curtiss Robin. The trip went routinely, but on a similar venture to Charleston the next day Dolson had gone only a few miles before he had to make a forced landing in a field near Tallulah, Louisiana. The same thing happened again the next day at the same place, this time with Dixon as pilot. On a third try on June 21 in a different plane—an open-cockpit Travel Air—Dolson and McBride finally made it as far as Atlanta, from where they subsequently flew to Charleston and then back to Monroe. Initial plans had called for each pilot to make a total of five round trips east and west from Monroe, but there was little enthusiasm for such a complicated procedure once the circuit had been tried. As Dolson later recalled, he knew that a mandatory thirty-day probationary period when only mail could be carried would be imposed upon the company by federal authorities before passenger service could commence, "so I intervened with C. E. Woolman and Pat Higgins and we cut the familiarization down to that one trip."[9]

At some point in June, as currents of excitement pulsed through the Delta organization and the city of Monroe made preparations to usher in the new home-based service with appropriate fanfare, a delegation of airport officials from Dallas visited Monroe and Selman Field. The Monroe *News-Star* warned that Dallas, already the point of convergence for four different airlines and divisional headquarters for three of them, was trying to lure Delta away from its northern Louisiana home. Whatever inducements the visitors had to offer, however, were to no avail, for Delta was still too firmly tied to the local scene to abandon it as a base of operations.

On July 1 the Monroe Stamp Club announced with pride that it had prepared a memento for the coming inauguration of the airmail service, scheduled for Independence Day: a triangular cachet enclosing the figure of an airplane with the words "July Fourth, 1934, First Air Mail" and featuring the name of the pilot. The inaugural flight took place as planned; at the controls of the seven-passenger Stinson-T, with its 100-mile-an-hour cruising speed, was Don Dice, who thus earned seniority over the rest of Delta's new pilots. The occasion was attended by officials of Delta, Monroe, West Monroe, and Ouachita Parish, plus a crowd of enthusiastic onlookers. The Stinson, bound for Dallas and limited to official nonpaying passengers, carried C. E. Faulk and his son Robert. After being loaded with mail from the Monroe area, which was stamped with the new cachet, the plane climbed into a blue sky and disappeared into the west.[10]

As Dolson later recalled, the eastbound flight that took off from Dallas later the same day made it as far as Birmingham with Tip Schier as pilot and was then canceled because of thunderstorms. In the understandable confusion that followed, Dolson, who was supposed to have inaugurated the Atlanta-to-Charleston run, ended up flying his plane in the opposite direction, to Birmingham, from which point Schier took it on to Monroe so that the westbound mail from the Atlanta area would not be delayed. Fortunately, the opening of the Atlanta-to-Charleston route had itself been postponed for several days because of uncompleted facilities east of the Georgia capital; on July 7 Dolson finally inaugurated that run and successfully completed the circuit back to Atlanta, thus marking the first full operation on route 24 under the Delta insignia.[11]

Delta's postal service was regulated by the Air Mail Act of 1934, which had become law on June 12. Repealing all previous airmail legislation, the new statute was designed to fix compensation in a more orderly manner while at the same time facilitating increased economic regulation of the airline industry as a whole. As a result of its passage, jurisdiction over carriers was now divided among the United States Post Office Department, which controlled contracts, routes, and schedules; the Interstate Commerce Commission, which had charge of rates and payments; and the Bureau of Air Commerce, which retained its previous authority over airway regulations and the licensing of pilots and planes. The act lowered the airmail rate from eight to six cents per ounce, limited all routes to a total of 29,000 miles, and made the postmaster general referee of all proposed mergers and transfers of contracts. Probably its two most far-reaching provisions were the mandatory separation of airlines from any association with aircraft-manufacturing firms and the creation of a special commission to study and recommend more competent supervision of civil aviation. The new law continued the recently awarded temporary contracts for a fixed time but also provided for their indefinite extension if the service rendered by the existing carriers proved satisfactory. On August 22, 1934, for example, Delta's contract for route 24 was extended to July 3, 1935. Four months before that term expired, the Post Office Department informed the company that it could apply for an indefinite extension and warned that failure to do so would throw the route open to rebidding as soon as the current authorization ended. Delta responded with an immediate application for indefinite certification, which was soon approved.[12]

Another significant milestone had been reached on August 4, 1934, when officials of the United States Commerce Department authorized the beginning of passenger operations, ending the month-long probationary period required under existing government procedures. Because of the length of route 24 and the relatively slow airspeeds of planes during this period, the company apparently had already decided to divide its system into two divisions, going east and west from Atlanta, for on August 5 two Stinson-Ts took off from the Georgia capital—one bound for Charleston, the other for Dallas–Fort Worth—to begin the new service. The Atlanta-to-Charleston inaugural must have been something of a disappointment, for when the Delta plane touched down in the South Carolina city it had no passengers aboard, though an account published in the Charleston *News and Courier* indicated that some travelers were expected to be picked up at Columbia and Augusta on the return trip. On August 7 the same newspaper reported that three passengers had arrived in Charleston aboard Delta's incoming flight the previous day and that seven had enplaned when the Stinson took off for Columbia on its way back to Atlanta. By the end of 1934 the company had attracted a total of 1,464 travelers on its entire system; it was hardly an army, but considering the limited carrying capacity of the Stinsons and the fact that the firm had been transporting passengers for less than five months, it was a fair beginning.[13]

For over a year operations proceeded fairly routinely, if not always smoothly. On the Atlanta-to-Charleston run, as Dolson later recalled, "passengers were scarce . . . there were no beacon lights and . . . no emergency landing fields east of Atlanta." At that time an airway normally had beacon lights at fifteen-mile intervals and emergency landing fields no more than fifty miles apart. Consequently, when the Department of Commerce eventually discovered that Dolson and other Delta pilots were operating "largely in darkness" on some of their runs east of Atlanta, they compelled the company to change its schedules to comply with existing federal regulations. Elsewhere along route 24, however, improvements were the order of the day. At Selman Field, for example, the parish police jury and the Monroe city government pooled their resources to build a new steel hangar, one hundred feet square. It was begun in September 1934 and completed by December; only the addition of lights and paved runways was still required to make Selman as modern as any field serving a comparable area and conducting similar operations. Agitation for these improvements was well underway by the summer of 1935, when Woolman and his associates were preparing to add night airmail service. Pat Higgins had begun softening up local resistance to making the necessary public outlays; in a February speech before the Monroe Kiwanis Club, he had warned that the city might lose its air transportation altogether because of the lack of airport lighting and inadequate drainage of unpaved runways. The requisite assurances must have been forthcoming, for in the following month C. E. Faulk announced that night service was to be inaugurated in May.[14]

The service would include an important new feature. Delta was for the first time in its history acquiring brand-new planes: two low-winged Stinson-A trimotor models designed for airmail, passenger, and express service on short-hop lines with relatively small airports. With accommodations for two crew members and eight passengers, each could cruise at about 160 miles an hour. This purchase and Faulk's accession to the presidency of the firm were not unconnected; the dignified bespectacled publisher put up nearly half of the $22,000 down payment that permitted these ships, which cost about $34,000 each, to be added to the Delta fleet. Faulk and Woolman watched them being constructed at the Stinson Company's Michigan factory while Laigh Parker was inspecting night-flying radio equipment in Chicago. Equipped with soundproof cabins and reclining seats upholstered with leather-edged whipcord, the Stinson-As were much more luxurious than their high-wing Stinson-T predecessors, but they were also somewhat anachronistic in being mostly fabric-skinned at a time when other manufacturers were introducing all-metal craft and in using three relatively small engines when the trend was toward the use of twin power plants with much greater individual capacities. Nevertheless, Delta was proud of the new planes and took pleasure in showing them off to federal aviation officials in a series of publicity flights over Washington, D.C., before formally placing them in service on the company's route system.[15]

Despite the May target date specified by Faulk, the inauguration of night service was delayed. Not until late June were all airports along the Delta route, except for the less profitable Atlanta-to-Charleston leg, provided with the equipment required by the Department of Commerce, and even then the installation of ceiling lights for fields east of Jackson remained to be completed. On July 11, however, the company did receive special permission to carry one of its first celebrities—actress Gail Patrick—on a complimentary night flight to her father's deathbed in Birmingham. Four days later a regular permit was finally received, and night passenger service began immediately.[16]

By this time the company's newest aircraft had already been pressed into service. On the morning of July 2, without fanfare of any sort, a Stinson-A, upon which Delta officials had bestowed the name The Georgian, arrived at Monroe from Dallas with Andy Dixon in the cockpit and nonrevenue passengers Faulk and Oliver aboard. Somewhat later, having been delayed by weather conditions, the other new Stinson, The Texan, flew in from Atlanta with George Cushing at the controls. Formerly a vice-president of Eastern, this highly experienced pilot had been swept out in Eddie Rickenbacker's rise to the post of general manager in that company. Signing on with Delta in March 1935, Cushing was destined for prominence within the organization. The arrival of the Stinson-As also heralded another new development: although they did not specifically require copilots and Delta had flown without second crewmen on all previous types, the firm had decided to provide them for the new craft, hiring men with pilot's training but using them mainly as handymen.[17]

On the night of August 14, 1935, at about 11:00 P.M., Delta's Stinson-A NC-14599—*The Georgian*—was cleared from Dallas for the run to Shreveport. The flight was listed on the schedule as "trip 4"; the pilot was Andy Dixon, and the handyman, or "courier," was Herbert Bulkeley. On board were two passengers—Birmingham businessman Paul A. Ivey and Atlanta grocery-store employee J. W. Thompson. It was a fine night for flying, with unlimited ceiling and visibility beyond a twelve-mile radius. In the calm darkness the three engines of the aircraft, equipped with Smith-Lycoming controllable propellers, were clearly audible to listeners on the ground. One of the new Stinsons—just which of the two is uncertain—had already experienced "prop trouble" a few nights before, but the problem had been diagnosed as an isolated instance, and both ships had continued in service.

Somewhere near Gilmer, Texas, close to the Louisiana border, the propeller blade of the plane's left outboard motor suddenly snapped and flashed away; the resulting unbalanced condition caused the left engine to wrench loose and fall. Down below, some people who were still awake on the hot August night became aware of the strange pitch of the motor sound; "the pilot was then in difficulty," according to the Department of Commerce's subsequent statement of probable cause, "and was at that time maneuvering the plane . . . for an emergency landing in a cotton field nearby." The doomed ship maintained its easterly course briefly and then turned left, bearing west, to make an approach to the cotton patch in a vain attempt to land. There were no eyewitnesses to the actual crash, though the sound of the engines was heard by several people still up at the moment of impact; then, almost immediately, flames lit the sky. A photograph taken in daylight shows a twisted airframe, like the skeletal remains of some large beast, and the charred hulks of two engines, the whole set in the midst of cotton plants just beginning to reveal white fiber. Curious folk from the area encircle the wreckage. Investigators from the Department of Commerce offered the informed guess that "the pilot, while attempting to complete an emergency landing, lost control of the plane due to the absence of the weight of the left outboard motor and resulting disturbed airflow over the wing." The missing engine and the broken blade were both discovered less than a mile from the crash.[18]

It was a heavy blow to the fledgling airline; Robert Faulk remembered particularly that his father wept over the loss of Dixon, for whom he had a special fondness.[19] Making the episode all the more galling was the difficulty encountered as company officials wrestled with the financial and legal ramifications of the crash. The chattel mortgage for the aircraft and Delta's promissory note were held by a Chicago-based finance company. Complex negotiations ensued as Delta attempted to collect on its insurance from a firm with headquarters in New York and at the same time to obtain a temporary replacement from the Stinson Company while a new plane of the same model was being constructed as a permanent substitute. For weeks an acceptable settlement seemed unlikely as Woolman and Faulk fired off a barrage of telegrams and received another volley in exchange; by December, however, an agreement was reached. The Commerce Department had concluded that the Smith-Lycoming propellers were improperly mated to the Stinson-A, and so the Stinson Company agreed to refit all of Delta's existing Stinson-A engines with a new variety—of a Hamilton Standard controllable type—mainly at its own expense. The settlement with the survivors' kin apparently was directly between Delta and these persons and was, in at least one case, in the neighborhood of $25,000.[20]

Whether because of the accident or the fact that the new Stinsons were already semiobsolete, Delta soon decided to acquire some really up-to-date planes. After it had phased out the old Stinson-Ts (in December 1935) but before the -As were gone (March 1937), the company switched to Lockheed 10-B Electras; deliveries began in December 1936. The Electra, an all-metal craft with two Wright Whirlwind engines, retractable wheels, and a distinctive twin-tailed configuration, could cruise at 180 miles an hour; it carried two pilots and ten passengers. This plane had been widely adopted by such larger lines as Pan American, Northwest, and Eastern, and its acquisition marked a major step forward for Delta. Years later Dolson commented that the Electra had brought the company decisively out of the barnstorming stage for the first time and had raised it to the status of a full-fledged airline. Faulk again played a key role in making it possible for the company to modernize, lending $150,000 for the purchase of three glistening silver ships. These new planes would touch down on solid pavement at Selman, for the parish and city governments again combined in 1935 to modernize the field, providing runways and taxi strips of asphalt covered with a thin surface of finely crushed stone, which incoming pilots could see for miles on a moonlit night.[21]

Unlike the old Stinson-Ts and -As, the new Lockheeds were specifically designed for operation by both pilots and copilots, forcing the company to add extra personnel. One of the early copilots, destined to become a veritable institution in the Delta family, was Fritz Schwaemmle, a former military flyer who had most recently been employed by Eastern, holding a variety of positions in that company until Rickenbacker had assumed command and dismissed a number of veteran staff members to make room for his own friends and associates. Schwaemmle, then stationed at Newark, New Jersey, took a chance and drove all the way to Louisiana to seek employment with Delta. His daring paid off, and this thoroughly seasoned flyer was too happy to have a job to complain unduly about the menial duties of a copilot, which included loading and unloading baggage, filling out countless airmail forms, and serving passengers box lunches, each of which usually contained two sandwiches, fruit (apple, banana, or orange), a small cake, and a thermos of coffee. Looking back several decades later, he remembered his early days with Delta as a time when relations with passengers were close because there were not too many aboard to chat with. He also remembered that the runs between Charleston and Fort Worth were often extremely bumpy because of the thunderstorms that were common in the Southeast. Fortunately, there were adequate lavatories on the Lockheeds, and the problem of airsickness was thus somewhat alleviated.[22]

Another new copilot, Thomas Prioleau (Pre) Ball, who ultimately rose high in the company hierarchy, came out of a barnstorming background; he had followed local fairs from one southern town to another taking passengers up for brief rides at five dollars each. Subsequently he had become co-owner, manager, and pilot for the Hawthorne Flying Service in Charleston, as well as airport manager in the same city. In 1934 he joined Delta as Charleston station manager. It was difficult to make a success in aviation as an independent during the depression, and Ball ultimately struck out in a new direction, driving to Atlanta through "the worst ice storm in twenty years" in the winter of 1936 to begin flying for Delta in the newly acquired Electras. Within twenty-four hours he had flipped a coin with another new employee, Charlie Ingram, to determine which of the two would take off on the morning flight and thus win the coveted seniority that would result. Ball called it wrong, but this loss was an untypical episode in what would become an illustrious career.

Until August 1939, when he won his captain's wings, Ball flew mostly on the run between Atlanta and Fort Worth, working under most of Delta's veteran pilots. The trip took six to seven hours, depending upon the total number of stops; occasionally he also served on the shorter east end of the route between Atlanta and Charleston. Electras were also used on that run, and the crews might alternate because of sick leave, vacations, and other contingencies. Ball came to know most of the company's passengers in the late 1930s, especially while serving as copilot. Like Dolson and Schwaemmle, he recalled that Delta's clientele consisted largely of businessmen, along with a few entertainers and people having to reach their destinations quickly because of family emergencies. In the virtually empty skies the planes could fly at almost any altitude, but on the eastbound runs they would normally cruise at 3,000, 5,000, or 7,000 feet while westbound planes flew at 4,000 or 6,000 feet. Occasionally a plane might detour via some out-of-the-way town if the weather were bad, but, given a mainly clear path, the pilot would fly a straight course. Rarely did crew and passengers see another plane in flight, except perhaps when they crossed the north–south route of Chicago and Southern, which flew the airmail artery connecting Chicago, St. Louis, and New Orleans.[23]

Whatever their individual status and seniority, as a group Delta's pilots were a colorful lot, who needed plenty of courage and resourcefulness to perform the tasks demanded of them. Flying over a region whose sudden semitropical thunderstorms were proverbial, they often encountered trouble coming in for landings at the small airports of that day, particularly at night when bad weather was closing in. Because navigational aids did not always function dependably before very-high-frequency equipment was introduced after World War II, pilots often had to "fly by the seat of their pants," depending upon landmarks that were not always visible when needed. Schwaemmle later remembered, for example, how difficult it could be to fly into Birmingham, with its surrounding hills and industrial smog, when the ceiling was low.[24]

When passengers were aboard, the crews naturally took every precaution to allay their fears, but sometimes, when there were no

The Stinson-A was flown by Delta from 1935 to 1937.

The Lockheed Electra, Model 10-B, flown by Delta from 1936 to 1942.

The site of the 1935 Stinson accident at Gilmer, Texas.

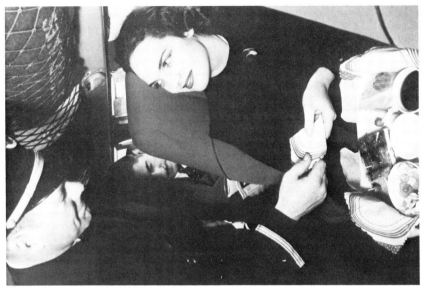

Copilot Jack Slaton serves a box lunch on the Lockheed Electra.

Captain George Cushing in the cockpit of a DC-3.

The DC-2-120, flown by Delta between 1940 and 1941.

Delta replaced its DC-2s with DC-3s in December 1940, and the venerable aircraft flew the Delta colors until October 1960.

Delta opened the doors of its General Office at the Atlanta Airport in 1941.

Vultee "Vengeance II" dive bombers undergoing modifications in World War II.

Stewardess LaJuan Gilmore on DC-2.

passengers, risks might cheerfully be assumed for the sheer joy of battling the elements. On one occasion when Dolson was flying an Electra on the westward run to Dallas, with a comparative fledgling named John Van Vuren in the copilot's seat, the last passenger left the plane at Shreveport, and the two men flew the final lap to Texas alone. Suddenly Dolson noticed a "mighty wild thunderstorm" to the northwest, and Van Vuren remarked that he had never flown into one that bad. Dolson's response was immediate: "Okay brother, let's go!" This adventure nearly turned out to be a serious mistake, for, as Dolson reminisced years afterward, "that was about as bad a thunderstorm as I've ever tangled with. We actually entered it at about 2,000 feet and finally got tossed out of it at about 7,500 feet."[25]

On yet another occasion Dolson was even more forcibly reminded that danger is an ever-present companion in the life of a pilot. On August 27, 1936, while he was taking off from Atlanta on a test flight aboard a Stinson-A, a mechanical failure rendered the plane uncontrollable when the wheels had barely lifted from the ground. Dolson emerged from the resulting crash landing with a broken back. Undaunted, he returned to work following a lengthy recuperation.[26]

Such men had no trepidations about standing up for their rights as they conceived them, as Woolman learned with displeasure in 1935, when Dolson and other captains were instrumental in forming the Delta chapter, Council 44 as it was officially designated, of the Air Line Pilots Association (ALPA). In view of his southern background and highly paternalistic outlook, it is not surprising that Woolman believed labor unions unnecessary in a properly conducted enterprise. On the other hand, Dolson and his fellow pilots were not satisfied with a pay scale averaging less than half that of larger lines in the industry; they persuaded ALPA to intervene when route 24 came up for renewal in Washington. Forced to acquiesce in a pay raise, Woolman nevertheless did not allow the episode to prevent him from recognizing Dolson's ability, as is clear from the fact that the latter was subsequently promoted to a succession of higher positions within the company. Nevertheless, as Dolson later stated, "I don't think he ever forgave me for getting that union started on Delta." In 1936 Delta management recognized a company local of the Air Line Mechanics Association International (ALMA) to bring that segment of its work force in line with those of other airlines in the industry.[27]

While the pilots flew the planes and the mechanics serviced them, the traffic department did its best to attract patronage. The varied, sometimes prosaic, but often interesting life of the personnel involved can be glimpsed from the Atlanta district traffic manager's files for 1935 through 1937. Oscar Bergstrom, who held the post, went to work for Delta in September 1934 at a salary of $110 a month. His main duties consisted of promoting ticket sales in his district; handling promotion, advertising, and public relations; and coordinating the efforts of the stations in his assigned area, which included the cities from Birmingham to Charleston. Naturally, he attended numerous civic-club meetings and traveled a great deal. Much of his time and effort were spent in securing the names of regular, lapsed, or potential passengers from Delta agents and other sources. In 1936, for example, the society pages of the Atlanta *Constitution* revealed that Jeanette Farmer of LaGrange, Georgia, was to leave shortly for San Francisco to take a cruise around the world. Going far out of his way to be of service, Bergstrom wrote her a long letter offering to come to LaGrange, which was about sixty miles away, to help her with her itineraries. Delta's "new, sixteen hour service" from Atlanta to San Francisco, with interline transfer to American for the Dallas–San Francisco leg, he assured Farmer, would enable her to complete the first lap of her "round-the-world journey in the most comfortable and convenient way."

Bergstrom's records do not reveal whether Farmer became a Delta customer, but his keen interest in her trip showed clearly the extent to which the airlines, increasingly aware that mail revenue could no longer be their main source of income, as it had been in the past, were courting any and all available passengers, regardless of their occupations. The realities of the situation were clearly borne out by the way in which Delta sought the patronage of the celebrated fan dancer Sally Rand. Whatever her reputation among people with traditional moral values, Rand nonetheless received a courtesy call from Delta representatives Bergstrom and Judd while she was performing at a "nude ranch" near Fort Worth. Later Bergstrom wrote to her that they were "disappointed when you could not accompany us to town for a bite to eat. As you know, Delta and its organization has always tried to give you the best service for your security and convenience. I hope that whenever you are traveling down south . . . Delta Air Lines shall have the pleasure of serving you." In reply, Rand was equally cordial: "I am most grateful for the service Delta has rendered me in the past."[28]

Together with his immediate superior, Laigh Parker, who had

organized the traffic department and kept a watchful eye on it from Monroe, Bergstrom did his best to keep Delta personnel in his district on their toes. In June 1936, for example, he complimented Frank W. Hulse, then station manager in Augusta and later to become chairman of the board of Southern Airways, on the way his revenues were holding up and expressed gratification that he was losing passengers only because of the lack of available space. Parker, on the other hand, was more critical and reproved Hulse at about the same time for failing to keep pace with Columbia and Charleston stations, each of which had recently produced business exceeding five hundred dollars in one month. "With a little additional traffic effort," Parker urged, "you should be able to put Augusta at the head of the list in June." Occasionally Bergstrom and Parker did not see eye to eye in other respects as well. In October 1936 the former recommended that when potential customers asked about return flights from Atlanta to Birmingham they should not be quoted the most popular flight but informed only about the one with the lowest load factor in order to build it up. Parker vetoed the idea; if a customer discovered later that there had been another flight at a more favorable time, he pointed out, it might alienate him from flying again with the firm. This concern for passenger good will, stressed by both Woolman and Parker from the outset, was to continue as a special feature of Delta's conduct of business.[29]

One of the duties that fell to Bergstrom was responding to complaints about unexplained cancellations of reserved spaces; occasional unavailability of weather forecasts, which led customers to seek alternative transportation; the presence of drunken passengers who were sometimes allowed to board against regulations; and even the unpleasant odor of the cleaning fluid used on the Lockheeds. Some of the complaints, he found, were based on misunderstandings and faulty perceptions, while others were downright unreasonable. One Atlanta passenger, for example, insisted that it was the company's duty to wake him at his hotel and to prepare him gently for the bus ride to the airport. Instead of being in his room when Delta placed a call, however, he was already up and in the hotel restaurant eating breakfast. When paged and reminded that the Delta bus would leave at its appointed time a few minutes later, he demanded that the driver wait until he finished his meal. The bus departed without him, but, after he had deluged the company with telephone calls, he was informed that the vehicle would return to pick him up. Still not satisfied, he demanded a taxi to take him to the airport at

Delta's expense. In the interest of good will, operations manager Higgins approved a refund for the resulting cab fare. Perhaps this response was being "generous to a fault," but it indicates the lengths to which the company was willing to go to accommodate its clientele.[30]

Delta was equally responsive to other complaints. One passenger who wrote that Delta's meals aloft were poor when compared to those of other airlines—particularly United—received from Parker a quick assurance that "our entire luncheon service will be revised within the next week or so."[31] But there were also compliments. A professor at the University of North Carolina wrote to express her "heartfelt appreciation of your service and the many courtesies we received from everyone in your organization" and announced that she looked forward to the possibility of flying Delta again in the future. Lee Forbis of Greensboro, North Carolina, whose wife had recently traveled on a Delta plane, reported that "in all her travels she has never been [better] taken care of or shown more courtesy than by your staff. . . . It will be a pleasure to us both to recommend our friends to your line."[32]

Credit for such passenger approval, but also blame for criticisms, logically rested upon the shoulders of Parker, the company's overall traffic chief. Certainly he cannot be faulted for laziness. With his hands firmly on the controls of the complex traffic setup, he traveled widely in performance of his various functions. One of Woolman's most trusted associates, he did not hesitate to offer whatever advice he thought necessary to the efficient running of the company, and he occasionally dispatched somewhat peremptory memoranda to Woolman himself. At one point during the hectic period preceding the resumption of airline service in mid-1934, he instructed Woolman to be in touch with the airport manager at Birmingham "without fail" about arrangements to use the facilities there, to write to Atlanta District Supervisor J. H. Bondurant about procurement of supplies and equipment required to open the Delta office in that city, and to hire an "additional secretary to report to duty not later than Tuesday the 3rd" of July. Once the mail service was underway, Parker wrote Woolman to "warn" him about "the heavy load that Judd will be carrying once the passenger traffic begins" and to suggest an applicant named Fred Dick as a suitable assistant. Woolman seems not to have been offended by Parker's occasionally blunt manner; he hired Dick, who later became a Delta copilot.

Before passenger service was resumed in August 1934, Parker

went up and down the line making sure that all was ready. No detail was too small to escape his attention; from Dallas, for example, he wrote to Woolman reporting about the steps he was taking to make sure that ships would be washed out and sprayed with disinfectant in the event of anyone's having suffered from airsickness. He also arranged for airplanes to be taxied back and forth between the storage hangar and the boarding gate each day so that "the pilots will not have to be running back and forth from one end of the field to the other," explaining that this scheme would also "enable the pilots to go to town in the same cab with the passengers." Several days later he wrote from Jackson to inform Woolman of his discovery that crews serving Delta planes could not put gasoline into the fuel tanks through strainers (to make sure that water would be kept out) "without standing on the leading edge of the wings." He therefore suggested that such men should use shoes with soft soles and also urged procurement of padded ladders to minimize the likelihood of damage. He had inspected the westbound plane from Birmingham, which had been serviced with unpadded ladders, and reported that it looked "as though someone had taken a rasp and filed the leading edge of the wing fabric." Woolman apparently appreciated Parker's constant watchfulness and promised to look into his suggestions about ladders "as soon as possible," but he also expressed concern about another aspect of Parker's recent advice, commenting that "our payroll for the month has increased at an alarming rate and we are going to have to be very careful of additional appointments."[33]

Although he felt free to give advice, Parker also constantly sought Woolman's reactions. In proposing names for the Stinson-As that would inaugurate night airmail service in 1935, for example, he informed his chief that "the idea of the 'Owl' and the 'Night-hawk' have been abandoned as per your suggestion, and in the absence of any final word or decision on the use of 'The Georgian' and 'The Texan' we have not gone into the naming of the two runs." This deference to Woolman's wishes extended even to relative trivia, such as the racks used to hold schedules in ticket offices; Parker noted that the cheapest cost sixty-six cents apiece in quantities of 150 or forty-six cents in lots of 250. Woolman approved naming the planes The Georgian and The Texan but, thrifty as ever, thought the price of the racks "rather high"; he suggested that Parker should "pass them up this time as I have some ideas which I think will work out O.K." The records fail to indicate what makeshift arrangement Woolman had in mind, but his correspondence with Parker shows again and again that he wanted a hand in all decisions large and small. Because Parker understood this point, Woolman placed special trust in him.[34]

As Delta's chief overseer of traffic and sales, Parker was also in charge of advertising and public relations. At the time when preparations to launch night airmail service were underway, he reported to Woolman from Atlanta that he had "made a radio talk today over WSB and had my 'pitcher' took by the Journal and Georgian Staff photographers." Apparently a recent photograph had not flattered him, for he expressed hope that the picture taken in Atlanta would turn out better than a previous one showing him assisting one of the company's early celebrated passengers—Eleanor Roosevelt—from a Delta plane.

Despite his many activities, Parker did not at that time rank among the highest-paid Delta executives. In 1936 Woolman was making $416.67 a month as general manager; Higgins came next at $350, followed by Coad at $300, and President Faulk at $250. Parker received $225, the same as W. C. Miles, maintenance superintendent in Atlanta. Some other monthly salaries paid by the struggling airline in those depression years included $60 to Frank Hulse at Augusta; $130 to Bergstrom in Atlanta; $15 to J. O. Bennett, a black porter who worked part time in Birmingham; $100 to R. C. Berry, a radio dispatcher in Shreveport; $100 to A. D. Clark, a mechanic in Dallas; and $160 to H. L. Stamets, a hangar foreman in Atlanta.[35] The rationale underlying these salaries is not apparent, but no surviving evidence reveals discontent.

In any event, Parker clearly earned his salary; it would have been difficult not to do so under Woolman's constant scrutiny. This brief overview of his activities offers only a glimpse of his many contributions to the company's early development; it could be extended almost indefinitely. One touchy but necessary task was lobbying with state governments over such matters as relief from gasoline taxes; early in 1935 Parker was occupied in trying to make such arrangements in Alabama, Georgia, and South Carolina. In late November and early December of 1936, he was in California, promoting traffic among agents of the various lines connecting with Delta at Dallas–Fort Worth. In checking out airline rivalry on the West Coast, he discovered that TWA and American were interested in "sewing up the Florida–Southeast travel" from San Francisco "so that United will not take it via Chicago." Parker, of course, was receptive to the idea, which would mean more traffic over Delta's own system. All in all, the trip was gratifying, and he reported to Woolman that he had "found the entire industry out here more receptive and more cordial than at any previous time." In Los Angeles he gave an open house for traffic bigwigs and "had a few misgivings when I first decided to have them all in together"; but he was reassured when he saw American's Max Kline with his arm around the shoulders of TWA's Oswald Cocke. "The party," he concluded, "was a tremendous success." [36]

Parker's optimism was well suited to the enterprise of which he had become so important a part. Although calling Delta itself a "tremendous success" at that point would have involved considerable hyperbole, much had indeed been accomplished in the short time since the firm had won its airmail contract and regained the status of a passenger line. New capital had been secured, largely from Faulk; capable assistants such as Parker had been added to the payroll; sleek modern Electras had replaced the antiquated Stinson-Ts and -As; a core group of capable pilots had been recruited; an unfortunate accident had been weathered; and the company was successfully maintaining around-the-clock schedules across the Southeast. If one considers especially that the nation as a whole was still struggling to escape the worst economic crisis in its history, with the end not yet in sight, it was a good record. But Woolman and his associates were too preoccupied to look back as they conducted the day-to-day business of running an airline. It would require all their attention to keep up with changes in the few years remaining before they and the country were plunged into World War II.

CHAPTER 5

On to Atlanta

URING THE LATE 1930s Delta consolidated the gains that it had made since winning its airmail contract in 1934 and established itself as a small but successful regional airline. It also experienced, and adjusted to, a series of significant changes. Responding to the development of new aircraft and pressures from the airline industry as a whole, the United States government established a new regulatory framework for commercial aviation which would have a profound future effect upon all American carriers, Delta included. Meanwhile, Delta encountered a number of internal problems as it sought to keep its equipment and facilities abreast of rising demand for its services. By 1940 these circumstances dictated a shift of the firm's headquarters to a new corporate base.

Because of the inevitable expenses involved in getting started, it is not surprising that Delta's airline operations were only beginning to show yearly balances in black ink in the last few years of the 1930s. Despite receipts of about $500,000 in airmail payments from the federal government, only the earnings of the dusting division enabled the company to show a modest profit of approximately $9,500 for the two-year period ending June 30, 1936. During fiscal 1937 the airline finally squeezed out of the red, posting profits of almost $5,000; the dusting operation earned more than three times that amount. In the following year, however, the tables were finally turned, as passenger, mail, and express revenues yielded a favorable balance of nearly $46,000 and the dusting side of the enterprise actually showed a small deficit. By the end of the decade the transition was complete. Airline earnings of $51,000 far outstripped the $16,594 profit from agricultural spraying in fiscal 1939.[1] (For these and other statistics on Delta's growth during the period, see Appendix 1.)

Rising passenger demand offers a clue to the airline's gradual upward trend in profits. In fiscal 1935, 4,104 people traveled aboard the company's orange-and-blue Stinson-T planes; this figure rose to 8,357 in fiscal 1936, during which the company introduced the Stinson-A. Despite the switch to the more modern all-metal Lockheed Electras, enplanements climbed only slowly to 11,519 in fiscal 1937, but this lag was perhaps traceable to the deep business recession of that year and also to a series of fatal air crashes that received headlines (though none involved Delta) and dampened public enthusiasm for flying. The upward trend was intensified in fiscal 1938, however, as 19,480 people boarded Delta's ships; two years later, by the end of fiscal 1940, the figure had jumped to 40,068. Year by year, passenger revenue came closer to equaling mail payments and finally exceeded them in fiscal 1940, when the company grossed $455,920 from fare-paying travelers, compared to $424,449 from the postal authorities.[2] (See Appendix 1.)

A passenger who boarded Delta's daily flight 2 at Fort Worth in the late 1930s would depart at 9:20 A.M. central time. If his destination happened to be Atlanta, he would arrive there at 5:10 P.M. eastern time, after having stopped at six intermediate points along the route. The one-way fare was $38.50, a round trip $69.30. In his seat pocket the traveler would find a variety of reading materials, courtesy of Texaco, which provided Delta's aviation fuel and lubricating oils. Some of them, like a booklet entitled *Welcome Aboard*, quite naturally reflected the interests of the donor: "The smooth, stable motion of an air-liner in flight gives a pleasing sensation of comfort and security. . . . Equally conducive to a relaxed frame of mind is the knowledge that the ship's engines, whose roar outside has been dulled to a purring in the sound-treated cabin, are fully and effectively lubricated at all times." Also included was a reprinted article from the *Saturday Evening Post*, explaining in detail how a modern passenger plane flew safely, scientifically, and dependably between points many hundreds of miles apart with the aid of sophisticated instrumentation and the most up-to-date communications devices.

After reading these materials the reassured passenger could relax with a crossword puzzle, again provided by Texaco. Three across, reflecting this, required a nine-letter synonym for "lightning-action gasoline" (Fire Chief), and forty-six down demanded a six-letter answer to the question "What chassis lubricant lasts twice as long?" (Marfak). If one of the passenger's children had come along for the trip, he could amuse himself by playing with a paper doll of banjo-eyed Eddie Cantor clutching a placard advertising his radio show, *Texaco Town*, aired every Sunday night over the Columbia network. Meanwhile, the passenger could follow the progress of the flight by referring to a detailed map of Delta's Trans-Southern Route or check his schedule for information about the various lines to which the company offered connecting service: Braniff, Chicago and Southern, Eastern, and American. Upon arriving at Atlanta, for example, he might transfer to an Eastern flight bound for Washington, D.C., or New York City.[3]

Delta's traffic division continued to work hard to attract passengers and promote the company's reputation as a progressive, successful enterprise. In April 1938, for example, Parker held open house at the Southeastern Aviation Conference in Montgomery; his expense account totaled $75.98 for such items as "6 quarts Rittenhouse Rye at $1.70 per Qt.—$10.20 . . . 10 cases (1 doz. to case) Sparkling Water at .80—$8.00 . . . 34 dozen hors d'oeuvres at $.75 per dozen—$25.50 . . . 4 porters at .25 each (setting up ballroom)— $1.00; 4 bar boys (3 at $1.00 each—1 at $2.00)—$5.00." Later that year Parker received a gratifying letter from Wayne Parrish, editor of the influential journal *American Aviation*. Parrish expressed appreciation for the hospitality he had received during a recent visit to Monroe and stated his admiration for Delta's "whole set-up," about which he intended to write a series of articles in his magazine. He became a warm friend of Woolman and for many years heaped praise upon Delta in his columns and editorials—nationwide publicity of a type that money could not buy. As the company became increasingly better known, Parker's appointment calendar attested to its growing status; by the early 1940s he was being forced to turn down speaking engagements because he could not accommodate all the opportunities that came his way. By that time his many services to the firm had earned him promotion to vice-president in charge of traffic and a seat on the board of directors.[4]

As the company spread its wings, an opportunity arose which, had events proceeded differently, might have transformed its own development and significantly altered the subsequent history of American commercial aviation. In 1938, bowing to federal regulations requiring separation of corporate ownership in air transport and the manufacture of aircraft components, General Motors agreed to surrender its controlling interest in Eastern Air Lines. In his autobiography Eddie Rickenbacker, then Eastern's general manager, later described how automobile-rental magnate John Hertz was granted an option to acquire control of the line for $3 million, only to have GM board chairman Alfred Sloan relent, at Rickenbacker's behest, and give the latter a chance to enter the bidding. Rickenbacker finally managed to organize sufficient financial backing to prevail

over Hertz, thus laying the foundations for a career at the helm of
Eastern that was to become legendary throughout the industry.
According to the recollections of Charles Dolson and veteran Delta
engineer Arthur Ford, however, there was yet another figure angling
for control of Eastern Air Lines at the time. This was Delta's own
president, C. E. Faulk, who offered approximately $3 million after
learning of GM's desire to unload. Learning about Faulk's move,
Rickenbacker allegedly used it to impress upon his business contacts Eastern's intrinsic value, thus winning the backing that ultimately decided the issue. In view of the bitter competition that was
to develop between Delta and Eastern in later years, it is interesting
to speculate how different the future of the two firms would have
been had Faulk been able to unite them.[5]

The same year, 1938, did produce a piece of federal regulatory
legislation that vitally affected the development of Delta and every
other American airline. Partly because of the overlapping jurisdic-
tions that it had created, the Air Mail Act of 1934 had failed to bring
order out of the chaos that had followed the Black committee hearings and the fiasco of the army's airborne postal service. In addition
to the problem of divided control, there had been a tendency toward
overstringent regulation, as if Washington were determined to ensure that no echo of the Brown era would be heard, whatever the
other unfortunate consequences. A series of fatal crashes in the mid-
1930s, one involving the death of a United States senator, Bronson
Cutting, had shaken public confidence in air travel, and a severe recession in 1937 and 1938 had further impaired the financial structure of many carriers. Wanting to be delivered from the control of
the Post Office Department, representatives of the airline industry,
acting through their collective instrument, the Air Transport Association, worked to secure what would amount to a new federal
charter for commercial aviation—one that would protect the interests of existing carriers and promote their future development. Contributing to the urgency of the situation was the appearance of the
Douglas DC-3, the first airliner capable of earning profits by carrying passengers alone. Up to this time, an airmail contract had been
an indispensable condition for survival in the industry; now, any
interloper with sufficient capital to purchase DC-3s could threaten
existing trunklines.[6]

Since the debacle of 1934 President Roosevelt himself had been
understandably hesitant to promote further change in the industry,
but he and other government officials ultimately were persuaded to

accept the need for new legislation. The Civil Aeronautics Act of August 22, 1938, sponsored by Senator Pat McCarran and Representative Clarence Lea, superseded all previous laws affecting the airline industry. Under the new statute, perhaps the most important in the entire history of American aviation, the regulation of air transportation fell to a tripartite agency known as the Civil Aeronautics Authority (CAA), composed of a five-member board appointed to formulate and oversee the execution of policies involving safety and economic development; an administrator charged with promoting air commerce, regulating air traffic, and establishing airways; and an independent Air Safety Board, charged with investigating airplane accidents and suggesting safety procedures.[7]

The new legislation guaranteed previously operating airlines reauthorization to conduct business over their former routes in the form of certificates of public convenience and necessity (CPCN), to be issued by the CAA. In order to retain these, carriers had to furnish evidence of satisfactory performance during a "grandfather" period from May 14 to August 22, 1938; this, however, was basically a pro forma procedure. On September 23, 1938, Delta applied for a permanent CPCN for route 24. After hearings by the CAA, it became the first airline to win reauthorization, on February 25, 1939.[8]

In 1940, using powers granted to him under a highly controversial governmental reorganization act passed during the preceding year, President Roosevelt revamped the tripartite system established by the Civil Aeronautics Act. Under the new arrangement the old Civil Aeronautics Authority was replaced by a Civil Aeronautics Board (CAB) which exercised both economic regulatory functions and the powers previously held by the Air Safety Board. An administrator of civil aeronautics, reporting to an assistant secretary of commerce, was entrusted with various responsibilities including oversight of the federal airways system, the development of airports, the issuing of airworthiness certificates for aircraft, and the certification of pilots. As a quasi-legislative and judicial body, the CAB was responsible to the Congress, though for housekeeping purposes it was placed in the Department of Commerce. The operations of the administrator of civil aeronautics, however, now fell squarely within the executive branch of the government. The new system was vigorously assailed by critics in Congress, the media, and the airline industry itself, but the president, who had been trying for years to bring independent regulatory agencies under a greater degree of administrative supervision and believed that the tripartite aviation

DELTA ROUTE SYSTEM
1938
(CONFIRMED BY "GRANDFATHER" AWARD,
FEBRUARY 25, 1939)

scheme of 1938 was too complex to work properly, was adamant. In any case, the plan he established was to continue in effect without significant alteration for nearly two decades.[9]

Although it would take time for the full impact of the new federal regulatory system to become apparent, its significance for Delta and every other American airline was profound. From 1938 onward, no carrier could operate over a given route without securing certification from the CAA or its successor, the CAB. Once service was established over such a route, it could not be abandoned without formal permission. No new carrier could enter commercial aviation without official sanction, nor could any merger between existing airlines take place without similar approval. All tariffs and charges for the transport of passengers and goods had to receive government approval, and various questionable practices, such as the issuing of rebates, were expressly prohibited. The manner in which the business affairs of air carriers were managed was subject to strict federal inspection. While certain functions, such as scheduling, were left up to the initiative of individual carriers, the overall result was a dramatic increase in the degree of regulation imposed upon commercial aviation. On the other hand, the threat of potentially ruinous competition was averted and fundamental ground rules were provided under which the industry could develop in an orderly manner. Whatever its drawbacks and disadvantages, it was a system under which Delta was destined to flourish.

While the industry settled down under its new governmental charter, Delta carried out related internal adjustments. In 1938, for example, to insure full compliance with emerging federal regulatory criteria, the company set up a more highly structured system of pilot training headed by the veteran George Cushing, who was designated chief pilot. As Dolson later recalled, Cushing "worked very hard at setting up a pilot training program and administering it . . . he contributed a lot toward upgrading the proficiency of the Delta pilot group." The value of such work was indicated by the fact that the company maintained an excellent safety record throughout the late 1930s and early 1940s, suffering no fatal accidents; in this respect it surpassed the performance of the industry as a whole, which underwent a round of fatal crashes in 1940 and early 1941. Delta did, however, have one close call on December 22, 1939, when the firm's ship 22, an Electra, made a difficult but successful landing at Shreveport in a driving rain. As the plane taxied toward the terminal at five miles per hour, pilot Lee McBride applied his right wheel brake and speeded up the engines to swing it to the right and position it in front of the main building. The wheels skidded on soaked grass, and the craft lurched into a forty-foot radio antenna. The jolt sent McBride's head through the side cockpit window, fortunately with only minimal injuries. One passenger, a noted radiologist, suffered a bruised side; damage to the Electra amounted to about $10,000. The accident was directly attributable to the fact that the Shreveport field, alone among those served by Delta at this time, had no paved runways. Unlike the old Stinsons, the heavier planes that had now become common throughout the industry required firm surfaces.[10]

Delta once again moved to update its fleet. In 1939, responding to increasing passenger demand, Woolman and other company officials concluded that the firm needed larger aircraft. Although the Lockheed Electra had represented a great advance over previous Delta equipment, it was not fully competitive with other available models, such as the Boeing 247 and the Douglas DC-2 and DC-3. Accordingly, Delta purchased four DC-2s from American early in 1940 and placed them in service on the daytime flight between Atlanta and Fort Worth. A sleek twin-engine model that the Douglas Aircraft Company had introduced for the first time in 1934, the DC-2 was larger and somewhat faster than the Electra, and it could accommodate fourteen passengers instead of the Lockheed's capacity of ten. As in the case of the Stinson-A, however, it was already semiobsolete when Delta acquired it and would soon be phased out in favor of its much-improved successor, the legendary Douglas DC-3.[11]

With the DC-2, Delta also introduced its first female cabin attendants who, as on other airlines at the time, had to be registered nurses. The first group went into training under the direction of Delta's pioneer stewardess, Laura Wizark, who had held a similar position with American; the new stewardesses were in service by March 1940. One member of this pioneer contingent, Birdie Perkins, had been assistant night supervisor of nurses at the South Highland Infirmary in Birmingham, Alabama. Though her recently-widowed mother begged her not to go into a new and unusual occupation that looked somewhat dangerous, Perkins was lured chiefly by a prospective salary of $110 a month, compared to a previous $60. She met the requirement of being unmarried, but barely squeezed under the cutoff age limit of twenty-six years. Hired in February 1940, she began her training under Laura Wizark after receiving a physical examination and a fitting for uniforms—navy blue for the winter, beige for warm weather. Years later, she recalled that the two-week training regimen included instruction in food service, ticketing, scheduling, passenger relations, and meteorology; in addition, there was a requirement that each trainee had to learn to make—at least on paper—an instrument landing approach. The trainees faced a probationary period of six months and were warned that making passengers angry meant immediate dismissal.

Delta was following an industry trend in employing female cabin attendants; the newer aircraft being introduced by American carriers were designed for third crew members, and copilots could no longer perform double duty as stewards. The hiring of stewardesses was also well calculated to appeal to the wives of businessmen, who constituted the majority of Delta's revenue passengers before World War II, just as they did with other trunklines. Should their spouses have chronic health problems or become sick in flight, such women were reassured in advance by the presence of a registered nurse. Potential health emergencies were not the only reason that Delta and other airlines at first required stewardesses to have nursing qualifications; it was also found that highly disciplined people were essential in the sensitive area of passenger relations.

After completing her training, Perkins was tapped for the flight marking the inauguration of Delta's new stewardess service from Atlanta west, with Wizark and Woolman aboard. The other inaugural flight from Dallas–Fort Worth east was served, quite appropriately, by a Texas-born stewardess, LaJuan Gilmore. Tension was compounded on the scheduled inaugural day, March 15, when the engines of the Atlanta DC-2 failed to warm up, forcing a postponement. Charles Dolson remembered that the Texas plane, which he was to fly, got bogged down the same day in CAA red tape, forcing abandonment of the flight. At the Atlanta airport, an hour before the rescheduled inaugural flight on March 16, flight dispatcher Alex Rainouard took Perkins aside and told her that he had arranged for her to be the first stewardess to fly for Delta, but at that moment she was too keyed up to appreciate the significance of seniority. With George Shealy at the controls, the nearly full DC-2 was airborne on schedule, ten minutes before the Texas stewardess took off from Fort Worth. Perkins was so jittery during the flight that Wizark finally left the plane at Shreveport to ease the pressure. Nevertheless, Perkins performed her duties successfully and felt like a seasoned veteran by the time the plane made its final touchdown at Fort Worth and she could relax before the next day's return flight to Atlanta. She later recalled that in contrast to the 1970s, when flight attendants and pilots are given accommodations in the same motels, Delta stewardesses in the 1930s were housed in one hotel and pilots in another—presumably to protect the virtue of the former.

The new stewardesses quickly found that their jobs offered something less than constant glamour. In a day of nonpressurized cabins and relatively slow airspeeds, the crews were exhausted after a DC-2's normal five-hour flight between Atlanta and Fort Worth. On the short hop from Atlanta to Birmingham, which took approximately fifty-nine minutes, box lunches only were served because the cabin had to be tidy on arrival, but even so the flight attendants had to rush to serve the meals and clean things up. On longer flights the passengers were generally served ham, potato soufflé, and thermoses of coffee. Although most of the passengers were businessmen, women were not rare and children often traveled. (Eight years was then the minimum age at which the company allowed children to travel alone.) At this time alcoholic beverages were not allowed on board; looking back three decades later, Perkins believed that this ban explained the differences between the more easily pacified passengers who flew in the early years of her career and those who came along in the postwar period. She pointed out, however, that some passengers of the earlier era did try to "sneak a nip" from time to time from flasks inside their shirts. Only once, however, did she have to ask a captain to turn back to the last stop and have a drunken passenger ejected.[12]

While the stewardesses became accustomed to their new routines, Delta updated its contracts with the unions representing its pilots and mechanics. On June 1, 1940, management signed a new agreement with the Air Line Mechanics Association; this contract, like another one executed two months later with ALPA, contained elaborate provisions for seniority rights, definitions of job categories, and stipulations governing wage scales. Each agreement was automatically to be renewed annually unless one of the parties gave notice of termination within the final thirty days of each year.[13]

Amid these developments, Delta neared a major turning point in its history. Despite the strong ties that bound it to the Monroe area, the company was rapidly outgrowing the Louisiana city. Notwithstanding the nearby natural-gas and cotton fields, it did not rank among the greatest southern industrial or commercial centers nor provide access to sufficient capital for constant expansion. As a result, the company to which it had given birth would soon be forced to move its main offices elsewhere; indeed, some shift in the direction of Atlanta was already in evidence. As early as 1936, the company's maintenance base had been moved to the Georgia capital, and most of its pilots were concentrated there. Operations chief Higgins had by that time established his office in Atlanta, and of the thirteen Delta captains and seven copilots, five captains (George Cushing, E. C. [Boss] Davis, Charles Dolson, George Shealy, and George Whittier) and three copilots (including Fritz Schwaemmle) had made it their home. It was a logical arrangement because Atlanta was the hinge of the system, where the eastern and western divisions met. McBride and Schier were among the minority still residing in Monroe; Dice and Ball were stationed in Dallas.[14]

Sentimental ties made Woolman and the other company officials reluctant to leave their northern Louisiana base. (In the late 1970s Delta's shareholders still held their annual meetings at the Central Bank in Monroe because of this attachment.) There was perhaps a related fear that the closely-knit feeling that was one of the company's greatest strengths might be lost in a larger community. Then, too, the very nature of the company's stock ownership limited its horizons. In its application for a certificate of public convenience and necessity in 1938, Delta presented evidence that more than 70 percent of its stockholders were registered voters of Ouachita Parish, Louisiana. Although technically a public corporation, it was actually much closer in style to a private firm: its stock was simply not offered on the general market. At this time, only 50,000 shares of common stock were authorized under Delta's corporate charter. As the certificate application showed, less than half this total had actually been issued by 1938; a large percentage was held by Woolman and Faulk, by the Biedenharn family, and by other closely related investors, some with preemptive rights. This situation reflected a cautious, though sound, approach to corporate ownership; among its virtues was that it rewarded Faulk for his financial services and compensated company executives for the frugal salaries that they had been forced to accept in times of economic blight. Certainly it was not an uncommon practice among fledgling corporations dominated by a small group of investors who wanted to retain control but promote a modest degree of growth at the same time. On the other hand, vigorous expansion would require much greater capital and a somewhat different approach. Such realities precipitated a series of interrelated crises at the end of the decade, making a change of head-quarters inevitable.[15]

In December 1939, when Delta decided to buy the DC-2s, it offered for sale, mostly to local investors, 13,184 shares of its authorized total of common stock. Because of the restricted nature of the purchasing clientele, the management did not believe it was making a public offering and consequently did not feel it necessary to register the issue with the Securities and Exchange Commission. Of the total number of shares issued, 11,587 went to directors, other officers, and third persons at $15 each; 1,597 were sold to rank-and-file Delta employees at $10 each. The company reaped $189,775 from the sale, which was used to purchase the four Douglas DC-2 transports from American. It seemed to be a straightforward and unexceptionable transaction.[16]

An Atlanta stockbroker, Richard W. Courts, Jr., was one of the few persons from outside the Monroe area who bought stock in this sale, which lasted until March 8, 1940. Courts, who had steered many of his clients' investments into bus transportation and was himself on the board of directors of the Greyhound Company, had become convinced that the airline industry was emerging from its pioneering stage and was ripe for expansion. Deciding to become an underwriter in the field of commercial aviation, he had toured the country to familiarize himself with various carriers. Because he had known Rickenbacker since the 1920s, he had hoped to establish a relationship with Eastern, but that firm already had its own brokerage arrangements. While looking about for other possibilities, Courts visited Monroe and was especially impressed with the hardworking Delta management. After taking a block of the 1939–40 stock issue, and unaware of the number of those who had subscribed, he told Woolman and his colleagues that he would like to serve as underwriter if and when Delta ever tried to raise major amounts of capital. He also warned the company that it should consult with him before it did so in order to avoid infringing the Securities and Exchange Law, explaining that many southern lawyers, particularly in small cities, were still not accustomed to operating under its provisions.[17]

In the summer of 1940, responding to increasing passenger demand as the prewar preparedness drive began to dispel the remaining traces of the depression, Delta's board of directors decided to purchase new airliners. Two options were available: six DC-3s from Douglas or seven Model 18 Lodestars from Lockheed. The decision

to buy the former type ended a prolonged discussion among personnel about whether the company needed the larger of the two—the
DC-3, with its 25,200-pound gross weight—or the faster—the 200-
mile-per-hour Lockheed. Delta's pilots, whom Woolman consulted
in the course of making up his mind, generally favored the DC-3,
which had been introduced into commercial passenger service in
1936 by American Airlines and had rapidly demonstrated economies
of operation unmatched by any previous transport plane. Although
its cruising speed was only about 185 miles an hour, it had a capacity
of twenty-one passengers, in contrast to the Lodestar's fourteen, and
its unprecedented dependability would ultimately lead some admiring aircraft aficionados to call it "the most remarkable piece of
machinery ever built." The decision to acquire it was surely one of
the soundest moves in Delta's corporate history, and the sturdy
ships were to bear the company's insignia across the southern skies
for nearly two decades.[18]

However abundantly justified this purchase proved to be, the
DC-3s cost a great deal of money—approximately $115,000 each.
Financing them was a formidable problem, but the company faced
yet another difficulty. At about that time it lost its lease on hangar
space that it had rented from Eastern at the Atlanta airport, which
forced Woolman and his associates to begin parleying with city
officials for the airline's own facilities. These negotiations culminated in an agreement on November 4, 1940, under which the company signed a twenty-year lease for a hangar and adjoining office
building to be erected immediately. The city of Atlanta agreed to
furnish $50,000 toward the hangar, with Delta supplying the rest of
a total cost which ultimately came to $127,250. The company also
consented to pay a rental of $2,500 a year, in monthly installments,
for the new facilities. Adding to the firm's financial straits was the
need to liquidate $145,000 worth of notes and other current debts,
acquire new radio equipment, and purchase a Link trainer to help
get its pilots ready to operate the DC-3s.[19]

The money with which to meet all these obligations obviously
had to come from somewhere. At this juncture the board of directors
turned to Courts and, with his advice, soon decided that the time
had come to modify the somewhat private nature of its stock holdings and to reach out for a significant increase in capital. The first
step in the process was a move to increase the limit of Delta's common stock from 50,000 to 500,000 shares, to which was connected
a four-for-one split designed to keep control in the hands of the origi-

nal stockholders after the new issue went into effect. Under this plan Delta's existing owners would wind up with 200,000 shares, and an additional 60,000 would be marketed at a public sale handled through Courts as underwriter. The remaining 240,000 shares would remain unsold for the time being, pending future contingencies. This move represented a turning point in the firm's financial development; the proposal was discussed and approved at a stockholders' meeting on September 9, 1940. At a subsequent board meeting on November 1 the directors took a further step toward going fully public by voting to abolish all preemptive rights of previous shareholders to subscribe to the company's stock.[20]

While waiting for the fruits of these arrangements to be harvested, Delta negotiated a $500,000 loan from the Atlanta-based Trust Company of Georgia, with which it had already established a credit relationship. This loan was granted on January 16, 1941, by which time the first of the company's new DC-3s had already arrived. In accordance with a shrewd but perfectly legal procedure, the plane was delivered to Cushing in Las Vegas in order to avoid California sales tax. As his surviving flight logs show, Dolson had his first instruction in flying the new plane on December 11, 1940, and was qualified as a DC-3 pilot on December 26. Together with Cushing and Schier, he headed west on January 1, 1941, to accept delivery on three more of the new ships and ferry them to Atlanta. "I was the first to get away," he later remembered, "and actually brought my DC-3 from Las Vegas to Fort Worth on January 4, 1941."[21]

Shortly after the beginning of the New Year another milestone in the company's development was passed. In a case decided by the CAB on January 30, 1941, Delta acquired certification for a highly important new route from Atlanta to Cincinnati by way of Knoxville, Tennessee, and Lexington, Kentucky, along with an eastern extension of the same artery from Atlanta to Savannah. Delta already had tried without success to add such cities as Memphis, Tallahassee, Jacksonville, and Tampa to its system, though it had managed to add the small Texas city of Tyler as a stop between Dallas and Shreveport. The firm's efforts to win entry into Cincinnati were bitterly contested by such airlines as American, Eastern, and Pennsylvania Central Airlines (PCA); the CAB finally split two to one in Delta's favor. The federal agency at the same time denied the company a further extension of the new route to New Orleans. A related move by Woolman to acquire Marquette Air Lines, a small line connecting St. Louis, Cincinnati, and Detroit, through merger, proved similarly abortive. Nevertheless, the addition of Cincinnati and the other three cities represented a major breakthrough for Delta, which had established for the first time a foothold in the highly populated Midwest.[22]

Everything appeared to be going extremely well, but a serious snag suddenly arose to threaten the entire structure that Woolman and his colleagues had worked so hard to erect. In his capacity as underwriter in charge of marketing the 60,000 shares recently authorized by the company, Courts discovered that the earlier sale of stock, consummated in the period from December 1939 to March 1940, had infringed Securities and Exchange Commission regulations concerning the number of people who could participate without it being adjudged a public issue. In addition, some of the buyers had resold their stock, thus unwittingly becoming underwriters under SEC rules. There was no implication that Delta had knowingly broken the law; its legal advisers in Monroe were simply unfamiliar with the technicalities surrounding the operations of a firm that was all too plainly outgrowing the city that had been its birthplace. On the other hand, as Courts pointed out, the SEC was sure to become aware of the earlier issue when Delta attempted to register the new one, and officials of the company would in fact become liable to criminal prosecution.

In this emergency Courts appealed to the SEC, which agreed that the Delta management had proceeded unknowingly. The threat of criminal prosecution was lifted, but the company was obliged under the amended Securities Act of 1933 to offer publicly to buy back the 1939–40 issue from all purchasers, whether of the first or second instance. The offer was to include cost price plus interest at 6 percent per annum from the date of purchase, less a dividend of a dollar per share paid in June 1940. Delta, having already become committed to proceed with its loan from the Trust Company of Georgia and still owing for other lines of credit endorsed by President Faulk, would have been in a shaky position if a substantial number of buyers had seen fit to rescind their stock purchases.[23]

Nonetheless, early in January 1941 letters went out from Delta to the individuals involved, explaining the situation and offering a choice between rescinding or affirming the original purchase. This letter was canceled a few weeks later because of certain omissions in the accompanying prospectus; obviously, the company's legal advisers were still having trouble navigating unaccustomed seas. A revised prospectus went out with a new letter on March 25; it gave

DELTA ROUTE SYSTEM
1941

each purchaser until April 26 to rescind or affirm. A lack of response by the latter date would be taken to indicate that the original purchase was to be honored. Fortunately for the company, there were no rescissions, and this first dark cloud evaporated. But another soon took shape: Courts experienced great difficulty in attracting buyers for the new stock issue. Delta's financial plight deepened: indications mounted that fiscal 1941 would produce the company's first deficit in several years, and representatives of the firm approached the CAB for an increase in its mail rate. Looking back many years later, Courts recalled that the crisis reached a point at which Delta faced being unable to meet its payroll. The storm finally passed when he succeeded in persuading tobacco heir R. J. Reynolds to take a substantial block of the new issue. The rest was subscribed by various other clients, and by May 1941 the worst of the crisis was over.[24]

It was during this period of challenge and response, marked by decisions to purchase new aircraft, complex stock transactions, and continuing financial crises, that the most significant decision of all was made. In May 1940 Delta's directors were still planning to renew the company's lease with Ouachita Parish and to continue using Selman Field as its main base of operations. Ten months later, on March 1, 1941, the corporate headquarters were moved to Atlanta. The minutes of board meetings during that period provide almost no clues to how this fateful choice was made, but the logic of events was inescapable. Atlanta's commercial importance and its role as terminus for the recently acquired Cincinnati route undoubtedly weighed heavily in the outcome; Courts later remembered advising Faulk early in 1941 that Delta must move to Atlanta if it wanted to expand its system. On the other hand, it seems likely that this sage counsel merely helped to hasten a foreordained move. The final resolution of the matter undoubtedly left Monroe and Ouachita Parish feeling like rejected lovers, and the newspapers of the area gave the move no special play. Local residents later recalled that most of the stockholders would have preferred Dallas as a company base, but the trend toward Atlanta was already unmistakable, and Woolman persuaded the directors to accept it.[25]

Significant personnel changes also took place in this period of crisis and decision. Laura Wizark returned to American after having built the Delta stewardess service; she was replaced by Birdie Perkins. Late in 1940 death by cancer took the veteran operations chief, Pat Higgins; George Cushing moved into the slot and was replaced as chief pilot by Charles Dolson. The new routes resulted in a shuffle among the company's flight personnel as some copilots became full-fledged captains and new recruits filled their former places on the right side of the cockpit. The runs to Savannah, Knoxville, and Cincinnati were successfully inaugurated and developed, with Pre Ball taking the maiden flight into the Ohio city. Then, as Dolson put it succinctly, "Things rocked along in pretty routine fashion until December 7, 1941."[26]

And so the prewar years came to an end. Once again the company had experienced perhaps more than its share of difficulty, and fiscal 1941 would produce a deficit of almost $86,000 (see Appendix 1). By this time, however, surviving crises had become almost a way of life for Woolman and the Delta family. There was also much evidence of positive achievement. The firm had a much improved fleet, including the impressive new Douglas DC-3s. A capable group of stewardesses had been recruited, and a well-trained cadre of pilots was compiling an outstanding safety record. Gross revenues for fiscal 1941 had exceeded the million-dollar mark for the first time, and the number of passengers had climbed to 58,208, up by 18,140 over the previous year (see Appendix 1). The route system had been substantially expanded with the addition of the airways leading to Cincinnati and Savannah. Above all, Delta now had a new corporate home whose location, population, and financial resources augured well for sound future development. In short, there was abundant reason for optimism—but suddenly a much more important crisis had arrived.

CHAPTER 6

Wartime Interlude

THE SHADOW of World War II had begun to darken Delta's future well before the Japanese attack on Pearl Harbor catapulted the United States into that awesome conflict. Late in 1940, while Nazi war planes were firebombing such English cities as London and Coventry, the board of directors in faraway Louisiana prepared to sell Delta's four DC-2s to the British Purchasing Commission. After the Douglas craft had departed for overseas service, Woolman was authorized to contract with the same potential buyer for the sale of four Lockheed Electras "if and when the company is able to replace same." But this second deal was not consummated, and the Electras never saw service with the RAF. Instead, most of them ultimately were sold to another customer, who had battles of his own to fight: Uncle Sam.[1] For Delta, as for every other American airline, the events of December 7, 1941, produced a sudden emergency situation in which regular operations had to give way frequently to the demands of the life-and-death struggle against the Axis.

At first glance, one might be tempted to credit World War II with transforming Delta from a distinctly modest enterprise into a thriving carrier ready to spread its wings in the period of dramatic growth that took place after 1945. Certainly every aspect of the company's business showed impressive gains during the war years, no matter what index is used. Between 1941 and 1945 assets climbed from less than $400,000 to more than $4.5 million, and working capital increased more than sixty times over, from approximately $50,000 to a sum in excess of $3 million. During the same period Delta accumulated an earned surplus of nearly $850,000. Company statisticians plotted graphs of upward trends in passenger totals, revenue miles flown, payloads accommodated per revenue mile, and quantities of airmail carried by Delta's small but dependable fleet of silver-winged DC-3s. New routes were added, and, despite inevitable wartime personnel headaches, the roster of employees grew in both numbers and experience. By 1945 Delta was a strong organization planning confidently and aggressively for a promising future.[2]

World War II also transformed the southern economy, enhancing the financial prospects of the region from which Delta's profits were mainly derived. Shipyards, aircraft plants, and ordnance works sprouted from one end of Dixie to the other, and a surge of growth took place in the manufacture of petroleum products, metals, chemicals, and a host of other commodities. The massive Oak Ridge plant of the celebrated Manhattan Project, lying squarely athwart Delta's air route from Atlanta to Cincinnati, was only the most dramatic of the many new installations that brought workers swarming into southern cities and war-spawned industrial complexes, thus augmenting the region's technical and managerial skills. The personal incomes of southerners rose by no less than 250 percent, fueling a formidable expansion in the area's purchasing power and capital resources. A different and much more highly urbanized South emerged during the war years, still somewhat underdeveloped by the standards of the rest of the country but nevertheless entering the "takeoff" stage that leads to sustained economic and technological growth.[3]

Delta was bound to benefit from these broader changes, both during and after the war. It also profited from the fact that the South possessed more military bases in proportion to its size and population than any other part of the United States, an advantage that would continue throughout the extended Cold War period to follow. Furthermore, like all other commercial airlines, Delta stood to gain from the high mobility of defense workers and their families, as well as from massive movements of armed-service personnel, which not only increased wartime revenues but also accustomed more people than ever before to travel by air, thus swelling the ranks of prospective postwar passengers.[4]

Despite these considerations, the importance of World War II in Delta's development, great as it was, should not be exaggerated or allowed to obscure the importance of underlying trends. For all its drama and undoubted bearing upon the future, the period between 1941 and 1945 was in some respects a heroic interlude in a story whose plot had already been substantially laid down. The acquisition of route 54 from Atlanta to Cincinnati, for example, had established the link between the Southeast and the populous Midwest that would dominate Delta's evolution over the next two decades.

Similarly, the decision to purchase the spectacularly successful DC-3 had inaugurated a pattern of aircraft purchase from Douglas that would persist well into the postwar era. Furthermore, the expenses associated with this move had forced a decisive shift in corporate financing, which significantly enhanced the company's prospects for subsequent expansion. Most important of all, Delta had already transferred its headquarters to Atlanta, a move with profound future consequences. The role which the human and economic resources of the Georgia metropolis would play in the firm's development was incalculable, while for its part Delta became a major force in the city's dramatic rise. From the beginning, it was a mutually happy relationship.

Delta thus entered World War II with the foundations for future growth already established. During the next four years it simply built upon them by making effective use of available aircraft and equipment, following a strategy of debt liquidation and other prudent fiscal policies aimed at eventual expansion of peacetime operations. Inevitably, adjustments had to be made as commercial aircraft were withdrawn for military use, key personnel were inducted into the armed services, and normal peacetime schedules were curtailed. In addition, a freeze on new route applications was ordered by the CAB, though it was removed late in 1943 and the company resumed its prewar policy of aggressively seeking to expand its system. Subsequently, as the government relaxed restrictive priorities, Woolman and his associates began to add more planes and to dream of a greatly enlarged postwar fleet. Early in 1945 they successfully accomplished a sale of new stock, which, together with the firm's wartime earnings, fueled an ambitious program. Without an appreciation of this underlying continuity, the events of the war years, important as they were, cannot be seen in proper perspective.

At the time of the Japanese attack on Pearl Harbor, the company had barely settled into the new office and hangar facilities that had been built with the cooperation of Atlanta officials. The municipal airport, then known as Candler Field, lay south of the city on a plot of land that had once been a swamp encircled by a racetrack. Established in 1925, it had gradually taken shape as a base for individual aviation enthusiasts, as well as for a succession of enterprises including Florida Airways, Pitcairn, Eastern, and Delta. Local leaders and the WPA strived to keep it up to date by providing hangars, paved runways, a beacon tower, and a cream-colored administration building, but the resulting terminal bore little resemblance to the massive complex that is familiar to passengers today. As Delta's new home, the airport became the focus for a variety of activities, most of which were connected in one way or another with the nation's war effort.[5]

In addition to carrying out regular airline operations, which were vitally important in moving military personnel and government officials, Delta contributed to winning the war by performing a number of special high-priority services for the army and the navy. In May 1942 the company headquarters in Atlanta was designated a temporary Army Air Corps Modification Base under a contract that remained in force for two years. The purpose of this program was not to manufacture planes but to speed the output of bombers, pursuit planes, trainers, and other military craft: in order not to delay production processes at the original factory, final changes were made, special equipment installed, and certain improvements incorporated at various modification bases. Often, for example, modifications depended upon whether a bomber was to be deployed in a tropical region or in a colder climate.

Working in a leased hangar across the street from the main Delta complex, under the supervision of chief engineer John F. Nycum, crews of technicians modified more than nine hundred planes. A good example of their contribution to the war effort was Delta's installation of long-range fuel tanks on sixty P-51 Mustangs, perhaps the greatest of all World War II fighter craft; the ability of such planes to support Boeing B-17s and other heavy bombers over Berlin and other German cities during the latter stages of the conflict was a clear sign that the days of the Third Reich were numbered. Another significant service to the modification program occurred in the winter of 1944 when a series of quick alterations were required on forty-five B-29 Superfortresses being built by the Bell Aircraft plant in nearby Marietta, Georgia. A team of Delta employees was "drafted" for the job and went back and forth every day between Atlanta and Marietta for six weeks making changes on the bombers' electrical and cooling systems, landing gear, and engine components. Delta took pride in the fact that its modification center was the last of its type in the country to be closed by the government, in November 1944.

Meanwhile, other Delta employees repaired or overhauled more than a thousand engines, in addition to large numbers of propellers and aircraft instruments, for the Air Service Command, using the experience and skills that they had gained from working on commercial planes to devise special techniques for rapid handling. An engine brought into the shop was systematically attacked by a team of mechanics, who stripped it down, placed the hundreds of components on roller-mounted racks, and completed the entire process of inspection, cleaning, replacement, repair, and reassembly within a matter of hours. For this work Delta won a special commendation from the government upon completion of the contract in June 1944.[6]

Delta was also proud of the teaching programs that, as a participant in the Airlines War Training Institute, it conducted for both military personnel and civilian pilots. Under the supervision of chief pilot Floyd Addison, replacing Dolson during his period of wartime service in the Naval Air Transport Command, such Delta veterans as John Van Vuren instructed graduates of army flying schools in instrument flying before they went on active duty, reflecting the United States War Department's recognition of the airlines' progress in ensuring air safety. Each of 123 officers received almost three hundred hours of training under the Delta program. A Delta pilot, Captain Edward F. Smith, designed an improved cockpit hood for teaching students the art of "blind" flying; fitting into the left side of a DC-3's V-shaped windshield, it resembled a venetian blind with the shutters arranged vertically. Combined with a cloth hung between the two seats in such a way as to allow only the instructor in the right-hand seat to see out, the device attracted national attention and gained Smith a citation from the company.

From July 1942 to December 1943, Delta's maintenance division provided special instruction for 252 mechanics recently graduated from military schools, where theory rather than actual practice had been stressed. After having had the opportunity to work side by side with veteran Delta employees, it was hoped, the trainees would return to the army with the skills "to do one or two things right and understand them thoroughly." The standards were strict, and the first graduating class of 25 men earned grades ranging from 77 to 88 on a 100-point scale after each had received about 240 hours of supervised guidance. Occasionally one of the alumni would write from a far-off theater of war to tell how valuable the training had been.[7]

Probably Delta's most dramatic contribution to the war effort was in transporting, for the Air Transport Command, military supplies and servicemen returning from overseas (including wounded veterans on litters) to various destinations under a contract that began in May 1942. Army cargo planes, one of them a former Delta ship converted for war service by the company's own mechanics, were used in this type of activity; the normal daily runs went from Atlanta to Dayton, Miami, and Oklahoma City, though special flights went as far afield as San Francisco, Seattle, and even Fort St. John in northwestern Canada. The planes ordinarily carried blood plasma, surgical supplies, C rations, small arms, and other military items; parts for the B-29 Superfortress were also flown from the Bell Aircraft plant at Marietta to a midwestern base on the Oklahoma City run. Some missions, however, were less directly related to the war, as in one emergency when an entire telephone system had to be flown to Baton Rouge in the aftermath of a disastrous fire. The occasions on which human cargo was carried revealed the most tragic costs of the war, as exemplified by a pathetic combat victim who had lost his arms and legs and was just recovering from a bad case of pneumonia as well. He weighed just seventy-six pounds when put on a Delta-operated plane in Miami for delivery to a hospital.[8]

Cargo services began to wind down in the summer of 1944, but Delta was among the last airlines still flying for the Air Transport Command when the army took over exclusive operation of its own routes in September. By that time Delta crews had logged nearly 2.5 million miles in this branch of operations, aggregating 6,632,975 passenger miles, 4,894,816,000 pound-miles of cargo, and 9,718,000 pounds of mail.[9]

Although with each passing year the dusting division figured less significantly in the total volume of Delta's operations, it could also lay claim to a part in the national victory effort. In addition to helping to sustain agricultural production through the eradication of pests, its low-flying biplanes were familiar sights in and around military bases in Alabama, Mississippi, Arkansas, and Louisiana, where they conducted extensive spraying operations for malaria prevention and mosquito control. Despite Delta's vigorous prewar efforts to modernize its passenger fleet, efforts that would be quickly resumed after 1945, Woolman remained something of a traditionalist about crop spraying. "The most satisfactory airplane . . . which is standard in our operations," he replied at one point to an inquiry from aviation designer and manufacturer Lloyd Stearman about the characteristics of dusting ships, "is the old Keystone Puffer."[10]

Induction into the armed forces affected every level of Delta's organization, including top management; by mid-1944 the firm had 187 stars on its service flag, 6 of which were gold. The highest-ranking company official to depart was Laigh Parker, who had been a captain in the Officers' Reserve Corps before the war and rose to the rank of colonel in the Air Transport Command before it was over. He saw duty in western Europe, Africa, Russia, and the Middle East, where he handled the air-transport phases of the Cairo and Teheran conferences. Ultimately he received the Legion of Merit for the skillful way in which he had put his Delta experience to use in determining priorities for the shipment of cargo to areas of vital need, serving as a liaison between the ATC and other branches of the military, formulating policies and procedures for the operation of newly established bases, and organizing a worldwide system of airborne evacuation of sick and wounded personnel. Correspondence between Woolman and Parker surviving from those years indicates how sorely Parker was missed on the home front. At one point Woolman complained that administering an airline operating as close to capacity as Delta was "is a pretty fair job in itself but the government work is taking about 80% of my time. . . . I wish you were here to help push and shove." On another occasion, after relating some details about his daughter Martha's recent furlough from her duties as a WAVE, looking "a little prettier than usual," the Delta executive informed Parker that "the air was truly balmy when we rolled home listening to Fibber McGee and Molly's program. . . . We only needed your presence to have completed the evening."[11]

Various Delta pilots answered the call to duty, among them John Henry (Luke) Williamson, a longtime veteran of both the dusting and airline divisions. As an army stunt pilot with Claire Chennault and H. S. Hansell, Jr., he had been one of the Three Men on the Flying Trapeze, who had flown with their wings joined together by thirty feet of cord and had done "everything in the book," along with "some things that weren't." Later, as a dusting pilot, he had terrified his associates by his willingness to swoop down to altitudes so low as to seem nothing short of suicidal. "Listen, Luke," a friend once told him, "you can do a good job without flying so low. Three feet from the ground is low enough." After having resigned a reserve commission in the late 1930s so that he could fight as a Flying Tiger in China under Chennault, he was finally sent home because the U.S. State Department deemed his presence detrimental to relations between the United States and Japan. He became an airline pilot until he was called to active duty in the air corps in 1942. After serving as a "light" colonel in troop-carrier operations in the North African campaign, he returned to his old stamping grounds, the Orient—this time at Washington's behest. While serving again under Chennault, he flew Vice-President Henry A. Wallace on several trips in China and was decorated for flying "the Hump" between that country and India. From China he wrote to Woolman in 1944: "As you know I am back with the 'old man' and I am sure glad to be 'on his wing' again. . . . Immediately he put me in complete charge of all his transports on this side of 'the Hump.' . . . I want to thank you for the Christmas bonus." The last was a reference to an annual holiday gift, averaging about twenty-five dollars, which Delta had granted to employees since 1939.[12]

Another Delta airline veteran, George Shealy, became a bomber pilot and in November 1944 accomplished a feat of a type that later became an almost hackneyed theme in fiction and television dramas: he nursed a crippled Boeing B-29 from Tokyo to Saipan after losing two of his four engines in a bombing run. A conference with his crew resulted in a decision not to abandon ship, and everything possible was then "chopped out and thrown overboard." In describing the adventure, Shealy later remarked that the plane was so light "it practically floated in the air by itself."[13]

By the summer of 1942 all senior Delta pilots with military experience had been recalled to active duty. Some of the departing pilots never returned, for one reason or another; old-timer Tip Schier, for example, died of a heart attack. But most came back, the richer for their many experiences. Among them was Fritz Schwaemmle, who had served as pilot and briefing officer with the Air Transport Command in practically every theater of operations until he returned stateside and became chief of navigation and briefing for the ATC in Washington. His duties, which included devising quick but thorough methods of visual presentation, helped to prepare him for his later work with Delta—as director of information services—after a severe eye infection unfortunately terminated his flying career in 1949.[14]

During the early stages of the war, Delta also lost many clerical and maintenance workers, whose services were hard to replace; management hired increasing numbers of women for jobs that had once been exclusively male. "Uncle Sam takes the man and Delta takes the wife," the company's employee magazine quipped in 1943 in a story about how Don McLaughlin and Raymond Graham, clerks in the Atlanta stockroom, had entered the armed forces and been replaced by their respective spouses, Anita and Hazel. Surprised observers commented frequently about the capable way in which women took over mechanical tasks. For example, an article entitled

"Engine Overhaul" appeared in the same magazine late in 1943; it was written by Dorothy Curtis, a Delta employee who reconditioned the ignition-wiring systems of airliners, army cargo planes, and other craft in the company's repair shop. Typical of the attention paid to this aspect of Delta's wartime operations was a newspaper article, "Atlanta Women Repair Airplane Motors," accompanied by photographs of female maintenance workers performing jobs once monopolized by men. "Of course this is strictly a man's field," the essay quoted Woolman as saying, "but women, darn 'em, have a way of doing things. . . . They're good! They have an amazing grasp of the mechanical, they have nimble fingers and they are capable of learning quickly." One such worker, twenty-three-year-old Margaret Mathews, had been spotted as a potential mechanic by a shop superintendent who admired the way she was running a filling station after her husband went off to war. Tired of dealing with customers who tried to wheedle more gas than their ration coupons would allow and were also careless about paying their bills, she was happy to turn the care of her four-year-old son over to his grandmother and go to work for Delta. By mid-1943, fully one third of Delta's employees were female, compared to fewer than 10 percent before the war. In the main reservations department in Atlanta, the staff was almost totally composed of women, "in contrast to a large majority of men previously," as the firm's annual report put it.[15]

In this and many other ways, Delta, like all other American airlines, adapted itself resourcefully to the demands of an emergency situation without parallel in the previous development of commercial aviation. Early in 1942 the federal government issued stringent guidelines that left the country's air-transport system in the hands of private enterprise but placed it in effect under the operational control of the War and Navy departments. The CAB stopped hearing new route applications. Schedules were ruthlessly pared, round-trip discounts and other travel inducements were suspended, and rigid priorities were established for different classes of passengers and cargo. To dovetail remaining schedules and maximize efficiency, timetables were no longer arranged for the convenience of travelers, and passengers often found themselves arriving at or departing from airports in the wee hours of the morning instead of at times to which they had once been accustomed—if they were lucky enough to get on a plane at all and to reach their destinations without being "bumped" at intermediate stops by travelers with higher-priority classifications.[16]

The key to survival for airlines lay in the effective use of available aircraft, particularly after the military demanded that 221 of the approximately 434 transport planes in commercial service at the beginning of the war be turned over, by sale or lease, to the armed forces of the United States and its allies. Before the United States' entry into the war, Delta had been operating five DC-3s and four Lockheed Electras; six DC-3s had also been ordered to replace the Electras and to accommodate the increased business expected on the company's recently expanded route structure. Shortly after Pearl Harbor, however, the government requisitioned one of the DC-3s, for use in military cargo operations. In the summer of 1942 the Electras were also taken, and by that time any hope of acquiring the additional DC-3s had long since gone by the boards. Under the circumstances there was nothing the company could do but make the best of what it had until August 1943, when a reconverted military DC-3 was pressed into service on an added round trip between Atlanta and Fort Worth and also over a newly opened route between Shreveport and New Orleans. From that point Delta received no authorization for more planes until July 1944, when it was permitted to add a sixth DC-3; a seventh arrived in September of the same year. These ships were not always easy to wangle; Woolman reported to Faulk at one point that "while in Washington we got the seventh airplane after quite a round."[17]

By the end of the war, conditions had loosened up considerably, and ten Delta ships were flying the southern skies, but for most of the period it had been a story of desperate efforts to keep a tiny fleet of planes aloft as many hours of the day and night as human ingenuity could contrive. Winston Churchill's famous statement after the Battle of Britain, that "never had so many owed so much to so few," had its own special application around Delta headquarters, as repair crews scrambled to keep the company's "big silver ships" in the sky. In 1943 a newspaperman captured the special character of wartime aviation: "Engines never wear out in an air line," he observed. "There won't be air line boneyards where the engines lie rusting in the rain as there are automobile boneyards where the hulks of worn-out cars lie smothered in weeds. An airplane engine never wears out for before long there's hardly any part of the original engine left—new parts are added as required, and the engine that speeds the big ships through the air is as fluid in its way as the changing air currents and clouds that are its elements."[18]

In this highly charged atmosphere, productivity soared to previously undreamed-of heights, as a vastly increased number of wartime passengers, made up mainly of service personnel and other priority travelers, competed for the severely limited number of seats available. The pressure sometimes became intense, as agents at the company's ticket offices could testify. On numerous occasions they had to telephone potentially irate businessmen to say, "This is Delta Air Lines calling. . . . We must inform you that the government has requisitioned your space on the flight this evening for priority use." Responses to this sort of news ranged from patriotic understanding to a petulant "Why didn't you call sooner?" or a threatening "Wait until after the war!"

For those who managed to hang on to their prized tickets a different type of drama might be in store. For example, on one night flight a seaman from the merchant marine suddenly woke up, "glanced out the window and went white with terror." Distraught, he went around the plane snapping out the other passengers' reading lights until stopped by a stewardess. Apparently "the motion of the plane, the sealike appearance of the air and the clouds outside, had made him think he was still aboard his tanker. Automatically he had blacked out the plane so that enemy subs couldn't sink it." Other, lighter moments revealed how the 21-passenger DC-3s encouraged emergence of a type of community feeling that is difficult to duplicate on today's giant superjets. One Delta stewardess, Dorothy Hills, described a soldier who boarded her plane with a huge lemon pie and insisted that each passenger eat a slice. Margaret Tucker recalled a flight on which the travelers included twenty GIs and a mother with "the most beautiful baby I ever saw." Several of the servicemen were fathers who had not seen their own children for a long time, and the woman's lap remained empty throughout the entire trip. One jarring note was supplied by a black USO official's complaint to Woolman about being accommodated in a lone seat up front. He was not satisfied to be told that this arrangement spared him possible embarrassment from the behavior of other passengers. Not surprisingly, in this respect the company's policies reflected its southern origin and route structure; they would change in the coming postwar era.[19]

Whether dramatic, heartwarming, or merely routine, most wartime flights were jammed. Statistics of passenger enplanements compiled by Delta's clerks and bookkeepers throughout the war years give a picture of impressive growth and reveal clearly why the company's financial condition steadily improved. In 1941 over 79,000 persons flew Delta, the firm's highest total up until then. Passenger traffic escalated sharply under the impact of wartime conditions, and in 1944 all previous records were eclipsed, as 164,287 travelers boarded Delta's expanding fleet of DC-3s. By August 1945 the fighting was over, and the mammoth leap to 274,823 passengers in that year must be viewed as partly reflecting a new era of peacetime growth; but it was also traceable to the large number of service personnel returning home and in that respect showed the continuing impact of the war.[20]

Even more significant are figures indicating how efficiently and productively Delta used its equipment, for, once basic costs were met, profits mounted rapidly with each additional seat occupied. In 1941 Delta was accommodating an average of 6.3 passengers for each revenue mile flown, and its passenger-load factor—the number of seats filled out of the total quantity available—was 43 percent. By 1944 its increasingly crowded DC-3s had an average of 18.7 travelers aboard per revenue mile, and the passenger-load factor had risen to 90.4 percent.[21]

This dramatic gain in productivity constituted the bedrock upon which the company's financial progress ultimately rested. Late in the war a report issued by the CAB showed that Delta led all other American airlines in making use of available resources. Its planes, for example, flew an average of 14:02 hours a day, against an industry figure of 11:39, and covered 1,903 miles a day in contrast to the industry mean of 1,793. By that time costs were mounting as new equipment was added and mail subsidies ceased, which made it all the more imperative to keep the company's planes in the air as long as possible and as fully loaded as the market would permit.[22]

Because of the greatly increased demand for transport and the reduced number of planes available to meet it, high use and productivity were to a certain extent built into the wartime situation for every American air carrier. Nevertheless, the unusual nature of Delta's accomplishments in this vital aspect of operations reflects something atypical about the company. In part, it is traceable to Woolman's managerial outlook and style; to an extreme degree, he believed in and communicated the need for a dynamic husbanding of resources, so that every Delta employee could see the relation between his individual efforts and the well-being of the organization for which he worked. As he ceremoniously retrieved rubber bands and paper clips in company offices or scavenged for safety wire and other small parts on the floor of a repair hangar, he effectively dramatized the crucial difference between using resources and wasting them. His compulsive thrift, unlike the miser's passion for squirreling things away, was not static but kinetic; it was deeply related to the impulse that kept a Delta plane flying farther and longer, on the average, than any other firm's planes—at lower cost and as fully loaded as possible.[23]

And it paid off. Like other American corporations, Delta stood to make money during World War II, which more than anything else finally pulled the United States out of the worst depression in its history. Like other companies, Delta operated under various constraints that limited its gains from wartime demand, and it derived only modest earnings from the services that it rendered to the government. Following a policy of making no excessive profits from military contracts, for example, Delta voluntarily refunded $64,250 to federal authorities in the fiscal year ending in mid-1943, and its earnings amounted to less than 4 percent of costs. Within this overall perspective, however, Delta could report with justifiable pride at the end of the war that it had achieved "one of the highest profits per ton mile of all domestic airlines." Additions to surplus over the preceding four years had aggregated nearly $1.75 million; allowing for dividends and other adjustments, including a downward revision of the amount that it had expected to retain from the sale of aircraft to the government at the beginning of the war, there still remained $847,823 to help brighten the postwar outlook. Equally commendable was the wartime improvement in the ratio between Delta's assets and liabilities, which amounted from 1.2:1 in June 1941 to a much more comfortable 3.2:1 in mid-1945.[24]

To some degree, Delta's improved financial position reflected a retroactive increase in mail pay granted by the CAB in January 1942, substantially augmenting revenues for this aspect of the company's operations during that particular year. The effect of this development, however, was only temporary, for subsidy support was soon withdrawn and mail revenue actually decreased in both 1943 and 1944. By the end of the conflict a typical Delta DC-3 earned more than five times as much per year from passengers as it did from postal receipts, underscoring the progress that had been made since the days when airmail alone made passenger service a viable proposition.[25]

Despite heavy losses through induction and the difficulty of securing and training capable new personnel, the number of Delta employees mounted rapidly in response to wartime needs. By mid-1944 the company had about 875 people on its payroll, in addition to 187 in the armed services, for whom places were assured upon their return from active duty. At that time it took about 111 people to keep one DC-3 in the air. Particularly hard to find and keep in the face of military demands were pilots, who had to meet stringent physical specifications and possess commercial licenses, instrument ratings, at least one thousand hours of flying experience each, radio-telephone operator's licenses, and familiarity with night-time operations. The company had to have ten of these highly trained men for every airliner in service.[26]

Five stewardesses were also required for the operation of each intensively used Delta plane. Company requirements specified that each cabin attendant must be at least twenty-one years old, from 5' to 5'5" tall, from 100 to 115 pounds in weight, in excellent health, and unmarried. In addition, each candidate had to have at least two years of college education, replacing the former demand for credentials as a registered nurse, and had to possess the characteristics of an energetic debutante. Those who made the grade were required to undergo special training, including memorization of routes and familiarization with aviation terminology, meteorology, and other subjects about which passengers were likely to ask questions, as well as instruction in the arts of passenger service, ticket handling, and record keeping. In 1944 the company announced the graduation of its largest class to date: nine young women, all from below the Mason-Dixon line. According to a contemporary article in the aviation magazine *Trade Winds*, Delta deliberately hired "sugar voiced" stewardesses whose accents were "as typical of Dixie as 'cawnpone,'" in order to enhance its image as "the Airline of the South."[27]

Keeping each DC-3 in flight also required about seventy ground-station and maintenance personnel, including station managers, field agents, cargo handlers, behind-the-counter ticket officials, and the mechanics and repairmen who kept the planes airworthy. Also in this group were skilled radio operators and a highly select category —the flight-control dispatchers, who were intimately acquainted with conditions all over the growing Delta system and had the responsible task of ordering changes in plans and even canceling flights when necessary.[28]

The company also estimated that for each of its aircraft it had to have approximately twenty-six employees in such departments as sales and reservations, accounting, purchasing, public relations, and personnel. Many of the sales and reservations workers were stationed in the ticket offices that Delta maintained up and down its network of routes. Mostly women, they made reservations either by telephone or across the counter, kept tabs on the availability of seats on various flights, and in other ways directed their "concentrated effort toward seeing that Mr. John Q. Public remains happy"— sometimes a tough job under wartime conditions. The accounting department, which in 1937 had been limited to three people, grew rapidly with the volume of wartime operations. By the spring of 1944 thirty-three staff members were needed to handle the financial accounts of the company, the enormous volume of clerical work pertaining to the military contracts, the preparation of official reports for such governmental bodies as the CAB, and the increasingly complex payroll, not to mention a bewildering array of tickets, flight coupons, airmail and express forms, baggage manifests, and refund claims. In addition to such longtime Delta family members as comptroller L. B. Judd, general auditor R. H. Wharton, and revenue auditor J. J. Medaries, its staff included young Ike Lasseter, who joined the company as revenue clerk late in 1941, earned a law degree by attending school at night, and won a promotion to auditor before becoming an air-force cadet in 1944.[29]

As a reflection of the tense wartime atmosphere surrounding many of the company's operations, a new department was established; it was composed of security guards, who watched for evidence of spying or sabotage and kept unauthorized people off Delta premises. "I must confess that I have not made any definite plans for my future in aviation," stated guard L. M. Hunt in an article that makes interesting reading in light of the Cold War developments and antihijacking precautions that were to follow in the years ahead. "Being strictly a wartime measure, I cannot foresee a future for our department in the company's postwar plans."[30]

The growing size and complexity of the Delta organization made necessary a more systematic presentation of its image to the public and also required increased emphasis on effective internal communications to maintain the closeknit family feeling that had been so much a part of the enterprise from the beginning. In 1941 James H. Cobb, who had worked for the Associated Press and been executive secretary for the Savannah municipal government, joined Delta to organize a public relations department. In addition to directing the firm's advertising, he supervised the development of a new in-house magazine which grew out of a monthly mimeographed newssheet, the *Delta Dispatcher*, conceived by several Atlanta employees. Like many informal ventures of a similar nature, this volunteer effort had been shortlived, and Cobb's department officially launched its permanent successor in May 1942 with a single-page fold-over pamphlet captioned "You Name It," offering a cash prize to the employee suggesting the best name for a company paper. From the various entries received, the name *Delta Digest* was chosen, and a publication destined to become a company institution was born. By April 1943 it was a regularly printed quarterly, and in 1945 production was established on a monthly basis. From the start *Delta Digest* made a noteworthy contribution to employee morale, and it was also valuable as a means of keeping in touch with personnel in the armed services.[31]

It was a growing and increasingly complex organization, therefore, that carried out its varied operations during the war years at the red-brick Delta complex and the nearby Atlanta terminal, with its Romanesque arcades, its "sturdy tower with distinctive corners of glass brick up all three floors," and its runways, from which about fifty commercial flights took off each day, bearing the insignia of the only two airlines to share its facilities—Delta and Eastern. Theirs was not the only activity, of course, for there was also the interminable drone of military aircraft over the busy airport and its adjacent "rolling suburban countryside," where pine trees and corn-stalks sprang from the "healthy red earth," as the Delta magazine described it. By late 1942 the $150,000 structure that housed Delta headquarters, only recently said to be "the most complete building of its type and the largest hangar in the Southeast," was already bulging at the seams, and it became necessary to make some additions. A one-story wing was built on to the southwest corner to provide more space for engine repair, and a two-story annex was constructed on the north side of the hangar to provide badly needed room for the fast-growing accounting staff and adequate washroom facilities for the ever-increasing number of female employees. As Woolman liked to say, "the only monotonous thing about the aviation industry is the constant change."[32]

Morale ran high, not only because of wartime patriotism, but also because of policies calculated to enhance employees' welfare. A Delta group-insurance plan that had been instituted in 1936, the first of its kind to make no extra charge for flight personnel, was broadened to include hospital benefits for the immediate members of workers' families. A credit union that had been organized in 1940 continued to function, extending small loans to employees (normally fifty dollars on an employee's own signature, with one co-signer required for each additional fifty dollars) and paying 6 percent interest on membership deposits. A significant innovation in the company's welfare provisions occurred in 1943, when the directors authorized a pension plan yielding retirement benefits to pilots and female employees at age sixty and to all other male workers at age sixty-five. Every member of the Delta staff who was twenty-two years of age or older was automatically covered after his first year of service. The general absence of friction throughout the organization was underscored by the prevalence of good relations between management and the union representing the pilots. Although the Delta mechanics had at first evinced little enthusiasm for their union, established in 1936, interest increased in wartime with the influx of mechanics personnel from the auto and other unionized industries. Wage increases were virtually frozen under wage stabilization, and the union "served more as a voice for the union than for the usual labor-management relationship," as Delta personnel officer Robert H. Wharton later recalled. Yet a new contract granting increased wartime benefits other than wage increases was negotiated with the Delta chapter of the Air Line Mechanics Association in 1944 without apparent difficulty.[33]

Continuity remained a strong feature of Delta's corporate management. In 1942 L. B. Judd, whose career was deeply rooted in the formative years of the company, took Laigh Parker's place on the board of directors when Parker entered the armed forces. Otherwise, the board remained in 1945 exactly as it had been four years earlier: President Faulk, Vice-President Malcolm Biedenharn, Secretary McHenry, Treasurer Oliver, and D. Y. Smith exercised general oversight in Monroe, while Vice-President and General Manager Woolman and Assistant Secretary Judd represented the active management. With rare exceptions, the periodic meetings of the group continued to be held in Monroe, even though Atlanta had become the nerve center of the enterprise; in this way the firm's ties with its place of origin were reinforced. Faulk and Woolman, who together held approximately 44,000 of the 198,384 shares of outstanding stock, were the dominant figures. Faulk played a prominent role in the development of basic financial strategy, but the conduct of day-to-day operations rested firmly, as always, in Woolman's hands.[34]

Meanwhile, in Washington, E. V. Moore continued to represent the company's legal interests and to maintain contact with governmental agencies. In addition to keeping up with the bewildering array of federal offices and bureaus spawned in the national capital under wartime conditions, he was constantly busy helping to promote Delta's efforts to acquire new routes after the CAB, which had frozen applications at the beginning of hostilities, relented in mid-1942 and consented to proceed with applications that had actually reached the examiners by the time of Pearl Harbor. This decision resulted in a reopening of Delta's petition for a route from Shreveport to New Orleans by way of Alexandria and Baton Rouge. Hearings on this proposed run dated back to September 1941; Braniff, Chicago and Southern, and National all were in competition for the award, even though the route permitted access to New Orleans only from the west. The company won a highly gratifying victory when the CAB ultimately decided in its favor early in 1943.

The actual opening of the new connection was delayed temporarily until an extra DC-3 was released to Delta by the army after military authorities decided that the added service would be beneficial to the war effort. Once these hurdles had been cleared, Delta was finally able to begin flights from Dallas–Fort Worth to New Orleans by way of Shreveport on October 15, 1943. Service to Baton Rouge and Alexandria was inaugurated the following month. As the state capital of Louisiana and a major oil-refining center, Baton Rouge was an important addition to Delta's growing network of destinations, and soon the company's DC-3s were skimming over the campus of Louisiana State University and the celebrated skyscraper capitol constructed by Huey Long. At the municipal airport, Harding Field, Delta set up accommodations of sorts in a small, olive-green terminal known affectionately to pilots as "the farmhouse," surrounded by army tents and ground crews noisily at work on fighter planes. For Woolman, who had once lived in Baton Rouge and had been associated with the university there, gaining access to the community must have afforded many sentimental satisfactions.[35]

Alexandria, too, was a worthy prize. A city of some 30,000 people, it was the trade and distribution center for an area with a population of more than 500,000, and the eight military camps and airfields nearby made up what was reported to be the largest concentration of armed-service personnel in the world outside of actual combat areas. Delta was the first commercial airline to establish service there. The local airport, where Delta occupied a tiny three-room terminal, swarmed with B-17 Flying Fortresses, which roared over the area on training flights day and night.[36]

The importance of these two cities to Delta, however, was vastly overshadowed by that of the bustling colorful seaport near the mouth of the Mississippi, with its Latin traditions, its French Quarter, its annual Mardi Gras, and its strategic location as the gateway to Caribbean markets, which Woolman hoped one day to penetrate. Not without reason New Orleans called itself the "air hub of the Americas," for it was already served by National, Eastern, Chicago and Southern, and Pan American; it was also excellently situated in relation to Houston, St. Louis, Havana, Mexico City, and other large urban centers at every point on the compass. Civic leaders appreciated the way in which Delta helped to fill in this radiating network of air routes, and newspaper coverage was enthusiastic when Delta officials arrived for a ceremonial visit marking the inauguration of service to Dallas and Fort Worth in mid-October. Despite the wartime atmosphere, it was a gala occasion for Woolman and his associates—including Faulk, who happened to be a connoisseur of such local delicacies as shrimp remoulade and trout marguéry at Galatoire's. Soon Delta was able to announce that it had attained the highest use rates ever reached on a new route, for flight 41 from New Orleans to Fort Worth showed an average load factor of 95.4 percent during the first two weeks of operation and actually reached a nearly incredible 98.8 percent for a one-week period in late November—an auspicious start for Delta's relationship with a city whose importance to its subsequent development was to be enormous.[37]

This new artery, however, was not the only prize Delta was after. At a meeting of May 31, 1943, in anticipation of the reopening of hearings on a wide variety of new routes, the directors gave Woolman and his aides full authority to file applications for whatever connections they thought advisable without seeking specific approval from the board in each instance. Armed with this wide discretionary power, Woolman created a new planning and research department under the direction of Edward Marion Johnson, who had seen prior service with Delta in 1939 as a marketing consultant during the CAB proceedings that had resulted in winning the route from Atlanta to Cincinnati. A Kansan who had been manager of the

New York Press Association, Johnson had an impressive background as a newspaperman and transportation analyst. One of the various posts that he had held was that of assistant to Joseph B. Eastman, coordinator of transportation in the early Roosevelt administration; this experience had given him valuable government contacts.[38]

After quickly assembling a five-member staff, Johnson plunged into the task of preparing plans, charts, tables, and graphs for a series of route applications which plainly indicated that Delta was "thinking big" about postwar expansion. "My! The work that is ahead for that fellow to do!" Woolman remarked in a letter to Parker early in 1943, describing the favorable impression that Johnson had created in the company organization. In a contemporary photograph, Woolman, his suspenders showing under the vest of a rumpled business suit and a document perched precariously on his left knee, discusses his postwar visions with Johnson in the corner of a cluttered office, surrounded by filing cabinets and a litter of papers. They had put together a series of proposals that may have seemed audacious at the time; yet almost every one of them was destined to materialize. The annual report, released later that year, contained a map showing no fewer than ten prospective new routes for which Delta was seeking certification. Looking back, one can see that the most important was the projected route—not to be won without a struggle—from Atlanta to Washington, Baltimore, Philadelphia, and New York by way of such intermediate points as Asheville, North Carolina. Delta also jumped into the developing campaign to break Pan American's monopoly on foreign routes, joining a lobbying group known as the Airlines Committee for United States Air Policy; with the exception of United every important domestic carrier took part.[39]

Despite possible outward appearances to the contrary, the maze of new air routes envisioned by Woolman and Johnson was not plotted without plan or purpose. As explained in the following year's annual report, it was intended to provide through service to destinations frequently visited by southern travelers without "the hazards attending . . . dependence on connecting traffic" and to "establish an overall service pattern that will contribute to the development of new uses for air transportation in the era of industrial expansion, which authorities in general are predicting for the South." Following this rationale, in early 1944 exhibits were completed for an upcoming CAB hearing on a proposed new route from Birmingham to Oklahoma City, for which Delta, American, Braniff, Chicago and

Southern, Continental, and Eastern were contending. By April a similar array of documentation had been prepared for proceedings on extending the New Orleans-to-Shreveport route to Kansas City.[40]

Although initial signs were encouraging, the eventual outcome of these two applications was highly disappointing. On May 30, 1944, the examiners recommended that the CAB award Delta a route from Birmingham to Memphis and in August moved favorably on the company's proposed artery from Shreveport to Kansas City. The CAB's public counsel subsequently urged that Delta receive temporary certification to operate a 1,775-mile route from New Orleans to San Juan via Havana, using Douglas DC-4s; he also favored giving Delta a new route from Chicago to Savannah via Cincinnati.[41] In the end, however, matters did not go well before the CAB itself, which was free to reject any or all recommendations made by its own subordinates. Particularly galling to Delta was a decision by the CAB on January 15, 1945, to override its examiners and to award a route from New Orleans to Tulsa and Kansas City to Mid-Continent Airlines after a hotly contested argument resolved by the margin of one vote. The three members favoring the rival carrier, relying on an argument that was to become distressingly familiar to Delta, declared that Mid-Continent was still receiving an airmail subsidy and needed to be strengthened. Further disappointment was in store for Delta when the CAB also denied it any share of a projected route from Birmingham to Oklahoma City by way of Memphis. Nor, in the end, did Delta secure Caribbean air lanes, additional southeastern connections, or the coveted routes to the major cities of the Northeast. Like the seven golden cities of Cíbola, which had beckoned to the Spanish conquistadores of earlier times, the lucrative markets stretching from Washington to Boston would long remain an elusive goal.[42]

While these issues were being argued, Delta pushed ahead on several other fronts to strengthen its postwar position. In November 1944 it established a new air-cargo department under the supervision of Paul Pate, a lanky veteran of the motor-freight business who had joined Delta as a traffic analyst late in the preceding year. A quiet man, who knew "how to be still and let a prospective air shipper talk himself into a contract," Pate scored quick successes for the new division by transporting three commodities in particular: newspapers, shrimp, and tomato plants. The company successfully flew Georgia fantail shrimp in dry ice from Savannah to Atlanta, heralded by an advertising campaign featuring a winged crustacean known as

Steve the Shrimp. Of all its cargo-carrying achievements in 1945, however, Delta leaders were proudest of having transported 160,000 tomato plants from Tifton, Georgia, to Bowling Green, Ohio, for the H. J. Heinz Company. A DC-3 crew led by Floyd Addison took custody of the plants on May 9 and rose skyward while the entire Tift County Chamber of Commerce, anticipating the profits that would result from the new service, "cheered us off as though we were carrying plasma to their sons in battle," as a subsequent report put it. Accompanied by two specialists from the United States Department of Agriculture, the plants were monitored closely during the flight to test the effects of temperature, humidity, and other conditions. Much to the gratification of everybody concerned, they arrived in excellent shape. Beside winning favorable publicity for the company in such magazines as *Time*, the feat promised considerable future rewards, for the raising of tomato seed plants in Georgia was a $2.5-million-a-year business.[43]

As the end of the war approached, the traffic and sales department was enlarged to keep up with expanded operations and to take advantage of an anticipated peacetime boom. The number of ticket offices was increased from seven to sixteen; new ones were opened in Alexandria, Baton Rouge, Charleston, Columbia, Columbus (Ga.), Fort Worth, Knoxville, Monroe, and Savannah. As wartime priorities were lifted and the schedule of daily flights correspondingly increased, a much expanded promotional campaign was instituted, featuring displays in such nationally circulated periodicals as *Time*, the *New Yorker*, and *Nation's Business*. The Burke Dowling Adams advertising agency, which had the accounts of many aviation enterprises, was engaged to help with this aspect of Delta's growing business, and the company also began advertising more frequently in the local newspapers of the cities that it served. In one respect, however, it bucked a trend among competitors by declining to lower its passenger rates, reasoning that its average fare of five cents a mile was already one of the lowest in the industry.[44]

To keep up with anticipated peacetime demand, particularly if Delta was successful in obtaining some new route authorizations from the CAB, Woolman and his advisers recognized that a major expansion of the company's equipment was imperative. Long experience during the war had confirmed the continued viability of the DC-3, and arrangements were made with the Defense Plant Corporation to lease five more of these dependable planes, in addition to the ten that the firm was already operating. With longer routes in prospect if the C A B should act favorably on one or more of Delta's interregional applications, the management also decided to acquire a fleet of Douglas DC-4s, which had been designed in the late 1930s and pressed into service as C-54 military transports when first produced in 1942. These four-engine planes, which could accommodate more than twice as many passengers as the DC-3, rapidly proved themselves under difficult conditions all over the world and came to play a prominent role in Delta's postwar operations.[45]

An expanded and modernized fleet would obviously cost a great deal of money, especially when Delta began purchasing new DC-3s and DC-4s instead of merely leasing them. During the early years of the war the loans that had financed the purchase of Delta's original DC-3s had been systematically repaid, and the annual report for 1943 announced to the stockholders that the corporation had "no outstanding notes and mortgages." Furthermore, wartime dividends, though paid regularly throughout the entire period, were deliberately kept at the modest level of fifty cents a share in the interest of accumulating funds for long-range postwar expansion.[46]

Nevertheless, the earned surplus of $847,822 that the company had built up by the end of the war would not have gone very far toward meeting all its needs for new and larger planes had it not been supplemented by the proceeds of a stock issue approved in December 1944, at which time only 198,384 shares of the 500,000 limit authorized in the reorganization of 1940–41 were actually outstanding. Under a plan conceived by the directors, 99,192 additional shares of stock, equivalent to one half-share for each share outstanding, were delivered to the current stockholders, thus keeping the proportion of ownership approximately the same in face of the impending issue of 102,424 shares to the public in order to secure funds for postwar expansion and a broader base of ownership in the firm's "present and prospective route territory." In February 1945 this sale was carried out, increasing the number of shares outstanding to 400,000 and yielding nearly $2.1 million to the company after expenses, the stock having brought $22.50 a share on the market. A contemporary photograph shows W. F. Broadwell of Courts and Company handing Woolman a check for $2,099,692 while Franklin Nash, trust officer for the Citizens and Southern Bank, looked on. Together with $297,576 transferred from Delta's earned surplus, these transactions gave the firm ample funds for new equipment and still left a substantial cash reserve for contingencies.[47]

By summer 1945, therefore, Delta was in an excellent position for future growth, and the only element missing was a major addition to the company's route structure such as had occurred with the winning of the Cincinnati run just before the war. This element was not long in coming. On August 22, 1945, during what one contemporary account called a "quiet, sultry summer afternoon," Catherine FitzGerald and C. E. Faulk sat in FitzGerald's office reminiscing about old times when suddenly, at about 3:30, the telephone rang. As she listened to the voice at the other end, the secretary's eyes widened. Gesturing excitedly and trying to take shorthand notes at the same time, she began "gasping, laughing, trying to say six things at once." Coming over the line was the news that Delta, in a contest among twelve airlines, had been awarded the longest single new route ever granted by the CAB since its inception in 1938—a 1,028-mile run from Chicago to Miami. As he comprehended what was happening, Faulk, "dignified, white-haired picture of a Southern gentleman" that he was, could not restrain himself and "let out an Indian war whoop audible all over the floor." Within moments the halls of Delta headquarters were full of excited employees yelling: "Chicago to Miami! Chicago clear to Miami!"

So loud was the commotion that workers downstairs thought a fire had broken out. Faulk hastily assembled a meeting and formally announced the "superlative news." One of the happiest people present was Johnson, who after more than two arduous years as head of the planning and research department finally had a triumph to celebrate. As he "stood in the hall and waved his arms and shouted," fellow staff members thronged around him to shake his hand. Ironically, the person most responsible for the breakthrough was not there; Woolman had gone to Buffalo with Cushing and heard the news on a radio broadcast while he was cruising over Ohio in a small Lockheed plane that the company had acquired for management use. In his exuberance, Cushing indulged in a bit of aerial acrobatics when the announcement came over the air. "I never want to be flying with George Cushing again when a new route is awarded," he quipped upon returning to Atlanta, throwing in some extra words of praise for "the efficiency of the seat belts in the Lockheed."[48]

Coming only weeks after the end of the war, the Chicago-to-Miami award created what a leading contemporary aviation magazine described as "a new link over which the raw materials and agricultural products of the South could be exchanged with the manufactures of the industrial North." Even more important, it gave Delta access to the second largest city in the nation and a highly desirable passenger route with enormous potential for the type of vacation trade previously enjoyed only by such lines as Eastern. Delta soon capitalized upon this advantage in advertisements billing the company as the "Trunk Line to Sunshine."[49] Delta was still not a giant, as airlines went, but it had abundant reason to face the dawning postwar era with confidence.

CHAPTER 7

New Vistas, New Planes, and New Routes

ELTA'S STUNNING NEW route victory launched a postwar era marked by vigorous expansion of the company's fleet and the acquisition of additional airways resulting from further action in cases argued before the CAB. During this period the firm also became involved for the first time in extensive competition with other carriers, including Eastern, a firm with which it was destined to carry on one of the classic rivalries in American business history. Responding creatively to the challenges of these years, Delta began to acquire a status in the industry as something more than a small distinctly regional airline.

Soon after World War II was over, Delta's board of directors affirmed a basic transformation that had been working, like yeast, since the early days of the enterprise. On October 29, 1945, the company's name was changed from Delta Air Corporation to Delta Air Lines, Inc., a move subsequently ratified by the stockholders at their annual meeting. However subtly, this change amounted to a "rite of passage," reflecting the altered sense of identity that had emerged over the years, as the transport of passengers, mail, and goods had come to eclipse crop dusting, once the mainstay of the firm but now a mere appendage to its ever-expanding operations.[1]

In another change the aging C. E. Faulk, a victim of failing eyesight, became chairman of the board, and C. E. Woolman was elevated to the rank of president. Woolman, who also retained the title of general manager, had, of course, been the main executive at Delta since its birth, but the board's formal acknowledgment nevertheless confirmed the dwindling importance of northern Louisiana businessmen in the company's development, though they had once been deeply involved in day-to-day decisions. The new title also gave Woolman the personal gratification of status equal to that of such pioneers as Eddie Rickenbacker at Eastern, C. R. Smith at American, Ralph Damon at TWA, and Carleton Putnam at Chicago and Southern—airline chiefs with whom he had long dealt as an acknowledged peer and respected competitor.[2]

Outwardly, the biggest Delta event in the opening months of the postwar era was the official inauguration of the new route from Chicago to Miami. In accordance with long-standing custom, the formal opening was marked by a series of special VIP tours. On November 23, 1945, a delegation of newspapermen from various cities along the greatly expanded route 54 boarded a Delta DC-3 and flew to Miami to enjoy some deep-sea fishing and to luxuriate in the Florida surf. "I spent yesterday chasing anti-freeze," wrote one Cincinnati editor in a statement well calculated to enhance the lure of Delta's new "Trunk Line to Sunshine" among readers back home. "Today I will chase dolphin, barracuda and sailfish in the warm water off Miami Beach."

After this tour had been completed, the same Delta ship flew from Chicago to Atlanta, picked up the city's chief executive, William B. Hartsfield, and headed south on the first lap of a ceremonial tour billed as the "Mayors' Special." At the Florida terminus the reigning Miss Orange Bowl, Libby Walker, rechristened the DC-3 *City of Miami*, smashing a bottle of orange juice over its nose. Following this ceremony the plane flew north along the route to Chicago, picking up mayors and other dignitaries from Miami Beach, Jacksonville, Brunswick, Augusta, Greenville, Spartanburg, Asheville, Knoxville, and Cincinnati. Each mayor was allowed to sit beside Miss Walker until the next one boarded, and the flight to Chicago was described as a "hilarious trip," despite some icing conditions, which forced an unscheduled stop in Indiana.

Regular service from Chicago to Miami commenced on December 1, 1945; four months later the inauguration of the Chicago-to-Charleston run was observed with a ceremonial flight during which flowering azalea plants were given to the mayor of each city along the route. Another community was added to the Delta system later in the same year, when the bluegrass capital, Lexington, Kentucky, which had been included by the CAB in the original Atlanta-to-Cincinnati award of 1941 but had lacked the necessary facilities for service, finally completed its preparations for commercial operations. The opening of new stations up and down the line added impetus to the company's accelerating growth, and the Delta payroll swelled from 982 to 2,350 during the fiscal year 1945–46 alone. Optimism soared throughout the organization: "It's not out of place for Delta to aspire to be the outstanding airline in the country for passenger service," the company magazine boasted at one point, as it invited novices to share with seasoned veterans "the same pride in saluting off the ramp the roaring, pulsating beautiful winged machine . . . power in the sky, dispatched by Delta!"[3]

Delta's postwar exuberance was shared by the industry as a whole. Under the spur of wartime conditions, commercial aviation had become for the first time a generally profitable business, and it was widely expected among airline officials and federal regulators alike that the upward trend would continue, that an increasingly air-minded public would fill the seats of a burgeoning domestic fleet as it traveled over the vast new route mileage authorized by the CAB. It was a short-lived dream—but it was pleasant while it lasted.

Thanks to the CAB's willingness to certify such carriers as Delta for operation into major urban centers from which they had previously been excluded, unprecedented competition reigned throughout the airline industry immediately after World War II. The new run from Cincinnati to Chicago, for example, pitted Delta directly against American. Delta was fortunate in that instance because the demands of American's passengers for nonstop service from Chicago to Washington had forced the company to eliminate some stops at Cincinnati. Capitalizing on this situation, Delta scheduled four nonstop flights from Cincinnati to Chicago and back each day, compared to two by American in one direction and only one in the other. Delta thus established itself strongly in this market, but the provision of as many flights as possible inevitably ran up costs, as well as revenues.[4]

Delta's chief competitor in the postwar era, however, was not American but Eastern, at that time riding the crest of its popularity under the leadership of the charismatic Eddie Rickenbacker and by far the most profitable carrier in the skies. During the 1930s the interests of Delta and Eastern had been complementary rather than divergent, and relations had been cordial. Rickenbacker, for example, had expressed deep regret about the death of Delta operations chief Pat Higgins in October 1940; correspondingly, after Rickenbacker had suffered an almost fatal injury as the result of an air crash in February 1941 near the Atlanta airport, Woolman had wired, "Eddie, this is indeed a tough break but we are pulling for your speedy recovery." On the other hand, the personalities of the two executives differed significantly; both had a patriarchal style, but Woolman had a common down-to-earth touch, while Rickenbacker tended to be lordly and sometimes downright arrogant toward Delta as a firm much lower on the commercial aviation totem pole. After the CAB awarded Delta a Chicago-to-Miami route in 1945, relations between the two firms became intensely competitive and sometimes bitterly so.

Although Eastern did not serve Cincinnati, it operated over a prime route from Chicago to Miami by way of such intermediate points as Louisville, Atlanta, and Jacksonville. Pitted against this Goliath, Delta acted decisively to establish the first nonstop service between Chicago and Miami in November 1946, forcing Eastern to counter with similar runs of its own two months later. For a time Delta did extremely well, partly because it beat Eastern to the punch in inaugurating four-engine service and partly because it scheduled more flights at peak demand times than Eastern did; in March 1947, for example, it carried 3,895 passengers between these terminal cities, compared to Eastern's 3,065.

By September, however, the tables had been turned, and Eastern was accommodating nearly three times as many passengers over the route as Delta was. Furthermore, its lead continued to widen until, within a year, Delta's share of this particular market was down to a mere 14 percent of that enjoyed by its powerful adversary. Similarly, although Delta did consistently well in competing with Eastern for traffic on the short run between Atlanta and Jacksonville, it had much more difficulty in maintaining a strong position in the Atlanta-to-Miami market. The company also experienced tough going in the three-cornered rivalry with Eastern and National for the Jacksonville-to-Miami trade, where it steadily surpassed National but fell far short of attracting the number of passengers who flew the route on Rickenbacker's "Great Silver Fleet."[5]

The fact that wealthier Eastern had the resources to put many more planes into service between various cities along the route from Chicago to Miami than Delta could afford accounted for part of the shift in fortunes between the two lines, but the ups and downs in the competition for nonstop traffic were primarily caused by changes in the type of equipment that each contender was using. Before the war Delta had chosen aircraft primarily on the basis of what it could afford to buy, with as much attention as possible to comparative operational costs and the relative "short hop" nature of its route structure. After the war it also had to consider what other airlines—particularly Eastern—were using, and the choice of equipment became a prime weapon in competitive strategy. This was a game at

DELTA ROUTE SYSTEM
1946

which Delta ultimately came to excel, a fact that explains much of its long-range success.

Delta got off to a good start in the postwar race for advantage by being the first airline in the East to put the Douglas DC-4 into service. As they jockeyed for position at this particular starting gate, airline executives pondered whether to wait for brand-new DC-4s to roll off the production line or to purchase reconditioned military-surplus planes. Douglas persuaded three airlines—National, Western, and Northwest—that they should wait for new planes, on grounds that they would actually receive quicker delivery. Both Eastern and Delta, on the other hand, chose to recondition C-54 cargo planes, the military version of the DC-4, which they acquired from the government for about $90,000 each. Once this decision had been made, an airframe manufacturer had to be selected to perform the actual conversion work. Both Republic and Martin offered lower labor rates than Douglas, but Delta engineers, led by J. F. Nycum, persuaded Woolman to choose Douglas anyway because it had created the plane to begin with and controlled the supply of parts on which other producers would have to depend. Accordingly, Delta set up a technical staff at the Douglas plant and in September 1945 dispatched Nycum to California to coordinate the conversion process with Douglas engineers and assembly crews. Eastern, on the other hand, chose Martin to do its reconditioning and wound up putting its DC-4s into service later than Delta.[6]

In Atlanta, chief pilot Charles Dolson, who had gained considerable experience with the navy's R5D version of the C-54 during the war, trained such veteran Delta flyers as T. P. Ball, George Shealy, and John Van Vuren for duty on these ships, using recently acquired military planes still awaiting conversion. Meanwhile, at the Douglas plant in Santa Monica a tense drama was taking place as Nycum, who got along very well with both management and workers, tried to complete the conversion of Delta's first ship before a brand-new DC-4 being built for National came off the line. The race was neck and neck, except that the Delta plane was waiting for a cabin-heating system that was in short supply. As Nycum later put it, "something very strange transpired" on the day when National was to take delivery; "it appeared they were now short a heating system and Delta was complete," and so it was the Delta liner that took off for the East Coast and the honor of initiating DC-4 service in that part of the United States. Underscoring the irony, the total cost of

Delta's reconditioned ship was only $225,000, whereas National paid about $420,000 for its new one.[7]

Engineer Arthur Ford, who took charge of further Delta conversion work at the Douglas plant after Nycum had seen the company's first DC-4 through the process, later reminisced about the revolutionary significance of this particular model for American commercial aviation generally. It was the earliest four-engine craft to see service in large numbers on domestic airlines after the war; its greatly expanded range, more than two thousand miles without refueling, permitted carriers to provide nonstop connections between widely separated major cities, instead of subjecting passengers to the series of "ups and downs" at intermediate points that were necessary in the smaller DC-3s. Delta therefore scored a real coup when, on February 14, 1946, it landed its first DC-4, in its smart new colors, at Fort Worth after the first leg of a cross-country flight from Santa Monica. With operations chief George Cushing at the controls, it flew on, being admired by crowds at other Delta cities along the route to Atlanta. At Jackson nearly a thousand people turned out to see the ship, and a Chicago and Southern agent was heard to exclaim, "Roll that big thing out of sight before our passengers get a complex!" When the plane finally arrived in Atlanta on the night of February 16, even employees of arch rival Eastern poured out of the terminal to gawk at it. After the inevitable training and familiarization process, the plane was placed in revenue service in March. It was followed quickly by others completed in California under Ford's prodding; by June seven of the craft were carrying the Delta insignia through southern and midwestern skies.[8]

The early arrival of the DC-4, which could cruise at 215 miles an hour, as opposed to about 175 for the DC-3, permitted Delta to get in on the tail end of the 1945–46 winter vacation season and thus to win a short-lived but nevertheless profitable advantage over Eastern in competing for the coveted Chicago-to-Miami trade. In another move aimed at the long-haul passenger, Delta officials had deliberately designed the interior of the plane to accommodate only forty-four people, instead of its theoretical load of sixty, thus providing plenty of room for stretching and walking around.[9] Quite soon, however, the glory days of the DC-4 ebbed, and the plane became just another workhorse of the air as the limelight switched to newer and more glamorous models. Unfortunately for Delta, one of these models bore the distinctive colors of Eastern Air Lines.

It was the Lockheed Constellation, which had been conceived in 1939 at the instigation of Howard Hughes and developed during the war as the C-69 military transport. A pressurized plane that cruised at more than three hundred miles an hour, it possessed a range in excess of three thousand miles and could accommodate up to eighty-one passengers. It offered a number of advantages over the unpressurized, slower, and slightly smaller DC-4, and it represented the first really modern postwar passenger liner. TWA first put it into service late in 1945. Unfortunately, the early L-049 model had a tendency to catch fire in midair; after several incidents, including a crash near Reading, Pennsylvania, in July 1946, all "Connies" were temporarily grounded by the CAB. Such difficulties, however, were eliminated in the improved L-649 and L-749 models, and the plane became highly popular with postwar passengers. Although Eastern Air Lines eventually acquired nineteen DC-4s, the first of which went into service in June 1946, Rickenbacker decided not to purchase the DC-6, which Douglas was developing to compete with the new Lockheed liner. Instead, Captain Eddie persuaded Hughes, who held priority rights in putting the first Constellations into service, to let Eastern have ten of the craft. Pleased with their performance, Rickenbacker placed orders for ten more and subsequently played an influential role in developing the plane's elongated successor, the L-1049 Super-Constellation.[10]

Delta was slow to appreciate the formidable threat posed by the Constellations that Eastern put into the sky for the first time in June 1947. Earlier in that same year, Woolman had casually informed Carleton Putnam of Chicago and Southern that Delta had not yet ordered any DC-6s or Constellations, noting that "insofar as our present operations are concerned, we have very few places where we could advantageously use them." After Eastern had introduced Constellations on the Chicago-to-Miami run, however, the public quickly showed its preference for the speedier pressurized service that they provided, and Delta's position in this market deteriorated swiftly. Within three months its share of the traffic had dropped to 36 percent of Eastern's share, and it kept right on plunging until September 1948, when Delta carried only 189 people between the two cities; Eastern carried 1,377. Faced with such ruinous competition, Woolman and his advisers made an agonizing reappraisal and reached the inescapable conclusion that new planes would have to be purchased. Typical of the facts that they faced was a memorandum by publicity chief James H. Cobb citing a survey of company agents in Chicago and Miami, who reported that they could sell space on the firm's DC-4's only when seats were not available on Eastern's Connies. Advertising slogans emphasizing that Delta's DC-4s had only four seats across instead of five, that users of the Lockheeds had to pay premium fares, and that Delta was friendlier and more courteous than Eastern fell on deaf public ears. "A lot of passengers we had last winter have deserted us," Cobb told Woolman. "Maybe it is unwise to try to compete with EAL and more economical to keep our present equipment and go after local business—you are the best judge of that—but I do know that we are losing the long-haul stuff in spite of our best advertising and sales efforts."[11]

Hoping to interest the Delta management in buying a reported half-dozen or more Constellations at about $800,000 each, representatives of Lockheed visited Atlanta on a demonstration flight in one of the new liners, which broke all previous speed records between Dallas and the Georgia capital. Betty Morton, a Delta stewardess who had served as a WASP during the war and was supposed to have logged more hours in the cockpit than many of the company's copilots, was allowed to fly the big four-engine craft on a publicity cruise over the city.[12] Lockheed's sales efforts did not sway Woolman and his advisers, however, and the company finally announced in February 1948 that it was adding five DC-6s to its fleet instead.

The most important reason for this move was that Delta wanted to avoid the "me too" position of copying Eastern, but a number of other considerations also favored the DC-6. Delta had by then used three generations of Douglas aircraft, the DC-2, DC-3, and DC-4, and the firm had been highly satisfied with their performance. It was second nature for Delta pilots to fly them and for company maintenance crews to work on them. Over the years Delta had established close rapport with the Santa Monica organization; Arthur Ford later recalled playing volleyball with workers at the plant during leisure hours and then hastily showering and dressing to attend an executive dinner hosted by Donald Douglas himself. More pragmatically, Delta pilots did not like the cramped cockpit of the Constellation, and its gracefully tapering fuselage, however pleasing aesthetically, did not seem to be as efficient for the accommodation of passengers as the cylindrical body of the Douglas ship. Although the speed and range of the Constellation and the DC-6 were quite similar, the $630,000 cost of the latter was significantly lower than that of the Lockheed plane. The clinching argument, if one was needed, was that the cockpit of the Constellation, though cramped, had been designed for three crew members—pilot, copilot, and flight engineer—and, under CAB regulations, required such a crew. The DC-6, on the other hand, was designed for the customary two-man operation and therefore seemed by far the more economical choice.[13]

Selecting the DC-6 did, however, involve one drawback. The plane had been developed principally at the behest of American and United, which between them had ordered more than eighty of the craft. Other deliveries were slated for Braniff, National, Sabena, and Panagra. Not until December 1, 1948, did the first Delta DC-6 take off on its maiden commercial flight; until then the firm's DC-4s had to face the murderous competition of Eastern's Connies. Nevertheless, there were some consolations, despite the licking that the company was forced to endure. Like the Constellation, the DC-6 had to go through a painful debugging stage; the biggest problem was the possibility that, during fuel transfer between the main and auxiliary gas tanks, gasoline might overflow into the air scoop for the cabin heating and pressurization system, which could lead to disastrous fires. This flaw caused one of the worst calamities in domestic airline history when a United DC-6 crashed in flames on the rim of Utah's Bryce Canyon late in 1947, killing all fifty-two people aboard. The emergency landing of a flaming American Airlines DC-6 at Gallup, New Mexico, shortly afterward led to the voluntary grounding of more than a hundred of these ships by the trunk lines that had purchased them. By the time that the planes were gradually returned to service in the spring of 1948, after having received appropriate modifications, their owners and the Douglas Company had lost approximately $13 million. Although United and American lost more money than the other carriers involved, the disruption of DC-6 service was especially hard on National, which was not large enough to absorb the resulting deficits without immense strain and was also involved just then in a crippling pilots' strike.[14]

Being obliged to wait its turn was a lucky thing for Delta: by the time that the company's first DC-6 rolled off the line at Santa Monica, the plane had been so modified that it had become a highly dependable airliner. On October 3, 1948, this first plane was officially christened the *Flying D* by movie actress Linda Darnell of *Forever Amber* fame, in a ceremony conducted at the Douglas plant by beaming Delta and Douglas officials. Then it roared off for the East Coast with Dolson at the controls, on what was deliberately intended to be a record-smashing flight to dramatize Delta's new ability to compete with the Constellations on equal or superior terms. Crossing the continent nonstop with newspaper people from cities along the Delta system and various company VIPs aboard, the plane attained speeds averaging 360 miles an hour; it landed at Jacksonville after 6 hours, 43 minutes, and 10 seconds in the air. Although NAA rulings required that New York be the eastern terminus of flights claiming official transcontinental records, the company nonetheless claimed to have broken all previous records for a flight between the West Coast and Jacksonville and basked in the adulation that newspapers heaped upon the *Flying D*. To symbolize this new departure in performance capabilities, the plane was decorated in a new red, white, and blue color scheme chosen in a company-wide competition which Larry Keith, district cargo traffic representative in Chicago, had won. It looked like a lady in a new dress, therefore, when it landed at night after the final leg of its journey to the company's headquarters and "parked triumphantly in center position at the Atlanta airport." Put into service after the customary prepping and soon joined by four others of its type, the ship became a familiar sight on Delta's express runs. By mid-1949 the DC-6s accounted for nearly 300,000 miles a month, about three times the total flown by the firm's DC-4s. More important, the new model won back many customers and was credited by management for the record earnings soon announced to stockholders.[15]

Besides being pressurized and featuring such technological innovations as reversible propellers for quicker landing stops and a thermal or "heated wing" deicing system for greater all-weather dependability, Delta's DC-6s incorporated a special cost-cutting capability that had already been achieved with the DC-4s. Soon after the introduction of four-engine aircraft, the Delta management had decided that there was no reason why a truck or cargo plane had to carry a new engine to a stranded airliner that had been forced down somewhere because of engine failure. Instead, Nycum and the engineering staff worked out a plan to demonstrate the ability of a Delta DC-4 to operate safely on three engines while returning to the Atlanta maintenance base from the scene of such an incident, provided that only a pilot and a copilot were aboard. CAA certification was obtained for this procedure after a series of tests conducted at Columbia, South Carolina, in November 1947; it resulted in the reduction of out-of-service time by hundreds of hours. For its DC-6s Delta arranged with Douglas to obtain certification for three-engine ferry operation at the factory while the plane was still being built, thus scoring an industry "first." The same characteristic was stipulated by the company in subsequent contracts with Douglas and other airframe manufacturers.[16]

In another important respect, however, Delta failed to realize an anticipated economy from the DC-6, though this particular disappointment ultimately turned into an advantage. As previously noted, Delta had purchased the DC-6 partly because it was designed to be operated by a two-man cockpit crew. During 1947 and 1948, however, the CAB came under increasing pressure to require both the Douglas craft and the new Boeing 377 Stratocruiser to carry flight engineers, as well as pilots and copilots. Understandably, Lockheed and the airlines that used its Constellations did not want to see other manufacturers and carriers gain a competitive edge by introducing planes that were just as large and fast as the Connies but required only two men in the cockpit. Various unions whose membership and treasuries stood to grow if the proposed ruling were put into effect also quite naturally favored passage. The Air Line Pilots Association (ALPA) was divided but nevertheless predominantly in favor of the controversial regulation, and the Airline Flight Engineers Association (AFEA) of the AFL, of course, strongly supported it. The Transport Workers Union of America, an affiliate of the CIO, went even further, demanding that two more crew members, a navigator and a radio operator, be required, in addition to a flight engineer.

Reflecting the views of most airline managements, the Air Transport Association (ATA) strongly opposed the move; big carriers like American and United led the fight. They pointed out that, historically, flight engineers had been used to perform such tasks as repairing and servicing planes at "isolated or inadequately manned stations"; controlling engine power in certain types of aircraft in which the pilots could not see or reach the appropriate controls; carrying out airborne maintenance on such planes as the Boeing 314 Flying Boat, the design of which permitted flight engineers access to the engines during actual flight; or keeping a close eye on fuel consumption on extremely long or transoceanic runs. None of these conditions prevailed on domestic routes, the ATA pointed out, especially since the advent of automatic carburetion, devices for measuring fuel flow, and torque meters for the direct reading of engine power. To the leaders of most domestic trunk lines, except for TWA and Eastern, which were committed to the Connies and naturally wanted competing airlines to bear the costs associated with having three men in the cockpit, the pressure for flight engineers seemed to be featherbedding pure and simple.[17]

The Delta management naturally fought the requirement for flight engineers. So did most of the firm's pilots, who, despite their ALPA membership, heavily opposed the move in a survey conducted early in 1947. Later that year Dolson, after testifying against the proposal at CAB hearings in Washington, correctly predicted to Delta officials that extra personnel would not be required on DC-4s. He also believed that a rule stipulating the presence of flight engineers on DC-6s was only a marginal possibility at that point, but events proved him wrong. The CAB ultimately responded to intensified pressure by ruling that, after December 1, 1948, a third crewman holding a flight engineer's certificate would be required on every four-engine airliner with a takeoff weight exceeding 80,000 pounds, including both the Boeing Stratocruiser and the Douglas DC-6.[18]

There was enough leeway in the ruling, however, for a managerial move by Delta that was to pay off handsomely in the future. The CAB did not stipulate that the third crewman had to be only a flight engineer or to spend his time in the cockpit solely in that capacity. Despite the strong opposition of AFEA, which wanted to maximize job potential for its members, the CAB allowed the third seat to be occupied by a pilot who had also been certified as a flight engineer. Although this move would represent considerable added expense, in that a pilot required more extensive training and received higher pay than a flight engineer, it was a move that the Delta management decided to make.

To Dolson and Ball, by that time vice-president of operations and chief pilot respectively, putting members of two different unions in the same cockpit seemed likely to create dissension and arouse conflicting purposes, partly because the flight engineer would hold a dead-end position and would never be able to aspire to the status and pay of a full-fledged airline captain. As there was no possibility of repairing or adjusting most airplane parts in actual flight anyway, the presence of a "pilot engineer" was much more valuable than that of a "mechanic engineer." In addition, the use of mechanical engineers, they argued, would divert good maintenance personnel from the company's repair shops and create the risk of rivalry and hard feelings there, as well as in the cockpit. Woolman accepted this reasoning, and it became a settled Delta policy that the third crew member be a fully qualified pilot who also possessed a flight engineer's certificate. The promotion route was to run from flight engineer to copilot to pilot, a route that has been followed since 1948. The judgment of Dolson and Ball was vindicated in later years when Eastern and other airlines experienced the predicted dissension and suffered costly strikes, whereas Delta escaped and flourished. Ultimately the Delta approach became standard throughout the industry.[19]

Another important move by Woolman and his advisers during this period, though not as crucial to Delta's long-range fortunes as the decision to use pilot engineers, nevertheless spared the company a great deal of anxiety and unnecessary expense: a decision not to go through with the purchase of a plane that later performed disastrously for another airline. In later years Nycum argued cogently that "the choice of the right equipment at the right time and in the correct quantities has played a large part in Delta's success." He also emphasized that "we have been extremely fortunate in never having purchased an airplane which proved unsuccessful, while most of the carriers have suffered one or more such experiences."[20] What he said is true, but events could all too easily have turned out otherwise.

After the war Delta, like all its competitors, looked around for a short-haul aircraft to replace the indomitable but aging DC-3. At that time Lockheed, whose Electras and Lodestars had vied so strongly in the prewar market, had nothing to offer in the way of a new twin-engine transport, nor did Boeing, whose earlier model 247 series had seen much service with such lines as United, PCA, and Western.[21] Taking advantage of this opportunity, the Glenn L. Martin Company, which had previously specialized in military aircraft and had built no passenger planes of note other than the famous "China Clipper" flying boats designed for transoceanic service in the 1930s, decided to get the jump on the rest of the industry by moving rapidly into production of a medium-sized airliner patterned on the firm's World War II B-26 bomber. Although Martin consulted with American Airlines, it committed the serious blunder of putting the plane into production without first making and testing a prototype. An unpressurized ship designed for simple loading and unloading and for takeoff and landing at relatively small airports, the new craft received CAA certification before any postwar rivals. In a hint

These women at Delta's World War II modification base in Atlanta are altering an Army Air Force Douglas A-20 attack aircraft for service on a fighting front.

George Cushing, Captain J. H. (Luke) Williamson, and Chief Flight Superintendent Alexander Rainouard pose in front of Delta's C-47 military cargo plane,
1942.

C. E. Woolman, Atlanta's Mayor William B. Hartsfield, and Captain George Cushing, then in military service, during expansion of General Office Building in 1943.

C. E. Woolman (*fourth from right*) and C. E. Faulk (*second from right*) join the celebration at the completion of the General Office's first expansion program in 1943.

The Atlanta reservations office, 1943.

Accounting personnel at front desk in 1943. *Left to right:* J. J. (Spic) Medaries, revenue auditor; L. B. Judd, comptroller; and R. H. Wharton, general auditor. Others in the room include Truman Haygood, J. T. Maples, Ike Lasseter, and Todd Cole.

Applications for new routes are discussed in 1943 by C. E. Woolman and E. Marion Johnson, director of the company's Planning and Research Department for twenty years.

Paul W. Pate, cargo manager, directs the first shipment of tomato plants from Tifton, Georgia, to Bowling Green, Ohio, in 1944.

For years Woolman reserved the privilege of personally presenting service pins to long-time personnel. Nip Hill, who became a supervisor in stores and celebrated his fortieth anniversary with Delta in 1975, is shown receiving his ten-year pin in 1945.

Dr. B. R. Coad and Woolman in Miami in 1945.

of the nightmare to come, American backed out of its plans to buy the plane, but orders were secured from PCA, Northwest, and two South American lines. Thus began the history of the ill-fated Martin 2-0-2.[22]

The prospect of dealing with an airframe manufacturer located on the East Coast and of beating its competitors to the punch with a new twin-engine transport, just as it had done with the DC-4 in the four-engine class, appealed strongly to Delta. During the summer of 1946 Woolman made a tentative commitment to buy ten 2-0-2s and to take an option on ten more; deliveries were to begin in September 1947. A contract specifying a unit price of $237,500 was submitted to Delta on September 10, 1946, and articles touting the new ship appeared from time to time in the *Delta Digest*.[23]

But things gradually went sour. At the behest of PCA, Martin eliminated a forward passenger entrance ramp that Delta had wanted and substituted a "cargoveyor," which diminished its sales appeal to operations chief Cushing. Meanwhile, Woolman attended a meeting at Washington in January 1947 and picked up disturbing scuttlebutt that the new "Martinliner" was not going to be quite the plane that the manufacturers were predicting. "I certainly hope this ship doesn't turn out to be a dud," he informed Chicago and Southern's Carleton Putnam in a worried letter after his return. Shortly thereafter, at Woolman's request, Cushing sent Delta engineer Walter Englund to Baltimore to take a close look at the craft; he received a highly discouraging report, emphasizing above all that the ship was structurally weak. "So much is made of weight and space saving," Englund declared sarcastically, "that one would think they were designing a piece of luggage instead of an airplane." A few months later Dolson and Nycum visited the plant to test-fly the plane and came away with negative reactions. Dolson criticized various features of the cockpit and also noted that faulty directional stability gave the plane a tendency to "hunt" while coming in for a landing. "It does not bore straight for the runway as does a DC-4 or -6," he commented. With this buildup of ominous signs, Woolman took comfort in the knowledge that the contract submitted by Martin lay still unsigned on his desk, but he regarded his word as his bond and hated to renege even on a tentative arrangement. Key advisers, however, persuaded him that the Baltimore firm itself was not producing the sort of plane that had been promised, and at some point in the late spring or early summer of 1947 Delta abandoned all plans to acquire the Martin ship.[24]

A stitch in time. . . . After the plane had been certified by the CAA, certainly a mistake in hindsight, and placed in service on Northwest Airlines, a serious flaw developed. On August 29, 1948, one of Northwest's Martin 2-0-2s crashed in a thunderstorm near Winona, Minnesota, when the left wing tore loose outboard of the engine; all thirty-seven people on the plane were killed. Investigation traced the disaster to a flange between the inner and outer wing spars; it had developed cracks under fatigue, and Northwest's entire fleet of 2-0-2s was grounded while Martin performed necessary modifications. Even after that troubles with the aircraft were not over. Several fatal crashes in 1950 and 1951 resulted in more groundings and the ultimate refusal of Northwest's pilots to fly the plane. The company finally managed to sell all its Martinliners after suffering great financial losses.[25]

Delta had thus avoided a major debacle, but it still faced the problem of finding a successor to the DC-3. One possible answer, the Convair 240, was rejected because of its limited range. For a time, Douglas contemplated building a new medium-sized transport; in view of future developments, it is curious that it was to be known as the DC-9, but the California firm eventually decided to forgo the project because of excessive development costs and a belief that the day of jet passenger service lay just around the corner. Martin recovered at least partially from the failure of the 2-0-2 by developing its 2-0-2A and 4-0-4 series, but Delta was not a prospect after narrowly escaping disaster once in its dealings with the Baltimore firm, and the fact that Eastern became heavily committed to the 4-0-4 gave Woolman added motive to avoid the plane. There is some evidence that he also considered the Saab Scandia 90A-2 after returning from a vacation in northern Europe, but then, as later, Delta resisted the lure of foreign-built airplanes.[26]

One remaining possibility for Delta was the so-called Super DC-3, a reconditioned version of the basic DC-3 design projected for 1949, with enhanced seating capacity and higher cruising speed. Despite a personal visit to Atlanta by Donald Douglas, Sr., Delta balked at a $234,000 unit price tag for modifying planes that Delta would have to supply; it decided to conduct its own face-lifting program on the dependable twin-engine craft. Accordingly, ship 48 of the Delta fleet was thoroughly modified by company maintenance crews: a forward bulkhead was moved up to provide room for a cabin with twenty-eight seats, the main passenger door was redesigned to eliminate the need for a separate boarding ramp, a new heating and cooling system was installed, the floor was strengthened, and the exterior trim was made more attractive. The interior was further improved by the provision of foam-rubber seats and headrests, more colorful upholstery, walnut-paneled bulkheads, and more efficiently placed baggage compartments. When the plane entered service in the spring of 1950, the seat pockets contained a booklet on the cover of which was the caricature of a DC-3 with a smiling feminine face and long eyelashes. It told how Woolman had looked everywhere to find a substitute for the familiar Douglas plane before saying: "Sweetheart, you've got admirers all over the world . . . and I think you rate a new spring outfit. Go to a beauty parlor and get the works. If we like it, we'll fix up all your DC-3 sisters." Passengers were asked to vote on the new design and decided resoundingly in its favor, after which the rest of the fleet received the same treatment.[27]

The result of Delta's decisions on equipment in the immediate postwar era, therefore, was an all-Douglas fleet, which in mid-1950 consisted of six DC-6s, six DC-4s, seventeen DC-3s, and three C-47 cargo planes. This augmented capacity—twenty-two more aircraft and about five times more seats than the company had had available at the end of the war—reflected not only the need to serve customary markets and to compete vigorously with other lines for traffic from Chicago to Miami but also the addition since 1945 of several new destinations to the ever-growing Delta system.

During the postwar years Delta continued the vigorous expansion program that had been signaled by creation of the research and planning department in 1943. Although it received far less than it wanted, the company still came out well in the Southeastern States Case, involving a complex network of new routes stretching from the Ohio valley to the Atlantic Ocean and almost to the Gulf of Mexico, which was decided by the CAB early in 1947. Complicating the situation as the major trunk lines jockeyed for position was the presence of smaller contenders, "feeder lines" run by new companies equipped mainly with war-surplus DC-3s and seeking routes connecting minor population centers with the larger points served by established carriers. Fearing that the so-called feeders would ultimately become trunk lines in disguise, further diluting revenues in a postwar market that was not as rosy as anticipated, Delta joined forces with other "grandfather" lines to fight the new firms. Comparing the upstart airways to the short-line companies that allegedly had produced a "chaotic condition" in the railroad industry, Delta's E. V. Moore reminded the CAB that none of the feeders had "one

dollar's air line investment to protect and enhance, or even a scin-
tilla of public responsibility to preserve and develop." Where, he
demanded to know, was there any compelling need for the "purely
local experimental service of the new applicants" in preference to
Delta's "seasoned and matured proposals for local expansion of its
existing service?" Face to face with the feeder-line menace, Moore
even found a few kind words to say on behalf of Eastern.[28]

But all to little avail, for the concept of feeder service had gained
ground steadily throughout the war and was viewed in Washington
as an idea whose time had arrived.[29] The principal casualty of
"feederitis," from Delta's point of view, was the company's hope of
winning an extension of its Chicago-to-Cincinnati route eastward
through a chain of cities in West Virginia, Virginia, and the Carolinas. Instead, the CAB awarded the route to one of the most promising of the new feeder lines, Piedmont Aviation. Piedmont was
also awarded access to Louisville, which Delta had wanted to add
as an alternative stop on its route from Cincinnati to Lexington.

In the Deep South, however, Delta fared much better. There the
aspiring feeder line, Southern Airways, was certified for operation
over routes connecting a variety of smaller points, including Tuscaloosa, Alabama; Valdosta, Georgia; and Greenville, South Carolina,
to such centers as Memphis, Birmingham, Atlanta, and Jacksonville,
but the CAB also added five other cities to the Delta system. As
alternative stops on its grandfather route from Atlanta to Meridian,
the company was authorized to serve Columbus, Georgia, a major
textile-manufacturing center and home of the large army infantry
base at Fort Benning; Montgomery, capital of Alabama and a focus
of trade and distribution; and Selma, smaller but a major blackbelt
Alabama city that had not previously had commercial air service.
On the run from Atlanta to Savannah, Delta planes were certified to
fly in and out of Macon, a textile and agricultural-marketing center
that had once housed temporary headquarters for Huff Daland
Dusters. Perhaps most important of all, because of its busy industrial plants, thriving tourist trade, and key location in the heart of
the TVA region, was Chattanooga, which came into the Delta system as an intermediate stop alternating with Knoxville on the route
between Cincinnati and Atlanta. Eastern already provided service
between Atlanta and Chattanooga, but the CAB had decided that
Chattanooga's need for direct air service to Cincinnati was the overriding consideration.[30]

Delta also scored a partial victory in another case decided by the

CAB in 1947, though again it failed to win its major objective. The big prize, for which numerous airlines were contending, was a jumbo route stretching from New Orleans to various points in the industrial Northeast, including the juiciest plum of all, New York City. Delta put extraordinary efforts into its argument, and hopes soared in Atlanta during April 1947, when a CAB examiner recommended that the company be given a route from New Orleans to Atlanta by way of Hattiesburg, Meridian, and Birmingham, continuing to New York City with stops at Washington, Baltimore, and Philadelphia. Predictably, however, the examiner's report was fiercely attacked by a swarm of other airlines, and the CAB finally decided, in January 1948, not to award the coveted route to anybody. This decision was especially galling to Delta, which also suffered a further blow: the CAB had granted PCA access to Atlanta on a route leading from Bristol, Tennessee, to New Orleans. Soon thereafter the same company, under the new name of Capital Airlines, was to win certification from Atlanta to New York. Woolman would have to wait nearly a decade to realize his dream of gaining entry to what he liked to call America's Main Street.[31]

Looking back, it may seem that the CAB had given Delta only a poor consolation prize: a short run from New Orleans to Meridian with Hattiesburg as an intermediate stop. Nevertheless, as knowledgeable buyers of aviation securities recognized, the advantages of this apparently minor link were far from negligible. Up to that time, all Delta flights into New Orleans had had to come from the west, for the 1943 CAB decision establishing the route from Shreveport to the "Crescent City" by way of Alexandria and Baton Rouge had not authorized its continuation eastward and the turnaround of Delta planes caused extra expenditure. The new link to Meridian permitted Delta to compete with Eastern on flights from New Orleans to Birmingham and Atlanta. Furthermore, the new award permitted Delta to offer the first through-plane service between New Orleans and Cincinnati to be certified by the CAB.[32]

Delta also failed to obtain CAB permission to enter several other potentially lucrative markets during the late 1940s. The doors to Memphis and Kansas City remained locked, as Eastern fought doggedly to block Delta's expansion northwest of Birmingham. Similarly, against the combined opposition of Eastern and National, Delta had no luck in gaining access to St. Petersburg and Clearwater or certification for direct flights between Miami and such major cities as Dallas, New Orleans, and Birmingham. The CAB, however, did add a few smaller communities in Texas and Indiana to the Delta system in this period. In addition, Delta won the right to stop at both Chattanooga and Knoxville on the same flight from Atlanta to Cincinnati, though it was banned from purely local traffic between the two Tennessee cities because of the existing service provided by Capital.[33]

From a long-range perspective, the biggest gains scored by Delta before the CAB during the late 1940s came not from permanent additions to its own route structure but from two pioneering arrangements under which the company agreed to share its routes and equipment with other airlines, at least temporarily. After World War II, while the majority of CAB members proceeded to award large amounts of new mileage to various carriers in order to encourage competition, a minority argued that the orderly development of commercial aviation would be better served by promoting the interchange of equipment on existing routes. Precedents for such action existed in the railroad industry, where a growing trend toward standardization of rolling stock and facilities had produced a number of cooperative arrangements aimed at cutting costs and avoiding duplication. In the airline industry itself, United and Western had collaborated during the late 1930s to provide through sleeper service between Los Angeles and the East, by means of an agreement under which pilots and crews belonging to the two lines took over the operation of each other's planes at Salt Lake City, an arrangement that ultimately proved unsatisfactory to United and was abandoned. Despite this somewhat unencouraging precedent, the basic idea continued to appeal to federal authorities who were afraid that expanding new route mileage would only drive down load factors, lead to overspending on new equipment, and otherwise multiply the problems of the trunk lines in the disappointing postwar market. Early in 1947 the CAB began a retreat from its expansionist philosophy, authorizing an interchange of equipment between Pan American and Panagra at the Canal Zone. Later that same year it took corresponding action on the domestic scene, approving an interchange agreement between Delta and TWA.[34]

This important arrangement arose partly from the CAB's action in awarding Delta and Eastern significant new air routes from the Great Lakes area to Miami in 1945. Eastern had received a route from Detroit to Miami via Cleveland and other intermediate stops; this threatened TWA, which already provided service from Detroit to Cincinnati, where its passengers could make southbound connec-

DELTA ROUTE SYSTEM
1948

INTERCHANGE ROUTES

------ with TWA

– – – with American

tions with Delta. Recognizing this, the CAB indicated that it would be favorably disposed to an interchange between TWA and Delta that would make it unnecessary for travelers to change planes at Cincinnati. Representatives of the two firms had heated discussions over various practical difficulties involved in implementing the plan, but in the end the mutual advantages led to an agreement, approved by the CAB over Eastern's opposition at the end of 1947 and put into effect on June 1, 1948. TWA personnel were to take charge of Delta planes at Cincinnati for northbound flights to Columbus, Dayton, Toledo, and Detroit. Later, Delta crews flew TWA ships south from Cincinnati to such cities as Atlanta, Miami, and Dallas.[35]

By the time this arrangement went into operation Delta was about to enter into an even more significant interchange proposal that would once again pit Woolman against his personal rival, Eddie Rickenbacker. Throughout the postwar period the CAB had come under increasing pressure to authorize through-plane service between various southeastern cities and the Pacific Coast. The revenue potential of such service was obvious, and its lure drew many airlines into what eventually became one of the most hotly contested route cases in the history of American aviation. Because of the CAB's growing disinclination to award major new route mileage, the chances were good that the problem would be solved at least temporarily by resorting to the interchange method. The two airlines most likely to be adversely affected by such a solution were Eastern and National, both of which wanted their existing systems extended westward to California; the logical beneficiaries would be Delta, already flying passengers to Fort Worth, and American, currently certified to take them on to such destinations as Los Angeles and San Francisco.[36]

Woolman had long wanted to expand the Delta system westward, and fruitless conversations involving an interchange with American had taken place right after the war. Matters finally got moving again in October 1948, when C. R. Smith sent Woolman a cordial letter reiterating the desire of American's management for such an arrangement and pledging that his company would cooperate fully with Delta on "any sensible program to get the job done." The timing was propitious. Although Delta and American were competing for traffic between Chicago and Cincinnati, relations between the two lines were friendly. Both used the same equipment, DC-6s, that would service the interchange route. American had no immediate plans to expand in the Southeast and was eager to stop any western incursions by Eastern or National. Under the circumstances alliance was a natural, though temporary, expedient, and an interchange agreement between the two companies was signed less than a month after Smith's letter had reached Woolman.[37]

Partly because of its members' own inclinations and partly because TWA, United, and Western strongly favored this interchange over an invasion by Rickenbacker, the CAB moved in 1949 with what one Delta lawyer called "unprecedented speed." Objections from Eastern and National were brushed aside in Washington, and the process from start to finish lasted only eight months. Although the board's authorization was not permanent—new route awards would still be considered—it was nevertheless a significant victory, which Delta and American moved quickly to exploit. Less than three weeks after the CAB made its decision, a party of federal officials and company executives, headed by Smith and Woolman, made a circuit of the entire route from San Francisco and Los Angeles to Miami. Speaking at Miami after a trip punctuated with gala luncheons and dinner celebrations, Smith called the interchange plan "so simple it should have been done years ago," and Woolman, as a CAB official looked on approvingly, told how the arrangement had brought about the first southern coast-to-coast air service "without adding one mile of new route, nor any additional expense." Passengers soon flew between Atlanta and Los Angeles in less than twelve hours and without change of plane.[38]

The consummation of the interchange agreement with American climaxed a remarkable period of expansion for Delta since it first won the Chicago-to-Miami route in 1945. The presence of Delta pilot W. Lee McBride at the controls of the American Airlines DC-6 flagship *Wyoming* when it landed at Miami International Airport with Smith, Woolman, and their fellow dignitaries aboard proved that Delta was recognized as a worthy associate by the largest trunk line in the industry. And the arrival of Delta ships at the bustling airports of San Francisco and Los Angeles soon provided another sign of the company's broadening range. The Atlanta *Journal*, praising the interchange as "another evidence of the progressiveness of an alert Southern enterprise," commented that it was "a far cry back to the days when Delta began flying six-passenger, fabric-covered ships."[39] And so it was.

CHAPTER 8

Stormy Weather and Brightening Horizons

FOR DELTA the postwar period was not just a succession of jousts with Eastern and other competitors, a string of generally profitable decisions on the acquisition of new aircraft, or a series of limited but encouraging victories in its constant efforts to add new route mileage. Expansion brought anticipated problems, but it also brought unexpected headaches. As they tried to cope with these difficulties, Woolman and the other company officials could find some satisfaction in knowing that they were not alone. For the airline industry as a whole, the dominant character of the immediate postwar years changed quickly from great expectations to crisis.

The causes of the crisis were intricate but readily understandable given the advantage of hindsight. The total passenger miles flown by the trunk lines soared from 3,408,290,000 in 1945 to 6,068,315,000 in 1946, but the anticipated profits from this expansion were largely devoured by the cost of new equipment, the expense of training pilots to fly more complex airplanes and ground crews to service them, the overhead associated with inaugurating new routes, and the need for rapid increases in personnel throughout the industry. Complicating everything was the start of an inflationary spiral, attended by the dropping of wartime controls, which was to become more and more familiar to businessmen and consumers through the succeeding years. The process of adjusting to these conditions had only begun when the industry's demand curve flattened rapidly; total passenger miles rose only slightly, to 6,307,690,000 in 1947, then dropped to 6,277,932,000 in 1948, before struggling upward to 6,562,580,000 in 1949.

It was not much consolation that the railroad passenger business, against which airline executives traditionally measured their progress, was falling off steadily throughout the period; the winner of the postwar "Transportation Derby" was clearly neither the locomotive nor the airplane: it was the automobile. Seasonal variations in traffic added to the problems of the airline industry, as did occasional strikes and periodic sensational air crashes, which alarmed prospective customers. Furthermore, although demand was far below previously anticipated levels, the nation's airport facilities proved, in many instances, inadequate to the needs and comfort of travelers, which led to bad publicity for the industry as a whole. Amid all these difficulties the domestic trunk lines sank deeper into the red, accumulating deficits totaling more than $47 million in the three-year period from 1946 through 1948.[1]

Of all the nation's airlines, only Eastern, which enjoyed a particularly favorable route structure connecting numerous large cities and a long-established vacation trade from northern points to Florida, earned consistent profits during this dismal era. Of the remaining carriers, Delta did far better than most. Nevertheless, throughout the winter months of 1945–46 it incurred a series of losses connected with acquiring new aircraft, training personnel to operate them, developing the new Chicago-to-Miami route, and adjusting to a forty-hour work week without lowering take-home pay. The company finally did manage to earn a net addition to surplus of slightly more than $362,000 by the end of the 1946 fiscal year. During fiscal 1947, however, Delta could not escape the fate of most carriers, and it experienced a net loss of approximately $310,000, despite strenuous economy moves, including a payroll reduction from 2,700 to 2,100 employees. Rising costs, partly connected with a major expansion of company headquarters in Atlanta, accounted for part of the deficit, as did a spell of what the company's annual report called "some of the worst weather in Delta's operating history," which hampered winter vacation traffic. Basically, however, the difficulties with which Woolman and his colleagues were struggling were general throughout the industry. The picture was much better by mid-1948, and the firm showed a net profit of almost $205,000 for the fiscal year just ended.[2] (See Appendix 1.)

Compared to most of the trunk lines, which as a group had incurred a deficit of more than $11 million during the first eight months of 1948 alone, Delta had done very well indeed, but the anxieties of the period nevertheless show up clearly in surviving company correspondence. "Our passenger loads have fallen off so much during the past three months that it has put us in the red in spite of everything we can do," Woolman moaned at one point to B. R. Coad, who was himself complaining about the sagging revenues of the dusting division. "If misery loves company we ought to be fairly happy," Woolman informed Coad on another occasion, noting that the weather had been improving and that a fare increase was in prospect but that both the pilots and the mechanics were demanding higher pay. "If it isn't one darn thing," he complained, "it is two."

Writing from Monroe during the summer of 1947, C. E. Faulk seemed as worried that in July nearly half Delta's available seat miles had gone unsold as he was about impending eye surgery. "I know you are doing your best and I do not want to appear too critical," he told Woolman, "but I think it would be a good idea for you to take the Traffic Department, from Mr. Parker to the lowest employee, and if they can not improve this situation I suggest you take off some of the flights." Less than a month later Faulk was in New York City only days away from his eye operation, but he still found time to inform Woolman that he was "not very well pleased with the present operations on Delta. . . . There must be some trouble in the Traffic Department, or the public just does not want to ride. My casual observation is that the Traffic Sales Department is at low ebb."[3]

Woolman tried to reassure Faulk while parrying suggestions that he did not like. He was particularly loath to reduce schedules, arguing that Delta "can't haul the people if we don't have the flights nor can you bop the flights on and off on a day's notice." But Faulk was not the only director who was concerned about the company's problems; Atlanta financier Winship Nunnally, who had been elected to the board in 1947, pointed out to Woolman in the spring of 1948 that the cost of gasoline had gone up by 48 percent, materials by 35 percent, and salaries by 64 percent. He suggested requesting CAB approval for elimination of unprofitable towns and routes and for reduced passenger services on DC-3 flights, including elimination of stewardesses and free meals. Although a bit extreme, his proposals were in some respects similar to the "air coach" strategy that was to become popular on some airlines, including Delta, not long after.[4]

Like many other airlines in a period of disappointing passenger revenues, Delta found some consolation in the growth of its air-cargo operation, which had begun on an experimental basis late in the war. Before 1941, when Eastern, American, TWA, and United had taken the lead in forming a jointly operated subsidiary known as Air Cargo, Inc., to provide large-scale freight shipments, domestic airlines had generally limited their cargo operations to the transport of lightweight items requiring fast delivery—canceled checks, motion-picture film, and highly perishable goods. The war had familiarized trunk-line operators with the handling of heavy freight, and the years immediately following the conflict found all carriers scrambling to establish themselves in this line of activity amid vigorous competition with such newly founded all-cargo enterprises as Slick Airways of San Antonio and the Flying Tiger Line of Burbank, California. Under those conditions air freight mushroomed from less than 5 million tons in 1945 to 125 million tons in 1948, by which time the certified passenger carriers had managed to capture a majority of the cargo traffic.[5]

Delta inaugurated regularly scheduled cargo service on August 15, 1946, after publishing tariffs and procedures covering items ranging from goldfish to heavy farm and industrial machinery. Under the leadership of Paul Pate, whose work with the company's previous unscheduled cargo deliveries has already been described in Chapter 6, the venture was off to a good start, capturing the patronage of such customers as the Chevrolet Division of General Motors, Procter and Gamble, and C. S. Fred of Lebanon, Ohio, the "Mushroom King of America." Delta planes flew 16 million pound-miles of cargo during the first month of the new service, and by mid-1947 the company was already handling more air freight than air express, with a volume of 290 million pound-miles in July alone. The business grew apace, and an all-cargo C-47 was added to supplement the capacity available in the freight bins of regular passenger ships. By mid-1950 air freight was adding a badly needed $500,000 or so a year to Delta receipts. The service was vigorously advertised; one popular display featured a scantily clad female dancer, some representative Delta cargo rates, and a limerick:

> A talented lassie named Alice
> Who danced every night at the Palace
>   Broke one vital string
>   But solved everything
> With a spare she AirFREIGHTED from Dallas.[6]

Only one thing, however, would put Delta firmly in the black—more passenger revenue—and the company went after it with a sales effort unprecedented in its history. "Get that one *other* passenger," Parker admonished a special meeting of district traffic and reservations managers in Atlanta during the winter of 1945–46 as the profit picture began to darken. He pointed out that one more passenger on every Delta flight would bring in almost $375,000 in additional annual receipts. Unremitting emphasis on such themes had led by November 1947 to the largest general sales conference yet held by the firm. Woolman, Parker, and other company officials challenged personnel from thirty-two cities around the system to fill more seats on Delta airliners and launched a program for the coming year that was to feature such strategies as organization-wide sales contests, all-out efforts to promote the vacation trade, and a "passenger of the month" plan to recognize travelers who patronized Delta regularly. But the postwar slump continued for one more year, and the number of revenue passengers actually declined from 528,687 in fiscal 1947 to 493,608 in fiscal 1948. (See Appendix 1.) Despite this decline, the company did have the satisfaction of boarding its two-millionth passenger on April 23, 1948; Miss Anna Grace Green of Atlanta was presented with gifts, including, appropriately enough, some Amelia Earhart luggage from Rich's. At another yearly sales conference in Atlanta in October, Parker took a hard line, warning the assembled personnel that "we've got to put out or get out" and stating that from then on it would be a matter of "sell or bust."[7]

As Woolman had lamented to Coad in 1947, demands from pilots and mechanics were compounding Delta's managerial woes. In 1945 pilots had begun putting pressure on all airlines over such issues as pay rates and working conditions on the four-engine planes that were already being planned for and purchased throughout the industry. No satisfactory terms resulted from negotiations between individual carriers and the ALPA, so an organization called the Airlines Negotiating Committee (ANC) was formed in December 1945; it was to be the official bargaining agent for thirteen enterprises, including both major trunk lines and such smaller companies as Delta, Braniff, PCA, and Chicago and Southern. Despite ALPA objections to dealing with such a common front, the CAB approved the new arrangement and sanctioned the ANC to deal with all aspects of pilot's pay and working conditions from the management side of the negotiating table.[8]

Still seeking to parley with individual firms, the ALPA first approached Delta in July 1946, asking for changes in the company's contract with its pilots. At issue were provisions affecting such matters as minimum base pay, mileage pay, travel expenses, and vacations. Delta responded by pointing out, through ANC, that the agreement currently in force was not subject to alteration before August 1, 1947, but that ANC would be glad to discuss any changes that might be adopted on or after that date.[9] Serious negotiations were slow to begin, and at one point in the fall of 1946 the ALPA, in an apparent effort to avoid direct dealings with the ANC, threatened to invoke mediation under the Railroad Labor Act. Finally, after months of desultory sparring, direct bargaining between ALPA and ANC got underway in April 1947; they proceeded, slowly but apparently without undue acrimony, to an individual settlement between the pilots' organization and Delta.[10]

Among the issues that had to be resolved was Delta's independent action on pay rates for pilots of four-engine aircraft. In July 1946, at the time of the opening gambits in the three-cornered game being played among the ALPA, Delta, and the ANC, an emergency board constituted by President Harry S. Truman to investigate working conditions in the airline industry recommended new pay rates for the pilots of TWA, at that time the only carrier whose ALPA chapter was actually on strike. The board also urged that disputes between pilots and other airlines, including Delta, be referred to the ANC for negotiation and that the rates suggested by the board for TWA be adopted as a basis for discussion. Delta's management, for its part, had pledged to make pay increases retroactive to the initiation of its own four-engine operations. When the ALPA dragged its feet on negotiating with the ANC, Delta unilaterally adopted the recommended TWA rates in September 1946 and distributed paychecks, which most Delta pilots cashed. The company completed retroactive payments by the spring of 1947.

This and other outstanding matters were finally settled in a contract between Delta and ALPA effective October 1, 1947. The pay rates were generous; captains, for example, were granted minimum base compensation substantially higher than that originally demanded by the ALPA ($2,200, as opposed to $1,600, for the first year in rank, with $200 increments for each year of additional service). The base pay, of course, was substantially augmented by supplements for hours spent in the air; mileage flown, computed according to the differential speeds of the DC-3 and DC-4; and the gross weight of the aircraft operated. Whatever heated words may have been exchanged while these details were being hammered out, the company's ALPA chapter did send Woolman a warm letter at the end of the process, expressing their "thanks and appreciation" for the cooperation that he had extended in reaching the agreement.[11]

The relations between Delta's management and union organizations seeking changes in working conditions for mechanics, however, took a different course. By the time that the company's previous contract with this segment of its work force came up for renewal in 1947, the United Auto Workers (UAW-CIO) had absorbed the Air Line Mechanics Association and was now the bargaining agent. The situation was further complicated by the claim of still another labor organization, the International Association of Machinists (IAM), to jurisdiction; the increasing success of IAM representatives in organizing Delta mechanics forced UAW-CIO into a belligerent mood. When Delta balked at demands by the latter, a wildcat strike ensued in May 1947. In part, this was a stratagem by UAW-CIO to stall an election which it stood to lose. Only a part of the work force joined in the walkout, which occurred while Woolman was on a business trip to Washington. Delta officials had tried to delay matters until his return, but the strikers did not heed their requests. Speaking for management, Parker branded the strike "illegal and unauthorized" and insisted that it violated a state law calling for thirty days' notice.

Some mechanics stayed on duty, and supervisory personnel helped to keep the airline functioning without any disruption of schedules. Meanwhile, charges and counter-charges were exchanged between labor representatives and company officials. The UAW-CIO alleged that Delta had refused to consider a wage increase while comparable carriers had granted substantial pay hikes for mechanics. As picketing intensified, Delta went to the Fulton County Superior Court seeking an injunction against strikers who, the company claimed, had molested workers refusing to participate in the walkout. Under the terms of a state law prohibiting mass picketing, Judge Bond Almand granted a temporary restraining order limiting the number of pickets that the union could have at one time to two—one at the airport administration building and the other at the downtown Delta ticket office. In the face of this court order and the split in the work force itself, the participating workers called off the strike in June.[12]

Negotiations were later resumed, but they had once more come to naught by September. A wage increase, which Delta unilaterally granted to its employees, took much of the steam out of this potentially volatile situation. An election was held in the fall of 1947 under NMB procedures, but there were few Delta votes for either UAW-CIO or IAM. By that time also the existing contract had long since expired, and the company, no longer restrained by its provisions, simply terminated its relationship with the UAW-CIO. When another effort was made in 1949 to organize the mechanics, it met with defeat, apparently because of a "grass roots" campaign by

Delta's inaugural flight to Miami in December 1945 is christened by the Orange Bowl Queen, Libby Walker.

The arrival of Delta's big four-engine DC-4 in 1946 attracted large crowds at the Atlanta Airport.

A $1,000,000 expansion program in 1947 added additional office space, new hangar and shop area, and a separate engine test cell.

Delta's Board of Directors in the late 1940s. *Seated, left to right:* L. B. Judd, C. H. McHenry, C. E. Faulk, M. S. Bieden-harn, E. H. Gerry. *Standing:* Winship Nunnally, R. W. Freeman, C. E. Woolman, R. J. Reynolds, Laigh Parker.

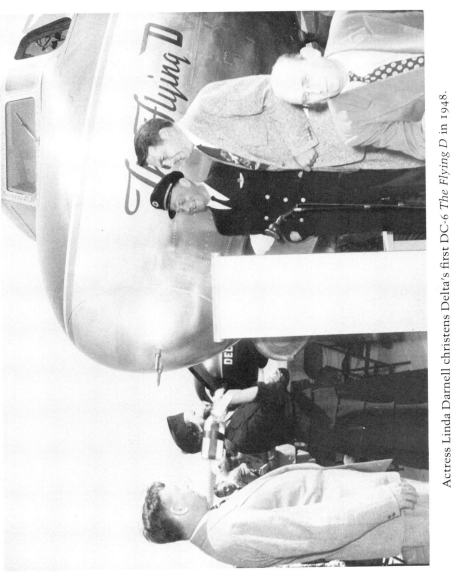

Actress Linda Darnell christens Delta's first DC-6 *The Flying D* in 1948.

The handshake between C. E. Woolman and C. R. Smith, president of American Airlines, symbolizes the first linking of the Southeast and the West Coast via the Delta–American Interchange Service, initiated September 25, 1949.

Catherine FitzGerald is surrounded by well-wishers on her twenty-fifth anniversary with the firm. *First row, left to right:* G. J. Dye, C. P. Lyle, O. B. Deere, John L. Sutton, T. P. Ball, C. E. Woolman, Miss FitzGerald, L. B. Judd, Jack King, J. M. Langford. *Back row:* J. T. Harper, Tom Oster, C. P. Knecht, Charles H. Dolson, Floyd Addison, Fritz Schwaemmle, Laigh Parker, George Shealy.

Delta's first DC-6, with new paint scheme, takes to the air in 1948.

antiunion employees. Surviving documentation makes it impossible to determine how much spontaneity there was in this counteroffensive, but Woolman, though certainly no proponent of unionization, was careful not to seem heavy-handed in dealing with representatives of organized labor. In May 1949, for example, he was contacted informally by Paul Chipman of the International Association of Machinists about alleged discrimination against a mechanic who had not shared in a general pay increase that the company had recently granted its employees. According to Chipman, "my only conference with you impressed me with the opinion that you sought to avoid discrimination against any employee." Woolman thanked Chipman for this commendation, assured him that it was not the policy of Delta to discriminate, and promised that the matter would be "thoroughly investigated." [13]

In the midst of these labor problems and gloomy economic developments, death stalked Delta in one of the most singular tragedies in the history of the United States airline industry. On April 17, 1947, H. R. Bolander, Jr., a rising executive who had joined Delta as Woolman's personal assistant after serving as vice-president and general counsel for Chicago and Southern, wrote to several municipal officials in Macon, Columbus, Montgomery, and Selma in order to make final arrangements for a survey trip that he and other company leaders were about to take, to help prepare scheduled airline service into these cities. He was signing his own death warrant. Five days later, on the morning of April 22, he and seven companions approached the Muscogee County Airport at Columbus, Georgia, in a Delta C-47 piloted by operations chief George R. Cushing, a veteran of more than eleven thousand hours in the cockpit. Shortly before, a private pilot named J. C. Fussell had taken off from the nearby Columbus municipal airport, headed for the Muscogee field on a short hop in a war-surplus BT-13 training plane.

Fussell was an experienced aviator, who had flown many missions for the Civil Air Patrol, but when he neared the airport, at about the same time that the Delta plane was coming in to land, he failed to fly a correct approach pattern and apparently did not keep a careful lookout for nearby craft. The field had no control tower then, and the barrel fuselage of the BT-13, with its relatively long nose, probably made it impossible for Fussell to see what was under him. As he too prepared to touch down, he did not realize that Cushing's ship was directly below. Suddenly Fussell's plane settled on the empennage of the C-47 just forward of the rudder and vertical fin. In what must have been an instinctive reaction as he felt his craft going out of control, Cushing applied power and rose to an altitude about 150 feet above the runway with the BT-13 lodged on his tail. Both aircraft crashed to the ground. Flames quickly consumed the interlocked planes, and the billowing smoke attracted some two thousand people, who were held back by military police from Fort Benning. A Roman Catholic priest tried to approach the wreckage to pull out possible survivors and administer last rites, but the searing heat was simply too intense. One veteran pilot on the scene declared that "there was no chance for anyone to be alive." Eight ambulances were assembled, and, after the flames had been extinguished and the wreckage could be entered, they carried the nine bodies away in solemn procession.[14] No airline in the United States, before or since, has lost so much executive talent and experience in so short a time —a matter of minutes.

Of more immediate importance, however, was the heartbreak that devolved upon families and friends of the accident's victims. Telegrams and letters of condolence poured into Atlanta as a grief-stricken company tried its best to recover from the shock. James H. (Jimmy) Doolittle, a famed leader of the Tokyo Raiders during World War II and an old friend from Woolman's South American days, summed up most of the messages when he said, "It is most unfortunate and indeed the irony of fate that after the magnificent record of safety and sound operations you and your boys have established through the years [these] . . . lives should be lost through a cause entirely outside their control." Gone, aside from Cushing and Bolander, were J. V. Little, Atlanta district manager; L. T. Campbell, superintendent of communications and head of a staff famed throughout the organization for never requiring operations personnel to "wait anywhere for communications to catch up"; E. A. (Bill) Rainouard, chief flight superintendent, noted for his "trigger-quick" but accurate decisions; C. S. Berry, superintendent of aircraft construction, who was probably the occupant of the copilot's seat on the ill-fated flight; John L. Schneider, superintendent of stations, just recently returned from a tour of duty in the army air force; and Lindley W. Camp, an Atlanta attorney and former solicitor general of the State of Georgia, who had represented the company in various local matters.

Charles Dolson, whose direction of the Pacific branch of the Naval Air Transport Service during the war had given him an excellent background for his new responsibilities, was quickly appointed operations manager, and by the end of the year he had moved up to Cushing's former rank of vice-president; peppery T. P. Ball was promoted to Dolson's previous slot as chief pilot. In a letter acknowledging Faulk's expression of grief and sympathy ("I know you were as deeply hurt over the terrible tragedy as I am") and expressing concern about replacing those who had died, Woolman voiced regret that some of the publicity over the accident, though mainly fair, "has given the implication that our whole top side had been wiped out, which of course is not true." To Faulk, Doolittle, and others, he stressed that Delta was "blest by having competent assistants whom we were able to promote, men who have had ten years or more with the company and are thoroughly familiar with their respective jobs and company policies." Certainly, he reassured Faulk, "we need not worry as to the determination of the entire force to carry on."[15]

An official report issued by the CAB in August 1947, after a thorough investigation of the accident, found no fault with the procedures followed by Cushing and attributed the accident to negligence on Fussell's part. The company could also point to the fact that it had not had a fatal accident in more than eleven years and almost 575 million passenger miles. Because the Columbus flight was not scheduled and the C-47 carried only men on official corporate business, Delta's record of flying without a revenue passenger fatality since 1935 continued unblemished a while longer.[16]

But that record, too, was soon blotted. Shortly before 11:00 P.M. on March 10, 1948, a Delta DC-4 sat poised on the right-hand north–south runway at Chicago municipal airport, ready for a night flight to Cincinnati and Miami. There were four crew members and nine passengers aboard. After what appeared to be a normal takeoff roll, it climbed into the sky—then suddenly assumed an abnormally steep, almost vertical, angle of attack. Personnel in the control tower saw instantly that the ship was in trouble and had already begun to telephone emergency rescue services when the plane apparently stalled and then dropped off to the right. It recovered for a moment, then plunged into the ground with a terrific impact, bursting into flames in a field to the north of the terminal. One section of the craft split off from the rest and escaped catching fire immediately, which enabled witnesses to rush to the scene and drag a few people out of the wreckage while ambulances and other vehicles struggled through deep snow covering the field. One passenger, Mrs. Tripolina Meo of Chicago, survived, despite extensive injuries. Everyone else on board died, including pilot Lee Hollaway, first officer J. S. Disosway, purser Marvin G. Hairston, and stewardess Sue L. Young.[17]

Woolman received several sharp queries from people who claimed to be regular passengers of Delta; they wondered whether the accident had resulted from improper handling and insufficient care by the airline. "As a Delta passenger you are certainly entitled to ask the questions you raised," he replied. "Our safety record is one of the best in the industry. Until the accident we had operated 750 million revenue passenger miles and transported just under 2 million passengers in regularly scheduled operations, without a fatality to passengers or crew during a period exceeding 12 years. We have been conservative in our operations, putting safety ahead of anything else and this will continue to be our goal." Candidly admitting that the cause of the accident was a mystery to him, he provided such details as he could about the investigation then being conducted by the CAB and gave assurances that Delta followed strict maintenance schedules and adequate personnel training policies in its quest for safe and dependable operations.

Despite intensive investigations by the CAB, the ATA, and Delta officials alike for more than a year, the cause of the crash remained unclear. Theories were tested involving such possibilities as the interference of ice with control cables and the inadvertent engagement of the mechanism designed to lock the elevators in place against the possibility of sudden wind gusts while the plane was on the ground, but all appeared improbable. Hollaway was a veteran of nearly 10,000 hours of flying time, and during his wartime military service had been assigned as personal pilot to high-ranking government officials. There was no evidence that the plane had been overloaded at the time of takeoff. A CAB report, which was finally released on June 14, 1949, stated simply that "the probable cause of this accident was the loss of longitudinal control of the airplane. The cause of the loss of control remains undetermined."[18]

Frustration about not knowing the cause of the Chicago crash, coupled with the fact that Delta had just received several awards for its outstanding safety record, made the fatal accident all the more distressing to company officials. So did continuing difficulties in escaping the postwar financial doldrums, which sometimes seemed to stretch on forever. One of the most persistent headaches was the never-ending inflationary spiral, which repeatedly caused prices to outstrip cost projections. In 1946, for example, Delta had been forced to expand its headquarters for the second time in less than four years. A contract was signed with the Austin Company of Cleveland, Ohio, to construct a new administration building and additions to the existing shops and hangars for $852,000, but within four months this figure had ballooned to $1,013,578. Ultimately the new facilities were completed; they were formally opened in the summer of 1947 by festivities that included a barbecue for employees and an open house for the local public. Visitors were shown a lobby and reception room paneled in bleached walnut and a new hangar capable of servicing three or four DC-4s at once. But rising prices had forced Woolman to make some draconian decisions, including one to forgo air conditioning, at least temporarily, even in the executive offices.

By 1948 the costs of parts and supplies had risen 25 percent above 1947 levels, thanks partly to inflation and partly to the impending arrival of the DC-6. Despite a careful program of cost control worked out by purchasing agent H. D. Wigley, the burden of the company's spare-parts inventory rose from $650,000 to about $1 million. Also indicative of hard times was the fact that pay raises were few and far between; in 1947, for example, only two company officers received salary hikes—one amounting to $200 and the other to a mere $75. Most airline presidents took small raises that year, despite prevailing adversities, but Woolman's annual salary of $18,000, far below the industry average, remained the same.[19]

New equipment, new facilities, and rising costs, added to the demands of a growing route structure, made it imperative that the company raise large amounts of new capital, both through borrowing money and issuing new stock. By late 1946 the transfusion provided by a major stock issue authorized nearly two years before had been largely absorbed, thanks to such expensive operations as the opening of the Chicago-to-Miami route and the acquisition of the DC-4s. Delta turned, as did the larger trunk lines at about the same time, for its first recourse to negotiating a sizable credit agreement with a consortium of banks, which would permit withdrawal of funds as needed over an extended period. Under a plan devised by L. L. Gellerstedt, executive vice-president of Citizens and Southern in Atlanta, eleven banks, of which eight were located in the South, joined in pledging $5 million, which Delta could borrow over a five-year period for new equipment of all kinds. In the accompanying publicity much was made about the fact that $4 million of the total was to come from financial institutions located in Dixie, which Woolman cited as "full evidence that the South is in a new era of financing its own enterprise."[20]

Despite its scope, this arrangement, which went into effect late in 1946, was insufficient for the outlays that would be required in the future. Discussions of the need for a broader financial base were complicated by the facts that Delta stock was not widely held and that company officials wanted to keep it that way. The idea of listing Delta stock on the New York exchange was broached on a number of occasions, but, on the advice of Richard Courts and other counselors, the board decided to seek SEC approval for a limited sale similar to those of 1939–40 and 1944–45. After receiving preliminary indications from the SEC that such a sale would be permissible under certain conditions, the board agreed to authorize the issue of from 50,000 to 100,000 shares of new stock, which would bring the number of shares outstanding to a maximum of 500,000. During May and June 1947 Courts negotiated a sale of the full 100,000 shares to various investors at a unit price of $22, on terms that netted the company $1,679,546.[21]

At the time that this issue was approved, the directors also authorized the selection of as many as five new members once the stock sale had been completed. On June 11, 1947, four new directors were elected in a move to broaden the base of financial leadership within the company; this move reflected the gradually diminishing role of Monroe investors in the firm's continuing development. One of the directors chosen was R. J. Reynolds of Winston-Salem, North Carolina, the tobacco magnate and aviation enthusiast who had invested heavily in the 1944–45 stock issue; another, who became a shareholder for the first time in the new expansion and who was destined to play an increasingly important part in company affairs, was R. W. Freeman of New Orleans, president and director of the Louisiana Coca-Cola Bottling Company. The third newcomer to the board was Winship Nunnally of Atlanta, a prominent Coca-Cola stockholder and member of the Trust Company of Georgia's executive committee, who had himself flown single- and multiple-engine planes since receiving his pilot's license in 1929. The fourth member chosen in 1947 was the first Delta director ever to come from outside the South, which showed the extent to which the company was by then attracting the interest of investors in the country's largest money markets; he was Edward H. Gerry, a New York City real-estate executive connected with the Harriman family. One year later the fifth director was added: Courts was elected to the board, emphasizing the firmness of Delta's Atlanta base and the role that Courts had played in making Georgia the company headquarters.[22]

The willingness of important investors to purchase 100,000 shares of Delta stock during a year in which the company announced its first annual deficit since 1941 and nearly every trunk line in the country was deep in the doldrums could not help but encourage Woolman and other Delta officials. Nor was the expression of financial confidence that it represented misplaced, for, although fiscal 1947–48 turned out to be another disappointing year, Delta's fortunes did improve, and the airline industry as a whole stood on the verge of a major upswing, which finally took shape in 1949. By the end of the decade the picture was brighter than at any time since the end of the war, and Delta was experiencing record profits.

The first dramatic improvement in Delta's financial health came through a development that was personally distasteful to Woolman, who hated to see his firm return to the status of a subsidized carrier. On the other hand, faced with the facts of life, he had no alternative but to follow the lead of other relatively small airlines and approach the CAB for a mail pay increase, which was ultimately granted in September 1948. As a result, Delta obtained $907,428 in back pay for the period from September 9, 1947, to March 31, 1948. A sliding scale was thereafter applied; under it mail pay rose or declined in inverse proportion to the company's passenger load factors. Making the bitter pill more palatable to Woolman, the CAB pointed out that Delta's costs in 1946 and 1947 had ranked among the very lowest in the industry and that the company had made strenuous efforts to keep off subsidies before seeking a mail pay increase. Nor was Delta alone in requiring government assistance, for Chicago and Southern and Continental had already been granted higher mail rates, and Braniff, which had been hurt by the temporary grounding of the DC-6s in the winter of 1947–48, received a subsidy from the CAB along with Delta.[23]

In any event Delta's subsidy, however helpful, was only temporary; it came to an end in October 1951, when a new compensatory scale went into effect after extended congressional hearings covering the airline industry as a whole. Meanwhile, a much more desirable boost to the fortunes of Delta and other carriers had occurred because of a general upsurge in passenger revenues that was clearly underway during the first half of 1949. This rise was somewhat paradoxical, in that the American economy was undergoing a recession at the time, but the airlines were benefiting from some special circumstances, including a much better safety record since the first wave of postwar equipment had undergone modification and considerable improvement in passenger services at new airport facilities throughout the country. Atlanta had played a prominent role in the latter development, opening a new air terminal in May 1948 amid ceremonies attended by Woolman, Rickenbacker, and J. H. Carmichael, the energetic new president of Capital Airlines. Pleased by the fact that the Atlanta city fathers had thriftily made a serviceable temporary terminal out of an older structure, Woolman described the entire project as "the finest bit of municipal spending I've ever seen," and Rickenbacker delighted local sensibilities by declaring that Eastern would be glad to have such a terminal at any of the eighty-seven cities served by his Great Silver Fleet. "And that includes New York City," he added by way of emphasis.[24]

The airlines helped to stimulate the recovery by adding some new services of their own, including special fares of four cents a mile on special no-frills "sky-coach" runs. Delta at first eyed this innovation somewhat suspiciously, partly because it had purposely designed its DC-4s and DC-6s to accommodate relatively limited numbers of passengers in the interests of comfort. It was soon forced to jump on the bandwagon, however, particularly after Eastern began to offer sky-coach service late in 1949. By the following April, Delta had already carried almost 15,000 coach passengers, though this figure placed it only seventh among the ten carriers that had experimented with the new strategy. Delta also joined in the drive to improve facilities, investing heavily in more attractive ticket offices and equipment for the speedier processing of reservations. Its employee magazine bristled throughout the late 1940s with articles describing the constant efforts up and down the system to provide ever better passenger services, reduce turnaround time at terminals, and get planes to their destinations on schedule. Along with other carriers, Delta had been working with the CAA ever since the end of the war to implement improved instrument-landing systems for greater passenger safety, and by September 1950 eighteen cities on its varied routes possessed the required new equipment. Finally, the company had done its best to provide fast and attractive planes to meet the needs of the traveling public, as its gleaming new DC-6s and revamped DC-3s clearly indicated.[25]

Such moves, which reflected general trends throughout the industry, paid off. During 1949 airline revenues climbed rapidly and produced an aggregate profit of more than $13 million after taxes, compared to a loss of almost $5 million the year before. In 1950 passengers continued to take to the skies in record numbers, even before the outbreak of the Korean war created new demands on the country's sixteen domestic trunk lines, which finished the year with unprecedented net profits totaling more than $36 million. With load factors going up and airliners operating at greater efficiency after what had amounted to a painful postwar shakedown, receipts were finally outpacing costs. Freight and express shipments by air stood at an all-time high, while the number of passengers was rapidly approaching parity with that which moved on Pullman cars over the nation's railways. The "Air Age" that had beckoned in 1945 was becoming a reality.[26]

Delta shared in this boom. During calendar 1949 more than 525,000 people flew on the company's planes, reversing a two-year downward trend and eclipsing the previous record of 508,405 set in calendar 1946. In 1950 Delta attracted 637,386 passengers, exceeding the number that it had carried during its entire history before 1945. Earnings followed a similar course, rising to $639,440 after taxes at the end of fiscal 1948–49 and reaching a new high of $815,751 during the following twelve months. Productivity also rose dramatically; this rise was highlighted by the company's vastly increased volume of service in 1950, with only twelve more employees (2,093) than it had had three years before. (See Appendix 1.) Thanks especially to the DC-6, Delta was effectively competing with all its rivals, including Eastern, over the full length and breadth of its route system.[27]

Although Delta, along with the rest of the industry, was obviously emerging from a painful period of postwar readjustment, the company's celebration of its twentieth anniversary as a passenger carrier, on June 1, 1949, was relatively restrained. Birthday cake was provided to passengers all over the system, and mayors of cities along the firm's network of routes proclaimed Delta Day; newspapers carried glowing editorials, and friends sent flowers and telegrams to company headquarters. At a banquet climaxing a spring sales meeting in Atlanta, Catherine FitzGerald, the first employee ever to be hired by Huff Daland Dusters, cut a three-tiered birthday cake at a head table graced by a model of the 1929 Travel Air, while C. E. Woolman and L. B. Judd looked on. The *Delta Digest* noted how much things had changed since the time when it had taken all day to fly from Texas to Georgia in the fabric-covered ships at ninety miles an hour and how much the company had grown since it had "pioneered its route across the South." The prevailing mood of quiet confidence was echoed several months later in another article in the same magazine:

We've got a medium-sized airline, but with the latest and finest of equipment capable of serving our system. We operate in an area, let's face it, where the population, and hence the traffic potential, is considerably below other areas of the country. With one or two exceptions, we don't have access to the great revenue producing cities of the country. But we've kept up with the best. We've always had the most modern equipment of which we could be proud. There are other carriers in similarly thinly populated areas which can't boast of our equipment. For the most part, we have operated in the black—not too deep in black, but black just the same. We enjoy the almost universal admiration and respect of the industry for a well-run, economical and efficient airline.[28]

There was some hyperbole in this statement, for only recently Delta had discovered all too painfully what it was like to lack "the most modern equipment" and pit outmoded DC-4s against Eastern's Connies. There was also a note of wry humor: the reference to the "almost universal" respect enjoyed by the company was undoubtedly inspired by Eddie Rickenbacker's disparaging remarks about airlines that received mail subsidies. He had recently made a public offer to a congressional committee to take over Delta and five other carriers because of his ostensible concern for the American taxpayer. Woolman, who had testified before the same body about conditions and prospects in the airline industry, was understandably nettled by the offer and wrote to a fellow executive that "Of course, the Senate Investigating Committee is always open season for all the screwballs. Frankly I don't think anybody pays any attention to Rick's blabber."[29]

Nevertheless, Delta's condition gave Woolman grounds for legitimate pride as he neared his twenty-fifth anniversary at the helm of the enterprise. This milestone was reached on May 1, 1950, when rank-and-file employees crowded into the main repair hangar at Atlanta to give their chief executive a surprise party and to present him with varied mementos and a tribute in the form of a song to the tune of "I've Been Working on the Railroad"; he was also given a new Cadillac in lieu of the traditional twenty-five-year pin, which he had refused to authorize for himself. In the numerous congratulatory messages that flowed in from around the country, one theme was stressed with particular frequency: the apparent cohesion of the Delta organization, which obviously impressed many observers throughout the industry. Sidney Stewart, President of Chicago and Southern, spoke for many when he told Woolman: "If I could build up the morale in our company that you have in Delta I would feel pretty happy about it." Other messages emphasized the degree to which the images of Woolman and Delta had become entwined over the years. In the words of an Atlanta banker, "the history of Delta is indeed the history of C. E. Woolman."[30]

In sum, though the postwar years had been much more difficult than anticipated in 1945 amid victory celebrations and after the winning of the Chicago-to-Miami route, the company had successfully negotiated a series of tests and attained a degree of maturity on the way. Its position was not unlike that of a young adult who had passed through a trying adolescence and had emerged with strengthened pride and a firmer sense of identity. The comparison could be extended even further, for just ahead, after abortive attempts to form enduring relationships with several other prospective partners, lay a corporate marriage.

CHAPTER 9

Looking for a Partner

THE EARLY 1950s found Delta a much larger and more securely based carrier than the tiny regional enterprise that it had been only a decade before. Its enhanced size and status was emphasized by improved profits and the arrival of new aircraft, which it soon deployed to fly its increasingly profitable network of airways. Nonetheless, Delta remained a firm serving too many relatively small communities and too few really major markets to make optimum use of its new equipment. If it were to continue thriving—particularly if and when the piston era reached its close and jet planes entered commercial use—it needed a better mix of long-haul and short-hop routes and a substantially augmented volume of traffic. The most likely way to obtain these goals was by absorbing another airline in a merger. Delta therefore began looking about for a suitable partner—but it would prove to be a difficult quest.

Although Woolman and his associates had not experienced financial difficulties of the same magnitude as those that had for a time threatened the very lives of some other commercial airlines, the healthy profits reported to Delta stockholders in a succession of annual reports between 1949 and 1952 could have come only as a massive relief after the economic tribulations through which the firm had just passed. As the number of people boarding the company's DC-3s, -4s, and -6s multiplied and cargo totals swelled, impressive profits were registered in virtually every category of operations. Passenger revenues in fiscal 1952, for example, climbed to almost $24 million, more than twice the amount earned just three short years before. Net earnings, perhaps the most crucial indicator of corporate well-being, soared even more dramatically, rising steadily from $639,440 in 1949—itself a Delta record at the time—to a precedent-smashing $1,650,450 in 1952.[1] (See Appendix 1.)

In the midst of these gains, the company also suffered losses, which, though not of a financial nature, were nonetheless deeply regretted. Two leading representatives of the old order moved on. On August 31, 1951, after several years of declining health, Chairman of the Board C. E. Faulk passed away at a local hospital in Monroe, Louisiana. A scant four months later Comptroller L. B. Judd, who had been with the firm since 1928, died suddenly of a heart attack on the day after Christmas, while driving back to Atlanta from a visit to his mother in Mississippi. His post went to another old timer, Chief Accountant Todd G. Cole, who had joined the organization when its headquarters were still in Monroe. These deaths were a sobering reminder of the lengthening years separating the still regional but increasingly cosmopolitan company from the tiny firm that had reckoned its profits mainly by the amounts of dust the "puffers" had sprayed.[2]

As old and familiar faces disappeared, new ones came along. "The family seems to get larger all the time, and it isn't as easy as it once was to know everybody," the company magazine pointed out in 1951 after employees throughout the system had celebrated Delta Family Day with appropriate festivities following the most successful winter season in the firm's history. In 1952 the payroll listed 2,722 people, compared to 2,093 in 1948. (See Appendix 1.) One sign of the times, reflecting the desire of employees at the Atlanta headquarters to foster a sense of togetherness amid the rapid expansion, was a "grass roots" move to acquire a tract of land at nearby Allatoona Lake to be used by Delta personnel for boating, fishing, picnicking, and other recreational activities. Thus began the development of Cushing Memorial Park, named for former Vice-President George Cushing, which would play an increasingly important role in the social lives of company members as the years went by.[3]

Satisfactory annual reports notwithstanding, management officials had to tackle the perennial problem of enlarging and updating the Delta fleet. The modernization of the company's seventeen DC-3s, begun in 1950 and nearing completion late in 1951, was nevertheless only a stopgap measure; sooner or later these venerable birds would have to be replaced by faster and more efficient models, even on the short hops serving smaller cities in the route system. Similarly, the six DC-4s still in use in mid-1952 were long outdated and had to be disposed of as quickly as possible if the firm was to enjoy the maximum advantage from their remaining resale value. Furthermore, although Delta added a seventh DC-6 early in 1951, even such relatively recent airliners gradually would have to be replaced to meet the competition provided by the Lockheed L-1049 Super Constellation after Eastern put it into service late in the same year.[4]

The long-awaited successor to the firm's DC-3s, and to its DC-4s as well, finally appeared, in the form of the Convair 340, a rugged twin-engine craft developed in 1951 and introduced into commercial service by United Air Lines in the following spring. Capable of cruising at 250 miles an hour, compared to the DC-3's 178 and the DC-4's 218, it could accommodate forty-four passengers, and, unlike the two older models, it was pressurized and air-conditioned. One of the Convair ships, when tested on Delta's route between Dallas and Atlanta, reached its destination almost an hour earlier than would have been possible in a DC-3. A contract to purchase ten of the new planes, which cost about $600,000 each, was executed by Woolman in June 1951.[5]

Because of production delays, the first CV-340 did not arrive in Atlanta until December 1952. Pre Ball immediately took qualification flights in the craft with factory pilot A. P. (Speed) Wilson and then started training Delta skippers in its operation. By the middle of the next year seven of the new ships were in operation and thirteen others on order. These purchases were abundantly justified by performance, as the model became legendary for its airworthiness and phenomenal durability. With the advent of the CV-340s it was possible to begin disposing of older models. The DC-4s were the first to go; by mid-1953 all six had been sold. Ball ferried one of these ships to a new owner in Miami in February of that year. "It was sort of a sad day," he later remarked, "for we'd learned to like this old workhorse." The sale of the planes, plus one DC-3, yielded the company a handsome net capital gain slightly in excess of $2.75 million.[6]

Having decided upon the equipment that would be used for short runs and medium-range flights, Woolman and his advisers turned to the problem of meeting the competition from Eastern's new "Super Connies" on long hauls. Because Consolidated Vultee had nothing yet to offer in the way of a big airliner and Delta continued to enjoy its usual cordial relationship with Douglas, the choice was relatively simple. In April 1952 an initial contract was signed with Douglas for the purchase of four DC-7s; subsequently additional orders were placed. This new model, developed specifically to compete with the L-1049, was slightly faster than the Lockheed and would soon be officially touted as the "Golden Crown," the pride of the Delta fleet. Its engines, however, proved to be something of a disappointment, primarily because they tended to overheat while climbing and were much less reliable than those used in the DC-6.[7]

In any event, during the late 1940s and the early years of the 1950s

Delta moved ahead on a variety of fronts while the country adjusted to a vastly changed world, plunged into the prolonged Korean "police action," and elected a Republican president for the first time in almost a generation. Company airliners were sometimes temporarily diverted for supply service in the Pacific, employees were periodically called up to military duty, and the *Delta Digest* carried occasional articles on such disturbing topics as "What to Do if the A-Bomb Should Hit Your Home Town." But the armed conflict being waged halfway around the world was taken in stride. As the same magazine argued at one point, "If it is Russian strategy to break us economically by keeping us armed for a decade or so, then we must fool the Communists by demonstrating this country's ability to keep a war machine and a peacetime prosperity both going at the same time." This prescription, though a bit unrealistic in a nation not as "up for the game" as it had been in World War II, nevertheless seemed appropriate as new stations and ticket offices were opened up and down the Delta line, new airport facilities were dedicated in such places as Columbia and Baton Rouge, new groups of pilots and stewardesses were trained, and passengers were lured into the skies in record numbers thanks to expanded advertising campaigns, energetic sales conferences, and well-promoted vacation plans.[8]

With so much going on, it would perhaps be hazardous to single out one theme deserving closer scrutiny than the rest. Yet during the five years that began in 1948 one goal became increasingly paramount at company headquarters in Atlanta: significant expansion of the enterprise through acquisition of one or more smaller airlines. Every echelon of the organization, from the board of directors and Woolman down, was deeply affected in one way or another by a pervasive "urge to merge."

Delta was not the only airline to pursue an aggressive merger policy during this period; the pressures toward consolidation within the industry were general. Sagging postwar revenues made it increasingly difficult for smaller lines to survive. The superior profitability of long routes over short hauls and the mounting costs of new and larger aircraft intensified the desire to combine. Not only airline officials but government spokesmen as well caught the merger mood. The President's Air Policy Commission, in its report of January 1, 1948, entitled *Survival in the Air Age*, recommended that the CAB defer new route awards and encourage existing companies to consolidate. Later that year, in an important policy statement,

CAB Chairman Joseph J. O'Connell declared: "There are certainly a number of situations where a combination of carriers or routes would make economic sense. . . . I believe that the industry must give serious consideration to desirable mergers and consolidations. Some personal and some corporate ambitions will have to be relinquished."[9]

Delta needed no urging to proceed along such lines, and its record of relatively prudent postwar management at a time when over-expansion had been rampant in the industry put it in an enviable position to enjoy the fruits of consolidation without having to sacrifice the "personal and corporate ambitions" to which O'Connell referred. The chances were good that it would be the surviving corporation in any merger it was likely to consummate.

The forces impelling Delta toward a merger were cogently analyzed in an internal memorandum written late in 1948, after the company had failed to win certification for the route from Atlanta to New York. The anonymous writer reviewed the firm's progress in adopting the most up-to-date equipment but complained that the CAB had not given it a route structure to match its development on other fronts. As the document succinctly stated: "We are now 'too little to be big and too big to be little.' We are both a feeder and a trunkline. We can't operate DC-6's between Fort Worth and Charleston/Savannah making 17 intermediate stops on the way. We can't operate DC-3's between Chicago and Miami and hope to compete with Eastern Constellations. A few of our routes are trunk line routes, but there are too few in number and in length and in terminals for the most efficient operation." Now, the memorandum continued, the CAB was clamping down on new route authorizations, and the thinking of the industry as a whole was "that there should be only six or seven strong air transport companies." Under the circumstances, there was no doubt about the direction that the company had to take: it had to negotiate a favorable merger on its own initiative or risk being absorbed into a less desirable combination by the sheer force of events.[10]

At that point Delta had already been deeply involved in merger talks with a leading competitor for at least six months. On May 17, 1948, the board of directors had discussed "a tentative proposal from another air line that Delta consider a merger," had passed a series of resolutions emphasizing the desirability of "an appropriate combination with one or more air lines under terms satisfactory to Delta," and had empowered Woolman to appoint a committee with authority to negotiate such an agreement. The other airline turned out to be National, which had been founded in 1934 as a tiny enterprise connecting St. Petersburg and Daytona Beach and had grown under the autocratic leadership of George T. (Ted) Baker into an important southeastern carrier.

National's route structure effectively complemented that of Delta. In addition to crisscrossing Florida, linking such cities as Jacksonville, Orlando, Tampa, St. Petersburg, and Miami, it also flew westward from Jacksonville to New Orleans by way of Tallahassee, Pensacola, and Mobile. More significantly, National had scored a major triumph in 1944, when the CAB had awarded it a route from New York to Jacksonville, thus breaking Eastern's previous stranglehold on the vacation trade from New York to Miami. During the immediate postwar era Baker's line had received further largesse in the form of CAB certification to such points as Washington, Baltimore, Richmond, and Havana.[11]

On the other hand, National had been plagued with problems that had severely limited its ability to capitalize on its apparently formidable assets. Right after World War II it had lacked the equipment to offer Eastern much competition on the run from New York to Miami; when it finally did acquire DC-6s in 1947 they were immediately grounded by the CAB at the beginning of the winter season —the worst possible time—because of accidents in which the new Douglas craft operated by other airlines had been involved. To add to Baker's woes, his company had become embroiled in a bitter dispute with ALPA over the dismissal of NAL pilot Marston O'Neal after a landing accident at Tampa. Because of this and other grievances, National's pilots, together with a number of clerks and mechanics, went on strike early in 1948. Ugly incidents quickly began to occur, one involving a striker shot in the leg by a working machinist, and the walkout threatened to last a long time.[12]

Against this disturbing backdrop, negotiations between Delta and National got underway. The attractions for Woolman were many, especially as more people flew between New York and Miami every year than traveled over the entire Delta system. In addition, desirable economies could be achieved through pooling of equipment and consolidation of facilities in cities served by both lines. As Delta's research director, E. M. Johnson, pointed out, the thirty-one destinations on the National system had twice the economic importance of the thirty-six cities served by Delta. Furthermore, Woolman mused about one other possibility: that Capital might be drawn into a Delta and National merger as a third party, thus creating a giant combine that could compete with mighty Eastern on almost equal terms. Even more exciting was the far-out chance of a five-way merger among Delta, National, Capital, Colonial, and Northeast, a possibility that aroused speculation in at least one prominent industry periodical.[13]

But talks did not go smoothly. Throughout the summer of 1948 officials of Delta and National exchanged visits at their Atlanta and Miami headquarters and haggled about the valuation to be placed on the assets of the two lines as the basis for an exchange of stock. These discussions bogged down quickly, partly because National's position in the industry was deteriorating so rapidly as to place its entire future in jeopardy. The strike with which the company was bedeviled dragged on until late in the year. Even after a settlement was reached in November, following three weeks of secret negotiations involving federal mediators, lingering disputes retarded the process of knitting the divided and demoralized personnel into a properly functioning organization. Although the airline had continued operations with substitute pilots throughout the ten-month walkout, its revenues had sagged badly, and enormous losses, totaling more than $1,875,000, had accrued for the calendar year. To make matters even worse, at that moment the CAB instituted one of the most controversial and complex proceedings in its history when in September 1948 it began an investigation to determine whether it possessed the authority to dismember National's entire system and to parcel out its routes to other lines—including Delta, which was mentioned as a possible recipient of the artery from Miami to New Orleans. Along with other airlines, which feared the potential effects of the precedent that the CAB was seeking to establish, Delta strongly questioned the federal agency's right to break up an existing company. It took the view, however, that, if the breakup did occur, Delta ought to receive all National's predominantly southern routes.[14]

With the waters so thoroughly muddied, it is certainly not surprising that no merger agreement could be reached. Although published estimates put Delta's net worth in late 1947 and early 1948 at a figure only marginally higher than that of National, the mounting crises threatening to engulf Baker's floundering enterprise precluded a consolidation on anything approaching equal terms. In June 1948, for example, a member of Delta's board of directors wrote to Woolman that "because of the further deterioration of National's position, I believe we should get better than two to one." Such an adverse valuation of his NAL stock was totally unacceptable to Baker, however straitened his circumstances. In addition, there was the problem of the roles that Baker and other NAL executives would play in the merged company. He had given some prior indications of being willing to remain relatively inactive, but he publicly repudiated such an idea after the negotiations were underway, and the chances were slim at best that he and Woolman could coexist peacefully under one corporate roof.[15] It would have been like asking Douglas MacArthur and George Patton to share a command!

Nevertheless, negotiations continued into the closing months of 1948. The New York aviation-consulting firm of Charles A. Rheinstrom, Inc., was retained by both companies to work out a valuation of assets on which both firms could agree, but the effort came to naught. Shortly after the New Year, Woolman informed a fellow airline executive somewhat laconically that "Dick Courts paid a visit to Miami to try his hand at closing the deal but didn't feel that he accomplished much." That was apparently the last gasp. Several months later Delta's annual report for 1949 summed up the whole episode in two terse sentences: "During the early part of the fiscal year discussions were had with National Airlines looking to its possible acquisition by your Company. These negotiations were terminated after some months when mutually satisfactory terms could not be agreed upon."[16]

National managed eventually to escape dismemberment and tried for a time to form a working partnership with Pan American and Panagra, which would have brought it under the effective control of those powerful organizations. Delta and other lines fought the move, fearing the entry of such a strong carrier as Pan American into the traffic between Miami and the Northeast, and National ultimately backed away from the project. Baker then turned his attention westward, finally succeeding in establishing an interchange that made his company a third partner in the Florida–California portion of the southern transcontinental arrangement established by American and Delta in 1949. Because this move gave National a foothold in the fierce competition for an eventual CAB award of one-company service to the West and also diverted some westbound passengers from Delta's Miami-to-Atlanta and Atlanta–west routes, Woolman's forces resisted it, but to no avail.[17]

Meanwhile Delta became deeply involved in another abortive merger attempt, this time with Northeast Airlines. In a sense, it was a prophetic attempt, for the destinies of the two organizations would eventually bring them together, though not until 1972. In some respects Delta and Northeast had similar histories. Both had begun as small, struggling regional carriers, surviving as best they could without the federal patronage lavished upon larger, more favored companies. Delta, however, had grown into an increasingly successful enterprise which, in the late 1940s, was becoming something more than a regional airline. With Northeast the story was somewhat different.

Northeast had been born in the bleak days of the Great Depression, the same period in which Delta had been forced to revert to crop dusting to maintain a perilously marginal existence after losing out on a federal airmail contract. (During these years also, another line which was eventually to merge with Delta, Chicago and Southern, was struggling to establish itself as a tiny passenger operator on the Pacific Coast.) Unlike the other two enterprises with which its destiny would ultimately become linked, Northeast stemmed from the dreams of a railroad man, Laurence Whittemore, assistant to the president of the Boston and Maine. Believing that a railroad "should act as a transportation medium for its region . . . should run buses and trucks over the highways, locomotives over the rails, boats along the coast and across inland waterways, and planes through the skies," Whittemore persuaded the executives to whom he reported to involve the Boston and Maine in commercial aviation. Railroad leaders, however, were no longer the daring breed that had pioneered the transcontinental systems of the previous century, and the new aerial venture was organized in such a way that its routes generally paralleled the trackage of the parent company. Robert M. Mudge, who later wrote a history of Northeast, characterized this strategy as "a handicap that in years to come would prove nearly fatal. The airline was born and guided by conservatism in the very period that called for gambling and adventurism." [18]

Whittemore and his associates also decided to launch their new project in a compact with the only international airline in the United States at that time—Juan Trippe's Pan American Airways. Pan American was interested in cooperating with the Boston and Maine because the initial route to be operated by the New England venture —leading from Boston to Bangor with several intermediate stops— was potentially a key link in what Trippe hoped would ultimately become a giant artery spanning the entire north Atlantic. With the Boston and Maine providing traffic services and Pan American furnishing day-to-day management, planes, crews, and airmail contracts, the fledgling service was inaugurated on an experimental basis on August 1, 1931. Pan American planes bearing Boston and Maine insignia flew between Boston and Bangor while other aircraft from Trippe's organization carried their own corporate logo between Boston and Halifax, Nova Scotia, often battling the fogs for which the region was notorious. Three weeks after the joint enterprise began it suffered tragedy when a Sikorsky S-41 crashed in fog-shrouded coastal waters as it approached Boston, resulting in the death of a passenger and the loss of its mail.

Despite this accident, operations continued until the end of September; high load factors demonstrated a good potential for long-term success despite the weather hazards involved. But the officials of the Boston and Maine apparently resented the dominant role being played by Trippe and feared his ambitious goals, so the partnership came to an end. On behalf of the Boston and Maine, Whittemore cast about for more logical associates to whom to entrust the airline and found them in the persons of Paul F. Collins, formerly affiliated with the recently defunct Ludington Line, which had operated between New York, Philadelphia, and Washington; Eugene Vidal, another member of the Ludington organization; and Samuel J. Solomon, a businessman with whom Collins and Vidal had been associated previously. All had extensive experience in aviation. Collins was a pioneer airmail pilot who had also been general superintendent for Transcontinental Air Transport (TAT); Vidal, a West Point graduate, had likewise held an administrative post with TAT and was familiar with the traffic and advertising aspects of airline operation; Solomon had at one time been involved in airport management. Like Delta, the Ludington Line had fallen victim to Postmaster General Brown, who had awarded the Washington–to–New York mail contract to another bidder, Eastern; Whittemore had followed Ludington's struggles with interest and appreciated the expertise which Collins and Vidal could bring to the Boston and Maine's own aerial offshoot.

Meeting in a New York hotel room, Collins, Vidal, and Solomon decided to accept Whittemore's invitation and form a company to operate the New England service under contract with the Boston and Maine. Partly for publicity and advertising purposes, they enlisted a fourth partner, the famed aviatrix Amelia Earhart; collectively the group put up the shoestring figure of $10,000 with which to launch National Airways, as they called their new venture. Within the next four days they purchased from Eastern at knock-down prices two Stinson trimotors which had formerly belonged to Ludington; hired a small staff of pilots and maintenance personnel, again drawing upon the old Ludington organization; familiarized themselves with the routes they would serve in New England; and made publicity flights to and from the communities involved, with Amelia Earhart playing a featured role. On August 11, 1933, pilot Hazen Bean took off from Boston and proceeded to Bangor with Earhart and eight paying passengers aboard, thus formally inaugurating the career of the enterprise that ultimately became known as Northeast Airlines.

From this time until the United States entered World War II, the tiny enterprise, operating initially under a subsidy from the Boston and Maine, navigated the rugged routes from Boston to such points as Augusta, Concord, Montpelier, Portland, and White River Junction, pitting itself against the fogs, thundershowers, and snowstorms for which the New England weather was proverbial. Flying without radios and other instruments which were becoming standard on larger commercial airlines, the company's pilots, under the leadership of Chief Pilot Milton H. Anderson, learned through experience how to cope and came through the period with only one fatal accident. Financial aid was provided by a federal airmail contract in 1934 following the "reshuffling of the deck" under Franklin D. Roosevelt and Postmaster General James A. Farley which was also instrumental in advancing the fortunes of Delta during the same year. Ultimately Burlington and Montreal were added to the route system of Boston and Maine Airways, as the line was officially known throughout New England to capitalize on its railroad connections. Aided by publicity agent Herbert Baldwin, a former newspaperman with many contacts in the region, Amelia Earhart beat the bushes for passengers, giving complimentary flights to potential customers who had not previously ventured aloft and holding afternoon teas for women who might prevail upon their husbands to patronize the airline on subsequent business trips. On the other hand, the leaders of the enterprise, whether because of masculine pride or railroad caution, would not permit Earhart to play a significant role in normal flight operations and used her mainly as a drawing card; well before her eventual disappearance in the Pacific she had drifted away from the company.

In 1936 the fabric-skinned Stinsons were replaced by all-metal Lockheed Electras, again paralleling the experience of such small lines as Delta and Chicago and Southern. Predictably, there was a move to Douglas DC-3s later in the decade, but a dispute over financing these, coupled with ill-health on Collins's part, led to a management shuffle in which Solomon became president and the firm's stock was sold publicly for the first time. In a related development the corporate name was changed to Northeast Airlines, partly to provide a firmer identity and partly to reflect larger horizons associated with the fact that the company was seeking access to New York City.

The advent of World War II brought Northeast both opportunities and troubles. The company won a route to New York but found it difficult to compete with the incumbent carrier, vastly larger American, for traffic. The board of directors was badly divided over whether to stick to the familiar but geographically limited corner of the nation in which the company was then operating or to branch out and seek new routes to such destinations as Pittsburgh and Chicago. To complicate matters further, a major change of ownership occurred in 1944, when the CAB, which did not like having Northeast controlled by a railroad, forced the Boston and Maine to relinquish its holdings as the price of the new route to New York. Much of its stock was purchased by the Atlas Corporation, a holding company whose dominant figure, financier Floyd Odlum, was married to another famous aviatrix, Jacqueline Cochran, who became a member of Northeast's board of directors. The Atlas transaction merely led to further difficulties, however, because that company was heavily involved in the ownership of Consolidated Vultee and thus ran afoul of a federal prohibition against combining airline and aircraft-manufacturing interests.

Northeast's contribution to the war effort was both noteworthy and dramatic. Under a contract with the government signed in January 1942, the company established a military supply route to Goose Bay in Labrador which was soon extended to Greenland, Iceland, and Scotland. Thus Northeast became a pioneer operator over Arctic routes that, after the war, would be flown commercially by larger carriers. Flying up narrow fog-shrouded fjords to land on snow-covered airstrips in poorly mapped territory, coping with icing conditions which threatened to drag their ships down into the frigid waters of the north Atlantic, or making hair-raising emergency landings or takeoffs on crude obstacle-strewn runways, such Northeast pilots as the legendary Captain Peter Dana came through the conflict without a single serious accident.

In one particularly heroic exploit, a Northeast crew was marooned on a frozen lake in the Canadian wilderness for more than two weeks after coming to the aid of an American Airlines plane that had been forced down there in February 1943; in another, five courageous Northeast flyers were decorated by the United States government for successfully undertaking a hazardous thirteen-day volunteer mission to provide emergency supplies for a pair of remote Arctic outposts and to rescue a weather bureau observer who needed medical attention. Not without cause did Ernest K. Gann refer to the company as "plucky little Northeast Airlines" in recounting the performance of commercial pilots in such soul-testing situations as these.[19]

However much it contributed to corporate self-esteem, the company's proud wartime record could do little to cushion the difficulties that Northeast encountered in resuming normal operations once the conflict had ended. Persisting discord among board members over the wisdom of expansion moves pursued by Solomon led him to resign as president in 1945; Collins took over the post and followed a policy of standing pat within the firm's existing route structure. Failure of traffic to measure up to expectations and continuing inability to compete satisfactorily with American on the Boston–to–New York route resulted in serious financial losses, while the CAB pressed for an end to the control which Odlum held in the enterprise. Seeking a way out of its problems, Northeast tried unsuccessfully to merge with PCA in a series of on-again, off-again negotiations that had a damaging effect upon employee morale. After these collapsed in 1947, the CAB ordered Atlas and Odlum to reduce their Northeast holdings within eighteen months. A new president, George E. Gardner, who had previous managerial experience with Eastern, National, and Northwest, was given the task of working out a plan of consolidation with a suitable carrier.

After some inconclusive talks had taken place among Northeast, Eastern, and Colonial, the CAB extended its deadline, and Gardner turned his attention southward. By 1950 National was emerging from its postwar problems, and for a time it looked as if Gardner and Baker might work out what, from many points of view, would have been a logical consolidation. The two lines met at New York City, and a merger between them had been discussed as far back as World War II. Gardner himself had been executive vice-president of National and was familiar with its operations, which would have meshed well with those of Northeast, whose business peaked in the summer, when residents of New York City flocked to New England resorts, whereas National depended heavily upon the winter vacation trade between New York and Miami. Despite these considerations, negotiations reached a standstill in May 1950 after Northeast's board of directors rejected an offer by Baker to buy its assets and Baker in turn refused a counterproposal to sell his stock to backers of the New England enterprise.[20]

At that point Gardner turned to another potential southern project: merger with Delta. Throughout the summer months of 1950 Woolman, Gardner, and other representatives of the two companies shuttled back and forth among Boston, Atlanta, and the Atlas Corporation's New York City headquarters in a round of conferences, conducted quietly and without public fanfare, which seem to have attracted no attention from the rest of the industry. On the basis of recent airline history, there was little reason to suspect that a merger would be attempted by two lines that did not connect at a single point; indeed, their closest terminals were more than seven hundred miles apart. Nevertheless, by late August negotiations had reached the stage at which Woolman submitted a draft agreement to Northeast, followed in September by a visit by Gardner to Atlanta, during which remaining issues were resolved to the satisfaction of both parties.

The result was hardly a pact between equals: Northeast's net worth was about $5 million, compared to Delta's $12 million, and Delta stock stood at a ratio of approximately 4.5 to 1 over that of the New England line. In addition, Northeast had gone from 1942 to 1949 without a single profitable year and had only recently begun to edge precariously into the black. On the other hand, many factors drew the two firms together. Frustrated in repeated attempts to work out a merger with any other line and unsure how long the CAB would extend the deadline against which he was working, Odlum had much to gain from achieving a consolidation that would merge his interests into a larger more secure company instead of being forced to unload his holdings on the open market. As Delta was eager to expand and attracted by the opportunity to gain a smoother seasonal traffic flow in the process, it is not surprising that a meeting of the minds was reached.[21]

The merger agreement, made public on September 28, 1950, called for Northeast stock to be exchanged for that of Delta at a ratio corresponding to that between the book values of both companies at the time of closing. It contained a clause permitting "one or more additional companies whose participation appears to both Northeast and Delta to be desirable" to join in the merger at a future time, looking, no doubt, for a third partner such as Capital, whose route system would close the "missing link" between Atlanta and New York. If the CAB did not approve the union in two years, either party could withdraw on thirty days' notice. Both firms expected a difficult struggle for government approval of the pact, especially considering that both Eastern and National were sure to oppose it, but Woolman confided to one correspondent that "since the Board has been asking for mergers rather vociferously for the past several years and is also confronted with the problem of what to do with the smaller airlines we think it should receive a warm reception." Symbolic of the high hopes of both lines was the arrival in Boston in late October of a chartered Delta DC-6 carrying the Bulldogs of the University of Georgia, who had come to play an intersectional football game with Boston College.[22]

But the success of the merger effort hinged on one crucial condition, the fulfillment of which was far from assured. As Delta counsel D. Franklin Kell commented many months later, the CAB, sympathetic as it was toward mergers at that time, would probably have approved the union quickly had the routes of Delta and Northeast touched each other at any point. Recognizing that no consolidation of entirely disconnected lines would bring much benefit to either, officials of the two companies had written into the merger agreement a clause specifying that it would not go into effect unless Delta secured CAB approval for a route extending its system to New York City. In the latest renewal of that perennial quest, Woolman had filed for CAB approval of a projected artery that would have connected Columbia, South Carolina, and New York City by a line running through Fayetteville and Wilson, North Carolina; Washington, D.C.; and Philadelphia. Following the public announcement of its prospective union with Northeast, Delta moved to combine this route application with the merger proceeding on the CAB docket.[23]

Delta argued that such a route was necessary because Fort Bragg was located at Fayetteville and Wilson was a national tobacco market, but the coupling of this application with the merger proceeding put the CAB in an uncomfortable spot. Although the agency was on record as favoring mergers, it was also under severe pressure to refrain from certifying new routes, a fact of which lawyers representing National and Eastern were well aware. Despite Delta's hopes that the CAB would move rapidly, therefore, the agency dragged its feet on the matter. Not until September 1951 did it open the New England–Southern States Merger Investigation, marked by hearings at which reams of testimony for and against the projected union were presented by no fewer than twelve airlines and representatives of such entities as the National Association of Machinists, the New Orleans Chamber of Commerce, the states of New Hampshire and Rhode Island, and the New England Conference of State Aviation Officials.

The result was predictable, given prevailing circumstances. The CAB affirmed that it was concerned about the "weak route structure of the small airlines serving the east coast region of the United States," that it favored the "integration of the small northeastern carriers with the stronger southern carriers," and that it appreciated the substantial savings that would accrue to the federal government if the airmail subsidies necessary to support small airlines could be eliminated through the creation of larger consolidated companies. On the other hand, the board wanted to accomplish these objectives without creating new route mileage, and it was clear by that time that Delta's projected Columbia–to–New York artery was a dead letter.[24] Instead, CAB policy was pressing Woolman and his staff toward a more complex solution to the pressing problem of gaining access to New York: purchase of an existing route from another airline.

The company from which such a route might be obtained was Capital, then involved in a merger effort of its own. Mainly a mid-Atlantic and midwestern carrier, this enterprise possessed two southern routes. One of these meandered from New Orleans to New York City via a host of intermediate stops including Mobile, Birmingham, Chattanooga, Knoxville, Bristol, Charleston (W. Va.), Clarksburg, Morgantown, Wheeling, and Pittsburgh. The other twisted and turned from Memphis to Norfolk and Newport News with two spurs leading from Asheville to Atlanta and Greensboro to Washington, D.C., via Richmond. Having abandoned its old identity as Pennsylvania Central Airlines in 1948, Capital was making a determined effort to improve its fortunes under the aggressive leadership of a new chief executive, James H. (Slim) Carmichael, formerly head pilot at PCA. Through drastic cost slashing and sales promotion, coupled with the acquisition of new aircraft and the development of low-fare "sky coach" service, the company had earned profits in 1948 and 1949. Partly in an effort to encourage its recovery from the near disaster into which it had fallen before Carmichael took over, the CAB had granted route extensions to Atlanta and New Orleans. Even so, Carmichael believed that Capital was not large enough to compete effectively in the long run with such formidable opponents as Eastern. During 1951 he became involved in merger discussions with President Croil Hunter of Northwest Airlines, which ultimately resulted in a formal agreement, announced early in the following year.

It became clear as these discussions proceeded that the CAB might look favorably upon a sale of Capital's southern routes to Delta, which would give Woolman entry to both Washington and New York. Indeed, it was intimated that federal officials might even make approval of the Capital–Northwest merger conditional upon such a move. In that way, two strong consolidated firms, Delta–Northeast and Capital–Northwest, would emerge without the award of any new route mileage: a neat fulfillment of CAB objectives.[25] All these merger negotiations had come to resemble a giant poker game among skilled players, with the chips to be raked in by those with the best combination of skill and luck.

Yet another related possibility aroused excitement at Delta headquarters as Woolman contemplated his next ante. One of the floundering small northeastern airlines causing the CAB concern was Colonial, in an increasingly precarious situation because of high-level chicanery and mismanagement. Tracing its history back to 1923, when the Bee Line had started charter service out of Naugatuck, Connecticut, and through a number of corporate reorganizations in the following years, Colonial had put together a tangled network of Canadian and mid-Atlantic routes serving such major destinations as Montreal, New York City, Baltimore, and Washington, as well as a host of smaller ones including Albany, Syracuse, Binghamton, Scranton, and Reading. It also possessed a potentially lucrative two-pronged vacation route from New York and Washington to Bermuda. After a difficult postwar experience, in which it had lost money trying to develop the Bermuda routes, the line seemed to be making a good recovery under its chief executive, Sigmund (Sig) Janas, a dapper individual known throughout the industry for the carnation that he habitually sported in his lapel. In 1951, however, federal officials found that Janas was mulcting his company through kickbacks and other illegal practices, which led to his forced resignation and threw Colonial into turmoil. Foreseeing nothing but trouble if the line tried to survive as an independent carrier, the new managers tried to work out a merger with National and, when that failed, submitted proposals to a number of other possible partners, including Delta.[26]

It was surely an enticing prospect. Delta had little need for all of Colonial's meandering network and contemplated selling some of its less important routes to such tiny northeastern feeder lines as Robinson (soon to be renamed Mohawk) or Wiggins. But Colonial's major trunk lines and vacation routes, if added to the Northeast system and bound together with Delta's own system through the acquisition of Capital's southern routes, would connect such points as New York, Pittsburgh, Washington, Richmond, Norfolk, Charlotte, Memphis, Birmingham, Atlanta, and New Orleans and would contribute to a mighty aviation enterprise. The very idea sent the staff of Delta's research department scurrying for pencils to calculate the vastly enlarged volume of business that would result. After thinking it over, Woolman and his advisers decided against a direct approach to the new bosses of Colonial. Instead, George Gardner, aided by the Atlas Corporation's Radu Irimescu, an Odlum lieutenant, was to try to work out a merger between Northeast and Colonial while Delta attempted to persuade Carmichael to part with Capital's southern routes for an appropriate financial consideration.[27]

Preliminary discussions among Delta, Capital, and other interested parties concerning the two Capital routes in question, officially designated as CAM 51 and 55, had been going on for some time. In early February 1951, after it had become clear that Capital and Northwest were moving toward a merger, Woolman, Carmichael, Hunter, and Gardner had met in New York City to talk about a deal for the coveted arteries, but that and succeeding contacts had been inconclusive. Arguing that the routes would still be necessary to smooth out seasonal fluctuations in traffic even after the proposed merger, neither Capital nor Northwest wanted to lose them unless forced to do so by the CAB. In addition, Carmichael risked giving up an enormous chunk of his route structure and then being left with a drastically reduced airline if anything happened to prevent consummation of the merger with Northwest.[28]

After the CAB opened the New England–Southern States Merger Investigation in September, however, the plot began to thicken. Included in the issues to be discussed was the question of whether it would be in the public interest for a merged enterprise consisting of Delta, Northeast, and possibly Colonial to acquire the rights to routes 51 and 55 from Capital. Delta and Northeast formally amended their joint application for CAB approval, inserting a clause offering to purchase the routes at a fair price. Then, on January 29, 1952, Capital and Northwest publicly announced that they had reached a merger agreement under which Carmichael would become president and chief executive and Hunter would become chairman of the board. "Hearty congratulations," Woolman declared in a telegram fired off to Carmichael after hearing the news. "How soon can we start phase two?" Knowing full well that many hurdles still remained to be cleared before the announced merger could be approved by the CAB and the stockholders of the two lines, Carmichael replied that "there is many a slip twixt the cup and the lip; phase two begins when cup reaches lip."[29]

A furious round of activity ensued, as Woolman and his cohorts prepared and dispatched formal offers for routes 51 and 55 while Carmichael tried to fend off their proposals, preferring to wait and see whether the CAB would force Capital and Northwest to give up the crucial airlanes as the price of the projected merger. On February 12 Delta offered Carmichael $4 million for the two arteries, including the equipment and facilities required to operate them. This was rejected by Carmichael on the grounds that pursuing the matter at that time would delay the merger proceedings. Woolman's response was to raise the ante. Figuring that the routes and the tangible assets used in their operation might be reckoned as worth half the market value of Capital's outstanding common stock and calculating that the latter was $12,012,150, Delta management offered to pay $6,006,075. L. Welch Pogue, a former CAB chairman, whose Washington, D.C., law firm represented Delta in its various expansion moves, summed up Delta's strategy in a letter to Woolman:

In making an offer at this time it seems to us that we must be prepared to take a turn down and then win at the Board level by convincing the Board . . . that our offer is so fair (even when compared to any others that may be injected . , . such as one from National or from Braniff) and the resulting route structure which would be created by a combination of Delta–Northeast and Capital's Routes 51 and 55 is so predominantly in the public interest, that the Board's approval of the Northwest–Capital merger must be made conditional upon their accepting our offer, or alternatively, conditional upon disposing of the southern routes.

Responding to the new Delta offer, Carmichael claimed that Woolman was overlooking some $3 million in Capital debentures, which should be taken into account in computing an offer, and also demanded to know what specific tangible assets connected with the operation of the routes were wanted by Delta. Woolman replied that such questions could best be settled in face-to-face bargaining but indicated that adjustments could be made in the price if Capital wanted to retain some of the equipment involved. Carmichael's rejoinder was an angry accusation that under the Delta plan Capital would have to hand over about $3.75 million worth of tangible assets used in the operation of its southern routes, so that, of the $6 million Delta was offering, only about $2.25 million would be paid for the routes themselves. This, he submitted, was ridiculous, and he professed that "it is difficult for us to believe that your offer was made in good faith or was intended to be taken seriously."

Gardner, informed of Carmichael's letter, discussed it with Irimescu and suggested that "it should be answered in such a way as to educate Slim on the facts of bookkeeping." Woolman, however, took a different tack. Carmichael's "extremely vehement and not too factual" letter, he confided to Pogue, had been written largely to influence the CAB, to which the Capital executive had dispatched a carbon copy. Woolman thought that there was a good chance that this strategy would backfire and decided not to make an immediate reply. "I am under the impression," he told Pogue, "that if the members of the Board really analyze this letter it could do us more good than harm."[30]

Delta then moved that the CAB consolidate the Delta–Northeast and Capital–Northwest merger cases, in the hope that approval of the latter might be made contingent upon the sale of the southern routes to Delta. Throughout the following weeks representatives of the contending airlines waged legal warfare in Washington as the struggle moved through the prehearing phase. The combative mood must have been contagious, for in early April, Delta attorney D. Franklin Kell informed Woolman that a "battle royal" had taken place among members of the CAB over the issues involved. By May, Woolman and his advisers were considering the possibility of yet another financial offer to Carmichael, but late that month a new development suddenly cast an entirely different light upon the whole matter. Northwest's stockholders, to whom the merger agreement with Capital had been submitted for approval, failed to deliver the two-thirds affirmative vote required for ratification. CAB action on the planned union, which had thus been doomed, was suspended indefinitely. The "slip twixt cup and lip" that Carmichael had feared had become reality.[31]

There was obviously no longer any hope that Capital would part with its southern routes. But there was still one other possibility: that Carmichael might be lured into a full-scale merger with Delta. E. M. Johnson's planning and research department drew up a map calculated to give Captain Eddie Rickenbacker nightmares. It showed what would result from a consolidation of Delta, Capital, and Northeast: a gigantic network of routes leaving out virtually no major center of population east of the Mississippi river. As Johnson pointed out, such a firm would constitute the third-ranking domestic airline in the United States. The fact that Delta was by then already deeply committed to a merger with yet another company, Chicago and Southern, made the prospect even more awe-inspiring.[32]

But the idea of a merger with Capital died quickly. Perhaps Woolman thought by that point that all Delta's energies should be enlisted in the effort to merge with Chicago and Southern, which was proceeding well, instead of being diverted into yet another chancy venture. And so, though the merger agreement with Northeast continued in effect, pending a solution to the perennial problem of access to New York, hope that the union with Gardner's line would really be consummated began to fade. Nor did a merger that Gardner himself had hoped to work out with Colonial materialize. Instead, that financially troubled company struggled on for a few more years while National and Eastern vied to see which one would ultimately absorb it. Eastern finally won out in 1956. Meanwhile, Capital, soon to stake its corporate future on a risky experiment with foreign-built aircraft, went its independent way until the early 1960s, when it succumbed to mounting waves of red ink and was acquired by United.[33]

In the summer of 1952, looking back upon more than four years of hard bargaining with prospective partners in enterprise, Woolman might justifiably have been pardoned had he thrown up his hands and exclaimed, "What's the use?" On the contrary, however, he had no disposition to quarrel with fate or yield to despair. In fact, prospects were brightening, and the goal that had eluded him so persistently lay just around the corner, in the shape of the most natural partner of all, a line founded and guided by an executive who had come to be one of Woolman's closest friends—Carleton Putnam of Chicago and Southern.

CHAPTER 10

The Early Years of
Chicago and Southern

I
N 1931 while members of the Delta organization were struggling
in Louisiana to keep a tiny crop-dusting venture alive after their
failure to secure an airmail contract, a young New Yorker
named Carleton Putnam became infected by the same virus that had
led C. E. Woolman to try his hand at the airline game. A graduate of
Princeton University, studying for a law degree from Columbia, Putnam came from a substantial family background; he was the son of
a newspaper editor who had died in the Argonne in 1918, and his
paternal and maternal grandfathers were respectively a noted publisher and a justice of the New York Supreme Court. Under the
circumstances, it would not have been surprising had Putnam embarked upon, and achieved, a distinguished legal career.

But, just as fate had decreed that Woolman would not spend his
life advising farmers about crops and pests, so Putnam was not destined to argue cases in court or to breathe the rarefied air of corporate jurisprudence. Strolling along New York City's Fifty-Seventh
Street one day in 1930, he had chanced to see a small airplane, a
Curtiss Robin, in a display window. He quickly acquired it, found a
flying instructor, Ted Hebert, and took off with him to Arizona,
learning how to handle the plane on the way and completing his
basic training at Phoenix. Throughout the next year, as he continued
to pursue his law degree, he piloted the little craft here and there between academic terms on his own personal cross-country odyssey,
seeking a yet obscure destiny while battling his way through storms
and touching down at various scenic and historic places. Finally, in
a somewhat out-of-the-way location, he found what he was looking
for.

Putnam's future beckoned one night in 1931, when he was suddenly awakened in a North Platte, Nebraska, hotel room by a United
Air Lines plane approaching to land "with a full-throated roar that
gained steadily in volume." Hastily rising from his bed to take a

look at the source of this sound, which came "like thunder down the dark and out of the west," he managed to get to a window just in time to see the blue flame of the aircraft's exhaust as it passed overhead. Then, "like a phantom, it was gone." Writing about the experience years later, Putnam could only ponder, but scarcely explain, the subtle intoxication of spirit that could lead a person "to wake and listen to an airplane, and so make his life's decision on the instant and fall asleep content." He merely knew that, from that point on, he "wondered only how much money it would take to start an airline somehow, somewhere."[1]

Putnam was graduated from Columbia, and, while most of his classmates were seeking admission to the bar, he cast about for a way of breaking into the still infant field of commercial aviation. But the times were not propitious, and he found it extremely difficult to find what he was looking for. After earning a transport pilot's license, he swapped his single-engine Robin for a larger Bellanca and flew to California—an alluring frontier of opportunity even in depressed 1933. In Burbank, discussing the problems of the aviation industry with Robert E. Gross, president of the small, struggling Lockheed Aircraft Company, he learned about a virgin territory that might conceivably support an airline: Gross, not without a flicker of humor, suggested that Putnam buy another secondhand Bellanca and start carrying passengers between Burbank and San Francisco along a coastal route. In addition to lacking air service, this potential artery had no such accoutrements as lighting either. But, said Gross, "Why worry? Just fly in the daytime. Your pilots can decide about the weather when they reach it." After mulling over the dubious economics as well as the possible hazards involved, Putnam decided to take the plunge.[2]

Feverish with the airline virus, Putnam sought a second used Bellanca; he finally obtained one from orchestra leader Wayne King, famous for such favorites as "The Waltz You Saved for Me." He also made progress on the legal front: on June 14, 1933, Pacific Seaboard Air Lines, Incorporated, received its birth certificate from the state of California. Under the terms of its charter, it was to provide passenger and express service between San Francisco and Los Angeles by way of Monterey, Santa Barbara, and other intermediate points. As Putnam noted later, its right-of-way followed part of the old eighteenth-century mission trail initiated by the Spanish explorer-monk Junipero Serra. It was a colorful route—but would it attract even the few customers necessary to fill the five-passenger Bellancas? On June 25 Putnam flew the inaugural run south from San Francisco in a Bellanca that had been christened *Miss San Jose* with a bottle of prune juice by the queen of the San Jose Fiesta de las Rosas. As Putnam later recalled: "The mayors were at the fields for ceremonies at all stops. . . . Trophies began to accumulate, and flowers . . . Philadelphia would scarcely have sent its mayor to greet a secondhand Bellanca. But a secondhand Bellanca meant a lot, for example, to Paso Robles."[3]

Putnam knew that it would be unrealistic to expect much in the way of immediate financial return from his line and that he would be better advised to concentrate on "building an aviation career based upon a moderate investment." Nonetheless, like any beginning businessman, he kept anxious track of his customers. Every day that first summer he would nervously scan the sky for the telltale black speck of an arriving plane. As he subsequently remembered:

When we saw one, we would gaze intently . . . until we were sure it was indeed our Bellanca. As it circled the field, we would try to discern how many passengers were on board. Sometimes it would draw up at the gate and discharge a full load. On those evenings I went back to my hotel in a buoyant frame of mind, and all of us, until the next evening, found everything *couleur de rose*. But sometimes the ship would taxi directly to the hangar, and thus we knew there were no passengers at all. Then I returned to town . . . and examined my checkbook through dark glasses.[4]

William J. Fry, a veteran pilot who eventually flew for both Putnam and Woolman, later remarked that the air passengers who traveled in the late 1920s and early 1930s "possessed an underlying spirit of adventure, challenge, and a burning desire to participate in the new and growing air transport industry." These attributes were especially required of the hardy souls who came to Pacific Seaboard headquarters at Mills Field in San Francisco to gamble their professional futures as employees of a fledgling operation in an industry that had itself won only a small percentage of the transportation dollar. One such adventurer was a woman, Erma Murray. A native of Arizona, with a bachelor's degree from the University of California at Berkeley, she had worked for aviation pioneer Walter T. Varney and then for United Air Lines when United absorbed Varney's air service between Salt Lake City and Seattle in 1930. In 1933 she decided to join the Pacific Seaboard staff as bookkeeper. In time, she would assume even more responsible positions and became the unofficial historian of the airline that Putnam had founded. Like her Delta counterpart, Catherine FitzGerald, Murray was one of the small trailblazing contingent of women in the airline industry; Putnam characterized her as "demure but ever courageous." Another original employee was West Coast airline veteran Leland D. (Hap) Anderson, the first pilot hired by Putnam; he was soon followed by such flyers as Stewart W. Hopkins, who would figure in an important way in the union chapter formed by the company's pilots two years later. As in the early Delta organization, the wages earned from service in the cockpit were hardly munificent; as Anderson later recalled, Pacific Seaboard's two "regular" pilots in 1933 worked two days on and one day off for $100 a month; two "reserves" worked one day on and two days off for $50 a month.

In its efforts to survive the dismal depression year in which it was born, Pacific Seaboard flapped its somewhat feeble wings, straining to fly from this perch to that. In mid-October it began carrying passengers and newspapers to Sacramento; on November 1 it commenced the same type of service on a circular route from San Francisco to Stockton to Modesto and back to the Bay area. Later in November the line made a major adjustment: it stopped flying all the way to Los Angeles but expanded its San Francisco–Sacramento passenger and newspaper service to include Monterey. In the following February, however, it did another turnabout and restored service to Los Angeles while reducing other runs.[5]

As Putnam explained, the basic problem that caused all this switching back and forth was "the old trouble of spending more than we made." At times it appeared that the airline was approaching the eagerly anticipated point at which profits might replace losses, "yet always the extra income seemed to coincide with a little extra expense. The passengers were demanding this, and the agents were suggesting that." In addition, a third used Bellanca had to be purchased to ensure dependable service, and after an initial "honeymoon period" during the firm's early months the employees began to grow restive, demanding more than the mere adventure of pioneering.[6]

Putnam had decided in the beginning to try to survive without the political problems that he feared a mail contract might bring, but he soon concluded that the line had no alternative but to "pocket our pride" and turn to the United States Post Office Department. Although he found the idea of a subsidy distasteful, he took comfort in the fact that his struggling enterprise had made "an honest effort to succeed alone." After all, as he later argued, the railroads had had their land grants, frontier seekers their Homestead Act, and manufacturers their tariffs, following which all "had moved with almost untrammelled freedom to the attainment of their individual goals." His subsequent preliminary approach to federal postal officials in December 1933 was well timed, for shortly after the beginning of the New Year the dramatic events connected with Franklin D. Roosevelt's cancellation of existing contracts (see Chapter 3), the disastrous Army Air Corps experiment in flying the mail, and Postmaster General Farley's call for new bids piled one upon the other in fortuitous sequence for Pacific Seaboard.[7]

After Farley called for new bids on the various routes, Putnam and his colleagues studied the possibilities and eliminated all the ones requiring multi-engine aircraft. Of those remaining, they were particularly attracted by an advertisement, dated March 30, 1934, for a temporary carrier of mail "on the most advantageous schedules" over a route slightly more than nine hundred miles long, from Chicago to New Orleans by way of Peoria, Springfield, St. Louis, Memphis, and Jackson. The service would require one round trip daily and involve no night flying; a three-month period of service was stipulated initially, with the possibility of extension for two additional three-month periods or "portions thereof." The Pacific Seaboard brain trust finally decided that this was the opportunity they were looking for, reasoning, as Putnam later put it, that it was an "old, established trade route, level from end to end . . . stemming from the nation's second largest city and connecting it with the largest port on the Gulf. Moreover, I am not ashamed to confess that the glamour of two names appealed to me. Memphis and New Orleans."[8]

Under the terms set forth in the advertisement, the rate of mail pay was to be based on the airplane space made available by the carrier, each cubic foot being regarded as equivalent to nine pounds of mail. The resulting pay was not to exceed 45 cents per plane mile and would be based on the average load carried over the route each month. In order to arrive at a bid that would be both low and profitable, Putnam called on his original flight instructor to make a survey flight over the route from Chicago southward. As the tight deadline of April 19 loomed, Ted Hebert performed the task in only two weeks and brought the vital data to San Francisco, where he, Putnam, operations boss Pete Reinhart, and a young maritime lawyer named Amos Culbert put together a bid. It was packaged by April

10, and Hebert flew with it to Washington, arriving just before the deadline. The bid, amounting to 17.5 cents per airplane mile, was the lowest ever submitted for an airmail route up to that time and brought quick results. The newspapers reported it first: Pacific Seaboard had been awarded route 8 from Chicago to New Orleans. The contract was formally proffered on May 3 and signed on May 14. Pacific Seaboard had thirty days from the former date to inaugurate the service or to forfeit its performance bond.[9]

Putnam had strained his resources in order to manage the $50,000 bond. In addition, the service required the purchase of two more Bellancas. For Putnam it was thus "double or quits now, and I laid my wager on the table." The risk was great—but so was the opportunity, and the young executive could not afford to temporize.[10]

Of the original employees, Putnam, Murray, Anderson, and Hopkins led this reverse frontier movement, which for Murray meant going against a vow never to leave the West Coast. In Memphis the weather was humid, but the reception was less than warm. The Tennessee city had become used to the Stinson Trimotors that American had employed on route 8, and the Memphis *Commercial Appeal* editorialized that Putnam's Bellancas "may be his idea of the New Deal in airline transportation, but it looks like a cold deal to us."[11] Certainly the support that Monroe had provided to Woolman and his cohorts was conspicuously lacking. The cool treatment accorded Putnam by Memphis only compounded the tension of preparing for the June 3 deadline, but the company nevertheless set about fireproofing mail compartments, setting up overhaul and line-maintenance facilities, building an inventory, hiring new personnel, and seeing that the pilots were at least minimally familiar with the route. In his subsequent memoirs Putnam recalled that "the postal and aeronautical inspectors who had frequented my office still wore a tentative expression. . . . Theirs were among the friendlier faces on the jury as the defendant took the stand."[12]

On June 3 one Bellanca was to leave Chicago and a second to depart from New Orleans; the latter was scheduled to arrive at Memphis first. At Memphis, as at Paso Robles in the previous June, the mayor was on hand. Another member of the welcoming committee was Hugh McKellar, postmaster of Memphis and a friend of Putnam's; his brother Kenneth, a United States senator from Tennessee, had taken a leading role in the Black committee hearings. It was June, hot but clear, so that weather was not a factor in the mounting tension as noon—the scheduled time of arrival—came and passed with no sign of flight 2 from New Orleans. A telegram had arrived announcing the on-time departure of the Bellanca, but a call to Jackson later revealed that the plane had never arrived there. Fear hung in the air like humidity, for the flight was two hours overdue. No qualified pilot was available to take flight 1 on the southward continuation after it arrived from Chicago; airline veteran William Fry, who had applied for a job with Pacific Seaboard that same day, was quickly shown how to taxi the Bellanca, and he subsequently took it to New Orleans.

Twenty minutes out of New Orleans flight 2 had experienced engine failure, and pilot Ben Catlin had been forced to make an emergency landing west of Slidell, Louisiana, in a swamp on the north shore of Lake Pontchartrain. The crew and general traffic manager Paul Preston were soon rescued unhurt, along with the mail. The plane, however, had to be dismantled before it could be taken out of the swamp. It was a bad start, appearing to vindicate critics who objected to using single-engine aircraft without radios.[13]

Other problems dogged the new operation. For one thing, service charges along the route increased. In fact, because of total costs for the rest of 1934, the average net monthly loss was at least as high as the firm had experienced back in California without the mail subsidy to cut deficits. Putnam and his associates had hoped that the prestige of carrying mail would attract a sizable passenger clientele and enable the company to gain financial backing for new equipment and other expenses connected with expansion, but this backing was not soon forthcoming. Statistics document the gloomy situation that faced the enterprise. On December 31, 1933, Pacific Seaboard's books showed a total deficit of $29,116.70; only Putnam's advance of his own resources had kept the firm afloat. Further losses ran slightly more than $4,000 in January 1934 and averaged between $4,000 and $5,000 a month from February through April. In May, when the company moved from California to Memphis, red ink flowed even more copiously, and losses amounted to slightly more than $20,000.

The dreary roll call of deficits continued during the months that followed. Under postal rules the company could carry no passengers in its first month of mail service; it is therefore not surprising that in June it showed a loss of $8,825.47. This figure fell to $6,589.44 in July, when passenger service was reinstated, and sank below $6,000 in August as passenger revenue doubled; but then it soared above $8,000 in September as both mail and passenger receipts declined.

The strange roller-coaster ride continued in October with a sharp increase in passengers, and the net loss for the month fell below $5,000 for the first time since April. But losses mounted steadily in November (to more than $6,000) and December (to more than $9,000). For the period between June 1 and December 31, 1934, the net loss exceeded $50,000, revealing, if nothing else, that mail pay had not been the panacea for which Pacific Seaboard had hoped.[14]

As important as such losses were—and they could not continue indefinitely at that pace—there was another side to the picture. The heartbeat of the organization was stronger, if for no other reason than that it possessed a passenger and mail route with substance and promise. It could scarcely be denied, however, that the benefits were more potential than actual. In February 1934, for example, the Bellancas carried a total of sixty-nine passengers, yielding an average revenue per passenger of only $4.90. The miles flown that month totaled 17,472. Of travel expenses amounting to $287.00 Murray was paid $45.00 for the use of her personal car. The sum spent on advertising (in the *Hotel Greeter's Guide* and the *Official Aviation Guide*, on a few placards, and on one or two other items) came to $110.59. The line was at that time truly a peanut operation. In December 1934 it carried only fifty-two paying passengers. Furthermore, the load factors were extremely low—13.6 percent for flight 1, originating in Chicago, and 15.4 percent for flight 2 from New Orleans, and total passenger revenue was actually less than in February—$298.71 compared to $310.50. On the other hand, mail operations raised the total mileage figure to 48,075, and expenditures for advertising during December reached nearly $400. The peanut was growing, if ever so slightly, but the future was still in doubt.[15]

Toward the end of 1934 Putnam and his key advisers made some decisions that led to significant changes. By then it had become obvious that new planes, multi-engine types, would soon be essential, for the federal government had almost finished arrangements for lighting route 8. As soon as this lighting had been installed Pacific Seaboard would be asked under its mail contract to undertake night flying, which under the rules established by the watchdog of civil aviation at that time—the Bureau of Air Commerce—required multi-engined planes. But where would the money to buy such planes come from? Putnam? He had no resources left for such an investment. Stock sales? The public attraction was not there at the time, as Putnam discovered while flying back and forth across the country in the fall of 1934 seeking capital from bankers, corporation tycoons, and even a rail line. Putnam was prepared in desperation to surrender control if necessary, in order to keep the enterprise alive. His only selling point was that, under the Air Mail Act of 1934, there was a vague possibility of gaining a higher mail rate, but this argument failed to sway any potential investors, and the situation appeared almost hopeless as the Post Office Department began to pressure Putnam on the matter of new equipment.[16]

In the words of the adage, "Things are sometimes darkest before the dawn." A former army flyer, aviation experimenter, and air racer, who had met C. E. Woolman in Peru years before while on a sales tour in South America, happened at that time to be Shell Oil's aviation manager for the Memphis district. He sold Pacific Seaboard its gasoline. This man, James (Jimmy) Doolittle, had liked Woolman and had felt the same way about the people at Pacific Seaboard. Besides, if they should prosper, Shell stood to gain. He himself had no large amount of capital to invest, but he happened to know a wealthy businessman who was also an aviation enthusiast, and he succeeded in arranging a meeting between this gentleman and Putnam.

It turned out to be one of those situations, of a kind that Delta had also experienced, in which key situations and people came together almost miraculously. The potential investor was D. D. Walker, heir to a St. Louis dry-goods fortune, who had founded a fixed-base aviation company at St. Louis's Lambert Field and had been one of the bidders on route 8. Although Putnam appreciated Doolittle's initiative in bringing him together with Walker, he had experienced too many negative reactions from other possible backers to be optimistic about this one. Walker, however, came from pioneer stock and was not averse to taking a gamble. He listened to Putnam's proposition over dinner and cocktails in Putnam's room at the Park Plaza Hotel in St. Louis: if Walker would invest enough money for Pacific Seaboard to buy five second-hand Stinson Trimotors, Putnam would make him vice-president and general sales manager "at a substantial salary . . . to accrue from the first month the company made a profit." Walker would also receive 20 percent more in stock for his investment, pro rata, than Putnam had received for his. During the course of their conversation, Putnam discovered something about Walker that had not been characteristic of his previous encounters with prospective investors; as he expressed it some years later, "Here was a man who wanted to follow his investment into action." With hardly a break in the deliberations, Walker took out his checkbook and pen, wrote in the amount of $60,000, and handed over the check to Putnam, assuring him that funds to cover it would be deposited by the next afternoon. It was enough to purchase the needed planes and to cover some of the winter's losses. Again, as in North Platte, Nebraska, a hotel room had been the scene of a drama with profound consequences for the future.[17]

At the turn of the year the obsolete and incongruous name Pacific Seaboard was abandoned. Putnam thought that the new name on which he and Walker had decided—Chicago and Southern (C & S)— had "a suggestion of railroad substance and stability." Of the old executive group (Putnam, now treasurer, as well as president; Reinhart, in charge of operations; Culbert, with the title "assistant to the president"; Murray, the auditor; and Preston, in charge of traffic) all but Preston took part in the renamed company. At some point early in 1935, however, Reinhart went back to his first love, flying, and was replaced as operations chief by Bruce E. Braun. Braun was, in Putnam's words, "a large, thick-set man in his early forties, dynamic and forceful, a powerhouse of energy . . . he had both seasoned practical judgment and personal drive." Coming from the Bureau of Air Commerce for the Chicago district, he, like Putnam and C. E. Woolman, was willing to gamble on the future of air transport and had sufficient courage "to abandon his government career and associate himself with a small airline that had never earned a cent, and might soon go bankrupt." Putnam retained only the presidency, and the post of treasurer was swapped back and forth between Walker and Culbert for the next seven years. During the same period these two men also shared the secretary's portfolio, except for an occasional interlude when somebody else, such as Braun, held it for a month or so. This relative informality in the exchange of managerial "hats" was also epitomized in the experience of another early C & S executive, Rogers Humphreys, who occasionally spelled Walker as chief of traffic. Back in the fall of 1934 Humphreys had given Putnam a check for $5,000—money he had put aside for his son's education— as a gesture of faith in the future of the enterprise; Putnam could not help but repose confidence in such a dedicated staff member. On the board of the redesignated company were Putnam, Walker, and Culbert. Other important figures who came aboard in 1934 or early 1935 and were destined to play major roles in the company were R. L. (Doc) Anderson, brother of pilot Hap, whose forte was maintenance; R. S. Scrivener, a Memphis native with a background in banking, who had worked for Curtiss-Wright in his home town; and pilots Victor L. Hoganson and Charles Quinn.[18]

The precise distribution of ownership in the reconstituted firm is difficult to determine. Each monthly financial statement for that year simply listed the amount of common stock issued as 35,000 shares, without stating who held how much. In an exhibit dated May 20, attached to an application for extension of the mail contract, Putnam was listed as the only person holding more than "5 per centum" of the stock, but the document also stated that Walker, Humphreys, and other unspecified parties would have significant holdings at some future time. By the end of 1935, when a plan of reincorporation (about which more will be said later) was being put through, Putnam was listed under the category of "officers accounts" as holding $172,543.35, Walker $65,000, and Humphreys $5,000—precisely the amounts of cash that they had invested earlier.[19]

Another crisis surfaced in 1934 and lasted well into the following years; it was almost as important as that surrounding the acquisition of new operating capital. A new mail rate was imperative if the company was to survive. It is a tribute to the vagaries of the legislative process that, under the Air Mail Act of 1934, the Interstate Commerce Commission, in its efforts to calculate a fair return to an airline, could not set rates for individual carriers that exceeded their original contract rates, regardless of increasing equipment costs. Under this manifestly unjust stipulation, the ICC investigated the mail-rate situation in the airline industry in the fall of 1934; among those called to testify in Washington was Erma Murray. In its deliberations the ICC determined that Putnam's struggling firm should receive twenty-nine cents a mile, based upon two round trips a day. That rate, however, could not go into effect unless Congress repaired the existing airmail statute. Bills to amend were accordingly introduced by Senator Kenneth McKellar of Tennessee and Representative James Mead of New York. C&S continued to lose money as the legislative mill ground with its accustomed slowness and Putnam spent long hours in the national capital lobbying with congressmen on behalf of his firm and the industry as a whole. Sometimes these meetings were as heated as Washington's climate. At long last, while Putnam waited anxiously in the gallery, the Senate put the final legislative stamp on the amendment in August, and another major hurdle had been negotiated.[20]

But this action did not provide an overnight cure for the beleaguered company's problems. For one thing, the newly acquired Stinsons were already outmoded in many respects, as Delta had also
found. As in Delta's case, C&S could not immediately afford the
Douglas DC-2, but, like Woolman's firm, it began planning to acquire the next best thing—the Lockheed Electra. Nevertheless, despite this problem and the net loss suffered in 1935, glimmerings
of progress began to appear. Mail revenue increased, as did passen-
ger-related income; in July, as passenger revenue soared to a record
$9,297.42 and the adjusted mail rate took effect pending congres-
sional sanction, the first net profit showed on the books—a grand
total of $2,971.40. However unimpressive this figure may appear
from a later vantage point, for Putnam and coworkers struggling to
survive in the depths of the depression it represented a shaft of light
in almost unrelieved gloom. "The problem for us," recalled Putnam,
"had altered from urging desperate hopes upon individual gamblers
to presenting a standard participation to the average investor."[21]

Even before these faint stirrings of hope surfaced, the company
had one vital asset that should have been attractive to both potential
customers and investors—its safety record. With the exception of
the embarrassment caused by flight 2 on June 3, 1934, it had experienced neither a serious accident nor a passenger fatality—an impressive performance in view of the dearth of airway refinements
along its California routes, the lack of radio communications (until
the advent of the Stinson-Ts), and the fact that the angle of its new
artery down the Mississippi Valley subjected its aircraft to more prolonged severe weather than Delta planes underwent.

But this enviable record suffered a setback in May 1935, not long
after C&S had begun night flying. At 10:00 P.M. on May 28 the
firm's Stinson NC-10894 was cleared at the Chicago airport for a
flight to Springfield, Illinois, with pilot John B. Lynn at the controls
and only one other person, nonrevenue passenger Paul Gardner of
Wichita, Kansas, aboard. The night was clear, and no bad weather
was anticipated, but a short time later witnesses near Nilwood,
Illinois, noticed the plane, somewhat off course, approaching from a
northwesterly direction and just skimming some treetops. Ahead,
within a thickly forested area, several gulleys yawned. Apparently
Lynn saw the trap into which he was heading, for he made a sharp
turn to the right, but he was flying so low that—at least so it seemed
from marks later discovered on the site—the down-swinging right

wing struck ground at a spot where its green navigation light was later discovered embedded in the earth. In the Bureau of Air Commerce's subsequent accident report, it was said that the plane "cartwheeled and came to rest with fuselage upside down and with the tail pointing in a direction opposite to the approach." The precise reasons for the crash, which killed both Lynn and Gardner, remain obscure, though some ground fog, normally not hazardous on a flight of this kind, had apparently been encountered along the way. In any event, the Stinson had failed to follow a direct flight path on the Springfield portion of its run to St. Louis and had lost altitude before reaching its fatal rendezvous. The bureau's report concluded merely that "the probable cause of this accident was an unintentional collision with the ground while flying at too low an altitude."[22]

There is no evidence that this enigmatic accident impeded growth, for only a month later the first significant upswing in passenger revenue occurred, and the first tiny but nevertheless precious profits were recorded on the firm's books. By that time Putnam had again embarked on a search for financiers whom he could impress with C & S's prospects. At long last, in St. Louis, he found an amenable group: I. M. Simon and Company, a small but highly reputable firm of investment bankers. Spokesman John Longmire had a manner "both kind and shrewd," giving Putnam the feeling that "he liked to see young men get ahead, but not too easily nor too quickly." In negotiations that went on from October to late December a second investment firm was brought into the picture—Lawrence Stern and Company of Chicago.

Finally, on December 18, an agreement was reached, and vital changes soon ensued. The first one came at the end of the year, when C & S was reincorporated in that hallowed corporate home, Delaware. The new charter called for two types of stock, convertible preference and common, granting the company authority to issue 50,000 shares of the former at $10 a share and 300,000 shares of the latter with no assigned par value. On December 31, 1935 the old corporation transferred its assets, including the contract for route 8, and as well as its liabilities, to the new Delaware company in exchange for common stock. This stock was in turn divided among the principal creditors of the old company, mainly Putnam, Walker, and Humphreys, who became principal shareholders of the reorganized firm, with a total of 85,100 shares of common stock.

All told, the stated capital and paid-in surplus allocatable to the

85,100 shares was $118,840.35 (assets of $155,517.49 minus liabilities of $36,677.14 transferred from the old company to the new). All these shares, however, were issued in the name of Carleton Putnam as sole voting trustee. All holders of common stock surrendered their voting power to Putnam under the new arrangement, which was, in the words of a later company history, designed "to insure continuity of management and control."[23] In related moves, Putnam, Walker, and Humphreys were each granted an option to purchase 25,000 additional shares of common stock in the future, though in 1936 they were collectively restricted to acquiring no more than a total of 3,000 shares at a unit price of $5. In addition, the Simon and Stern firms each received options on 12,000 shares of C & S common.[24]

One central purpose of this reorganization, as a stock prospectus issued in February 1936 indicates, was to provide expanded capital to purchase a fleet of Lockheed Electras and thus to make it possible to court passengers with faster and more modern ships at a time when the overall industry trend was away from too much reliance on mail revenue. In addition to supplying funds for four Electras, the issue was to bring in money for reserve equipment, radio apparatus, the training of crews, and fresh working capital. Finally, it would also permit the establishment of a contingency fund or "crash reserve," which the airline, of course, hoped would never have to be tapped.

Of the 50,000 preferred shares authorized by the new charter, 35,000 were to be offered to the public; the expected net yield was $315,000. This convertible-preference stock had various attractions: under certain conditions its holders were to "possess all voting power in respect of the affairs of the Company, and to elect new directors to fill any vacancy." If the company's net assets were to fall below the level prevailing in February 1936, convertible-preference owners could vote to dissolve it or sell, lease, or exchange any or all of its property, including the airmail contract. In the important matter of dividends, each share of convertible-preference stock would earn seventy cents per annum, subject only to approval by the board, whereas the common stock bore no nominal dividend rate. Upon voluntary or involuntary termination of the corporation, holders of preferred stock would receive payment before owners of common stock. These attractions were not only meant to lure buyers but were also part of a complex corporate setup that had been designed by the financiers, in Putnam's words, "to protect the stockholders from too prolonged failure on our part—which was a good way to protect us from ourselves." In addition to the stock options previously described, the two investment firms received between them 15,000 shares of common stock, fully paid and nonassessable.[25]

As president, Putnam headed the high-level managerial team that was preparing to put the new Lockheeds into operation. Other officers included Walker, finance; Humphreys, traffic; Braun, operations; and Culbert, legal affairs. The reconstituted board was composed of these five men, though curiously no one was designated chairman. The corporate nerve center had also been moved in September 1935 to new headquarters in St. Louis, as a gesture of appreciation to Walker and to ensure more convenient accommodations.[26] The company's first meteorologist, Leonard Scruggs, arrived in the same year, his job made somewhat easier by new equipment being acquired. Ground radio had been installed in 1935, and the first message was sent in January 1936. The Stinsons carried only receiving sets, however, and it was not until the inauguration of Lockheed service in May that conversations between ground and air could take place.[27]

When Robert Gross's Lockheeds went on the line—some three years after he had steered Putnam toward his maiden voyage—it seemed to the latter that they "shone like silver in clear, blue skies that spring. They darted into the traffic pattern around the airports on our route like new comets arrived in the solar system from outer space. They were so much quieter and more comfortable to ride in than the old Stinsons that, for a while at least, we all wanted to travel our own line constantly." The attractiveness of the new aircraft to passengers is illustrated by statistics for 1936 as a whole. From January through June, figures reflecting combined Stinson-Lockheed operations showed monthly losses broken only by a small profit in March, when there was a fairly sharp increase in both passenger and mail revenue. In May the number of revenue-producing passengers and the amount of passenger revenue almost doubled, whereas mail revenue decreased slightly. Passenger and mail levels then remained fairly constant for the rest of the year, and in four of the final six months (July, September, October, and November) the line made small net profits, ranging from a high of $5,624.63 in July to $593.14 in September. Such variables as weather and holidays undoubtedly played a part in the total picture, but the Lockheeds nevertheless seemed to have brightened the present and ensured a rosier future. Indeed, C&S was able to announce a fare reduction on November 1 and called attention to the fact that October 1936 had shown a 95 percent increase in passengers over those carried in the same month a year before.[28]

Still, the addition of new planes did not go off without one unfortunate hitch. On the night of August 5, 1936, Electra number NC-16022, continuing flight 4, which had originated in New Orleans, revved up its engines at St. Louis's Lambert field in preparation for takeoff. In addition to pilot Carl F. Zeier and copilot Russell C. Mossman, five passengers were aboard. A preflight weather report had indicated some moderate fog and haze in the area, which restricted visibility below optimum levels, but conditions were supposed to improve en route to Chicago, and there was no reason to expect unusual difficulty at any point in the flight. To the near north, however, the ceiling had lowered to only five hundred feet at the time of takeoff. Witnesses under the plane's flight path, experienced in the coming and goings of aircraft, knew by its navigation lights and the sound of its engines that it was flying at an unusually low altitude during its initial climb, but the engines appeared to be functioning normally. Suddenly, however, the lights vanished, and the drone of the engines died away. The plane had made a sharp turn to the left, heading back toward the airport, but, like the earlier Stinson, it was too low for the maneuver, perhaps because of a "decided tendency" of this Lockheed model to lose altitude when turning left. Whether the plane dipped or had strayed too low, the left wing struck and dragged on the ground. The resulting crash killed everybody aboard.

A subsequent investigation revealed no reason to suspect structural or material failure, and the possibility that weather conditions had caused the accident was discounted. No emergency message had reached Lambert, despite the fact that the plane's radio was in working order. Apparently some undetermined circumstance had persuaded the pilot to return immediately to the airport, with unfortunate results. As in the earlier accident, the precise cause was a mystery and would forever remain so.[29]

In the final analysis, however, 1936 was a year in which Putnam's dreams finally showed signs of materializing. Thanks partly to the reorganization and the acumen of such advisers as Longmire, financial losses fell to $17,083.37 but could be offset against a paid-in surplus of $25,000.[30] In the new St. Louis headquarters, things were still crowded, even though accommodations were better than those available in Memphis. Operations, flight control, reservations, and

Burke Dowling (Bob) Adams *(left),* long-time president of Delta's advertising agency by that name, discusses poster designs with James H. Cobb, Delta's first director of public relations and advertising.

Arthur Ford *(left)* and John F. Nycum together in the Engineering Department in the early 1950s.

Stations personnel in the early 1950s. *Left to right:* Finis Fox, C. B. (Speedy) Wilder, and R. J. Williams.

W. L. Miller *(left)*, head of Stores Department, confers with Purchasing's Wade Hobbs and Horace D. Wigley, in the early 1950s.

C. E. Woolman in merger talks with George E. Gardner, president of Northeast Airlines.

DC-7 aircraft were flown by Delta from 1954 to 1968. The DC-7B, pictured here, joined the fleet in 1957.

Members of Northeast Airlines crew marooned on Lake O'Connor, Canada, 1943.

Boston and Maine Airways, forerunner of Northeast Airlines, inaugurated service on August 11, 1933, with Stinson-T Model SM-6000 equipment, flying from Boston to Portland and Bangor, Maine.

Captain M. H. Anderson, pioneer Boston and Maine Airways pilot.

Northeast's early stewardesses wore pilgrim uniforms.

Northeast Airlines DC-3, shown flying over Revere, Massachusetts.

communications were all housed in one room in a miniature frame building known as the "doghouse." At the terminal building C&S shared the ticket office with TWA and Bowen Airlines, a small enterprise that, unlike C&S, did not survive this strenuous period. Putnam, Braun, Walker, Culbert, Murray, Scrivener, and others occupied executive offices in a nearby hangar, which quite naturally did not afford the most luxurious accommodations. As *Sky Steps*, the in-house periodical of C&S, recreated the atmosphere some years later, "in the doghouse, days and nights were hectic. Putnam, Braun, Walker, Culbert . . . often stood by on radio while flight superintendents . . . were up working the planes." Despite the hardships, the company was successfully turning a difficult corner.

As business improved, new problems arose. In the words of *Sky Steps*, "One day Braun and Walker, substituting on reservations and radio, mixed up some reservations and sold space without space available. Then it was that Central Space Control was born in 1937."[31] Over the next few years a decentralized system evolved, which combined flexibility with greater accuracy. Each city along the route controlled a certain number of seats, which would be released to the next city if they remained unsold upon the departure of a given flight. In addition, a city reservations office could call down the line to request seats allotted to other stations. As airline veteran George E. Shedd described the complex setup many years later, "On a Chicago–St. Louis–Memphis–Jackson–New Orleans route, Chicago reservations might have been unable to confirm a seat from Chicago to New Orleans from their own allotted space. They could, however, confirm the Chicago–St. Louis portion and secure the St. Louis–New Orleans seat from St. Louis reservations. They might also get a St. Louis–Memphis seat from St. Louis, a Memphis–Jackson seat from Memphis and/or a Jackson–New Orleans seat from the Jackson office." However primitive the system may appear now, in a computerized age, it nevertheless worked. "Most reservation offices," Shedd recalled, "were equipped with a six- or eight-sided table with a Lazy Susan type arrangement in the center on which the control charts and reservations cards were set up so each agent at the table had ready access to them."[32]

The business recession of 1937 slowed the firm's upward climb to some degree, but the new Lockheeds proved their worth, affording increased dependability of operations over a region posing formidable meteorological problems. Delta's ships, which bisected the flight path of Putnam's planes in the lower Mississippi valley region, penetrated the severe weather fronts sweeping west to east and moved through them in a comparatively short time. In contrast, the C & S craft, flying northward or southward, had to stay in these lengthy fronts—especially if they were slow-moving—for much longer times. Both airlines, of course, sometimes had to interrupt or cancel flights because of bad weather, but performance statistics show that C & S was usually able to take the elements in its stride. In the period from January through May 1937, when spring spawned violent weather across the Gulf coastal plains and up into the midlands, C & S planes were forced to land because of inclement weather only twice. The company also achieved a commendable record of coping with "station delays," which held up departures because of mail-handling problems, mechanical failures, passenger difficulties, or adverse weather conditions. Only in January of this five-month period did C & S's record of on-time performance drop below 88 percent.[33]

A C & S sales manual, dated September 1, 1938, illustrates how sophisticated the line had become, compared to its primitive operations five years before. Putnam led off with a mood piece describing the attractions of the firm's Valley Level Route to old and prospective customers:

From the brisk pace of Chicago's Michigan Boulevard to a stroll at twilight through New Orleans' Vieux Carre . . . in the short span of seven hours! Below your window the panorama unfolds its colorful, changing story of climate and enterprise, of custom and tradition. . . . St. Louis [later in the manual there was a photograph of a C & S Electra winging above a bridge across the Mississippi against a backdrop of clustered downtown buildings and a riverboat moored to the shore], city of music lovers . . . Memphis, Queen of the Deep South, largest inland cotton market in the world, warm-hearted home of Southern graciousness and carnival gaiety; Jackson [photographs showed a C & S Electra parked near a terminal building like a southern mansion and another climbing above the terminal, hangars, and trees], capital of Mississippi, historic landmark of Confederate days. And then New Orleans [more prosaic photos of an Electra over the delta, followed by a photographic tour of the impressive, modern airport, revealing how far the development of such facilities had come from the dirt-runway, ill-lighted days of less than a decade before] . . . a great Pan-American gateway with docks piled high with sugar and bananas, spices and hemp. . . . Here, the iron lace work of some Pontalba balcony looking downward on the Place d'Armes, you may visualize the glamour of a golden long ago.

Putnam also extolled unhurried hours of fishing and idling in the southern sun, convenient connecting train schedules to inviting

Gulf Coast resorts at such places as Biloxi and Pass Christian, and a variety of pleasures, including "golf, boating, tennis, swimming, and never-to-be-forgotten moonlight rides along white shell roads."[34] Eastern and National had Florida at the end of their rainbows, and Putnam was attempting to do the best he could with the lesser-known Mississippi Gold Coast at the end of his.

The same sales manual reveals various aspects of the company's policies and service in the late 1930s. Like most other lines, C&S offered a 15 percent reduction on air-travel cards and 10 percent on round-trip fares. Any ticket entitled the purchaser to the carriage of thirty-five pounds of free baggage. Lost or damaged baggage carried a liability of $100 unless a higher evaluation was declared in advance of a flight. The ticket agents at C&S offices, in such hotels as the Palmer House in Chicago or at airports, sold trip insurance at the rate of $5,000 for twenty-five cents. The company reserved the right to cancel reservations before a flight or en route; passengers would be entitled to refunds for their own cancellations only if the latter were made at least three hours before the flight. Pilots could remove passengers from a plane or refuse to admit them for safety "or other reasons."[35]

In 1938 a C&S passenger flying from Jackson to Chicago paid a one-way fare of $36.50. At some point along the way a meal of pineapple salad, fried chicken, potato salad, olives, pickles, buttered rolls, cake, hot coffee, and mints would be served by the copilot. During one such flight, Memphis automobile dealer Herbert Herff observed an episode that impressed him. It was mealtime and copilot Reed Knight (later chief pilot for C&S) was serving the trays and pouring the coffee. Another passenger, a woman, had in tow two young children and an infant in arms. (C&S encouraged family travel with half-fares for children under twelve years of age and free rides for children up to two years old if carried by parents or guardians.) After he had served the other passengers, Knight, without prompting, took the infant and held it so that the mother could eat her meal. Herff wrote to Putnam that "such voluntary interest and loyalty should not go unnoticed, and being an employer of a large number of people, I know how pleased you will be to receive these few lines of communication."[36]

The sales manual featured a gallery of C&S pilots who had posed rather self-consciously for the camera: Captains L. D. Anderson, Ben Catlin, S. W. Hopkins, and Charles Quinn, and First Officer Reed Knight. Underneath their pictures was the slogan "Caution Is a Part of Their Character." Resembling candidates for "most likely to succeed" in a college yearbook were photos, with accompanying biographical blurbs, of members of the executive staff: suave balding Putnam; bespectacled Braun, with the mien of an intelligent bear; long-faced Amos Culbert, looking like an "earnest young man"; and round-cheeked Walker, with a slightly amused smile. The pictures gave a collective impression of relative youth, befitting the management of a fledgling firm that was just beginning to become established securely after a trying series of birth pangs.[37]

Like other airlines, C & S was vitally affected by the Civil Aeronautics Act of 1938. Putnam thought that this statute was long overdue, for the previous system had reached "its logical and final absurdity" when, he recalled later, Eastern won a crucial route addition with the low bid of zero cents per mile. On the other hand, he had not always looked with favor upon the kind of regulatory body established by the new legislation. In 1935, testifying before the federal commission set up by the act of 1934 to make recommendations for the airline industry, he had spoken against the type of regulatory bodies that were ultimately created in 1938. These independent boards, he had reasoned, would be subject to pressures from larger vested interests, and small operators like himself would suffer. But increased security had made him change his mind about the proper nature and degree of the government's role.[38] In any event, C & S continued to develop satisfactorily under the altered statutory authority; passenger revenues and monthly profits grew at a modest rate through 1939. Meanwhile, the firm's dependence upon mail revenue declined, conforming to industry-wide trends. In February 1939 the company received its Certificate of Public Convenience and Necessity for route 8 from the CAB, and the transition to the new federal procedures was complete.[39] Few people flying the Valley Level Route that year could foresee any particular change in their own future prospects as a result of the outbreak of war in Europe. The flat land below was peaceful, except for the seasonal storms, and the country had already weathered almost a decade of depression.

As the depression drew to an end, important decisions were made about significant expansion in a peacetime context. The still shiny but no longer new Electras were reaching the limits of their depreciation, and it was decided to replace them with four Douglas DC-3s. After a survey of the financial terrain and some internal debate, the directors secured the necessary consent of three fourths of the convertible-preference stockholders, at a meeting on January 5, 1940, to seek a loan for the four new planes, instead of funding them with a stock issue, as had been done for the Electras. But a loan was not easy to find. Bankers in New York, Memphis, New Orleans, and even St. Louis were not eager to advance money to such a small company. United, yes; TWA, yes; American, yes. Eastern, certainly. But Delta, C&S—well. . . . Bankers in those cities would lend money toward the purchase of only three DC-3s and wanted 5 percent interest assuming the risk. After much difficulty C&S finally found an institution, the American National Bank and Trust Company of Chicago, with acceptable terms for lending a sizable amount toward the cost of four DC-3s, but the bank did not open its coffers without exacting an agreement, called a "trust indenture," by which the company mortgaged all its current property and all future equipment until the note was repaid. The rate, however, was a manageable 4 percent. This loan of $350,000 was augmented by depreciation reserves and working capital totaling $250,000, thus providing the $600,000 needed to buy the four new DC-3s. Although C&S had ten years to pay off the loan, the company determined not to take nearly that long.[40]

Another 1939 decision was to apply for a route extension from Memphis to Houston. As Putnam phrased it:

We tightened our belts and knocked on the Board's door with our Houston prayer. Tom Braniff followed suit, and so did Eddie Rickenbacker. Braniff was twice our size, and Rickenbacker's Eastern was one of the Big Four. We, on the other hand, introduced studies to show that the flow of traffic over the new route would fit better into our system than into either Braniff's or Eastern's, and we laid special stress on our need for greater mileage to compete properly with our rivals in costs and standards of service.

The wait for a decision, which produced a "prolonged feeling of suspense," lasted for more than a year.[41]

The thrill of receiving the DC-3s and putting them into operation relieved the suspense to some degree. On April 15, 1940, the first of these new planes was christened in St. Louis. Gleaming in sunlight and trimmed in the C&S colors of the time—black and orange—it was named *City of St. Louis* as Jan Smith, the city's reigning Veiled Prophet Queen, smashed a bottle of Booth's champagne on the nose of a propeller. With her on the makeshift platform were veterans Putnam, Murray, and Hap Anderson. Because the DC-3s required separate cabin attendants, the company began taking applications for stewardess training. Some two hundred young women applied; Putnam, Walker, and Braun were the selection board. What were they looking for? William J. Spangler, who soon joined C&S and became a pilot, recalled that in the 1940s the company had stressed the image of a well-bred young lady with the aura of the debutante.

After much deliberation, the selection board chose an initial group of thirteen women for seven weeks of training. It was not long before their beauty queen potential was revealed: Dorothy Travis, who had been selected for the post of chief stewardess, was named Miss National Aviation Forum, and another member of the group, Margaret Mellon, was named Miss American Aviation for 1940 at the National Air Carnival. C&S definitely attempted to draw a parallel between its stewardesses and the southern belle of regional lore (but not the headstrong Scarlett O'Hara of the recent novel and movie *Gone with the Wind*). On the back of the C&S schedule for November 1940 was the photo of a beaming stewardess with a meal tray, accompanied by a drawing of a classic smiling southern belle in front of a mansion; the copy promised "a cuisine influenced by the best traditions of famed southern chefs and stewardesses eager to be of service." Spangler believed that the stress on gentility for C&S stewardesses was logical in view of the fact that the passengers of the 1940s were by and large middle- and upper-class people with traditional values.[42]

On May 1, 1940, C&S inaugurated its DC-3 service with three round trips between New Orleans and Chicago every twenty-four hours; one round trip between St. Louis and Chicago was made on the Electras. The Lockheeds, however, were all removed from service in the fall of 1940 after the acquisition of a fifth DC-3; still another DC-3 was put into service in spring 1941. The fiscal year ending June 30, 1940, showed a net profit of slightly more than $29,000, but it had required income from an adjustment in the mail rate and sale of some Lockheeds to keep this figure from being a loss. Another factor, as Putnam reported to the stockholders, was the considerable preparatory and promotional expense involved in the acquisition of the DC-3s.[43]

Possible problems with stockholders threatened in the summer of 1940, when it was discovered that the firm's net current assets had fallen below $35,000, the figure prevailing in February 1936. Under the C&S charter such a turn of events placed all voting rights in the hands of the holders of convertible-preference stock, thus temporarily neutralizing the power of the voting trust. The directors moved quickly to remedy the situation by authorizing an issue of 65,000 shares of common stock, which yielded $487,500.[44]

Late in 1940 the portal to Houston was opened to C&S. A CAB order of December 6 awarded the company a new Certificate of Public Convenience and Necessity for route 53, providing service between Memphis and the Texas city by way of Pine Bluff, Arkansas, and Shreveport, Louisiana. The service became a reality on May 1, 1941, when a C&S DC-3 named *The City of Houston* took off from Memphis with the first passengers on route 53. Mail would not be carried until July; this requirement was a reversal of the former governmental restraint on transporting passengers over a new route until mail had been flown for a certain period. Reminiscing about the reception extended to C&S officials by civic leaders at a ceremonial dinner in Houston, where he was introduced by "the faithful Jimmy Doolittle," Putnam later recalled "how completely at one I felt with my Houston audience when I talked about the spirit of the old border, and the new frontier of the air." From the roof of his hotel that night he watched flames from distant natural-gas wells "whose glow had a smoky, lurid quality that suggested rich incense burning in a giant censer . . . here was the sign and emblem of the wealth and growth of Texas. Texas, of course, had cattle and fruits and other resources, but oil—black gold—was a distinctive, an odorous, a flowing wealth."[45]

Having come so far in only a few years from the shoestring days, Putnam had good reason to ponder an exciting future on that spring night, as he watched the distant fires licking the Texas sky. Meanwhile, thousands of miles away in Europe, flames of a different sort portended the entry of the United States into what was rapidly becoming a global holocaust. Within months the country was at war, and a new chapter in the development of C&S had begun.

CHAPTER 11

High Hopes and Rough Air

DESPITE THE ADDITION of the route from Memphis to Houston, Chicago and Southern's accounts for fiscal 1941 were splotched with red ink. To some degree this deficit reflected unusual circumstances in a nation still officially clinging to neutrality but in reality moving ever closer to the status of a full-fledged participant in the conflict; in September 1940 military maneuvers in Louisiana led to a temporary ban on night flying over the company's routes from Memphis to New Orleans and from Memphis to Houston. The adversities encountered by the firm may also have been partly owing to a series of fatal accidents that plagued the industry in late 1940 and early 1941, temporarily dampening public enthusiasm for flying. C & S, fortunately, was involved in none of these accidents, but its monthly passenger totals tapered off somewhat, and its load factors declined.[1] Putnam mentioned these considerations in his annual report to the stockholders at the conclusion of the fiscal year, and he also cited such factors as the expenses of opening the new route, increasing depreciation charges on the recently acquired DC-3s, and higher wage and tax outlays to explain the reasons for the $111,931 deficit registered by the enterprise. An additional financial drain resulted from C & S's move back to Memphis after half a decade in St. Louis.[2]

The return to the old base came about because C & S had outgrown its facilities at Lambert Field and nothing else was available. The Memphis city fathers were more inclined to appreciate the company than they had been in 1934 and hastened to construct a suitable hangar and office building at the municipal airport. The firm's operating base and general offices were therefore transferred down the river in stages between March and August 1941.[3]

Citizens of Missouri's largest city were probably too preoccupied with other matters to care much about this development; after all, the Cardinals were on their way to winning the National League pennant and most residents of St. Louis probably thought of C & S rarely, if at all. Even though the shadow of the war was often clearly discernible, it seemed remote as Chicago and Southern's DC-3s flew their accustomed rounds and Putnam and his cohorts planned and dreamed of new expansions. Then, on one fateful Sunday in December, people in Memphis, St. Louis, New York, and other cities across the land switched on their radios and learned that Pearl Harbor had been bombed. Suddenly the awesome realities of the world situation became all too real.

The experience of C & S during World War II was generally similar to that of Delta and other American carriers. The frenzy of wartime activities—in particular the rapid increase in mobility caused by massive transfers of armed forces, supplies, war workers, and dependents—both strained the resources of C & S and provided an unprecedented opportunity for the company, as it did for other lines. C & S, too, had to develop a split personality; it became a government contractor, flying military cargo and performing other defense tasks, while struggling to maintain civilian airline service with reduced equipment. It also had to focus—above the smoke of battle, so to speak—on the uncertain horizon of the postwar era.

Merely to generalize about the wartime experience of C & S, however, would be to miss much of its individual flavor. Seven days after Pearl Harbor the company set up a modification program for army air-force planes, with J. A. (Joe) Young heading the modification center at Memphis. A master of several trades, Young, after joining C & S in 1935, had risen from stock clerk to this new and demanding position. Soon such aircraft as the Bell P-39 Airacobra fighters were passing through the center to be specially adapted for service in particular theaters of war. Edward Bolton, who later became a supervisor in the engine shop at the Delta jet base in Atlanta, was employed by C & S as a mechanic just before Pearl Harbor and later worked on the P-39s. An Arkansas native, raised in Memphis, he had trained at the local Whitehaven School of Aeronautics. He had owned a filling station and had taken a cut in pay to join C & S, but he found the airline industry exciting. Interviewed years later, he expressed his belief that the modification of the Airacobras, fifty in number, was the first such work performed by any of the airlines. Although modifications and airline operations were separate functions, Bolton worked in both areas and sometimes in other types of defense-contract production as well.[4]

As was also true at Delta, the variety of work performed by C & S for the government included transitional and multiple-engine training for air-corps personnel, maintenance training for military mechanics who were to service war planes, extensive overhaul services for military engines, and training in airline navigation and meteorology for members of the armed services. Apart from the manufacturing side of the air-transport industry, which was turning out the "warbirds," the services performed by C&S and other airlines in the defense effort gave credence to the prophecies of such pioneers as Colonel Paul Henderson, former second assistant postmaster general, who, while earning a reputation as the father of night airmail in the early 1920s, had insisted that the development of commercial aviation was essential to a viable aerial defense.[5]

One of the most important services performed by C&S was the transportation of military cargo. William Spangler, who would eventually become a senior Delta captain, flying Boeing 747 jets by 1976, joined C&S during World War II and at first flew military cargo exclusively. A native of Missouri, though raised in Memphis, he came from a railroad family, and with this transportation background it was not surprising that he choose aviation. While attending Southwestern College in Memphis, he took part in the civilian pilot-training program. After completing thirty-five hours of training, he received a private pilot's license, and, when he reached his twenty-first birthday, C&S hired him. After a brief period of instruction by Reed Knight, he was ready to fly a DC-3; "Uncle Ben" Catlin was designated his check pilot. Following his first successful flight up and down the Valley Level Route, he spent several months assisting with the well-known cockpit mockup known as the Link Trainer by day and serving as reserve copilot by night. Eventually he checked out as a captain, but his age prevented him from qualifying for an unrestricted airline-transport rating (ATR). C&S, however, managed to secure a waiver that gave Spangler the right to fly aircraft carrying military cargo.

During the wartime rush Spangler received only minimal training, and his first full instrument approach occurred after he had earned his wings and had sat at the controls himself. But, as he later recalled, he learned by his own mistakes, in the tradition of pilots who "flew by the seat of their pants," and adapted to flying and its innovations as much through instinct and "feel" as through technical training. There still remained in many of the pilots of that era, systematic training notwithstanding, something of the barnstorming spirit that had animated the early Lindbergh or such daredevils as Bert Acosta. This vital spark undoubtedly accounted in part for some of the great fighter aces and dauntless bomber pilots of the war, and it also contributed to the success of a rapidly trained young pilot transporting vital military cargo.[6]

Hurried instruction was not the only problem in the cargo service. When this operation began in May 1942, crews were sometimes stranded at one point or another for several days awaiting orders from the army. They could not be given bonuses or paid under their normal contractual arrangements for this type of layover. Eventually such problems were worked out, perhaps mainly because the system had its informal, as well as its formal, aspects. Although army regulations and orders governed operations, the flights themselves were under neither direct military nor CAA control. The cargo planes took off when C & S dispatcher and company pilot agreed that weather and load conditions were right. The pilot did, however, file a military flight plan.[7]

In June 1942 the army "inducted" into the service two of C & S's six DC-3s. Federal payment for these planes did not ease the burden of operating with reduced equipment—a situation that lasted just over two years. The loss of the two planes resulted in the immediate elimination of one round trip between Chicago and New Orleans. One of the aircraft sold was converted by C & S into a cargo carrier and assigned to the company's military supply operation by the Air Transport Command (ATC).

Whatever the future was to bring, fiscal 1942 meant a financial bonanza for C & S, for there was not only a complete reversal of the deluge of red ink that had occurred in fiscal 1941 but also, as Putnam informed stockholders, it had been "possible to eliminate the deficit in the surplus account resulting from losses in previous years." The main reason for the improved situation was a CAB decision to award C & S $201,096 in retroactive mail pay. Other important factors in the "most successful year in the history of the line" were increases of 50 percent or more in passenger, express, and mail revenues over the previous fiscal year because of the dramatically improved utilization levels characterizing the whole industry at that time. Putnam attributed these increases partly to wartime expansion but also to "the normal upward trend of . . . traffic as the public becomes more accustomed to, and familiar with, the advantages of air transportation."[8]

By 1943 C & S had successfully adapted to the conditions governing an airline in wartime, one of which was a shortage of men in a traditionally male-oriented industry. The main exception to this orientation was, of course, the cabin attendants, and there was no shortage of young women there. In fact, by 1943 the original group of C&S stewardesses had been totally replaced by new people, without any apparent decrease in efficiency. Of the thirteen originals, all but one had become married, to physicians, airline pilots, servicemen, and others. Dorothy Travis, the first chief stewardess, had married Dr. Garrett Allen of Chicago; Bobbie Brace, C&S Captain R. Nelson of Memphis; Ruth O'Shea, Lieutenant T. P. Stewart; Margaret Mellon (Miss American Aviation of 1940), William Felvey of Chicago. Only one, Carmen Nesbitt, was not married; she was working with TWA's traffic division in Chicago. Other divisions of C&S also began to register increasing female participation. Endorsing this trend, the February 1943 issue of *Sky Steps* quoted a pioneer American aviatrix, Harriet Quimby, who had written in 1912: "There is no reason why the aeroplane should not open up a fruitful occupation for women. I see no reason why they cannot realize handsome individual incomes by carrying passengers between adjacent towns . . . taking photographs from above, or conducting schools for flying."

Although women did not pilot C&S planes, they filled a variety of other jobs that had been held mainly by males until the war. Mary Busch of St. Louis became one of the industry's foremost reservations managers, and Freddie Robertson took over as chief author of all company manuals. Elizabeth Folsom served capably as instructor in charge of Link training in the Memphis pilots' ground school, and Anne Beasley was appointed the first C&S district traffic manager. Other women became flight-control and radio operators, draftswomen, welders, riveters, and instrument experts. Erma Murray was proof that a capable woman could hold a responsible position in peace and war alike. In 1940 she had been appointed assistant secretary of the firm, and in 1943, at a banquet sponsored by the National Aeronautical Association (NAA) in recognition of the company's tenth anniversary, NAA President Gill Robb Wilson paid special tribute to her pioneer role, as well as to those of Hap Anderson and Carleton Putnam.[9]

In 1943 Anderson's rugged features were selected to represent "Every Person's United States Airline Pilot" in an advertisement sponsored by the ATA. This full-page color spread, which appeared in such national periodicals as *Life, Newsweek, Collier's, Saturday Evening Post,* and *Cosmopolitan,* was designed to emphasize the airlines' twin contributions to the war effort—as instruments of defense and as operators of an indispensable mode of transportation.

C & S took pride in this recognition and in the cadre of company employees who served in the armed forces. The firm did not lose a top executive, as Delta had lost Laigh Parker, to the armed services, but C & S Captain William (Bill) Fry rose to the position of director of training, with the rank of colonel and the status of command pilot, at the headquarters of the A T C's ferrying division, and veteran skipper Stewart Hopkins served as commander with the navy's Air Transport Service. A former stewardess, Catherine Bender, joined the WAVES and became an ensign in charge of a division of sailors at the New Orleans naval air station.

Several young C & S employees who had not previously served as pilots took flight training with the A A F and served with distinction. Former draftsman William R. Cubbins of Memphis, for example, piloted Boeing B-17s over Europe; he was twice shot down, escaping the first time and being imprisoned in Romania the second. He was released in 1944 when Romania joined the Allies. He came home with a Purple Heart and a Distinguished Flying Cross, as well as memories of flak peppering the sky, enemy fighters maneuvering like sharks, and damaged planes about to explode. Another company employee, W. J. McCoy, was released early because of wounds and reclaimed his job as station agent in Jackson. He had been a sailor on a landing craft that took marines into Guadalcanal and brought their wounded out. A victim of the same campaign, former Marine Corps tailgunner Edgar Franciscus, was wounded on Guadalcanal in an air raid; he joined the St. Louis reservations staff in 1943. Former C & S flight officer T. J. (Ted) Johnson flew a Navy R-5D transport plane into Saipan in July 1944 and wrote to Braun a vivid description of the terribly wounded young ground troops whom he ferried out. As he watched eighteen- and nineteen-year-olds being loaded aboard, "it wouldn't have taken much to draw tears." [10]

Even though C & S lost no top executives to the armed services, many of the old managerial group departed for other occupations during the war. Rogers Humphreys had already left to take up residence in the Virgin Islands before the conflict broke out. Late in 1942 Culbert went to American Airlines, and in 1943 Walker left to devote more time to his business affairs in Missouri. Such departures must have occasioned nostalgic moments within the organization. Humphreys, whose loyalty had led him, at a crucial moment, to invest in the firm some precious funds earmarked for his son's education, was gone. Walker, the financial savior, was gone. And Culbert, who had helped to nurture a fledgling operation into a respectable regional carrier, was gone. At the upper managerial level the only old timer left, beside the founder himself, was Bruce Braun; as always, Putnam continued to lean heavily on his wisdom and expertise.[11]

Replacements were chosen to implement the company's plans for the postwar period, for, as one newcomer later expressed it, "it appeared that a favorable solution to the war could be foreseen." He was Richard S. Maurer, a Yale-trained lawyer from Ohio. H. R. Bolander, Jr., who was elevated to general counsel to replace Culbert—and was, like his predecessor, a lawyer from San Francisco—had brought Maurer into the C&S organization from the CAB, where he had been serving on the general counsel's staff. Once appointed as Bolander's assistant, Maurer was well situated to make a timely contribution, for the CAB was encouraged by favorable war prospects to open hearings on new routes and the young lawyer's CAB experience certainly furthered the company's various applications for extension. "So many and so great were the possibilities," Putnam later reminisced in his memoirs, "both in the national and international field."

To prepare for new opportunities, the directors increased the firm's authorized capital stock to a half-million shares and then held a stock sale, the main purpose of which was to provide funds for additional aircraft when they became available and to pay off the old bank loan that had funded the earlier acquisition of the DC-3s. Seven firms were chosen as underwriters, including the old standby, I. M. Simon, and a newcomer that had already become deeply involved in Delta and would one day play a key role in the merger of that company and C&S—Courts and Company of Atlanta. The voting-trust mechanism continued to function; the main cash-raising aspect of the sale was to be the issue of 60,000 voting-trust certificates for common stock at $12.50 a unit, to fetch the company $660,000. In addition, approximately 50,000 shares of common stock were to be issued at $8.00 each, pursuant to certain options. To the holders of these options and all other shares of common stock, the trustee offered voting-trust certificates for the deposit of their shares with him. However this issue might turn out, voting control would remain in the hands of Putnam. Eventually the stock sale of 1943 raised $1,060,000.[12]

Another portal opened to C&S when the CAB granted the company a route between Memphis and Detroit via a string of cities across Kentucky, Indiana, and Ohio. Inauguration of the service was delayed until May 1945, when the end of the war in Europe and the availability of surplus DC-3s led the CAB to switch on the green light. In July 1944 the government returned the first of the expendable Douglas planes, and the C&S fleet began to increase steadily; it had twelve such aircraft by December 1945. In mid-1944 the government declared the firm's military contractual obligations at an end. By that time Reed Knight had been advanced to chief pilot and then to superintendent of flying, yielding his former post to Hap Anderson; along with Anderson's brother Doc, an engineering-maintenance specialist, these men could at last bend their efforts to airline business and prepare for the postwar period. Particular recognition of the company's maintenance expertise came in 1944, when *Aviation Magazine* granted C&S its coveted Maintenance Award for record utilization of aircraft during October and November of that year—two hours and forty-five minutes a day above the national average. The award also recognized a long list of pioneering C&S engineering developments, including a pressurized ignition harness perfected by Doc Anderson.[13]

With its north–south orientation, C&S had carried less priority military traffic than had lines such as Delta, whose main route coincided with the predominantly east–west flow of military movements. Nevertheless, C&S enjoyed profits in the war years from fiscal 1942 onward, although it had problems with rising costs and the Post Office Department's reduction of its mail rate from approximately thirty cents to thirteen cents per air mile cost it the subsidy. As, one by one, the surplus airliners were absorbed into the fleet, operating revenues increased, and postwar prospects were viewed through rose-colored glasses.

Buoyed by visions of expansion, Putnam launched a two-pronged campaign of his own to prepare for the postwar era. On one front he moved defensively. In speeches and pamphlets he repeatedly expressed his old, passionate belief that in a free-enterprise system the door to opportunity must remain open; the history of the airline industry, he insisted, illustrated that some doors, at least, were indeed still open. On the other hand, he noted in a speech delivered in 1944 at Houston that "today we have in the air transport industry four air lines doing 80 per cent of the nation's business and the twelve remaining lines doing the other 20 per cent" and predicted that "unless the tendency to concentration of power in the hands of a few great air lines is curbed, we will see the remaining carriers slowly starved and finally strangled." Such a result would mean the death of "the diversified opportunity" represented by the small carriers. He noted another threat to free enterprise in aviation, in the form of large railroad corporations seeking to run the airlines. Such a development, he argued, would lead to dependence upon "the old railroad mentality with its overwhelming preoccupations and investments upon the aging earth."[14]

On another front, Putnam took the offensive. Actually he made a counterattack, for United States Senator Pat McCarran of Nevada had proposed that in the postwar era all international routes become the monopoly of one combine, to be known officially as the American Flag Line, with all existing American carriers to have some share in its profits and management. One enterprise already controlled all existing American international routes—the line that C. E. Woolman had helped to establish in South America, which had soon gained a virtual if unofficial monopoly of American aviation interests on that continent—Pan American Airways and its half-owned subsidiary, Pan American-Grace (Panagra). Although other business interests periodically had attempted to challenge Pan Am's dominance, that company, with powerful support from the federal government, had managed to maintain its privileged position. Domestic lines had become preoccupied with continental problems; they knew that establishing overseas routes was an expensive proposition, requiring special equipment and diplomatic contacts that Pan Am already possessed. Thus Pan Am, under the energetic leadership of Juan Trippe, not only consolidated its dominance in Latin America but also pioneered in developing routes across the Atlantic and Pacific oceans.

Putnam was no more afraid to take on both a United States senator and one of the Olympian deities of the industry than Woolman was fearful of Captain Eddie Rickenbacker of Eastern. But, unlike Eastern—a company that Putnam likened to a shark that loved to "swim in the warm, inviting waters of competition"—which used every possible tactic of corporate warfare to maximize its advantages, Pan Am relished its monopoly position and did everything possible to safeguard its international preserve. Fearing that Trippe would dominate any consortium established under the McCarran scheme, whatever safeguards were involved, Putnam set his face resolutely against the plan.[15]

When the CAB unbarred the door to route applications in 1943, C&S joined practically every other American carrier in rushing to apply for both domestic and international routes. One of the prime

Carleton Putnam's Bellanca "Pacemaker" CN-300 with which C&S inaugurated service in 1933 as Pacific Seaboard Air Lines.

A C&S threesome in 1951. *Left to right:* George E. Shedd, manager interline and agency sales; J. J. Shad, general sales manager; Joe W. Meyer, general traffic manager.

C&S Lockheed Electra flying over St. Louis.

In 1940, C&S, striving to improve and expand service along the fast-growing Mississippi Valley route, changed equipment to the Douglas DC-3.

C&S headquarters at Memphis in 1942. In the background are USAAF B-25C "Mitchell" bombers modified by C&S.

Gathering of C&S personnel in the 1940s. *Seated, left to right:* Bruce Braun, vice-president–operations; Erma Murray, treasurer; Amos Culbert, vice-president–secretary-treasurer; Mr. and Mrs. Carleton Putnam, president; D. D. Walker, vice-president–traffic.

In the C&S hangar, with DC-3, in the 1940s. *Standing, left to right:* Charlie Broyard, John Kelly, Gene Neiner, Don Hettermann. *Kneeling:* Cecil Pierce, Don McLean, and Ray Stout.

C&S festivities at the St. Louis airport prior to the inauguration of the airline's first Caribbean service in 1946.

C&S pilots Stewart Hopkins *(standing)* and Hap Anderson share a moment of relaxation.

factors in this sudden industry-wide attempt to crack Pan Am's hammerlock on international routes was the fact that many of the exclusively domestic lines had enjoyed the opportunity to fly beyond the continental boundaries of the United States during wartime. C&S, for example, had sent cargo planes with troops and supplies to Dutch Harbor, Alaska, during the Aleutian campaign. Aside from its application to provide extensive new service in the Caribbean area, Putnam's firm sought permission to fly from Chicago to Singapore and Batavia via Alaska, on what would be "the shortest route between the East Indies and the West Indies." In pursuing his own challenge to McCarran's ideas, Putnam wrote to the senator that "I earnestly trust you will not permit the self-serving arguments of Juan Trippe, whose line is already gargantuan and surfeited with routes, to lead you inadvertently to perpetuate what must in all realism be called the Trippe Monopoly." Under the McCarran bill, he claimed, C&S would be only a "still, small voice on the board of a giant combine" ruled in a heavy-handed fashion by Trippe and the presidents of the "Big Four."

In the end, after intense debate, the challengers won, and the Pan American monopoly was cracked. No doubt Putnam's eloquence was a key weapon, for, though C&S did not receive the Polar Great Circle Air Route, it did obtain a major Caribbean route, which, after considerable diplomatic preparation, enabled it to commence service in the postwar era to such places as Havana, Port-au-Prince, Ciudad Trujillo, San Juan, Jamaica, and Caracas.[16] Thus fortified with an exciting new opportunity for additional profits and enhanced stature as an international carrier, Putnam's firm turned to problems connected with consolidating its postwar position.

As the war clouds began to evaporate and his plans for acquisition of new aircraft and route expansion came closer to reality, Putnam faced the need to revamp his organization in the areas left vacant by the departure of Walker and Culbert. As Richard Maurer later expressed it, "a talent hunt was begun." It netted former insurance and dairy executive Albert J. Earling, who soon became traffic boss; Colonel N. Henry Josephs, a New York lawyer with considerable experience in military flying, who became vice-president of finance and administration; and Harvey L. Williams, an executive with background in management engineering and sales, whose aviation experience went back to early airline days and who became executive vice-president. As might be anticipated, the arrival of new leadership had repercussions throughout the organization. Early in 1946

Bolander resigned as vice-president of administration to join Delta—
"perhaps as a result of conflicts that arose over these new work
assignments," as Maurer later put it.[17]

Maurer, who had become corporate secretary, replaced Bolander
as general counsel, and Braun remained as operations *jefe*. Once the
administrative shuffle had been completed, in 1946 C&S began an
ambitious program to quadruple available seats and to develop a
separate air-cargo operation. All this activity meant new facilities or
expansion of existing hangars, shops, and ticket offices, as well as
large additions to staff. The workhorse DC-3 was no longer sufficient; for service between major cities it was to be supplemented by
Douglas C-54 Skymasters, four of which C&S purchased for conversion to the civilian DC-4 model, each with a fifty-six passenger
capacity. Unlike Delta, which turned to Douglas to perform its
DC-4 modification program, C&S employed the Glenn L. Martin
Corporation of Baltimore to handle the conversions, which included
replacing the wartime Pratt and Whitney 1350 hp engines with
Wright Cyclone 9HD 1425 hp engines, in order to boost cruising
speeds to 300 mph. The DC-4s were also to be equipped with the
new Pioneer PB-10 autopilot, designed to reduce pilot fatigue and to
provide passengers with a smoother ride; each also carried the recently developed Hamilton-Standard automatic synchronizer for
propellers, crafted to achieve similar results. These changes represented a far cry from the days when Hap Anderson, Bill Fry, Uncle
Ben Catlin, and Stewart Hopkins had flown Bellancas. At the same
time, Martin agreed to sell C&S its new model 2-0-2, which was
intended as the ultimate replacement for the DC-3. The company
contracted to buy ten of these twin-engine planes, and took an option on seven more.[18]

As a sign both to its personnel and to the general public that a new
day was dawning for the company, C&S changed the uniforms of
pilots and stewardesses from the old blue-gray to navy blue and sent
the stewardesses to restyling clinics, or "charm schools," conducted
by expert Betty Coy. Makeup, posture, hairstyling, and deportment
were stressed, and attention was even given to ways in which a
stewardess could stoop to adjust the heat control of an aircraft while
keeping her "extremities out of the passengers' faces."[19] The company's aircraft received a face lift at the same time: a new color
scheme in lemon yellow, deep green, and cabin gray. A new trademark was also chosen: a rocket incorporating "C&S" and the slogan
"The Route of the Dixieliners." A new passenger-service manager

took charge of all ticketing and reservation functions in the major cities along the C&S route structure: Chicago, St. Louis, Detroit, Indianapolis, Memphis, New Orleans, and Houston. Many other elements were changed, from the timetable that a potential passenger could study and the comment form that he or she was to fill out at the end of a journey to the folded napkin and the silverware brought by newly retrained stewardesses with the meals served in flight.

While these moves were in progress, good news arrived from Washington, where in May 1946 Harry S. Truman had approved a number of recent CAB awards, including the Caribbean route giving C&S access to Havana and Camagüey, Cuba; Port-au-Prince, Haiti; Ciudad Trujillo, Dominican Republic; and San Juan, Puerto Rico. From Havana a second route led to Kingston, Jamaica; Dutch-quaint Aruba and Curacao; and Caracas, Venezuela. With a stroke of President Truman's pen, as it were, C&S acquired magnificent sunsets and the variegated blues, purples, and greens of the Gulf-Caribbean area to entice the tourist, where once it had been able to offer only the silted brown of the Mississippi river. Although various protocols remained to be negotiated before the new routes actually could be opened, the C&S system had potentially increased its mileage from 2,212 to 6,180.[20]

To help finance the expansion, the firm held another stock sale in the summer of 1946, offering voting-trust certificates for 170,000 shares of common stock. The proceeds were to be applied to the purchase of the Martin 2-0-2s; the expenses to be incurred in establishing the Caribbean route; new office facilities and a new hangar in Chicago, where management was planning to move the executive headquarters; air conditioning of facilities at various other airports; and an addition to the working capital. Ultimately the sale produced $3,060,000.[21]

Despite this intense flurry of activity, however, the anticipated millennium failed to arrive. In fact, C&S experienced more financial troubles, with accompanying organizational tremors, in the immediate postwar era than at any other time since the early struggles on the West Coast and in Memphis immediately after the company's move eastward. To some degree, the same troubles that beset C&S afflicted most airlines, large and small, in the postwar world. Labor problems and inflation were ever-threatening realities. The change to four-engine aircraft was extremely expensive, both in the initial purchase outlays and in subsequent maintenance costs. Most Americans still traveled by railroads, buses, and cars, whether on long journeys or short trips. The policies of the CAB fluctuated from time to time and were not always beneficial. The greatest days of the airline industry were still in the future.

But the pattern of developments at C&S had its own unique aspects. Although the new men—Williams, Josephs, and Earling—could not be accused of lacking either enthusiasm or vigor, they could be criticized for overambition, given prevailing conditions in the industry, as Richard Maurer later suggested. Thomas Miller, who came to C&S at about the same time as Maurer and initially was assigned to help prepare route applications, looked back at the immediate postwar years nearly thirty years later and observed that events of the period had led C&S to the verge of bankruptcy. He did not believe that the Williams–Josephs managerial team was actually irresponsible, however, for the industry's overall traffic estimates were projecting a tenfold increase in passengers. Unlike the traditionally prudent managers who led Delta, the C&S team was simply blinded by rose-colored glasses.

Two examples of this overoptimism occurred in Chicago. Because a plan to move part of the company's general offices to the Windy City was under consideration, a lease was signed with Union Carbide for a building next to its headquarters on North Michigan Avenue. The deal, consummated after prolonged negotiations, involved a commitment by C&S to perform extensive interior remodeling and to build a new façade for the structure, which was old and badly in need of renovation. If done on the scale originally contracted for, the repair work could have cost at least $1.5 million. Another example involved a contract for the erection of a large new hangar at Midway Airport; it was to cost $750,000.[22] Of course, Putnam and the C&S board of directors shared responsibility for these costly ventures, for the new managers were not empowered to act independently.

Two other expansionist policies helped to bring about a serious financial crisis in 1946; they involved the purchase of more aircraft than were actually needed—an eventual total of six DC-4s, coupled with plans for acquiring the Martins—and a sizable increase of personnel, with consequent upswings in salaries, wages, and other related operating expenses. In 1946 C&S had projected that it would fly 2.6 percent of the industry's total domestic passenger miles, but its traffic for that year fell substantially below this sanguine estimate. Rising costs, such as those associated with special operating and maintenance problems with the DC-4s, were not offset by proportional increases in revenues.

In Maurer's apt phrase, "it soon became evident that radical surgery was required." In the late summer of 1946 Williams and Josephs submitted their resignations and moved on. The choice of these men had proved disappointing, but the selection of their successors, coupled with a subsequent managerial realignment, was by contrast extremely successful and saved the company from impending doom. Putnam chose Sidney A. Stewart to be the new executive vice-president; formerly an officer in the Hamilton Standard Propeller Division of United Aircraft Corporation, he was named to his new post in September 1946. As Maurer later put it, he had "a history of strong and aggressive management in the aviation industry" and "recognized the severity of the problems with which he must deal at Chicago and Southern." He brought with him as treasurer Junius Cooper, whom Maurer characterized as "a lanky North Carolinian with a Scottish background and a brilliant, hardnosed approach to the airline's financial problems." Several months later Stewart obtained the services of yet another United Aircraft alumnus, W. T. (Tom) Beebe, as director of personnel—a tough job, for the company payroll had to be slashed.[23]

The new team launched into retrenchment and revamping with as much vigor as the old one had displayed in the expansion, or overexpansion, phase. But by then the skies were dark and growing darker. To C&S, as to various other smaller airlines in that period, it became obvious that the government had to come to the rescue with financial assistance, and the firm began to push hard for a change in its "service," or nonsubsidy, rate, established by the CAB in 1943. Writing an epilogue to the crisis some time afterward, Putnam noted that in 1947 "air transport . . . found itself plagued at every turn by a confused and hostile press, a suspicious Congress, and a divided regulatory Board, while its losses mounted and its securities crashed. Never was the cause more obvious, nor more generally misapprehended. Deprived of all normal, peacetime government aid during the war years because war traffic made it unnecessary, the industry was left to flounder without this essential support when peace returned."[24]

Such "essential support" was not easy to regain. While negotiations with the CAB went forward, the Stewart team performed painful surgery, trimming employees across the board, canceling the order for the Martins, curtailing flights, and renegotiating contracts. Under Maurer's direction, Miller became director of properties and quickly went to work, cutting back certain of the arrangements for facilities that had been entered into in earlier, more optimistic days. For example, he persuaded Union Carbide that the costly restyling of the old leased building must be cut back greatly if the solvency of C & S was not to be threatened. As a result, the estimated $1.5 to 2 million cost was reduced to a much more manageable $125,000. Construction of the new Chicago hangar was still in the beginning stages, and Miller persuaded the contractor to defer completion until C & S could pay for it. He then sold Delta on the idea of sharing the facility, with each company bearing half the cost. Other major commitments were also renegotiated.[25]

It was a long way back to some sort of financial normality. The consequences of the company's massive retrenchment were severe. The Memphis *Commercial Appeal* reported to its readers on November 28, 1946, that C & S planned within a matter of weeks to lay off 275 employees. This figure actually did not reflect the seriousness of the situation, for Putnam informed the stockholders that, by March 1947, the true figure would reach 600, out of a total payroll of 2,174. The necessity for such harsh action was obvious, for, as Putnam reported in a less than cheerful Christmas message, C & S had lost more money in the first eleven months of 1946 than it had earned in its whole previous history. The remedy was no less hard upon workers whose livelihoods suddenly ceased. As retrenchment proceeded, negotiations with the government over the company's domestic and international mail rates became the key to staving off complete obliteration. These negotiations turned out to be long and involved. Finally, on July 28, 1948, after a thorough investigation of the C & S financial situation, the CAB issued its decision on the domestic rate: C & S would receive $1,053,528 in retroactive mail pay for 1946 and 1947. Although this sum was not as much as the company had hoped for, it was still a godsend.

The CAB noted the defects in planning and execution that had turned out so badly in the postwar era, but it also commented favorably on the measures that Stewart's team had taken to correct the situation, for example, the fact that a cutback in the number of DC-4s from six to four and the accompanying cancellation of the Martin 2-0-2 purchase had brought the company's use of available flight equipment in 1946 and 1947 into line with the performance of other comparable carriers. The report also mentioned the impact of such adverse circumstances as a series of fatal crashes in the spring of 1947; though none had involved C&S aircraft, the accidents did have bad effects on the public's desire to fly during a normally peak traffic time and thus hurt Putnam's firm, along with the rest of the industry.

For the future, the CAB established a sliding mail rate for C&S which would yield a maximum level of pay at load factors of 56 percent and below, adjusted downward as such factors decreased. As Maurer subsequently recalled, this arrangement gave the company an "excellent motivation" for aggressive efforts to attract more passengers and was willingly accepted by the C&S management, but the resulting adjustment actually permitted a greater return on investment than the CAB was willing to subsidize, and the extra earnings realized on the firm's domestic operations were ultimately charged against the subsidy needs of its international services. As a result, the relief experienced from the CAB action, though welcome, was nevertheless limited. In spite of the return to subsidy, Putnam pointed out in the company's annual report for 1948 that, based on the rationale for mail pay laid down by federal legislation in 1938 and the overall level of services performed, there actually had been a decline of 78 percent in government aid since 1937, while the cost-of-living index had risen 73 percent.[26]

Still, the company could count its blessings. "By 1948," Maurer later noted, "blue sky began to reappear through the haze." In that year red ink began once more to give way to black in the company's profit-and-loss statements. The annual reports for the ensuing three years recorded further progress and the end of retrenchment. In 1949 the directors authorized the first dividend on common stock since 1945. Dividends were also paid in 1950 and 1951, increasing each time.[27]

Although C&S stockholders had reason to be happier, fresh problems demanded solution. The decision to forgo the Martin 2-0-2s and to cut down on the order for DC-4s, salutary as it was, could not change the fact that the DC-4s were rapidly becoming obsolete and would have to be replaced as soon as possible. The first aircraft with pressurized cabins were available, and a decision between Douglas DC-6s and Lockheed L-649 Constellations had to be made. Unlike Delta, C&S chose the Connies. Bill Spangler, who flew them for C&S, later praised this choice and pointed out that the triple-tailed

Lockheed, though not as big a money maker as the DC-6, was nevertheless a rugged aircraft with a good "feel." Don Hettermann, who began with C&S as a mechanic in 1946 and rose to become vice-president of technical operations with Delta, also claimed that the L-649 had better lift capacity than the DC-6, making it a better choice for the relatively short runways of the Caribbean; furthermore, he pointed out, it had an innovative detachable pod known as the "Speed Pack," permitting extra cargo. In any event, five Connies were ordered, and delivery was completed in 1951, the same year in which ten new Convair 340s, each with a forty-four passenger capacity, were ordered as eventual replacements for the DC-3s.[28]

Although C&S suffered no paralyzing labor strife during the period of postwar tribulations and renewal, there were problems nevertheless. As previously noted, the first air union—a chapter of the ALPA—was begun in 1935 but not officially recognized by management until 1940. During and immediately after World War II, partly because of unsettled conditions and increased pressure from organized labor—and possibly also because Putnam, however active, did not play as great a day-to-day role in his firm as the patriarchal Woolman did in the Delta organization—practically every segment of the C&S staff formed a chapter of the relevant union and succeeded in negotiating an agreement with the management.

Bill Fry, who later retired as senior Delta captain, many years after coming over in the merger with C&S, recalled that the relations between pilots and management under Putnam's leadership were "warm and cordial." The operations department, he declared, "made every effort to meet the pilots' requests." Fry, however, had been away on wartime military duty when conflict developed over an issue involving the pay differential between night and day flying— a contest decided in favor of the pilots by a neutral arbitrator. After the war difficulties occasionally arose in connection with such matters as the temporary discharge of a captain in 1946 for alleged bad handling of a DC-4 on takeoff and failure to file a proper report. After negotiations between company and union representatives a probation period was established for the pilot. Another conflict was triggered in 1949 when a mechanic was fired for carelessness in preparing an aircraft for flight. This kind of dismissal was painful for all concerned, especially since the mechanic was a wounded veteran of World War II, but, as a neutral arbitrator observed in upholding the company's action, the mechanic had been warned about carelessness several times before, and the safety of the traveling public had to be paramount. The stewardesses' union was not a docile group and seems to have grown more combative as good times returned in the late 1940s and early 1950s. Sometimes, for example, conflict over assignments threatening vested interests arose, as when the stewardesses based in New Orleans heard that their counterparts based in Memphis might be placed temporarily in Caribbean service. Their protest led to eventual compromise. Other grievances involved health problems and interpretations of sick leave and the definition of excessive flying in a twenty-four-hour period. Veteran C&S employee Ed Bolton later recalled other instances of hard negotiations between various union representatives on one side of the table and management officials, including Maurer and Beebe, on the other, but he emphasized that there was none of the bitterness that characterized labor relations in such firms as American.[29]

Whatever difficulties C&S experienced in the last years before 1950, they were minor compared to the crisis that had been met and overcome several years before. By 1951 the management team had been thoroughly overhauled and was obviously the best such group since the early war years. Braun had deferred retirement in order to help out during the tribulations of the immediate postwar era, but he finally stepped down in 1947, leaving Putnam alone to represent the company's original cadre of senior executives. The next year the founding father himself went into semiretirement so that he could move to Washington, D.C., and begin research on a book dealing with the early life of Theodore Roosevelt. He assumed the newly created position of chairman of the board, and Stewart, as a reward for his brilliant work in leading the company from darkness back into light, became president. Maurer was elevated to the rank of vice-president in 1950 and was soon joined at that level by Beebe and Miller.

Gradually, the old order passed away. In 1951 Putnam took a significant step away from previous policies by terminating the voting-trust agreement. In explaining this decision, he stated simply that "our financial condition is sound; our earnings and dividends have reached a gratifying level. The present management is able and confident of the company's future. The usefulness of the voting trust in securing stability and continuity of management and overall policy seems to me to have ceased."[30] Like the rest of the company's senior officers, he could take satisfaction in the fact that his once-beleaguered enterprise had "made it" after a hard pull. Furthermore, beginning in 1951, events were moving toward the absorption of Chicago and Southern into a stronger, more efficient unit, fully capable of still further growth and greater stability in the approaching jet age. The company had attained maturity, and corporate marriage with Delta lay just around the corner.

CHAPTER 12

Courtship, Engagement,
and Marriage

As EARLY AS 1935, when Lockheed Electras were considered
"big ships," C. E. Woolman and Carleton Putnam had carried on "occasional conversations on the subject of the com-
patibility of our views and policies and the smoothness with which
our managements could be integrated if circumstances should
someday seem propitious," as Putnam later put it in testimony before the CAB. In that day of localized operations, however, it had
seemed that relatively small airlines *could* enjoy "independent
growth to a status of self-sufficiency," and the talks never proceeded
very far. But, with the jet age lurking in the not-too-distant future
and long hops from one big city to another becoming increasingly
vital for the profitable use of large, four-engine aircraft, the "propitious circumstances" had finally arrived.[1]

The long-adjourned merger talks between Woolman and Putnam
were revived in the late spring of 1951, when, together with C&S
President Sidney Stewart, the two men met in Washington, D.C.;
they discussed the state of the industry in general and pondered how
their respective personnel could be combined should their companies be united. They discussed the same subjects once more in July,
savoring the heady prospects of a consolidation that might include
Delta, C&S, Northeast, and Capital's southern routes. Shortly after
that the chief financial officers of the two firms, L. B. Judd and Todd
Cole of Delta and Junius Cooper of C&S, tackled the thorny task of
determining comparative book values, a task made all the more
difficult because of the difference between Delta's DC-6s and the
Lockheed Constellations that were the pride of the C&S fleet. In all,
three meetings on this key issue took place, two in Atlanta and one
at the Memphis headquarters of C&S. Meanwhile, Delta operations
chief Dolson conducted a study of the C&S route structure and
flight schedules, in order to determine what economies might be
enjoyed in the event of a merger.[2]

By November 1 enough progress had been made so that an important conclave could be held in Atlanta; participants included Woolman, Putnam, Judd, Cole, Cooper, and two others whose presence indicated the start of a new stage in the negotiations. These were John R. Longmire, veteran C&S director and policy adviser from the St. Louis brokerage firm of Simon and Company, and Delta's longtime financial expert, Richard S. Courts. The discussions dealt in part with the relative values of Delta and C&S stock and the ratio at which an exchange might take place, as well as the tax liabilities involved in a merger. In its annual report for fiscal 1951, Delta had listed total assets, making due allowance for depreciation of operating property and equipment, of approximately $14.5 million; current liabilities and outstanding long-term indebtedness amounted to roughly $5.5 million. During the previous twelve months the company had earned about $1.6 million on gross revenues of $22,221,000. C&S operated on a calendar year; its forthcoming annual report for 1951 would show assets of approximately $11.5 million and liabilities slightly in excess of $4.5 million; its earnings would amount to about $1.1 million on gross revenues of $16.2 million. The ratio of Delta's profits to those of C&S over the preceding fifty months was 2.65 to 1, whereas Delta's book value and market value were pegged at ratios of 1.80 to 1 and 2.12 to 1 respectively over those of C&S.

Based upon these figures, one proposed course of action was a two-for-one exchange of stock, with assigned values per share of $25 and $12.50 for Delta and C&S respectively, which would have yielded a final purchase price of $6,375,000. Under this plan, the stockholders of C&S would receive either 255,000 shares of Delta stock or a combination of Delta stock and other securities. Another proposed arrangement, slightly more favorable to C&S, called for a settlement involving 102,000 shares of Delta stock and $4,075,000 in other securities bearing 6 percent interest.[3]

These proposals, however, were not satisfactory to C&S. As the November meeting revealed, a merger based on a simple exchange of stock or other securities at a specific ratio posed problems for Putnam's company, which was unique among domestic airlines in that the market value of its stock was below the firm's book value. The reasons were complex; they were traceable partly to the fact that a large block of C&S shares had long been held in a voting trust, which resulted in confusion in the minds of potential buyers about whether they were purchasing actual stock or merely voting-trust certificates. In addition, a decision by C&S management to list on the New York Stock Exchange and to forgo over-the-counter sales had resulted in a loss of support among southern and midwestern brokers, who specialized in unlisted securities. Even after the voting trust had been terminated, the listing of C&S common stock on the New York exchange had failed to yield anticipated results, because the company was "too little known to attract a following"; a public-relations campaign was just starting to pay off as the merger negotiations with Delta moved into high gear. Although the postwar history of C&S had admittedly been rocky, the company's officers did not believe that the current standing of its stock accurately reflected its actual performance or future prospects. On the other hand, a merger based strictly on book values was likely to be unsatisfactory to Delta's stockholders, who would logically want the relative market figures to be taken into account. The ultimate solution to the problem, involving the exchange of C&S stock for convertible debentures issued by Delta, was advocated by Courts and discussed at the November meeting, but no agreement was reached on the specifics, and further talks had to take place before the matter could be settled.[4]

Negotiations proceeded on into the winter. C&S, hopeful that its stock might rise in the near future, kept pressing for further adjustments in book values, which led to fresh discussions among Woolman, Stewart, Cole, and Cooper at Memphis in January 1952. Nor was this thorny issue the only matter impeding progress. Some C&S executives were loath to leave Memphis for Atlanta and were also nervous about how much weight they would carry in an enlarged company that might also include Northeast and part of the Capital system. Meanwhile, C&S was also pondering the possibility of merging with other airlines, including American, National, TWA, and Delta's arch rival, Eastern. Longmire reminded Woolman at one point that other suitors were in the wings and *"if we are going to ignore these proposals we simply must be sure that any deal we make with Delta is beyond challenging on the part of our stockholders."*[5]

The pressure on C&S to work out a plan of consolidation with one or another airline was intensifying at that time because the CAB, after long prodding from Congress, had just adopted a new basis for airmail payments, separating subsidies from regular mail pay. C&S, along with Braniff, Capital, Delta, National, Northwest, and Western, was placed in a category for which fifty-three cents per ton-mile was to be the normal domestic compensatory rate; anything above that figure was to be classed as subsidy. The CAB permitted C&S a sliding-scale rate, which yielded the line $1.27 a ton-mile in the first six months of 1952, but that arrangement was only temporary. In addition, C&S faced renegotiation of its international mail rates, which might further impair its prospects for dependable profits, even in the boom times that the industry was enjoying in the early 1950s. Thanks to the heroic measures taken by Stewart and Cooper, C&S had shown that it could weather the most trying circumstances; but where one regional line did well to survive, might not two joined together really flourish? [6]

All in all, the situation favored Delta as a marriage partner. Other considerations being approximately equal, the cordial relations that had long existed between Putnam and Woolman, as well as the general similarity of their business philosophies, augured far better for a happy union than a hookup with Baker and National, the other medium-sized airline in the picture. And senior C&S officials were much more likely to continue to wield strong influence in the Delta organization, even if Northeast were included, than in a consolidation with a giant of the airways such as American, TWA, or Eastern. Indeed, as Longmire indicated in a letter to Woolman, Putnam's policy was "to blanket out the consideration of any deals other than Delta," causing anxiety among major C&S stockholders in the St. Louis area, who believed that the company could strengthen its hand by dickering with at least one other carrier. [7]

The relationship between C&S and Delta developed further during the spring of 1952, when Stewart invited Woolman to accompany him on a trip to the Caribbean, where C&S had worked diligently to promote tourism to such swanky attractions as Cuba's palm-fronded Veradero Beach and the recently opened Tower Isle Hotel on Jamaica's north shore. Taking along Wayne Parrish, editor and publisher of the influential industry periodical *American Aviation* (President Ralph Damon of TWA had also been invited but could not go because of other commitments), they surveyed the prospects for increasing travel to the area and proceeded to Venezuela to interview leaders of that nation's burgeoning oil and mining enterprises. An unforgettable highlight of the tour was an aerial expedition aboard a DC-3 provided by the president of Linea Aeropostal Venezolana (LAV) to inspect the massive iron deposits near Ciudad Bolívar and to enjoy an aerial view of one of the world's most spectacular natural wonders: Angel Falls, a narrow ribbon of cascading water with a drop fifteen times that of Niagara, which plunged from a mesa six thousand feet high into a dense jungle area between the Orinoco and Amazon rivers in the Guiana highlands.[8]

The trip gave Woolman and Stewart ample opportunity to take each other's measure and to consolidate the progress that had already been made toward uniting their respective companies. Years afterward, Parrish remembered that Woolman was the aggressor on this trip, attempting to persuade a still reluctant Stewart of the merits of a merger. One of the reasons that Parrish had been asked along, he recalled, was to help talk the C&S president into the arrangement. The trip apparently had the effect Woolman desired.[9]

There were still, however, various hurdles to overcome. Courts was engaged in a protracted effort, involving inconclusive contracts with the United States Treasury Department, to convince Longmire that the debenture or combined debenture-and-stock deal that Delta was willing to offer would yield tax savings to C&S. Although Courts continued to insist on the soundness of his position, the C&S management remained unconvinced, and in mid-April Putnam wrote an urgent letter to Woolman warning that the company was under "a lot of pressure" from another possible merger partner, the identity of which he did not mention; it was in fact Eastern. Longmire favored considering this offer. "I think Delta should review its interest in C&S very seriously," Putnam warned. "All the ratios which we have discussed up to date must now be considered as obsolete and a fresh start made."[10]

This letter had the effect that Putnam wanted, and matters began to move swiftly. Delta clearly had to make an offer that would satisfy both Putnam and Longmire; it was made at a meeting at the Stevens Hotel in Chicago on April 23–24, 1952, which was attended by Putnam, Woolman, Courts, Cole, Pogue, Longmire, and L. R. Billett, a partner in the investment firm of McCormick and Company and a C&S director. Courts took an afternoon plane back to Atlanta on the first day of the conclave and thereafter kept tabs on the proceedings by telephone. Pogue, who remained, played a vital diplomatic role in keeping the discussion moving toward a settlement acceptable to both sides. The amount finally decided upon was $10 million, subject to minor adjustments depending upon relative book values at the time of closing. The negotiations were prodded a bit on the second day, when a rash of C&S stock sales, particularly in the St. Louis area, caused anxious stockbrokers to telephone Putnam, who revealed that merger talks were in progress. Putnam indicated later, however, that he had already decided upon $10 million as a fair price, one that he would be willing to accept. Eastern's offer was slightly higher, but Rickenbacker's line was interested only in what R. S. Maurer later called a "flat buy-out," which would have eliminated current C&S executives from playing any future role in the development of the firm. Also, Courts continued to argue that the tax advantages of a convertible-debenture deal with Delta, plus other capital gains that would accrue from such a plan, made the latter proposition financially preferable. In any event, the die was cast, and a preliminary merger agreement was ratified by both boards of directors on April 26.[11]

This agreement took the form of a letter from Woolman to Putnam, countersigned by the latter. It provided that the agreed-upon purchase price was to be paid by an exchange of C&S stock for Delta debentures bearing 5½ percent interest and convertible into Delta stock at the rate of $35 in debentures for each share. Stipulations for the redemption of the debentures at stated intervals were inserted. The precise form of the legal contract under which the debentures would be issued was to be spelled out in a subsequent definitive agreement, which both parties promised to expedite. The preliminary agreement further specified that the combined enterprise initially would do business as Delta–C&S Air Lines, although the surviving corporation, in the legal sense, would be Delta Air Lines; that Putnam would be chairman of the board; that Woolman would be president and general manager; and that Stewart would be executive vice-president. In addition, the new company was pledged to retain as many C&S employees "as is consistent with the efficient and economic performance of the expanded operation" and seniority lists were to be established "by collective bargaining or by such other method as the Civil Aeronautics Board may specify or approve."[12]

Throughout the next ten weeks, action proceeded on two main fronts, as the prospective partners, now officially engaged, initiated the procedures necessary to obtain the all-important CAB approval of their union while simultaneously negotiating the details of the definitive merger agreement. On April 28, 1952, Delta and C&S filed a joint application with the CAB for permission to merge; they wisely petitioned that the merger be considered separate from the increasingly unpromising effort to consolidate Delta and Northeast. In view of the fact that the Delta and C&S systems interlocked at no fewer than five points—Chicago, Anderson–Muncie, Shreveport, Jackson, and New Orleans—it would have been foolish to jeopardize the welding of two such obviously compatible systems by linking it to another merger proceeding predicated upon securing the perennially elusive access to New York.

By mid-May the CAB had assented to this reasoning; shortly thereafter it also gave other indications of favoring the new merger pact, ordering that the case be expedited and setting early dates for the filing of supporting exhibits (July 9), rebuttal exhibits (August 1), and the examiner's hearing (August 11). As expected, several parties filed petitions to intervene. In view of the fact that Delta's lawyers had so often challenged the advisability of permitting Capital's southern routes to be retained by the system that would result from that company's projected merger with Northwest, it is not surprising that Capital's attorneys now demanded that the Delta and C&S merger be conditioned upon transferring some of their routes —particularly the one between Birmingham and New Orleans—to another carrier. Quite predictably, National took much the same line. Nor was it at all unexpected that Eastern would insist upon a host of conditions, including its own absorption of every route that had ever been awarded to either Delta or C&S on the grounds that they were smaller than Eastern: Kansas City to Memphis (C&S), Houston to Memphis (C&S), Memphis to Detroit (C&S), Evansville to Chicago (C&S), Atlanta to New Orleans (Delta), New Orleans to Dallas (Delta). Nevertheless, the signs that such petitions would be denied appeared good.[13]

Meanwhile, representatives of Delta and C&S continued to hammer out the details of the definitive merger agreement, which had to be ratified by both companies before the July 9 exhibit deadline imposed by the CAB. The chief matters to be settled were the precise form of the debentures and the nature of the stipulations to protect the interests of C&S stockholders who would hold them. In a letter of May 16, Richard Maurer conveyed the wishes of C&S to Pogue in great detail; Pogue in turn informed Woolman that "a good many of the things he mentions will work out all right I think but there are some points which will require resistance." Pogue did not indicate exactly what demands were to be resisted, but it is clear that Maurer's letter provided the basis for the eventual agreement, which was approved by the boards of directors of both companies on July 8, just one day before the CAB deadline. In addition to specifying the denominations in which the debentures were to be issued, the document of July 8 required Delta to maintain a purchase fund as long as $5 million of debentures remained outstanding, imposed certain debt and dividend restrictions upon Delta until all debentures had been redeemed, established antidilution provisions to safeguard the $35 conversion price should Delta issue additional stock priced below that figure, explicitly subordinated the debentures to other obligations incurred by Delta in the normal pursuit of its business, and assured debenture holders of protection should Delta enter into any merger in which it was not the surviving corporation. The successful ratification of the agreement by both groups of directors brought to a triumphant end the long process of negotiation that Woolman and Putnam had begun many months before, and the brevity of the telegram that Woolman dispatched to E. V. Moore in Washington must have concealed great satisfaction: "Closed deal with C and S. All needs now is government approval." [14]

And so the two marriage candidates, now even more firmly bound together, entered upon the next stage of the merger process. On July 9 they submitted to the CAB three volumes of exhibits, representing mountains of work by the clerical staffs of both companies; this massive array of evidence was required under the terms of the Civil Aeronautics Act of 1938 in order to prove that the consolidation would be in the public interest. Would the proposed merger, the CAB wanted to know, result in a well-integrated route structure with efficient traffic flows and effective utilization of equipment? Would it impair any existing services rendered by either Delta or C&S? What effect would the merger have on their respective revenues? Upon their requirements for mail compensation? What adverse effects, if any, would it have upon other carriers? Would it create a monopoly in restraint of trade? What impact would it have on employees of the two companies? Did the proposed consolidation involve any hidden understandings or covert agreements not set forth in the merger contracts? Were the financial considerations upon which it was based fair to Delta and C&S stockholders? In response to such queries, the two firms had to submit copies of all agreements reached, lists of oral communications relative to the merger that had taken place between their respective officers, copies of written correspondence relevant to the negotiations, transcripts of the meetings of boards of directors and executive committees, lists of stockholders, information on stock options given to company officials, balance sheets covering operations during recent months, and reams of other data on route structures, equipment, schedules, traffic, air mail, express, freight, personnel, and labor relations. [15]

As the CAB digested these voluminous inputs, the two firms moved ahead with such vital matters as laying the groundwork for stockholder approval of the merger and preparing their employees for integration into a single organization. Ever mindful of what had happened when the Capital–Northwest merger had been presented to Northwest stockholders, Woolman and Putnam made sure that everyone who owned shares in Delta and C&S was kept well informed about the details of the consolidation and the benefits that would accrue from it. Aided by Georgeson and Company, a Wall Street firm with long experience in such matters, they also set about rounding up proxy votes.[16] Meanwhile, the in-house journals of both airlines kept their readers abreast of merger developments and showed how "Delta and C&S go together like ham and eggs," as one contributor to the *Delta Digest* put it. Referring to the jet aircraft that would begin to appear on the commercial aviation scene in the near future, another article warned that "Only the big lines will be able to afford them, and companies without them will get the crumbs." It ended by coupling a rhetorical question with a resounding note of affirmation: "Now do we want to be big, or will we be content to stand back while passengers fight to climb aboard our competitors' jets? Whoosh, let's be in front!"[17]

In Washington, spokesmen testifying for Delta and C&S before a CAB examiner at mid-August hearings pointed to various benefits that the merger would produce, as revealed in the joint exhibits submitted by the two companies. Through services would become available from Dallas to such cities as Detroit, Chicago, Havana, and Caracas; from Atlanta to Houston; from Detroit to Atlanta and Miami; from Detroit to Charleston; and so on. With a larger route system, equipment could be used much more economically. Had the merger been in effect during the twelve months preceding March 31, 1952, it was argued, the two companies would have realized an increase of about $7.3 million in gross revenues, yielding an addition of approximately $2.5 million in net operating income and at least $1.2 million more in net profits after taxes because of operational economies and expanded flight schedules. Because the CAB had made it clear that it would be particularly concerned about any adverse effects that the merger might have on employees, counsel for the two companies emphasized the new jobs that the enlarged traffic pattern would create.[18]

Critics and opponents of the merger also had their innings during the eight-day hearings. Predictably, Eastern opposed the consolidation on all counts; it was the only carrier to take such an unyielding stance. Denying that the proposed union would produce any public benefit, Rickenbacker's firm charged instead that it would create "a sprawling network of nonintegrated routes." Even if the merger were approved, Eastern contended, the combined company should not be permitted to serve Anderson–Muncie–New Castle, a key link in the projected new through-plane routes from Detroit, Toledo, and Fort Wayne to Cincinnati, Atlanta, Jacksonville, and Miami. Similarly, Eastern urged that the C & S route from Kingston, Jamaica, to San Juan not be transferred to Delta and sought also to have any new through service from Atlanta and Birmingham to Beaumont–Port Arthur and Houston banned. Predictable opposition to the merger was also voiced by the city of Memphis and the Memphis chamber of commerce, which feared the loss of jobs and revenues when C & S headquarters were moved out of that city.[19]

Other carriers were willing to see the marriage take place but pleaded for restrictions on the merged organization. Braniff, for example, urged the CAB to prohibit any new through service to Chicago or Havana from Dallas–Fort Worth. Capital continued to insist that Delta's route from Atlanta to New Orleans and the C & S artery from Memphis to Houston would not "properly integrate with the merged company." National and Pan American argued that C & S's Caribbean routes should be sacrificed as the price of consolidation with Delta, and TWA asked for a bar on additional through service between Cincinnati and Detroit. Meanwhile, a number of labor organizations, including the Air Line Pilots Association, the Air Carrier Communication Operators Association, the Air Line Stewards and Stewardesses Association, and the United Automobile, Aircraft and Agricultural Implement Workers of America (UAW-CIO) pointed out that C & S was highly unionized whereas Delta, except for its pilots, was not. These unions sought various "employee protective provisions" similar to those that had been stipulated in another recent airline merger, between Braniff and Mid Continent. The C & S stewardesses were apprehensive about what the merger would mean for them, because the Delta stewardesses were not organized. Finally, as we shall see in more detail later, one group of C & S pilots, represented by Stewart W. Hopkins and Thomas S. Bridges, opposed the merger altogether.[20]

While waiting for CAB officials to sift through all this testimony and to make recommendations to board members, Delta management pushed ahead with some financial moves designed to put the company in as strong a position as possible for the consummation of the merger and the subsequent business opportunities that would open up. From the time that the preliminary merger agreement had been signed in April, it had been obvious that a large block of Delta stock, estimated at about 285,000 shares, would have to be reserved to provide for the ultimate conversion of approximately $10 million in debentures. Since Delta was still committed to a merger with Northeast when and if a connecting link to New York City could be secured and since that merger would also require exchange of a substantial number of Delta shares for stock of the New England enterprise, it was deemed wise to increase Delta's authorized capital from its limit of 1 million shares to 1.5 million. Such a plan was ratified by the company's stockholders at the annual meeting in October. Liquidity was also promoted by the sale of 100,000 shares of stock for cash and by disposal of Delta's DC-4s under arrangements previously described. In addition, a massive credit arrangement was negotiated with twenty-five banks, under which $20 million could be borrowed at any time up to August 1, 1954, to finance the purchase of new aircraft. Among other benefits, these steps were well calculated to impress federal officials with the soundness of the company's capital resources as it moved toward completion of its union with C&S.[21]

Good news came in late September, when CAB bureau counsel Leslie G. Donahue, after analyzing all the testimony presented in the previous month, recommended approval of the merger in a thirty-one-page brief stressing the improved service that would be provided for the traveling public; the better use of facilities, equipment, and personnel; and the money to be saved the government through reduction and ultimately elimination of remaining subsidy payments to C&S.[22] The even more crucial report of CAB examiner William F. Cusick took somewhat longer to be filed, but it was well worth waiting for. On November 13 this seventy-four-page document swept aside all objections and reservations offered by intervening carriers and recommended the consolidation of Delta and C&S throughout the entire length and breadth of their existing route systems. The two carriers had already worked out a series of policies designed to protect employees from undue hardship or inconvenience in transfers to new locations because of the merger, to establish reasonable dismissal allowances, and to resolve other potential labor difficulties. These policies, with minor exceptions, were approved by Cusick, who noted that, though an estimated 398 people would be transferred because of the consolidation, only about 20, who were engaged in technical or professional jobs, would face termination because of it. The merger would, on the other hand, create more than 400 new positions. The report did strike one brief note of concern among company officials by its recommendation that the transfer of foreign and domestic routes from C&S to Delta be considered separately in the final disposition of the case, but this suggestion caused no difficulty in the end.[23]

Although both companies knew from past experience that a positive examiner's report did not guarantee affirmative action by the CAB—after all, Delta would long since have been certificated to operate into New York City had that been so—there was every reason for optimism as arrangements to knit both organizations into a single entity proceeded. A major step was the announcement that two veteran C&S officials would assume high executive posts in the combined enterprise once the merger had been consummated: Junius Cooper would become vice-president for finance, and Richard S. Maurer would become vice-president for legal affairs. In addition, Putnam, Stewart, and Longmire would serve on the Delta board of directors. During the next few months, Putnam and Woolman worked out a series of job assignments combining the managerial staffs of the two corporations, following the trend already established by the decisions involving Cooper and Maurer. In general, Delta officials held the top positions in the "line" groups—operations and traffic—while C&S people were assigned the leading roles in the "staff" categories—finance, law, and personnel.[24]

As was to be expected, some difficulties had to be ironed out, and certain concessions had to be made in the interest of harmony. One matter involved a protracted effort by C&S to secure CAB approval for an interchange agreement with TWA to provide through service from Houston to New York by way of Indianapolis and Pittsburgh. Delta feared that such an arrangement would weaken the combined company's chances to win access to New York from Atlanta after the merger had been completed, and Delta officers were never more than lukewarm toward the plan. Nevertheless, they respected the arguments, put forth by C&S officials, that the smaller company was honor bound to live up to its commitment to TWA. The interchange was finally approved by the CAB in mid-December.[25]

Of much more concern was the fact that some C&S employees, particularly one very active group of pilots, opposed the merger and were persisting, even after the publication of the examiner's report, in efforts to block it. Again, for reasons that involved no adverse reflection upon Delta, their opposition was not difficult to understand. Over the years, through many hardships, C&S had developed an enviable esprit de corps and a firm sense of organizational identity. There was bound to be shock and dismay among long-standing employees when it was announced that the company would be absorbed into a larger enterprise. The arduous struggle to escape from the recent financial crises that had plagued the firm, which was now beginning to pay off as black ink once more appeared in the ledger books, only intensified the frustration felt by some who argued that, in one way or another, C&S could prosper as an independent entity despite changing conditions that favored bigness in the airline industry. After all, Putnam had preached the virtues of small enterprise too ably for too many years for his subordinates to be unaffected by the message. The fact that C&S was heavily unionized and that Delta was largely not, naturally created further apprehension. Then, too, it was only human to dislike the prospect of transferring from a familiar locale to a new one, with the attendant disruption of neighborhood, church, school, and other social ties.

The men who flew the planes up and down the Valley Level Route were particularly apt to entertain negative feelings toward the consolidation. As Delta's longtime chief pilot, T. P. Ball, once observed, "Pilots don't like mergers." Probably no other occupational group in the airline industry is more fiercely attached to seniority rankings or more deeply imbued with a spirit of exclusiveness toward "outsiders." The pilots of Northwest had played a key role in scuttling the attempted merger with Capital by communicating their opposition directly to the stockholders, and it is not surprising that some skippers from Putnam's line attempted a similar role in their efforts to block the company's union with Delta. Led by such veteran flyers as Stewart Hopkins, Tommy Bridges, and William Spangler, they secured stockholder lists and wrote letters urging negative votes when the merger was presented for ratification. They took their case to Longmire, who listened sympathetically but counseled acceptance of the merger plan as a fait accompli; the pilots argued that a significant undeveloped traffic potential existed on the company's present routes, particularly in the Caribbean. Hopkins and Bridges, testifying before the CAB, denied that the situation warranted the "loss of morale, insecurity, hardships, seniority disputes and jurisdictional strife" that the merger would, in their judgment, produce. Undeterred by Cusick's eventual endorsement of the merger plan in

his examiner's report, the dissident group went ahead with the preparation of an "economic study" and brochure to be used against the
project in the upcoming stockholder ratification effort.[26]

Reminiscing nearly a quarter of a century later, Hopkins and
Spangler, who eventually served many years as Delta captains,
looked back upon the "pilots' revolt" in which they had participated
and expressed their satisfaction at its failure. From their later perspective, matters seemed to have worked out for the best. Hopkins
recalled a conversation with Woolman shortly after the merger had
been made final that convinced him that Delta's boss was sincerely
concerned about the welfare and professional interests of all the
pilots who served under him. But in late 1952 things were different,
and the situation had the leaders of both airlines worried. "I don't
think that we should treat this opposition lightly," Woolman wrote
to Putnam in mid-November as he reviewed the strategies being
pursued by the obdurate pilot group. "I am at a loss to know what
more we should do with the pilots," Putnam responded, adding that
"we have a core of about fifteen of our men who seem to be absolute-
ly adamant against the merger and with whom we can expect to do
little." Putnam hoped that existing differences between the pilots of
Delta and C&S over seniority rankings and other issues, which
were then being negotiated, could be resolved through arbitration, a
process that had proved necessary in the recent Braniff and Mid
Continent merger. As for the hard core of the opposition, however,
he declared that "I can see no course we can take except to gird up
our loins and present a clear case to our stockholders."[27]

Otherwise, matters went along nicely. Shortly after Cusick's
favorable examiner's report was announced, Pogue notified Woolman that final oral arguments might take place before the CAB by
mid-December, leading to the further possibility that the merger
might secure ultimate board approval by the end of the month. This
was a highly desirable objective because the timing of the approval
would coincide with the end of the C&S fiscal year and thus save
the considerable delay and expense associated with the new audit
that would otherwise be required. Writing from his Washington
office, Putnam assured Woolman that he was doing everything possible to convince CAB officials of the need to expedite matters.

With the help of Pogue and Woolman's special assistant, Earl
Cocke, these efforts were successful, and the merger moved ahead
with dispatch. The concluding session of oral testimony was held on
December 11, and by the time that the CAB adjourned for the holi-

days a unanimous decision in favor of the merger had been made by members Joseph P. Adams, Harmar Denny, Chan Gurney, Josh Lee, and Chairman Oswald Ryan. Putnam kept Woolman informed of what was going on and wrote just three days before Christmas that the main remaining question was whether President Truman's signature, necessary because C&S was an international carrier, could be obtained before the beginning of the New Year. Thanks partly to Adams, who was the only board member to remain in Washington over Christmas and who "worked without a break until the President had signed the documents and the formal approval order was issued," all hurdles were cleared, and official approval of the merger was publicly announced on December 31, climaxing months of hard work, tension, and suspense. Stewart, in a more or less routine letter to Woolman on that day, dealt with a continuing program to prepare stewardesses for combined operations and supplied a fitting comment on the occasion. The neatly typed salutation read "Dear C.E.," but Stewart crossed out Woolman's familiar initials and scrawled above them the single word "Boss."[28]

It was indeed a moment to be savored, but Woolman, Putnam, and their respective forces could not yet relax, for the proverbial million and one details remained to be attended to before the union of the two airlines could become final. Throughout the winter and into the spring of 1953, for example, committees representing both companies spent enormous amounts of time in the unglamorous but necessary job of standardizing the myriad procedures and forms connected with such matters as payroll practices, ticketing, preparation of freight receipts and baggage manifests, checking in of passengers, and organization of seasonal vacation tours. Differing approaches sometimes sparked vigorous arguments, such as the one that erupted over the question of whether passengers who changed planes within the Delta and C&S system should be issued only one ticket coupon, which had been the practice at C&S for reasons of simplicity and cost, or two, which Delta preferred because it facilitated better control of traffic and accounting.[29]

More crucial in the long run, perhaps, were negotiations at various levels on how employees of the two firms, from high management on down, were to be welded together on a department-by-department basis with appropriate job titles, responsibilities, and seniority rankings. In a number of instances it meant that a person who had been in charge of a particular function or office with one organization would now serve in a lower capacity. While this difficult and

emotionally taxing aspect of the merger was being attended to, officials in charge of operations laid plans for the eventual consolidation
of maintenance facilities; and the personnel departments, with an
eye to the employee-protective provisions laid down by the CAB,
devised policies governing transfers, moving allowances, losses incurred through the sale of real estate, and related matters. It was a
time of mingled tension and anticipation in both companies.[30]

The early months of 1953 were also filled with activity for the
legal departments and advisers of the two firms. Probably the most
crucial task was the preparation of detailed proxy statements to be
submitted to the stockholders for their all-important ratification
vote. These statements, which described the details of the merger as
clearly as possible, particularly the rights and restrictions that
would devolve upon the debenture holders, had to be approved by
the SEC, and it was not until the third week in March that they
were in final printed form ready to be submitted to the shareholders
for action. Looking back upon the results of the balloting in the attempted Northwest and Capital merger and anticipating that a relatively few votes might decide whether the necessary two thirds'
majority in favor of consolidation could be mustered among those
owning stock in C&S, officials of that company had done their best
to persuade remaining holders of the old voting-trust certificates to
exchange them for common shares so that they could vote on the
merger. By March 20 both sets of proxy documents were in the mail,
and officers of the two firms waited with some degree of tension for
the results to come in.[31]

But there were also lighter moments in the process that unfolded
after the CAB had made its decision in favor of the merger. In January, for example, Woolman, Stewart, and other dignitaries took part
in a gala flight marking the formal opening of C&S service to Puerto
Rico, Haiti, and the Dominican Republic through the New Orleans
gateway. In addition to enjoying the festivities, the two presidents
found time to "talk business" while reporters speculated about
the upcoming balloting among shareholders and about the effects
that the merger would have upon the destinies of both carriers.
An article in a leading business periodical, published the following
month after an interview with Woolman, reflected widespread chat-
ter in financial circles by pointing to the high costs still plaguing
C&S, despite impressive gains in revenue and net earnings under
Stewart's leadership, and asking whether the somewhat dissimilar
fleets of the two companies could be welded into a coherent profit-

making unit. But, as the writer noted, nothing seemed to be worrying "easy-going, weather-seamed Woolman," including the awaited results of the impending stockholder voting. Recent merger-related decisions, Woolman pointed out, had been endorsed by a whopping 87 percent of Delta's ownership, and every hurdle cleared in the consolidation process since the preceding April had resulted in improved quotations for C&S stock on the big board. In his estimation, the C&S shareholders were "too wise to vote against their own pocketbooks."[32]

Woolman was right on both counts. On April 22, at special stockholders' meetings held in Memphis and Atlanta, the results of the crucial referenda were announced. As anticipated, the merger proposal had sailed through Delta's family of shareholders with virtually no opposition, receiving 561,163½ favorable votes with only 76½ against. The tally in Memphis was not quite so overwhelming but nevertheless quite comfortable: 448,658 shares were recorded on the affirmative side, 5,996 opposed. Based on the total stock outstanding, Delta received a positive response of 93.5 percent, and C&S garnered 88 percent, both figures being far in excess of the two thirds' margin required.[33]

The last obstacle had been cleared, and there remained only a final week of frenzied paperwork before the formal closing took place. Thanks to the gains registered by C&S in preceding months, the principal amount of debentures authorized by the Delta board of directors was $10,942,600, and the necessary procedures were duly executed. Scores of notifications were sent to banks, so that existing C&S accounts could be transferred to the surviving corporation, and legal protocols were concluded with foreign governments throughout the Caribbean, so that a new business entity could operate the international mail routes served by C&S. Lawyers representing both firms checked and rechecked the corporation laws of Louisiana and Delaware to make sure that no possible technicality had been overlooked and put the finishing touches on a long and complex agenda of documents to be signed and countersigned at the official closing ceremonies.[34]

And so "M-Day" arrived at last on May 1, 1953, culminating so many months and years of mingled frustrations and achievements on the part of both airlines participating in the union. As they sat down to a festive luncheon at Atlanta headquarters, after all the signatures had been duly recorded, and watched Woolman, Putnam, and two stewardesses cut a cake topped by a pair of wedding rings symbolizing the merger, the directors of the new corporation had much to ponder.[35] For Putnam, Stewart, and Longmire, a loss of independent business identity promised a more secure future in an enterprise fully capable of exploiting the promise of the approaching jet age. For Woolman and his longtime Delta associates, five years of persistent and sometimes extremely discouraging merger efforts had finally paid off in a corporate marriage creating an aviation empire that encompassed a much wider range of southern and midwestern markets, in addition to a network of Caribbean routes. And everybody present had to agree that the two tiny enterprises that had begun life as Huff Daland Dusters and Pacific Seaboard Airlines had come very far indeed.

The first annual report of the combined enterprise, issued only a few months later, presented a detailed picture of its greatly expanded size and resources, including total assets of nearly $38 million; net profits for the preceding fiscal year of about $4.2 million; a fleet of fifty aircraft; and a route system whose 9,500 miles of airways made it the sixth-ranking domestic carrier in the industry. Its 4,281 employees represented vast managerial experience, formidable technological expertise, and a rank-and-file with a record of unusual loyalty based upon family-style traditions and the overcoming of many obstacles encountered along the way as Delta and C & S had risen from humble beginnings.[36] The scope of the organization was still modest as compared with the giants of American industry, or even with that of such large aviation enterprises as American, United, Eastern, and TWA. Nevertheless, the nucleus of a major airline had been brought into being, and future years would demonstrate that a solid foundation for substantial growth had been securely laid. The promise was great—but the problems were challenging.

CHAPTER 13

Shakedown Cruise

NEITHER DELTA NOR C&S had ever gone through a merger prior to the one that united them in 1953, and perhaps it was only to be expected that difficulty would be experienced in welding the two organizations together. In addition to predictable strains connected with relocating employees and combining the functions of previously separate staffs at stations up and down the route system, problems were encountered in integrating the pilot seniority list. Meanwhile, an even more threatening situation arose as declining passenger revenue, partly caused by a temporary decline in customer service, led to a corresponding drop in corporate profits. Amid these circumstances friction developed within the company hierarchy, and two highly placed executives formerly with C&S were gone by 1954. Nevertheless, these difficulties proved to be temporary, and by the end of its first fiscal year as a united enterprise the firm was showing encouraging signs of recovery.

"We're being watched," employees were warned by the retitled *Delta–C&S Digest* not long after formalization of the merger. Stewardesses and reservations clerks were instructed not to be "lip-lazy" and to pronounce the name distinctly, DEL-TAH CEE AND ESS, with the pride befitting the nation's sixth-ranking domestic airline. Actually the official corporate name continued to be Delta Air Lines, Inc., but the title Delta–C&S was to be used in public, partly to promote the morale of former C&S staff and partly to retain the image C&S had acquired among its southern and midwestern clientele. The designation "Delta Air Lines operating as Delta–C&S" was also used sometimes, further confusing the issue.

Regardless of what the firm was called, publicly or privately, the eyes of the industry were sure to be focused on it in the months ahead, the magazine went on to remind its readers. Bankers and investors would be anxious to know whether costs could be held down and profit levels maintained. The CAB, one of whose members had called the recent consolidation a "model merger," would want to gauge its impact from the point of view of future policy. Competitors would be quick to size up the performance of the expanded enterprise and to take advantage of any weakness. Passengers would be "waiting to see whether we continue our reputation for personalized service." Some of them, the article continued, "think the merger may make us too big to be nice."[1]

It would take "a lot of doing," the magazine emphasized, to fulfill the promise inherent in the merger, and the early results were not entirely encouraging. A period of difficult adjustment following "M-Day" actually was not unexpected. Although a merger is not quite as precarious as an organ transplant, the patient must still be watched closely for signs of rejection of the grafted body. There was thus a high degree of suspense at Delta. There were also moments of humor: replying to a sales pitch for the airline to purchase vitamins for its employees and to call them Deltamins, Woolman informed the pharmaceutical concern's vice-president that "we are so completely occupied in digesting our merger and a new fleet of airplanes that digestive pills would be more in order."[2]

In practice, the two corporate components remained virtually independent for a number of weeks. On May 17 the Delta component suffered its first fatal crash since 1948, when a DC-3 headed from Dallas to Shreveport fell in the vicinity of Marshall, Texas, during a heavy thunderstorm. The accident would have been tragic at any time, but it was particularly unwelcome—almost a bad omen— coming as it did less than a month after the merger. The captain, copilot, and seventeen passengers perished instantly, and the stewardess died of injuries after a race to a nearby hospital. Miraculously—for the plane was smashed and scattered when it struck the ground after ripping through a thicket of trees—one passenger survived: she was found sitting upright in a detached seat. The CAB investigation pinned the blame on the captain's decision to penetrate the storm, even though it would have been feasible to detour around it—a decision that violated both Delta and CAB regulations. One feature of the press coverage, noted by the *Delta–C&S Digest*, was that "no newspaperman asked whether the DC-3 involved was a former Delta ship or a former C&S ship. The public already looks upon us as a consolidated company and our future destinies are tied together."[3]

Some of the problems that arose during integration of the two firms had been foreseen, but others were unanticipated. One of these involved the number of employees in the new organization. Although the merger was expected to produce more jobs in the future as business grew, it had been predicted that at first the combined payroll would shrink temporarily, a prediction offered to the CAB as evidence of monetary savings promised by consolidation. But, to Woolman's disappointment, the shrinkage did not occur. "Contrary to our expectations," he informed all department heads on August 21, "our total number of people employed is now greater than the former sum total of the employees of the two individual companies." In a quick economy move he directed that thenceforth all payroll-change forms would have to be approved by the new executive vice-president, Sidney Stewart. "In the case of new employees," Woolman continued, "a memo explaining the necessity for hiring should be attached."[4]

One clearly anticipated problem involved the transfer of personnel from one place to another, particularly from Memphis to Atlanta. On August 11 veteran Delta personnel officer R. H. Wharton, Jr., reported to Woolman that sixty-six people had been transferred from the old C&S headquarters to the Georgia capital. Thirty-seven of them had owned homes in Memphis before the merger, of which twenty-nine had been sold, two were in the process of being sold, one was not up for sale, and five were still on the market. Delta–C&S had been obliged to underwrite six of the sales for amounts slightly below appraised values, resulting in a total outlay of $2,500; in addition, the company had underwritten second mortgages totaling $5,050 in three instances. As the company was protected by equity, it stood to suffer only "as a result of a drastic decrease in realty values." Obviously, this aspect of the merger had taken place with little financial strain for Delta, though Wharton pointed out to Woolman that "quite a number of houses" would be thrown on the market when a planned move of maintenance personnel from Memphis to Atlanta took place.

The immediate impact of the move was eased by liberal provisions under the company's policies governing hotel expenses for employees and their families, meal and automobile allowances, and the like. Each employee had forty-five days' notice before having to report to a new job location. Juanita Burnett (now Juanita Whiddon, a corporate record clerk for Delta) was a housewife when she and her husband, who was in radio maintenance and later in personnel, moved to Atlanta in July 1953. She looked upon the move as an adventure, and her husband accepted it as part of his job. George Shedd, later assistant vice-president for public relations at Delta, was a C&S hand who had reacted to the merger with surprise and apprehension when it was first announced. He had just bought a new house, and he subsequently experienced some difficulty in selling it. His experience was unusual, however, and he soon became happy with his new post. Others, however, did not adjust so quickly. Ed Bolton, one of the line-maintenance people in Memphis, was apprehensive about a new work environment, and his family did not look forward to leaving home, schools, and church. It took Bolton about a year and a half to make the psychological transition from being a C&S employee to feeling like a "Delta person." His experience was typical. Former C&S people tended to band together at first in the communities where they settled in the sprawling Atlanta area, but ultimately they came to share the "Delta family" feeling. The post–World War II era was one of increasing mobility in American society, and the social dislocations arising from the merger were certainly not unique. When Don Hettermann, a future Delta vice-president, came to Atlanta in August 1954, as part of the shift of maintenance personnel from Memphis, he found that things had settled down among former C&S people.[5]

Not all C&S personnel had to move, of course, and a few chose to find other employment. John Taber, who was in the C&S legal division at Memphis as director of properties, but found this function a part of the finance division in Delta, resigned effective August 28, 1953, "after careful deliberation over a period of at least three months." For those who did move or were troubled by the merger in general, adjustment was often made easier by Woolman's paternalistic approach. Pilot Bill Spangler and Don Hettermann later remembered that a talk with their new boss helped to alleviate much of their uncertainty; Woolman's knack of establishing rapport with the rank and file apparently never served the company better than during this difficult period of adjustment. Mrs. Charles Flesh, who described herself as the wife of "a small link in a large chain," was one of several former C&S employees' spouses who wrote in gratitude to Woolman. She pledged that "in appreciation of your leadership I am trying to cooperate 100% with you," and praised business, religious, and civic groups in the Atlanta area, who had "made us feel very much at home."[6]

In March 1954 Woolman sent a message to all remaining employees at Memphis, declaring that "one of the most pressing problems resulting from the merger has been the determination of the long range status of the Memphis maintenance base." He told of unsuccessful efforts to lease the facilities to an independent operator and concluded that "it now seems that by far the best solution to our problem is to continue the Memphis base only for the period necessary to maintain the Constellations." By late summer, part of the maintenance facilities no longer needed by the company had been leased, and disposal of the rest was under negotiation. As most maintenance personnel had already been transferred, the "Memphis problem," in both its psychological and physical aspects, was well on the way to being solved.[7]

Although Memphis posed the most intricate problem, it was not the only base that presented difficulties. At New Orleans, where both Delta and C & S had operated when they were independent, the process of integrating personnel from the two companies was particularly troublesome. It was not until December 1953 that the full dimensions of the trouble were revealed. An inspection team composed of Wharton, acting for Woolman; Finis Fox of stations; and Jim Turner of maintenance spent the first week of December in New Orleans to see what could be done. Integration of facilities and personnel had been ordered in October by J. G. Dye, superintendent of maintenance, but the December inspection revealed that "no real effort" had been made and that Delta and C & S personnel "were operating out of two different hangars." There was still confusion between maintenance and stations personnel about duties and responsibilities on the ramp. The principal bottleneck was the inability of the general foreman, a former C & S man, and his assistant, an old-time Delta employee, to get along. The inspectors found that the foreman had little rapport with other personnel, whether agents, pilots, mechanics, or stewardesses, but had outstanding technical competence. He was therefore assigned to paperwork involving technical matters and overall assignment of duties. His assistant, who enjoyed good relations with most personnel, was to "be given the direct responsibilities of the flight line, and to be in complete charge of that function at the station" with the necessary personnel to cover flight-line operations and the power to requisition additional people "out of the hangar area" if necessary. After pep talks and gripe sessions, at which the general foreman and his assistant were present, the investigators ordered that one of the hangars be vacated, operations concentrated in the other, and surplus equipment shipped to Atlanta. The local bosses promised to cooperate and to make New Orleans the best base in the system.[8]

At Chicago, another base where separate facilities had been combined, Wharton and C. B. Wilder, superintendent of stations, found in December that integration had proceeded much further than in New Orleans. Employee morale was high, and there seemed to be little friction or jealousy resulting from the merger. Still, some problems did exist. Pilots had complained about "organized confusion," and there were many flight delays. Captains trying to hand in their flight plans often had to go from one agent to another before locating the right one. Mechanics were uncertain how to obtain information about such essential functions as the fueling of aircraft. Prior to this time, the two companies had utilized different operational procedures and neither had attained the sophisticated functioning that expanded operations in the jet era would require. Wharton and Wilder attributed much of the confusion to cramped quarters—in contrast to excessive space in New Orleans. Doing their best to cope with the situation, they established better procedures for the filing of plans and reports and making sure that the crew of an outgoing plane knew what had been done to rectify any mechanical problems encountered during its previous flight. Wharton and Wilder discovered that many delays were not caused in Chicago but resulted instead from late arrival of incoming planes. All in all, they agreed that the Chicago personnel, who had been integrated only since October, were functioning much better than expected and under trying winter conditions.[9]

One of the major postmerger difficulties, again fully anticipated, arose from the introduction of new equipment and the phasing out of old at the same time that two fleets and two separate rosters of flight personnel were being integrated. Maintenance was especially troublesome. In July 1953 Wharton complained to Woolman about a report estimating overall manpower needs for maintenance. He was unhappy that it had been prepared by "top-side people" who had little day-to-day familiarity with maintenance problems. He recommended that the report be redrafted with more input from those down the line before it was submitted to Dye, Dolson, and William T. Arthur, who had come from C&S to be Dolson's assistant in restructuring operations. This request evidently was granted, but as late as February 1954 the matter was still being debated.[10]

Plans for the introduction of the new Douglas DC-7, the fastest airliner then available, caused more headaches. Later called "the piston-engined plane that almost broke the airlines" by Bolton, it was hailed by company officials at a "get-acquainted rally" in Atlanta in June 1953, at which the purchase of DC-7s was announced. In November, however, Vice-President and Comptroller Todd Cole expressed his concern about the absence of concrete planning for inauguration of service with the new craft. Atlanta and Miami, he pointed out, would have to share maintenance for ten more four-engine planes when the DC-7s were put into service; how much of the burden Miami could lift from Atlanta had to be determined. Besides, there was a potential pilot problem. Training for Convair operations had proved unexpectedly costly because of some last-minute changes in which some personnel already trained had been assigned to the wrong bases. This mistake ought to be avoided with the DC-7s, he argued. Furthermore, there were too many pilots, and some might have to be furloughed; until they were chosen, training was hampered because no one knew who should be included. Cole also pointed out that a plan to train flight engineers for the DC-7s, to replace pilots with inadequate flight-engineer training, was urgently needed. In an almost desperate tone, he stressed the need for cooperation among the traffic, operations, and finance divisions; quick action, he declared, would save a lot of money. After a training program for flight engineers was set for January, Dolson appealed to Parker for "reasonably accurate forecasts" about the operation of all aircraft after arrival of the fourth and tenth DC-7s. Using this information, officials would determine who was to be trained and who furloughed.[11] Somehow, it all got done.

Flight captains in general were a problem group immediately after the merger, and the "pilots' revolt" continued for some time. The principal object of the pilots' wrath in 1953 was the combined seniority list, which had been determined on March 27 prior to the official merger date by a union committee consisting of J. H. Longino and H. Averett, representing Delta pilots; Eugene Fletcher and John R. Reeves, representing C&S pilots; and William M. Leiserson, chairman and neutral member appointed by the National Mediation Board. On that day this committee met at ALPA headquarters and explained to the combined master executive councils of both unions the mathematical procedures used to prepare the list, obtaining their seal of approval. Almost immediately, however, protests arose from individuals, including Fletcher and one C&S member of the master executive councils, Joseph A. Meek. By the deadline of May 15 various pilot protests had been filed, and the committee then met again. Of the 141 protests, 94 came from C&S pilots and 47 from Delta pilots.

The mediators remained in session for about a week and finally rejected all protests. Both Delta and C&S representatives acknowl-

edged that errors had been made, though they could not agree on precisely what the errors were; both sides reiterated that the principles
on which the list was based were sound. They also agreed that revis-
ing the list would probably result in even more errors and called attention to the fact that 72 percent of those on the list had not raised
any objections. Some of the protesters were merely trying to protect
their positions on the list. The decision to let the list stand was
finally signed in Geneva, Switzerland, on June 11, 1953, by all members of the group except Fletcher, who did not wish to be a party to
any injustice.[12]

This majority action did not end the matter, however, and rever-
berations continued for several months. Captain Truman Outland,
an old C&S hand, tried to appeal the matter to the CAB, alleging
that ALPA President Clarence N. Sayen was violating contractual
rights by refusing to order adjustments in the combined seniority
list. But the CAB informed Outland that it had no jurisdiction in
this dispute.[13] Despite threats of legal action, the "revolt" eventually simmered down, and even Outland remained a highly valued
member of the merged company's staff.

As for labor relations generally, both Delta and C&S agreed during the merger negotiations that the existing labor contracts of the
various C&S unions would be honored for their stated durations
and then be subject to renegotiation. After the merger the new organization moved in the direction traditionally followed by Delta—no
unions except for the pilots. One by one, as the various contracts
expired, management served the proper notice of termination. Although some protests were raised, especially by the parent unions,
most of the old C&S hands accepted the new arrangement.[14]

One of the most crucial decisions affecting labor relations which
was implemented by Delta management in the immediate postmerger period involved a number of flight engineers who had previously served with Chicago and Southern. Delta had decided that
the third cockpit crew members mandated for large four-engine aircraft by the CAB in 1948 would be trained as pilot engineers who in
the normal course of their careers would rise to the ranks of copilot
and pilot. C&S, like many other airlines, had promoted its flight
engineers strictly from mechanics, with no training as pilots and,
therefore, no long-range possibility of advancement to pilot status.
In discussing this situation with Richard S. Maurer during the winter of 1952–53, while arrangements were underway to consolidate
the staffs of the two companies, Woolman had declared, "We must

never put a board on a man's head." What he meant was that a third man in the cockpit trained strictly as a mechanic would watch younger men rise above him while his own status was frozen. In time the resentment produced by this state of affairs would result in severe labor problems that Woolman was determined to avoid.

Accordingly, after the merger was implemented, all former C&S flight mechanics were advised by the Personnel Department that, while none would be fired and each would be guaranteed a ground assignment with equivalent pay, Delta intended to restrict its cockpit crews to persons with pilot training once the Constellations acquired in the merger had been phased out of the fleet. To soften the impact of this decision, those affected were told that if they chose not to accept a ground job they would be treated under the merger's employee protective provisions as if they had been fired. This carried with it a substantial benefit, for most of the former C&S flight mechanics had long seniority and could thereby qualify, if dismissed, for severance pay of one year's salary free of tax. As a result, most of the group resigned, took the severance pay, and found jobs as flight mechanics elsewhere. The move cost Delta approximately $250,000 but this turned out to be one of the wisest investments in the history of the firm when, later in the decade, the labor difficulties that Woolman had foreseen broke out on a number of airlines because of difficulties between pilots and flight engineers trained solely as mechanics, producing costly strikes while Delta remained unaffected by the controversy.[15]

The most serious postmerger problem facing the company was stated bluntly by Woolman in a letter to longtime Delta employee Esther Tarver early in 1945: "Quite frankly, the air line could use a few more cash customers." His comment and Cole's earlier plea that the training of flight engineers be organized quickly to save expenses reflected a decline in revenues that had struck with greater severity than had been forecast. By March 1954 what had at first seemed merely a slump in profits was turning into an actual deficit. The downturn caused deep concern not only within the merged company but also among stockholders, potential investors, and bankers holding company loans.

James H. Cobb, Jr., vice-president for public relations and advertising, had been one of the earliest to sound the alarm. In August 1953 he had sent Woolman a memorandum declaring that "the general tone of the June financial report was so pessimistic that it would do us great harm if one of these fell into the hands of a financial writer."

Cobb was referring to a financial statement that had showed the first net loss in many months, $196,866, including a loss in mail revenues for the first time in quite a while. The company tried to put as good a face on the economic picture as it could, but inevitably further sets of discouraging figures caused reactions. In October, Allen Stutts, vice-president of American National Bank and Trust Company of Chicago, responding to a report covering the previous three months, wrote Woolman that "the unsatisfactory operating results were a surprise to me and, of course, raised the question as to the cause and future prospects." Woolman tried to soothe his anxiety and that of other inquirers by pointing out that the first quarter of the fiscal year was a seasonally low traffic period and that this year it had been coupled with a "transition period" involving unusual merger-related expenses. Also the benefits of the new Convair service were not yet being fully realized. In spite of these and other difficulties, he continued, the net loss for the quarter was only $72,000. He warned that additional merger-related and equipment-integration expenses lay ahead and declared that improvement in the overall picture would depend largely on a seasonal pickup in traffic.[16]

One key to the disturbing traffic situation was a deterioration in the services provided to customers, particularly in the vital area of punctuality. The management acted promptly to arrest it. In addition to the inspection teams sent to New Orleans and Chicago, various committees were formed to deal with the problem, and Sidney Stewart undertook what was probably the most significant task of his brief tenure with Delta–C & S: coordinating the effort. A special "on-time" committee, composed of C. B. Wilder, Luke Williamson, Jack King, Charles Payne, Joseph Meyer, Thomas Miller, and Robert Johnson, began a detailed analysis of flight operations and made recommendations to Stewart on December 1, 1953. Among the findings were "somewhat unrealistic block-to-block flying times . . . inadequate ground times at certain stations . . . the practice of holding for late passengers and connections beyond reasonable times . . . apparent lack of enthusiasm and interest on the part of many of our people." The committee recommended precise corrective measures and expressed the belief

that much of the unenthusiastic and casual attitude displayed by many of our people results from the fact that our chief executives have been so absorbed with duties in connection with merger . . . that there has been an understandable tendency to let up on the day-to-day policing of our operations . . . unless all personnel from one end of the line to the other are impressed with the fact that the company considers even a single avoidable delay a serious matter, we are still not going to run our airline on schedule.

Earlier in the fall Woolman himself had called for reports of deficiencies from the various stations and sales offices along the routes. After personnel meetings at those bases, reports began to flow across his desk. The Birmingham sales manager, Asher Lane, Jr., reported that "we are enclosing a signed pledge which all of the gang have signed to redouble our efforts with renewed vigor to keep these errors at barest of minimum." From the pioneer base of Selman Field at Monroe, station manager R. F. Bonner reported that, although Selman had received no passenger complaints "reflecting growing pains or lack of service as a result of the merger," he and his staff were determined "to do a better job . . . and . . . get that extra passenger." From Shreveport the station manager and sales manager both admitted that "following May 1st, our service was not up to standard" but insisted that "our problems have been satisfactorily solved." The various meetings up and down the system throughout the fall of 1953 turned up a wide range of alleged deficiencies:

Better selection of magazines on flights. . . . The Company waits too long to replace a personnel vacancy. . . . Stewardesses talk too loud about oversales within earshot of passengers. . . . General Office apparently has lack of confidence in the field personnel. . . . Company should give policy on how much abuse we are expected to take from totally unreasonable passengers. . . . Bulletins not received by all departments affected. . . . Poor connections at Memphis causing complaints and loss of business.

Stewart channeled these complaints to the relevant divisions.[17]

W. D. Huff, passenger-relations manager, may have provided as much incentive for improvement as anybody, when he reported to Parker that, "Probably because of the increase in the number of passenger complaints mentioning the lack of interested attention and service at many of our stations, I have noticed a number of interesting passenger developments recently on the part of Eastern Airlines."[18]

In December 1953 the division heads met with Woolman and Stewart weekly on the assumption that "the initial phases of the merger are now behind" but that "substantial operational problems" remained.[19] But the clouds grew darker with the appearance of the second-quarter report. It showed a net loss of $3,615, compared to a net profit of more than $4 million for the comparable period in 1952. Banker H. Lane Young wrote Woolman in February, questioning whether the merger should have been attempted. He received in reply an admission that "Very frankly, the past half year has not lived up to our pro forma plans." The Delta executive cited "unforeseen increases in gasoline" and "sizeable wage increases," in addition to other factors already mentioned.[20]

Another difficulty confronting the troubled enterprise involved its mail rate. Ever since the passage of the Civil Aeronautics Act in 1938 mail-pay rates for carriers operating both domestic and international divisions had been computed separately, and this principle had been followed in the case of C&S. In 1952, however, the Post Office Department had launched a suit claiming that domestic profits earned by C&S in 1948–50 should have been taken into account in determining that firm's compensation for international mail and seeking, under this "offset" principle, a refund of $654,000. Despite an initial CAB denial of this claim, a federal circuit court of appeals sustained the Post Office's view in May 1953, and Delta–C&S in turn appealed to the United States Supreme Court. If the company's appeal failed it stood to lose a large sum of money. It was therefore a heavy blow when, on February 1, 1954, that tribunal upheld the circuit court's ruling. After recovering from the shock, Woolman wrote to one financier that "it is almost impossible for anyone to prognosticate the effect of the Supreme Court's decision at the present time." On the other hand, he said, "It does not call for any immediate or hasty action on our part." He was correct, for the Supreme Court had ordered the CAB to recalculate the mail pay that C&S should have received, and that process was bound to take time. Nevertheless, Delta–C&S stood to forfeit a substantial sum when the case was ultimately settled.[21]

As the post-merger shakedown period continued, there were thus more downs than ups, and it is not surprising that some relationships within the executive team began to go sour, culminating in March 1954 when Woolman and Stewart came to a parting of the ways. Soon afterward Junius Cooper also left. Little can be gleaned from surviving materials in Delta's corporate files about the precise reasons for this top-level split, but it seems clear that differing managerial philosophies, combined with the disappointing record of the newly merged organization in the first year, intensified what would have been a strained situation in any event. Both Carleton Putnam and Richard S. Maurer have testified to the unusual business acumen of Stewart and Cooper, whose competence in their respective areas of responsibility is beyond question. But, as Putnam later admitted, "I probably should have foreseen that bringing in Stewart as Executive Vice President under Woolman in the new organization would cause a clash of personalities, particularly as Woolman felt none of the urgency about retirement that I did." In premerger negotiations Woolman had talked vaguely about stepping up to board chairman, with Stewart taking over as president; perhaps, as Putnam put it, "Stewart may have anticipated a swifter unfolding of his ambitions for the future than were in Woolman's plans." Then, too, there were differences over such matters as the relative merits of aircraft: Woolman and other old-line Delta personnel had a well-developed predilection for Douglas, whereas both Stewart and Cooper preferred Lockheed. But this difference was in all likelihood only a contributing, not a decisive, factor.

Looking back more than two decades later, Maurer, who was intimate with the managerial styles of both Stewart and Woolman, underscored the importance of seeing the episode in historical perspective and understanding the differing philosophies that the two executives had gained from their previous experiences. Like Putnam, Woolman was a founding father, but, unlike Putnam, he had no outside interests that could lure him away from active management. Delta Air Lines was his life. His approach was patriarchal, and he consulted whom he pleased in reaching high-level decisions, expecting that subordinates would fall into line with his thinking. In these respects he was not much different from any other first generation airline pioneer. His outlook was both characteristic and understandable.

In contrast, Stewart was not a founding father but belonged to a second generation of airline executives who had come into the industry with a different attitude. Stewart looked upon himself as a member of a management team whose decisions were essentially collective and in which he maintained a relatively low profile. He believed in a clearly defined chain of command. Major decisions were to be reached after free-wheeling general discussions in which each participant had his say, often in a blunt and outspoken manner. Disagreement was welcomed and even expected, but, once a matter had been resolved, it was understood that all parties would unite and leave their differences at the office door. This approach, which had developed partly from military procedures adopted in World War II, was characteristic of a developing professional managerial style and was just as understandable in its way as Woolman's long-standing paternalism. It had become the standard approach at C&S when that firm was being rescued, under Stewart's leadership, from the near disaster of the early postwar period; ultimately it became deeply ingrained in the Delta organization itself under such later chief executives as Charles Dolson, W. T. Beebe, and David C. Garrett.

Such transitions take time, however, and in 1954 Delta was not ready for an abrupt switch. It is therefore not surprising that, in Maurer's words, "the amount of time consumed in making major decisions proved frustrating to Stewart." Cooper experienced similar feelings and had a hard time adjusting to patterns of interaction that had quite naturally been carried over from Delta's premerger experience. Under the new setup, for example, Comptroller Todd Cole formally was supposed to report to Stewart through Cooper, the chief financial officer, but in practice he did not. Woolman traditionally had maintained an "open-door policy," encouraging subordinates to come directly to him with their problems; it is not surprising then that Cole went directly to the top about certain matters, even though he upset the chain of command to which Stewart and Cooper had become accustomed. On the other hand, who can wonder that the former C&S officials became irritated?

And so matters proceeded toward their predictable outcome, and Stewart and Cooper resigned. As Putnam acknowledged many years later, "an important section of the merger pattern was upset. . . . But I cannot fault either the Board or Woolman for accepting these resignations, because I agreed that they had become inevitable." Stewart became vice-president of the Niles-Bement-Pont Company in West Hartford, Connecticut, and Cooper became chief financial officer of the Vitro Corporation of America in New York City. There was no need to appoint a successor to Stewart, whose position had been created especially for him; Cole assumed Cooper's previous responsibilities. Any concern about further departures by former C&S personnel was quickly allayed when Beebe moved up to vice-president for personnel in April, and Maurer was appointed to Stewart's vacant seat on the board of directors. As Maurer later recalled, "once this traumatic period of readjustment was passed, the remaining members of the C&S management team were rapidly assimilated into the Delta family in positions of increasing responsibility. . . . Woolman did conscientiously draw the former C&S group into his inner-councils and, over a period of years, let them advance in accordance with their abilities."[22] The extent to which Delta's top management roster was studded with names of former C&S

officials in the mid-1970s attests to the accuracy of Maurer's observation.

A brief crossing of swords did occur between Putnam and Woolman in April 1954, just before the board meeting at which Stewart's resignation was to be presented. Surviving documents do not indicate clearly that it was directly related to the resignations, though it may well have been; certainly C&S people were shocked, as a letter from John Longmire to Woolman a few days later indicates: he told the Delta executive that "debenture holders are quite disappointed." The only clue to the precise nature of the disagreement is contained in a letter from Woolman to Putnam on April 9: "I am very much concerned at having you state that our Board of Directors are dominated by me," C.E. declared. He also objected to Putnam's comment that the financial condition of the company was "far below" what had been predicted a year before, reminding Putnam that the forecast had been based on an overoptimistic expectation that the "initial integration steps" would be completed before the beginning of the new fiscal year.[23]

In any event, the friction between the two men soon abated. It had been a rough year, and it is not surprising that feathers were temporarily ruffled, but nothing like a real split between Woolman and Putnam ever took place. The firm's emergence into a more quiet time was undoubtedly facilitated by an improvement in the third quarter of the fiscal year, a signal that the worst pains of consolidation were past. In April, O. H. Swayze, an interested banker, wrote how pleased he was with "the very handsome net profits" for the first quarter of 1954. At the end of the fiscal year total profits stood at $1,305,949, although much of this figure resulted from disposition of flight equipment and was plainly marked as such. Recovery and operational improvements in the last two quarters had turned earlier red ink into a net gain (exclusive of aircraft sales) of $283,584.[24] However modest, this figure was nonetheless encouraging. By the summer of 1954 Delta–C&S was looking ahead, not behind.

CHAPTER 14

The Big Breakthrough

URING THE MID-1950S Delta completed the process of assimilation that had taken place since "M-Day" in 1953 and enjoyed the enhanced status that came with the expanded scope of its operations. On the other hand, though profits began climbing upward once more, it was obvious that the firm continued to need more long-haul routes leading to major urban markets if it was to achieve really satisfactory earnings. The company therefore waged an intensive struggle to win a long-standing Delta objective—access to the metropolitan centers of the heavily populated Middle Atlantic region. It was an uphill battle, but that only served to make the final outcome all the more pleasing.

One of the characteristic problems facing an airline after a merger is that of fleet standardization. The aircraft sales that had helped to keep Delta in the black during the difficult months of transition following M-Day reflected the need to consolidate the somewhat disparate assortment of planes belonging to the new firm and to plan for an efficient and well-balanced roster of equipment in the future. Fortunately, both Delta and C&S had been moving in the same direction, as far as medium-sized, twin-engine airlines were concerned; together they owned six Convair 340s at the time of the merger, and fourteen more were on order. For small twin-engine planes both companies had long used DC-3s, and their postmerger fleet included thirty of these venerable ships, of which three were used exclusively for cargo. Delta's fifteen DC-3 passenger planes, however, had been recently remodeled, and each provided accommodation for twenty-five people; the C&S craft were of the old twenty-one-seat variety. Delta was committed to phasing out the DC-3 as quickly as possible; shortly before the merger, ship 40, the first DC-3 ever purchased by the company, had been sold to Mohawk Airlines. In thirteen years of service it had logged almost forty thousand hours and had flown nearly five million miles, the equivalent of 198 trips around the world. Furthermore, all of Delta's DC-4s had been sold by M-Day though the last one was not delivered until July 1953.[1]

In the large four-engine category, however, Delta owned seven DC-6s, whereas C & S had six Lockheed L-649 Constellations. Delta was decisively committed to the DC-7 as its large four-engine luxury liner of the future, anticipating that this sixty-nine-passenger model, which was capable of flying at least fifty miles an hour faster than either the DC-6 or the Connie, would be the queen of the Delta fleet. Four DC-7s had already been ordered, and Woolman's appetite for more was whetted in mid-May when the first such plane made its successful maiden flight at Santa Monica. At a "get-acquainted rally" in Atlanta in June it was announced that the company had ordered six more DC-7s. Meanwhile, a seventh Convair 340 had arrived and seven more were slated to join the fleet in the next three months.[2]

The steady arrival of the new forty-four-seat Convairs permitted Delta to dispense with older craft, and the twelve DC-3s that had belonged to C & S were quickly sold. Next to go were the Connies, much to the displeasure of some former C & S pilots and personnel who loved the graceful ships. But their fate was sealed when the DC-7s began to arrive. On February 24, 1954, the company's first DC-7, christened *Royal Biscayne* by actress Piper Laurie in a ceremony at the Douglas plant in Santa Monica, roared across the continent to Jacksonville in six hours and twelve seconds, with Dolson and Ball at the controls and a party of newsmen, management brass, and federal aviation officials aboard. Later that spring three Constellations were sold to TWA. The other three remained in the fleet for about a year and were then leased to Pacific Northern Airlines for operations between Seattle and Alaska. "Luxurious new 69-passenger DC-7's are replacing the Constellations over Delta–C & S routes," the company magazine declared in announcing the transaction.[3]

As if to underscore this development, on April 1, 1955, the firm's newest DC-7, *Royal Caribe*, was christened with Venezuelan oil at Chicago and took off on a ceremonial flight to Caracas, picking up the mayors of New Orleans, Houston, and Atlanta, as well as other guests, on the way. Upon arriving at the Venezuelan capital after having trimmed one hour and forty-two minutes from the previous flight record, it was rebaptized by Mrs. Fletcher Warren, wife of the American ambassador, with water from Lake Michigan, climaxing a series of shorter ceremonies at such stops as New Orleans and Montego Bay. In a speech before the Caracas chamber of commerce, Woolman harkened back to his first visit to South America some thirty years before: "There weren't many airplanes then, and only a few hardy souls ventured aboard those that were flying." The old planes had indeed been a far cry from the regal *Royal Caribe*, with its pressurized cabin and mechanical air-conditioning system.[4]

Despite such festive occasions, Caribbean operations had been plagued with problems that helped to keep down revenues on the firm's international routes. In December 1954 Cole mentioned that the company had suffered a "substantial loss" on international flights during the preceding month because of a $15,000 decline in revenues (the passenger-load factor dropped from 36 to 34 percent) and an increase of $23,000 in expenses. In contrast, there had been a $134,000 decrease in domestic operating expenses. Cole attributed the increase in international expenses to high maintenance costs for the Constellations and Convairs still in Caribbean service, but there were other problems as well. One involved regulations imposed upon the company by foreign governments; Cuba, for example, would not allow Delta–C&S to operate planes from Havana to other Caribbean points or to Caracas unless the number of flights out of Havana matched the number coming into that city from Houston and New Orleans. Further headaches resulted because Pan American Air Lines had established itself firmly in the Caribbean years before other American lines had operated there. A Delta–C&S agent in Haiti, for example, complained to Tom Miller about what he considered excessive charges by Pan American for Delta's use of the airport at Port-au-Prince. PAA, he informed Miller, was guilty of "monopoly practices."[5]

While management officials coped with such matters as well as they could, life went on routinely throughout the system. One incident reflected in a wryly humorous way the growth of the space effort that was developing in the Southeast. In Birmingham, Delta sales representative Tom Hunter-Reay, a former RAF flyer, met a German scientist from the missile research facility at Huntsville's Redstone Arsenal. "Haven't we met before?" the scientist asked. Hunter-Reay, who had taken part in the first bombing raid on the V-2 installation at Peenemunde, replied, "Yes, but I was 6,000 feet up." This too was the era when the dreaded scourge of infantile paralysis was about to yield to massive medical research. In Montgomery, Delta–C&S employees donated blood to the Red Cross for use in producing gamma globulin to help check a polio epidemic there in 1953; a year later Delta–C&S planes were carrying monkeys from the Okatie Farms breeding grounds in South Carolina to the Cutter Laboratory at Berkeley, California, where the little animals were used in preparation of polio vaccine under the auspices of the National Foundation for Infantile Paralysis. After still another year a Delta–C&S plane brought the first shipment of Salk vaccine to the state of South Carolina.[6]

One by one, old pioneers continued to disappear from the scene. Travis Oliver died in his sleep in February 1955. Dusting veteran Hank Fraser had passed away a few months earlier. Other veterans advanced to positions of increasing importance. Charles Dolson was elected to the board of directors, along with J. Woodall Rogers, former mayor of Dallas. By January 1955 Richard W. Freeman had become chairman of the board; this forty-one-year-old Coca-Cola magnate from New Orleans had played an increasingly prominent role in the directors' deliberations during the merger period but had accepted the chairmanship only after considerable coaxing by Putnam, who wanted to step down in order to devote more time to writing a biography of Theodore Roosevelt. Putnam later remarked that "Woolman, not unnaturally, would have liked to consolidate power at the top among his old Monroe supporters from Delta's earliest days, but after the loss of Stewart this seemed to me a bit soon. ... Freeman was one of Delta's leading directors, he had a broad base and background in the northern middlewest as well as New Orleans, and wide business experience, combined with youthful energy."[7]

By May 1955 Woolman himself had been with the company for thirty years. On May 2 a large crowd massed in front of the main Delta hangars in Atlanta to watch him receive a book containing the names of all current Delta employees, a birthday cake, and a thirty-year pin set with a diamond and two rubies. In anticipation of a hoped-for route award then pending, a Delta stewardess also gave him a large key to New York City. Touched by this display of loyalty and affection, Woolman told the assembled throng: "I'm working for the finest group of airline people in the world. It's a privilege ... trying to live up to the example you people set for me." As usual, the common touch of which Woolman was such a master went over well.[8]

As he surveyed company affairs from his cluttered office at the Atlanta headquarters, Woolman had many things to be thankful for as 1955 neared its close. There had been no strikes, despite a flareup from the International Association of Machinists, which demanded an election to represent Delta's unionless mechanics. The mechanics showed little or no interest in such a ballot, and the effort fell through. Hard negotiations did develop, however, over a new contract with the pilots' union. In October these culminated in an agreement, the most important new feature of which was a supplement to the regular fixed-benefit retirement plan in force since the merger in 1953. This supplement, called a "variable-annuity retirement-income plan," was soon made available to employees at lower supervisory levels. As veteran Captain Dana Jones later reflected in commenting upon the history of pilot bargaining in the Delta organization, such negotiations often paved the way for benefits for certain other company employees, diminishing the degree to which Delta could be regarded as a "nonunionized" company.[9]

Woolman could also be thankful that there had been no recent fatal accidents. There had, however, been a near-tragedy in March 1955, and Woolman could take pride in the way the Delta crew had responded to it. Convair N-4810C, after making a routine takeoff from the Atlanta Airport, bound for Knoxville, was making a turn to the right when, at 1,800 feet, the rear emergency door blew open with a loud bang followed by a hissing sound. Stewardess Claire Randolph informed Captain Ray Crocker, Jr., about the situation; he quickly radioed the Atlanta tower and was cleared to return for a landing. Meanwhile, First Officer Vic Hewes hurried into the passenger cabin to investigate the source of trouble and arrived in time to see the door fly off. It struck the horizontal stabilizer and, in Crocker's later words, "the ship went into a steep dive . . . accompanied by severe buffeting of the elevator cables." Crocker managed to arrest the dive and, with the help of Hewes, who had made his way back to the cockpit, prepared for an emergency landing. Although she had received a blow on the head from the initial lurch of the plane, Stewardess Randolph calmly reassured the passengers. The plane was more or less level as it approached a runway, but it was "porpoising" badly and Crocker chose to attempt a belly landing because he feared that to lower his wheels "would change the attitude and I would lose what little control I had." He set the craft down safely and Randolph and Hewes quickly herded the passengers out and away from the plane. Not one of them was injured. One of the passengers, Staff Sergeant Jimmy Sparkman, assigned to a United States Air Force fighter squadron based in Tennessee, wrote to

Woolman praising the crew for its cool performance and declaring that he would be willing "to fly on Captain Crocker's plane at any time."[10]

Two positive developments that Woolman undoubtedly mused upon indicated that the company was making progress in overcoming any remaining feeling that it consisted of two separate components. One sign of the successful amalgamation of C&S into the Delta organization was the rapid redemption, under policies adopted by the board in 1955, of the principal amount of the 5.5 percent convertible debentures that had been such a prominent feature of the merger plan. Another sign was a decision to eliminate "C&S" from Delta's operating title upon the recommendation of a committee composed of old C&S hands Maurer and Beebe and veteran Delta executive Parker in the summer of the same year. The committee pointed to the confusion created by the new operating name; some members of the public were confusing C&S with the Atlanta-based C&S (Citizens and Southern) Bank. It was agreed that keeping "C&S" in the title was no longer necessary for the morale of former C&S personnel, for it appeared that "most former C&S employees now use the single name 'Delta' in referring to our company." Because the premerger routes and organization of Delta constituted the larger part of the merged company, the committee commented, "it would thus appear that the name of the dominant entity would be most logical. The single name 'Delta' has already been adopted by a large part of the public, and is already being used in referring to the merged company." In yet another move to unify the organization, the phasing out of the old Memphis base was completed, enhancing operational efficiency.[11]

Woolman also had reason to be happy about the figures for the fiscal year that ended on June 30, 1955. Unlike the returns for the previous twelve months, the reported net income of $2,166,025 was attributable only in a minor way to the sale of aircraft. The addition of more DC-7s and the inauguration of daylight coach service in December 1954 had brightened the financial picture, but it was "less impressive," the *Delta Digest* had candidly admitted, when one realized that this amounted to a net return of only 3.2 percent of gross revenues. Emulating a strategy followed by many other corporations, the board of directors adopted an "incentive compensation plan" at a meeting held on October 19, 1955. Officers and employees bearing executive responsibility and prime accountability would receive a bonus depending upon the extent to which the company's operating profits exceeded 5 percent of operating expenses, with a maximum bonus the equivalent of four months' salary.[12]

Such measures, however, could do little to improve Delta's earnings unless the company could find some way to overcome one of the basic problems that had made the acquisition of C&S so necessary and still persisted despite the recent merger: the company needed more long hauls to major cities to make up for the heavy expenses of serving so many smaller communities on relatively unprofitable short hops. As Woolman was so fond of pointing out, the firm needed access to "Main Street America"—the business, financial, and government centers of the Northeast. In short, it was imperative to break Eastern's monopoly on service between Atlanta and New York.

Delta's relationships with most other airlines were amicable. Woolman enjoyed a pleasant association with W. F. Patterson, president of United, with whom he shared an occasional fishing trip. He also felt a great deal in common with Continental's flamboyant and aggressive chief executive, Robert F. Six, who like himself had built a successful enterprise from humble beginnings and infused it with a family spirit similar to that which pervaded the Delta organization. Essentially, Woolman and Six were both mavericks who commanded respect because of their accomplishments, whatever their fellow airline executives may have felt about their individual styles. From time to time the two men discussed merger possibilities, but neither was willing to see the other's firm emerge as the surviving corporation and nothing came of the idea. In the case of both United and Continental, of course, good relations were facilitated to some extent by the fact that their route systems complemented that of Delta rather than competing with it. Likewise, Woolman usually got along well with American's C. R. Smith, with whom he shared a common patriarchal touch and a mutual interest in the interchange which the two lines maintained between the Southeast and the Pacific Coast. Smith kept track of developments within the Delta family and sent an occasional note to mark an occasion. Upon learning about Oliver's death, for example, he wrote to his widow saying that he had "long been an admirer of Travis Oliver for he was a man of vision for aviation in the days when men of courage were scarce." On another occasion he had praised Woolman warmly concerning Delta's recovery from its postmerger financial doldrums:

"That's a fine first quarter statement and I congratulate you on it. You have done a great job for Delta." [13]

With Eastern, however, it was a different story; company correspondence during the postwar era reflected the growing animosity between the forces arrayed under Rickenbacker and Woolman. In October 1954, for example, newly elected director Woodall Rogers notified Woolman that Rickenbacker, while speaking to a group of prominent businessmen and city officials in Dallas, had expressed Eastern's interest in serving Love Field; Rogers asked whether Delta should counter by declaring its willingness to schedule more flights into that facility. Woolman replied tersely that "the schedules we operate into and out of Dallas . . . seem to me to speak volumes, and this is not just a temporary situation." The boss did not react so defensively when he learned that Eastern might be concealing some of its earnings; he informed director Edward Gerry that he had told the CAB "very forcibly" about a rapid write-off policy on modern equipment that Eastern had adopted. At lower managerial levels the rivalry between the two firms was felt just as intensely. In December 1954 Laigh Parker reported to Woolman that Eastern had doctored the facts and "compared bananas with pears" in attempting to "lay some stress on EAL's DC-7s as being superior to those of ours and National's." Parker was concerned lest Eastern appear superior to Delta in any area. When he learned that Rickenbacker's line was thinking about putting tape-recorded music in its DC-7s, he advised Dolson that Delta should look into doing the same, "as we could 'spike their guns' on this one feature . . . if we could make it available on our DC-7s before they get theirs in service." [14]

Above all, however, Delta resented not being able to compete with Eastern for the highly profitable traffic between Atlanta and the metropolitan centers of the heavily industrialized and urbanized northeastern states. In October 1950 *Time* magazine carried a story telling how, after a meeting of airline executives in Washington, D.C., a scramble had ensued to get taxis. Woolman had jammed into the last space in the last cab in sight, and Rickenbacker had asked the Delta president if he might ride a short distance on Woolman's lap. Woolman replied, "Well, Eddie, I've been helping support you for years, so I might as well do it some more." His remark, the article explained, was a not-too-subtle reference to the fact that Delta had "long served as feeder . . . into Eastern Air Lines' lucrative routes from Florida to New York and New England." [15]

As Woolman and his colleagues never tired of pointing out, every other trunk line conducting an appreciable part of its business east of the Mississippi—a list that included American, Capital, Colonial, Eastern, National, Northeast, Northwest, TWA, and United—enjoyed access to the New York and Washington areas; only Delta lacked it. The stakes involved were indicated by the fact that at this time nearly 45 percent of all air travelers in the country began or ended their journeys in this immensely lucrative corridor. Furthermore, as Delta reminded the CAB, passengers living in New England, the Middle Atlantic states, the Midwest, and the Far West all had the advantage of competitive service from their areas to the nation's "Main Street," whereas, with only a few exceptions, those living in the South and Southwest did not:

The South and Southwest still—nearly 17 years after the establishment of the Board—are almost wholly dependent for modern air transport service to the Northeast upon the two separate monopolies of Eastern Air Lines and of American Airlines. These areas are still denied the benefits of effective competition enjoyed by other important areas of the Nation. . . . During the life of the Board the South and Southwest have been forging ahead in industrial and economic development. They are growing faster than other areas of the nation. Their progress is dramatic. Their dependence upon transportation ties to other areas is increasing. Their air traffic to and from the Northeast has doubled in less than ten years. Some of the heaviest domestic traffic flows are here. Widespread competitive air service authorizations have been granted in other areas where the traffic is lighter. Relief from monopoly is needed here.[16]

"Our network of Southern cities just cries for an outlet into Washington and New York," the company magazine declared late in the summer of 1953, reminding its readers that five years earlier Delta had lost out in efforts to win a route from Atlanta to New York, despite a favorable recommendation from a CAB examiner. The editorial in which the statement appeared was a response to the CAB's recent decision to receive applications for new routes between the Southwest and the Northeast. Like virtually every trunk line in the country, Delta had quickly submitted a sheaf of applications in the hope that they would be consolidated in the proceeding despite the fact that some fell outside the parameters the CAB had in mind. In addition to seeking an extension of its existing route between Fort Worth and Atlanta, which would then proceed through Charlotte, Washington, Baltimore, and Philadelphia to New York, the company wanted to close gaps in its system between Birmingham and

Memphis and Miami and Havana; to open a giant air artery from San Antonio to New Orleans by way of Houston, continuing to Detroit through Nashville and Cincinnati; and to fly from Chicago to Minneapolis–St. Paul.[17]

Because of the importance of this case and the many carriers involved, it is not surprising that preliminary maneuvers took a long time and that hearings before the CAB did not begin until September 8, 1954. By that point the issues had been fixed, and some of the secondary objectives that Woolman and his advisers had hoped to achieve had been set aside. Still very much alive, however, was the question of whether Delta could obtain the coveted route from Atlanta to New York, and the company responded by mounting an unprecedented effort to win this goal. "Months of careful planning and hard work have gone into the preparation of Delta's exhibits," the employee magazine pointed out; they included more than three hundred pages of documentation. Nine other scheduled and two nonscheduled carriers had also entered exhibits, and more than eighty state and local governmental agencies and business groups were intervening. In addition to the inevitable opposition of Eastern, which naturally wanted to preserve its long-standing monopoly of traffic between Atlanta and New York, Delta also faced stiff competition from both Braniff and Capital. The former, Delta lawyers argued, was essentially a southwestern operator and could not hope to provide the connecting service to the multitude of southern cities that their own firm could offer; Capital, on the other hand, was primarily an east–west carrier and had failed dismally to develop the potential of its existing north–south routes, some of which had been abandoned entirely. Also, the lawyers declared, Delta had amply proved its ability to compete with such giants as Eastern and American and possessed more modern equipment than either Braniff or Capital. Granting the route to Delta would permit better use of existing facilities and personnel, cut costs, and promote the financial stability of the firm as it continued to liquidate the debentures resulting from the recent merger.[18]

Above all, Woolman's attorneys argued that it was high time to provide competition for Eastern's existing services north of Atlanta. A parade of witnesses appeared before the examiners to complain about the provisions made for the traveling public by Rickenbacker's line. Mayor William B. Hartsfield of Atlanta pointed out that his city had only three nonstop flights a day to New York, compared to six to Chicago. Eastern, he stated diplomatically, was a good airline, but it was not good for Atlanta to have all its eggs in one basket, as far as services to New York were concerned. What would happen, for example, if Eastern were to be shut down by a strike? An executive representing Rich's Department Store testified that company policy forbade more than ten of its officers to travel on any one flight. Because it was not unusual for forty such officers to go to New York in a single weekend, some were forced to go by train because there were insufficient nonstop flights at appropriate times. He also complained about a "lack of fast and accurate information by telephone or at the Eastern ticket counters" and pointed out that Eastern did not notify passengers about delays or cancellations. Finally, he declared, Eastern's food was not up to par, and competition would help to raise standards in this respect.

A high official of the Genuine Parts Company testified that eight of his executives made five or six round trips between Atlanta and New York a year and that he considered Eastern's existing service "very inadequate." On his own preceding seven trips he had been put on "stand-by" four times. On one occasion, when he and his wife had flown into New York from London, they had missed an Eastern flight and had been informed that they could not obtain a nonstop reservation for two days. In addition, one of the company's employees had barely made it to his mother's funeral on time because accommodations were not available on Eastern.

Maurer, reporting to Woolman about all this testimony, expressed particular pleasure at the effectiveness of Robert Snodgrass, president of an automobile-finance company with fifteen branches in the South. "He gave one or two personal examples of poor experiences at the hands of Eastern and was not broken down in any degree on cross examination," Maurer stated. Another witness, Arthur Harris of the Atlanta Paper Company, which had fifteen or twenty employees "traveling constantly by air," was "quite vitriolic about the inadequacies of Eastern's services," so much so that one of Rickenbacker's lawyers charged that he was actually a Delta stockholder. Harris "emphatically denied" the claim.[19]

Altogether, nearly a hundred people, representing forty cities, appeared on behalf of the company over a three-week period in the autumn of 1954. In a letter to Woolman in November, E. V. Moore expressed a firm belief that "this is the best prepared case, and in the main best presented case that Delta has ever had before the Civil Aeronautics Board." On the other hand, Moore warned, the company had presented a good case in 1948 and had lost, despite a favor-

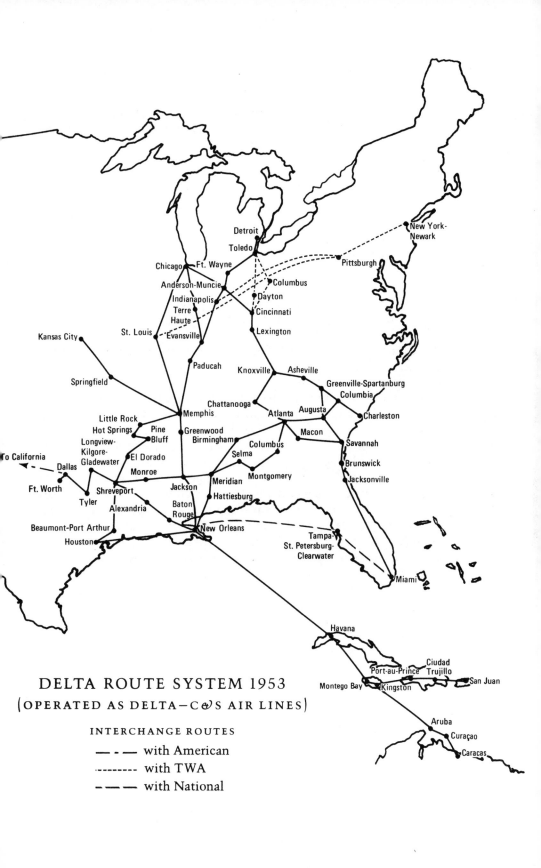

DELTA ROUTE SYSTEM 1953
(OPERATED AS DELTA—C&S AIR LINES)

INTERCHANGE ROUTES
— · — with American
·········· with TWA
— — — with National

able examiner's report. "In the present instance I think beyond a doubt that the Examiner will recommend the extension of Route 24 from Atlanta to New York," Moore confided, adding that "the major problem, it seems to me, will be to see that we don't lose the decision this time."[20]

Although he was mistaken about the precise sequence of events, Moore's cautionary mood turned out to be justified. The hearings dragged on until December 15, followed by the preparation of legal briefs for submission to the examiner. Because of the sheer volume of the material to be digested, four months were allotted, and a deadline of April 15, 1955, was imposed. Aside from the research and writing required of the company's legal staff, these four months produced a flurry of other activities. A related case was also in progress: Delta and other carriers, including Northeast, were fighting for a route from Miami to Boston. Perhaps fearing that its still-pending merger agreement with Delta would prejudice its chances of victory, Northeast gave the required thirty-day notice to be released from the pact that Woolman and Gardner had negotiated in 1950, and in January the CAB was formally notified of this cancellation. During the same month Oklahoman Ross Rizley was appointed to a vacant seat on the CAB and, after Senate confirmation, became chairman. While the Delta brief supporting the company's application for the route from Atlanta to New York was being prepared, exhibits were also being gathered for presentation in the Miami-to-Boston case. The latter were filed April 8, and hearings were to begin in June. As the bureaucratic process took its leisurely course, company attorney D. Franklin Kell tried to reassure employees that there was no cause for worry, that Delta would soon break Eastern's stranglehold on the route to New York. "Surely the Civil Aeronautics Board will not ignore the dynamic growth that has taken place in the southern tier of states during the past decade and allow this monopolistic air transport situation to continue to exist," he predicted.[21]

Matters did not proceed as smoothly as Kell hoped, however. The company's brief was filed in April, along with those of other parties active in the Southwest–Northeast case. Among the documents submitted to federal officials was the brief of the CAB's own bureau counsel, which contained both good and bad news for Delta. The good news was that a route to New York had been recommended; the bad news was that the artery was to run from San Antonio to New York by way of Austin, Houston, Alexandria, Shreveport, Monroe, Memphis, Nashville, Knoxville, and Washington, with various restrictions designed to protect other carriers serving some of the same points. If this proposal were upheld, the company's hopes of being able to provide service from Fort Worth and Dallas to New York by way of Atlanta and Washington would be dashed. "We were extremely pleased to have a favorable recommendation from the Bureau Counsel, inasmuch as it is obvious therefrom that he recognizes the public need for an extension of our system into the Washington–New York area," Kell stated in his monthly column in the company magazine. "However, we believe the Examiner will determine, on the basis of the evidence we introduced, that the route recommended by the Bureau Counsel should be authorized in such form as to permit us to provide, in addition to a service through Memphis and Nashville, direct services from Atlanta and all of our other Route 24 cities west thereof, to and from the Washington–New York area." [22]

Kell was correct that the examiner's report would be forthcoming in "three or four months": it was issued in late August, by CAB official William B. Madden, but it was a bitter disappointment. Eastern was recommended for two routes between Dallas–Fort Worth and New York; one was to proceed through Memphis, Nashville, and Pittsburgh, the other through Memphis, Nashville, Knoxville, and Richmond. American was to receive a route between Nashville and Houston, which would enable it to compete with Eastern all the way between Houston and Washington and New York. Most galling to Woolman and his associates, however, was the recommendation involving Capital, which was to receive extensions that would permit it to operate a route leading from New Orleans to New York by way of Mobile, Birmingham, Atlanta, Charlotte, Washington, and other cities. Delta was to be shut out completely. [23]

Although acknowledging that the report was a "keen disappointment," the Delta management refused to despair, pointing out that the CAB followed the counsel of its examiners in only about 60 percent of all route cases. Company attorneys filed exceptions to the examiner's recommendations early in September and prepared briefs to be presented to the board later that month. Meanwhile, Woolman and his staff organized a massive campaign to bring public pressure to bear upon the CAB. They emphasized, for example, that implementation of Madden's plan would leave twelve rapidly growing industrial metropolitan areas in Texas, Louisiana, Arkansas, Mississippi, and Alabama without any direct service to Washington or New York and six other important regional centers without competitive service. Three state capitals—Baton Rouge, Montgomery, and Little Rock—would remain dependent upon one airline for accommodations to Washington, whereas Austin and Jackson would have no direct access to the heavily populated Northeast. Soon newspapers all across Dixie were bristling with editorials complaining about layovers and missed connections that would continue to plague southern businessmen and political leaders unless Delta's application were approved. Should Woolman's forces lose their fight, the Meridian *Star* averred, "We shall see airline restrictions definitely harmful to our growth, as have been those unfair freight rates which for a quarter of a century throttled back . . . our section of the nation." A leading Shreveport daily pointed out that the new routes for American and Eastern bypassed a vast strip of the southern heartland: "Under these recommendations Shreveport and this territory of 29 major cities and 26,000,000 people would be left in the position of a hole in a doughnut so far as one-line service to and from the major business and air traffic arteries of the East are concerned." The Jackson *State-Times*, seeing a threat to the Mississippi capital's "mercurial growth," expressed a common sentiment in an editorial that concluded, "we implore the CAB to reject the examiner's recommendation."[24]

The CAB was also deluged with letters from irate southern businessmen, many of whom sent carbon copies to Woolman. Typical was one from a frequent air traveler named James P. Furniss; it recited a long list of past inconveniences and ended with a ringing vote of no confidence in Capital's ability to render effective competition to Eastern's service north of Atlanta. In addition to a blind copy, which he sent to Woolman, Furniss mailed carbons to Georgia senators Walter F. George and Richard B. Russell, as well as Congressman James C. Davis. "Mr. Woolman—thought this might add another coal to the fire," he stated in an appended handwritten note. Another advocate of the Delta cause, R. B. Wilby of Atlanta, invoked deeply cherished traditions of free enterprise in a letter to the CAB. Wilby branded the examiner's recommendations as "startling" and declared:

If I understand the purpose of CAB it is not to reverse the normal American system by greatly limiting competition, but rather to encourage it. If there were no CAB it is self-evident that Delta and Eastern would be competing between Atlanta and New York. Certainly you should have more sound reasons than appear upon the surface of it thus to interfere with the normal natural working of a competitive marketing system which is supposed to be the very backbone of the American industrial system.[25]

By late September it appeared that Delta's campaign was showing results. "I just returned from Washington a few days ago and understand that these letters are making a real impression on the Powers That Be," Woolman informed N. F. Fiske of Augusta, Georgia, president of the Fine Products Corporation, who had written to Rizley urging that the CAB disregard Madden's report. Added to the weight of business pressure and editorial opinion was the solid support of prominent political leaders. From one end of the Deep South to the other, mayors, congressmen, and senators communicated to CAB officials their dissatisfaction with the examiner's recommendations; typical was a letter to Rizley from powerful Louisiana representative Hale Boggs, pointing out that the controversial report ignored the needs of Shreveport, Monroe, Alexandria, Lafayette, and Baton Rouge, all of which would have direct connections to Washington if Delta's application were approved. Equally helpful was Mississippi's veteran senator, John Stennis, who pressed the claims of Jackson and Meridian for direct service to the Northeast.[26]

Throughout the mass of testimonials on Delta's behalf that descended upon the CAB, the note of regional identification and pride was strong. Never had affection for Delta, the "Airline of the South," been more apparent or more instrumental in advancing the company's fortunes. In the words of an editorial in the Selma Times-Journal, Delta was "born and bred in the South" and "best knows the South's needs." Capital, by contrast, was looked upon as something of an interloper, owned and operated by faraway interests.[27]

When members of the CAB met on October 12 for three days of oral arguments before rendering a final decision in the Southwest–Northeast case, they were confronted with an array of business and political leaders who had come to testify on behalf of Woolman's company. There was no overlooking the degree to which Dixie stood behind Delta. Leading off the parade of witnesses for the firm was Senator Russell Long of Louisiana; he was followed by Georgia Congressman James C. Davis and Mayor William B. Hartsfield of Atlanta, who declared forcibly that Delta could provide the "effective competition" needed to improve his city's air services to New York. Delta's attorneys demonstrated that the company's proposals would provide better connections to the Northeast for at least twenty-six cities across the South, including twelve that currently lacked any direct access to Washington and New York. Public interest in the proceedings was reflected in unprecedented press coverage and the presence of overflow crowds throughout.[28]

Telegrams and letters continued to pour into Washington as the CAB retired to make its long-awaited decision. "I think we made a splendid showing for the record and, certainly, have had marvelous support from the entire area we serve," Woolman wrote shortly afterward to John A. McDorman, district manager for Kaiser Aluminum in Atlanta. All that could be done now was to "await the decision of those five good men which, according to rumor, should be forthcoming by the first of December. . . . In the meantime, keep your fingers crossed."[29]

The decision came even earlier than Woolman had hoped and fully demonstrated the effectiveness of Delta's intensive drive: the CAB granted the company 1,075 miles of new routes, including the coveted artery from Atlanta to New York by way of Charlotte, Washington, Baltimore, and Philadelphia. Although Eastern in particular received far less than the examiner's report had recommended—it gained only access from Atlanta to Pittsburgh and lost its monopoly on traffic between Atlanta and New York—the CAB followed what might best be described as a strategy of "something for everybody." Capital, for example, received an extension of its existing route 51, which enabled it to operate between New Orleans and New York on a line duplicating much of Delta's new route. Similarly, Braniff received a plum that the examiner had earmarked for Eastern, winning certification from Dallas–Fort Worth to New York by way of such cities as Memphis, Nashville, and Washington. American won a route from Houston to Pittsburgh and also gained entry into Columbus, Ohio. TWA received access to Tulsa and Oklahoma City, and even tiny Ozark Airlines obtained a three-year certification to serve Paducah, Kentucky, another city that Eastern had wanted to add to its sprawling system.[30]

This omnibus package was not put together without some soul-searching among CAB members, two of whom (Harmar Denny and Chan Gurney) favored awarding Delta the route between Atlanta and New York but filed a dissent from the decision on Capital, charging that it represented "uneconomic competition contrary to the public interest." Delta, however, had every reason to be jubilant about a victory that crowned more than a decade of striving. Sweetening the outcome even more was the CAB's decision to allow Delta to fly directly from New Orleans to Houston, thus permitting it to offer through service to New York from both Houston and Dallas–Fort Worth. From near and far, congratulatory messages flowed into the corporate headquarters. "Justice has triumphed," wired S. Olive Young, an account executive at Atlanta radio station WAGA; "Am confident Delta will continue to soar to new heights." "Congratulations on breaking the New York barrier," said a telegram from an admirer in New York; "Couldn't have happened to a nicer and more deserving guy." Perhaps most expressive of all was a message from Mary Ann Leatherwood, the stewardess supervisor at Delta's Miami base: "We have waited years for our run to New York—We made it—Just a word to tell you that the Miami stewardesses are 100 percent behind you—Our jubilance cannot be transmitted."[31]

As Woolman said in telegrams to various friends and associates, Delta had special reason to celebrate Thanksgiving Day 1955. At one stroke the company had gained access to four major northeastern cities, representing one fifth of the nation's retail sales and manufacturing activity and one third of its wholesale sales, bank deposits, and postal receipts. Because of this single route acquisition the Delta organization stood to grow by at least 20 percent. The ultimate impact of the victory was incalculable. Soon a multitude of plans to inaugurate Golden Crown service to the Northeast were underway, and the company magazine was full of articles describing the manifold attractions of the new destinations. Yet such was the pace of change that, amid all this activity, the airline stood on the verge of an equally significant watershed. The same issue of the *Delta Digest* that described the maiden flights to Washington, Baltimore, Philadelphia, and New York also notified employees that the company had placed a $28.5 million order for a fleet of six Douglas DC-8 transports. For Delta, the breaking of the "New York barrier" was also a signal that the jet era was about to begin.[32]

CHAPTER 15

Into the Jet Era

C RUCIAL though it was, Delta's struggle to gain access to the
metropolitan centers of the Middle Atlantic states was not
the only matter of critical importance facing the company in
the mid-1950s, and its successful resolution coincided with the
reaching of an important decision in the never-ending process of
keeping up with technological change. For the American commercial aviation industry, the long-awaited jet era was about to dawn;
for Delta, as for other airlines, preparations for it would dominate
the rest of the decade.

Continuing a long-established practice, Delta inaugurated its
newly authorized service into and out of the Washington–New
York corridor in a festive mood. In Atlanta, on February 1, 1956,
Mrs. Helen Woolman christened a DC-6 headed for the Northeast
with a giant bottle of Coca-Cola; in New Orleans on the same day,
Mrs. Chep Morrison, wife of Mayor Delesseps Morrison, smashed a
container of Mississippi River water on one of the propellers of a
northbound Golden Crown DC-7 while a jazz band played in the
background. Meanwhile, in New York City, opera star James Melton provided music of a different sort at ceremonies marking the
initial southbound flight of a Delta airliner. Later that same day, in
Washington, Coca-Cola splashed again, as Leoma Naughton, Miss
Press Photographer of 1956, broke a bottle over the ship's fuselage
while Melton and Woolman looked on.[1]

Operating on the new skyways created an immediate need for additional aircraft. Early in 1956 Delta ordered five Convair 440 Metro-
liners, representing an improved version of the manufacturer's
dependable CV-340, but these planes, along with ten more DC-7s,
would not begin arriving until summer. Delta thus had no alternative but to look around for used planes, ironic considering that, having already disposed of all the L-649 Constellations acquired in the
C&S merger, it found itself obliged to purchase from Pan American
four relatively antiquated craft belonging to the earlier L-049 series.
Maurer pointed out to Woolman that the contract under which

three of the L-649s had been leased to Pacific Northern Airlines
(PNA) contained a cancellation clause permitting their recall, but
Woolman vetoed the idea; he had given verbal assurance to the president of the Alaskan firm that such action would not be taken. On
the basis of this promise PNA had, in turn, sold its earlier planes,
and the line would thus face ruin if Delta recalled the Connies.
Woolman insisted that his word was his bond, and that was that.
However creditable to Woolman's honor, the decision was a costly
one, for the obsolescent L-049s required extensive overhauling to
make them even marginally competitive with newer models, and
they ultimately proved difficult to dispose of once they were no
longer needed.[2]

Mere mention of the L-049s still caused some Delta executives to
wince more than two decades later, but veteran engineer Arthur
Ford pointed out that the episode had been beneficial in that it had
alerted management not to move too hastily in a similar matter.
Shortly after the outmoded Constellations were acquired, it became
clear that Delta's cargo operations had outgrown the C-47s used for
that type of business. Because no new freighters were available, the
best alternative was the Curtiss C-46, another transport of World
War II vintage. In Miami the company located five such ships, which
had come from an aviation graveyard near Calcutta, India, but Ford
convinced Dolson that buying them would create a problem similar
to that of the L-049s; he received permission to conduct a search of
his own. His quest led ultimately to Taiwan, where Civil Air Transport (CAT), a cargo carrier originally founded by such notables as
Claire Chennault, was trying to sell five C-46s that were in much
better condition than the planes in Miami. Although flying these
planes across the Pacific Ocean required temporary installation of
extra fuel and oil tanks, contract pilots ultimately did ferry them all
the way to Miami, where a series of modifications were performed
to bring them up to the same standard of reliability required of the
company's passenger ships. This purchase was a highly successful
venture, in that the cost of the C-46s amounted to only about
$200,000 each and the planes performed dependably for a number of
years.[3]

Fleet modification is a never-ending process in the airline industry, and Delta spent nearly $3.5 million in 1956 and 1957, installing
such improvements as weather-avoidance radar systems in its
planes, most of which were soon sporting the characteristic black
plastic nose that housed the scanning mechanism. Delta also began

to update its seven DC-6s, once the company's pride but increasingly used only for relatively short hops or Flying Scot coach runs. The continued utility of these planes was proved when the company leased five additional DC-6s toward the end of the 1950s, but luxury travel had become identified with the newer Golden Crown DC-7s.[4]

All these developments were, however, overshadowed by the impending advent of the jet era. During the 1930s, while Delta was plying its trans-southern route with Stinson trimotors and Lockheed Electras, engineers in Great Britain and Germany had pushed ahead with the development of experimental planes powered by gas turbines, in which the combustion of fuel mixed with hot compressed air caused rotor blades to revolve. Because the air was expelled from the rear of the engine at a much higher velocity than it was taken in, propulsive thrust was produced. By 1941 Allis-Chalmers, General Electric, and Westinghouse had begun work on similar power plants in the United States. Relatively few jet aircraft saw combat during World War II, but by the end of that conflict the essential groundwork had been laid for developments that would revolutionize aviation.[5]

During the late 1940s and early 1950s, larger and more powerful jet engines were developed for military use by the United States, Great Britain, and the Soviet Union. Among them were the Pratt and Whitney J-57, which powered the Boeing B-52 bomber, and the General Electric J-79, first used in the Lockheed F-104 fighter; both engines were to figure in Delta's future. Work also progressed on airframe modifications to facilitate flight at the greater speeds permitted by jet propulsion: the swept-back wing, underslung engine pods, leading-edge flaps, and other innovations first developed in Germany and eagerly seized upon by the victorious powers after the war.

Despite experience with these developments, the prospects for applying jet technology to commercial aviation were still uncertain. The advantages of being able to whisk passengers from city to city at speeds approaching that of sound had to be weighed against a number of potential drawbacks. Jet engines, for example, use more fuel than their piston-driven counterparts, and planes equipped with them require longer runways. Because of the continual use to which commercial airliners are subjected, standards of safety, reliability, and frequent maintenance require careful scrutiny. It was correctly anticipated that jet transports would cost much more than the most advanced piston-driven types, whereas outlays for newly acquired

Editor Wayne Parrish *(front)* poses on the steps of a C&S Constellation with Delta's C. E. Woolman and C&S's Sidney Stewart during Latin American tour in 1952.

Robert Bolander (*standing*), C&S vice-president and general counsel, poses with Al Earling (*left*) and R. S. Maurer, 1946. Bolander later joined Delta as Woolman's special assistant.

C&S officials in the early 1950s. *Seated:* R. S. Maurer, secretary and general counsel; W. T. Arthur, vice president–operations; Sidney A. Stewart, president; Junius H. Cooper, vice president–finance. *Standing:* T. M. Miller, general traffic and sales manager; W. T. Beebe, personnel director.

An important milestone in C&S history was the purchase of new 300-mile-per hour Constellation L-649s in 1950.

Convair 340 operated by Delta–C&S after the 1953 merger.

Merger Day finds Delta–C&S buttons being pinned on C. E. Woolman by Bettye
Williams of C&S and on Carleton Putnam by Mary Edmonds of Delta.

Merger Day, May 1, 1953, saw signs like this in Delta and C&S cities.

Board of Directors meeting in 1955. *Seated, left to right:* Laigh Parker, C. H. McHenry, C. E. Woolman, Woodall Rodgers, Carleton Putnam, R. W. Courts, Winship Nunnally. *Standing:* R. S. Maurer, D. Y. Smith, E. H. Gerry, C. H. Dolson, R. W. Freeman, R. J. Reynolds, J. R. Longmire.

fleets of DC-7s and Super Constellations would have to be written off with unaccustomed haste should commercial jet models burst suddenly upon the scene. Airline executives wondered whether the first generation of commercial jet planes could come close to equaling the efficiency of the best postwar piston craft, which performed safely and economically at costs that were highly predictable. Meanwhile, aircraft manufacturers pondered the risks of introducing ships that departed significantly from time-tested traditional designs. Breaking into the market with an unsuccessful plane that had cost many millions of dollars to develop could bring even such well-established firms as Boeing and Douglas close to ruin.[6]

By the early 1950s, however, the British aviation industry was forcing the hands of nervous American executives. Using a relatively small jet engine created during the war, the de Havilland manufacturing company decided to produce a thirty-six-seat airliner known as Comet I; BOAC bought the plane and inaugurated the first jet passenger service anywhere in the world in May 1952. An enlarged version, the forty-eight-seat Comet II, was introduced the following year, and a seventy-six-seat model, to be known as Comet III, was planned for delivery in 1956. Convinced of the plane's promise, Pan American ordered three and took an option on seven more. Eddie Rickenbacker also announced that he was thinking of acquiring the plane for Eastern. Suddenly the jet age in commercial aviation had begun—and American manufacturers were still waiting at the starting gate.

The dramatic British effort to seize supremacy in jet aviation was doomed to disaster, for in 1953 and 1954 Comet airliners were involved in a series of fatal crashes caused by cracks in the fuselage brought on by metal fatigue after repeated pressurization. As a result, the plane was abruptly withdrawn from service, and the much-heralded Comet III was never put into commercial production.[7] American manufacturers, however, had no way of anticipating these events, and in 1953 they were already scrambling for positions in what threatened to be a fierce struggle to retain the dominance that the United States had long enjoyed, both domestically and internationally, in the sale of commercial aircraft.

The first American airframe manufacturer to move decisively in response to the British threat was Boeing, which designed the prototype of a jet-propelled ship that could be used either as a military tanker or as a commercial transport. The tanker model, known as the KC-135, was developed first; Pan American ordered six of the passenger variety late in 1955. By that time Boeing had learned about the initial specifications of the rival jetliner that Douglas was preparing; consequently it decided to enlarge its own prototype, which would require the use of entirely different tooling from that employed in building the tanker fuselage. Not until the end of 1957, therefore, did the Boeing 707, the first American jet transport, take to the air. Deliveries to Pan American began the following August.[8]

Boeing's decision to develop a jetliner had forced Douglas, Delta's long-established supplier, to make a difficult decision of its own. Unlike Boeing, which had been mainly a builder of military planes and which had done poorly with its only entry into the postwar commercial market, the model 377 Stratocruiser, Douglas had long dominated the passenger field with a spectacular series of piston-driven ships, from the DC-2 through the DC-7. In 1954, for example, Douglas transports flew 81 million of the 164 million passenger miles flown each day by the world's regularly scheduled airlines. As historian John B. Rae has observed, it was "only natural that Douglas should have wanted to keep things as they were as long as possible before launching into the expensive and technically uncertain field of jet airliners." But, when American Airlines, long a lucrative client of Douglas, ordered thirty Boeing 707s in 1955, executives in Santa Monica had no alternative but to act. In the words of Donald Douglas, "We had to go into the building of the DC-8 . . . or else give up building airplanes." Although the firm had no chance of putting a jet transport into the air as quickly as Boeing, it could aspire to create a superior one and could hope that the splendid reputation of its previous models would persuade established customers, including Delta, to wait for its new jet, rather than to buy the Boeing 707. Plans for the DC-8, to be powered by four Pratt and Whitney engines modeled upon the military J-57, were announced in June 1955.[9]

Lockheed exercised still another option that was open to manufacturers and airlines in that transitional era: the turboprop engine using both a propeller and a gas turbine, which drove the propeller through a set of reduction gears. Such an engine is considerably lighter than a piston engine of equal power, and it is capable of much greater speed, though not as much as a jet power plant. On the other hand, the turboprop engine is an extremely complex piece of machinery requiring significant modifications in propeller design and posing potential maintenance problems. Still, it held the promise of efficient performance on mid-range flights at speeds above four hundred miles an hour, and both Douglas and Lockheed contemplated reequipping DC-6s, DC-7s, and Super Constellations with it.

Just as they had taken the lead in developing jet transports, the British led the way in the turboprop field, with the Vickers Viscount, a four-engine craft put into commercial service in 1953; it was ordered in large quantities by Capital Airlines. Among American manufacturers of aircraft engines, the Allison division of General Motors showed most interest in developing a turboprop engine for commercial use to compete with the Rolls Royce Dart, which powered the Viscount. Lockheed, doubting that it would be able to prevail against both Boeing and Douglas in a competition involving jet airliners, pinned its hopes on developing an acceptable turboprop craft. Beginning in 1954, its representatives submitted three designs to American Airlines, the first featuring British engines and the other two Allison power plants. Final plans for the resulting plane, a four-engine model known as the Lockheed L-188 Electra (not to be confused with the much smaller piston-driven Model 10 and Model 12 Electras of prewar vintage) were made public in 1955. American ordered thirty-five of the projected new craft and Eastern ordered forty.[10]

Eastern's decision to acquire the Electra made it imperative for Delta to bring itself abreast of technological change; otherwise it would face ruinous competition on some of its most important long-haul routes. Of the various alternatives available, one appears never to have been considered seriously; although Continental and Northeast eventually followed Capital's lead and ordered the Vickers Viscount, there is no evidence that Delta gave British turboprops more than a passing glance. Chief Pilot T. P. Ball, among others, opposed such a move:

For whatever it was worth, I certainly put in as much as I could against the Viscount, because of its foreign manufacture and the fact that I just didn't believe that it made a lot of sense to buy an airplane and an engine that we couldn't get parts for in this country and on which service information would be difficult. These objections were later overcome by Rolls-Royce and Vickers, but at the time that we were prospective customers they were very important factors.[11]

Woolman himself showed little interest in the Viscount but leaned strongly toward the new Lockheed Electra. His overriding concern was the wait of nine months or more anticipated between Eastern's first deployment of Electras and the earliest date at which

Delta could hope to acquire jet aircraft. But there were other arguments in favor of the Electra as well. Many experts at that time believed that the jet engine would be decisively superior to the turboprop variety only on extremely long flights and that the turboprop would be more efficient and economical on route systems like Delta's own, which linked major population centers only 500 to 800 miles apart. That the initial cost of a turboprop plane was appreciably less than that of the jetliners Boeing and Douglas were building—the Electra, for example, cost $1.8 million, compared to at least $4.5 million for the DC-8—strengthened such arguments. Other than the ill-fated Comet, no jetliner had yet entered regularly scheduled service on any of the world's airlines, whereas by the summer of 1955 turboprops had been in commercial operation for more than two years. When such giant enterprises as American and Eastern were placing large orders for the Electra and Capital was swinging solidly behind the Viscount, the temptation to climb aboard the turboprop bandwagon was readily understandable.[12]

Within the Delta organization, however, there was a good deal of skepticism about turboprop engines in general and the Lockheed Electra in particular. In the view of veteran engineer John Nycum, for example, the turboprop had "all of the complexities of the propeller aircraft *plus* the new and untried jet engine—with its own development problems." Although it was true that jet engines had not been tested thoroughly under commercial conditions, such power plants as the J-57 and J-79 had performed well in military service. Nycum feared that, as soon as jet aircraft appeared on commercial airways, their superior speed and freedom from propeller vibration would make turboprop planes obsolete; under the circumstances, the Electra was likely to be a "short-lived airplane." Ball was equally emphatic in opposing the Electra, whose Allison engine he later described as "connected to a fantastically complicated gear box and then to a massive and equally complicated four-bladed propeller." He recalled:

The turbo-prop Electra was never an airplane in which I had the slightest interest. I knew that it was a very nice flying machine from a pilot's point of view, but I just could not see buying a turbo-jet engine, connecting that engine to one of the most complicated gear boxes that the world had ever seen in order to drive a propeller which itself was so complicated mechanically and electrically that it took hours of classroom study to understand. So it seemed to me that a cleaner, clearer decision would be to pass up the geared turbo-prop engine airplane and go straight to a pure turbo-jet which at this particular time would be either the Boeing 707 or the Douglas DC-8.[13]

The final decision, however, was not for Ball or Nycum to make; it belonged to Woolman, who continued to favor the Electra as the quickest and most economical means of countering the competitive edge that Eastern would gain by introducing the same airliner. In the fall of 1955 a committee consisting of Woolman, Dolson, Cole, Ball, and Nycum visited Boeing, Douglas, and Lockheed to take a good look at what each manufacturer had to offer.[14] Snow was already falling as the group arrived in Seattle to test-fly the Boeing prototype, which, with various modifications, ultimately became the 707 jetliner. "We were extremely impressed," Ball stated later. "The performance of the machine was just simply fantastic. . . . In addition, its maneuverability and excellent approach and landing characteristics were also outstanding."

Various considerations, however, led the committee to be wary. Delta had never done business with Boeing and was skeptical about the company's postwar record in producing passenger planes. In the years ahead Boeing would provide excellent service to commercial carriers, but in 1955 its reputation was chiefly military, and Woolman feared that this orientation would impair its responsiveness to civilian customers. In addition, the Boeing pilot at the controls of the prototype was unwilling to put the plane through certain basic maneuvers—steep turns, stalls, and recoveries—to which Delta had subjected previous ships it was considering for purchase. Although the 707 ultimately proved to be an excellent ship, Boeing engineers were not yet completely sure about its aerodynamic characteristics. Finally, there was a matter that particularly bothered Todd Cole, who as Delta's comptroller was already deeply concerned about the cost of jet operations. On the instrument board of the prototype was a "Veeder counter," which, like a taxicab meter, clicked incessantly, recording the fuel being consumed during the flight. "As this thing ran constantly and the numbers rotated at a very high rate of speed, it really impressed Todd when he realized that he was actually seeing the kerosene going through those engines and at that fantastic rate," Ball recalled later. "He was very impressed, but not favorably, I'm sure."

The itinerary led next to Burbank, California, where Lockheed sales representatives made what Nycum later summed up as an "effective presentation" of the merits of the forthcoming Electra turbo-prop. But Lockheed was deeply committed to producing planes for American and Eastern under a contract that gave it little latitude to meet the needs of other potential customers. It therefore offered Delta only three Electras, the first of which would arrive well after Eastern had put the plane into service. Woolman had hoped to order at least ten of the turboprops and was angered by the Lockheed proposal, whereas Nycum and Ball were quietly elated. Delta was not the only carrier to find Lockheed so heavily committed to Eastern and American that it could not promise early delivery of any considerable number of Electras to other airlines; National had a similar experience. In any event, the visit to Burbank was distinctly disappointing.[15]

So the committee continued on to the familiar surroundings of Santa Monica to consult with Douglas engineers and executives, whom they knew and trusted from long years of experience. By this time Pan American and United had committed themselves to the DC-8, but Pan Am, with its transoceanic routes, required planes equipped with advanced Pratt and Whitney JT-4 (military J-75) engines, which would not be available for delivery as soon as the smaller JT-3 (the commercial counterpart of the military J-57). Along with United, Delta could use the JT-3 and would therefore be able to obtain early delivery dates. Furthermore, because of Delta's status as a long-established customer and the warm relations between the two companies, Douglas was willing to do its best to meet Woolman's needs.

It is not surprising, therefore, that after the committee returned to Atlanta things moved in favor of Douglas, though not without anxiety about the lead that Eastern was likely to gain by putting its Electras in the air before the DC-8s would arrive. At a meeting of the board of directors on January 27, 1956, Parker, Dolson, and Cole reported on the "traffic, competitive, operational, and economic aspects of the turbine-powered aircraft being offered by Douglas, Boeing, and Lockheed." After a luncheon break and "extended discussion" of the issues involved, a resolution was moved by Woolman and accepted by the board: management was authorized to purchase a maximum of eight DC-8s and "such number of Lockheed Electra aircraft (between zero and fifteen) as its judgment dictates." The door was still ajar should something happen to improve the prospects for quicker and larger deliveries from Lockheed, but it was becoming increasingly likely that Delta would move directly into the jet age and bypass turboprops completely. On February 14, 1956, Delta announced the order of six DC-8s, with delivery to begin in June 1959. The authorization to purchase the Electras soon became a dead letter.[16]

Although they had no way of knowing it at the time, Delta's worried leaders were pursuing a fortunate course. A prototype of the Lockheed Electra flew for the first time in December 1957. The manufacturing and certification process took two years, and on January 12, 1959, Eastern put the new ship into service on its run from New York to Miami. After less than a month, however, one of American's new Electras crashed, and during the next year both Braniff and Northwest experienced fatal accidents with the plane. Federal investigations revealed deficiencies in the wing and engine installation, and Lockheed was forced to undertake a modification program costing approximately $25 million. Meanwhile, airlines using Electras were allowed to operate them only at greatly reduced speeds—ultimately only 295 miles an hour, instead of the normal cruising speed of 400 miles—which severely hampered their ability to compete with older piston-driven craft. As one of the principal airlines involved in the development and use of the Electra, Eastern suffered greatly from this turn of events. Even when they operated satisfactorily, turboprop planes could not compete in the public eye with the principal assets of jet aircraft—speed and the comparatively smooth ride that resulted from the absence of propeller vibration and operation at high altitudes. By the early 1960s it was already clear that the Electra and the Viscount were obsolescent.[17]

This ultimate vindication of Delta's decision was, however, still in the future when, in early 1956, the company prepared for the arrival of the DC-8s. Gearing up for jet operations posed formidable problems for all airlines, as Delta officials clearly recognized before committing themselves to this challenging and uncertain course of action. On December 2, 1955, Arthur Ford and other company engineers had submitted to management a lengthy summary of the characteristics of the DC-8 that differed from aircraft previously used by the firm. They concluded with a sobering but accurate assessment:

The results of this very brief study indicate that the jet transport proposed herein is to be a new and radically different type of airplane, both from the standpoint of the power plant and the fundamental changes in the basic airplane systems. It is going to necessitate a great deal of educational footwork as a prerequisite for its introduction into airline service. All phases of the operation will be affected—engineering, maintenance, flight operation, ground handling, overhaul; all will have to earn their stripes from scratch.[18]

For the previous several years, Ford had been establishing a uniform system of methods and training procedures to replace the confusing patchwork that had evolved over the years before the C&S merger. As a result of his efforts, paperwork had been reduced substantially, a series of standard practice manuals had been published, and a centralized training school had been set up for the first time in company history. His work had laid the foundations for a massive instructional effort that was launched to prepare Delta employees for the jet age.[19]

Because of the need for a highly experienced person in California to oversee the planning and assembly of the DC-8s, Nycum was sent to the West Coast, and Ford took charge of the engineering department. Ford's successor as superintendent of methods and training was David C. Garrett, who would in time become Delta's president. A South Carolinian who had received a bachelor's degree in business from Furman University in 1942 and had served as a flight engineer with the United States Air Force in the Pacific Theater of Operations, he joined Delta in 1946 as a reservations clerk in the marketing division. Rising to manager of the company's downtown reservations office in Atlanta in 1951, he then enrolled in evening courses at Georgia Tech, pursuing a master's degree in industrial management. The next few years tested his determination and capacity for hard work as he successfully completed courses in basic engineering, financial analysis, and planning while pulling together the western half of Delta's marketing system after the merger with C&S in 1953; in order to keep up, he became an expert in speed reading. He received his degree in 1955 and was soon putting his training to use in the immense task of educational planning required if personnel throughout the company were to be ready for the arrival of the jets.[20]

Increasing the magnitude of Garrett's task was a decision by Delta management to introduce not one, but two, new jetliners. As prospects for acquiring the Lockheed Electra receded, Woolman pondered the possibility of acquiring a medium-sized jet plane for service on mid-range route segments while the DC-8 was used on long hauls. His desires coincided with the plans of Howard Hughes, who had belatedly recognized that TWA could not successfully pit Lockheed Super-Constellations against the Boeing 707s that Pan American was going to use on transoceanic runs. As always, Hughes was incapable of thinking small; after ordering more than thirty 707s from Boeing in 1955, he concluded that a new mid-range jet was desirable for TWA's domestic routes and turned to Convair to develop such an aircraft.

The resulting plane initially was designated the CV-600 Skylark but subsequently renamed the CV-880—according to Jack Zevely, Convair's sales manager, because of "the 880 meetings we had with Howard Hughes over its construction." As befitted an aviation pioneer known for setting world records, Hughes wanted the new ship to be the fastest commercial plane in the air, and it was designed for a top cruising speed in excess of 600 miles an hour. It was to be powered by four CJ-805 (military J-79) engines developed by General Electric, marking that company's debut in the commercial jet field after it had built more than 31,000 jet engines for military use. The plane would be capable of taking off and landing on 5,000-foot runways, making it possible to operate from every major airport in the country. Initial plans also called for a distinctive exterior with gold-tinted skin panels, because of which it was to be officially named the *Golden Arrow*. It was an exciting ship to contemplate, and Delta was further enticed by the prospect of being one of the first two airlines to introduce it. An extra inducement was the initial price of $3.5 million, low by comparison with either the Boeing 707 or the Douglas DC-8, but Convair was willing to settle for a lower price in the interest of attracting customers. The upshot was a preliminary agreement with Convair and General Electric, announced June 20, 1956, under which Hughes committed himself to buy thirty of the craft for TWA and Delta contracted to purchase ten.[21]

There was thus much for Garrett to coordinate in the fall of 1956, when he assumed his new responsibilities. In November, Delta sent two representatives to a conference at Santa Monica to discuss ways in which Douglas could assist airlines in the training and familiarization process required for the introduction of the DC-8 into commercial service. In addition to suggesting such obvious educational aids as motion pictures, slide transparencies, scale models, cockpit trainers, animated panels, study guides, and maintenance manuals, Delta joined United, Eastern, Pan American, and Japan Air Lines in asking that groups of employees be given systematic courses of on-site instruction at the Douglas plant before actual delivery of the aircraft.[22] Throughout the next two years Garrett, working with such

Delta officials as C. B. (Speedy) Wilder, director of technical operations, planned and supervised the flow of personnel between the East and West coasts as the DC-8 took shape.

Preparations were also made for the CV-880. On March 11, 1957, Garrett was the opening speaker at ceremonies marking the inauguration in Atlanta of the Delta–General Electric Jet Familiarization School, the first of its type to be established by a commercial airline. During 1957 classes concentrated on jet-engine fundamentals; in the next two years they became increasingly specialized, leading to detailed study of the CJ-805 engines that would power the new Convair ship. Because plans for these engines were still classified, much time had to be spent working out the necessary military security clearances before Delta personnel could be trained in their operation and maintenance. R. C. Reese and Harry Wardell, two seasoned instructors from General Electric's jet engine plant at Evendale, Ohio, were the first faculty members, and twenty-six Delta employees made up the initial class; these first students would in turn become instructors and pass along their knowledge in a program designed ultimately to reach every person in the entire organization. "In approximately three years," it was claimed, "there should be complete saturation of every pilot, flight engineer, stewardess, maintenance person and even reservations people on the principles of the turbojet with the same degree of understanding as they now have of piston engines."[23]

After the necessary manuals and study guides had arrived from Douglas, classroom training totaling nearly 250 hours per person was set up for maintenance workers, in order to familiarize them with the airframe and the electronics system of the DC-8. Minimum passing grades on examinations were 80 percent for nonsupervisory personnel and 90 percent for supervisors. Courses aimed at providing "conversational knowledge" about the DC-8 were established for other employees. Following General Electric's lead, Pratt and Whitney conducted lecture courses and maintenance demonstrations with the JT-3 engine, and one technical-training instructor went to Tinker Air Force Base for firsthand experience in overhauling its military equivalent, the J-57. After returning to Atlanta, he taught classes attended by about six hundred workers based in the city and an equivalent number from other stations in the system. On-site instruction at the Douglas plant was underway by early 1958, and soon scores of key staff members were shuttling back and forth between the Deep South and California, getting ready for the arrival of the jets. Pilot training was begun at the factory in February 1959, and during the next few months ground crews throughout the system were trained in loading, unloading, fueling, and servicing the new ships.[24]

Meanwhile, the eagerly awaited jetliners gradually took shape in California. "How are you coming on my DC-8's?" Woolman inquired in a letter to Donald Douglas, Sr., in May 1957, on the eve of ceremonies marking the dedication at Long Beach of a new twenty-million-dollar complex in which the aircraft were to be assembled. "Your DC-8's are coming along fine," Douglas replied, adding that "the basic materials for your order are due in our plant by July this year, and by September there will be a sufficient number of parts showing up that we might be able to have your picture taken with them."[25] Throughout the following year Woolman received regular progress reports culminating in the news that the first ship in the series had been rolled out of its construction hangar on April 9, 1958. Many months of waiting remained as the new model was subjected to the rigorous test flights required by federal regulations, but the announcement was nevertheless heartening. Delta engineers had followed every step of the assembly process, to the accompaniment of reams of technical memoranda passed back and forth across the continent. As the final delivery date drew ever closer, Woolman and other Delta executives referred frequently to a constantly growing "jet aircraft planning schedule," setting deadlines for gathering an endless variety of items, ranging from spare parts to buffet apparatus and linen supplies, which had to be on hand as soon as the company's first jetliners took to the air.[26]

While the DC-8 was being assembled at Long Beach, work on the Convair 880 got underway in San Diego. By July 1957 Delta and TWA officials were able to admire the luxurious design of the cabin interior in a full-scale plywood mockup. The next few months were taken up with tooling, wind-tunnel testing, training supervisory personnel, acquiring materials, and examining specimen units from the various structural systems of the aircraft. Work on the first subassemblies of wing components was in progress by the end of the year, and major assembly began on April 10, 1958. Matters proceeded smoothly, and by October the first ship in the series was approaching structural completion as the wing was mated with the fuselage. On December 15, two weeks ahead of schedule, the glistening new plane was rolled out in ceremonies attended by more than a thousand people, and on January 27, 1959, it took off from San

Diego's Lindbergh Field on a seventy-six-minute maiden test flight. The testing process continued into February, and Convair pilots and engineers lavished praise on the craft for its engine performance, acceleration, speed, and climbing characteristics. By then the idea of a gold-tinted exterior had been dropped as impractical, because Alcoa could not guarantee that the anodized aluminum panels would perfectly match one another. The ship seemed to be living up to expectations otherwise, however.[27]

Delta's existing maintenance and overhaul facilities were inadequate for servicing the new ships being built on the West Coast. In May 1956 Dolson pointed out the problems that would be involved in planning the extensive new facilities required and urged that preliminary studies begin. With the new construction projects that would be taking place at terminals throughout the Delta system in preparation for the jet age and with the expansion of Delta's general offices in Atlanta, the company's facilities staff had its hands full keeping up, and the help of outside consultants was required. Taking everything into consideration, Dolson predicted that planning a new jet base would take about one year; another year would be taken up in securing bids and awarding contracts; and eighteen months would be needed for actual construction. If the proper facilities were to be ready when the jets arrived, things had better get moving. "An early decision is very important," he concluded.[28]

Dolson's memorandum was prophetic. In addition to the steps he outlined, the company had to negotiate an agreement with the Atlanta city government under which a large tract of land would be provided at the municipal airport and bonds issued to finance construction of the new jet base, which in turn would be leased to Delta under a long-term arrangement. An agreement was ultimately reached; the city contracted to issue $6.5 million in airport revenue certificates and Delta pledged to install $3.5 million worth of equipment for a giant new facility to be located on a fifty-acre tract of land, but these and other preliminaries took a great deal of time, and it was early 1959 before actual work at the site was well underway.[29]

Preparing for jet operations also required unprecedented outlays of capital for equipment and facilities. Fortunately, the last of the debentures issued in connection with the C & S merger had been retired by the end of 1955, facilitating to some degree the heavy borrowing that lay in store. A revolving credit agreement with a group of twenty-five banks, for $30 million, was approved early in 1956.

Later that spring the company decided to issue 125,000 shares of new stock, after making provision to safeguard the interests of existing stockholders by declaring a 25 percent stock dividend. SEC approval had been secured, and the sale took place in July, netting approximately $4.3 million. By that time the CV-880s had been ordered, and the company was committed to new equipment worth a total of $110 million, necessitating further credit negotiations over the next few years. By 1959 arrangements had been made with four insurance companies for a loan of $25 million, and the revolving credit agreement of 1956 had been amended to permit borrowing up to $35 million.[30]

Getting ready for the jets thus involved a series of complex preparations reaching into every echelon of the Delta organization. Then, on July 22, 1959, after more than three years of waiting, Delta's first DC-8 took off from Long Beach at 9:06 A.M. and made the 2,497-mile trip across the continent to Miami in four hours and forty-three minutes, flying at speeds averaging 530 miles an hour and breaking previous records for the route. T. P. Ball was in the pilot's seat, and Delta veterans Lee McBride and James H. Longino formed the rest of the cockpit crew. Rain was falling when the plane arrived, but it remained on the runway for an hour while a long line of company employees stood under umbrellas waiting to look inside. Then the DC-8 took off for Atlanta on another record-breaking flight lasting just a few seconds over seventy-eight minutes. Sandy Howell, a Delta stewardess in the crowd awaiting its arrival, tried to be calm about the occasion but did not succeed: "I really got butterflies when I saw the silly thing come in," she told reporters later. "Just think, it's ours!" Nip Hill, a truck driver standing on the ramp, probably caught the essence of the moment as eloquently as anybody: "All the pride and glory of Delta Air Lines is right there," he murmured as the ship touched down. "She's the queen of the skies."[31]

After nearly two months of certification flights and pilot-qualification activities, Delta was ready to inaugurate commercial service on the new ship. With United, it had been one of the first two airlines to take delivery of the craft, and both lines put it into service on the first day that FAA regulations permitted it to be operated, September 18, 1959. Because of the time differential between the East and West coasts and the vagaries of the weather, the Delta DC-8 was in the air several hours before its United counterpart. In christening ceremonies at Idlewild Airport, Mrs. Woolman failed in four tries to break a bottle of champagne against one of the plane's engine pods and finally gave both container and contents to officials of the New York Port Authority as a memento. Then, shortly before 10:00 A.M., the big jetliner took off for Atlanta, with Captain Floyd Addison in control, arriving one hour and thirty-four minutes later. With mayors from the Atlanta suburbs looking on, the two Woolmans, husband and wife, jointly wielded another champagne bottle to rechristen the ship for the return flight; they succeeded in smashing it against the plane on the third try, though C.E. cut his hand in the process. Far away in San Francisco, a United DC-8 had been held up by bad weather but finally took off for New York a few minutes after 11:00 A.M., Pacific standard time. Woolman hailed the flight of the Delta plane as "an indication that air transportation is keeping pace with other industries in the South's march of progress," and the *Delta Digest* exulted in the fact that the company had become "the first airline in the world to fly the Douglas DC-8 on a scheduled flight."[32]

For the next several months Delta had the satisfaction of pitting a growing fleet of DC-8s against Eastern's propeller-driven airliners. The decision to settle for the less powerful JT-3 engine had paid off, because Rickenbacker had held out for the JT-4 and was accordingly forced to wait longer for deliveries. In addition, the JT-4 turned out to be highly intensive in its use of fuel, and its design was such that planes equipped with it could not be refitted with the more efficient fan-jet engines that soon became available for commercial aircraft. Delta's new ships, however, could be altered in this fashion, and thus the company gained an additional competitive edge. Meanwhile Eastern suffered from the speed restrictions that federal authorities had imposed upon the accident-prone Electras. Even when they were not tied up in the modification program that Lockheed was forced to undertake, these turboprops were temporarily slower than the DC-7s and had the extra handicap of a bad public reputation.[33]

Delta soon had yet another formidable competitive weapon. By February 1960, the Convair 880 was ready for delivery. Under the original plan, TWA was to place the first of these speedy ships in commercial service, reflecting the leading role of Howard Hughes in developing the aircraft. At that point, however, the Hughes financial empire was in temporary disarray, and its leader was in seclusion.

TWA was staggering under the impact of enormous losses and frequent changes in upper-level management, and Hughes was vainly attempting to arrange a $265 million loan from a consortium of bankers to cover his massive orders of aircraft from Boeing and Convair, without losing his absolute control over TWA. As a result of the impasse, deliveries of CV-880s to TWA could not begin. Having guided the design and development of the ship, Hughes was bitterly opposed to allowing another airline the distinction of being first to place it in service, but Convair, itself facing financial disaster as a result of the troubles in which Hughes found himself, was understandably eager to complete whatever sales it could, and Delta did not hesitate to claim the planes for which it had contracted.[34]

On February 6, 1960, Ball and Longino, who had come to California several weeks earlier to complete pilot training for CV-880 operations, received their ratings to fly the craft, and two other Delta personnel, Dick Tidwell and Brian Bolt, won certification as flight engineers. "What a celebration we had that night!" Ball later recalled. "We were prepared to leave San Diego with our newest treasure—the fastest commercial jet aircraft in the world!" On February 8, Woolman arrived in San Diego, accompanied by various Delta officials and guests. There ensued a series of hurried consultations between Woolman and representatives of the Hughes interests, in which Woolman made it clear that Delta needed the new ships as soon as it could possibly have them and intended to take delivery without further delay. Underlining the irony of the situation was the fact that a group of CV-880s made for TWA were roped off in a parking area adjacent to the Convair plant; nobody was authorized to accept them.[35]

On February 10, 1960, therefore, J. V. Naish, Convair's president, presented Woolman with a golden key to the cockpit of Delta's first CV-880 in ceremonies at Lindbergh Field. Shortly thereafter, at 1:11 P.M., the new plane took off for Miami on a flight that established a commercial speed record between California and Florida, one that was still standing seventeen years later. It averaged 665 miles an hour and, thanks to favorable tail winds first encountered over Arizona, actually reached a ground speed of 779 miles an hour at one stage of the trip. "We crossed the State of Texas from its westernmost edge to the Gulf of Mexico . . . in fifty minutes," Ball quipped, "which I say reduced Texas to its proper size!" Just three hours, thirty-one minutes, and fifty-four seconds after leaving San Diego, the plane touched down at Miami, having sliced nearly half an hour from the previous record between the two points set a month earlier by a DC-8. After being hailed by city representatives and several hundred spectators, the new craft continued on to Atlanta for another enthusiastic reception. A contemporary photograph shows Ball, Longino, and Tidwell, along with stewardess Maryanne Kowaleski, beaming in front of a placard welcoming home "the undisputed speed champion."[36]

Three months later, a solid nucleus of pilots and flight engineers had been trained, aircraft certification tests had been completed, and a second ship had arrived from the West Coast. On May 15, for the second time in less than a year, Delta had the honor of introducing a new model into scheduled service by putting the CV-880 on the run between Houston and New York. Indeed, because of continuing difficulties with the tangled finances of Howard Hughes, Delta enjoyed a monopoly on the plane until December 1960, when Northeast Airlines, which had leased a few of the aircraft originally intended for TWA, became the second carrier to deploy it. Being the sole operator of the craft involved problems, as well as advantages, because Delta had to contend with all design and manufacturing irregularities without being able to consult with any other airline. Ultimately each of the first five ships received from Convair had to undergo a series of modifications, which were carried out by the manufacturer at Delta's Dallas maintenance base, to insure operations at a satisfactory level of schedule reliability. Nevertheless, the new planes caught on well with both pilots and passengers, particularly because of their speed. As Ball later recalled:

These were great days for our flight crews as far as competition with our Eastern friends was concerned because we flew this aircraft [the CV-880] from New York to Atlanta to Miami and over the Miami–Chicago route, and it was a great thrill for the Delta pilots to be able to climb to altitude and cruise right past the fastest thing that Eastern had flying. We took great pleasure in telling the passengers over the PA system that if they would only look to the left or right-hand side, as the case might be, they would see the Eastern Air Lines aircraft that . . . we were now passing.[37]

For Delta, therefore, 1959 and 1960 were truly halcyon years. Significant milestones in the company's development were passed one after another. On June 21, 1960, the huge new jet base was officially dedicated at a gala ceremony, climaxing more than four years of planning and construction. With more than nine acres of space un-

C-46D, in service with Delta's cargo division from 1957 to 1966.

George E. Bounds was director of public relations and advertising for C&S and later director of advertising for Delta–C&S.

Delta goes on the big board. Pictured in 1957, when Delta stock is first listed on the New York Stock Exchange, are *(left to right)* C. E. Woolman, Bettye Jo Rogers, Betty Beck, and G. Keith Funston, Stock Exchange president.

Mrs. C. E. Woolman gets an assist from her husband in christening Delta's first jetliner, the Douglas DC-8-51.

DC-8-51 photographed with personnel complement required in 1959 for operating each jet.

Delta's chief maintenance and overhaul facility at Hartsfield Atlanta International Airport has been expanded in three phases, from nine acres of floor space under roof in 1960 to thirty-six acres in 1978.

Convair 880, first introduced by Delta in 1960.

T. P. Ball receives clearance papers from a Hollywood starlet for record-breaking delivery flight from San Diego to Miami in 1960.

der roof, the facility was dominated by a gigantic hangar whose doors alone were four stories high and almost twice the length of a football field. Among other components, the complex housed a jet-engine test center, within whose massive concrete walls engines could be run at full capacity while electronic equipment checked every aspect of their operation. Mayor William B. Hartsfield praised the company's initiative and looked forward to another significant occasion in the following May, when Atlanta would itself dedicate a greatly expanded terminal to accommodate what had become the fifth largest volume of air traffic in the United States. "The ocean of the air has no shoreline, and our great modern terminal, soon to be completed, puts us at the gateway of the world," Hartsfield declared. "The future of Atlanta will hinge on how we manage this great asset—the Atlanta Airport."[38]

Some of the episodes as Delta pressed forward into the jet age were attended by feelings of nostalgia, as on October 29, 1960, when the last of the company's venerable DC-3s, ship 42, made its final flight from Knoxville to Atlanta after accumulating more than 56,000 hours—more than six years—in the air. One of the original five DC-3s purchased from Douglas in the winter of 1940–41, it had flown approximately nine million miles and had carried an estimated 400,000 passengers since its maiden flight on January 18, 1941, with Tip Schier in the cockpit. Appropriately, Schier's granddaughter, Gail Airoldi, a recent graduate of Delta's stewardess school, was cabin attendant on the old ship's final mission, and Birdie Perkins Bomar served as honorary stewardess. Thus ended an era that had begun December 23, 1940, when the first Delta DC-3 took to the air on a flight from Atlanta to Birmingham. "We can't help having a soft spot for them," commented veteran Delta pilot Luke Caruthers. "No matter how many trips out, they always came chugging home with you."[39]

But, though one era had ended, another had just as decisively begun. By mid-1960 the company already possessed six DC-8s and three CV-880s, and nine more of the latter were scheduled to arrive within the ensuing year. Delta, which had so strongly considered going for the turboprops, was advertising itself as "the airline with the big jets" and vigorously opposing the use by competitors of the term "prop-jet" for turboprop planes. "Delta means the *most* jets to the *most* places" was the way one advertising display put it, referring to an imposing list of destinations. Los Angeles was the last city named in the advertisement, and its inclusion in the list was particularly important, because it heralded approaching victory in another route case, fully as significant as the one that had opened the way to Washington and New York half a decade earlier.[40] Having already chalked up an extraordinary series of breakthroughs, Delta was poised to record yet another.

CHAPTER 16

On to the Coast

THE ADVENT OF jet aircraft, which were especially well suited to carrying large numbers of passengers at extremely high speeds over very long distances, accentuated the advantages to an airline of having many nonstop long-haul routes between major population centers. If Delta wished to derive maximum advantage from its newly acquired fleet of DC-8s and CV-880s, it could not afford to rest content with the fruits of its hard-fought Atlanta–to–New York route victory. Major new markets were essential, and the company set out to gain them.

During the late 1950s and early 1960s, therefore, Delta continued its traditional policy of vigorously seeking new route authorizations. In December 1958 E. M. Johnson, Delta's veteran planning and research director, compiled a list showing that the company, which was included on no fewer than forty-three CAB dockets, had far more applications outstanding than any other carrier; arch rival Eastern, which ranked second in this category, was involved in only half as many proceedings. Johnson had qualms about the unwieldiness of Delta's roster of cases and suggested a "mopping up job" to consolidate the list, but there was no question that the firm's aggressiveness was continuing to yield dividends. During the same month the cover of *Delta Digest* showed eight gaily wrapped packages under the corporate Christmas tree, signifying the number of new destinations added to the route system during the previous year.[1]

As usual, expansion had required arduous effort and the capacity to endure temporary setbacks. Under the terms of the company's New York route award, Delta's southbound passengers had to change planes in Atlanta before continuing to Florida. In early 1956 Eastern and National were the only carriers enjoying direct access from New York to Miami, and a case was in progress in which Delta and five other contestants were seeking to become the third airline to be admitted to this lucrative vacation market. Delta representatives worked hard to secure support from cities that would benefit from their company's selection; they pointed out to the CAB that a logical route could be formed merely by filling an eighty-nine-mile gap between Delta cities in the Carolinas. Their hopes were buoyed on April 3, 1956, when CAB examiner Thomas L. Wrenn recommended that Delta be awarded a route from New York to Miami and, in the process, be given access to Tampa and St. Petersburg.[2]

But Wrenn's advice was disregarded. In a split decision handed down in September 1956, the CAB gave Northeast Airlines authority to fly from New York to Miami for a period of five years, on grounds that this award would enable Northeast to survive without federal subsidy. There was some consolation in the fact that Delta was granted entry to the Tampa–St. Petersburg–Clearwater area, but even this access was soon withdrawn; the CAB, upon reconsideration, decided to incorporate issues involving service to these cities in a massive proceeding known as the Great Lakes–Southeast Service case, which was just beginning in the fall of 1956.[3]

The principal matters at stake in this new case were the question of whether additional competition was needed in the Chicago-to-Miami trade shared by Delta and Eastern and the disposition of new routes and connecting services in a sprawling fifteen-state area bounded by Chicago, Detroit, and Buffalo on the north and Miami on the south. As if these issues were not enough to ensure a long and complicated struggle, three other closely related cases were also in progress. One of them, the TWA Route Transfer case, had arisen from the fact that TWA, which had been transformed since World War II from a domestic airline into a worldwide carrier, had voluntarily agreed to give up its route from Detroit to Cincinnati in exchange for authorizations that would strengthen its transcontinental services. Meanwhile, in the Great Lakes Local Service proceeding, a swarm of feeder lines were fighting for route extensions in a belt of states stretching from Virginia to Illinois. Finally, another series of additions to existing route patterns south of the Ohio valley was under discussion in the St. Louis–Southeast Service case.

Since most of the country's airlines were involved in one or another of these deliberations and since so many overlapping issues were being debated at once, many months of legal maneuvering were required before the final decisions could be made. Along with Eastern, Delta fought vigorously to convince the CAB that no new competition between Chicago and Miami was necessary, while a group of other carriers, particularly National and Northwest, sought just as diligently to invade this rich market. Defensive efforts were also required against feeder lines trying to usurp midwestern routes that had been served over the years by Delta and C&S. Taking the offense, the company argued that its long-standing interchange agreement with TWA made it the logical recipient of that carrier's route from Detroit to Cincinnati, and asked that Columbus, Dayton, and Toledo be added to Delta's route 54. It also sought access to Cleveland and Pittsburgh as key points on a projected artery from Detroit to Charlotte. Finally, Delta wanted to add Louisville as an intermediate stop between Cincinnati and Lexington, and it urged the addition to its route system of four cities in Florida: Tampa, St. Petersburg, Orlando, and West Palm Beach.

After the customary hearings, examiner's reports, petitions, and counterpetitions had been negotiated and endless reams of testimony and statistical data sifted and analyzed, the CAB decision in the Great Lakes–Southeast Service case was finally handed down on September 30, 1958. For Delta, there was both good news and bad news, as was probably inevitable in such a complex proceeding. The chief disappointment was the board's concurrence with examiner William Cusick that more competition was needed on the Chicago-to-Miami run, though Cusick's recommendation in favor of National was reversed and Northwest received the prize instead. In addition, Capital won authority to fly from Buffalo to Miami via such cities as Cleveland, Pittsburgh, Atlanta, and Tampa and St. Petersburg, giving yet another carrier access to the Florida vacation trade.

But there was still much for Delta to rejoice about. Confirming the company's position in the TWA Transfer case, the CAB added Columbus and Dayton to the Delta system, putting them on route 54, along with Toledo and Detroit, and thus giving Delta a direct line from Detroit to Miami in competition with Eastern. Although Cusick had suggested putting Indianapolis and Louisville on Northwest's new Chicago-to-Miami route, the CAB added them instead to Delta's route 54, thus giving the firm access for the first time to Kentucky's largest city and increasing its potential for attracting traffic bound for the southeast; previously Delta had been able to serve Indianapolis only on the old C&S route 8 from Detroit to Houston.

A long-standing Delta objective was achieved when the CAB filled an obvious gap in the company's route system, allowing it to fly from Savannah to Charleston. Far more significant for the future, however, was the award to Delta of Orlando and West Palm Beach, along with final confirmation of access to Tampa and St. Petersburg;

all these cities were added to route 54. Although Northwest was also authorized to serve Tampa and St. Petersburg, the addition to the Delta system of these two points, which ranked second only to Miami in the Florida vacation trade, promised Woolman's firm considerable new revenue.[4]

There was more bad news than good for Delta in the decision handed down by the CAB in the St. Louis–Southeast Service case. TWA was awarded a route from St. Louis to Miami via Nashville, Atlanta, and Tampa–St. Petersburg, creating a situation in which no fewer than five airlines were competing for passengers between Atlanta and Miami. Furthermore, TWA's existing western routes permitted it, after the CAB decision, to provide one-stop transcontinental service between California and Florida via St. Louis. Delta believed that this feature of the decision prejudged issues involving southern transcontinental service, soon to be decided in one of the most important cases ever contested before the CAB, and it led several other trunklines in successfully challenging the board in a federal court suit. As a result, restrictions were ultimately imposed upon TWA, lessening the competitive potential of the California–St. Louis–Florida route, but the other features of the St. Louis–Miami award remained intact.

Delta did gain one important advantage from the St. Louis–Southeast case, however: the CAB filled in what was perhaps the most glaring gap in its entire route structure, permitting the firm, at long last, to fly between Birmingham and Memphis. Delta could now offer direct service from Kansas City to Atlanta and Florida. Combined with the new route authorizations from the Great Lakes case, this important link gave Delta access to markets that had, in 1956, produced approximately $36 million in passenger revenue. However badly Delta management may have felt about being forced to share Florida vacation traffic with three new competitors, it still had emerged from a series of complex legal battles with some worthwhile gains.[5]

Delta suffered several outright defeats in other cases argued before the CAB during this period. Continuing previous efforts, it tried to penetrate one of Northwest's traditional preserves, the heavily traveled route between Chicago and Minneapolis–St. Paul, but this goal remained as elusive as ever; Capital and Eastern were selected instead. Delta also sought unsuccessfully to add Bradenton and Sarasota to its Florida network and to obtain a route from Atlanta to Toronto by way of Pittsburgh and Buffalo in a case ultimately won

Detroit
Toledo
Chicago • Ft. Wayne
Anderson-Muncie
Indianapolis
Terre Haute
St. Louis
Evansville
Kansas City
Springfield
Paducah
Little Rock
Hot Springs
Longview-
Kilgore-
Gladewater
To California
Dallas
Ft. Worth
Tyler
Alexandria
Beaumont-Port Arthur
Houston

New York-
Newark
Philadelphia
Pittsburgh
Baltimore
Washington
Columbus
Dayton
Cincinnati
Lexington
Knoxville
Asheville
Charlotte
Greenville-Spartanburg
Columbia
Chattanooga
Memphis
Atlanta
Augusta
Charleston
Greenwood
Birmingham
Macon
Columbus
Selma
Savannah
Monroe
Montgomery
Meridian
Brunswick
Shreveport
Jackson
Hattiesburg
Jacksonville
Baton Rouge
New Orleans
Tampa-
St. Petersburg-
Clearwater
Miami
Havana
Montego Bay
Port-au-Prince
Kingston
Ciudad Trujillo
San Juan
Aruba
Curaçao
Maracaibo
Caracas

DELTA ROUTE SYSTEM
1956

INTERCHANGE ROUTES

------ with TWA

- — - with American

— — with National

by Eastern.[6] These, however, were only minor skirmishes in comparison with an epic struggle that was taking shape in the West. In a case fully as important to Delta's destiny as the protracted battle of the mid-1950s to gain entry to Washington and New York, Delta mounted an all-out drive to win independent access to the Pacific Coast.

The Southern Transcontinental Service case, described by one Delta official as "the most complex and bitterly contested route case in the history of the Civil Aeronautics Board," grew out of dissatisfaction in Texas with service to Los Angeles and San Francisco on airways that had long been monopolized by American, at that time the largest trunk line in the nation. Responding to a formal complaint by the city of Dallas, the CAB began prehearing procedures in May 1956. Delta was one of nine airlines that took part in what came to be known as the Dallas-to-the-West Service case. These firms were attracted by the business opportunities afforded by the burgeoning southwestern states, the population of which had grown by nearly ten million people in the previous fifteen years. After considering various possibilities, Johnson and his research staff plotted a zigzag route leading from Dallas–Fort Worth to Amarillo, El Paso, Albuquerque, Phoenix, Las Vegas, San Diego, Los Angeles, and San Francisco–Oakland. Delta also indicated its willingness under a "catch-all" clause to serve other points, including Lubbock, Santa Fe, and Tucson.[7]

Delta argued that its existing stake in the southwestern traffic, resulting from the interchange agreements with American and National, plus the fact that it could feed passengers from thirty eastern and Latin American cities through the Dallas–Fort Worth gateway, made it the logical choice to provide competitive service to the Pacific Coast. After a series of protracted hearings and legal arguments, however, CAB examiner Wrenn (who had earlier favored Delta's application in the New York–Miami proceeding) recommended Continental for the new western route. Delta's superior connections to the east, he argued, were not germane in a case aimed simply at improving service between Dallas and the Southwest. Furthermore, an award to Delta, which would automatically terminate the company's existing interchange with American, would have a far greater adverse impact upon American than a decision in favor of Continental.[8]

Wrenn's recommendation, however, soon became a dead issue. Two of the airlines involved in the Dallas case, Eastern and National, had been critical of the proceedings, in which they were at a disadvantage because neither of their existing systems connected with Dallas and Fort Worth. Realizing that their applications had little chance of success because of the gaps between Dallas and their closest outposts, San Antonio and Houston respectively, they feared that a decision in favor of any other carrier would prejudice their own chances of gaining access to the Pacific Coast when and if the CAB ever got around to granting transcontinental operating authority between California and Florida. American had similar concerns, for it wanted eventual transcontinental certification to Florida, superseding existing interchanges with Delta and National, and was understandably averse to seeing any of the parties in the Dallas case break the Texas-to-California monopoly and secure potential advantage in the competition for an eventual coast-to-coast route at the same time. Finally, other Texas cities, particularly Houston and San Antonio, also wanted better connections to the West and stood to gain if the scope of the Dallas case were expanded.[9]

These considerations soon led to a restructuring of the entire proceeding. Two weeks after Wrenn's report was released, the CAB responded to a request from Houston by launching an investigation of that city's air transport needs, which soon grew into the Southern Transcontinental Service case. After a prehearing conference had been held and massive inputs obtained from interested parties, an order was issued on August 5, 1958, defining the scope of the proceeding and consolidating the issues previously included in the Dallas case. At stake in the new case was a series of long-haul authorizations connecting every major metropolitan area between Miami, Jacksonville, and Atlanta in the east and San Diego, Los Angeles, and San Francisco in the West. The enormous growth of the Sun Belt during the postwar era guaranteed that competition would be intense, and no fewer than eleven carriers entered the fray, including American, Braniff, Capital, Continental, Delta, Eastern, National, TWA, and Western.[10]

In this battle of giants, Delta proposed to connect Miami and other Florida cities, via the Tampa–St. Petersburg gateway, with Pensacola, Mobile, and New Orleans, eliminating in the process its existing interchange with National. From New Orleans the projected Delta artery would lead to Houston and Dallas–Fort Worth and then proceed over two branching segments to El Paso via Lubbock and San Antonio. From El Paso the route would continue to Albuquerque, Tucson, Phoenix, Las Vegas, San Diego, Long Beach,

Los Angeles, and San Francisco–Oakland. Most of the other airlines involved in the case had equally ambitious goals. A major concern for Delta was the possibility that it might be forced to share traffic on its grandfather route from Dallas to Atlanta and its long-standing artery from Dallas to New Orleans as a result of the proceeding.[11]

One of Delta's earliest moves as the transcontinental battle got underway was to engage outside counsel to assist Maurer's staff of attorneys, already severely burdened by the requirements of the other cases in which the company was involved, to fight what was sure to be a protracted and extremely demanding struggle. Late in 1957 the law firm of Pogue and Neal, which had served Delta so ably in the C&S merger and various route cases, including the long campaign to gain access to Washington and New York, reluctantly withdrew from its relationship with the firm because its heavy volume of business with Delta prevented it from serving other potential clients. In addition, an older client, Western Air Lines, was now trying to expand its system eastward, raising the prospect of conflict of interest. The parting was entirely amicable, and Delta shortly added to its own legal staff one of the ablest young lawyers then working for Pogue and Neal, James W. Callison, but the loss of the counsel formerly provided by the distinguished Washington partnership was nonetheless deeply felt. It was highly fortunate, therefore, that, after a thorough search for a suitable successor, Delta succeeded in retaining Chapman, Walsh and O'Connell of Washington and New York to represent the company in the crucial transcontinental proceeding. Two members of the legal firm were to be particularly helpful: Joseph J. O'Connell, who, like L. Welch Pogue, was a former chairman of the CAB, and Robert Reed Gray, a former navy pilot with particular expertise in aviation law.[12]

The closing months of 1958 were largely spent amassing the enormous volume of statistical and interpretive data required for Delta's formal proposal, showing why the economic needs of the states covered by the case could best be satisfied by the new air services that Delta wished to establish and giving detailed information on the types of schedules the company would maintain, the nature of the equipment that would be used, the new facilities required, the number of new employees who would have to be hired, the costs of the operations involved, the diversionary impact on other carriers if Delta's plans were adopted, and a host of related matters.

Delta approached the task as a general staff prepares for a major battle. "During this period the lights in Planning and Research burned far into the night and calculators continued to grind out the answers through most weekends," William V. Costello, Johnson's chief assistant, later recalled. By the time the data were ready for submission to the CAB in January 1959 they filled a bound volume of approximately 400 pages, each of which represented dozens of preliminary work sheets and endless hours of computation. Hardly had this task been completed when copies of the proposals of the other airlines involved in the case arrived; these proposals had to be meticulously analyzed for possible weaknesses, and rebuttal exhibits had to be prepared to challenge them. This work was finished in April, when Delta sent the CAB another 150 pages of material calling into question the calculations of its opponents.[13]

Delta hoped that the comprehensiveness of its proposal, coupled with the care taken in preparing it, would pay off. The company had plotted an ambitious series of nonstop and long-haul connections between major population centers, clearly indicating the seriousness of its intent to offer strong competitive service throughout the entire area covered by the proceeding. Capitalizing on the fact that it was the only passenger carrier in the Southeast still maintaining an all-cargo division—both Eastern and National had reduced previous operations in this area—it drew up a schedule of transcontinental freight services carefully calculated to appeal not only to business firms but also to military shippers and officials in the rapidly developing space program. It also planned to offer accommodations to as many thrift-class and coach passengers as possible, pledging to back this policy up with massive advertising efforts aimed at the vacation trade. The company's ability to carry through on these proposals was sure to be questioned by competing airlines in the hearings that lay ahead, but Delta management believed that, if the proposals could be defended successfully under cross examination, the firm would be in a good position to win preferment over the rest of the field.[14]

While the basic proposal was painstakingly assembled, various departments girded for a series of regional hearings to be held by the CAB beginning in May 1959; at these hearings representatives of municipal governments, chambers of commerce, aviation committees, business firms, and military installations located in the regions affected by the case would spell out their needs and wishes for additional service. Drawing upon its long experience in new route acquisition, Delta organized an intensive public relations campaign, combining the resources of the legal, planning and research, information services, and civic affairs departments. A detailed reference manual was prepared for mass distribution; it set forth as clearly and concisely as possible the nature and background of the case, the proposals submitted by the various carriers involved, the specific features and advantages of Delta's own proposal, the various steps the CAB would follow in conducting the proceeding, and the manner in which petitions and exhibits should be filed with the proper authorities. It was periodically revised and expanded as the case went on and was supplemented by radio and television interviews, news releases, press conferences, and magazine articles.[15]

Frequent contacts with municipal organizations, influential leaders, and military officials were maintained by a cadre of Delta representatives, including Maurer, Rox, and Callison of the legal department; Johnson and Costello from planning and research; Miller from traffic; and Earl Cocke, the company's energetic vice-president for civic affairs. Johnson alone traveled approximately 35,000 miles on such missions. Typical of this phase of the proceeding was a trip by Miller and Rox to Birmingham, Jackson, and Shreveport in January 1959 to demonstrate Delta's commitment to providing these cities with better service to the Pacific Coast. Partly because the CAB was known to be interested in strengthening smaller carriers, rather than the Big Four, in the southern transcontinental market and partly because Delta believed that the witnesses would have an easier time under cross examination at the upcoming civic hearings if they appeared neutral, rather than single-mindedly supporting the company, the two Delta emissaries were instructed not to press municipal leaders to support Delta over other carriers but merely to make sure that a strong case was presented, proving the need for the services that Delta hoped to provide and endorsing Delta's fitness to render them.

This approach seemed effective. At Jackson, Miller and Rox debated with Robert Ramspeck of Eastern before the chamber of commerce; among other issues, they discussed merits of Delta's DC-6s and DC-7s versus those of the Lockheed Electra, which Eastern was just beginning to deploy. At Shreveport they confronted Ramspeck again, along with a representative from Braniff. Miller and Rox did their best to persuade leaders in all three cities to testify that Delta's existing services on the route between Dallas–Fort Worth and Atlanta were adequate. On the larger issues of new transcontinental connections, however, they made no effort to secure endorsements of Delta at the expense of any other airline. At Jackson, for example,

Miller stressed that the company had been serving the city for thirty years and was willing to let the record speak for itself. Similarly, after the Shreveport encounter Rox informed Maurer: "We emphasized heavily that the City and Chamber should not support Eastern, Delta or Braniff by name, but should support a need for one-carrier service to the west coast. This was particularly impressive to the members of the Aviation Committee . . . since Eastern had just spent about 20 minutes saying that the Chamber should support Eastern."[16]

The CAB's regional hearings took place in May and June at Houston, Los Angeles, and Miami. Gray conducted the questioning of witnesses for Delta, assisted by Maurer, Rox, and Callison. Although the company did its best to bring out testimony affirming the quality and adequacy of its existing services, it continued to focus on the needs of the represented interest groups for improved access to points that Delta was seeking to add to its system, without attempting to force witnesses to take sides on behalf of any particular carrier. Keeping the questioning as general as possible, Delta counsel believed, would minimize the chances of losing existing advantages east of the Mississippi and preserve Delta's excellent chances of winning new route mileage west of Dallas–Fort Worth.

Hearings at which the participating airlines could defend their specific proposals under cross examination by the other companies involved commenced in Washington in July. In accordance with customary procedure, airlines spoke in alphabetical order, and the first four lines to take the stand were American, Braniff, Capital, and Continental. Because attorneys from so many carriers were taking turns questioning witnesses, the proceeding moved slowly, and it was not until early August that Delta's testimony began. The presentation of the company's case was entrusted to such veteran witnesses as Costello, Miller, and Laigh Parker, who defended the route proposals and the complex traffic and scheduling arrangements that they entailed, and Cole, who fielded questions pertaining to anticipated costs and other fiscal matters. Because of the vast scope of the issues, the pressure on each witness, high in any proceeding, was particularly intense in this case. Costello later commented:

When one realizes that the gain or loss of millions of dollars in potential future revenue is at stake, it is not difficult to understand why an atmosphere of tension and emotion pervades the hearing room, and the hearing is suddenly characterized by rough and tumble tactics not usually evident during the civic portion. . . . It is difficult to avoid a case of nerves as the witness finds himself reviewing his exhibits and trying to recall the many details of each estimate he has made. A part of this ... is the haunting thought that in spite of all the care and precaution with which such work is done, a significant error in calculation or judgment has crept into the exhibits and that a lawyer of the opposition is gleefully awaiting his opportunity to demonstrate the error and thereby seriously weaken or bring about the collapse of the entire proposal.[17]

As anticipated, Delta's witnesses were questioned intensively about the viability of the company's thrift-fare proposals. American also contested the firm's capacity to provide projected cargo services, and Eastern tried to advance its own case for gaining a share of the Atlanta-to-Dallas traffic by attacking various features of the Delta–American interchange operation. Led by Maurer and O'Connell, Delta attorneys were always on hand to raise points of order and object to repetitive or improper questioning. After two weeks of cross examination in what Costello later called "a time of little sleep, hastily eaten meals at odd hours and the constant pressure of too much to do and too little time in which to do it," the Delta group felt confident that it had come through the ordeal in good shape. The company's lawyers then returned to the offensive as Eastern, National, and other carriers took the stand. Finally, on October 24, 1959, after seventy-four volumes of transcript totaling an estimated fifteen million words of testimony had been collected, the hearing phase came to an end.[18]

All parties, including both carriers and civic groups, then had to prepare legal briefs for submission to the CAB examiner, Edward T. Stodola, by February 18, 1960. As this process got underway, representatives of the competing airlines worked overtime to marshal as much public support as possible for their respective positions. As usual, Delta and Eastern fought each other with all the resources at their command. Rickenbacker himself took part in the battle, with a series of speeches to local groups, in which his appeal as a former racing driver, war hero, and survivor of epic ordeals was exploited to the fullest. Writing to Johnson from Arizona on November 25, 1959, Costello described a speech that Captain Eddie had made in Phoenix, "carrying the 'raft' on one shoulder, a racing automobile on the other and dangling the Medal of Honor out in front." Obviously, rivalry between the two firms was as strong as ever. Continuing its previous strategy, Delta urged municipal leaders to remain neutral about the choice of carrier and to stress their needs for competitive services on routes that Delta wished to acquire. This approach was apparently successful, for more than half of sixty cities or interest groups summarized in a memorandum by Maurer on March 8, 1960, took a neutral position between Delta and Eastern on major route issues or named no carrier at all, though twenty-three favored Eastern, National, American, or Braniff for various awards. In another encouraging development, the CAB's own Bureau of Air Operations, which filed a brief with the examiner, recommended Delta for a transcontinental route from Florida to California, though it advised imposing a mandatory stop at Atlanta, which would seriously impair Delta's ability to compete with any carrier that might be granted direct access from Miami to the Pacific Coast.[19]

In its own brief, Delta reviewed at length its historic involvement in service to the West, stressed its proven ability to compete effectively with major airlines, and argued that it would suffer greater diversionary impact than any other carrier should the CAB rule against the company's proposal. As opposed to the more limited Dallas–West Coast case, there was no question that the connecting services Delta could offer to a large number of eastern and Caribbean destinations were germane to the present proceeding, and the company's brief made the most of them. Delta also defended its projected thrift-fare and cargo operations and pointed with pride to its past record in promoting vacation travel. The massive jet-aircraft procurement program in which Delta was currently engaged was stressed, and weaknesses in the proposals of other airlines were highlighted. Finally, Delta called attention to existing imbalances that would be perpetuated and extended if any of the Big Four were to win the proceeding. In conclusion a flourish of trumpets was sounded: "Delta meets all the standards relied upon by the Board in the past for selection of carrier. No other carrier applicant can make this claim! Delta will meet *all* the needs of *both* the southern transcontinental and inter-regional markets and will be an aggressive and effective competitor with American west of the Texas gateways. The necessity for the selection of Delta is clear!"[20]

Having received the mass of briefs and exhibits produced by the carriers and civic parties, Stodola went to work sifting the enormous body of evidence in order to reach his examiner's decision, which was issued on June 20, 1960, after the relatively short span of four months. This document represented a major victory for Delta, in that the company was recommended for an extension of route 24 to the Pacific Coast. From Dallas–Fort Worth the new artery was to lead to Lubbock and Albuquerque, whence two separate airways

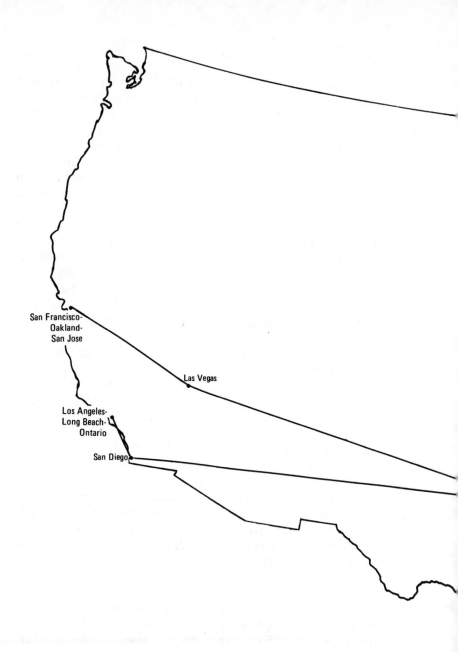

San Francisco-
Oakland-
San Jose

Las Vegas

Los Angeles-
Long Beach-
Ontario

San Diego

DELTA ROUTE SYSTEM 1961

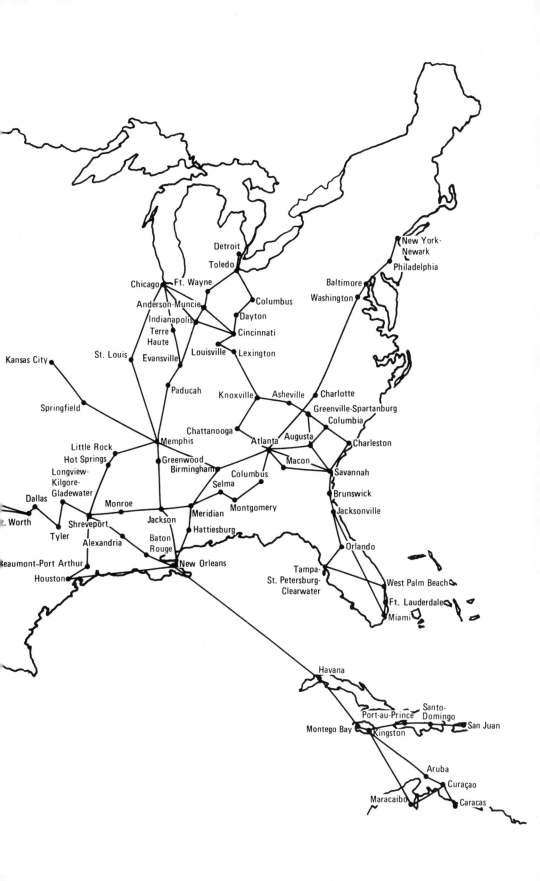

would go to San Francisco and Oakland via Las Vegas and to Los Angeles and Long Beach via Tucson, Phoenix, and San Diego. Delta was naturally delighted by this development but also disappointed because Stodola's plan would not allow the company to fly from Florida to California without stopping in Atlanta and because it also would deny a route to the West via Tampa–St. Petersburg, New Orleans, Houston, San Antonio, and El Paso. Furthermore, Delta flights between Los Angeles and San Francisco would be impossible if the examiner's report were upheld. In other extremely unwelcome developments, Stodola had advised granting Braniff a route from Dallas to Miami via New Orleans; giving National rather than Delta authority to fly from Houston to San Francisco via Dallas, Fort Worth, Lubbock, Albuquerque, and Las Vegas; and certificating Eastern to operate between Atlanta and San Antonio via Birmingham, Jackson, Shreveport, and Dallas–Fort Worth. Nevertheless, Delta's main objective of extending route 24 west of Texas to the Pacific had been recommended.[21]

As on many past occasions, however, there was no guarantee that any of the examiner's conclusions would be ratified by the CAB. The next step, therefore, was the submission of briefs to the board by all carriers and civic parties. Each firm argued in favor of recommendations with which it agreed and took exception to those deemed objectionable. Delta's brief, filed on August 26, 1960, presented evidence on the company's enormous stake in the westward extension of route 24 but argued that the addition of operating rights between Los Angeles and San Francisco was also vital to ensure satisfactory load factors in the upcoming era of large jet transports. It strenuously opposed giving a Dallas–New Orleans–Florida run to Braniff, claiming that this award would seriously undercut Delta's historic stake in these markets, established since 1943. It also strongly urged the board not to grant to Eastern rights between Atlanta and Texas, the weakest segment under dispute in the entire case from the point of view of passenger flow. Finally, Delta continued to press its claim to a western route through Houston and San Antonio and particularly opposed granting National authority to fly from Houston to Dallas–Fort Worth.[22]

Oral arguments before the five-member CAB commenced on September 26, 1960, and lasted three days. Then, after the most hotly contested proceedings in its history, the board withdrew to ponder the mountains of exhibits, briefs, recommendations, and testimony that had been amassed. It took almost six months for the decision to be hammered out, while the industry waited in suspense. At last, on March 13, 1961, the news was released. Delta was one of the two major beneficiaries, winning 2,789 new route miles along two separate airways to the Pacific Coast. One of them led from Dallas and Fort Worth to Los Angeles and Long Beach via San Diego. The other led from the same Texas cities to Oakland and San Francisco via Las Vegas. Nonstop authority between Atlanta and California was also authorized, along with numerous one-stop connections between eastern and western points.[23]

Maurer, whose leadership of the legal division had contributed so greatly to the outcome, happened to be at the Detroit airport when the news came in, and he learned about the decision from Delta ticket agents who were excitedly passing word up and down the counter. Hastening to the nearest telephone, he called Gray in Washington; Gray confirmed the reports and told him that a copy of the CAB decision was already on a plane bound for Atlanta. When he returned to Atlanta that night, Maurer was met at the airport by his entire legal staff, whom he accompanied to headquarters in order to study the decision in detail. Then they telephoned Woolman at home. As was to be expected, the boss was in a jovial mood. Over the years, when asked about how things were going, C.E. had developed a habit of striking a "poor boy" pose by answering, "I never felt better, and I never had less." This time, Maurer recalled years afterward, there was a different twist. In reaction to the award that fulfilled one of his lifetime dreams, he exclaimed to Maurer, "I never felt better, and I never had more."[24]

There were, predictably, some disappointments for Woolman and his associates. National, the other big winner in the case, did receive operating rights from Miami to Los Angeles and San Francisco, which Delta had wanted for itself, and Continental had won the privilege of serving San Antonio, El Paso, Tucson, and Phoenix on a new route from Houston to Los Angeles. Delta was gratified that Stodola's recommendation of a Houston-to-Dallas run for National had not been upheld and that no new service was authorized between Atlanta and Dallas–Fort Worth but displeased that Eastern had been granted the Miami–Tampa–New Orleans–Dallas route that the examiner had earmarked for Braniff.

Any regrets about these aspects of the decision, however, were decisively overshadowed by jubilation over the fact that Delta had been transformed from an essentially regional trunk line into a transcontinental carrier. As news of the CAB action spread through

Atlanta headquarters on March 14, a crowd of about two thousand employees assembled in the jet-overhaul hangar to hear a beaming Woolman announce the award. As a symbol of the victory, Dolson presented C.E. with the same key to New York City that had been used at the champagne christening marking the inauguration of the company's jet service to that crucial destination, topped by a placard bearing the slogan, "California, here we come via Delta." This line was quickly taken up as a chant by the excited throng. In his remarks, Woolman stressed that the triumph had resulted from collective effort and said, "I'm proud to be associated with a group of people like you."[25]

In accordance with CAB procedures, the decision reached in March was not final until petitions for reconsideration had been heard from carriers and civic parties dissenting from various features of the awards that had been announced. American, for example, protested that the decision would result in revenue losses for it far beyond what the board had projected and, along with Braniff, continued to plead for the Dallas-to-Miami route that had been granted to Eastern. TWA wanted restrictions imposed upon Delta's right to provide transcontinental service to passengers from points north of Atlanta without changing planes at that city, and National opposed a feature of the decision that extended Delta's route 24 to Jacksonville and Orlando, thus making possible one-plane transcontinental service from those points to California via the Atlanta gateway. Both National and Delta challenged another provision, which forbade them to offer local service between Las Vegas and San Francisco.[26]

After deliberating on these and other pleas, the CAB issued a final order on May 26, reaffirming the basic provisions of the March decision, including the crucial transcontinental awards to Delta. There were some minor adjustments. Delta, for example, was upheld in its right to carry passengers from Charlotte and other points north of Georgia to the Pacific Coast without a change of planes in Atlanta, though on such flights the company was obliged to make at least one stop between Atlanta and Dallas. The "closed door" between Las Vegas and San Francisco was retained but only on a temporary basis, pending disposition of a Pacific–Southwest local-service proceeding. National's petition that Jacksonville and Orlando be placed on that company's route 39, rather than on Delta's route 24, was denied. At last, after more than three years of strife, the Southern

Transcontinental Service case was officially over, and Delta could begin to harvest the fruits of its victory.[27]

As congratulatory messages poured into Atlanta, the company prepared for the customary gala events to mark the beginning of service over the new routes. On June 1, 1961, a DC-8 loaded with southeastern dignitaries took off from Atlanta for Los Angeles on a preinaugural flight, arriving in four hours and eight minutes. After being greeted by a Dixieland band and a crowd of well-wishers, the passengers refreshed themselves at the Los Angeles terminal with champagne and strawberries, then embarked on a schedule of activities that included visits to Disneyland and to the Cocoanut Grove night club. Meanwhile, the plane took off for the East with a large party of Californians, who touched down first at New Orleans, where Delta board chairman Richard Freeman hosted them at dinner at the Old Absinthe House, and then proceeded to Atlanta. Later in June a planeload of guests representing the media were taken on a three-day preinaugural trip to Las Vegas, where they visited such local attractions as the downtown Casino Center and the Dunes, Sahara, Sands, Thunderbird, and Desert Inn hotels. "Las Vegas definitely knows that Delta has arrived," the manager of Delta's news bureau subsequently reported to Woolman, noting that company billboards had been posted along the Strip.[28]

Regularly scheduled service to Los Angeles began on June 11 with three jet flights; the first, in a DC-8 commanded by Floyd Addison, carried the Woolmans and was greeted by a large crowd, including an old friend of the company, Donald Douglas. In a symbolic gesture, the plane carried a Confederate flag, the flag of the California Republic, and the Lone Star flag of Texas, picked up in ceremonies at Dallas. Service to Las Vegas began July 1, with daily DC-7 flights via Birmingham, Jackson, Shreveport, and Dallas. Because of the need to obtain more jet planes and the inadvisability of trying to compete with existing American Airlines schedules until the new planes arrived, service to San Francisco did not begin until October, preceded as usual by preinaugural flights that enabled dignitaries from both ends of the route to enjoy the customary round of banquets, nightclub tours, and visits to scenic attractions. During the same month jet service between Orlando and Los Angeles began, facilitating the movement of personnel between Cape Canaveral and rocket installations on the West Coast. The following spring the CAB removed the "closed door" restriction between Las Vegas and San Francisco, further enhancing the value of that particular route.[29]

In the midst of these events an editorial in the *Delta Digest* invoked the words of an old hymn familiar to generations of worshipers in the southeastern Bible Belt, which the firm had served for so long. The writer acknowledged that some of the lines were mawkish and that the melody to which they were sung was "not beautiful as a Bach fugue is beautiful." Nevertheless, both words and music summed up admirably Delta's vibrant mood as the company looked back upon all that had transpired since the mid-1950s. "Count your blessings," the hymn began. "Name them one by one."[30] For Delta, there were a great many blessings to count.

However important the company's victory in the Atlanta–to–New York case had been in Delta's rise to greatness, it was the successful outcome of the West Coast case which gave it the means to become a truly major airline. Given the enormous postwar growth of the Sun Belt and the popularity of the tourist attractions with which California and Nevada abounded, the market potential of the routes leading to Los Angeles, Las Vegas, and San Francisco was incalculable. Furthermore, the vast distances stretching between these places and Delta's eastern cities provided ideal conditions for the distinctive economics of jet transportation to work in the company's favor; a comparatively few planeloads of travelers bound nonstop from Atlanta to Los Angeles, for example, would result in far greater earnings than a much larger number of short-hop up-and-down flights between a string of small cities located only a few hundred miles apart. Furthermore, Delta could, and would, use its many connections with relatively small southeastern and midwestern communities to funnel traffic into such nodal centers as Atlanta, thus collecting passenger pools for the long nonstop runs where the greatest profits were to be gained. Now, more than at any previous time, the company's system had a highly advantageous mixture of cities with varying populations, locations, and resources, all adding up to a recipe for success; and Delta was poised to enter the ranks of America's foremost commercial airlines.

CHAPTER 17

Coping with Problems
in an Age of Transition

FOR DELTA the dawning of the jet age was not solely a matter
of planning and implementing service, sending newer swifter
birds hither and yon over parts of its route system; nor was it
solely a matter of waging such regulatory battles as the fierce struggle for a route to the West Coast. New problems arose, and old problems persisted. Some challenges, such as climbing inflation and
growing public demand for in-flight liquor service, were products of
the times, spawned by an affluent society grown increasingly more
complex with the spread of industrial technology and accelerating
change. Others, such as a series of difficult pilot negotiations,
seemed to run counter to prevailing trends.

During the 1950s labor-management relations in the United
States were generally good. Indeed, between 1953 and 1964—roughly from the time of the Delta and C&S merger to the early years of
jet operations—man-days of production lost because of strikes in
the United States went over .03 percent for only one year, 1959.[1] In
the airline industry, however, labor strife increased as the 1950s
waned, and strikes began to have a significant impact on the relative
standings and economic health of the leading airlines. Space does
not permit discussion here of all the factors involved, but one especially noteworthy development was the battle between the Airline
Pilots Association (ALPA) and the Flight Engineers International
Association (FEIA) over the status of flight engineers on turbine-
powered aircraft. So bitter did this conflict become that in some airlines flight crews actually drew chalk lines on the cockpit floor to
mark their territorial preserves. Because it was unionized to a much
smaller degree than most carriers, and because its management had
wisely chosen to avoid having two separate unions represented in its
cockpit crews by opting for pilot engineers rather than flight engineers (see Chapter 7), Delta had less reason for concern than its major competitors and came out of the decade with its labor relations

in excellent shape. Nonetheless, there were some anxious moments along the way.

Delta's first negotiations with ALPA after the C&S merger had been concluded in December 1955 with no undue amount of friction. The contract signed at that time was to continue in force until June 1, 1957, and was to renew itself automatically on that date if neither party wished to reopen negotiations; if changes were sought, however, at least sixty days' notice was required. In January 1957 the Delta chapter of ALPA indicated to management that it intended to reopen negotiations. Company records do not indicate that Woolman or his associates felt any apprehension at that point, but the situation changed somewhat in March, when Clarence N. Sayen of ALPA's national office forwarded a copy of the proposed changes in the 1955 contract. The minutes of the meeting held by Delta's board of directors on April 25, 1957, characterized these initial demands as "fantastic." The consensus, following a gloomy analysis by Dolson, was that "the current negotiations will be much more difficult than in the past."

The changes proposed by ALPA fell into two main categories: general terms of employment and matters pertaining to the pilots' grievance committee, known as the "system board of adjustment," which had been established under the 1955 contract. In addition, the pilots sought to modify their existing retirement income plan, particularly by making it fully noncontributory.[2] Shortly before the issues were joined across the bargaining table in mid-April, Delta's payroll supervisor estimated that the monetary demands alone, involving various categories of compensation, would require an added annual outlay of $7,482,522 per year. The categories in which the greatest increases were sought were longevity pay; pay for operational-duty time for first pilot, copilot, and second pilot (pilot engineer); and pay for trip hours. This last category led all others, with a projected figure of $2,869,620; the cost of increased longevity pay was estimated at $868,076. Added operational-duty pay would require more than $2 million each year.[3]

Looking back upon the episode two decades later, management officials and pilots alike recalled that neither side wanted a strike. Here, as on other occasions, Delta benefited from having an unusual degree of rapport among the different echelons of the organization. Nevertheless, handwritten notes surviving from the negotiating sessions reveal the size of the gulf separating the two interest groups. On August 22, 1957, having sampled opinion among the Delta pilots, Ralph L. Harkenrider of the ALPA employment agreements department summed up the talks that had been held thus far by informing management representatives that his organization no longer felt "in position to negotiate" because of remaining disparities between the contending parties. The pilots, he contended, had made "all proposals . . . we have listened to your objections and tried to reconcile differences." If one more round of conversations did not produce agreement, he stated, the discussions would collapse. Moments later Dolson, who had once played a leading role in founding Delta's ALPA chapter but now sat on the other side of the table, said, "Afraid we can't do anything with it, Ralph," whereupon Harkenrider responded, "I'm sorry you can't, I really am." A three-week recess was then agreed upon, giving each side time to reevaluate its position and to study the results of concurrent contract negotiations involving other airlines, which might be helpful in resolving the Delta impasse.[4]

During the recess ALPA appealed to the National Mediation Board (NMB) to intervene in the Delta negotiations. Still feeling that direct "one-on-one" discussions might yield results, management reluctantly agreed to the idea, but was gratified when the NMB took the same position and recommended that more talks take place before mediation was commenced. On September 17, therefore, representatives of the two parties met again. Apparently their respective positions had softened in the interim, for progress now began to take place. By September 19 things had proceeded to a point at which discussion centered upon such relatively minor matters as the way in which pilots were reimbursed for such expenses as lodging and taxi fares while away from home; Harkenrider was trying to secure concessions in this area to compensate for Delta's refusal to budge on the union's demand for a noncontributory retirement plan. Sensing that a breakthrough was within reach, W. T. Beebe of the management team asked, "Can we assume from this discussion that the rest of . . . [the company's] proposal is acceptable?" "Just about," Harkenrider replied, ticking off various items on which ALPA was prepared to agree. The next day Dolson sent a terse message to the various Delta stations: "Tentative agreement reached in pilot contract negotiations this date with regard to pay items." It took several more weeks to iron out all details and put them into draft form. By November, however, agreement had been reached on all the matters in dispute, and ALPA withdrew its application for NMB intervention.[5]

The 1957 contract was to continue in force until April 10, 1959, with automatic renewal provisions similar to those agreed upon in 1955. There was also periodic need to interpret and reinterpret aspects of the settlement. Writing on June 26, 1958, to Captain Stewart Hopkins, chairman of the master executive council (MEC) of Delta's ALPA chapter, Dolson mentioned "problems which continue to plague us in relation to . . . the current pilot agreement." Dolson went on to state that "most of the inequities existing in the present contract are, I believe, compensated for by economic safeguards. I believe this was foreseen by the negotiators." The blunt-speaking former pilot added, "In my opinion, the present situation is the result of pilots not really wanting what they thought they did. This is not unusual." It may have been that Dolson was conditioned by then to see things only from a managerial point of view, but his statement also may have reflected the old adage "It takes one to know one." The pilots were ever zealous for gains and what they perceived as their rights, although the fact that they had never struck perhaps indicates that, like most other Delta employees, they shared the unusual loyalty that pervaded the company's patriarchal structure. When the Delta MEC met in April 1958, it aired various pilot concerns. One of these had to do with retroactive pay due under the terms of the contract of 1957 but delayed by the intricacies of processing checks in an era when the firm was just beginning to install more up-to-date data-handling equipment. The MEC immediately got in touch with the relevant company office, which expressed regret over the delay and promised that the checks would be forthcoming in a few weeks. The pilots accepted the delay.[6]

Such willingness to give management the benefit of the doubt contrasted sharply with the experience of several other carriers at the time. In 1958 several presidential emergency boards held hearings and made recommendations in an effort to avert a clash between various trunk-lines and employee groups over such issues as the "third crew member" controversy between pilots and flight engineers and dissatisfaction with pay scales. In attempting to deal with the first of these problems, the federal panels recommended that the third crew member, on most airlines a flight engineer without pilot training, receive such training for service on turbine-powered aircraft and that there be a combined seniority list for pilots and flight engineers. When such companies as Eastern tried to implement this advice they met stiff employee resistance. Soon work stoppages began to erupt throughout the industry over this and other issues. Capital was struck by its mechanics, whose union refused to accept an emergency board's recommendations for a pay hike. Responding to this initial walkout, five airlines—Capital, United, TWA, American, and Pan American—announced a mutual-aid pact, subject to CAB approval, in which they pledged to extend financial help to any participant closed by a strike. Despite ALPA objections, the CAB approved, but the pact failed to deter employees from taking strike action. Before the end of 1958, Eastern was struck by both its flight engineers and its mechanics. The former objected to a company requirement that flight engineers should have pilot training on turbine-powered craft, in line with federal recommendations; the latter wanted more pay than the emergency boards suggested. TWA's mechanics walked out for the same reason, and dissatisfaction with salary scales and a desire that the third cockpit-crew member have pilot training, among other issues, also led American's pilots to strike.[7]

While these bombs were exploding throughout the industry, Delta remained relatively secure for two main reasons: its nonunion tradition and the wisdom of Woolman's decision, following the C&S merger, to continue to insist on the use of pilot engineers. In August 1958, when jurisdictional conflict between the FEIA and ALPA was about to explode, Richard W. Freeman, chairman of the board, had written Delta's president: "I am more than ever reminded of the very smart decision you made some three years ago that all Flight Engineers are to be qualified Pilots. It is certainly indicated that this issue is leading to real trouble." Once the issue erupted, its effect on Eastern, combined with that firm's other labor problems, brought direct benefits to Delta. Replying to a question about how the company's business had been affected by the wave of airline strikes, Woolman commented: "As might be expected, our business during the Eastern strike increased very substantially. There is no question but that many people were introduced to Delta service as a result of the strike. . . . If we continue to provide the proper standard of service, there is no question but that we will retain a lot of the 'strike patronage.'"[8]

To the firms that suffered them, the airline strikes were extremely costly. The Eastern walkout of 1958, for example, lasted thirty-nine days and grounded all services, in the middle of the profitable Florida winter tourist season. Problems involving the status of flight engineers continued into the 1960s and were settled in various ways by the different airlines affected; the ALPA's position in favor of pilot engineers tended to prevail.[9] To some extent, Delta looked on from the sidelines, but in a period of industry-wide strife the flight-engineer, wage, and other problems, leading as they did to new strikes and new settlements, could not help but bring indirect pressure on the company to grant increased benefits to its own personnel, even those who were not organized.

In April 1959 Vice-President Beebe reported to Woolman that James Hoffa's International Brotherhood of Teamsters was vigorously attempting to organize the airline industry. According to Beebe's contact, the Teamsters thought that "Delta was just the kind of company they would like to tackle since Delta was anti-union." This news was confirmed by a Teamster insider whom Beebe knew personally. Teamster organizers had visited various Delta cities in March 1959 and had made contact with company employees, seeking a chink in the company's armor—a station where willing recruits could be signed up immediately. Such a place would provide a base of operations and "give their drive momentum at the other cities." Beebe stated that Hoffa's agents had not discovered such a chink yet, but he warned that they would probably keep trying.

In July, Beebe reported continuing Teamster probes. He also noted that the Air Lines Stewards and Stewardesses Association, affiliated with ALPA, was "very active among our stewardesses in Miami, Atlanta, and Memphis." John L. Sutton, director of flight personnel, however, had held meetings with the women, which had "resulted in the union organizing drive losing momentum." All in all, Beebe commented to Woolman, "employee relations are certainly being subjected to the most severe tests of recent years because of all the union organizing activities." Nevertheless, he was "encouraged by the strength of our people's convictions up to this point."[10]

By late 1960 the Teamster drive had abated so far as Delta was concerned, apparently owing to Delta's having met most of the economic expectations of the employees at whom Hoffa's efforts were aimed. Beebe, however, expressed to Woolman his continued concern that ALPA, from which a dissatisfied older stewardess group had recently defected, would attempt to replace it with a new subsidiary for flight attendants and would make "an intensive stewardess union drive on Delta. . . . The company is presently conducting a series of stewardess meetings . . . and all bases will be covered in the next thirty days." He summarized the general labor situation in commercial aviation: "There has been and continues to be substantial labor unrest in the industry, including strikes by various unions against Southern Airways, Continental, Northwest and Braniff Airlines. . . . I think it is safe to predict that the next 12 months may bring additional labor turmoil in our industry. In the long run, this all works against Delta because the settlements made with the union reflect themselves in Delta costs."

Despite Beebe's fears, new attempts to organize Delta's stewardesses were no more successful than the earlier Teamster drive had been. In addition, the company was fortunate in its relations with Delta's ALPA chapter. The mood was relaxed in 1959 as negotiations began for a new pilot agreement that would take into account the inauguration of service with turbojet equipment. Indeed, the company took the lead in reopening negotiations over the pilots' contract on all counts except the sections dealing with the seniority list and the systems board of adjustment. At the January 1959 meeting, Dolson told the board of directors that no particular difficulties were anticipated over the new contract, and there apparently were none. Instead of starting out with extreme demands and then compromising, the two sides evidently began in moderation. Although pay rates were higher in the new contract, signed on April 10, 1959, and provisions reflecting the advent of jet equipment had been incorporated, changes were few in comparison to those that had generated strife in the 1957 negotiations.[11]

One issue, however, still lingered from the 1953 merger. In the spring of 1958, more than two hundred pilots on the company's roster of approximately seven hundred appealed to the CAB to review the seniority list put together more than six years before. This group, consisting mostly of former C&S personnel, claimed that tension persisted over alleged inequities resulting from the postmerger agreement negotiated with the help of ALPA. Claiming that the charges were not justified, Delta management pointed out that the integrated list had not been injected into discussions involving the pilot contracts negotiated in 1955, 1957, and 1959. After hearing both parties, the CAB declined to review the list, and the problem subsided.[12]

Beebe had been correct, however, in anticipating that conditions in the industry generally would get worse before they got better. At one point early in the new decade, six airlines were shut down by strikes, including Eastern, which was suffering a second walkout. Delta continued to benefit from the resulting extra business, and indeed its facilities were almost overburdened. When conditions eased somewhat in March 1961, the company placed an advertisement in several leading newspapers, in which Woolman likened its situation to that of "a husband unexpectedly bringing home two dozen guests for dinner. Every available aircraft was put into service. Extra sections were scheduled on every route possible. Reservation phone calls multiplied over, and over, and over." He praised passengers for their patience and expressed gratitude "to our Delta employees, who forgot quitting hours and just worked on . . . and on." All in all it was one of the shrewdest advertisements that Delta had ever used. Now, Woolman informed the public, "We hope you will fly Delta again soon, to experience the full quality of our service via phone, at ticket counters, and in the air."[13]

Though the labor picture probably had caused Delta executives to take an occasional aspirin and Woolman to bury himself more intently in his off-duty hobby, raising orchids in his own hothouse, Delta had nonetheless emerged relatively unscathed from a period of strife that seriously affected other less fortunate carriers. But headaches were experienced in other areas as well. Among other things, "demon rum," though not as serious as labor problems, direct and indirect, also produced anxiety. Years later, in reflecting on her pioneer role as a Delta stewardess and on her observations as a passenger since, Birdie Perkins, now Mrs. Richard Bomar, remarked that service of alcoholic beverages by airlines had produced marked changes in passengers as a group—from relatively well behaved and thus easy to control to often quarrelsome and very difficult to manage. Dolson, however, disagreed, arguing that by serving liquor the airlines had acted to limit intake and to exert more control. Certainly before Delta seriously considered serving alcoholic beverages on its aircraft in the late 1950s, there had been various unfortunate incidents associated with liquor.[14]

In the period 1951 to 1957, when no alcohol at all was permitted on board Delta aircraft, several rather nasty episodes with possible legal ramifications had occurred, sometimes even forcing emergency landings. One such incident in 1951 began as an apparent heart attack; once on the ground, however, the afflicted passenger seemed to be only a belligerent drunk and ended up being hauled off by police after having berated the Delta crew, threatened to sue the airline, and verbally assailed law-enforcement officials on the scene. In addition, minor episodes sometimes caused embarrassment to passengers and crews and required the exercise of firmness, judgment, and tact. Cabin attendants, who bore the brunt of these episodes, were naturally skeptical about the wisdom of serving liquor as a normal part of trips aboard the company's planes, but during the 1950s pressure to adopt such a policy, arising from passengers' wishes and the policies of competitors, became ever stronger.[15]

Various domestic airlines, including American, United, Eastern, Northwest, and TWA, had begun serving alcoholic beverages by 1957; transoceanic flag lines, such as Pan American, had been serving liquor much longer. For a time Delta steadfastly resisted growing pressures to change, even when they came from powerful voices within the company. In June 1955 Director Winship Nunnally wrote Woolman suggesting that a maximum of two cocktails per passenger be served on each flight. Although he personally felt that liquor and flying did not mix, Nunnally argued that "we have to adjust our practices to what the public demands, providing there is no serious objection." The considerations prompting his advice became clear when he mentioned that he had observed Eastern serving drinks on its flights from Atlanta to New York and United dispensing cocktails on its routes to the West Coast. Because Delta was then seeking access to the heavily urbanized Northeast and would soon become involved in a massive attempt to penetrate such populous markets as Los Angeles and San Francisco, perhaps the time had come to cater to metropolitan tastes. E. H. Bishop, Miami district sales manager, urged the same policy, suggesting that wine be served on certain Miami-to-Chicago flights. The "'elegance' of the normal meal service is enhanced considerably with an appropriate wine," Bishop stressed.[16]

But the advice of Nunnally, Bishop, and others did not immediately prevail, for the lure of the elegant and the cosmopolitan was counterbalanced by the attitudes prevalent in Delta's base of operations —the South, with its Bible-belt orientation. In July 1957 the *Christian Index*, official organ of the Georgia Baptist Convention, praised Delta for its no-alcohol policy. Prominent pastor Louis D. Newton of Atlanta endorsed an open letter, written by the executive secretary of the Florida Baptist Convention to its 400,000 members, expressing satisfaction that no liquor had been offered on a recent Delta flight, in contrast to his experience on other airlines. Baptist conferences in other southern states wrote, in a seemingly well-organized campaign, to commend Delta for its stand and to urge it not to give in to the growing trend toward serving liquor on flights.[17]

Nor were Baptists the only denomination to urge Delta to "continue to fly dry," as one Presbyterian minister in Houston put it. At least one clergyman, Lindsey D. Boyd, pastor of a Baptist church in

Gainesville, Florida, showed some appreciation of Delta's unenviable position. He was aware, he indicated, that there was a "diversity of opinions" on the issue and acknowledged that the company management was "caught in the middle." Boyd further mentioned a poll among airline passengers, in which some 80 percent favored serving alcoholic beverages in flight. Woolman replied that he doubted the accuracy of such a poll but admitted having received a "good many requests for such service." On the other hand, he informed an Atlanta lay Baptist who praised Delta for its stand, "We intend to resist giving this service, unless . . . we find that the great majority of our passengers prefer it, which somehow I cannot believe will be the case." [18]

It is difficult to tell whether Woolman, no teetotaler himself, was deeply convinced of this assessment of public opinion or merely "whistling 'Dixie,'" but, as the months passed, various passenger surveys showed that more and more of Delta's passengers wanted in-flight liquor service. At the beginning of March 1958 the firm was the only regional or trunk carrier not serving alcohol on its domestic routes. By that time Delta had acquired access to New York, and on the potentially lucrative flights from Houston to New York it was being outdistanced by Eastern, which was averaging thirty passengers per departure to Delta's fourteen. Delta gave rose corsages to women, provided knitted slippers for comfort en route, and furnished Corona cigars for men, but to no avail: Eastern served liquor. Finally, on March 8, Woolman bowed to the inevitable, and the decision was made to sell liquor (some lines provided it free) on Delta's nonstop flights 770 and 771 from Houston to New York. Only two drinks per passenger were to be served per flight, and they were to be sold only in a short space of time before lunch or dinner. Further evidence of the reluctance with which this limited experiment was undertaken was the manner of serving: stewardesses handed out cards with the menus, after which those wishing to order—some 65 percent in March alone—received sealed miniatures and had to mix their own cocktails. Even this conservative approach had a salutary effect on business, however, for Delta sales personnel in Houston notified various firms whose employees had previously flown Eastern on the New York run and were gratified to report that such personnel had begun to switch to Delta. [19]

As expected, a volley of protests greeted this change in company policy, with southern Baptists firing most of the ammunition. The *Christian Index*, in an editorial on March 6, had urged its readers to

Mr. Woolman looks at the portrait, painted by Anthony Wills of Houston, presented to him by the company's one thousand pilots in 1964. *Left to right:* Captain Truman Outland, who made the presentation, Mrs. Outland, Woolman, Robert Griffith, Fritz Schwaemmle.

These members of Delta's first stewardess corps came to Atlanta on Woolman's fortieth anniversary to present a DC-2 model to the boss. *Left to right:* Sybil Peacock Harmon, Laura Wizark Baker, Woolman, LaJuan Gilmore McBride, Birdie Perkins Bomar, and Inez Jackson Gibson.

Final flight of Delta's last DC-3 in 1960. *Left to right:* First Officer D. T. Rounds, Stewardess Gail Airoldi, Captain H. G. Rowley, and Honorary Stewardess Birdie Perkins Bomar.

Charles H. Dolson (*right*) presents symbolic key to C. E. Woolman in celebration of Delta's victory in Transcontinental Route Case, 1961.

Delta introduced the DC-9-14 in 1965. This is the DC-9-32, which joined the Delta fleet in 1967.

The DC-8-61, which joined the Delta fleet in April 1967.

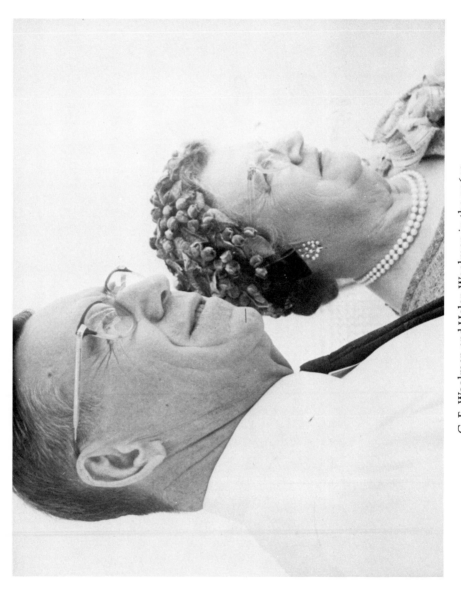

C. E. Woolman and Helen Woolman in the 1960s.

The Lockheed L-100 "Hercules," which succeeded the C-46 as Delta's cargo carrier in 1966.

A 1925 Huff Daland Duster, reconditioned by Delta employees as a memorial to C. E. Woolman and presented to the Smithsonian Institution in 1968. On the platform are *(left to right)* Charles H. Dolson, S. Paul Johnston, Catherine Fitz-Gerald, Stuart Tipton, and Gene Berry.

"Fly Delta if You Fly," encouraging people going to the impending annual meeting of the Southern Baptist Convention in Houston to patronize Woolman's company. The following week, after the firm's change of policy on the flights from Houston to New York had been announced, the *Index* headlined an editorial with the words "Goodbye, Delta; We Are Sorry" and suggested that enough protests might bring about a reversal of the decision. On March 24, Laigh Parker wrote a long reply to the *Index*, pointing out that on 99 percent of Delta's flights no alcohol was served, despite diversion of business to competitors who served liquor over the same routes. Delta hoped to keep it that way, he stated, but "the severity of the criticism and the harshness of the condemnation . . . from some of our ministerial friends and a number of your readers offers us little encouragement to continue our efforts in that direction."[20]

One of the most unenviable tasks in the entire controversy fell to Delta sales representative Lorenzer Jones, who had been trying to promote business for the Houston meeting of the Southern Baptist Convention. Earl Cocke, Jr., Delta's vice-president for civic affairs, frankly informed Woolman and those who had supported his decision that "we let Lorenzer Jones down something terrible . . . in the fast action in making this change." Jones, who had not been informed of the decision beforehand, was stuck trying to defend his integrity to his Baptist contacts.[21]

Another tough aspect of the move was the anguished reaction it produced among members of the Delta family, many of whom were ardent temperance advocates. Here Woolman again displayed his masterly personal touch. The new policy had been a business decision, he explained, however reluctantly adopted, and Delta's success had been built on shrewd business decisions. But, as one interesting exchange of correspondence indicates, Woolman characteristically did not adopt a "like it or lump it" approach in defending the new policy to unhappy employees. Stewardess Patricia Southard wrote to him on September 7, 1958, about a rumor that Delta would soon serve liquor on all first-class flights. "If it is," she said, "I feel Delta is making a bad mistake . . . is lowering their standards to do business." Her letter clearly epitomized the loyalty toward the company that characterized its rank and file: "Mr. Woolman, I've worked for Delta for 5 years and I've always been proud of my company because they deal fair and square with everyone. This in turn was passed on to the people." Now, perhaps because of the same loyalty, she felt impelled to speak out on what for her was clearly an issue of conscience. When the other airlines were serving liquor and Delta was not, she asked rhetorically, did that not make Delta "a little stronger, a little more like God would want us to be?"

Ever the diplomat, Woolman replied that, although the rumor was not entirely correct, Delta was indeed planning an extension of its liquor service. He explained at length why Delta was being forced to change its no-drink policy, pointing out that the number of people who patronized the firm because of that stand "has not been numerous enough to offset the effect of the business we have lost." Continuing to emphasize pragmatic realities, he mentioned "the very heavy financial commitments Delta has made to assure that we have the finest equipment available with which to provide service equal to or better than that of our competitors" and stressed that, "in recent months, our profit has amounted to the equivalent of the patronage of only one-half passenger per aircraft mile flown." He hoped that Southard could understand why, at a time when the country and the airline industry were in the throes of a serious recession, the decision to serve liquor had to be made. "I personally have resisted it to the point where it is no longer advisable," he told her, "but I am glad you wrote me as you did as it has given me the opportunity to outline the problem with which we have been faced. Thank you for your expression of loyalty to Delta and for the contribution you have made in the last five years to our success. I hope we can continue to merit such."[22]

Gradually the controversy simmered down. Occasionally a patron would protest, and Woolman would patiently reply. One letter received in May 1959 complained that the serving of drinks seemed to take precedence over other aspects of service by the cabin crew. Woolman admitted the problem but maintained that stewardesses were instructed to give the needs of nondrinkers "prior consideration in their choice of beverages, magazines, pillows, etc." By that time, however, public demand was altering Delta's initially conservative approach to the serving of alcoholic beverages; the company was offering liquor on most flights and the "card with the menu" approach had been discontinued. Despite the pleas of a vocal minority, the change of policy had been accepted enthusiastically by most passengers and was here to stay.[23]

As was characteristic in an industry that practiced considerable self-regulation and was constantly under the scrutiny of federal officials, alcohol was served in accordance with standard policies designed to ensure safe and efficient operation. Under an agreement signed with the Air Transport Association on June 27, 1958, the number of drinks remained limited to two per passenger for each flight, nonstop or segmental. Guidelines laid down in Washington after the creation of the Federal Aviation Agency (FAA) in the same year further diminished the risk of untoward incidents resulting from the behavior of inebriated pasengers. An FAA regulation of March 10, 1960, strictly prohibited the consumption of alcoholic beverages aboard an airliner unless they had been served by the carrier operating the plane. No such beverage was to be served to any person who appeared to be intoxicated. The FAA requested Delta and other lines to provide information about this policy to travelers in "public relations folders normally provided all passengers . . . in the pocket in the back of each passenger seat." The administrator of the FAA, Ellwood R. (Pete) Quesada, stressed that the agency expected "to pursue vigorously any report of a violation." During the 1960s letters and memoranda in Delta's files continued to detail occasional "drinking incidents," but they do not appear to have represented any more significant a problem than the company had experienced before 1958.[24]

The Federal Aviation Agency (later Federal Aviation Administration) came into being in 1958, with the passage of the Federal Aviation Act. This act came about in part because of serious organizational problems in the old setup with respect to the effective functioning of the CAA. It had to "run the gauntlet of the CAB, the Defense Department, and a maze of interagency panels." What seemed to be needed was a "single agency with consolidated structure and binding jurisdiction." Because of the "gloom of an air transport industry facing tremendous equipment costs and the worst profit picture since the . . . late 1940's," the CAA was felt by its critics to be "too lightweight an organization with too limited a charter to provide a commanding leadership." The act of 1958 created a Federal Aviation Agency in the place of the CAA; the new FAA was answerable only to the Congress and the president. The economic regulatory provisions of the 1938 act were incorporated intact in the new legislation, which differed from its predecessor mainly in the area of air safety (in response to a series of crashes in 1958) involving both commercial and military aircraft. The FAA was granted more power to ensure better air safety. The CAB's power to prescribe air-safety rules passed to the administrator of the FAA: an important switch that meant that this official issued the very rules and standards that he and his agency enforced. The CAB, however, retained its economic regulatory powers and continued to retain full responsibility for investigating aircraft accidents and fixing their causes.[25]

Woolman and Quesada, the first FAA administrator, became good friends, and the company's relationship with the new agency was reasonably smooth, despite an early complaint by Dolson that a swelling number of FAA regulations and inspections was proving costly to the airlines without apparent commensurate benefits. The operations department was particularly critical of FAA training-flight procedures, which, as will be discussed later, led to a series of tragic accidents involving Delta and other carriers. Nevertheless, the firm had no difficulty supporting most of the directives that came from Quesada's office. Responding to the FAA's regulation of March 1960 governing the service of liquor on airline flights, Woolman told Quesada "we anticipate that it will be rigidly adhered to by our personnel. . . . Delta Air Lines has favored the adoption of an industry code with respect to the serving of alcoholic beverages aloft."[26] Similarly, Delta cooperated with the agency in its controversial regulation of March 15, 1960, mandating sixty years as the cutoff age for pilots flying large aircraft in airline operations, although, as Beebe told Woolman, "the Air Line Pilots Association will take the FAA to court immediately to test this new regulation." ALPA did as Beebe predicted, but the United States Supreme Court eventually denied its appeal.[27]

A particularly critical area in which the FAA and Delta cooperated was that of noise abatement. The noise problem was not new in airline history, but it had been intensified by the introduction of jets. As Quesada told Woolman early in 1960, the FAA was very concerned about growing public dissatisfaction with noise levels around airports and wished to work closely with individual airlines, ATA, and ALPA to secure remedial action. In Quesada's words, "the future of our air commerce may well rest on the success of our mutual efforts."[28]

Despite Quesada's hopes, the problem proved extremely complex, and cooperation among carriers, special-interest groups, and federal agencies was not always forthcoming. The airlines were often caught in the middle between governmental officials and infuriated citizens living near airports such as the Atlanta terminal or Idlewild in New York, where sleep was disturbed and church services disrupted by arriving or departing aircraft or by engine tests at jet-maintenance facilities. In the absence of established mechanisms for resolving the issue, such episodes often led to private damage suits, which, though results generally favored the industry in the early jet days, did involve time and expense.[29]

Delta, like other lines, attempted to deal with the problem by means of a variety of expedients, none completely successful. Responding to the complaint of a family living near the Atlanta jet-maintenance base, Fritz Schwaemmle took the members on a tour of the facility and pointed out the steps taken to "reduce or confine" the noise, such as installing thick masonry walls, putting sound suppressors on engines, and employing sound engineers for future planning. The family seemed impressed. Later, an improved test cell was designed to muffle the sound of test operations still further. When J. H. (Jack) Gray, veteran manager of the Atlanta airport, complained in August 1960 that airport personnel were being forced to go home ill from the revving of Delta's jet engines near the terminal, the company took additional corrective measures: engines would "be positioned with compass readings as near due north as practical" in order to aim the noise away from airport buildings, and tests would be stopped entirely if the control tower advised that they were impeding the operation of the airport. A month later G. J. Dye, Delta's superintendent of maintenance, dealt with the problem of excessive noise at night by issuing orders that, at the airport itself, the test stand not be operated between 7:00 P.M. and 7:00 A.M. and that engines on aircraft not be run up between 10:00 P.M. and 6:00 A.M.[30]

Delta's major noise problem in the early jet era occurred, however, not at Atlanta but at Idlewild. In October 1960 John R. Wiley, director of the aviation department of the Port of New York Authority, wrote Woolman, complaining in strong language that Delta had "repeatedly and continuously flouted our jet noise criteria." He went on to specify the nature of the violations, described previous communications with Delta personnel about the situation, and ended with a threat to revoke Delta's permission to operate jet aircraft at Idlewild.[31]

As the ALPA safety chairman for the New York region commented, the Port Authority had itself contributed to a chaotic situation at Idlewild by withdrawing from a unified program of noise abatement established with the help of ALPA, ATA, and federal officials and by making individual agreements with various airlines in an attempt to impose its own standards. The latter, based on the findings of a consulting firm that had surveyed the problems of communities near the airport, were considered a threat to air safety by

ALPA and ATA, particularly in that they required a momentary reduction of power during takeoff. Just why Delta was singled out by the Port Authority for violating its rules is not clear, for a number of airlines disagreed with the new rules. It is possible, however, that Delta's extreme safety consciousness led its pilots to operate in accordance with ALPA–ATA criteria, rather than with Port Authority standards.

For a time Delta and the Port Authority continued on a collision course, and the Port Authority took its case to a New York state court. Delta succeeded in having the proceeding transferred to a federal district court, but in the end the company had to reach an accommodation with the Port Authority. In a letter of November 4, 1960, Woolman promised the Port Authority's legal counsel that "we believe we can demonstrate to your satisfaction that Delta Air Lines can and will conduct its operations so as to conform to your rules and regulations . . . and it is our intention to cooperate with you in every reasonable effort to attain this goal." Woolman continued, however, "Nothing in this letter concedes the legality or reasonableness of your rules and regulations." On the basis of the company's subsequent noise-abatement performance at Idlewild, the Port Authority withdrew its suit from federal court early in 1961.[32] All in all, it was a distasteful episode, in which Delta had been forced to walk a tightrope between the vital necessity of ensuring the safety of its passengers and public pressure to cut down on aircraft noise.

One major problem that beset Delta in the period of transition from pistons to jets was not peculiar to the commercial aviation industry but instead reflected the state of the American economy as a whole. By the mid-1950s Delta had emerged from the traumatic postmerger period and was beginning to exemplify what the consolidation had been intended to produce—financial health, even a rosy glow. From 1955 to 1956, as the annual report for the latter year showed, "The volume of service rendered, gross revenues, and earnings all reached new highs." Operating income for the twelve months ending June 30, 1956, was $7,951,000, compared to $5,696,000 in the previous fiscal year, an increase of 40 percent. Earnings per share of stock soared to $4.70, up from $2.62 in 1955. Net income after taxes more than doubled from $2,166,025 to $4,677,966. The story for the year ending June 30, 1957, was not quite so glowing: operating income dropped to $6,085,000, earnings per share fell to $2.34, net income from operations after taxes slumped to $2,539,000, and total earnings were down to $2,621,585.[33] (See Appendix 1.) The situation was not desperate, but the glow was dimming.

In December 1957, in an address before the American Society of Mechanical Engineers in New York City, Dolson blamed three factors for a continuing downturn in the new fiscal year: "lower load factors, higher costs, and our inability thus far to obtain approval for increased fares." He was referring to the rejection by the CAB in August 1957 of a request from Delta and several other airlines for an interim 6 percent raise in domestic fares pending final disposition of a general fare investigation begun in 1956. Woolman, speaking in Chicago after the CAB turndown, summed up the situation by declaring that the airlines were "providing 1957 service in ultramodern, air-conditioned, faster and more comfortable planes at 1938 rates."[34]

When Dolson made his speech, the United States was suffering the most severe recession to hit the country since the end of World War II. As the annual report for 1958 pointed out, the situation was worsened by "political unrest in three of the five Caribbean countries served by your Company . . . [and] South Florida's worst winter in half a century . . . sharply reducing the traffic of every airline serving the state." The CAB provided some relief early in 1958 with an interim increase of 4 percent in passenger rates plus $1.00 per ticket, amounting to 6.6 percent overall; effective August 1, 1958, a 3 percent federal tax on air freight was also repealed by Congress, but the lawmakers failed to remove a 10 percent levy on passenger travel. Figures in the 1958 annual report reflected the dismal picture: total earnings slumped to a quarter of what they had been for fiscal 1956; no dividend was paid for the June 1958 quarter; net income from operations after taxes fell below $1 million. There was some consolation, however: the 1958 annual report predicted that the recession was "bottoming out."[35]

Delta's directors continued to withhold dividends in 1958 and the first quarter of 1959. There were, of course, some protests from stockholders, but Woolman defended the decision in terms of financial exigency. The introduction of liquor service was also defended as a recession-fighting move. To attract more passengers, the company offered first-class "royal service," featuring an extra stewardess, music, complimentary champagne, and specially expedited baggage handling, among other luxury items. External factors helped: the strikes that continued to deal crippling blows to Eastern and other lines diverted business to Delta, and in October 1958 the CAB granted the industry a second interim fare increase of 3.5 percent. These factors combined to reverse Delta's slide. The figures for the year ending June 30, 1959, indicated that the company, like the nation as a whole, was emerging from the gloom of recession. Net income from operations after taxes and other charges soared to $4,062,000. Dividend payments were also resumed in the second quarter of 1959, and earnings per share rose to a healthy $3.62.[36] (See Appendix 1.)

Symbolic of bluer skies and the transition to jet service was the introduction in 1959 of the now familiar red, white, and blue triangular symbol known affectionately throughout the company as the "widget." Noting the similarity of the swept-wing configuration of the company's new jet aircraft when seen overhead to the Greek letter Delta, Richard S. Maurer discussed this resemblance with Burke Dowling (Bob) Adams, director of the firm's advertising agency, which in turn designed the distinctive trademark. The blue upper portion of the triangle pointed skyward, representing the apex of professional achievement; the white middle portion, forming a broad inverted V, represented the swept wing of a jet plane; and the red base, which suggested the exhaust behind the jet, also represented the firm's solid foundation and "the flame of leadership that keeps the point headed upward."[37]

Delta's performance for the year ending June 30, 1960, was somewhat disappointing, though not because of any general business recession, and no stringent actions such as the suspension of dividends were taken. Total earnings and net income from operations were off by more than $1 million each, and earnings per share fell to $2.53. In his explanation of the downturn Woolman pointed out that the strikes against major competitors which had benefited Delta in the previous year were now over. The advent of jet operations in the twelve months just ended had also required "advance personnel staffing and rapid expansion of that service." Unit costs of operations had not varied greatly from those of the 1959 fiscal year, however, and that was some consolation. In addition, the economic scene had been stabilized somewhat by the CAB's final determination in the general fare investigation that airlines could raise passenger fares by 2.5 percent plus $1.00 per ticket, effective July 1, 1960, superseding previous interim raises. Although this final arrangement saw Delta lose a share of the interim increases that the firm had previously gained, it nevertheless represented an increase over the old level and provided a stable price framework within which Delta could earn a more acceptable return on investment than had been possible before 1958.[38]

Increased efficiency offered another way of maximizing profits and providing better service at the same time. Anticipating the inauguration of jet service, Delta had established a scheduling committee in 1957; it was a genuine innovation, unlike scheduling committees in the industry generally. Largely because of the recommendations of a specialist in organizational techniques, Otis Kline, the new group was not the creature of the traffic and sales division, as in most airlines, but was composed of vice-presidents from finance, traffic and sales, and operations, assisted by key subordinates. As a result, much broader input could be brought to bear on one of the most critical areas of company service.[39]

Another recently established group, the customer-relations committee, addressed itself to an area as basic as scheduling. Born out of difficulties in the immediate postmerger period and providing a fairly accurate barometer of the general ups and downs of business, the committee was headed by T. P. Delafield, director of customer services. Normally, it had the pleasant task of selecting from various departments the recipients of periodic customer-service citations, who received certificates, single shares of Delta stock, and letters of commendation from Woolman. But the committee also had the unpleasant job of gathering statistics on customer complaints, categorizing them, and making suggestions for alleviating the difficulties involved, which were then passed along to appropriate units, including the scheduling committee. As a result of the adjustments that had to be made with the introduction of the jets and the other problems faced by the company in the late 1950s, the complaint picture was critical by 1960. In a report to Woolman late that year, Delafield mentioned "problems created by a continuing high level of operating irregularities, equipment substitutions, and off-schedule performance" and listed steps that might be taken to rectify them, including better sharing of information with passengers, reduction of mechanical delays, expedited baggage handling and check-in procedures, and other improvements. The testimony of rank-and-file Delta personnel, such as Gerald H. Rance of Detroit reservations, reinforced top-level concern. "Several times when I have tried to sell the Jet," Rance reported, "the passenger has said, 'thanks, I've heard about it. It's never on time.'" By March 1961, however, Delafield was able to discern an improvement in the "overall quality of service provided." A few months later he was pleased to inform Wool-man that "continued progress in schedule performance and decline in other operating irregularities, coupled with high employee morale at all levels, appears to be producing for us, currently, as fine a standard of customer service as we have attained in recent years."[40]

While customer services gradually improved throughout the first half of 1961, another problem was finally settled by an unwelcome development. After years of litigation, the Delta–C&S offset mail-rate case (see Chapter 13) was finally settled in federal court, and Delta was obliged to refund to the United States Post Office Department $1,651,863 of mail subsidies considered in excess of need for C&S's operations between 1946 and 1952. Beginning in April 1961, Delta paid this amount in monthly installments extending over a three-year period.[41]

Another problem arising indirectly from the C&S merger involved Caribbean operations. In 1957 Delta realized its first profit from service in that area since the merger, but increasing political instability in Cuba, the Dominican Republic, and Venezuela soon produced another flow of red ink. In 1956 Fidel Castro landed in Cuba and launched his revolution against the Batista dictatorship; after a shaky start, he succeeded in overthrowing Batista on January 1, 1959. Thereafter, as Castro converted the revolution into a Marx-ist one, Cuban relations with the United States deteriorated. It was within this context of violence and tension that Delta's Cuban operations grew increasingly impossible. On December 29, 1958, Batis-ta's plain-clothes police at Havana had forced their way aboard a Delta aircraft piloted by veteran Ben Catlin and had removed two American nationals, allegedly for discussing the revolution. After Castro took power, it soon became evident that Delta and other American airlines were no longer welcome on the island. Delta be-gan cutting down its personnel at Havana and restricted its Cuban ticket sales. Toward the end of 1960, the Castro government began to reduce the service of the state airline, Cubana, to the United States. This move signaled the end of American service to Cuba. The termination of Delta's flights to that troubled island came in 1961.[42]

The difficulties in the Dominican Republic arose in part from the disintegration of dictator Rafael L. Trujillo's rule in the 1950s, but the deterioration of the country's economy, connected with the de-cline of island-hopping tourism in the Greater Antilles generally, led Delta to suspend its Dominican operations in 1960, even before

Trujillo was finally assassinated. Although operations continued in Venezuela, which had also experienced a great deal of turbulence in the 1950s, Delta was caught temporarily in the middle of a diplomatic crisis when the Venezuelan government began to interfere with American airline operations, in violation of the existing bilateral aviation agreement between the two countries.[43]

Closer to home, a tragedy related to the beginning of jet operations temporarily thrust other problems into the background. On May 23, 1960, one of the company's new Convair 880s crashed and burned just after taking off on a training flight. The takeoff roll seemed normal, as did the liftoff, but seconds later the plane assumed too steep an angle of attack, banked left and right, and then crashed, killing all aboard. In the next few days, while an investigation was being launched, somber rites were conducted for instructor-pilot James H. Longino, captain-trainee Henry L. Laube, who had been at the controls, captain-trainee William F. Williams, and Bryan E. Bolt, who had served as flight engineer. Although there were some indications that Laube might have suffered a heart attack, leading to loss of control of the plane, the medical report could not positively confirm or eliminate that possibility. The CAB could suggest as a probable cause only that the craft had stalled for unknown reasons. It was the second enigmatic accident in recent years in which a Delta plane had been involved, although the earlier one, resulting in the loss of a Delta DC-7, had not involved company personnel. The plane was being operated by a National crew on a segment of the Miami–New Orleans interchange route when, in the early morning hours of September 16, 1959, it had plunged into the Gulf of Mexico some hundred miles short of its destination. Bits and pieces of wreckage and some bodies had been recovered, but they had not been sufficient to provide an answer. Despite speculation about the possibility of a bomb carried aboard by a passenger flying under an assumed name, the CAB listed the cause as unknown.[44]

Natural deaths took pioneers John (Luke) Williamson, Carl McHenry, and Laigh Parker. Williamson, whose colorful career had included flying Delta crop dusters as well as airliners and who had flown as one of Claire Chennault's Three Men on the Flying Trapeze, was only fifty years old at the time of his death in 1957. Probably the biggest blow to Woolman was the death by cancer of Parker on December 23, 1959. One of the few confidants of the Delta chief, Parker had helped to infuse life into the company as its traffic man when Delta was regenerated as an airline in 1934. His stature was attested to by his three terms as president of the Air Traffic Conference of America. Another indication that the old order was passing was the death of the quiet McHenry, longtime secretary of the company; like Parker, his career had spanned the full range of Delta operations from crop dusters to jets. He died on March 22, 1960.[45]

The company's board of directors, whose changing composition reflected the inexorable demands of time, lost two of its members in the passing of McHenry and Parker. Another veteran member left the group in 1959, when R. J. Reynolds declined to stand for reelection and was succeeded by investment banker Emery Flinn. The company's enduring ties with its Louisiana birthplace were affirmed in 1960 with the election to the board of Monroe attorney George M. Snellings, Jr., a longtime friend and associate of Carl McHenry, but death removed yet another director when Woodall Rogers passed away in 1961.[46]

For Delta the late 1950s and early 1960s thus brought both tribulation and triumph. Nevertheless, the company had weathered the transitional era far more successfully than many of its competitors. Though he could scarcely have predicted the unprecedented growth that the next few years would bring, Woolman clearly recognized, on his thirty-fifth anniversary with the firm, that the problems were far outweighed by the opportunities that beckoned in the dawning jet age. In a message to Delta employees, the boss told them: "Last night and the night before Mrs. Woolman and I sat up until nearly midnight reading, and sometimes re-reading, those hundreds of wonderful congratulatory messages. . . . When we finished we decided we're indeed very rich (and I am not referring to dollars) and that Delta was very rich, in having such wonderful, such fine, and such dedicated people as members of its family."[47]

CHAPTER 18

The Soaring Sixties

URING THE YEARS after 1961 Delta reaped the abundant harvest of a series of highly favorable developments that had taken place in the previous decade. The merger with C & S, new route acquisitions, and the move to jet aircraft, along with the fortunate circumstances that had led to bypassing the turboprops, all combined to raise the company to the status of a major airline. Finally, but significantly, Delta had managed to escape costly work stoppages that had plagued most other carriers, including its most important competitor, in the late 1950s, and it continued to enjoy similar good fortune during the early and middle 1960s while strikes recurred periodically on other lines throughout the industry.

As a result of these factors, along with the company's recovery from the 1957–58 slump, Delta's profits skyrocketed to levels that would have been unimaginable only a few years before. A net income after taxes of $4.6 million in 1961 was soon dwarfed as passengers enplaned in unprecedented numbers and operating revenues swelled from year to year. By 1965 earnings had increased fivefold, amounting to $23 million; this was followed by a dramatic jump to $34.5 million in 1966 and a precedent-shattering $49.2 million in 1967 as strikes on five other airlines intensified the flow of traffic over the Delta system. This situation, however, was clearly recognized as a windfall, and company officials were pleased when the return of more normal conditions produced profits of $36 million in 1968, $39.2 million in 1969, and $44.5 million in 1970. (See Appendix 1.)

Altogether, earnings over the ten-year period from 1961 through 1970 aggregated $267 million, more than ten times what the firm had earned in its entire previous history. Delta was not the only airline to register record gains during what was a prosperous decade for the industry as a whole; National, for example, posted impressive profits under the leadership of its new president, L. B. Maytag, Jr., who had bought the line from Baker in 1962 and had built up the formidable traffic potential of the company's new route from Miami to the West Coast. Other carriers did well too; in fiscal 1964, TWA's earnings rose by 85 percent, Northwest's by 105 percent, and Braniff's by 372 percent. But Delta had made a smoother transition to jet operations than most trunk lines and recorded consistently high profits while those of many other carriers ebbed and flowed. Eastern's performance was particularly spotty; it lost money heavily during the early years of the decade as labor problems and the unpopularity of the Electra took their toll, recovered for a few years under new management, but slipped back into deficits in 1968 and 1969.[1]

In response to the questions of a reporter from the Los Angeles *Times* in the summer of 1965, Woolman attributed his company's surging revenues partly to the new transcontinental route and partly to the phenomenal economic growth of the South; the Mississippi Valley, he observed, was fast becoming the American Ruhr. NASA's Gemini program had also given a substantial fillip to travel and cargo shipments across the Sun Belt.[2] The basic reasons for the dramatic growth of profits for Delta and other carriers, however, lay in the fundamental characteristics of jet transportation. Jet planes were far more attractive to travelers than piston-driven types. They flew at much higher altitudes, thus getting "above the weather" and giving passengers much smoother rides, and there was less noise or vibration inside the cabins. Above all, they were roughly twice as fast as earlier models, cutting down enormously on travel fatigue and making certain types of trips possible for the first time. A family with limited vacation time at its disposal, for example, could go farther away from home without losing entire days reaching and returning from its destination. Businessmen could go to far-off cities in the morning and be back by night, thus saving their companies the expenses of hotel accommodations and extra meals.[3]

But this convenience was only part of the story. While jet aircraft offered the public speed and comfort, they gave the trunk lines much more attractive cost-profit ratios than piston-driven planes. In the words of Robert Oppenlander, who rose rapidly during this period to become Delta's chief financial officer, they "flew twice as far twice as fast," thus permitting phenomenal gains in equipment use and productivity. Instead of burning high-octane aviation gasoline, they ran on kerosene, which at one point in the early 1960s was selling for as low as eight cents a gallon. Their engines, fundamentally simpler than piston types, required much less frequent maintenance, and their greater reliability cut down on ferry flights to shift partly disabled planes to repair bases. The benefits of these operational characteristics were passed on to the consumer in the form of lower fares, thus enhancing the appeal of jet travel and leading to further expansion of markets.[4]

Translated into operating statistics, these circumstances brought Delta 9.4 million passengers in 1967, as opposed to 3.2 million in 1960, an increase of 294 percent. On the other hand, operating expenses for each mile flown by the company's planes actually declined by approximately 17.3 percent. It was small wonder, therefore, that the firm enjoyed unprecedented profits. Even though it followed its traditional custom of plowing most earnings back into future operations, dividends to stockholders increased more than four times over the same period, while stockholder equity rose dramatically from $6.93 to $26.12 per share. Meanwhile, investors received frequent splits, which steadily augmented the value of their holdings; the climax came with a three-for-one split in 1967. The once penny-ante organization was now a blue chip in the solid company of such lines as American and United.[5] It is not hard to understand why proud Captain Eddie of Eastern, once head and shoulders above formerly regional Delta, had little to say about his rival in his memoirs.

One consequence of the flood of new business that accrued to Delta during this period was the need for radically improved data processing. Many years before, shortly after moving its headquarters to Atlanta, the company had acquired electronic accounting machines to facilitate its expanding payroll operations. Although the equipment was updated in the 1950s, by the end of that decade it was no longer adequate to handle the complex variables involved in computing pilot pay scales based on speed and weight of aircraft, mode of propulsion, differentials for night and day flights, and adjustments for flying over water or land. In addition, the maintenance department urgently needed to modernize procedures for acquisition, inventory, and reorder of its rapidly mounting volume of spare parts. After a feasibility study by a select company committee, Delta acquired its first programmable digital computer, an IBM 650, together with a high-speed printer with an output of six hundred lines a minute. These machines were very successful and convinced management to apply modern data processing techniques to other operations.

At that time reservations were still handled manually, requiring mountains of file cards, cumbersome retrieval procedures, and endless hours of effort to perform even the most routine tasks, such as preparing tickets, changing passenger schedules, and keeping track of cancellations and no-shows. Along with American Airlines, Delta pioneered in reservations management by working out with IBM the so-called Sabre system, using two large IBM model 7074 computers and a variety of other cybernetic devices to handle alphabetical as well as numerical information, in order to reduce operations that had once taken as much as thirty minutes to mere fractions of a second. Following two years of programming and more than seven thousand hours of testing, the new system, given the trade name Deltamatic, was installed in a converted engine-overhaul building near the company headquarters; it was operational throughout the entire organization by the end of 1964.

Even this modernization proved to be a stopgap measure, however, for by 1968 the system was already overloaded, and it was taking Delta agents as long as forty seconds to respond to customer requests. Accordingly, a separate computer facility, the Greenbriar Center, was constructed on a site adjacent to Interstate 285 west of Atlanta, and an IBM 360/65 system with a memory four times as large and internal speeds five times as fast as the IBM 7074 was installed. Under the leadership of W. A. Atchison, a former military cargo pilot who also had training in mechanical engineering and industrial management, the new complex not only served a constantly growing reservations network but also performed a number of added functions, including the preparation of flight plans, the dispatch of aircraft, and the continuous monitoring of all Delta flights from takeoff to landing. The Greenbriar Center also contained an ultramodern simulator facility, with constantly updated electronic equipment, in which the responses of Delta pilots to hypothetical in-flight contingencies were regularly checked. Eventually, cockpits replicating to the smallest detail those of the company's planes were connected to computers that minutely analyzed every aspect of a pilot's performance, making it possible to practice a given procedure over and over again; outside the cockpit windows, displays simulating runways and landmarks at the various airports in the Delta system could be switched on and off to facilitate in a highly realistic way the rehearsal of taking off, cruising at altitude, and landing under all kinds of ceiling levels and weather conditions.[6]

Another Delta innovation in marketing and sales had occurred in the early jet era; it was based on an idea of T. M. Miller, who had taken Laigh Parker's place as Delta's chief marketing officer. Miller

Owly Bird and Early Bird at Jet Base Open House in 1968.

One of the fleet of prop jet Viscounts bought by Northeast in 1958.

Northeast utilized the Fairchild Hiller FH-227C in small New England markets.

Inauguration of Northeast service to the Bahamas on May 15, 1968. Bahamas Premier Lynden O. Pindling and his wife *(seated, center)* participated in welcoming ceremonies. Francis W. Sargent, Governor of Massachusetts, is seated at Mr. Pindling's left.

Delta's Early Bird and Owly Bird welcomed the Northeast Yellowbird to the merged company in 1972.

Delta and Northeast became one company in 1972. *Left to right:* Bill Michaels, W. T. Beebe, George B. Storer, Sr., and David C. Garrett, Jr.

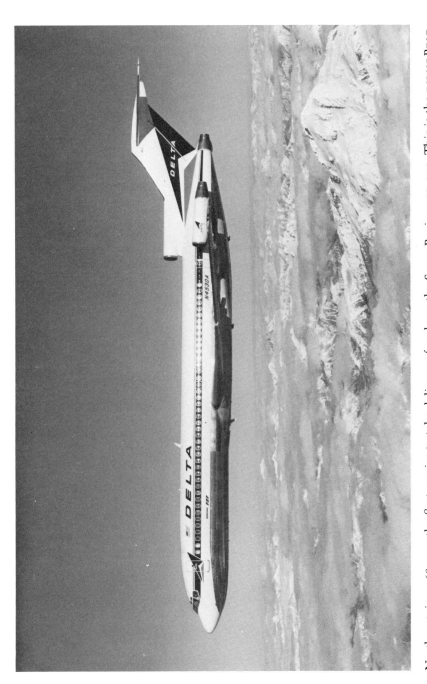

Northeast, in 1968, was the first carrier to take delivery of and use the Super Boeing 727-295. This is the newer B727-232 in flight over Mount Baker in the Pacific Northwest.

The largest jetliner ever designed for commercial use, the Boeing 747, flew Delta's colors from 1970 to 1977.

had noted that in the period between 10:00 P.M. and 4:00 A.M., when lower night-coach fares were in force under CAB policy, flights through Atlanta were scattered throughout the time frame, accommodating relatively few passengers although carrying a considerable amount of mail and cargo. He brought Woolman a set of trial schedules, proposing that a number of planes would leave their points of origin between 10 P.M. and 4 A.M. in such a way as to converge on Atlanta between 5:00 and 5:30 A.M. These planes could then take off in various directions between 6:00 and 6:30 A.M., still qualifying to carry passengers at the lower night-coach fare. Though designed to involve only about fourteen planes during an initial trial period, the plan still required a considerable increase in staffing to fly and to service these planes while they were bunched at the Atlanta airport. Woolman, Miller later recalled, was at first reluctant because of the costs involved, but finally agreed to the proposal. Miller's confidence that revenue would far exceed expenses was quickly borne out, and in the next few months the Atlanta airport was the busiest in the Southeast in the early morning hours. The concentration of planes on the ground at Atlanta to attract passengers through lower rates was next planned for arrivals during the 11:00 to 11:30 P.M. time frame, so that these aircraft could move on to their various destinations during the midnight to 12:30 A.M. period. This program, too, was a striking success, and Delta took the national lead in flights originating in the late evening and early morning hours at discount fares. To promote the new services, the trade names Early Bird and Owly Bird, suggested by Miller, were adopted and used widely in Delta's advertising. These flights contributed heavily toward enabling Delta to reach levels of aircraft utilization and revenue ton-miles in excess of its size relative to other airlines.[7]

As usual, however, Delta made its most obvious innovations in the vital area of new aircraft acquisition. Aided by rising profits, which helped pay off the cost of its first jet transports quickly and to buy more planes of the same type without incurring unduly high debt levels, the company moved swiftly to build an ultramodern fleet. By 1965 it had sixteen DC-8s, all equipped with fan-jet engines, and an equal number of CV-880s. The company was also nearing a decision to acquire the DC-8-61, a stretched version of the basic model, which had been renamed the DC-8-51. Dubbed the Super 61 by Douglas, the new craft was 187 feet long and could accommodate 195 passengers. Woolman initially was skeptical about the plane until Arthur Ford and other Delta engineers devised an effective visual means of showing that only a minor fraction of the ship's added carrying capacity would be absorbed by increased costs. A model was prepared in which 125 seats, corresponding to the number in the conventional DC-8-51, were painted gray. Of the remaining seats, 7 were painted red to signify the added cost of operating the aircraft, and 63 were painted bright green and marked with large dollar signs. The boss was convinced. Furthermore, as Miller pointed out at a management conference in 1967, the company could alternate regular and stretched DC-8s on the southern transcontinental and Great Lakes-to-Miami runs, depending on seasonal traffic fluctuations, thus optimizing operating efficiency. By 1970 Delta had thirteen DC-8-61s and twenty-one DC-8-51s.[8]

Although the company was pleased with the speed, comfort, and maneuverability of the CV-880, the plane was highly fuel-intensive. In addition, as one Delta official later put it, Convair "tinkered" too much with the plane by introducing new models, which made it difficult to plan for a standardized fleet of these craft. Therefore, although the firm retained the sixteen ships it had already purchased, no more were ordered. Nor was Delta much tempted by Convair's newer and even faster airliner, the CV-990, which seemed to offer satisfactory operating economy only on nonstop transcontinental flights.

At that time Delta also shunned the Boeing 727, introduced in 1963 after attracting large orders from Eastern and United. This series of planes was destined to be phenomenally successful, but the earliest model, known as the 727-100, struck Nycum and other Delta engineers as having too short a range for a relatively large ship, even though it offered fuel economy superior to that of the CV-880. Another consideration was that, like all the other jet planes of that early period, it required a three-man cockpit crew. Having decided that the DC-8 and CV-880 best suited the needs of its long-haul and medium-range routes, Delta was becoming increasingly interested in helping to develop a smaller jetliner that would replace such twin-engine piston craft as the CV-440 on shorter segments, thus enabling the company to move toward an all-jet fleet. If a craft of this type could be designed to fly with a two-man crew and still carry as many passengers as some four-engine propeller-driven ships, it would offer truly outstanding operating economy.[9]

At that time the British had a twin-engine jet nearing completion in the form of the BAC One-Eleven, but Delta as usual shied away from acquiring a foreign-built craft. Instead, during 1961 and 1962 Arthur Ford conducted a series of discussions with Edward Burton, vice-president for engineering at Douglas, leading ultimately to the creation of a new jet transport known as the DC-9. Various configurations were analyzed, including one version featuring four small jet engines mounted in a tail compartment, and approximately 1,300 pages of specifications were drawn up. Because the plane was intended for frequent short hops from relatively small airports, with numerous takeoffs and landings each day, Ford and Burton were particularly concerned about reliability and deliberately stressed the use of redundant systems so that the failure of a single component would not require an interruption of service. In addition, the two engineers tried to select the best equipment from the various jetliners then in service. As the basic power plant, for example, they settled upon the Pratt and Whitney JT8D-5 engine, which was demonstrating exceptional reliability in the Boeing 727.[10]

As the planning proceeded, other carriers became involved in the discussions, which sometimes resulted in conflicting points of view. There was some pressure for a plane only slightly larger than the CV-340 and using a relatively small jet engine based on Pratt and Whitney's military TF-30, but Delta insisted that traffic levels in small cities were already outgrowing the capacities of current twin-engine craft and held out for a bigger ship. Early in 1963, Douglas held what Ford later described as a "let's go ahead and move" meeting at which Delta was represented by Ford, Dolson, Nycum, and Ball. Shortly thereafter, Donald Douglas, Sr., went in search of orders. Believing that he needed substantial commitments before production could begin, he planned to approach American first because of its stature as one of the two largest firms in the industry. Ford, however, urged him to begin instead with a visit to Woolman, who was virtually certain to opt for the new plane.

Accepting this advice, Douglas brought various members of his staff to Atlanta and obtained a preliminary letter of intent, signed by Woolman on March 13, 1963, to purchase fifteen DC-9s at a unit price slightly in excess of $3 million. Douglas subsequently failed to secure an order from American but decided to go into production anyway, and Woolman's offer was accepted on April 16. While the final details of the purchase agreement were being hammered out, a team of Delta engineers including Ford and Julian May went to California to help Douglas employees complete the design process, working steadily from early morning to late evening throughout a three-month period. As Ford later recalled, they did not even stop for Memorial Day weekend.[11]

Designed to take off from a 5,300-foot runway and to land in even less distance, the resulting ship was approximately 104 feet long, and its wing span of 89 feet, 5 inches was actually less than that of a DC-3. Yet it could carry from fifty-six to eighty-three passengers, depending upon the seating configuration, giving it substantially greater capacity than existing twin-engine piston craft and, indeed, rivaling the four-engine DC-6. Delta's DC-9s were built to carry sixty-five people, with twenty in the first-class compartment and forty-five in the tourist cabin. Two aft-mounted turbofan engines gave the plane a maximum speed of 560 miles an hour, thus permitting a drastic shrinkage of time between small stations on the company's route system. The cockpit, carefully designed on the basis of elaborate time and motion studies, required only a two-man crew. Woolman saw the ship as the jet-age equivalent of the DC-3 and anticipated that it would be Delta's short-haul workhorse for many years to come. "Douglas," he pointed out to one reporter, "has never built a bum airplane."[12]

The advent of the DC-9 did threaten to create a problem in labor relations, but Delta fortunately escaped unscathed. Although nationally various members of ALPA wanted a three-man crew for the DC-9, several Delta pilots were invited to inspect the plane while it was being built and succeeded in convincing their colleagues in Delta's ALPA chapter that safety did not require more than a two-member cabin crew for the new craft. Besides, with the pilots already benefiting from Delta's prosperity, featherbedding did not appear necessary. Later, led by veteran pilot B. B. Barclay, the Delta delegation to the 1964 ALPA convention spearheaded a successful move to exclude the DC-9 from a list of planes for which three-man crews would be demanded.[13]

Partly because of the advance planning that had gone into it, the new aircraft took shape in California with unaccustomed speed. On January 12, 1965, a hangar door opened at Long Beach in response to a filmed signal from United States Secretary of Commerce Luther Hodges in Washington, D.C., and the first DC-9 was rolled out to be admired by more than six hundred invited guests. On February 25, a month ahead of schedule, the ship took off on its initial test flight. Five ships were used in an extensive test program conducted by twelve pilots and forty engineers, and things went so smoothly that the plane was ready for Delta's acceptance flight by September 8, three months ahead of earlier estimates. On October 7, with Ball and McBride in the cockpit, the company's first DC-9, christened the *Delta Prince* with a bottle containing water from twenty cities that it would serve, took off for Atlanta on a trip lasting four hours and nineteen minutes of flying time, with a fueling stop in Dallas. While a high-stepping band from the Atlanta suburb of College Park struck up "Dixie," Woolman appeared in the doorway of the craft and waved to a welcoming crowd, which later inspected the gleaming new acquisition. The plane was officially certified by the FAA on November 23, again ahead of schedule, and on December 8 Delta for the third time in recent years introduced a new model into commercial service with a round trip from Atlanta to Kansas City via Memphis. Within a week, service had begun to seventeen other cities, many of which had not enjoyed jet transportation before.[14]

Delta had already exercised an option to double its initial order of fifteen planes, and by 1970 the company possessed seventy-five DC-9s, showing clearly the way in which the ship had lived up to expectations. Of this fleet, seventeen planes belonged to the initial DC-9-14 series, and the rest were a stretched version designated as the DC-9-32. The development of the expanded model again demonstrated the dynamics of Delta's longstanding rivalry with Eastern, which ordered an eighty-nine-passenger ship known as the DC-9-31. Despite its increased capacity, this plane still had only one buffet compartment, located up front, and two lavatories, situated in back. Sensing an opportunity to gain competitive advantage, Woolman instructed Ford to arrange with Douglas for the interior of the expanded Delta model to have two buffets at either end and lavatories located both fore and aft. Because the buffets facilitated quicker meal service on short flights and required less walking up and down the elongated aisle, the arrangement proved popular with passengers and cabin attendants alike.[15]

The steady expansion of jet service throughout the decade sealed the fate of the company's piston-driven ships. Elimination of the DC-7s, which had always been plagued by high operating costs, was completed by February 1968, and Delta's few remaining DC-6s were phased out by the end of the same year. Next to go were the durable CV-340s and CV-440s. Whatever nostalgia was caused by the departure of these tough old birds, many of which still had years of feeder-line service ahead of them, was mitigated by the markedly lower unit costs of jet operation and the satisfaction Delta took in its image of technological progressiveness. By the end of April 1970, Delta had an all-jet passenger fleet.[16]

The cargo fleet also underwent face-lifting during this period. By 1965, particularly because of the demands of the space program, freight shipments had outgrown the capacity of the C-46s acquired in 1956, and the search for a suitable replacement was underway. Company officials temporarily considered buying three used DC-6 cargo planes, but memories of the hastily purchased L-049s of the late 1950s still lingered, and precipitate action was avoided. Instead, Ford consulted with Lockheed, whose plant at nearby Marietta, Georgia, had produced large numbers of C-130 Hercules turboprop cargo planes for military service. These planes had proved exceptionally reliable, and Lockheed was eager to introduce the ship into scheduled domestic service with commercial carriers. Because Delta would be the first carrier other than an Alaskan airline to fly the craft, it was able to negotiate a highly favorable contract to purchase three new planes at a unit price of $2.7 million, with the right to sell them back to Lockheed if they proved unsatisfactory.

Until the advent of the Boeing 747 and the Lockheed L-1011, both of which offered ample cargo space in their belly compartments, the L-100, as the Hercules was designated for civilian use, was highly suitable for Delta's needs. Its distinguishing feature was a large rear-loading hatch through which up to twenty-five tons of palletized cargo could be deposited in a capacious hold. During the summer of 1966, Ford, May, and other Delta engineers, again disregarding holidays, designed a handling system and other modifications to meet commercial, as opposed to military, requirements; Ford later recalled that the basic concepts were worked out on his dining-room table on the Fourth of July. The result was an industry first, in that truck-sized vans prepacked with cargo could be loaded into the plane and transferred directly to ships, railroad cars, trucks, or other aircraft upon reaching their destination.

Because the plane was already in production for the armed services and fully certified for commercial operations, it did not take long to adapt it for Delta, and the company put it into service on September 15, 1966. The last pallet of cargo to be loaded that morning slightly overlapped the tail gate, whereupon "freight agents went to work with muscle, oaths, pinch bars, and anything else they could find." The hatch was finally closed, and the Hercules took off for Chicago to inaugurate a highly successful new era for the company's cargo division. By 1970 the C-46s were gone, and a fourth L-100 had been added to the fleet.[17]

Steady acquisition of aircraft was accompanied by an expansion of physical facilities. By the middle of the decade, for example, the new jet base, which had seemed so enormous just a few years before, was already inadequate, and a project that would nearly double its size was begun. When completed in mid-1968, the enlarged complex, with sixteen acres under roof, was admired by a crowd of ten thousand employees and visitors, who trooped through a mile-long series of attractions during a two-day open house.[18] During the same period a new ground training center was constructed, with classrooms, living quarters, flight-simulation equipment, and a technical library for pilot and stewardess trainees.[19] By the end of the decade, the recently completed Greenbriar Center was already being expanded to accommodate the company's accounting, treasury, purchasing, and internal-audit personnel, who had become much too numerous to be accommodated any longer at the main headquarters. For Paul Pate, the former cargo chief who was now vice-president in charge of properties, it was a never-ending battle to keep the firm from bulging at the seams.[20]

New planes and facilities required heavy outlays of money, but the unprecedented profits garnered by the firm, along with sales of used aircraft, provided part of the capital required, and the rest was obtained without difficulty under revolving credit arrangements with banks and insurance companies. As late as 1967 the firm's outstanding long-term debt stood at only $89.7 million; representing approximately 52 percent of equity, it was one of the lowest levels in the entire industry, many carriers having reached ratios of 150 to 200 percent. During the next few years, massive orders for new superjets to meet the needs of the coming decade required a fresh wave of borrowing, which raised the company's long-term obligations to $229.9 million by mid-1970, but in a related move the firm's permissible capitalization soared from 8 million to 25 million shares under a plan approved by the board of directors in 1967.[21]

The roster of employees was also growing by leaps and bounds. In 1961 the Delta payroll had included some 8,290 people; by 1970 there were approximately 20,500. (See Appendix 1.) Continuing efforts dating back to 1936, when Delta had negotiated its first group-insurance plan with Aetna, the company in 1964 announced an updated schedule of fringe benefits, which included an airline-industry first: a guarantee that surviving dependents would receive up to half a deceased employee's gross monthly salary. Other aspects of the package included substantially increased life-insurance, medical, and disability coverage. A conversion feature facilitated continued medical coverage after retirement.[22]

During the 1960s the makeup of Delta's work force began to change to some degree, in response to the growing movement toward racial equality. Before that time, virtually all jobs above the lowest levels on commercial trunk lines were limited to whites. Paradoxically, despite the segregationist heritage of the region, southern-based airlines tended to hire more Negroes than their northern or western counterparts, simply because local traditions identified certain tasks, like cleaning aircraft cabins or carrying baggage, as suitable for black employment. Nevertheless, the pattern of discrimination was nationwide. As a careful study has indicated, aviation had an "elitist character," which made it "the most exclusionist of transportation industries." An intense concern for safety led to technical standards that, considering the educational opportunities available to blacks, kept avenues of upward mobility closed to them and thus reinforced social prejudices. The strong passenger orientation of the industry, fostered by federal regulations severely limiting price competition, led carriers to accept, and cater to, the sometimes stereotyped expectations of the traveling public for cabin-service and cockpit personnel. Before the 1960s, for example, there were only three black stewardesses in the entire industry, the first of whom was hired in 1957, and two black pilots, one of whom flew for a cargo carrier and the other for a helicopter service.

Not until John F. Kennedy became president of the United States in 1961 was federal pressure exerted upon airlines to take affirmative action toward equal-employment opportunity. Under a Plans for Progress program spearheaded by Vice-President Lyndon Johnson to promote the hiring of blacks in American industry generally, the nation's largest domestic trunk lines and flag carriers began to take positive steps in this direction, prodded by the President's Committee on Equal Employment Opportunity (PCEEO) and such successor agencies as the Office of Federal Contract Compliance (OFCC) and the Equal Employment Opportunity Commission (EEOC). Ultimately the National Alliance of Businessmen began a program, in which Delta and other airlines participated, to reduce hard-core unemployment among blacks and to provide slots for them in higher-echelon positions.

As was perhaps inevitable in an area involving deep-seated social attitudes, progress was slow. By the end of the decade, for example, fewer than 100 of the 33,000 pilots flying for the nation's air carriers were black, and the estimated 900 black stewardesses employed throughout the industry in 1971 constituted only about 3 percent of the total figure. Some positions were hard to fill because of the difficulty in locating qualified black applicants, and special training programs had thus to be established; in other cases, companies hoping to promote existing black workers found that skycaps in particular were disinclined to change jobs because they were already making substantially more money than was paid by many theoretically more prestigious positions. As a group, southern-based airlines moved somewhat more slowly than their counterparts elsewhere. Nevertheless, significant change did take place. A portfolio of pictures in the 1968 annual report showing Delta personnel going about their everyday tasks highlighted the fact that the company's middle-level ranks were being integrated. By 1970 the company had 361 black employees working in jobs to which they had not traditionally enjoyed access. The list included 2 pilots, with 2 more in training; 52 stewardesses; 89 reservations agents; 22 mechanics; 8 traffic agents; 3 station agents; 1 lead reservations agent; and 182 service agents.[23]

The increasingly pervasive role of the federal government was also reflected in another area of employee relations after the passage of the Civil Rights Act in 1964. Title VII of this legislation was ultimately determined by the EEOC to prohibit airline rules requiring stewardesses to resign in the event of marriage. In April 1966 a question addressed to the editor of Delta Digest asked why the company had not followed the recent example of certain other carriers in rescinding this type of regulation and wanted to know whether there was any hope that such action would be taken in the future. Although not specifically ruling out a change in official policy, the reply, apparently reflecting the views of management, stressed that the work routine of a stewardess imposed "a more irregular pattern of living than perhaps any other job in which girls are normally employed"; dwelt at length on how this pattern could create conflicts between an employee's job and her home life, with consequent impairment of her morale and attitude toward passengers; and mentioned various hazards and embarrassments that could occur to pregnant cabin attendants whose responsibilities involved "nearly constant walking and lifting in an aircraft 30,000 feet in the air sub-

ject to abrupt and unexpected motion." Nevertheless, by the following year the firm had adopted a new rule permitting married
stewardesses to remain with the company. Perhaps making the best
of a situation about which strong misgivings had been held, the
annual report for 1967 pointed out that Delta now employed approximately twelve stewardesses for each plane in its fleet and that the
changed regulation would enable the company to "keep these highly
trained young women longer at their jobs."[24]

Another federal regulation about which the company had much
graver reservations resulted in a tragic accident on March 30, 1967,
when a Delta DC-8 carrying five pilots and an FAA instructor
crashed near New Orleans while on a training flight. Involved was
a requirement that, in order to be certified to operate a four-engine
aircraft, a pilot must be able to execute a landing approach using
power from only two engines, both on the same side of the plane.
Although somewhat hazardous, this maneuver was not excessively
difficult in piston-driven ships, for the propellers were allowed to
keep spinning so long as the engines were throttled back to a "zero
thrust" condition and the resulting air flow past the wing provided
a degree of residual lift. In addition, because of the straight wings
characteristic of piston planes, vertical deviation or yaw did not pose
a major problem, and power could be recovered more quickly by advancing the throttles. A jet plane, however, was quite different. Yaw
was a much more serious problem because of the swept-back wings,
and the acceleration time of a jet engine that had been throttled back
was comparatively slow. There were no propellers to supply residual
lift, and the manipulation of landing flaps was also highly intricate
when power on one side was lost.

Such problems had already resulted in the loss of DC-8s and Boeing 707s by American, Pan American, and TWA before the Delta
accident occurred, but the FAA had made no change in its procedures, despite remonstrances from individual carriers and the operations committee of the Air Transport Association. Never before,
however, had the cost in human life been so high. In addition to the
five Delta pilots and the FAA official aboard the DC-8 at New Orleans, thirteen people on the ground were killed when the plane
ripped through several houses and part of a motel complex. At the
hearings conducted by the National Transportation Safety Board
(NTSB) following the accident, Delta maintained that it would
never again cooperate with FAA in imposing the "two engine out"
requirement and listed alternative training procedures that it was

willing to substitute. The official report adopted by the NTSB blamed the incident partly on errors in judgment on the part of the pilot trainee and partly on inadequate supervision by the instructor pilot. Nevertheless, Delta's stand, coupled with the unusually high level of casualties and property damage caused by the crash, seemed to have an effect, for the controversial maneuver was subsequently dropped from training flights by the FAA.[25]

Delta's pilots, the only truly unionized segment of its personnel at the advent of the jet era, continued periodically to reopen contract negotiations during the 1960s. In negotiations stretching over ten months in 1961, management agreed to make heavier contributions to the cost of retirement coverage. The "third cabin member" controversy, successfully avoided by Delta in the past, cropped up briefly in 1962, when a position paper by Delta's ALPA chapter called for a new arrangement respecting turbine-aircraft pilot training and assignments to end a condition under which pilot-flight engineers might go years without having the opportunity to pilot an aircraft, yet under existing contractual arrangements they might make more money than copilots. Subsequent contract settlements appear to have eased these problems by establishing new pay scales and making other adjustments. All in all, pilot demands were relatively tame, compared to those voiced in the 1950s.[26]

Continuing its past tendencies, Delta was involved constantly in CAB litigation during the 1960s. Two particularly important cases argued early in the decade involved merger proposals of unprecedented magnitude. Having overcommitted itself on the Viscount turboprop and fallen hopelessly in arrears to its British manufacturer, Vickers-Armstrong, Limited, Capital Airlines was faced by the alternatives of merger or bankruptcy. Choosing the former, it worked out a pact with United, which thus stood to become the nation's largest air carrier. The agreement was presented to the CAB on an "all or nothing" basis; disapproval of any of its features would void the contract, leaving Capital at the mercy of Vickers, which clearly intended to foreclose.

Along with Eastern, Delta stood to suffer from the transfer of Capital's southern routes (which by then had been largely abandoned) to a mammoth enterprise fully capable of developing their competitive potential. Examiner Thomas Wrenn, however, refused to "fragmentize" the case by admitting evidence on such specific issues and ultimately recommended that the board approve the proposed consolidation in toto. Delta continued to fight as the case came before the entire board, urging that the merger be disallowed unless some arrangement could be made to dispose of Capital's route from Washington, D.C., to Atlanta and New Orleans. In addition, the company strongly attacked the proposed consolidation as monopolistic and pointed out that a number of heavily traveled routes would have little or no competitive service if it were approved. Though conceding that such arguments would possess some merit in a normal proceeding, the CAB decided that the consequences of allowing Capital to go bankrupt would be too grave to contemplate and upheld Wrenn's finding. Still refusing to surrender, Delta appealed the verdict in federal court, but to no avail.[27]

After having been defeated in this protracted struggle, Delta waged another in 1962 and 1963 to persuade the CAB to reject a merger proposed by the two one-time leaders of domestic airline service, American and Eastern. Strikes, unfortunate choices of equipment, and competition over routes that it had once monopolized, among other factors, had diminished the strength of American, and its profits had dropped off after its failure to obtain a southern transcontinental route in 1961. Eastern's plight was worse, for much the same reasons. Its service, according to an Eastern executive, was "widely considered inferior to its competitors." Both these lines were intense competitors of Delta, and Eastern was its traditional rival; Delta thus strongly opposed the merger, pointing out that such a union would control 35 percent of the country's trunk-line business. Richard Maurer and Frank Rox led Delta's legal assault on the proposal with the argument that it would violate federal antitrust acts, reverse the CAB's commitment to foster competition, and motivate other unwise mergers. In its battle Delta had many allies among other trunk lines, various labor unions, and the CAB's own Bureau of Economic Regulation. Following an unfavorable Hearing Examiner's report, the proposal was withdrawn and a major threat to Delta's well-being was averted.[28]

While the outcome of the American and Eastern merger was still hanging fire, Delta entered a number of new route applications, beginning what was to be a somewhat frustrating period in its dealings with the CAB. With but a few exceptions, its system was to remain unchanged until the end of the decade. Nevertheless, the company remained as aggressive as ever in seeking fresh destinations for its sleek new jets. If its route map had an increasingly familiar look as the years went by, it was not for want of trying to have it otherwise.

Having already made a substantial contribution to the space program through the transport of passengers and freight to and from such centers as Orlando and Los Angeles, Delta moved in 1962 to secure operating authority between Huntsville and the West Coast via Dallas and Fort Worth. Despite the opposition of American and Southern, CAB examiner Merritt Ruhlen supported the proposal on the grounds that the needs of the space effort outweighed the potential diversionary impact that such an award would have upon other carriers. But the board ruled otherwise, finding that Southern would suffer severely from diversion if the award were approved and that existing connecting services with American at Memphis were adequate. For Delta, then as later, the door to Huntsville remained closed.[29]

The company soon scored its only new route victory of the mid-1960s, however, by helping to establish the first through service between the southeastern United States and Europe. In May 1963 Delta and Pan American joined in an interchange proposal under which Pan American crews would take charge of Delta planes arriving at such international gateways as Washington and New York bearing trans-Atlantic passengers from Atlanta and New Orleans. The aircraft would then proceed to London or Paris, without subjecting the passengers to a change of plane. The fact that both companies used DC-8 equipment facilitated the plan technologically, and Miller, Delta's vice-president of traffic and sales, pointed out that it would benefit travelers from forty-one cities, who at that time had to use sometimes roundabout connecting services. After a year of deliberations the CAB approved the idea, though limiting it to the Washington gateway. Implementation of the agreement required the acquisition by Delta of several DC-8-33s with the heavy JT-4 engines required for trans-Atlantic flights, but it represented a significant breakthrough and gave the company a valuable basis for what would ultimately develop into a major bid for an independent Delta route from Atlanta to London. Under the interchange service, which began May 29, 1964, passengers could fly from New Orleans and Atlanta to London four times a week and to Paris three times a week.[30]

From that point until late in the decade, the pickings were slim, as Delta was rebuffed in a series of important route cases. In the Pacific Northwest–Southwest Service Case, which began in 1965, the company tried to secure entry into Portland and Seattle but failed; instead Eastern received a route from St. Louis to the Pacific Northwest.[31] Delta was similarly disappointed in its persistent efforts to

secure a direct route from Boston and New York to Miami. The admission of Northeast Airlines to this market in 1956 on a temporary
five-year basis had not been followed by anticipated gains in traffic.
As always, Delta's most logical argument was that it needed only an
eighty-nine-mile extension of its existing routes to give it an un-
broken connection between New York and Florida. Nevertheless,
the company was unable to convince the CAB of the merits of its
case when the coastal artery came up for renewal. In the end, Northeast won the permanent authority for which it had been fighting so
long, and Delta came away empty-handed.[32]

Further disappointment lay in store in the complex Trans Pacific
Route Investigation opened by the CAB in 1966. Though traffic
across the Pacific Ocean had grown immensely since World War II
and the advent of jet aircraft promised to revolutionize transport in
the area, an earlier effort by the CAB to assign new route authorizations had been frustrated by presidential disapproval, and the certificates possessed by United States flag lines remained essentially as
they had been in 1946. As a result, foreign carriers such as BOAC,
Qantas, and Japan Air Lines were making incursions serious enough
to affect the American balance of payments. Delta's request was
modest in comparison with those of other competitors, but the CAB
granted only TWA's request to provide competition for Pan American in the central Pacific, focal point of Delta's ambitions. Delta
also lost out in an attempt to link the American South with Hawaii;
the defeat was compounded by Braniff's gaining access to Atlanta for
the first time.[33]

Delta suffered a string of other route defeats in the late 1960s. It
failed to gain access to Minneapolis–St. Paul, Albuquerque, and
Bermuda and also lost an important battle for a route from Miami to
London.[34] The company had entered some of these cases knowing
that its chances were slim and may have operated partly on the assumption that losing a few cases might increase its hopes for preferment in subsequent ones. Nevertheless, it had strongly desired several of the prizes that had been awarded to other carriers and had
fought hard for them. It was a relief, therefore, when the tide finally
began to turn late in the decade, even though some of the victories
that the company won had some undesirable side effects.

For example, there were mixed results in an important international case decided by the CAB in 1968, establishing a series of new
routes in Latin America. Despite the cessation of service to Havana

and periodic turmoil in such trouble spots as Haiti and the Dominican Republic, tourism had grown enormously in the Caribbean, and competition for new CAB authorizations was intense. Delta did score worthwhile gains in this proceeding, including permission to provide direct service from Puerto Rico, Venezuela, and Jamaica to Los Angeles and San Francisco either nonstop or via Houston and New Orleans. In particular, the nonstop authority between San Juan and Los Angeles, at this point the longest single new route ever granted to the firm, would prove highly valuable in future years.

On the other hand, the same proceeding produced some setbacks as well. Delta was not unduly displeased when the board removed its authority to serve Aruba, Curaçao, Kingston, Port-au-Prince, and Santo Domingo, which for various reasons it had not developed as intensively as other Caribbean vacation spots. What did hurt, however, was the CAB's denial once again of access to the Caribbean through the Miami gateway, a much more direct and lucrative funnel than New Orleans. In a dissenting opinion, CAB Vice-Chairman Robert T. Murphy urged that Delta's Chicago-to-Miami route be extended to Jamaica, but the rest of the board did not concur. Apparently, some long-cherished goals were destined to remain perennially elusive.[35]

The same pattern of mixed results was apparent in the Gulf States–Midwest Points Service Investigation, launched in 1967 to determine the need for new services between ten important pairs of cities in a twelve-state area stretching from Ohio to Texas. As a result of the decisions finally handed down in September 1969, Delta was subjected to new competition in the Chicago–Memphis, Chicago–New Orleans, and Houston–Detroit markets. Because of the growth of traffic in recent years the company took no exception to the admission of other carriers to these airways, but it did hope to be compensated by receiving new authorizations of its own under a so-called offset principle. Following this logic, CAB examiner James S. Keith recommended that Delta be granted a new route from Dallas–Fort Worth to Detroit, which, among other features, would have given the company access to Cleveland for the first time. The board demurred, however, and awarded that prize to Braniff.

On the other hand, Delta did win a consolation prize. In his examiner's report, Keith had suggested that the company be given access to Huntsville on an alternate routing between Chicago and New Orleans. Once again, the CAB kept Delta out of the Alabama rocket center, this time by deciding in favor of Eastern. But the final order did admit Delta for the first time to Nashville, an industrial, financial, and political center whose population had been growing rapidly in recent years. In addition, as the nation's leading center of country-and-western music and home of the famed Grand Ole Opry, it offered some potential for expanding Delta's ever-growing vacation traffic. On August 1, 1969, one of the company's new DC-9s inaugurated service to the Tennessee capital with appropriate ribbon-cutting ceremonies.[36]

One result of the Gulf States proceeding was the intensification of Delta's long-standing rivalry with Eastern, which won nonstop rights between Chicago and New Orleans and would also have been installed in the Chicago-to-Memphis market had not the board on reconsideration put Southern on that segment in competition with Delta. An even more significant development soon took place, however, in the Southern Tier Nonstop Competitive Investigation, in which Eastern won a major award at Delta's expense by securing separate long-haul routes from Atlanta to Dallas–Fort Worth and Los Angeles. By the end of the decade, Delta and Eastern were thus competing over thousands of new route miles, and one of the most fiercely competitive relationships in American business history had become even more heated.[37]

Although it was not anticipated at the time, two other results of the CAB's Southern Tier deliberations, seemingly considerable victories for Delta, were destined to produce a good deal of frustration. One, the award of a nonstop route from Miami to San Francisco, turned out to be much less lucrative than expected when market forecasts proved misleading and heavy traffic failed to develop. The CAB also admitted Delta to the busy Miami-to-Houston market, but this move, which undoubtedly would have provided the company a great deal of profit in years to come, was successfully challenged in court by Continental. In the long run, Delta's only important gain from the entire proceeding was a nonstop authority from Miami to Kansas City, which gave an extra fillip to its midwestern vacation trade.[38]

In 1969 and 1970, however, Delta did win two clear-cut victories, adding important new markets to its route system. Affirming the recommendations of examiner William Cusick in a case fiercely contested by eight other airlines, the CAB selected Delta for a nonstop route between Dallas–Fort Worth and the rapidly growing southwestern metropolis of Phoenix. Eastern again was a strong contender for this authority, but Delta won preference by projecting schedules that offered the Arizona capital five new flights a day, substantially expanding the eastward connections provided by American, the existing carrier in this market. Service on what turned out to be a profitable route began on October 1, 1969, as the *Delta Digest* reported enthusiastically on the attractions offered vacationers by the area's scenic wonders, dude ranches, ghost towns, lost mines, golf courses, Indian handicrafts, and superabundant sunshine.[39] The following April, despite claims by Eastern that the award would cause a serious diversion of that company's revenues, the board granted Delta access to two other significant markets as a result of the North Carolina Points Service Investigation: Greensboro–High Point–Winston-Salem and Raleigh–Durham. In addition to providing the company with a variety of new nonstop routes connecting Chicago, North Carolina, and Miami, this decision also authorized turnaround flights between Charlotte and New York City for the first time. Service on the new routes began on June 15, using the company's new stretched DC-9-32s.[40]

Even if they did not compare in importance with earlier triumphs in the New York and southern transcontinental cases, Delta's newest accessions were nevertheless pleasing, coming as they did after nearly a decade of disappointment in CAB route proceedings. In part, the firm had been paying the price of its own success, for the board, following a strategy that previously had worked in Delta's favor, was trying to strengthen smaller or weaker carriers and to establish competition on routes that historically had been dominated by one particular airline. It was hard for Delta to claim that it needed strengthening when, as Ralph Wiser of the CAB pointed out in one examiner's report, the company's rate of return on investment for 1966 amounted to 24.63 percent. Similarly, it could not and did not deny the justification for authorizing new competitive services in such markets as the heavily traveled route from Chicago to New Orleans, where, according to a 1966 CAB survey, Delta attracted about 93 percent of the passengers flying between those two cities.[41]

Indeed, considering the rationale underlying many of the board's decisions, it is perhaps remarkable that Delta achieved any new routes. Delta was now a major airline in every sense of the word, and it is not surprising that its system was growing less rapidly. Furthermore, the company could afford to be philosophical about occasional setbacks in route investigations, for its burgeoning profits clearly indicated that it was growing where it really counted. By 1970 it had become anachronistic to talk of the industry's Big Four: they had become the Big Five. For C. E. Woolman the dreams born when there were only a few crop-dusting planes had finally come to fruition. But the dreamer was no longer around to enjoy the results of his labors.

CHAPTER 19

C. E. Woolman: End of the Route

THE PASSING of the piston era in American commercial aviation coincided with the end of a period in which the nation's largest trunk lines had been guided by a remarkable group of highly paternalistic executives who had become living legends throughout the industry. In 1960 Howard Hughes, already a recluse, lost control of TWA and spent most of the following ten years trying to retrieve his former power in a series of fruitless legal battles. In 1962 George T. (Ted) Baker sold National to Lewis B. Maytag, Jr., went into retirement, and soon died of a heart attack. Between 1963 and 1968 such giants as W. F. Patterson of United, Eddie Rickenbacker of Eastern, and C. R. Smith of American relinquished command of their respective enterprises.[1] Delta was to prove no exception to this trend.

So thoroughly had the identities of Delta and C. E. Woolman become interlocked that by the early 1960s it was difficult to mention one without thinking about the other. The reminiscences of Woolman's daughter, Barbara Woolman Preston, indicate how completely her father immersed himself in company affairs; among other things, she later recalled that she and her sister never shared a picnic with their father—a sin of omission all too common among male parents in twentieth-century American culture. But perhaps it was to be expected from the founder-patriarch of a pioneer enterprise, an airline that he had nurtured, as if it were a child, from the scrabble of dusting a few fields. Mrs. Preston also recollected that she and her sister could not count on awakening in the same room in which they had gone to bed because Woolman often brought home an "offloaded" passenger to spend the night, necessitating a change in sleeping accommodations.

What few hours Woolman spared from the affairs of the enterprise he had created were spent with his wife, Helen, who bore with infinite patience and a saving sense of humor the countless irritations imposed by his dedication to the company. Barbara Preston feels that her mother was a special bulwark for her father, that underneath the folksy charm he was shy, and that Helen enabled him to meet the world socially. Fortunately, he had a place for seclusion other than his residence, with its frequently jangling phone whose number he insisted on listing in the phonebook: a greenhouse erected on his Northside Drive property in northwest Atlanta. Here he raised orchids, which became part of his mystique. He presented them to company secretaries, to the sick, to graduating stewardess classes, among others, and the women who received them viewed the gift as a special tribute. Veteran flight attendant Sue Myracle recalls her thrill on being handed her orchid at graduation in the early 1960s. But orchid cultivation—his main hobby of the last Atlanta decades—was something Woolman shared with his wife. Helen kept the records in the intricate process of breeding and crossbreeding.[2]

Like many other hard-driving executives, Woolman refused to confront his own mortality and believed himself indispensable to the company over which he wielded a benevolent dictatorship. But his workaholic habits could not help but exact their toll. Early in 1958, when he was in his mid-sixties, he painted a somewhat humorous picture of himself in a letter to an acquaintance from Monroe days whom he had not seen for years: "I am about 10 lbs. heavier, the steps are getting steeper, my arms shorter, and the telephone books are printed apparently in a much finer type than they used to be." Several months later, after an unusually severe siege of illness, he told another old acquaintance that "two severe cases of Flu started me on the downgrade and I wound up in the hospital for the first time in my life."[3]

The boss made a slow but steady recovery from this assault on his once robust constitution, complaining to one friend that a mandated diet meant "blue-john for milk and, in fact, . . . eliminates anything of pleasure in eating or joy in anticipation."[4] Later in 1958 he departed for a projected trip around the world, only to be stricken by a heart attack while visiting India. Fortunately the medical care he received there and in Atlanta following his return, along with the constant attention and comforting presence of his wife, helped him pull through this ordeal, and by early 1959 he was once more in active command in his office on the northwest corner of the company headquarters.[5]

Outwardly the corporation showed no evident anxiety about the capacity of its chief executive to carry on as usual. Behind a confident public façade, however, there was much concern. With Woolman having suffered one coronary and two bouts with influenza during the same year, it was only natural to fear that further crises loomed ahead. Meanwhile, the state of the boss's health was beginning to place a strain upon decision-making processes throughout the organization. For decades he had insisted on having the final word on every significant move; as former board chairman R. W. Freeman has reflected, he was "of the old time management school and he didn't really believe in T.O.s [tables of organization] and flow of authority." Opinions vary concerning the extent of his inclinations toward autocracy; veteran marketing executive T. M. Miller, for example, has emphasized that considerable autonomy was allowed within the company's operating divisions once it was understood that all significant departures from standard procedure had to be discussed with Woolman in advance. Similarly, Freeman has pointed out that Woolman was not a tyrant; he simply regarded loyalty to himself as being synonymous with loyalty to Delta. Nevertheless, a heavy paternal hand was ever present, its power buttressed by the indisputable fact that Delta had risen from humble origins to the status of a major airline under its sway. Now the grasp of that hand was weakening; as Charles Dolson has pointed out, senior executives on the scene in Atlanta had no alternative but to make important decisions while Woolman lay incapacitated halfway around the world, and this tendency persisted to some degree after his return. In Dolson's words, "we didn't point out to him all the little things we were doing without getting his approval."[6]

Though unable to face the certainty of his own ultimate departure from the scene, Woolman had always encouraged his top executives to groom potential replacements in their respective divisions, particularly since the Columbus plane crash of 1947 in which a large group of Delta officials had been wiped out at one stroke. Whenever possible, talent was to be identified and nurtured within the company itself, but if he considered it necessary to depart from this general rule Woolman was prepared to go outside, as he did in the late 1950s to secure a strong backup person for the talented Todd Cole in the finance division. While making plans for the establishment of the jet base, Delta had secured advice from Cresap, McCormick and Paget (CMP), a prominent consulting firm; in the process, W. T. Beebe and other Delta executives were impressed particularly by Robert Oppenlander, a young CMP representative and graduate of MIT and the Harvard Business School, and soon thereafter Oppenlander accepted an offer from Woolman to join the company as comptroller. Despite a pervasive sentiment within the Delta organization against going outside the firm for high-level personnel, things worked out successfully and within a few years Oppenlander became treasurer of the corporation. The wisdom of his selection as Cole's understudy became even more apparent in 1963 when Cole accepted the challenge of playing a leading role in the efforts of Malcolm A. MacIntyre, Eastern's president, to reorganize that struggling enterprise and moved over to Delta's traditional rival as executive vice-president for finance. Oppenlander was quickly elevated to Cole's former position and became a key factor in the firm's subsequent growth.[7]

It was one thing for Woolman to keep a keen eye on possible successors to his senior vice-presidents, but grooming a potential replacement for himself was another matter entirely. Following the death of Laigh Parker in 1959, R. W. Freeman became Woolman's closest business confidant. Wishing to step down as board chairman and seeing the need for a more tightly structured managerial setup, Freeman tried for a long time to persuade Woolman to take his place and turn the day-to-day management of Delta over to a president and heir apparent. Predictably, Woolman resisted the idea. Having been the boss so long, he simply could not let go. Symptomatic of his outlook was the tenacity with which he clung to the title of general manager as well as that of president of the corporation; those who knew him well concur that the former was even more precious to him than the latter. Apparently it was impossible for Woolman to conceive that anyone could completely fill his place; then, too, he may have appreciated the difficult position in which any publicly designated successor would find himself while the founding father was yet alive. In any event, Woolman had long held a firm resolve, which he expressed quite clearly to James Montgomery of the Atlanta *Constitution* on one occasion: "When I leave the company, I'll go to the cemetery."[8]

On the other hand, Woolman could do nothing to alter the fact that each passing year imposed further limitations upon his energies. In April 1962 he suffered a heavy personal blow when, following a protracted struggle with cancer, Helen Woolman died. A loner by nature, underneath the incessant whirl of his business activities, and, as his close personal confidant Wayne Parrish has observed, a man with many acquaintances but few intimate friends, C.E. was now deprived of his main source of emotional support and lived by himself at the old family residence with only a staff of housekeepers. Possibly because of a deep but unarticulated need for companionship, he frequently gave his chauffeur the day off and asked one or another of his top executives to drive him home at night. Television helped to some extent to fill up the empty hours when he was not working in his office; suddenly Dolson discovered that he had to be sure to know what NBC's *Today* show had predicted and relate it somehow for the boss to Delta's own specialized weather forecast. As for the raising of orchids, painful memories made it a much less satisfying avocation. On one occasion Richard Maurer brought Woolman home for the night and was asked in for a drink, after which the two men went back to the greenhouse to look at the flowers. Maurer noted that many of the plants were drooping and seemed neglected, whereupon Woolman replied that since Helen's death his heart was no longer in the cultivation of orchids. So he clung to the daily routine of running the only thing on earth which continued to hold meaning for him: Delta Air Lines.[9]

Yet as his vitality flagged it became increasingly necessary to deal with a contingency that, however difficult it was to confront, must have lurked constantly at the back of his mind. Though he did not adopt Freeman's advice that he institute a reorganization that would have reduced his responsibilities substantially, he did ultimately make a move which, like so many compromises with reality, was probably ill-fated from the start. On July 25, 1963, Delta's board of directors, at Woolman's initiative, elected Earl D. Johnson as executive vice-president and a director of the firm. Johnson's credentials were impressive: among other things, he had been president and vice-chairman of the board of General Dynamics and under secretary of the United States Army. Freeman and Woolman had come to know him as a result of Delta's acquisition of the CV-880, manufactured by General Dynamics' Convair subsidiary, and it was undoubtedly flattering to Woolman that such a person was willing to come into the Delta management in a position subordinate to himself. Whether or not Johnson's title indicated that he was the official heir apparent is not completely clear, but it is noteworthy that it was exactly the same designation that had been conferred upon Sidney Stewart at the time of the C & S merger and that only two other Delta executives had ever possessed anything like it: Cole, who had borne the title of executive vice-president for administration, and Dolson, who had the title of executive vice-president for operations when Johnson came aboard.

In any event, things did not work out. It was hardly to be expected that senior executives who had worked long and faithfully to advance the fortunes of the corporation would be enthusiastic about the appointment to an obviously prestigious position of an outsider who, whatever his previous experience in the airframe industry, had none whatsoever in airline management. In addition, Johnson's role, like that of Stewart before him, was by its very nature ill-defined: he had no responsibilities within the company's operating divisions and any real power he could have exercised would by definition have had to be delegated to him by Woolman; but he apparently believed, like Stewart, that he would soon come to share a substantial part of Woolman's command authority. In this, however, he was wrong; Woolman was temperamentally incapable of surrendering the ubiquitous role he had played over the course of four decades. Looking back upon the episode, some Delta officials later recalled personality clashes which did not help an already unfortunate situation, while other employees remembered Johnson as a man of considerable charm. Veteran executive secretary Marjorie Langford, for example, recounted a flight on which Johnson went out of his way to exchange courtesies with her and her family, displaying a charisma somewhat akin to that of Woolman himself. Under other circumstances Johnson might have achieved an enduring place within the organization; given the understandable tensions surrounding the issue of who Woolman's ultimate successor would be and the firm's long tradition of promoting from within, however, his departure was practically inevitable, and within less than a year Delta had bought up his contract. It was expensive, Freeman later recalled, but it would have been even costlier to keep him.[10]

Freeman was correct, however, in believing that the Johnson appointment would eventually bring about a closer realization of his own ideas. By bringing a potential successor into the firm, Woolman had implicitly acknowledged that a leadership transition was underway, and after Johnson left it was difficult to return to the previous status quo as if nothing had happened. It was crucial to reassure present stockholders and potential investors alike that the progress of the most profitable trunk line in the industry would continue uninterrupted if and when its chief executive, now approaching seventy-five years of age, found it impossible to remain at the helm. In the spring of 1964 Thomas M. Miller, whose scheduling efforts had produced the Early Bird–Owly Bird system and other successful innovations, was promoted to the rank of executive vice-president for marketing, putting him in a special category along with Dolson immediately under Woolman. In July 1964 Miller was also elected to the board of directors, along with Sears, Roebuck executive Charles H. Kellstadt, but this did nothing to clarify the fundamental issue. Despite pressure from his closest advisers, who sympathized deeply with his situation and yet felt an equal need to safeguard the future of the enterprise, Woolman could not bring himself to take decisive action. During the mid-1960s, however, two more heart attacks, neither of them severe enough to keep him away from the office for very long, added fresh urgency to the problem.

Finally, on November 1, 1965, matters began to be resolved. Freeman, a tower of strength to the company ever since he had taken over the chairmanship of the board from Putnam in 1954, relinquished that post as he had so long desired to do. Into his place moved Woolman, who reluctantly gave up his title of president and general manager but received a new one, that of chief executive officer. This designation, which was already being used by other airlines but was new to Delta, meant that Woolman was still the boss. In theory, he was to focus specially on the area of general planning; in actuality, he could not help but continue his involvement in all aspects of Delta's operations. Succeeding Woolman as president of the firm was Charles Dolson, whose service to the corporation as a captain, chief pilot, and operations head stretched all the way back to the company's inauguration of airmail flights in 1934. He was to focus on the day-to-day aspects of running the airline, performing the functions that in the earlier days of the industry had devolved upon the official holding the title of general manager. Because such a designation was no longer in fashion and Woolman's emotional attachment to it would have precluded it from being given to another person in any event, it was simply dropped. In related administrative developments, Freeman was appointed chairman of Delta's finance committee, thus assuring his continued involvement in important company decisions, while David C. Garrett, whose work in planning for the arrival of the jets had clearly indicated that greater things were in store for him, took over Dolson's former post as vice-president of operations.[11]

Though many responsibilities continued to be exercised as before, these moves represented more than a mere reshuffling of titles, for they strongly suggested that Dolson would be Woolman's successor and helped assure Delta's investors and the business community in general that an orderly transition was in prospect in the event of Woolman's death. As the firm's overall performance indicated, and as future developments would continue to demonstrate, the com-

pany had no shortage of managerial talent. In addition, the inescapable tensions associated with carrying out their functions as
effectively as possible despite the sense of worry that each of them
could not help but feel, far from drawing them apart, actually drew
Woolman's top subordinates even more closely together.[12]

While company officials struggled with the problems created by
Woolman's advancing age, certain nostalgic rites of observance
emphasized the fact that Delta was increasingly an historic entity
as well as a modern corporation whose prime business was transporting people and things in up-to-date jets. Marking the firm's
thirty-fifth anniversary as an airline in June 1964, the *Delta Digest*
featured a photographic montage showing the first tile-roofed headquarters building at Monroe, the Atlanta general office building and
hangar in 1941, and the sprawling complex that constituted the current company headquarters. The technological changes that had
occurred during the same period were revealed clearly by pictures
of all the aircraft Delta had operated from the Travel Air to the
DC-9. In other scenes from the past, Pat Higgins posed beside a
Travel Air in June 1929; Woolman stood beside a row of "Huffer-
Puffers" in the early 1930s; a beaming Woolman and a soberly con-
templative Putnam accepted slices of cake from Delta and C&S
stewardesses on "M-Day," May 1, 1953; passengers boarded a DC-8
for the first commercial flight of that Douglas model on September
18, 1959; and Woolman showed evident glee as he and Dolson, the
latter smiling in a somewhat restrained manner, held an outsized
key in 1961 at a victory rally celebrating the award of the long-
sought route to the West Coast.[13]

In the fall of 1964 a ceremony occurred which must have affected
Woolman deeply: the Delta pilots, on behalf of themselves and
their families, presented the boss with a large oil painting of himself, which now hangs in the reception lobby of the company headquarters. The presentation was made by Captain Truman Outland,
once a leader of the C&S "pilots' revolt" at the time of the 1953
merger. In April 1965 Delta's pioneer stewardesses held a twenty-
fifth anniversary observance; Laura Wizark Baker was there, along
with six other originals including Birdie Perkins Bomar. Along with
selected successors from various periods of Delta history, they wore
the uniforms of their respective times.[14]

The following month, five of the original stewardesses came to
Woolman's office on the occasion of his fortieth anniversary as an
employee of the firm and presented him with the model of a DC-2,

the plane on which they had first flown with Delta in 1940; these members of the company's "clipped wings club" posed amiably for the camera alongside the large rawboned Woolman, who combined the look of an aging farmer and an airline executive full of years and honors. Early in 1966 it was Catherine FitzGerald's turn to be honored on her fortieth anniversary with Delta and its dusting predecessor. As she glowed with a beaming Irish smile, Woolman affixed to her lapel both a jeweled Delta pin symbolizing the anniversary and one of his now rare orchids, commenting that she had joined Delta's Huff Daland predecessor while still a schoolgirl in upstate New York and moved to Monroe with the inauguration of crop dusting there in the early 1920s. "She was a little timid," he recalled, "but she stuck to her knitting, and stayed with us through thick and thin. . . . She's been a part of Delta through it all. She never wavered, never looked back. Delta is her way and her life." [15]

Nostalgia affected more than ceremonies marking anniversaries and the like; Woolman also clung to something that had long become obsolete in terms of profitability, but which had carried the company financially in the period of its earliest airline operations: the dusting division, which continued to be directed by the most significant pioneer in the history of aerial spraying techniques, Dr. Bert R. Coad. As was clearly indicated in one of Coad's periodic reports, dusting remained what it had been ever since the 1930s—a miniscule appendage of the mammoth enterprise it had spawned:

After several weeks of wrestling with high winds, turbulence, snow, etc., in the [Texas] Panhandle, we finally emerged with a gross of approximately thirteen thousand dollars. . . . On the other hand, the vetch work, after three false starts, fizzled out, and we abandoned the effort. We have been waiting all month for a start on our fire ant contracts, but, as usual, when dealing with the government, there have been delays. . . . Cotton has been getting off to a slow start here after being planted late, and we will be at least two weeks behind expectations in getting into any swing in the cotton fields. [16]

Then, in February 1966, another link with the seedtime of the corporation snapped when Coad, who had suffered for years with various health problems, died. Woolman rarely saw his former close associate, whose headquarters were located in Bryan, Texas, but was nonetheless crestfallen by the departure of a man whom he had continued to regard as "a devoted friend." [17] In June 1966, in a speech at Charleston, South Carolina, Woolman paid tribute to Coad, emphasized his own role in the development of aerial crop dusting, and indicated stubbornly that the work of the agricultural division would continue: "I was a farm-extension agent for Louisiana State University back in the early 1920s," he recalled, "when . . . I formed a strong and permanent dislike for the boll-weevil. Dr. B. R. Coad . . . and I formed a fighting team which grew and expanded over the years . . . a close and continuous association until Dr. Coad's death only a few short weeks ago." Indulging in a bit of hyperbole, the boss claimed that "our Dusting Division . . . still makes a considerable call upon our time and energies," even though the airline bulked much larger in the total corporate picture.[18]

Early in September 1966 Delta executives were informed that Woolman would be temporarily out of town to attend a meeting in Wyoming of *Los Conquistadores del Cielo*, an organization of aviation personalities to which many airline executives belonged. While there, he also intended to do some fishing. Charles Dolson also planned to attend the meeting and expected to leave in Woolman's company but was informed at the last minute that something had come up to prevent the boss from going and that he should proceed by himself. From Cheyenne, Dolson rode with Wayne Parrish to the ranch where the meeting was to take place.[19]

From the beginning, Woolman's projected Wyoming junket had been an elaborate subterfuge created to hide from all but a select few the fact that he was really slated to go elsewhere for a much different purpose: he was to have surgery in a Houston hospital to correct a threatening aneurysm. Both of his daughters, Barbara Woolman Preston and Martha Woolman Taylor, knew. Catherine FitzGerald, his private secretary, knew. Delta's Houston sales manager also knew, for it was he who had made the arrangements. So Woolman went to Houston, accompanied by Barbara, and had the operation on September 7. He seemed to come out of it in such good shape that his daughter soon returned to Atlanta. Then, on September 11, 1966, as suddenly as a plane's wheels touch a runway upon landing, he died.[20]

As secretaries Mary Helen Payne and Mildred Crout later recalled, the news produced profound shock and even outright disbelief throughout the Delta family, from executives down through the rank and file. Charles Dolson, who had accepted a ride back to Atlanta from the *Conquistadores* meeting with President Floyd Hall of Eastern in a private jet, learned of it only upon reaching the Atlanta airport the day after the death had occurred; his initial reaction, which subsequent events proved correct, was "that he was going to have to do a lot of things he had not done before." One of his first tasks was to arrange to bring the body back to Atlanta. Richard Maurer was at home when he received a call telling him of Woolman's passing. Unlike Dolson, he did not immediately think of the consequences, possibly because he was not the likely successor; instead, he was preoccupied with the need to make funeral arrangements and notify those persons who should be informed by some more personal means than mere announcements in the public media.[21]

The intensity of the sorrow felt by the rank and file demonstrated the depth of Woolman's appeal throughout the Delta organization. Secretary Rosemary Wadewitz had last seen the boss just before he left for Houston; she was due to be hospitalized at any moment to have a baby and recalled that he joked with her about the imminence of her departure. She heard of his death in the hospital from a radio next to her bed and was filled with grief remembering how kind and fatherly he had been to her. In later years she remembered his conscientiousness in such things as personally answering customer complaints. Secretary Mary Johnson recalled poignantly how Woolman had called her his "birthday twin" because both had been born on October 8. Switchboard operator Diane Stanford and her husband were entertaining company when public-relations official George Shedd called her with the somber news and asked that she come immediately to her post at company headquarters. She later recollected telling her guests that "Delta has died." After returning to her station she was inundated by calls in which men as well as women often broke down and wept. They recounted to her their memories of some thoughtful Woolman comment, some joking remark, some kindness, some occasion when he sent an orchid as an indication of personal regard. She remembered switchboard monologues—for she mainly listened—as an outpouring, a verbalization of love and grief from the "family." She wanted to tell someone her fond recollections of him but it was her duty to answer and listen.[22]

Like many other Delta employees, Stanford was fearful for the future, but not for the financial aspect—only for the close-knit morale factor. Would the spirit go with Woolman, who had epitomized the family closeness in his paternalistic role and his rapport with the rank and file? Others, such as secretary Helen Thones, reacted the same way. Both Stanford and Wadewitz feel it took them about a year to accept the reality of Woolman's death. The pilots, who had known of Woolman's heart condition, were still stunned by the abruptness of his departure from the scene.[23]

On a rainy Tuesday morning, September 14, an estimated fifteen hundred to two thousand mourners crowded into Atlanta's First Presbyterian Church to attend a brief funeral service, following which Woolman's body, which had been flown from Houston in a Lockheed Hercules cargo plane, was laid to its final rest at Arlington Cemetery in the nearby suburb of Sandy Springs. Telegrams and letters of condolence poured into the company headquarters, while other tributes appeared in periodicals and newspapers. Among the latter, an essay written by James Montgomery, business editor of the Atlanta *Constitution*, was particularly noteworthy. It pointed out that on the first day of trading on Wall Street after the announcement of Woolman's death, Delta stock actually closed up by nearly six points. In Montgomery's view this reflected an awareness among knowledgeable investors that no large technologically oriented enterprise in such a complex field as commercial aviation "is or can be a one-man show in today's economy," and that once-dominant chief executives had now become essentially "figureheads" dependent upon the expertise of key subordinates. Delta was "one of the last of a vanishing species—a large modern corporation stamped with the towering personality of a single individual." Nonetheless, despite Woolman's stature as "an exceptional human being, legendary in life for his integrity and wit as well as for his management skill," the company he had founded was already a team-managed enterprise whose future was not likely to be imperiled by the loss of his leadership. In truth, he had been more dependent upon it in the recent past than it had been upon him; in Montgomery's eyes, Woolman's stubborn refusal to contemplate retirement provided "convincing evidence that he was in his later years sustained by the organization he fathered."[24]

Events following the funeral bore out the accuracy of these observations. On September 15 Delta's board of directors met to select a new chief executive officer. In an atmosphere free from any hint of anxiety they made the logical choice, Charles Dolson, who committed himself from the outset to emphasize team leadership. During the final years of Woolman's life, looking ahead to the inevitable day when the patriarch would no longer be on the scene, W. T. Beebe had worked out an organization chart corresponding to the realities of the decision-making process that was gradually emerging at Delta

underneath Woolman's ostensible one-man rule; this quickly became the model upon which procedure was based as the firm moved
toward a record income of $49.2 million for the fiscal year that
ended less than ten months after the founding father's death.

A color photograph in the 1967 annual report showed Delta's new
collective leadership assembled in a confident mood in Woolman's
old office. Grouped around Dolson were the five major division
heads: Miller for traffic and sales, Beebe for personnel, Maurer for
legal affairs, Oppenlander for finance, and Garrett for operations. In
every respect they epitomized the image of what they were: salaried
professional managers of the type that had long since taken command of America's largest business corporations and were now
coming to the forefront in commercial aviation. During the next
two years there occurred a wave of promotions as the division heads
were formally designated senior vice-presidents and a cadre of longtime Delta employees moved into vice-presidencies and assistant
vice-presidencies under them, filling the positions characteristic of
a functionally managed enterprise with a clearly articulated assignment of responsibilities. An indication of the change that was taking
place was the fact that in mid-1967 Delta had only three assistant
vice-presidents; within a year there were thirteen; by mid-1969,
twenty-four. Since Woolman's death, Beebe, Garrett, and Oppenlander had also been elected to the board of directors. Meanwhile,
the pace of the company's development quickened. Fiscal 1969, for
example, brought record highs in three important categories: operating revenues, revenue passenger miles, and cargo ton miles.[25]

Other indications of change appeared quickly during this period of
transition from paternalism to newer concepts of corporate management. The crop-dusting operation to which Woolman had clung so
devotedly for sentimental reasons was now sold to United Services,
Factors, and Guarantors for $88,000; ultimately its real estate was
acquired by the city of Monroe, Louisiana. In another move reflecting the same practical outlook, the stockholders voted on January
28, 1967, to change the state in which Delta was incorporated from
Louisiana, its birthplace, to Delaware. The annual report that appeared later that year assured its readers that this was "a technical
change only, for efficiency in the legal and tax structures of the company and in no way involved any move of personnel or property."
Nevertheless, it was a symbol of the times.[26]

Still, Delta did remain mindful of the need to preserve vital elements of the Woolman heritage. Annual meetings, for example, continued to be held at Monroe, emphasizing deeply meaningful links with the corporate past. The same stockholders meeting that endorsed moving the firm's legal home to Delaware also ratified the election to the board of Bernard W. Biedenharn, the Monroe businessman who in his younger days had rented hangar space from the hard-pressed dusting organization for his Gypsy Moth. Although the executive offices at the Atlanta headquarters became a bit less Spartan than they had been under Woolman's administration, their accoutrements remained considerably more modest than those found in the posh managerial suites of many large American corporations. Above all, the new leadership, steeped as it was in the experiences of the Woolman era, recognized the need to nurture the close-knit "family feeling" that the patriarch had worked so hard to sustain among Delta employees.[27]

One series of events in particular demonstrated the regard Delta felt for its departed founder. In November 1966 two antique survivors from Huff Daland's original fleet of crop-dusting planes were crated and shipped to Atlanta in moving vans. After studying them carefully, a team of Delta employees, led appropriately by mechanic Gene Barry, who, like Biedenharn, began his relationship with Delta in the early 1930s, selected one of the craft and stripped it to its barest components. A thorough process of restoration was then commenced. Six months later, the finished product was rolled out for public admiration prior to being shipped to the Smithsonian Institution as a permanent memorial to C. E. Woolman. A shining biplane bearing the distinctive triangular emblem of the dusting service, with its puffing god of wind, it was hailed by Dolson as a fitting symbol of the humble origins from which Delta had emerged. An article in the *Delta Digest* compared it to an ancient gladiator, saying that "It fought a battle well, helped save the economy of a whole area, and helped bring to life the jobs we have today."

On January 18, 1968, the plane was presented officially to the Smithsonian in a ceremony held at the Arts and Industries Building in Washington, D.C. On the platform were Dolson; Catherine Fitz-Gerald; Gene Berry; Stuart Tipton, president of the Air Transport Association; and S. Paul Johnson, director of the National Air and Space Museum. Dolson summarized the highlights of the company's history, and Berry pointed out various technological features that made the craft so suited to the work it was designed to perform. Tipton spoke about Woolman himself, saying that he "saw aviation in terms of people." Johnson, accepting the plane after a brief statement of presentation by FitzGerald, declared that he considered it to be "one of the finest jobs of restoration that I have seen in this country or in Europe." Thus, before an audience of approximately seventy persons, including Woolman's daughters and grandchildren, the little duster joined a select group of historic aircraft and spacecraft including the Wright brothers' first airplane, Lindbergh's *Spirit of St. Louis*, and John Glenn's *Friendship 7*. As the *Delta Digest* commented, "It is flying now in the highest cotton."[28]

For Delta, an era had ended and a transition of crucial importance was successfully underway. Understandably reluctant to relinquish command of the enterprise to which he had devoted his life, one of the industry's most significant pioneers had passed on, leaving behind a legacy whose essence Tipton's words captured as well as any. In the years ahead, when questioned about what made Delta unique, company executives would invariably begin by saying that it was a "people-oriented airline."

CHAPTER 20

Acquisition and Consolidation

D ELTA ENTERED the 1970s with a flurry of activity, and the
early years of the decade witnessed a series of developments
highlighted by the purchase of a new fleet of wide-bodied
planes and a major addition to the Delta family resulting from merger with another airline. During the next few years these gains were
digested and the company pursued a massive fleet standardization
program that substantially reduced unit costs of operation in the
face of rapidly mounting fuel prices and other inflationary trends.
Acquisition was thus matched with consolidation.

As if to symbolize the size its operations had attained by 1970,
Delta was preparing, as the decade began, to inaugurate service with
the largest passenger plane ever built. Several years earlier, in a
move to counter the sales appeal of the Douglas DC-8 Super Sixty
series, Boeing had decided to create a revolutionary wide-bodied
"jumbo jet," which would become famous as the 747. Featuring a
number of ideas gleaned from the Seattle firm's unsuccessful effort
to win a contract to build the giant C-5A military transport, the new
ship was to be powered by four Pratt and Whitney JT-9D engines
possessing a total thrust of 164,000 pounds, carry up to 490 passengers and 60,000 pounds of freight and luggage in a fuselage nearly
232 feet long, and cruise at 625 miles per hour with a ceiling of
45,000 feet. Pan American was the first customer, ordering twenty-
five of the aircraft in April 1966.

Early the following year, Arthur Ford visited the Boeing plant at
Renton, Washington, where the new airliner was being assembled,
and returned to Atlanta impressed with its potential. Shortly thereafter, a large party of Delta officers and directors visited the Renton
facility; their initial reaction to the unfinished plane was one of
speechless amazement. From the outset, Delta management agreed
that under foreseeable market conditions, and especially because of
the company's predominantly short- and medium-haul route structure, there was no need for such an enormous ship over the long run.
On the other hand, circumstances dictated the temporary acquisi-

tion of a limited number of 747s. Two of Delta's competitors, American and Northwest, had decided to purchase the plane, and the consequences could be highly unwelcome if these companies used it to compete with Delta's DC-8s and CV-880s on the routes from Chicago to Miami and Dallas to the Pacific Coast. Accordingly, in April 1967 Dolson announced that a decision had been made to purchase three of the ships, which cost $20 million each, with plans to acquire two more at a later date. It was the first time Delta had ever bought a plane from Boeing, and the purchase marked the beginning of a significant relationship with the Seattle firm.[1]

Preparations for the Boeing 747 included the installation of more than two million dollars in new ground equipment at the six cities and three alternate airports from which the massive ship would operate. As usual, the *Delta Digest* reported significant milestones such as the rollout of the initial 747 in late September 1968 and the maiden inspection flight on February 9, 1969. When the ship entered commercial service for the first time with Pan American late that year, two Delta representatives were aboard: E. L. Hamner, vice-president of stations, and J. L. Ewing, manager of the company's news bureau, who wrote that it was difficult to describe the experience because "there is no way to compare it to air travel as we know it today. It is more of a feeling of flying across the country in your living room." After almost one year of waiting, Delta finally received its first 747, which was flown from Seattle to Atlanta on October 2, 1970, with T. P. Ball in command and B. B. Barclay in the copilot's seat. Twenty-three days later it began scheduled service between Los Angeles, Dallas, and Atlanta; by the end of the year two other 747s had arrived and flights had begun to Chicago, Detroit, and Miami.[2]

While discussing the 747, Delta management had also pondered the best long-range solution to the problems and opportunities presented by the advent of wide-bodied jet aircraft. One possibility was the DC-10, which Douglas engineers had begun to design at the behest of American Airlines for service on medium-haul domestic routes. While conceived as a smaller plane than the 747, this model, to be powered by three General Electric CF-6 turbofan engines, would nevertheless have a spacious interior laid out in the emergent wide-bodied pattern and seat more than two hundred passengers. The other alternative was the Lockheed L-1011 TriStar, planned along similar lines in response to American's specifications.

Delta liked both planes, but circumstances ultimately favored the

Lockheed entry. Despite the technical success of the DC-8 and DC-9, Douglas had encountered serious financial problems in developing them and experienced a series of annual deficits when sales fell below expectations. The result was a merger with the McDonnell Aircraft Corporation in 1967. With Donald Douglas, Sr., no longer in charge and C. E. Woolman now dead, the close personal ties that had bound the two firms together were weakened. In addition, Lockheed, anxious to reestablish itself in the commercial field following the troubled history of the L-188 Electra, had decided to encourage a maximum of customer input; it therefore launched a program of elaborate discussions with operations, maintenance, and passenger-service representatives from various airlines, including Delta.

The result was a ship beautifully tailored to meet prevailing needs. Its guidance and navigation equipment was especially remarkable; embodying the latest advances in computerization, the TriStar would include many new cybernetic features including an automated landing system that could adjust to changing wind conditions without the need for pilots to make frequent corrections by hand. McDonnell Douglas was also slower to commit itself decisively to going ahead with the DC-10 than Lockheed was with the TriStar and could not provide Delta with the production schedules it wanted. Finally, and perhaps most important, the new Delta management team wanted to do its best to stimulate competition in the airframe industry and believed it would be good strategy to encourage Lockheed at this point. Accordingly, in April 1968 Delta signed the largest contract in its history by ordering twenty-four TriStars for a total price of $360 million. Deliveries were scheduled to begin in the fall of 1971.[3]

Production of the TriStar was soon underway at Lockheed's giant assembly complex at Palmdale, California. Dolson and other Delta officials would have preferred the ship to have American-made engines, but Lockheed had decided instead upon the Rolls-Royce RB-211 power plant. Matters proceeded smoothly and the TriStar made its first test flight on November 16, 1970. Early the following year, however, Rolls-Royce collapsed financially and went into receivership on February 4, 1971. For months the fate of the TriStar, and indeed of the Lockheed Aircraft Corporation as a whole, hung in the balance as representatives of American banks, the airlines that had committed themselves to the L-1011, and Lockheed itself persuaded the British government to guarantee loans permitting the reorganized engine manufacturing concern to stay in business. Meanwhile, the United States Congress debated the merits of guaranteeing similar loans to Lockheed. Even if these efforts were to succeed, a delay in deliveries was a foregone conclusion, and Delta officials were understandably anxious about the situation. At a special meeting of the board of directors on March 28, 1971, therefore, a decision was made to order five DC-10s from McDonnell Douglas as a temporary measure pending further developments. A contract was soon executed specifying deliveries in late 1972 and early 1973.

Over the strong opposition of various legislators, including Senator William Proxmire of Wisconsin, a bill was approved by Congress in August 1971 under which Lockheed was permitted to borrow $250 million from banks under the protection of the Emergency Guarantee Loan Board. Related developments in Great Britain saved Rolls-Royce from extinction, and a plan was worked out under which Lockheed's airline customers further insured the future of the TriStar by making payments totaling $100 million over and above the advances specified in initial contracts. These emergency allotments were credited against the delivery price when the planes were ultimately completed, and Lockheed reimbursed the carriers for interest charges incurred in obtaining the funds ahead of previously anticipated schedules. Delta's share of this arrangement came to $20.4 million. The price of the plane itself was also increased, as was the cost of the Rolls-Royce engines. Because of the delay that had occurred while these issues were being resolved, Lockheed was forced to alter its delivery plans and production did not begin on Delta's first L-1011 until late 1972. Nevertheless, the TriStar had been saved.[4]

During the spring of 1971, however, another project that would have added a dramatic new member to the Delta fleet later in the decade died on the floor of Congress. Eight years before, in a speech at the United States Air Force Academy in Colorado Springs, President Kennedy had announced that the United States government would support the design and production of a supersonic jet transport to compete with the projected Anglo-French Concorde. Soon thereafter the FAA invited proposals from a group of airframe and engine manufacturers, resulting in a competition won late in 1966 by Boeing and General Electric. Believing that the company would have to acquire a modest number of these planes in order to maintain its competitive position, Delta management reserved three delivery positions for the aircraft and, in accordance with FAA stipulations, advanced $1 million per plane as risk money to supplement the funds being spent by the government and the manufacturers during the development of a prototype. As the project moved forward, however, it met a firestorm of opposition critics who looked upon the venture as wasteful, unnecessary, and potentially dangerous to the environment. Led by Proxmire, who chaired a crucial series of hearings on the issue in 1970, enemies of the SST finally succeeded in cutting off appropriations for the venture; the final blow came in May 1971, when the Senate failed to concur with the House of Representatives in an attempt to reverse earlier action that had cut off funds for the controversial aircraft.[5]

Delta officials took the outcome philosophically, for the Boeing 2707, as the plane had been designated, was far better suited for long transoceanic runs than for the company's route structure. Any regrets about its fate were mitigated quickly by the contemporaneous events that insured the survival of the Lockheed L-1011. Besides, Delta was deeply involved at this point in a matter of much more importance to its growth and welfare than the collapse of the American bid to create a rival to the Concorde. For the second time in its history, the company was poised to acquire Northeast Airlines, the prize that had proved so elusive in the early 1950s for want of a connecting link at New York City.

The fact that Northeast still survived in 1971 was something of a miracle. The tiny New England–based trunk line had banked heavily on the 1956 CAB award that gave it a five-year certificate to fly from New York to Miami via Washington (see p. 284) as the answer to its chronic financial problems, but events did not match expectations. The firm had ordered a fleet of new DC-6s, hoping to use these on the Miami run pending the arrival of five British turboprop airliners scheduled to be completed in late 1957, but deliveries were slow and Northeast executives finally opened the route with two secondhand DC-6s hastily acquired from another carrier. One of these crashed shortly after takeoff from New York's LaGuardia Airport on February 1, 1957, with the loss of twenty passengers; the incident, which ultimately became the subject of a book and a television documentary, gave the company bad publicity at the very outset of service on a new route crucial to its welfare. Two more fatal crashes in 1957 and 1958 led to an FAA investigation of Northeast's entire pilot force and the adequacy of its training program. Ultimately, George Gardner, who had become chairman of the board since negotiating the abortive merger with Delta earlier in the decade, was forced out and replaced by an executive from the parent Atlas Corporation. In a related move, James M. Austin, previously an officer with Capital, became president of Northeast, which was still losing money despite the new Florida operation.[6]

In 1959 Northeast acquired ten Vickers Viscount turboprops and leased a Boeing 707 jetliner, but heavy losses continued and merger negotiations were begun with TWA. This brought Howard Hughes into the picture, and the Hughes Tool Company soon began making large loans to Northeast in anticipation that the consolidation would take place. In addition, Northeast was permitted to lease six of the newly built Convair 880s that originally had been intended for service with TWA but had not been delivered to that airline because of its tangled relations with Hughes. Despite these measures, Northeast's losses continued to grow. Then, during the winter of 1960–61, Hughes was forced to give up control of TWA and put his holdings in a voting trust. For the time being, the merger talks collapsed.

Pressures mounted as creditors demanded payment of overdue obligations while Eastern and National, Northeast's competitors on the route from New York to Miami, made a proposal to dismember the embattled corporation, reserving the Florida artery for themselves while parceling out Northeast's New England routes to Mohawk Airlines. Austin resisted this humiliating maneuver, but the only alternative seemed to be another approach to Hughes, this time with the idea that the Hughes Tool Company take control of Northeast by acquiring the Atlas holdings. Despite intense opposition from Eastern and National, the CAB ultimately decided to approve this procedure; all that stood in the way was renewal of Northeast's certification for the route from New York to Miami, without which the Hughes enterprise was unwilling to close the deal. Meanwhile, financial aid from the Hughes Tool Company was resumed.

In mid-1962, however, the CAB dealt Northeast a devastating blow when, by a three-to-two vote, it decided to terminate the company's Florida authority, as well as its right to operate commuter services from Boston to Philadelphia and Washington. There was a furious response as an outpouring of letters and telegrams from New England denounced the board's action. Employees of the beleaguered airline organized a massive petition campaign, ultimately collecting nearly 250,000 signatures for submission to Congress, and a media drive dramatized the company's valiant struggle for life. Pressure from Senator Edward M. Kennedy and other spokesmen for the northeastern region resulted in hearings before the Aviation

Subcommittee of the United States Senate on the effect the CAB ruling would have upon the New England economy; meanwhile, the United States Justice Department filed a petition for reconsideration citing the need to insure adequate competition on the Florida route. Morale within the Northeast organization suffered when the company's entire fleet of Viscounts was sold at auction to satisfy the demands of creditors, but the fight continued. When the CAB refused to alter its original verdict, a preliminary stay was secured from the United States Court of Appeals for the First Circuit in Boston permitting the company to continue flying the disputed routes, followed by a decree setting aside the board's findings and ordering the case to be reopened. Heartened by the resilience shown by the firm, Hughes Tool went through with its plan to acquire the Atlas holdings and continued to advance funds to Northeast on a limited basis.

Nevertheless, the situation became desperate once more in December 1964, when the CAB, having reheard the Florida route case, again reached the same decision when the same members cast the same three-to-two vote. The controlling Hughes interests became disheartened by this turn of events, and Northeast's board of directors prepared to accept a joint offer by Eastern and National to pay the firm $15 million, in return for which the company would drop its court battle, accept the loss of the Florida route, and revert to the status of a small regional feeder line. This act of surrender was prevented only by a stockholder suit that produced a restraining order from the Suffolk Superior Court of Massachusetts enjoining the board from taking such action. The United States Circuit Court of Appeals then intervened once more and required the CAB to hear the case for a third time. While a plan of employee ownership was discussed, the CAB again decided against Northeast's renewal application, only to be thwarted by renewed action in appellate court.

This impasse was finally broken by events that transpired in the spring and early summer of 1965. CAB chairman Alan Boyd became under secretary of commerce for transportation and the term of Chan Gurney, another member of the board, expired. Their departure removed two of the three officials who had opposed Northeast's application. With the balance of power now decisively changed, business interests which had previously shied away from the Northeast situation became convinced that the airline had a future. One of these was the Storer Broadcasting Company, which operated a thriving chain of radio and television stations in nine major metropolitan areas throughout the United States. Its chief executive, George B. Storer, Sr., had long wanted to enter commercial aviation and had once made an unsuccessful attempt to acquire National. On July 30, 1965, Storer Broadcasting acquired control of Northeast Airlines by purchasing the majority interest previously held by Hughes Tool Company. Not long thereafter the CAB turned about-face and gave the company permanent certification from New York to Miami. Somehow, against all the odds, Northeast had survived.

George Storer moved quickly to update Northeast's fleet, which consisted mainly of DC-3s and DC-6s at the time he assumed control. The former were replaced by the Fairchild Hiller 227, a high-wing turboprop seating forty-three persons and designed primarily for small airports. For longer runs the company obtained the Douglas DC-9-31 and the Boeing 727-95; it also ordered the stretched version of the latter, the model 727-295, which Boeing began to produce in 1966. Trying to create a fresh image to present to the public, Storer selected a yellow, black, and white color scheme for these new acquisitions, and began advertising them as the "Yellowbirds." Customer services were improved and the roster of personnel was expanded, topped by a new chief executive, F. C. Wiser, formerly a vice-president with American Airlines. Encouraged by the transformation that had taken place, the CAB responded by awarding the firm a number of important new routes: Boston to Bermuda; New York to Freeport and Nassau in the Bahamas; Montreal to Miami; and Burlington, Vermont, to Chicago via Cleveland and Detroit. By the end of the decade yet another artery had been added that would figure significantly in future events: Miami to Los Angeles.

But the company lacked the capacity to digest so much so soon, and once the excitement of fresh beginnings wore off it was the same old story. For the first time in many years, Northeast showed a tiny profit—approximately $1,000—in 1966, but this glimmer was quickly extinguished by a wave of deficits from 1967 through 1970 totaling nearly $50 million. Desperate efforts at retrenchment were instituted as orders were canceled for the Lockheed L-1011 and service was suspended to various local markets in New England. The route award from Miami to Los Angeles represented a familiar formula as the CAB tried to shore up a faltering enterprise by granting it a supposedly lucrative plum in the hope of compensating for the flow of red ink elsewhere, but this was no more successful than the 1956 decision to allow Northeast to fly from New York to Miami.

As things went from bad to worse, Storer revamped the carrier's top management, installing as president and chief executive officer Bill Michaels, who was also president of the Storer Broadcasting Company and whose background was exclusively in newspapers, radio, and television. More and more, Northeast was administered as an appendage to the parent organization, with key decisions being made by men who had little or no experience in a bitterly competitive industry full of seasoned airline professionals. Michaels was frank to admit this; as he declared at one point, he and some of his fellow executives wanted to "get back to running a business with which our officers and directors feel they have reasonable familiarity and competence, rather than a business which poses a continuing drain on both our capital resources and our manpower attention."

As Northeast's financial condition worsened, speculation arose in the financial community that the company might be forced to seek merger with a larger carrier as the only way out of its woes. During the summer of 1969 R. C. Crisler, a Cincinnati stockbroker who was a mutual friend of George Storer and Delta director Charles H. Kellstadt, approached Storer about the possibility of a merger between Northeast and Delta. At this time Northeast was competing with Delta and other airlines for a route from Miami to Los Angeles, and Storer realistically feared that taking part in merger discussions with any carrier would unfavorably prejudice his firm's chances of winning such an award from the CAB. He therefore rebuffed Crisler's overtures but promised that he would get in touch with him if he ever changed his mind.[7]

Despite an examiner's report recommending that Delta receive the route from Miami to Los Angeles, the CAB awarded it to Northeast on September 18, 1969, solely on the grounds that the smaller carrier needed strengthening. On its part, Northeast had assured the CAB that it did not contemplate merging with any other airline. At a meeting of Northeast's executive committee held only six days later, however, projections were discussed indicating that the company was headed for losses of nearly $18 million during the current fiscal year despite the Los Angeles route victory. Shaken by this forecast, Michaels stated that Storer Broadcasting could not cover such deficits indefinitely and indicated that "drastic measures" might have to be taken, "up to and including looking for a merger partner." Michaels soon persuaded Storer to begin discussions with interested airlines, and on October 9 Storer called Crisler in fulfillment of his earlier pledge.

Crisler had never possessed any authority to speak in behalf of

Delta, but the company nevertheless responded quickly to his tip that Northeast was ripe for merger. On October 10 Dolson and Robert Oppenlander visited Storer and other Northeast representatives at Storer's Florida home for preliminary discussions. As befitted seasoned executives contemplating a series of hard bargaining sessions, the Delta spokesmen were careful to restrain any enthusiasm they may have felt at this point and the talk did not proceed beyond generalities. According to Storer's subsequent recollections, his visitors showed no great desire to continue negotiations, and upon being contacted by Crisler shortly thereafter to see how things were going he expressed disappointment about Delta's apparent lack of interest.

In actuality, behind its poker-faced approach, Delta wanted badly to work out a deal under the most advantageous terms it could obtain. The company had fought hard on two occasions to gain a direct route from New York to Miami only to see it ultimately given to Northeast, and Delta looked upon the current situation as a golden opportunity to acquire the coveted artery, along with a variety of other routes with considerable revenue potential. On the other hand, Delta officials were in somewhat of a quandary about how to calculate the terms under which they might offer to acquire a failing enterprise with a negative net worth and rapidly shrinking assets. After studying the matter, Oppenlander decided that the best way of arriving at a formula was to try to capitalize the potential value to Delta of Northeast's route structure in terms of assumed revenues, costs, and profit yields. On this basis, it was ultimately determined that the best offer the company could make would be an exchange of stock under which six shares of Northeast would equal one share of Delta. These terms were presented to Storer at a meeting held on October 27 in Dolson's office, but the broadcasting executive indignantly rejected them.

Storer had already opened negotiations with two other carriers, Northwest and TWA. After the unsuccessful meeting with Delta officials on October 27, the talks with Northwest intensified. Delta management realized they were in progress, but doubted that Northwest's canny chief executive, Donald W. Nyrop, would arrive at a formula more generous than the six-for-one ratio Dolson had offered. Assuming that there was still ample time for further negotiations, Oppenlander decided that the only possible way of working out better terms to offer Storer would be for a team of Delta analysts to visit Northeast headquarters in Boston and examine the firm's accounts. On November 11, having heard nothing from Northeast since October 27, Dolson telephoned Storer and made arrangements for such an inspection trip. Later that same day, however, it was publicly announced that a merger agreement had been reached by Northeast and Northwest embodying a five-for-one stock exchange and the assumption by Northwest of a ten-million-dollar debt owed by Northeast to Storer. It is possible that Storer may have been unaware of the progress his representatives were making with Northwest negotiations at the time he received Dolson's call, or he may merely have been refraining from tipping his hand. In any event, Delta officials were caught by surprise at the sudden turn of events and were understandably nettled that Dolson had been led to believe the situation was still fluid at the time of his telephone conversation with Storer.

Predictably, many parties intervened in the ensuring hearings as the CAB considered the Northeast–Northwest merger plan. National, one of Northeast's chief competitors, came out flatly against the entire proposal and urged that Northeast's routes from New York to Miami and from Miami to Los Angeles should not be transferred to the surviving carrier even if the merger were approved. Similarly, Allegheny and Mohawk fought against the transfer of active or dormant routes between various points in New England, the Middle Atlantic states, and the Midwest, while Pan American opposed the transfer to Northwest of Northeast's vacation routes to Bermuda and the Bahamas. Braniff, Continental, and Western asked the CAB to prohibit single-plane service linking the route from Miami to Los Angeles with Northwest's existing artery from Los Angeles to Hawaii. A group of Northeast stockholders objected to the five-for-one exchange ratio specified in the plan, while labor organizations, already upset about massive layoffs being conducted by Northeast as the company desperately tried to cut expenses, wanted to delay the consolidation until stringent protective provisions were agreed upon.[8]

Delta, disappointed by Northeast's success in reaching agreement with Northwest, naturally hoped that the CAB would not approve the merger and asked that the board investigate the possibility of a Delta–Northeast consolidation at the same time it considered the existing Northeast–Northwest pact. As another alternative, it suggested the dismemberment of Northeast and a subsequent parceling out of its routes to various airlines, along with provisions designed to protect Northeast employees against loss of their jobs. Should the board ultimately decide against a Delta–Northeast merger, Delta argued that it should get the route from Miami to Los Angeles on the grounds that this artery had been granted to Northeast only to strengthen that carrier and that originally Delta had been recommended for the award by the CAB examiner. Above all, Delta stressed that it had been parleying with Northeast during the fall of 1969 and had been trying to keep negotiations alive on the very day the pact with Northwest was announced. There were two willing partners for Northeast, it insisted—not just one.[9]

When Delta's initial moves were rejected and the CAB began to consider the Northeast–Northwest merger on its own merits, Delta joined other carriers in arguing against the transfer of key routes to the surviving carrier, particularly the one between Miami and Los Angeles. While cross-examining Storer, for example, Delta attorney Frank Rox did his best to show that Northeast had already been looking for a merger partner in the summer of 1969 while its application for the Miami–Los Angeles artery was pending and had been using the possibility of receiving such an award as "merger bait" despite giving the CAB assurances to the contrary. In addition, Rox pressed Storer for an admission that Delta had been trying to keep negotiations open on the day the merger agreement with Northwest was released to the press. Storer, however, disclaimed any recollection of Dolson's telephone call.[10]

Although Delta's strategy failed to prevent the CAB from approving the Northeast–Northwest merger, it may nevertheless have served its purpose well. On December 22, 1970, confirming previous recommendations by its own bureau counsel and examiner, Robert L. Park, the board gave the projected consolidation its official blessing but specifically excluded the route from Miami to Los Angeles from transfer to Northwest despite threats from Nyrop that this would terminate the entire arrangement. The CAB did not question that Northeast had acted in good faith in assuring the board that it was not contemplating merger with any other airline just before the Miami–Los Angeles award was made final in 1969. On the other hand, the route had been granted to the company solely because of its dire financial plight, and this rationale had been destroyed when, less than a week later, Northeast's executive committee had begun discussing merger possibilities with Northwest, an exceptionally profitable carrier. To transfer the route to Northwest under these circumstances would set a bad precedent encouraging other airlines to base future merger negotiations on the prospective outcome of pending CAB cases, and this could not be allowed. Despite subsequent pleas for reconsideration the board refused to retreat from this position, though it did indicate that Northwest, along with other carriers, would be free to apply for a route from Miami to Los Angeles in a reopened hearing. These terms were unacceptable to Nyrop, and on March 10, 1971, Northwest formally terminated the merger agreement. To its consternation, Northeast found itself still doing business as an independent trunk line.[11]

But not for long, for Northeast's financial condition was now even more desperate than it had been fourteen months earlier when the merger agreement with Northwest had been announced. Despite heroic economy measures, Northeast had lost $10.7 million in 1970 and another substantial deficit was inevitable in 1971. Reflecting this situation, the value of Northeast stock had plummeted. In November 1969 Northwest would have had to issue $47 million worth of securities to acquire Northeast under the agreed-upon five-to-one exchange ratio; by the time the merger agreement was terminated this figure had shrunk to $25 million. Because of the need to bail out the airline, Storer Broadcasting had lost nearly $2.7 million in 1969; it managed to record a profit of $3.8 million in 1970, but this was far below the level of earnings to which it had been accustomed before the acquisition of Northeast in 1965. Ultimately, Northeast might drag the parent company into bankruptcy. It was imperative that a new merger partner be found, and quickly.[12]

Shortly before Northwest formally canceled its merger plans, Eastern Air Lines approached George Storer about a consolidation of interests. Eastern, however, was playing for high stakes. Sensing that Storer's increasingly serious plight might induce him to sell out entirely, it proposed to acquire Storer Broadcasting and thus get Northeast as part of a much larger package. Its plan was further complicated by the fact that it wanted to resell some of Northeast's assets to National in accordance with the dismemberment scheme Eastern and National had been proposing for years. Storer feared that this complex transaction, which required the approval of both the CAB and the Federal Communications Commission, would take as long as two years to complete; in addition, though he was eager to get out of commercial aviation, he had no desire to lose control of his broadcasting venture or merge it with any other corporation, particularly an airline. Although he vacillated sufficiently at one point to encourage Eastern and National to draw up a formal proposal, these discussions ultimately came to naught. TWA also expressed renewed interest in a merger, but it too was more eager to effect a consolidation with Storer Broadcasting than to acquire Northeast alone. Two other carriers, Braniff and Continental, were at least mildly interested in acquiring Northeast, but talks with them never got beyond generalities.[13]

Of all the firms that contemplated acquiring Northeast if the merger with Northwest fell through, only Delta was prepared to offer terms that Storer was likely to take seriously. At a meeting of Delta's board of directors on January 28, 1971, Dolson and Maurer pointed out the strong likelihood that Northwest would withdraw from its agreement with Northeast, and a resolution was passed authorizing contact with Storer if this occurred. Northeast, however, took the first step. Two days before Northwest formally abrogated its agreement, Stuart Patton, Northeast's vice-president for legal affairs, telephoned Charles Kellstadt, the Delta director who had helped to arrange the abortive discussions that had taken place in October 1969. How serious had Delta been, Patton wanted to know, in telling the CAB that it would be willing to negotiate a merger with Northeast if the proposed consolidation with Northwest failed to materialize? Kellstadt quickly contacted Maurer, who telephoned Patton with assurances that Delta was ready to reopen discussions as soon as the merger pact between Northeast and Northwest had been formally terminated. Within a week after Northwest's subsequent cancellation of the agreement, an exchange of financial data between Northeast and Delta was underway.[14]

Because of the situation that had arisen concerning the telephone call he had made in an effort to keep the 1969 merger talks going, Dolson felt it inappropriate to take charge personally of the fresh discussions now in prospect. In addition, by March 1971 Delta was deeply absorbed in attempting to cope with the problems caused by the financial collapse of Rolls-Royce and the resulting jeopardy in which this had placed the future of the Lockheed L-1011 program, requiring enormous amounts of managerial time and effort. The company therefore decided to secure outside help in attempting to reach an understanding with Northeast and retained the services of two investment bankers from the Atlanta branch office of Reynolds and Company, John Ellis and Jay Levine, as negotiators. Ellis and Levine were well known to Delta because of their earlier employment with Courts and Company, which Reynolds had recently acquired. In addition, Reynolds had handled some previous financial transactions for Storer. The arrangement therefore promised to be a good way of "carrying the ball back and forth between the two main players," as one Delta executive later put it.

So far as Delta was concerned, the main points to be resolved were the stock exchange ratio, which because of Northeast's continuing losses was bound to be even more unfavorable to Storer than the one offered in 1969, and the extent to which Delta would provide interim financing to Northeast while a merger plan was pending before the CAB. Though these issues were also crucial to Storer, the broadcasting magnate also wanted badly to recoup at least part of the substantial sums he had loaned to Northeast in order to keep the company afloat. Delta was willing to assume all of Northeast's obligations to "outside" creditors, but insisted on regarding Storer's loans to the enterprise as equity capital, the face value of which would have to be compromised substantially in any final settlement. Fortunately, Ellis and Levine justified the wisdom of their selection as intermediaries by working out a means of resolving this issue. Acting on the premise that the successful completion of a merger between Delta and Northeast would lead to a rise in the stock of the surviving carrier, they proposed that a substantial number of options be issued to Storer to purchase Delta stock at a specified price within a given number of years after the merger was consummated. The approval of this strategy in principle by both Delta and Storer removed an important stumbling block to the success of the negotiations.

As Ellis and Levine continued their efforts to arrive at terms on which both sides could agree, Maurer and Oppenlander personally entered into the conversations and matters approached resolution. One area of disagreement involved Storer's desire that the price of the options he was to receive should be determined by the market value of Delta stock at such time as the CAB approved a merger between the two carriers, while Delta held out for a figure 5 percent above the closing price at the time of execution of a letter of understanding. There was also considerable discussion about ways of reducing the expenses George Storer would incur in registering Delta securities obtained through the merger; the possibility of an offer by Storer to purchase stock from Northeast's minority shareholders at a specified price; and the extent of Northeast's representation on the Delta board of directors. Mindful of the way in which CAB restrictions on the route from Miami to Los Angeles had stymied the Northeast–Northwest merger, Storer also needed to be assured that

Delta would consummate an agreement with Northeast even if the board were to impose the same limitation again.

Finally, on April 22, the Storer executive committee indicated tentative approval of the way in which most of the outstanding issues had been resolved. Delta responded by requesting that Storer, Michaels, and other Northeast representatives be present in Atlanta the next day to consider a possible formal proposal. On the morning of April 23, 1971, Maurer outlined to Patton the specific features of the plan Delta management had approved for submission to its finance committee, which was to hold its regularly scheduled meeting later the same day, and notified him that Delta would if necessary accept the same sort of restrictions that the CAB had imposed in the Northwest merger case regarding the route from Miami to Los Angeles.

At noon the Delta finance committee approved the proposed set of merger provisions including a formula under which ten shares of Northeast stock would be exchanged for one share of Delta; the issuance of warrants to Storer entitling the latter to purchase 500,000 shares of Delta stock at a unit price of $48, exercisable until April 30, 1978, to liquidate all of Northeast's indebtedness to Storer; an agreement on Delta's part to advance up to $6 million in operating funds to Northeast pending consummation of the merger; and the nomination of Storer and Michaels to Delta's board of directors. Representatives of Northeast Airlines and Storer Broadcasting, meeting at a nearby motel, voted to accept these terms. By the end of the afternoon a letter of intent had been signed by all parties and news of the merger was released to the public. A definitive agreement was executed and signed within three weeks with the approval of the boards of all three companies.[15]

Moving with alacrity, the CAB opened hearings dealing with the proposed merger on May 12. Predictably, Eastern and National flatly opposed the consolidation and argued that in any case none of Northeast's routes should be transferred to the surviving corporation. The long-haul coastal routes leading from Boston, New York, and other cities to Florida, they contended, should return to the status of two-carrier competition; Delta's acquisition of these arteries would cause harmful diversion and inflict unwarranted hardship on both of their companies. Accordingly, they urged that a far better solution to what Eastern called the "East Coast–Florida excess capacity problem" would be their long-standing plan under which Eastern and National would jointly acquire Northeast and parcel out its route system among themselves. Eastern also charged that under the Delta–Northeast merger agreement Storer Broadcasting would recoup substantial losses for which it had already secured tax benefits and claimed that its own merger proposal to Storer had been more reasonable than had been represented in opposing testimony. No other airline contested the Delta–Northeast marriage in principle, but various carriers argued for the nontransfer of various routes to Delta, including the ones to Bermuda and the Bahamas as well as the artery from Miami to Los Angeles which had been so important in the Northeast–Northwest case.[16]

Buttressed by the support of thirty-nine state and municipal intervenors who endorsed approval of the merger, Delta pointed out that the CAB had twice upheld the need for three-carrier competition on the long-haul Florida routes by granting Northeast access to them, and that the board had already denied the validity of the "excess capacity" argument in the Northeast–Northwest case. Delta also presented numerous statistics indicating that the growing volume of traffic on the coastal arteries over the years and Northeast's record of success in attaining a sizeable share of participation in these markets, despite the financial and equipment difficulties under which it had labored, proved the public necessity of transferring them to the surviving company. The claims of the other airlines were countered principally by recourse to the argument that they had already been rejected by the CAB when it had conditionally approved the Northeast–Northwest merger agreement. With regard to the route from Miami to Los Angeles, Delta contended that the board had amply preserved the integrity of its decision-making processes by refusing to transfer the artery to Northwest and pointed out that its own merger with Northeast had been entered into long after the conclusion of the 1969 transcontinental proceeding, removing any possible impropriety in transferring it to Delta at the present time.

Above all, Delta stressed that the public interest would be well served by CAB approval of the new merger. Unlike the situation that had prevailed in the early 1950s when the two lines did not connect at a single point, they now met at no fewer than thirteen terminals and shared eleven major common markets. The integrated system resulting from the merger would create 283 new single-carrier connections between cities and provide first competitive service in 48 markets. Significant economies would be achieved by eliminating duplicating facilities, but ample employment opportunities would remain to prevent loss of jobs to Northeast personnel, particularly because Delta would reinstitute some suspended services and terminate arrangements under which maintenance of Northeast aircraft engines had been farmed out to another carrier. Delta would advertise service on crucial routes far better than Northeast had been capable of doing and provide ultra-modern wide-bodied jets that the smaller company had been unable to afford. New England's air transport needs would be much better provided for as a result of resuming lapsed schedules and opening up new traffic patterns to the South and West. Finally, Northeast's minority stockholders would benefit by salvaging a reasonable share of their investment in a company that all too clearly was headed for collapse if the merger with Delta were to fail. The only other conceivable alternative, dismemberment of Northeast by Eastern and National, would produce a drastic shrinkage of competitive services on a variety of key routes and more layoffs for Northeast employees.[17]

These arguments proved persuasive. After oral testimony had been concluded on July 27, the various participants in the case submitted briefs to examiner Arthur S. Present, who withdrew to study the issues involved. His recommended decision, served three months later, acknowledged that consummation of the merger would have an adverse impact upon Eastern and National, particularly because of Eastern's persistent financial problems. On the other hand, he maintained, Eastern had "a large system over which to absorb the more intensified competition from the surviving carrier," while National was fundamentally healthy and would suffer no undue strain in meeting the challenge posed by Delta's entry into the East Coast–Florida route pattern. In any case, public interest in preserving competition over the heavily traveled arteries flowing into Miami and other Florida cities made Delta's acquisition of Northeast far preferable to the anticompetitive dismemberment plan proposed by Eastern and National. Northeast was clearly in extremis and likely to go bankrupt if the merger were disallowed, exposing employees and stockholders alike to disastrous consequences. The proposals of other carriers for the imposition of route restrictions had no more merit in this proceeding than when they had been advanced and dismissed in the Northeast–Northwest merger case. The examiner's verdict was clear: "on balance, . . . the proposed merger is consistent with the public interest . . . and should be approved."[18]

The filing of exceptions to Present's conclusions and further legal maneuvering by the intervening parties were followed in due course by the board's own study of the matter, but nothing occurred to change the outcome of the case. On April 24, by majority vote, the CAB approved the merger; by May 19 a decision embodying its findings had been rendered and presidential ratification, necessary in this case because of the foreign routes operated by Northeast, had been obtained. The merger agreement had already been endorsed overwhelmingly by Delta's stockholders at the previous annual meeting in October 1971, and on June 16, 1972, Northeast's stockholders took similar action.

The merger was consummated formally on August 1, 1972, with appropriate observances at various points on the combined route systems. In Boston, Northeast personnel looked on with mingled feelings as a large Yellowbird symbol was removed from the ticket counter at Logan International Airport to make way for the Delta logo; in Chicago, the first Northeast crew to land at Midway Airport was warmly welcomed by Delta employees and presented with a layer cake. In Atlanta, Northeast President Bill Michaels joined hands with W. T. Beebe and David Garrett, who had become Delta's two top executives following the recent retirement of Charles Dolson. Together they held aloft a large broadside bearing the caption "Now Delta, a great airline, becomes even greater!" The cover of the *Delta Digest* for the same month featured a rooster and an owl, emblematic of the company's Early Bird and Owly Bird services, with their wings draped in welcome around a Yellowbird clutching a travel bag. After nearly forty years of pioneering accomplishment and bitter struggle, Northeast Airlines had passed into history.[19]

For Delta, there was one major disappointment. Despite all the arguments company lawyers had been able to muster, the CAB had decided that Delta's consolidation with Northeast was a long-range result of the decision to seek a merger taken by Northeast executives shortly after the Southern Tier Case in 1969, and that the same logic that had rendered it inadvisable to transfer the Miami–Los Angeles route to Northwest in 1971 still prevailed. As a result, Delta's new certificate for route 27 prohibited the company from operating this transcontinental segment. Hearings were soon reopened on the ultimate disposition of the controversial artery, and in 1973 a CAB examiner recommended that it be assigned to Pan American. His advice was not implemented by the board, however, and after three more years of legal maneuvering Western was selected as the recipient. This verdict was in turn challenged in court by Delta and other carriers.[20]

Another issue still unresolved at the time the Delta–Northeast merger was approved was whether Delta, as the surviving carrier, should be required to provide service to a number of small New England points whose traffic potential was inadequate to support profitable operations. Northeast had already been permitted to delay or to suspend flights to these communities, whose needs were to be the subject of a pending New England Service Investigation. Two CAB members had dissented from the decision approving the merger, arguing that Delta should be forced to clarify its intentions regarding these markets before the consolidation was authorized, but a majority of the board had disagreed.

Following consummation of the merger, evidence was heard in the New England Service Investigation and a decision was reached in July, 1974. Delta retained full authority to serve such cities as Burlington, Manchester, and Worcester, which could be accommodated economically with jet aircraft. The company's obligation to serve such points as Augusta, Lewiston, Nantucket, and Martha's Vineyard, however, was suspended for a five-year period during which a test could be made of the adequacy of operations conducted by a new regional carrier, Air New England. Simultaneously, another group of destinations including Bar Harbor, Rockland, and Laconia was deleted from Delta's certificate altogether. Despite continuing dissent from the same two CAB members and the pleas of civic parties who argued that Delta service to the deleted points should merely be suspended, leaving the company with a residual obligation in these markets, a majority of the board continued to affirm the July decision in an order on reconsideration handed down in October 1974. The state of Maine then took the case to court and won a technical victory in 1976 when the board restored Bar Harbor and Rockland to Delta's certificate on a suspended basis. Actual service, however, continued to be provided by commuter lines.

Despite this minor change and the board's continued refusal to permit the company to fly passengers from Miami to Los Angeles, the outcome of the New England Service Investigation was a considerable triumph for Delta, which thus managed to acquire most of Northeast's highly desirable long-haul routes without having to assume a tangled web of unprofitable local service operations. Even the CAB members who voted in the majority conceded that in view of Delta's status as the most profitable airline in the industry and its assumption through the merger of such prizes as the artery from Boston and New York to Miami, "it would seem only fair to require the carrier to serve northern New England markets as well, even at losses which it could in any case easily absorb." On the other hand, those officials concluded that forcing an unwilling carrier to conduct operations that could not possibly yield a return on investment would "produce only grudging, ineffective service, ultimately subsidized by Delta's passengers on other routes."

Critics of the decision argued that such reasoning failed to take sufficient account of the federal subsidies that might be required to support feeder and commuter operations over Northeast's old local routes, charged that the CAB had been "ambushed," and grumbled that Delta had been permitted to "get away with it," in the words of one industry official. Nevertheless, the board persisted in its belief that the main goal—adequate service to important transfer points for travelers from small New England communities—could be provided best by local and regional carriers charged with this specific purpose, and this was the point of view that prevailed. On its part, Delta responded to critics by pointing out that in the merger proceedings it had simply pledged to continue operations to all points then being served by Northeast until such time as the CAB was prepared to render its final decision in the New England Service case, in which proceeding the company would spell out its views as to which of the smaller New England points should continue to be designated as "trunkline" cities.[21]

While the legal division worked on these remaining regulatory issues, Delta embarked upon the process of knitting together two formerly separate organizations. There was no transfer of senior officers to Delta as had been the case two decades before when the firm had merged with C&S. Nevertheless, the Delta organization had to absorb approximately 2,800 former Northeast employees, and this was bound to cause some difficulties.

As in any merger, seniority lists had to be integrated, and this proved troublesome just as it had after 1953. Following a well-established procedure, the new pilot seniority list was based on length of service adjusted to take cognizance of the ratio between the number of pilots belonging to each airline. Negotiated by representatives of Delta's and Northeast's pilot unions in 1972, it was ratified by ALPA but subsequently renounced by a group of former Northeast pilots who charged that their representatives had exceeded the authority delegated to them. Several lawsuits were brought against Delta and ALPA, but all were ultimately dismissed and the 1972 list stood. Even more difficult to settle were disputes involving the adoption of an integrated seniority list for flight attendants. Negotiations between stewardesses representing the two organizations broke down after completion of the merger when the group chosen by the former Northeast flight attendants demanded a list based strictly upon length of service without taking into consideration the disparity between the number previously employed by each airline and the larger aircraft types operated by Delta. After Delta management unilaterally adopted a seniority list based upon both criteria, a series of legal proceedings ensued, complicated by efforts of the Transport Workers' Union, which had previously represented Northeast's flight attendants, to enter the litigation. After the CAB had dismissed an initial complaint by the Northeast group, the case was taken to court and ultimately went into arbitration. A final verdict was still pending in mid-1978.[22]

In other respects, however, the welding together of the two organizations went smoothly. Cecil Brown, who joined Delta's long-range planning department after serving as director of public affairs for Northeast, pointed out one reason why: Delta had already gone through one merger and was well aware of the problems involved; consequently, it had planned elaborately for the various contingencies that were likely to occur after consummation of the union with Northeast. In particular, the personnel division worked diligently to assist former Northeast employees in disposing of property and acquiring new homes, coping with moving problems, and adjusting to new surroundings. As this potentially difficult process got underway, the *Delta Digest* urged company old-timers to remember when they had been in the same situation and do everything possible to make the newcomers feel welcome. As Brown also indicated, the pride taken by Northeast employees in the way the tiny New England carrier had weathered a succession of storms was mingled with the realization that the company all too clearly had been headed for bankruptcy; there was satisfaction in belonging at last to a strong organization offering a secure future. As one former Northeast employee put it, "These past years have been a struggle; uncertainty about the future hung over us. That's all past now. I find I walk down these same airport corridors with a new proudness. I hold my head high and I feel right up there with National and Eastern. No longer do I feel we are at a disadvantage. I'm part of a company with big jets like theirs and our new route system is some eyeful."[23]

Even without permission to fly the Miami–Los Angeles artery,

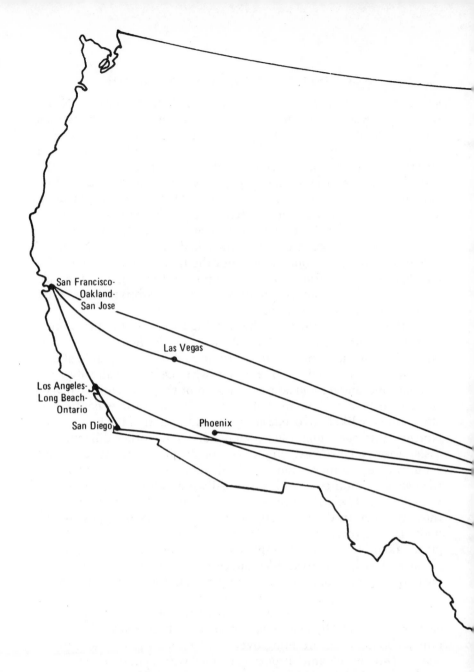

DELTA ROUTE SYSTEM 1972

INTERCHANGE ROUTE

------ with Pan American

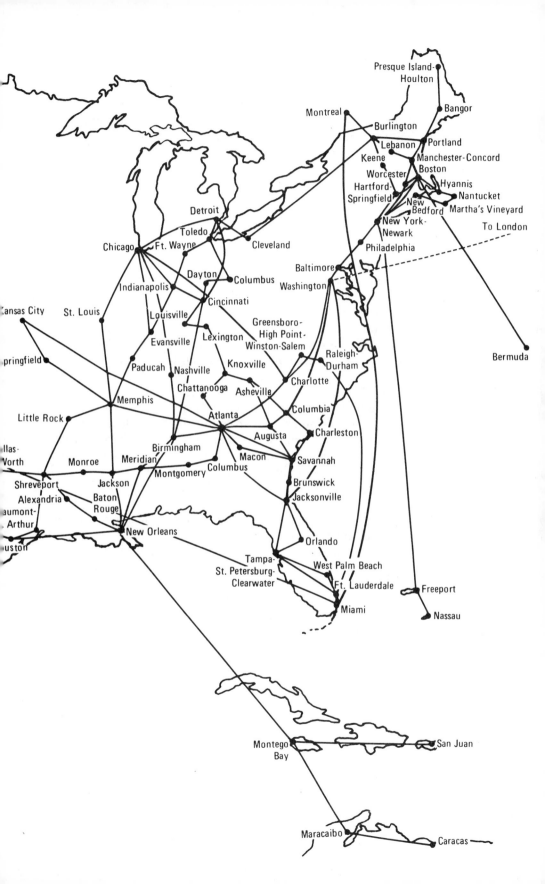

Delta's new route structure was indeed impressive. After more than a decade of relatively modest gains in CAB cases, the company had suddenly secured access to such major metropolitan centers as Boston, Cleveland, and Montreal; acquired long-denied airways connecting New England and the East Coast to Florida; entered the vacation markets of Bermuda and the Bahamas; and added a group of smaller but nonetheless profitable regional centers including Burlington, Hartford–Springfield, Manchester–Concord, Portland, and Worcester. Furthermore, unlike its experience immediately following the C&S merger, the company registered handsome gains from these latest acquisitions within a matter of months. Net earnings in the first year of consolidated operations climbed to an all-time record of $66 million, almost exactly twice the amount garnered separately by the two companies in fiscal 1972; substantial increases were also posted in operating revenues, which passed the $1 billion mark for the first time; passenger traffic, which rose 15 percent; and cargo receipts, which mounted 17 percent. As the firm's annual report for 1973 indicated, there could be no doubt that the Delta–Northeast merger had been a resounding success.[24]

But there was one tragic note. On July 31, 1973 one of the DC-9-31s obtained in the merger flew from Burlington to Boston under the type of adverse meteorological conditions for which New England was proverbial; thick fog shrouded much of the region. The plane stopped en route at Manchester to pick up some passengers who had been stranded there due to the cancellation of another flight because of the weather, and then proceeded on its way to Logan International Airport, where a dense fog was rolling in from the sea and visibility was approaching zero. After several delays, the ship was cleared to make an instrument landing. At about 11:08 A.M., eastern daylight time, it crashed into the seawall on its approach to runway 4R, about 165 feet off course and approximately 3,000 feet short of its intended touchdown point. Visibility was so bad that the wreckage remained smoldering at the end of the runway for almost ten minutes before airport officials realized a crash had occurred. It was by far the worst air disaster in Delta's history; dead were eighty-two passengers, five crew members, and a pilot who was aboard as a cockpit observer. One other passenger, who almost miraculously managed to crawl free of the wreckage after the fuselage bounced onto the runway and burned, died in a hospital nearly six months later. There were no survivors.

As is often the case, it was difficult for federal investigators to identify the precise cause of the accident, but the resulting report stressed how "an accumulation of discrepancies, none of them critical, can rapidly deteriorate, without positive flight management, into a high-risk situation." As the Delta plane came toward the airport, the FAA flight controller was rectifying a potential collision course between two other aircraft and hence did not provide clearance instructions in accordance with standard procedures. For the same reason, timely release of the DC-9 to tower control was delayed. In the confusion, the jetliner's airspeed was too high throughout most of the approach. Meanwhile, as was revealed by tapes surviving the crash, the cockpit crew was having difficulty obtaining satisfactory readings from the flight direction instruments. Furthermore, perhaps because of its concern over discrepancies between instrument readings and instructions from the ground, the crew apparently had neglected to monitor the altimeters during the final part of the approach. The presence of the extra pilot flying as an observer may also have caused confusion in the cockpit. In any event, the result was catastrophic, and the crash marred a company record of having gone more than twenty years without a passenger fatality.[25]

The accident highlighted the fact that the plane involved had not been built originally for service with Delta and had required modifications to its guidance system to bring it in line with company standards. This in turn reflected one of the most immediate problems resulting from the Northeast merger: the need to systematize the unwieldy assortment of planes produced by the combination of the two fleets. As of August 1, 1972, Delta found itself operating twelve different aircraft, powered by eight different types of engines. The roster included three varieties of DC-8s, three of DC-9s, and two of Boeing 727s, plus the Boeing 747, Convair CV-880, Fairchild Hiller 227, and the Lockheed L-100 cargo plane. Two other models, the DC-10 and Lockheed L-1011, were on order. In the interest of standardizing operations, holding down parts inventories, and reducing maintenance costs, it was imperative to bring a measure of order into this potentially chaotic situation.[26]

Recognizing the seriousness of this problem, Delta management had already worked out a long-range policy under which the bulk of its fleet would ultimately consist of three or four types of aircraft, corresponding to the varying sizes and lengths of its markets and route segments. A vital consideration affecting the development of this plan was the desire, reflecting both the firm's deeply ingrained cost consciousness and the rapidly intensifying national concern about energy conservation, to eliminate older planes that consumed excessive amounts of fuel. Coupled with fleet standardization was a continuing drive to rationalize schedules as much as possible; combined with wise selection of aircraft, this permitted expanded passenger and cargo carrying capacity without a corresponding increase in expenses. Carried out under the quiet but relentless prodding of David Garrett, who became president of the firm after the retirement of Charles H. Dolson in 1972 and who would ultimately become chief executive officer in 1978, the program became a key element underlying Delta's phenomenal success in achieving record-breaking profits later in the decade.

To service smaller markets and short-to-medium hauls, the company decided upon the stretched DC-9-32 with its highly efficient JT8D-7 engines. Northeast was already using the DC-9-31, owning four outright and leasing ten others from a subsidiary of Storer Broadcasting. These ships used the same power plant as the DC-9-32 but had a less satisfactory cabin layout for passenger service; they were therefore disposed of as quickly as possible after completion of the merger and were largely gone by 1974. Even quicker to go were Delta's original DC-9-14s, which were becoming too small for the company's needs. Under an agreement announced in August 1972, all thirteen of these craft were sold to Southern Airways under terms specifying deliveries as rapidly as they could be replaced by new equipment. By mid-1973 only six were left and these disappeared soon thereafter. As the decade wore on, the number of DC-9-32s in the Delta fleet gradually decreased as traffic built up over the system, and by 1977 the firm operated fifty-six as opposed to sixty-three five years before. Nevertheless, the model continued to meet certain needs better than any other plane available, and this, coupled with its exceptional reliability, seemed to guarantee that it would remain part of the Delta scene for a long time to come.

For medium-sized markets and mid-range hauls Delta chose a plane that was already playing an important part in Northeast's operations prior to the merger, the Boeing 727-200. Possessing a seating configuration which made it more competitive than the CV-880, it was also much less fuel intensive than the Convair plane and had by 1970 become the largest-selling jetliner in the world. Its attractiveness to Delta was enhanced by the fact that it used the same JT8D-7 engines as the DC-9-32, though with some advanced features further reducing noise levels and smoke emission. In March

1972 Delta announced an agreement to purchase fourteen of these ships, contingent upon the successful outcome of the merger with Northeast, which was itself operating thirteen under lease from Storer. Boeing simultaneously agreed to buy all sixteen of Delta's CV-880s, and these ships were gone from the company's fleet by the end of 1973. As always, qualms were felt about the departure of a plane that had earned a proud reputation in its years of service with the firm. "Like the thoroughbred it is, it started fast, ran a beautiful race, and finished in the money," wrote Delta pilot Paul W. Bennett in a nostalgic tribute: "It had class." But such regrets were outweighed by the superior performance of the new Boeing liner, and the company quickly contracted to acquire more of them. In January 1974 a significant milestone occurred when the thousandth 727 produced by Boeing joined the Delta fleet. By 1977, when eighty-eight of the ships bore the company's insignia, it was Delta's chief workhorse.[27]

The arrival of the 727-200 also permitted Delta to dispense with the seven DC-8-33s it had obtained in 1964 to facilitate flights to Europe under the interchange agreement with Pan American. These too were sold to Boeing along with the CV-880s. Because of the high fuel consumption of the JT-4 engines with which the DC-8-33s were equipped, the company was glad to see them go. On the other hand, the remaining two models in this series, the DC-8-51 and DC-8-61, still possessed considerable utility and their JT-3D turbofan engines provided satisfactory efficiency under prevailing energy conditions. There was thus less hurry about replacing them. In October 1974 Delta signed an agreement with FBA Aircraft, a broker, for the sale of its entire fleet of twenty-one DC-8-51s, to be delivered periodically as Boeing 727s and Lockheed L-1011s arrived to replace them. Nevertheless, a few of these ships were still flying Delta skyways in 1977, their usefulness prolonged by the company's acquisition in that year of a new route to Tulsa and Denver. Meanwhile, the firm continued to retain its thirteen DC-8-61s, whose carrying capacity provided a desirable margin between passenger revenues and operating costs. While considered supplementary to the company's core fleet, these ships were likely to remain in service for the foreseeable future.[28]

By mid-1972, once it had become clear that production of the Lockheed L-1011 TriStar would continue, Delta committed itself anew to this wide-bodied jetliner as the third member of its core fleet, handling long-haul runs in high-density markets while the

DC-9-32 and Boeing 727-200 provided for the bulk of the company's other traffic. The five McDonnell-Douglas DC-10s that the firm had ordered in 1971 for insurance purposes while the fate of the TriStar still hung in the balance would now be operated only as a stopgap while the L-1011s were being built, and an agreement was therefore announced in June 1972 transferring the ultimate purchase rights to these ships to United Air Lines. Delta's first DC-10 arrived in Atlanta in October 1973, and scheduled service began on runs up and down the East Coast on December 15 of that year. Together with the Boeing 747s acquired earlier in the decade, they kept the company fully competitive on routes requiring the largest available aircraft, pending the arrival of the TriStars. Then, their mission accomplished, the DC-10s were turned over to United, from whom Delta had been leasing them. By May 1975 the last DC-10 was gone from the Delta fleet.[29]

Throughout 1973 Delta's TriStars took shape at Lockheed's Palmdale facility in a final assembly building large enough to hold six Houston Astrodomes. Representatives of the company's Quality Control Department monitored the process closely as the ships progressed through ten positions on the fuselage assembly line, swallowed up miles of hydraulic lines and electrical wiring, went through mating with wings and tail components, received their three Rolls-Royce RB-211 engines, and were fitted with ceiling panels, carpeting, and seats. Of special interest was the installation of the plane's complex electronic and cybernetic equipment, for this model was the most highly automated and computerized airliner ever built. Because of this, it would be able to fly more precisely plotted air routes than any other commercial plane and execute landings when the ceiling was zero and there was only seven hundred feet of runway visibility. It was also superior to other aircraft with regard to environmental impact; while two and a half times as powerful as those of the first generation jets, its engines produced hardly any smoke and made significantly less noise than such planes as the DC-8.[30]

In October 1973 Delta finally received the first of the TriStars it had ordered five years before. The first one, which arrived on October 12, was flown across the continent under the command of veteran pilot C. A. Smith, who had become vice-president of flight operations upon the retirement of T. P. Ball in 1971. The first officer on the flight, Captain Jack McMahan, was one of only two pilots in the entire nation—the other being an inspector for the FAA—certificated to fly all three jumbo jets currently in service: the Boeing 747, DC-10, and L-1011. Asked to compare these models, he praised the maneuverability of the DC-10 and the overall design of the 747 but stressed the sophistication of the TriStar's guidance and control system, which had brought the ship all the way from California to Atlanta without the need for manual intervention. All in all, however, he remarked that "flying the three planes is sort of like going with three sisters. They have the same backgrounds but different personalities."[31]

Delta inaugurated scheduled service with the TriStar on December 15, and by mid-1974 the fleet included ten of these giant jetliners; further additions brought the total to twenty-one by 1977, with still more to come. From the outset their performance was extremely satisfactory, not only because of their reliability and popularity in passenger service but also because of their ability simultaneously to carry large quantities of cargo in their belly compartments. By the beginning of 1975, though comprising only 8 percent of the Delta fleet, they were already transporting 25 percent of the company's freight shipments. This contributed importantly to the fleet standardization program, because the Lockheed L-100s purchased in 1966 had now become expendable and were all sold by the end of 1974. Arrival of the TriStars also prompted the company to begin dispensing with its Boeing 747s, two of which were soon sold to Flying Tiger Lines. The other three remained in the fleet a while longer but were likewise gone by 1977, the last one making its final flight for the company on April 23 of that year from Las Vegas to Atlanta under the command of Captain Beverly Dickinson, who had been in charge of Delta's first scheduled 747 flight earlier in the decade.[32]

Two more casualties of the fleet standardization drive were the Fairchild Hiller 227s and Boeing 727-95s inherited from Northeast. The fate of the former was sealed by the 1974 CAB decision permitting Delta to suspend or eliminate service to small New England communities, leading to quick disposition of these high-wing turboprops. Partly because of arrangements with Storer Leasing Corporation, which was ultimately absorbed by Delta in 1977, the 727-95s were disposed of less swiftly, but by the middle of that year only four of these craft were left and they too were scheduled for imminent departure.[33]

During the five years following consummation of the Northeast merger, therefore, Delta carried through a program of standardization resulting in what was possibly the most modern and efficient fleet in the airline industry. As of November 1977 the average age of its planes was only 5.3 years. With the exception of a handful of DC-8-51s it entered 1978 operating only four basic models of aircraft: the DC-9-32s, Boeing 727-200s, and Lockheed L-1011s, which made up its core fleet, and the DC-8-61s, which were used mainly on economy coach runs in high-density markets. In addition to permitting substantial reductions in fuel consumption and maintenance costs—the company calculated, for example, that twenty-one of its Boeing 727-200s had saved nine million dollars in producing the same services as the older models they had replaced—the modernization plan had also led to remarkable levels of mechanical reliability. Thanks to the care that had been taken in their design, Delta's DC-9-32s operated with a reliability factor of 99.28 percent, meaning that only 0.72 percent of departures were delayed because of mechanical reasons; the corresponding figures for the 727-200 and L-1011 were 99.24 and 97.43 percent, with the latter being considered outstanding for a large wide-bodied plane. Equally important in an era of rapidly rising fuel costs, the Delta fleet was by 1977 burning the same amount of kerosene as it had used five years earlier but producing 2,113,798 revenue ton miles as opposed to 1,276,211.[34]

The progress of the fleet standardization program highlighted what for Delta had been a constant theme throughout the early and mid-1970s: matching expansion with assimilation. Having absorbed a small but nevertheless important trunk line, and substantially expanded its fleet, it had fortified its status as one of the industry's Big Five and at the same time achieved higher levels of efficiency and productivity. Thus it preserved an organization that was still lean despite its size and apparently well prepared to meet the exigencies of a world in which the conservation and careful husbanding of resources was increasingly crucial.

The DC-10, leased by Delta in 1972 to fulfill the expanding need for multi-range jetliners.

The Lockheed L-1011 TriStar, which joined the Delta fleet in 1973.

Flight crew, led by Captain Dana Jones (*left*) stands on the wing of a newly delivered Delta L-1011.

Senior vice-presidents with top executives in 1978. *Seated, left to right:* Robert Oppenlander, finance and treasurer; W. T. Beebe, chairman of the board; D. C. Garrett, Jr., president; R. S. Maurer, vice-chairman of the board and secretary; Ron Allen, personnel. *Standing:* Frank Rox, flight operations; James Callison, general counsel; J. A. Cooper, marketing; Hollis Harris, passenger service; Hoyt Fincher, technical operations.

CHAPTER 21

Enduring Traditions and Changing Times

F OR DELTA, as for the airline business generally, the mid-1970s posed a number of formidable challenges, highlighted by unprecedented fuel price increases and other inflationary trends that made it difficult to hold down costs. A severe recession in 1974 caused further headaches, while difficulties experienced by the federal government in formulating a comprehensive energy policy and a strong congressional move to alter the regulatory structure under which commercial aviation had developed over several decades made for an uncertain future. Nevertheless, Delta came soaring through the period with record profits and fresh victories in important new route cases. As the decade neared its end and the firm approached its fiftieth anniversary as a passenger carrier, there was no sign that the forward impetus that had brought it so far since its first tiny Travel Airs had taken to the sky in 1929 had lost any of its unremitting thrust.

Despite a temporary slowdown during the recession in 1975, Delta benefited from a constantly growing demand for air travel which raised passenger enplanements from approximately 20.5 million in fiscal 1972 to 28.8 million in fiscal 1977. Translated into dollar amounts and coupled with other sources of income including cargo and mail receipts, this trend produced a dramatic growth in operating revenues from $883.5 million to $1.7 billion over the same six-year period. Operating expenses also increased substantially, jumping from $816 million to approximately $1.6 billion: the impact of this trend was particularly severe in fiscal 1975, when revenues increased by only $150 million while costs mounted by $212 million in the wake of the Arab oil embargo and sharply escalating fuel prices. Still, Delta reported net earnings of 49.2 million in that year, representing a considerable decrease only because in fiscal 1974 the firm had posted the highest profit ever garnered up to that time by an American airline—$90.6 million. By 1976 recovery was clearly underway with a net income of $70.2 million, and in fiscal 1977 Delta once more eclipsed all previous profit records for the industry by earning an unprecedented $93.2 million. From fiscal 1972 to 1977 inclusive, its total earnings were almost $400 million.[1] (See Appendix 1.) As one reporter put it, Delta is "not the country's biggest airline; it doesn't have the most flights or fly the most passengers. It just makes the most money."[2]

Making money seemed to have become a Delta tradition by 1977; by that point the company had gone three decades without an annual deficit. This fact in itself had an important bearing upon the nature of the management under whose guidance Delta recorded consistent profits while some other carriers experienced a more irregular pattern of financial peaks and valleys. At Delta there had been no necessity for periodic administrative shakeups or the appointment of new high-level executives with radically different ideas. Thus, despite going through a succession of economic and technological changes since the days when it had been only a small regional trunk line using piston-driven equipment, Delta had benefited from a high degree of inner stability.[3]

This continuity was evident in the makeup of the management team that guided the company through the era of rapid growth that followed the death of C. E. Woolman in 1966. Charles Dolson, who had been with the firm since 1934, served as president until January 1970, when he moved up to chairman of the board. Dolson was succeeded as president by W. T. Beebe, the veteran personnel official who had joined C & S in 1947, entered the Delta organization in the 1953 merger, and had risen to the rank of senior vice-president for administration. In November 1971 Dolson retired from active employment while Beebe became chairman of the board and chief executive officer. At this time David C. Garrett, senior vice-president for operations since 1967 and a Delta employee since 1946, assumed the presidency. At Beebe's insistence, partly to facilitate orderly transitions of power within Delta's leadership structure, a rule was adopted by the board of directors requiring all senior officers to retire at age sixty-five unless extremely compelling circumstances dictated their retention.[4]

The composition of the board of directors itself reflected both Delta's continuity with the past and a conviction on the part of management that in a public company whose executives owned relatively little stock, board membership should be representative of stockholder interest. Accordingly, of the seventeen board members in 1978, only five—Ronald W. Allen, W. T. Beebe, David C. Garrett, Richard S. Maurer, and Robert Oppenlander—represented active management. Two others, Charles H. Dolson and T. M. Miller, were retired executives. Of the remaining ten who formed a solid majority of "outside" members, seven had long associations with the firm: Bernard W. Biedenharn, R. W. Courts, Richard W. Freeman, Edward H. Gerry, John R. Longmire, Carleton Putnam, and George M. Snellings, Jr. Two of the newer members reflected the Northeast merger: Bill Michaels, a Storer Broadcasting Company executive who had served as president of Northeast prior to its acquisition by Delta, and Stuart W. Patton, a Miami attorney who had been Northeast's vice-president for legal affairs. The most recently elected member of the board was Jesse Hill, Jr., an outstanding black business leader and president of the Atlanta Life Insurance Company. Two veteran directors, Charles H. Kellstadt and Winship Nunnally, had died earlier in the decade, as had George B. Storer, Sr., whose age had made him ineligible for reelection in 1972 after serving briefly on the board. Another longtime member, Emery Flinn, had chosen not to stand for reelection in 1975 and had been named director emeritus.[5]

Long experience with the company was also reflected by the senior vice-presidents heading the company's major divisions, which were expanded from five to six in 1972 when operations were split into two separate units. At the end of 1977 these officers included Richard S. Maurer, who had been in charge of legal affairs since the C & S merger and whose airline career began in 1943; Robert Oppenlander, who had succeeded Todd Cole as chief of finance in 1964 after joining Delta as comptroller in 1958; Joseph A. Cooper, who had followed Thomas Miller at the helm of marketing in 1973 after holding various posts with the company during 18 years of service; Hoyt Fincher, who had taken charge of technical operations in 1971 after many years of employment in maintenance and production control; Hollis Harris, an engineer who had joined the firm in 1954 and had been selected to oversee the newly created passenger service division in 1972; and Ronald W. Allen, a former methods and training specialist who had been hired by Delta in 1963 and had become Beebe's understudy before succeeding him in charge of personnel. Together with Beebe and Garrett, the group collectively possessed 212 years of executive experience. Having risen from lower positions with either Delta or C & S, they dramatized the potential that the company's policy of promoting from within held out to rank-

and-file employees, who knew that they too could aspire to top leadership positions in the organization. In addition, their firsthand experience with lower-echelon tasks enhanced their credibility throughout the divisions they administered.[6]

Without exception, all of these men had joined Delta during Woolman's lifetime; it is therefore not surprising that their style and outlook reflected his enduring influence to a considerable degree. Nevertheless, the way in which they ran the company differed from Woolman's managerial philosophy by emphasizing collective leadership rather than one-man rule. Under the new approach, which began under Dolson and was well established by 1977, leadership of the corporation became essentially a function of the eight top officers including Beebe, Garrett, and the six senior vice-presidents. Each of the vice-presidents was encouraged to consider himself a generalist and to take an active interest in the affairs of every division of the company. Should circumstances make it necessary, it was hoped that any senior executive could step into the position of chief executive officer without difficulty. Formally speaking, Maurer and Oppenlander reported to Beebe and the other four senior vice-presidents to Garrett, but in practice these distinctions were of limited importance. What mattered most was the smooth flow of information among members of the team and the ability to arrive at collective decisions quickly and harmoniously.

At the heart of the system were meetings held every Monday morning at which the current problems of every division were discussed and matters requiring decision thoroughly aired. All questions of general concern to the firm were similarly explored and policies decided upon. Formal votes were avoided, the goal being to arrive at a mutually satisfactory consensus. In the event of disagreement unresolvable by any other means, Beebe retained final authority and it was expected that ranks would close after a decision had been reached. Brief daily meetings were held to make sure that all members of this group were abreast of the latest operating statistics and aware of any sudden developments that might require attention.[7]

Although this managerial style differed radically from that practiced by Woolman, the impact of the founding father's influence was still much in evidence throughout the company's six major divisions. Nowhere was this more observable than in the highly conservative policies followed in finance under Oppenlander's supervision. The firm, for example, pursued a long-established practice of owning rather than leasing most of its planes and depreciating equipment rapidly over ten years to a residual value of 10 percent. Acquisition costs were amortized over the shortest possible period, and outlays relating to new route cases, pilot training, and keeping a satisfactory inventory of spare parts were also written off quickly. While costly over the short run, these policies provided a hedge against the possibility that aircraft might become obsolescent more quickly than expected and enabled Delta to sell used planes while they could still command favorable prices; during the five years ending in 1977 the company sold eighty-six planes without suffering a loss. Similarly, owning aircraft outright gave the firm substantial tax benefits in the form of investment credits. These were spread out over the entire life of the equipment rather than claimed immediately, again passing up short-run benefits in order to obtain the long-run advantage of smoothing out peaks and valleys in the company's earnings.

As had also been customary throughout the Woolman era, Delta kept dividends low in the interest of plowing most of its earnings back into operations and thus promoting the capital appreciation of its stock. Also characteristic of the Woolman heritage was the firm's constant effort not to allow debt to exceed equity despite its aggressiveness in obtaining the most up-to-date equipment possible. In 1977, for example, its long-term obligations amounted to $237.5 million while stockholder equity was $620.5 million. In the interest of quick debt retirement, and also because of its faith in the continued profitability of its future operations, the company pursued a moderate course regarding the retention of disposable cash and made no effort to hoard large sums of liquid capital. Partly as a result of this, it was able to minimize long-term interest payments.[8]

Intense cost-consciousness, another legacy from the Woolman years, had an especially profound effect upon policy development in the technical operations division, which bore the brunt of the rapidly intensifying energy crisis. In the twelve months following June 30, 1973, the price of kerosene rose by no less than 86 percent; another substantial increase took place in fiscal 1975. Meanwhile, the federal government imposed an allocation system limiting airlines to 90 percent of the fuel they had used in 1972. The resulting double bind created what Hoyt Fincher, senior vice-president, later described as the most formidable problem ever to hit the division he headed, outranking in seriousness even the transition from piston to jet aircraft.

One response to the situation was an immediate intensification of the fleet standardization program; fuel-hungry DC-8-33s and Convair 880s were replaced as quickly as possible by Boeing 727-200s equipped with highly efficient JT-8D-15 engines. Meanwhile, older planes in the same Boeing series were retrofitted with this improved power plant. Reduced cruising speeds were put into effect; the use of simulators was expanded in pilot training; and new ground handling techniques were instituted to conserve fuel in moving planes from one location to another or warming up their engines prior to flight. Dispatchers monitored ever more closely the amount of kerosene put aboard an aircraft for a given route segment in an effort to reduce the amount of unnecessary weight the ship would have to carry, and schedules were curtailed in some markets where there was limited demand. As a result of these measures the company achieved a 9 percent increase in fuel efficiency during fiscal 1974 and registered a further slight improvement the following year. Nevertheless, costs continued to escalate because of rising prices, jumping $91 million in fiscal 1975 alone.[9]

During Woolman's lifetime Delta's marketing division had been consistently innovative and aggressive, thanks particularly to the imaginative scheduling and advertising policies carried out under Thomas Miller, who retired late in 1973 after more than thirty years of service. In addition to the pioneering Early Bird–Owly Bird strategy, Miller had developed a hub-and-spoke concept by means of which Delta funneled traffic from small and medium-sized cities to such nodal points as Atlanta, Memphis, Chicago, and Boston. This was extended by his successor, Joseph Cooper; by 1977, an intricate pattern of flights cross-connected at the Atlanta airport eight times each day, facilitating an enormous variety of travel patterns. It became a standard joke among southerners that "even when you die, whether you go to heaven or hell, you'll have to change planes at Atlanta." The system, however, yielded significant benefits to passengers by making possible many more connecting services than would otherwise have been possible, while for Delta it optimized load factors and conserved fuel. Its success went far toward explaining why the firm resolutely held on to a number of smaller cities such as Macon, Augusta, and Chattanooga instead of turning them over to feeder lines as some other carriers might have done.[10]

Another important marketing function, advertising, continued to bear the stamp of the down-to-earth practicality Woolman had done so much to inculcate. Despite coining a number of highly successful slogans, such as "Delta is ready when you are," and styling itself "the airline run by professionals," the firm placed as little reliance as possible on "image" advertising aimed at broad national recognition and concentrated instead on reaching local markets through newspaper advertisements, radio announcements, and outdoor signs conveying highly pragmatic information about destinations, fares, and departure and arrival times. During the last six months of 1977, for example, nearly 70 percent of the company's advertising budget was spent on this type of publicity; earlier in the decade, the proportion had been even higher. Delta also promoted bumper stickers extensively, particularly in the Atlanta area with its high concentration of company employees. Television publicity increased steadily throughout the 1970s as the firm sponsored such annual events as the Heritage Golf Classic and the day-to-day games played by Atlanta's professional athletic teams, but still accounted for less than 8 percent of the advertising budget in 1977.[11]

Constant attention to the quality of service rendered to the passenger had been another hallmark of Woolman's managerial philosophy, reflected in the boss's frequent admonition to his subordinates that they "put themselves on the other side of the counter." This continuing concern, along with the need to achieve better administrative balance within the company by reducing the massive number of employees in the operations division, resulted in the establishment of a new division, that of passenger service operations, in 1973. Hollis Harris, who had advanced through a succession of administrative posts in engineering, facilities, and in-flight service, was named to head up the fledgling unit, with the rank of senior vice-president. Under his supervision were all employees who dealt directly with passengers from the time they arrived at an airport until they reached their final destinations: sky caps, ticket-counter personnel, baggage handlers, gatehouse agents, cabin service workers, and flight attendants, among others. Food service, another key factor affecting customer satisfaction, was also under his charge. As might be expected, his job kept him constantly on the move attending to the proverbial thousand-and-one things that needed attention along the company's sprawling network of stations, but essentially it boiled down to one central preoccupation: motivating people to provide the high-quality performance that made so much difference in an industry in which service competition was traditionally intense. One gauge of his success was the fact that from

1974 to 1976 the CAB received only 2.07 complaints per 100,000 enplanements about the service provided by Delta—the lowest figure in the entire industry.[12]

Harris's responsibilities kept him in close contact with the personnel division, which handled employment, the establishment of uniform standards and procedures, the translation of such procedures into manuals, the training of flight attendants, and above all the crucial task of developing strategies for maintaining effective contact with employees and seeing that their morale remained high. Perhaps the most enduring legacy of all from the Woolman era was the company's constant solicitude about perpetuating a phenomenon that over the years had come to be known as the "Delta family feeling." A special concern of Beebe's during his years at the helm of the personnel division, this remained a primary objective under his successor, Ronald W. Allen.

Part of the problem faced by Beebe and Allen lay in the constant growth of the company's roster of employees, which could all too easily result in growing impersonality unless special efforts were made to avoid it. Another problem was the fact that a family needs a father-figure and none of the firm's officers, however capable and dedicated, pretended to possess that peculiar charisma inherent in Woolman's folksy charm and unique status as Delta's founder-patriarch. Conscious of the difficulty, the new managerial team did its best to keep Woolman's memory a living reality among the growing number of employees who had never known him personally. In addition, a carefully structured system was developed to replace the extremely successful though much less formal contact which had been maintained by Woolman during his ceaseless swings around the Delta route system. This plan insured that high-ranking officers of the company would meet each employee on a regular basis every twelve to eighteen months. A typical meeting, held at one of the cities served by the firm, would be attended by twenty-five or thirty employees who would be brought up to date on various aspects of Delta's current operations, finances, route applications, salaries, and other matters of interest. A question-and-answer session, often lively, would then ensue. During the second half of the meeting the visiting executive would excuse the local supervisory personnel for a candid session with the subordinates, thus furthering the "open door" policy of the Woolman era, which had enabled any employee to appeal personally the decision of his immediate superior concerning a grievance. To keep unnecessary faultfinding to a minimum the visiting brass held preliminary sessions with local supervisors before the general ones got underway to identify and discuss whatever problems, if any, existed at a particular station. After the general meeting was over, a wrap-up session would be held at which the results of the discussions could be evaluated by everyone concerned.[13]

Because of the size the Delta organization had attained by 1977, some long-cherished customs were reluctantly discontinued; Cushing Memorial Park, for example, was no longer large enough to accommodate the Delta Day outing which had once been held every summer for employees and their families. A yearly "Delta Night at the Braves," at which personnel from all over the system could watch Atlanta's National League baseball team in action, was instituted as a partial substitute. More important, however, were a series of annual award observances at which employees who had reached significant milestones in their service to the company would be invited with their spouses to come to Atlanta to be entertained at Delta's expense, concluding with a banquet which, because of the numbers involved, has come to be held at Atlanta's World Congress Center.[14]

When asked what made the corporation distinctive, senior Delta officials would typically begin by referring to the strong "people orientation" of the firm and the lengths to which it went in maintaining upward and downward communication throughout the organization. Such executives preferred to characterize Delta as a "pro-people" rather than an "anti-union" company, but much thought and effort was devoted to maintaining working conditions sufficiently attractive to blunt any desire on the part of the rank and file to organize. Although they stressed a belief that poor communications constituted a more potent stimulus to unionization than questions involving salaries and fringe benefits, they did not neglect to keep the latter as attractive as possible and also took pride in a policy of avoiding furloughs and layoffs even during the severe recession that struck the economy in 1974; pilots and stewardesses grounded during that period, for example, were given other tasks to perform, and the firm did its best to keep their compensation close to normal levels. Continuing a long-established tradition, Delta adhered to a policy of promoting from within the organization unless a given position was simply so specialized that no current employee could be found to fill it. Senior officials also liked to emphasize the company's success in retaining employees over the course of long careers and the large number of persons with recent applications on file for any new positions that would be available. Approximately 250,000 people were seeking jobs with Delta at the end of 1977.[15]

Throughout the 1970s the personnel division was deeply involved in efforts to intensify the hiring and promotion of women and persons from minority groups, reflecting the altered social environment affecting the conduct of American business generally. Under Beebe's leadership Delta was an active participant in the JOBS program inaugurated in 1968 by the National Alliance of Businessmen to provide permanent and part-time positions for the hard-core unemployed and disadvantaged youth; by early 1977 it had provided approximately nine hundred full-time and twelve hundred part-time jobs to men, women, and teenagers recruited through this program alone. In April 1973 the company entered into a court-sanctioned agreement with the Office of Federal Contract Compliance (OFCC) of the Department of Labor and the Civil Rights Division of the Department of Justice setting forth various provisions aimed at preventing discrimination in employment practices. Back pay settlements were specified in cases where financial loss had allegedly arisen because of delays in transfer and promotion, and a bidding system was established guaranteeing consideration for certain positions of minority applicants who could meet minimum qualifications, replacing previous criteria aimed at selection of "best-qualified" applicants. An affirmative-action plan submitted to the federal government in August 1973 spelled out long-term goals for improving minority representation in various employment categories, and veteran executive James A. York of the personnel division was designated as Delta's affirmative-action officer.

Changing government directives involving the inclusion of women in affirmative-action processes, along with disagreements between Delta and federal officials over goals and timetables in selected job categories, delayed the adoption of a formal affirmative action plan; negotiations were still underway in early 1978. Because of the difficulty of securing qualified personnel, the company insisted that established goals and compliance deadlines could not be set in some highly technical areas having a direct bearing upon public safety. Meanwhile, Delta continued to implement the 1973 settlement agreement and the number of minority and female employees in various job categories rose steadily, if slowly, throughout the five years following its adoption. Between April 1973 and January 1977, for example, total employment within the company increased from 27,250 to 28,753 persons, a gain of 5.2 percent. During this same period, minority (primarily black) employment rose from 3,059 to 3,640 persons, a rise of 19.2 percent, while the number of women employed jumped from 8,075 to 9,274, an increase of 14.9 percent. In addition, minority and female employees were transferred and promoted at a higher than average rate. Illustrative of the trend was a decline from 78.1 percent to 66.4 percent of minority workers in the occupational category of laborers, and significant increases—227 and 505 respectively—in the number of minority and female personnel among the firm's reservations and sales agents. Over the same period the number of minority employees working as flight attendants increased from 289 to 474.[16]

Progress was slower in some areas than others. In 1977, for example, the company had 16 black pilots, exactly the same number as in 1973. However, there were now 3 female pilots in what had long been an exclusively male preserve.[17] A list compiled by the personnel division at the end of 1977 showed 162 women in such job classifications as flight analyst, mechanic, investment analyst, and senior system planner for computer services. Delta, C&S, and Northeast had all had female officers or directors in the past, among them Catherine FitzGerald, Erma Murray, Amelia Earhart, and Jacqueline Cochran; following in this tradition in the late 1970s was Jeannette Easley, assistant vice-president for passenger service. Other women holding significant managerial positions included Frances Connor, director of economic research, and Jan Rake, who headed Delta's dining service system. Women had long held major responsibilities in the public-relations department, whose roster in 1977 included such persons as veteran staff assistant Harriette Parker and Linda Sherman, editor of the *Delta Digest*. One occupational area in which Delta had a much higher percentage of female professionals than was characteristic of the nation as a whole was the legal division, in which four of the seventeen staff attorneys were women.[18]

The impact of changing times was felt in other ways as well. The intense service orientation of the industry had led Delta, like other airlines, to impose dress and grooming standards upon its employees. Although these were relaxed to some degree in the face of changing social customs during the 1970s, some male personnel protested company regulations against beards and certain hairstyles. Similarly, some female flight attendants fought against weight restrictions whose enforcement had long been taken for granted.

Throughout the decade the company found itself involved in frequent litigation defending its existing policies. As of early 1978 the legal division had been successful in upholding management's position on these matters, and the company showed no sign of relenting.[19]

Members of the legal division and other representatives of the company also spent a great deal of time during the mid-1970s opposing a move that gathered force in Congress to bring about drastic alterations in existing legislation affecting commercial aviation. Arguing that the industry was insufficiently competitive as matters stood, proponents of change advocated that entry by carriers into new markets and exit from unwanted routes should be greatly liberalized, and that other steps should be taken in the general direction of laissez-faire to reduce the authority of the CAB in matters affecting fares, mergers, and licensing procedures. Although these moves were supported by a few airlines, including United and Pan American (which saw an opportunity to obtain long-desired entry into domestic markets), they were vigorously assailed by most carriers, including Delta, and by a number of civic, business, and labor groups who feared that they would create chaos on the nation's airways, deprive small and medium-sized communities of economical service, jeopardize air safety, foster increased concentration in the industry, and perhaps ultimately lead to nationalization. Because of its solid financial condition Delta felt few qualms about its ability to survive under virtually any conditions short of nationalization itself, and it supported the selective modification of existing statutes to enhance competition. Nevertheless, it strongly deprecated any fundamental alteration of a framework that in its view had "produced the world's greatest air transportation system, with more service, by more carriers, in more markets, with greater variety, with more competition, and at lower rates and fares than exist anywhere else or under any other regulatory scheme."[20]

As always, however, the most dramatic activities of Delta attorneys centered around the firm's continued aggressiveness in seeking new route awards. During the early 1970s the CAB spent much of its time investigating the tariff structure of the airline industry and followed a conservative course in allocating route extensions. Nevertheless, Delta did secure nonstop rights between Memphis and Miami and pursued a number of other objectives including the right to fly from Atlanta to Cleveland and from Chicago to Montreal. Although Delta was disappointed in these efforts, it did win a significant victory by the middle of the decade when the CAB granted it nonstop rights between Boston and Atlanta.[21]

By 1975 the tempo of new route cases had picked up significantly. In one of the most important of these cases Delta waged another of its epic battles with Eastern, this time for operating authority in the underdeveloped but potentially lucrative market between Atlanta and three western cities: Tulsa, Oklahoma City, and Denver. Up to this point the only direct link between Atlanta and Denver had been a severely limited interchange conducted by Eastern and Braniff; most of the traffic flowed indirectly by way of such places as Dallas or Chicago. The company suffered a temporary reverse when Ross I. Newmann, administrative law judge, selected Eastern in an initial decision, but counsel counterattacked vigorously and won the final verdict when the CAB awarded Delta the right to fly between Atlanta, Tulsa, and Denver, with Braniff securing an alternate route via Oklahoma City. Eastern protested vigorously and tried to have the new operating authority stayed pending reconsideration, but to no avail. On July 28, 1977, Delta commenced service to the new destinations with their manifold recreational attractions and business opportunities. There were now ninety-two cities on the firm's system, and total route mileage had increased to 32,785.[22]

By this time an even greater prize was almost within reach: London, England. In September 1973 the CAB had instituted the first comprehensive review of transatlantic air service since 1950, responding to changes that had taken place since that time including increasing competition from foreign carriers; growing congestion at northeastern international gateways; the emergence of dramatically new types of aircraft; and the rapidly developing energy crisis, which had already resulted in temporary approval of arrangements limiting competition between such existing flag lines as Pan American and TWA. Among the issues to be resolved in the case was whether, because of population shifts and economic growth in various parts of the United States, a number of new gateway cities should be designated for nonstop transatlantic flights. Predictably, the proceeding attracted a swarm of applicants, including Braniff, Continental, Delta, Eastern, National, Northwest, Pan American, TWA, and a group of lines involved strictly in cargo or charter operations.[23]

Unlike other trunk lines, which put together complex proposals involving multiple American and European points of origin and departure, Delta concentrated on only one pair of cities: Atlanta and London. The rapidly growing southeast, it stated, was long overdue

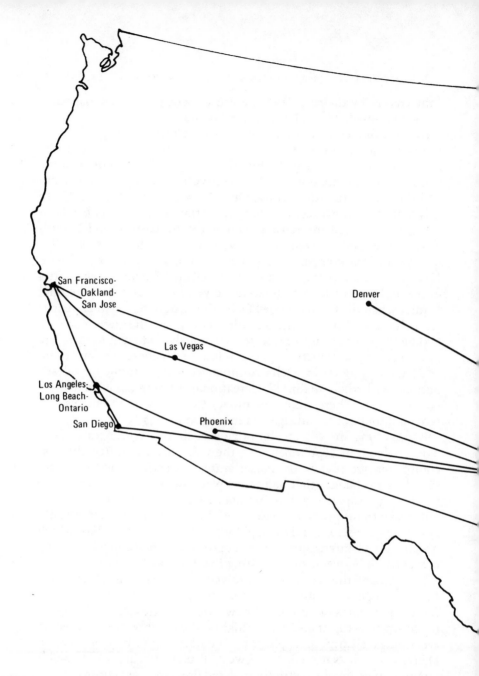

DELTA ROUTE SYSTEM 1978

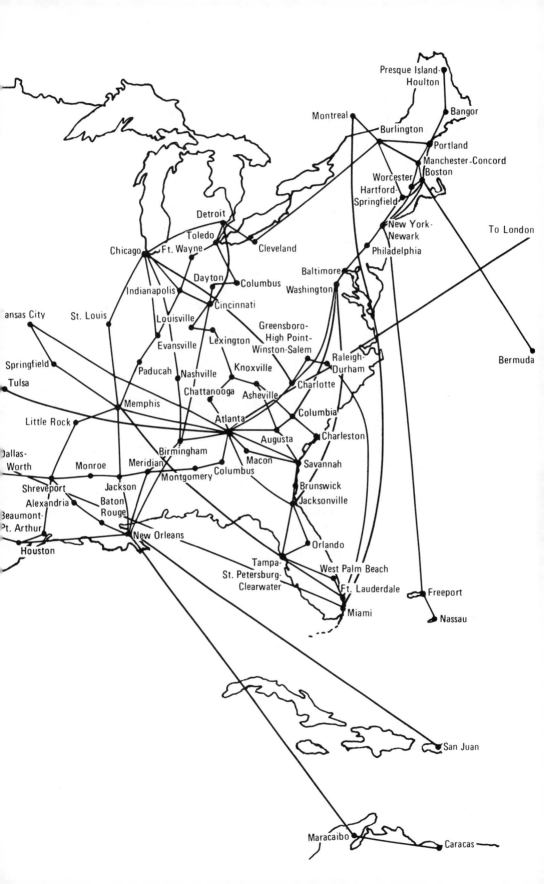

for a nonstop outlet to Europe; on the other hand, the region differed from other sections of the United States in that an unusually high percentage of its actual and potential demand for transatlantic service came from widely scattered communities rather than from a concentrated megalopolis. Atlanta, it argued, was the obvious collecting point for southern traffic to Europe, superior to Dallas–Fort Worth, Houston, or New Orleans; and Delta's hub-and-spoke operation was better calculated to gather a transatlantic passenger pool at Atlanta than the system of any other airline, including Eastern. Similarly, because of its status as the largest aviation hub in Europe and the prime destination of most southerners flying to that continent, London would be the best possible dispersing and gathering point on the other side of the ocean. As a further argument supporting its fitness for a London route, Delta pointed to its experience in operating an Atlanta-to-Europe interchange with Pan American and the fact that it had been operating offices in Great Britain for the past decade.

Newmann, who served as examining judge in this as well as the Oklahoma-Colorado case, rejected Delta's arguments and decided that no new American flag lines should be added to those currently flying the Atlantic. Agreeing that Atlanta should become a gateway to Europe, he chose Pan American to provide such service. In its rebuttal before the entire board, Delta stressed that Pan American had no connecting routes in Atlanta and therefore would be hampered in collecting southeastern traffic. To bolster its arguments, Delta used National's successful Miami-to-London route as an example of how a firmly based regional carrier could form a transatlantic passenger pool from a number of smaller cities; conversely, it attributed the failure of Braniff to develop a profitable operation from Atlanta to Honolulu on the fact that Braniff had no southeastern infrastructure on which to draw. Pan American, it indicated, would suffer the same fate.

Once more Delta was successful in persuading the CAB to overturn the recommendations of an examiner. On July 15, 1976, after nearly three years of hearings and other legal proceedings, in a four-to-one decision the board proposed that Delta be awarded a five-year certificate for a route from Atlanta to London, while Pan American was to receive nonstop rights to the British capital from Houston and Dallas–Fort Worth. As in all international cases, however, the verdict required presidential approval and this was not quickly forthcoming. On December 24, 1976, Gerald Ford returned the deci-

Captain Elmer Bennett *(center)*, Delta's senior pilot before his retirement in 1978, flew Delta's L-1011 on its inaugural flight to London. Beside him are John Moran *(left)*, who flew as check airman, and Ron Rice, who flew as first officer.

Ribbon-cutting ceremonies on the tarmac (ramp) at England's Gatwick Airport on May 1, 1978. *Left to right:* John Lovegrove, Delta's director of Europe, Middle East, and Africa; Flight Attendant Mary Lou Sears; Delta President David C. Garrett; Sir Kenneth Keith, chairman of the board of Rolls Royce; Sherry Cardinale, Philadelphia marketing representative; John Mulkern, chairman of British Airports Authority; and Flight Attendant Carolyn Cote.

Delta's Board of Directors at their October 1978 quarterly meeting. *First row:* R. S. Maurer, R. W. Freeman, W. T. Beebe, David C. Garrett, Jr., C. H. Dolson, R. W. Allen, Carleton Putnam, Robert Oppenlander; *second row:* R. W. Courts, John R. Longmire, George M. Snellings, Jr., Jesse Hill, Jr., Bill Michaels, B. W. Biedenharn, T. M. Miller, Edward H. Gerry, Stuart W. Patton.

David C. Garrett, Jr., and W. T. Beebe, 1977.

sion to the CAB unsigned, asking for further study of its economic impact. Despite Delta's pleas that the reconsideration be expedited as quickly as possible, the CAB subsequently decided to await the results of bilateral treaty negotiations between the British government and the incoming Carter administration, which were not concluded until early the following summer.

The results of these meetings, embodied in a protocol known as Bermuda II, paved the way for a resolution of the case and conferred an unexpected potential benefit to Delta when it was decided that the Atlanta-to-London market would be served exclusively by an American carrier for three years, at the end of which British Caledonian Airways would also be allowed to participate in it. In the reopened CAB proceeding various arguments were used by Eastern and other airlines in an attempt to reverse the board's 1976 findings or to defer a final verdict until more information had been gathered, but these maneuvers failed, and on October 21, 1977, the CAB issued a decision confirming most of its earlier recommendations including Delta's Atlanta-to-London route. After what seemed an interminable wait at the company's headquarters, President Carter added his seal of approval just four days before Christmas. In a statement hailing this welcome development, Beebe declared that it "practically assured Atlanta's future as a world city of major stature" and pledged that Delta would provide "the highest standards of intercontinental airline service."[24]

At the end of 1977 Delta looked back with satisfaction upon what Beebe unhesitatingly declared to be "the greatest year in the entire history of the firm." Management and employees alike took pride in a spate of articles that appeared in business periodicals praising the company and its leadership. Several indications of peer recognition were particularly satisfying. In December 1977 *Air Transport World* magazine named the company its "airline of the year" and *Dun's Review* selected Delta as one of the five best-managed enterprises in the nation. Not long afterward, the *Delta Digest* was named the best airline publication in the industry in a competition sponsored jointly by the Airline Editors Forum and the Air Transport Association. Yet another accolade was received when *Financial World Magazine* selected W. T. Beebe as chief executive officer of the year for 1978 and presented him with a gold medal in token of this honor. The editors of this prestigious publication stressed particularly Beebe's work in the area of personnel policy: "Not only does Delta turn in outstanding profit performances in good years and in bad—

it has also an unequaled record for avoiding layoffs even during recessions. As a result, Delta is known for the best employee morale in the industry."[25]

At a quarterly meeting of the board of directors held in late January 1978, Delta announced that it had earned $116.5 million during the previous twelve months, marking the first time in history that an American airline had exceeded $100 million in profits in a calendar year. A series of important administrative changes were also disclosed. Noting that only two more years remained before he reached Delta's mandatory retirement age of sixty-five, Beebe had urged the importance of initiating "an orderly transition of duties" and suggested that the time had come to make David Garrett chief executive officer of the firm. This proposal was ratified, with Beebe retaining his post as chairman of the board. During the previous six weeks, Beebe, Garrett, and Maurer had also discussed the need to broaden Delta's senior management group and achieve better balance between the company's main operating divisions. Pursuant to this aim, the board created a new senior vice-presidency for flight operations and announced that the position would be filled by veteran attorney Frank F. Rox, who had been working closely with the firm's pilots in recent years. Hoyt Fincher remained senior vice-president for technical operations, with maintenance as his chief area of responsibility.

In other related moves, Maurer was elevated to the newly established post of vice-chairman of the board, while continuing to serve as secretary of the corporation; succeeding him as senior vice-president and general counsel was James W. Callison, who had played a leading role in the campaigns for the Denver and London routes. In addition to enlarging the firm's top executive team from eight to ten members, the realignment facilitated the promotion of several younger persons into new positions of increased responsibility in the Delta leadership structure. In the judgment of Beebe, who had tirelessly promoted the concept of collective leadership and the subordination of individual roles to the needs of the organization as a whole, the steps that had been taken would give Delta a head start in making a successful transition to the time when he would no longer be active in the corporation's management. "If I could leave one thing to the business community," he told a reporter, "it would be Delta's senior staff concept."[26]

Throughout the opening months of 1978, however, attention at

Delta headquarters was focused chiefly upon preparations for the opening of the London route. After making a careful study of the options available, management decided that the best airliner with which to provide the new transatlantic service was the long-range L-1011-500 TriStar being planned by Lockheed; on January 23 Delta placed an order for five of these craft, becoming the first American carrier to do so. Deliveries, however, would not begin until May 1979. As a temporary substitute the company leased two L-1011-100s from TWA, which, though lacking the payload capacity of the upcoming L-1011-500 series, had a longer range than Delta's regular TriStars.[27]

The marketing division completed scheduling plans for the new route while these arrangements were being made. Delta would provide one daily round-trip flight to London; originating at New Orleans in mid-afternoon, it would proceed to Atlanta for an early evening departure and arrive at London's Gatwick terminal at breakfast time the following day so that travelers could attend morning business meetings or make a variety of connections to Europe, Africa, and the Middle East. The return flight would depart from London shortly after noon and be back in Atlanta by suppertime, with a continuation to New Orleans for an early evening arrival. The beginning and end of each round trip were designed to mesh with a large number of connections to southeastern and midwestern points through Delta's hub-and-spoke system.[28]

Delta issued a special medallion to commemorate the beginning of the new service; it featured a dogwood blossom, representing Atlanta and the southeastern states, surrounded by the Tudor rose of England, the leek of Wales, the thistle of Scotland, and the shamrock of Ireland. The advertising and public relations departments devised a series of displays featuring a "Peachtree to Piccadilly" theme, gathered and disseminated information useful to tourists, and prepared a special glossary of British colloquialisms for travelers who might not otherwise appreciate the vast difference between the meanings of various words in the two countries or comprehend the idiosyncrasies of English terminology for certain types of food or public accommodations. Meanwhile, dining service officials planned choice menus for passengers, including smoked salmon, Pheasant Galantine, Filet of Beef Wellington, and Cornish Game Hen Véronique.[29]

Perhaps nothing in Delta's fifty-year history had so captured the imagination of the company's entire staff as the opening flight to London, which took place on April 30, 1978. Traditional ribbon-cutting ceremonies were held at New Orleans, after which the newly leased TriStar with its partial complement of passengers flew on to Atlanta for a more elaborate celebration. As official hosts for the occasion the firm selected Vice-Chairman of the Board and Mrs. Richard S. Maurer, who gathered with 159 revenue passengers in one of the VIP "Crown Rooms" at Atlanta's Hartsfield International Airport. Stilton cheese and Scotch whiskey were served while bagpipes droned and a young lady danced in appropriate Highland costume. Georgia Governor George Busbee entrusted to Maurer an intricate glass dogwood sculpture, the work of the well-known Atlanta artist Hans Frobel, to be presented at the other end of the line to the Lord Mayor of London. Then the party proceeded to gate 51-A while the bagpipes struck up "Scotland the Brave." Before they boarded the shining L-1011-100, resplendent in its Delta insignia, Maurer and Busbee took part in a ribbon-cutting ceremony, assisted by two Delta employees dressed in a beefeater costume and the uniform of a London bobby.[30]

Many other employees, not on duty but eager to take part in this dramatic moment in the company's history, were on hand to see the flight off; they began cheering as the TriStar was tugged away from the embarkation gate. As the plane moved down the finger toward an exit lane it passed between two rows of Delta tugs, whose drivers had lined them up in a formation similar to that of cheerleaders greeting an athletic team as it takes to the field. While the giant Lockheed craft taxied toward takeoff position, Maurer experienced a surge of emotion he had rarely felt before in his long association with the firm.[31] Soon the plane was airborne in a cloudless Georgia sky.

In the captain's seat on the left side of the cockpit was Delta's most senior pilot, Elmer Bennett, who had joined Chicago and Southern as a reserve copilot in 1939. While growing up in St. Louis, he had seen the tiny Ryan monoplane in which Charles Lindbergh had made his epic 1927 flight from New York to Paris, and from then on his imagination had been captured by the idea of an aviation career. Two thoughts were uppermost in his mind during the inaugural flight to London. Like his boyhood idol, the Lone Eagle, he was taking part in an important first flight across the Atlantic, nonstop also but with equipment that would have been virtually unimaginable back in the days when the *Spirit of St. Louis* had spanned the Atlantic. In addition, there was a personal dimension: Bennett's ancestors had come across the same ocean from Great Britain as emigrants to the United States, but up until now no one in the family had ever returned to his former homeland. Now he was doing so under circumstances that his departed relatives could scarcely have envisioned in their wildest dreams. It was one of those things one felt, not simply in one's mind, but in one's very blood.[32]

In accordance with its flight plan, the TriStar flew across the Carolinas, crossed the Virginia line, and departed the American mainland in the vicinity of Norfolk at a speed exceeding six hundred miles per hour. Despite some open patches through which the dark ocean could be glimpsed far below in the waning twilight, the craft was now flying mostly over a cloud cover which blotted out the surface of the water. Dinner was served at about 8:30 P.M., and a motion picture was shown for the entertainment of the travelers: *Oh, God*, starring George Burns and John Denver. Then, while the passengers slept or mused upon the adventure in which they were taking part, the plane continued to speed through the night toward its destination. As the sun came up the big jet passed over Land's End, England's westernmost tip, and proceeded eastward over the English Channel with Plymouth and Brighton on its left and the French coast on the right. Hot towels were provided to freshen the travelers up, and a continental breakfast was served. Because of a low ceiling over Gatwick, Bennett made the decision for an automatic or "Black Box" landing. A retired Delta pilot on board as a passenger later expressed his confidence that Bennett could have landed manually with practically no ceiling, but the Delta veteran, drawing on the experience he had gained over the course of his thirty-nine-year career, decided upon the safest way. With its sophisticated electronic systems operating perfectly, the ship broke through the clouds at a few hundred feet above the ground in exact alignment with the runway. At 7:30 A.M. GMT, eight hours after departing from Atlanta, the plane was on the ground, just as its schedule had specified. It was drizzling, but this did not lower the spirits of the group that participated in more ribbon-cutting ceremonies at Gatwick's gate 18, including Sir Kenneth Keith, chairman of the board of Rolls-Royce, and David Garrett, Delta's president and chief executive officer. The company's inaugural flight to London thus passed successfully into history.

As Maurer had said at the ceremonies held earlier in Atlanta, it was "a proud day for the people of Delta Air Lines." Looking back over the half century that had elapsed since a crop-dusting enterprise had first taken to the skies as a passenger carrier, members of the Delta family could ponder a saga of accomplishment that was unique in the development of American commercial aviation. Alone among the industry's domestic Big Five, Delta had survived its earliest years without benefit of the potentially lucrative route structures granted to such enterprises as American, Eastern, TWA, and United in the heyday of Postmaster General Brown and the 1930 "Spoils Conference." Temporarily debarred from the southeastern route it had established, the company had returned in the heart of the Great Depression to begin its long rise to the ranks of the nation's largest and strongest air carriers. Guided by C. E. Woolman, and strengthened by the addition of Carleton Putnam's Chicago and Southern, Delta had gradually achieved a combination of route structure and ultramodern equipment which, aided by conservative financial policies and an extraordinarily loyal staff of employees, had made it the most consistently profitable airline in the country. After Woolman's death in 1966 the firm had cemented its position by acquiring Northeast Airlines, pursuing the highly effective management policies that marked the era of leadership under Dolson, Beebe, and Garrett, and following a strategy of fleet consolidation which paid off handsomely in terms of efficiency and operating costs. Throughout its entire history the company had excelled in the art of obtaining important new routes when it needed them, climaxed by the addition of the transatlantic airway to London.

Unlike the pattern of development experienced by many other airlines, Delta's history has been marked by consistent forward progress rather than by spasmodic "boom or bust." The company has endured some lean years but has never incurred major financial losses; to an extraordinary degree its corporate epic has been one long success story. As they look toward the future, the executives leading the firm as its fiftieth anniversary approaches see no reason why things should not continue the same way, particularly if they continue to adhere to the traditions established by its founding father. Officers of the firm stress their continuing alertness to the human factors that Woolman did so much to emphasize and remain committed to the aim of running a "people-oriented airline." This explains why, when expanding business needs led the company to construct an imposing new office building in 1978, just up the street from the smaller edifice which Woolman and his colleagues had occupied for so many years, Delta's senior management made it clear from the inception of the project that they had no intention of leaving the old headquarters for more elegant offices in the new structure. "Not on your life . . . it's just not in keeping with the way we run Delta Air Lines for that to happen," Beebe told an inquiring reporter. "We're going to stay right where we are."[33] Speaking in the same vein, Richard S. Maurer epitomized the feelings of Delta's leadership by saying, "Today, and in the days ahead, C.E.'s successors will be trying to maintain that lean, tough, service-oriented, family-style group of loyal Delta personnel that Woolman struggled so long and against such severe odds to develop. . . . To the extent that they can achieve C.E.'s ideals and goals, so the Delta family of tomorrow should grow and prosper."[34]

Appendixes

Appendix 1

DELTA AIR LINES, INC.
STATISTICAL DATA, FISCAL YEARS 1935–1977

Fiscal Year	Gross Revenues	Operating Expenses	Net Income after Taxes	Revenue Passengers	Revenue Passenger Miles	Number of Employees	Cargo Revenue
1935	$ 245,441	$ 261,871	$ (4,930)	4,104	1,200,034	—	$ 184,158
1936	431,281	445,996	599	8,357	2,372,819	—	315,918
1937	493,256	488,441	11,405	11,519	3,449,619	—	331,251
1938	615,472	569,543	28,425	18,480	5,200,797	—	372,667
1939	681,673	630,672	51,570	22,733	6,439,846	—	386,358
1940	893,920	826,649	60,306	40,068	10,282,192	242	431,901
1941	1,127,213	1,281,889	(85,715)	58,208	15,526,291	385*	433,777
1942	2,040,730	1,770,600	358,602	102,772†	29,800,968	549‡	701,951
1943	2,423,789	1,779,494	403,997	110,334†	35,613,463	833‡	625,507
1944	3,233,325	2,395,536	428,606	164,287†	51,844,000	875	582,878
1945	5,156,527	3,638,960	550,781	274,823†	84,877,000	982	850,005
1946	7,861,670	7,226,843	362,017	374,560	150,072,000	2,348	817,899
1947	11,488,836	11,910,491	(310,249)	528,687	222,704,000	2,081	775,873
1948	12,818,969	12,618,944	204,730	493,608	188,293,000	2,093	2,586,882
1949	15,227,845	14,281,956	639,440	518,481	201,711,000	2,119	3,038,250
1950	17,185,295	15,775,141	815,751	566,246	238,335,000	2,093	3,090,191
1951	22,220,999	18,889,201	1,631,798	759,803	345,246,000	2,362	2,401,951
1952	27,018,121	22,641,069	1,650,450	940,120	427,536,000	2,722	2,294,766
1953***	32,337,802	28,901,728	4,158,678	1,119,688	507,713,000	4,281	2,726,221
1954	50,333,882	48,296,311	1,305,949	1,675,900	769,653,000	4,257	4,334,452
1955	59,187,961	53,492,032	2,166,025	1,995,700	952,426,000	4,547	4,224,461
1956	66,599,937	58,648,758	4,677,966	2,261,770	1,080,267,000	5,294	4,533,000

Year							
1957	78,596,003	72,510,934	2,621,585	2,572,982	1,299,482,000	5,842	4,883,000
1958	88,172,695	85,631,084	1,063,155	2,728,220	1,408,857,000	6,058	5,704,000
1959	103,805,445	94,420,611	4,062,222	2,988,241	1,554,630,000	6,723	7,237,000
1960	120,191,225	113,460,589	2,839,083	3,241,511	1,757,208,000	7,567	7,752,000
1961	146,132,333	134,431,114	4,651,836	3,569,778	2,034,047,000	8,290	9,057,000
1962	169,777,000	154,671,000	6,985,000	3,768,707	2,393,991,000	8,783	10,897,000
1963	210,073,000	177,622,000	13,824,000	4,606,367	3,004,157,000	9,257	15,068,000
1964	224,672,000	189,871,000	15,694,000	5,964,269	3,353,842,000	10,283	15,564,000
1965	257,460,000	213,131,000	23,005,000	5,233,548	3,855,012,000	11,069	19,620,000
1966	318,930,000	253,092,000	34,554,000	7,556,422	4,997,958,000	12,971	24,039,000
1967	397,836,000	308,737,000	49,190,000	9,422,422	6,415,467,000	14,829	31,638,000
1968	431,562,000	363,140,000	36,134,000	11,783,372	7,116,095,000	16,500	32,141,000
1969	516,113,000	433,938,000	39,191,000	13,927,366	8,249,085,000	18,700	42,536,000
1970	622,129,000	529,179,000	44,527,000	15,784,053	9,397,913,000	20,500	50,786,000
1971	661,246,000	608,475,000	29,994,000	16,373,467	9,719,346,000	20,786	54,327,000
1972	757,569,000	682,117,000	42,169,000	17,880,837	10,609,729,000	21,309	59,408,000
1973††	1,049,699,000	928,940,000	65,995,000	23,702,870	14,449,748,000	27,500	76,323,000
1974	1,227,127,000	1,070,043,000	90,649,000	25,565,208	15,445,891,000	27,600	86,685,000
1975	1,377,030,000	1,282,000,000	51,880,000	25,831,631	15,916,860,000	27,800	85,388,000
1976	1,528,942,000	1,411,333,000	70,207,000	27,996,665	17,621,247,000	27,891	100,626,000
1977	1,719,645,000	1,578,464,000	92,380,000	28,811,966	18,042,339,000	28,527	114,800,000

Source: Delta Air Lines, Inc., Annual Reports; CAB, *Recurrent Report of Mileage and Traffic Data*

( ) represents loss
* CAB, *Annual Airline Statistics*, fiscal year 1941.
† CAB, *Annual Airline Statistics*, calendar years 1942–45.
‡ Figures shown are for calendar years; fiscal year figures were not available.
** Delta merged with C&S on May 1, 1953. The figures for the year ending June 30, 1953, reflect the operation of the merged system only since May 1, 1953.
†† Delta merged with Northeast on August 1, 1972. The figures for the year ending June 30, 1973, reflect the operation of the merged system only since August 1, 1972.

Appendix 2

GROWTH OF DELTA AIR LINES, INC.
COMPARED TO THE INDUSTRY
FISCAL YEARS 1950–1977

Fiscal Year	Industry Revenue Passenger Miles (thousands)	Delta Revenue Passenger Miles (thousands)	Delta's Percentage of the Industry
1950	9,202,212	238,335	2.6
1951	11,793,668	345,246	2.9
1952	14,216,180	427,536	3.0
1953	17,063,214	507,713	3.0
1954	19,084,726	769,653	4.0
1955	22,505,919	952,426	4.2
1956	25,986,870	1,080,267	4.2
1957	29,419,796	1,299,482	4.4
1958	31,506,071	1,408,857	4.5
1959	33,318,923	1,554,630	4.7
1960	38,113,648	1,757,208	4.6
1961	38,750,676	2,034,047	5.2
1962	42,453,796	2,393,991	5.6
1963	45,948,365	3,004,157	6.5
1964	54,207,816	3,353,842	6.2
1965	62,651,172	3,855,012	6.2
1966	76,455,988	4,997,958	6.5
1967	86,316,169	6,415,467	7.4
1968	106,574,264	7,116,095	6.7
1969	119,800,571	8,249,085	6.9
1970	128,895,419	9,397,913	7.3
1971	132,321,533	9,719,346	7.3
1972	144,240,463	10,609,729	7.4
1973	157,930,820	14,449,748	9.1
1974	164,982,985	15,445,891	9.4
1975	159,022,580	15,916,860	10.0
1976	172,271,180	17,621,247	10.2
1977	183,801,467	18,042,339	9.8

Source: Delta Air Lines, Inc., Annual Reports; CAB, *Recurrent Report of Mileage and Traffic Data.*

Appendix 3

HIGHLIGHTS OF
DELTA AIR LINES, INC., BALANCE SHEETS
FISCAL YEARS 1939–1977

May 31, 1939

Current Assets	$ 127,603.66	
Investments	10.00	
Property and Equipment	249,777.98	
Deferred Charges	17,474.59	
Total Assets	267,252.57	
Current Liabilities		$ 71,272.91
Tickets Sold, Unused		2,803.86
Common Stock and Earned Surplus		193,175.80
Total Liabilities		267,252.57

June 30, 1944

Current Assets	$ 1,668,698.20	
Stocks, Deposits (Travel Plan, Meter and Postage)	1,331.83	
Property and Equipment	625,279.13	
Prepaid Expense	28,379.04	
Total Assets	2,324,048.20	
Current Liabilities		$ 667,481.69
Capital Stock and Earned Surplus		1,656,566.51
Total Liabilities		2,324,048.20

June 30, 1949

Current Assets	$ 5,310,482.00	
Investments	154,805.00	
Operating Property and Equipment	6,800,718.00	
Deferred Charges	363,263.00	
Total Assets	12,629,268.00	

Current Liabilities		$ 2,751,859.00
Long-term Debt		2,925,000.00
Deferred Credits and Reserves		241,915.00
Capital Stock and Earned Surplus		6,710,494.00
Total Liabilities		12,629,268.00

June 30, 1954

Current Assets	$ 17,592,939.00	
Other Assets	2,854,438.00	
Operating Property and Equipment	26,076,080.00	
Property Acquisition Adjustment	993,591.00	
Deferred Charges	572,949.00	
Total Assets	48,089,997.00	
Current Liabilities		$ 8,861,111.00
Notes Payable		11,700,000.00
5½ percent Convertible Debentures		10,858,546.00
Deferred Federal Income Taxes		335,000.00
Reserve for Aircraft Overhaul		102,113.00
Capital Stock and Earned Surplus		16,233,227.00
Total Liabilities		48,089,997.00

June 30, 1959

Current Assets	$ 23,947,879.00	
Other Assets (Net Assets of Dusting Division and Other Investments)	388,270.00	
Property and Equipment	70,525,042.00	
Deferred Charges	565,709.00	
Total Assets	95,426,900.00	
Current Liabilities		$ 8,158,931.00
Notes Payable		35,000,000.00
Reserves and Deferred Credits		9,332,330.00
Stockholder Equity and Earned Surplus		37,409,576.00
Total Liabilities		95,426,900.00

June 30, 1964

Current Assets	$ 38,069,134.00
Other Assets (Net Assets of Dusting Division and Other Investments)	485,065.00
Property and Equipment	155,686,574.00
Total Assets	194,240,773.00

Current Liabilities	$ 28,408,942.00
Long-term Debt	47,679,762.00
Deferred Federal Income Taxes	41,135,000.00
Stockholder Equity and Earned Surplus	77,017,069.00
Total Liabilities	194,240,773.00

June 30, 1969

Current Assets	$ 89,791,000.00
Property and Equipment	542,296,000.00
Advance for SST Development, Being	
Amortized	2,178,000.00
Total Assets	634,265,000.00
Current Liabilities	$ 73,833,000.00
Long-term Debt	214,942,000.00
Deferred Credits	118,975,000.00
Stockholder Equity and Earned Surplus	226,515,000.00
Total Liabilities	634,265,000.00

June 30, 1974

Current Assets	$ 152,368,000.00
Property and Equipment	1,041,834,000.00
Other Assets	1,125,000.00
Total Assets	1,195,327,000.00
Current Liabilities	$ 176,777,000.00
Long-term Debt	345,119,000.00
Deferred Credits	229,605,000.00
Stockholder Equity and Earned Surplus	443,826,000.00
Total Liabilities	1,195,327,000.00

June 30, 1977

Current Assets	$ 216,740,000.00
Property and Equipment	1,259,146,000.00
Other Assets	15,933,000.00
Total Assets	1,419,819,000.00
Current Liabilities	$ 272,475,000.00
Long-term Debt	237,497,000.00
Deferred Credits	361,264,000.00
Stockholder Equity and Retained Earnings	620,583,000.00
Total Liabilities	1,491,819,000.00

Source: Delta Air Lines, Inc., Annual Reports.

Notes

AR	Annual Report of Delta Air Corporation (after 1945, Delta Air Lines, Inc.)
BF	Oscar Bergstrom Files
DD	*Delta Digest*
DGO	Delta General Offices
DPRF	Delta Public Relations Files
GAF	General and Administrative Files, Delta Air Lines
MF	Erma Murray Files
MHP	Carl H. McHenry Papers
MHR	Miscellaneous Historical Records, Delta Air Lines
Minutes	Minutes of the Board of Directors of Delta Air Corporation (after 1945, Delta Air Lines, Inc.)
PP	Laigh Parker Papers
TCP	Todd Cole Papers
WF	C. E. Woolman Files

CHAPTER 1 · *Takeoff*

1. The sequence of events leading up to the hypothetical, though typical, takeoff that follows is based on a series of interviews by Lewis and Newton of the following Delta personnel on December 10 and 15, 1976: Dana Jones, captain; Sue Myracle, senior flight attendant; Allen B. Epps, flight superintendent; William H. Kipp, lead mechanic; Jan Rake, systems manager/dining service; and Marcus Godwin and Richard Ryan, senior customer service agents.

2. Edna H. L. Turpin, ed., *Essays by Ralph Waldo Emerson*, p. 93.

3. Information on the early life and career of C. E. Woolman in this and succeeding paragraphs is taken partly from a file of obituaries and other materials about Woolman collected by the University of Illinois Alumni Association, Urbana, Illinois. Among many other sources see particularly "Delta History," leaflet published by Delta Air Lines c. 1951, in Delta Air Lines, General and Administrative Files (hereafter cited as GAF), Box M-4 (1951–52), folder marked "Delta Air Lines, Inc."; and "Meet Your Leaders: C. E. Woolman," *Delta Digest* (hereafter cited as *DD*), September 1950.

4. The brief treatment of early aviation and airline history in this chapter is based upon a number of works varying widely in quality and comprehensiveness. For two fairly recent comprehensive treatments, see R. E. G. Davies, *A History of the World's Airlines* and *Airlines of the United States since 1914*. Among many other volumes see also Henry Ladd Smith, *Airways*, still valuable despite its age; Elsbeth E. Freudenthal, *The Aviation Business from Kitty Hawk to Wall Street*, a hostile view; Arch Whitehouse, *The Early Birds*, a popular account; and Grover C. Loening, *Takeoff into Greatness*, written by an early aviation pioneer.

5. Information about the early life and marriage of Helen Fairfield Woolman is available in a file of newspaper clippings and other materials collected by the University of Illinois Alumni Association.

6. On the development of aircraft manufacturing in the United States see particularly John B. Rae, *Climb to Greatness*, an authoritative account; and G. R. Simonson, ed., *The History of the American Aircraft Industry*. A particularly valuable work

on the development of the airplane in the context of changing economic needs and circumstances is Ronald Miller and David Sawers, *The Technical Development of Modern Aviation.*

7. On the development of airmail, see particularly Benjamin B. Lipsner, *The Airmail,* by the founder of the airmail service in America; and Roger E. Bilstein, "Technology and Commerce: Aviation in the Conduct of American Business, 1918–29," *Technology and Culture* 10 (1969): 392–411.

8. Among other sources on the developments described here, see Laurence F. Schmeckebier, *The Aeronautics Branch, Department of Commerce.* On Henderson, see biographical sketch by Lewis and Newton in *Dictionary of American Biography,* supplement five.

9. "Delta Air Lines," *Delta Air Lines News,* n.d.; B. R. Coad to Harriette Speer, May 26, 1959, Delta Public Relations Files, Delta General Offices, Hartsfield Atlanta International Airport (hereafter cited as DPRF-DGO); *USDA Year Book, 1922,* p. 714; Coad, "Killing Boll Weevils with Poison Dust," *USDA Year Book, 1920,* pp. 241–52.

10. Kenneth Messenger and W. L. Popham, "From One to Five Thousand in Thirty-Four Years," *USDA Year Book, 1952,* pp. 250–51. The beginnings of aerial crop dusting in general have been thoroughly traced by Eldon W. Downs and George F. Lemmer in "Origins of Aerial Crop Dusting," *Agricultural History* 39 (1965): 123–35. The article, however, does not mention the role of C. E. Woolman.

11. Down and Lemmer, "Origins," pp. 124–219, 131, 133; C. R. Neillie and J. S. Houser, "Fighting Insects with Airplanes," *National Geographic Magazine* 41 (March 1922): 333–38; Julius A. Truesdale, "Spraying from Air," New York *Times,* January 8, 1922, VII, 4; Coad to Speer, May 26, 1959; John H. Van Deventer, Jr., "The Story of Keystone," *Air Transportation* 6 (January 19, 1929): 54–55.

12. Harold Rubin, "Boll Weevils Started His Air Line," *Dixie* (New Orleans *Times-Picayune* Magazine), February 13, 1955. Woolman apparently took little direct part in the actual experimentation Coad was directing; Brig.-General (ret.) Harold R. Harris, USAF, to Newton, August 22, 1974.

13. Downs and Lemmer, "Origins," pp. 129–31; *Aircraft Year Book, 1924,* pp. 75–82; B. Coad, E. Johnson, and G. L. McNeil, "Dusting Cotton from Airplanes," USDA Bulletin no. 1204 (January 1924), pp. 1–40; Coad to Speer, May 26, 1959.

14. Coad to Speer, May 26, 1959; *Aircraft Year Book, 1925,* pp. 59–60; Roger William Riis, "Commercial Crop Dusting," *Aviation* 18 (May 25, 1925): 573; Downs and Lemmer, "Origins," pp. 131–33; *Annual Reports* of the LSU Extension Service for 1925 (November, Circular no. 80, p. 3) and 1926 (June, Circular no. 87, p. 1); employment record card of Woolman, LSU Division of Cooperative Extension Service records, Baton Rouge, La.; Harris to Newton, August 22, 1974.

15. Riis, "Commercial Crop Dusting," p. 573; *Aircraft Year Book, 1925,* pp. 60–61; memorandum, "Contracts and Business Details (Confidential)" and "Memorandum with Regard to Establishing Units and the Dust Involved," Woolman Files, Delta General Offices, Atlanta, Ga. (hereafter cited as WF-DGO). Oliver I. Snapp, who was in charge of the United States Peach Insect Laboratory, Fort Valley, Georgia, took credit for initiating the use of aerial dusting in Georgia of peach orchards and, during the process that began in November 1924, for involving Coad, the Delta Laboratory, and Huff Daland: see Snapp, "Airplane Dusting of Peach Orchards," *Journal of Economic Entomology* 19 (1926): 450–59. He does not, however, mention Macon as headquarters for either Huff Daland or C. E. Woolman.

16. *Annual Report*, LSU Extension Service, 1925 (November, Circular no. 80), p. 88; "City's Aerial Development Given Impetus by Surrounding Localities," *Shreveport* (publication of Shreveport Chamber of Commerce) 7 (September 1927): 35; Fifth Annual Progress Edition, Monroe *News-Star*, 1928; *Aircraft Year Book, 1926*, pp. 71–72; W. E. Hines and Herbert Spencer, "Insecticide Control for Sugarcane Borer: A Report of Progress," Louisiana Agricultural Experiment Bulletin no. 201 (August 1927); notes, dated 1956, of interview, Speer with Coad, DPRF-DGO; Huff Daland report of cotton and sugarcane acreage assigned or to be assigned and assignment of units, April 12, 1928, and letter, with statistical enclosures, of Harris to Woolman, October 6, 1926, WF-DGO.

17. "Dusters Journal," ledger of expenditures, Huff Daland Dusters, 1925–29, WF-DGO; Harris to Woolman with statistical data, October 6, 1926; Van Deventer, "The Story of Keystone," pp. 54–55.

18. George N. Woolcott, "The Status of Economic Entomology in Peru," *Bulletin of Entomological Research* 20 (August, 1929): 227; "Dusters Journal," pp. 68–69; W. S. Reid to Harris, March 9, 1927; J. B. Pope, "Major Injurious Cotton Insects of Piura," typed report; "Standard Contract for Airplane Dusting Service in Peru"; Dan E. Tobin to Woolman, April 7, 1928; lists entitled "Peruvian Contracts—1928" and "Peruvian Contracts Signed Year '28–29"; Huff Daland deposit and withdrawal lists, National City Bank of New York, Lima, Peru Branch, all in WF-DGO.

19. The general story, of which the Huff Daland account is a part, of United States aviation diplomacy in Latin America in the 1920s and early 1930s is documented in Wesley Phillips Newton's *The Perilous Sky: U.S. Aviation Diplomacy and Latin America, 1919–1931*.

20. Harris to Robert W. Atkins, June 20, 1928, WF-DGO.

21. During a history spanning nearly four decades, Panagra operated routes extending from Panama down the west coast of South America to Santiago, Chile, and from thence across the Andes to Buenos Aires. Its development over the years was retarded by cross purposes between Pan American and Grace; ultimately, in 1967, its system was absorbed by Braniff Airways. *World Airline Record*, 7th ed., pp. 403, 445–46.

CHAPTER 2 · *The Emergence of Delta*

1. Edgar N. Gott to Harris, August 27, 1928, and draft of proposed concession, Huff Daland with Ecuador, 1928, WF-DGO; *El Comercio* (Lima), July 18, 1928; *El Telegrafo* (Guayaquil), July 17, 1928; copy of letter, R. S. Webber to Mrs. R. S. Webber, July 30, 1928, Woolman Scrapbook, and undated memorandum of C. W. Berl, WF-DGO.

2. Interview of Newton with Harold B. Grow, September 30, 1967; Stephen James Randall, "Colombia, the United States, and Interamerican Aviation Rivalry, 1927–1940," *Journal of Interamerican Studies and World Affairs* 14 (1972): 307; Woolman to Matthew Hanna, April 9, 1928, WF-DGO.

3. John C. Leslie, Pan Am History Project, to Newton, June 4, 1974; Harris to Newton, August 22, 1974; *El Comercio*, September 13, 1928.

4. Memorandum of Harris regarding "Disposal of Huff Daland Dusters," August 28, 1928, WF-DGO; Delta Air Corporation Charter of 1930, art. 8, in Minutes of the Board of Directors of Delta Air Corporation (hereafter cited as *Minutes*), vol. 1 (1930–40), DGO; agreement between Huff Daland Dusters, Inc., and Harris, Auerbach, Woolman, and Catherine FitzGerald, July 27, 1928, WF-DGO. Catherine FitzGerald was on

the original board as listed in the charter of 1930, but was not on the board in 1934 when Delta Air Corporation actually began operations as a mail-carrying airline: see *Minutes*, vol. 1, as cited above.

5. In a letter to Auerbach on August 25 (copy signed by Harris, WF-DGO), Harris refers to a board meeting of some sort "that we rushed our telegrams to." The telegrams are not in the Woolman Files, but Harris's letter seems to suggest that they contained a bid on the dusting assets made at a board meeting of Keystone held in New York City. Whatever group or groups were represented, the board meeting was held on August 24, shortly before Harris arrived in New York. Hoyt was there. Harris sent Auerbach a telegram on August 24 (copy, WF-DGO), stating the essentials of Hoyt's offer to sell out for $40,000.

6. Copy, letter, Edgar N. Gott to Harris, August 27, 1928; Harris to Gott, September 5, 1928, WF-DGO. Newton, *Perilous Sky*, has details of apparent friction between Gott and Pan American officials. As previously indicated, the new entity was chartered in Peru on September 4, 1928, under the name Peruvian Airways Inc. Equal shares were owned by Pan American and W. R. Grace and Company, the shipping firm in South America with which Pan American went into partnership for aviation purposes in the Andean region: see John C. Leslie to Newton, June 4, 1974.

7. Copy, letter with enclosures, Auerbach to Oliver, September 11, 1928; copy, memorandum, Auerbach to Richard F. Hoyt, September 14, 1928; copies of letters, Gott to Auerbach, both September 27, 1928, all in WF-DGO.

8. The option granted to Auerbach in the letters of September 27 read in part, "Huff Daland Dusters, Inc. . . . hereby gives you and/or your associates, the following option." It would seem that Auerbach interpreted the phrase "you and/or your associates" as giving him the leeway to dispose of the assets and reap the profit for himself. Possibly, therefore, he was on sound legal ground, despite the highly questionable ethics involved.

9. Copy, letter, Woolman to Harris, begun October 26, finished November 15, 1928; John S. Woodbridge to Gott, October 30, 1928; copy, telegram, Woolman to Harris, October 27, 1928, all in WF-DGO.

10. Letter, with enclosures, Auerbach to Woolman, October 24, 1928, WF-DGO.

11. Woolman to Harris, October 26 and November 15, 1928; Woolman to Harris, October 27, 1928; copy, letters, Woodbridge to Gott, October 29 and 30, and November 5, 1928, WF-DGO. It is not clear from these documents whether Woolman intended to sell the dusting equipment and purchase new equipment for the projected new enterprise or whether the term "sale" refers to the securing of financial backing in order to purchase the assets.

12. Copy, telegrams, Woolman to Thomas H. Huff; Woodbridge to Keystone Aircraft Corporation; and Travis Oliver to Gott, all November 8, 1928, WF-DGO. Also in these files, along with the copies of the telegrams noted above, was, on a Western Union telegram form, a note from Oliver to Woolman listing the names of the subscribers of the $12,000: they were Oliver ($2,000); Prentiss M. Atkins ($2,000); Carl McHenry ($1,000); D. Y. Smith ($2,000); Richardson ($500); Dr. Cole ($1,000); Abe Arant ($500); C. E. Slagle ($2,500); and George Sherrouse ($500). All of these were local planters or businessmen; Oliver, Atkins, McHenry, and Smith would become officers and directors of the firm.

13. Articles of Incorporation of Delta Air Service, Inc., filed December 3, 1928, Corporation Charter Book E., p. 28, Ouachita Parish Courthouse. An audit of Delta books by Cornell and Company, dated February 24, 1930, does not refer to the De-

cember 3 charter but instead says that the first charter was secured on December 6, 1928, with capital stock fixed at $150,000. A search of the parish records, however, did not produce such a charter.

14. Woolman to Harris, October 26 and November 15, 1928; Monroe *News-Star*, February 13; April 5, 18, and 25; May 1, 16, 22, and 31; June 1, 4, 8, 15, 16, 23, and 28; July 16 and 20; August 10 and 27; September 5, 12, 22, and 27, 1928. See also Charles A. Lindbergh, *The Spirit of St. Louis*, p. 477.

15. Copy, letter, Woolman to Harris, November 15, 1928, WF-DGO; Monroe *News-Star*, May 3, 1928; interview, Newton and Lewis with Gene Berry (hereafter cited as Berry interview), January 25, 1975.

16. Report of Leander Poole to Postmaster J. G. Bass, Birmingham, June 25, 1925; H. J. McNally to Woolman, February 21, 1929, WF-DGO. These files also contain a copy of a typed report, "Operations Cost Data on Travel Air Biplane and Cabin Monoplane," with the date 1/24/29 written on the cover.

17. Interview of Irene Fox by Lewis and Newton, September 19, 1974; Hot Springs (Ark.) *Sentinel-Record*, February 18, 1962; copy, letter and attachment, Woolman to J. S. Fox, May 23, 1929, and "Line up of ships and motors" as of June 6, 1929, typed sheet initialed C.L.H., WF-DGO. Eddie Holland of the State of Arkansas Division of Aeronautics supplied Lewis and Newton with a photocopy of the page of John Howe's logbook on which is noted the first official Delta flight, on June 17, 1929, by Howe from Dallas to Monroe.

18. "Birmingham: From Truck Farms to Three Generations of Airport Facilities," *DD*, December 1973.

19. Woolman to Gott, January 7, 1929; bill of sale from Huff Daland Dusters to Woolman and Harris, July 31, 1929; telegram of Harris to HUDADUS, Monroe, October 23, 1929; Harris to Woolman, December 3, 1929; Harris to Woolman, November 20, 1931, all in WF-DGO.

20. List of Delta stockholders, November 18, 1929, and cover letter and audit from Cornell and Company to Delta Air Service, Inc., February 24, 1930, WF-DGO.

21. Atlanta *Journal*, June 19, 1930; Delta Air Service, Schedules and Tariffs Effective June 17, 1930, DGO. Passengers leaving Fort Worth or Atlanta reached the opposite terminus in ten hours and fifteen minutes.

22. Woolman to Harris, April 1930, WF-DGO.

23. Resolution adopted by aviation meeting at Jackson, Mississippi, May 6, 1930, WF-DGO; testimony of C. E. Woolman, January 11, 1934, in U.S. Senate, 73rd Congress, 2nd Session, *Hearings before a Special Committee on Investigation of Air Mail and Ocean Mail Contracts* (hereafter cited as *Black Committee Hearings*), pt. 4, pp. 1597–98; Woolman to Harris, April 22, 1930, WF-DGO. The nature and significance of the McNary–Watres Act, and the manner in which it differed from previous airmail legislation, is ably explained in Smith, *Airways*, pp. 158–63 and passim. For an abridged text of the law, see Smith, pp. 377–79.

24. Resolution adopted by aviation meeting at Jackson, Mississippi, May 6, 1930, WF-DGO. The same files contain a list of the participants in this meeting, the minutes of the meeting, and prior correspondence pertaining to it.

25. Smith, *Airways*, pp. 156–69 and passim; for a defense of Brown's objectives and, to some extent, of his conduct in achieving them, see Smith, pp. 270–77. For other accounts of the McNary–Watres Act and the developments that followed, see Claude E. Puffer, *Air Transportation*, pp. 198–222, and John H. Frederick, *Commercial Air Transportation*, pp. 11–15.

26. Smith, *Airways*, pp. 167–68; testimony of C. E. Woolman, January 11, 1934, *Black Committee Hearings*, pt. 4, pp. 1599–1600. In his book *High Journey*, pp. 175–81, Carleton Putnam tells of an episode, related to him by Woolman, about how Woolman received a call from Seth Barwise, a Texas aviation pioneer, in which Barwise warned him about a meeting going on in Washington, D.C., sometime in the spring of 1930 at which Postmaster General Brown and representatives of the larger lines were discussing plans for dividing up airmail routes at the expense of the smaller independents. In all probability, this was the telephone tip to which Woolman referred in his testimony of January 11, 1934, though this cannot be proved conclusively from other sources. For biographical data on Broussard see *Biographical Directory of the American Congress, 1774–1971*, p. 645.

27. Testimony of C. E. Woolman, January 11, 1934, in *Black Committee Hearings*, pt. 4, pp. 1600–1601, 1606–7; *Airways*, p. 188; undated pencil copy of telegram from Woolman and C. V. Moore to J. S. Fox, approximately late May or early June 1930, WF-DGO.

28. Testimony of C. E. Woolman, January 11, 1934, *Black Committee Hearings*, pt. 4, pp. 1600–1602; Smith, *Airways*, pp. 147–55.

29. Smith, *Airways*, pp. 169–70.

30. Smith, *Airways*, pp. 188–89; testimony of C. E. Woolman, January 11, 1934, *Black Committee Hearings*, pt. 4, pp. 1603–7; testimony of Hainer Hinshaw, January 10, 1934, ibid., pp. 1585–87; telegrams of September 11, 12, 15, 16, 23, 29, and 30, WF-DGO. On the commencement of service between Atlanta and Fort Worth by AVCO's Southern Air Fast Express subsidiary, see *Air Commerce Bulletin* 2 (1930): 296.

31. Agreement of November 3, 1930, Delta Company Records, File A.

32. Articles of Incorporation of December 31, 1930, bound in *Minutes*, vol. 1 (1930–40), DGO.

33. Postscript to agreement of November 3, 1930, WF-DGO.

CHAPTER 3 · *Doldrums*

1. Woolman to Harris, April 22, 1930, WF-DGO.

2. Monroe *News-Star*, December 19, 1930.

3. Several company documents for early 1931 in the Carl H. McHenry Papers, DGO (hereafter cited as MHP-DGO) continue to refer to Delta Air Service as the company's name. This seems, however, to be unintentional misuse from old habit.

4. Interview of B. W. Biedenharn by Lewis and Newton, September 9, 1974.

5. Articles of Incorporation, Delta Air Corporation, filed December 31, 1930, Charter Book F, p. 322.

6. Material on Woolman in this and succeeding paragraphs is based largely upon interviews with persons who knew him well and a file of clippings and other memorabilia kindly supplied by the Alumni Association of the University of Illinois. Among materials in the file, see particularly "C. E. Woolman—An Air Pioneer," *Illinois Alumni News*, September 1941; Rubin, "Boll Weevils Started His Airline"; "From Cotton Fields to Skyways," *The AeROHRcrafter* (magazine of Rohr Corporation), November 1957; and "C. E. Woolman Is Dead at Seventy-six; Chairman of Delta Air Lines," from unidentified newspaper, September 1966. Mrs. Leo Hartman of Monroe is the source for the timbre of his voice in the early Monroe days (inter-

view of Mrs. Hartman by Newton, December 20, 1974); on the comparison between Woolman and Will Rogers, see undated Delta Air Lines news release, University of Illinois Alumni Association Files. The comments of Wayne Parrish are from an interview of Parrish by Newton, August 31, 1976.

7. Parrish interview; interview of Richard S. Maurer by Lewis and Newton, July 19, 1973; Rubin, "Boll Weevils Started His Airline"; interview of Elmer Culpepper by Newton, December 18, 1974; interview of C. B. McMahan by Lewis and Newton, September 11, 1974.

8. Putnam, *High Journey*, p. 179; interview of Esther Tarver by Lewis and Newton, September 11, 1974.

9. Interview of Barbara Woolman Preston by Newton, December 22, 1977; interview of H. L. Rosenhein by Newton, December 19, 1974; Culpepper interview; interview of Bernard W. Biedenharn by Lewis and Newton, September 9, 1974; memorandum by Maurer to Newton, June 16, 1975; interview of W. L. Alexander by Newton, December 19, 1974.

10. "Synonymous: Delta, Woolman," clipping from Chicago *Tribune*, March 18, 1963, Illinois Alumni Association Files.

11. Interview of Gene Berry by Lewis and Newton, January 25, 1975; Hartman interview; interview of Frank Breese by Lewis and Newton, September 10, 1974. Breese, now deceased, was a local Monroe-area historian who possessed a vast store of knowledge about the families and economic development, as well as the general history, of Monroe and Ouachita Parish.

12. Tarver interview; Hartman interview; interview of Charles H. Dolson by Lewis, September 16, 1975.

13. Notes, Speer–Coad interview, 1956; Hartman interview.

14. "Ouachita Parish, Louisiana, 1945, Resources and Facilities," State of Louisiana Department of Public Works and Ouachita Parish Planning Board, Baton Rouge, Louisiana, 1945 (hereafter cited as "Resources and Facilities"); interview of Frances French by Newton, July 15, 1973; unpublished mimeographed article, "The First Sixty Years of Central Savings Bank and Trust Company"; photocopy of unpublished article, "Ouachita National Bank, Organization and Development"; Hartman interview; Monroe *Morning World*, June 30, 1935. On the new runway, see also minutes, Ouachita Parish Police Jury, 1931–34, Ouachita Parish Courthouse, Monroe, Louisiana, meetings of July 15, 1931, p. 719, and August 31, 1931, pp. 729–30.

15. Berry, Biedenharn, McMahan, and Hartman interviews; chattel mortgage, dated June 1931 (apparently never executed), containing list of Delta planes and their value as of that date, Miscellaneous Historical Records, DGO (hereafter cited as MHR-DGO).

16. The cards on Murray, Palmer, Fullilove, Porter, Chance, Irvin, and de Yampert, among others, for 1931 are located in MHR-DGO. The invoices are to be found in these records also. The source for the English ownership of the Delta and Pine Lands Company is the Berry interview.

17. Delta Air Corporation invoices 11 and 13 (1931); 187, 199, 272, and 277 (1932); and 307 and 313 (1933), MHR-DGO; Delta Air Corporation statement of March 13, 1931, DGO.

18. There are month-by-month invoices for Biedenharn in the Delta Air Corporation invoices for 1931–34, MHR-DGO. These same invoices show storage charges for Faser's Travel Air and Miller's Stinson for various times in the same period.

19. Delta Air Corporation invoice 362 (1933), MHR-DGO. A number of similar in-

voices for Biedenharn, Faser, Miller, and several others are contained in these records.

20. Delta Air Corporation invoices 60 and 66 (1931), and 126 (1932), MHR-DGO. Various invoices in these records provide details on instruction, taxi, and photographic services rendered by Delta during the period 1931–34.

21. Interview of Irene Fox by Lewis and Newton, September 9, 1974.

22. Testimony of C. E. Woolman, *Black Committee Hearings*, pt. 4, p. 1607. See the record of the entire hearings for the revealing story that led to cancellation.

23. Smith, *Airways*, pp. 249–58.

24. *Minutes*, vol. 1 (secretary's copy), May 22 and June 11, 1934. According to James Noe of Monroe, Louisiana, a pioneer investor in Delta and former governor of Louisiana, politics played the decisive card in Delta's winning the contract, in that it was Senator Huey Long's importuning of Roosevelt and the latter's intervention that caused previously hesitant postal authorities to decide in Delta's favor: interview of James Noe by Newton and Lewis, September 10, 1974. According to Professor T. Harry Williams, Long's biographer, however, it is unlikely that Roosevelt would have done such a favor for Long at that time because their mutual antipathy was then at its height: Williams to Newton, October 6, 1975.

CHAPTER 4 · *The Return of the Airliner*

1. Historical memorandum prepared by Charles H. Dolson, 1975 (hereafter cited as Dolson memorandum).

2. Statements of Delta Air Corporation, December 31, 1931; December 1, 1932; and December 31, 1933, in duplicate set of corporate minutes, Corporate Records Office, DGO; Rosenhein interview; undated financial statement of Delta Air Corporation, copy supplied by Travis Oliver III, Ruston, Louisiana; Ouachita Parish Tax Records 1934, Ouachita Parish Courthouse, Monroe, Louisiana.

3. *Minutes*, May 22, 1934; interview of Robert Faulk by Lewis and Newton, December 10, 1976. Dolson later recalled that both he and McBride knew that Woolman was technically proscribed from holding a managerial position with Delta at this time, but that nobody filed a complaint against him with the Post Office Department; interview of Dolson by Lewis and Newton, March 4, 1974.

4. *Minutes*, May 22, 1934; Woolman to Central Savings Bank, May 23, 1934, General File, MHP-DGO.

5. *Minutes*, May 31, 1934.

6. *Minutes*, June 11 and 12, 1934.

7. Undated list of Delta personnel with biographical data, c. 1934, MHR-DGO.

8. It is difficult to reconstruct a fully accurate account of Delta's earliest pilot force. In his historical memorandum, Dolson recalls the seven airline pilots who began the mail service as himself, Dice, McBride, Schier, Conover, Dixon, and Shealy. A list of file cards in MHR-DGO on various employees of that period shows Sidney F. Whitaker as being hired on June 23, 1934; according to Dolson, he signed on as a dusting pilot at that time and entered airline service later in the year. The file contains no card on George Shealy, who according to Dolson was employed on July 1, 1934. The Monroe *News-Star*, June 20, 1934, states that as of that date Dice, Dolson, McBride, Dixon, and two other men—John Worttun and O. R. Haueter—were flying terrain familiarization missions in preparation for inaugurating the airline. The names of the last two are not in the file cards and do not appear on any Delta

records; Dolson later recalled that Haueter accepted a job with another airline shortly after he arrived in Monroe to work for Delta.

9. Dolson memorandum.

10. Monroe *News-Star*, June 19, July 1, 4, 5, and 8, 1934; envelope with cachet, Woolman Scrapbook; interview of Robert Faulk by Lewis and Newton, December 10, 1976. The eastbound flight, according to the *News-Star* of July 4, did not begin until later that day and originated in Dallas.

11. Dolson memorandum; Monroe *News-Star*, May 25 and July 2, 1934.

12. "Civil Aeronautics Board—Reply to Questionnaire of Legislative Oversight Committee," September 1958, Box A, Accession 62-A-154, Office of Administration, Management Division, CAB, R/G 197, Social and Industrial Section, NA; Smith, *Airways*, pp. 284–86; James A. Farley to Delta, March 8, 1935, and C. H. McHenry to Farley, March 11, 1935, both in General File, MHP-DGO; *Minutes*, March 30, 1935.

13. Monroe *News-Star*, August 5, 1934; Charleston *News and Courier*, August 5, 6, and 7, 1934; summary of operations over seven-year period ending June 31, 1941, in Annual Report of Delta Air Corporation, 1941, pp. 8–9 (hereafter cited as AR, with appropriate year).

14. Dolson memorandum; Proceedings of the Parish Police Jury, August 20, 1934, p. 1211, Ouachita Parish Courthouse; minutes, City of Monroe, City Hall, vol. 3 (1927–36), pp. 439–40; Monroe *News-Star*, August 21, September 23, and December 6, 1934, and February 21 and March 20, 1935; *Minutes*, March 31, 1935.

15. Dolson memorandum; *Minutes*, May 30, 1935; Kenneth Munson, *Airliners between the Wars, 1919–39*, pp. 86–174.

16. Monroe *News-Star*, June 25, July 1, 12, 15, and 16, 1935.

17. Ibid., July 2, 1935; Dolson memorandum.

18. Monroe *News-Star*, August 15, 1935; Dolson memorandum; *Air Commerce Bulletin* 7 (October 15, 1935): 92. In a historical memorandum prepared in 1974 (hereafter referred to as Ball memorandum), Captain T. P. Ball recalled that the account he received of the crash described the major cause as a broken piece of propeller slashing into the cockpit and killing the pilot.

19. Faulk interview. Hugh D. Reagan of the Auburn University History Department was a schoolmate and good friend of Thompson's and was deeply pained by his loss. He remembered that shortly before Thompson took the flight, the latter jokingly said that if the plane crashed it would likely come down in a cotton field. Interview of Reagan by Newton, June 1, 1975.

20. Various telegrams between Delta and Stinson, Delta and the Commerce Department, and Delta and Alro Insurance Underwriters, all in September 1935; notarized agreement between Delta and Stinson Aircraft Corporation, December 12, 1935; McHenry (for Delta) to Auto-Aircraft Acceptance Corporation, December 17, 1935, all in General File, May 1934–January 1943; MHP-DGO; *Air Commerce Bulletin* 7 (October 15, 1935): 92. Hugh D. Reagan is the authors' source for the settlement with the survivors' kin.

21. *Minutes*, October 1 and December 6, 1935; Munson, *Airliners between the Wars*, pp. 80, 167–68; Monroe *News-Star*, October 30, 1935. For a summary of periodic changes in and additions to Delta's aircraft, see also *DD*, June 1959 (thirtieth anniversary issue).

22. Interviews of Schwaemmle by Lewis and Newton, August 10 and December 18, 1973.

23. Dolson memorandum; Ball memorandum; interview of Ball by Lewis, January 15, 1974; Dolson interview, March 4, 1974.

24. Schwaemmle interviews.

25. Dolson memorandum.

26. Charles Dolson, Flight Log no. 7 (in Dolson's private possession), entry of August 27, 1936; interview of Richard S. Maurer by Newton, June 16, 1975.

27. Dolson memorandum; "Mechanics Sign Delta Agreement," *American Aviation* 1 (January 15, 1938): 8. Robert H. Wharton, retired Delta executive, states that the move for a mechanics' union began in 1936 (memorandum appended to letter of Wharton to Richard S. Maurer, November 16, 1976 [hereafter cited as Wharton memorandum]).

28. Oscar Bergstrom to Jeanette Farmer, December 17, 1937; Bergstrom to Sally Rand, August 6, 1935; Rand to Bergstrom, August 14, 1936; Oscar Bergstrom Files, DGO (hereafter cited as BF-DGO). On the passenger-courting moves underway in the industry generally at this time and the rationale underlying them, see Robert M. Kane and Allan D. Vose, *Air Transportation*, pp. 30–31.

29. Memorandum, Bergstrom to station manager, Augusta, June 9, 1936; Parker to same, June 16, 1936; Bergstrom to city traffic manager, Birmingham, June 29, 1936; memorandum, Bergstrom to Parker, October 12, 1936; reply, Parker to Bergstrom, October 14, 1936; all in BF-DGO.

30. M. P. Mull to Delta, Atlanta, October 30, 1936; memorandum, Bergstrom to Parker, December 21, 1936; Bergstrom to Parker, October 14, 1936 (two memos of that date); Bergstrom to Parker, November 11, 1936; Bergstrom to district traffic manager, Dallas, November 28, 1936, BF-DGO.

31. Bergstrom to Parker, November 3, 1936; Parker to Bergstrom, November 4, 1936, BF-DGO.

32. Elizabeth Bain to Bergstrom, October 7, 1936; A. Lee Forbis to Delta management, Atlanta, September 27, 1936, BF-DGO.

33. Memoranda, Parker to Woolman, June 30 and July 25 and 27, 1934; Woolman to Parker, July 28, 1934, Laigh Parker Papers (hereafter cited as PP-DGO), file covering period 1934–41.

34. Memoranda, Parker to Woolman, June 5, 1935; Woolman to Parker, June 7, 1935, ibid.

35. Memorandum, Parker to Woolman, June 7, 1935, ibid.; list of Delta employees by position, salary, and station, c. July 1, 1936, WF-DGO.

36. Parker to Woolman, January 24, 26, and 27, 1935; memorandum, Parker to Woolman, December 1 and 2, 1936, File 1934–42, PP-DGO.

CHAPTER 5 · *On to Atlanta*

1. Appendix 1 contains detailed operating statistics for Delta Air Lines from 1934 through 1977.

2. See Appendix 1. For passenger and other statistics by calendar rather than fiscal years, see also "Comparative Profit and Loss Statement, Seven Years Ended June 31, 1941," in AR 1941, pp. 8–9.

3. Packet of materials carried in seat pockets of Lockheed Electras operated by Delta, c. August 1938, in the possession of the Rev. Vernon Broyles, Atlanta, Ga.

4. Parker to Chet Stewart, February 10, 1937; itemized statement for party of April 15, 1938; Wayne W. Parrish to Parker, July 6, 1938; folder marked "Talks, etc."; memorandum, Robert W. Weeks to Parker, October 26, 1939; Parker to Charles Rochester, March 8, 1940, all in PP-DGO; Parrish interview, August 31, 1976; AR 1941, p. 1.

5. Edward V. Rickenbacker, *Rickenbacker*, pp. 217–22; Dolson interview, March 4, 1974; interview of Dolson and Arthur Ford by Lewis, August 28, 1975.

6. For varying treatments of the background and provisions of the Civil Aeronautics Act of 1938, see Arnold E. Bridden, Ellmore A. Champie, and Peter A. Morraine, *FAA Historical Fact Book*, pp. 34–35; Davies, *Airlines of the United States since 1914*, pp. 200–203; Frederick, *Commercial Air Transportation*, pp. 15–20; Kane and Vose, *Air Transportation*, pp. 31–32; and Smith, *Airways*, pp. 288, 357–62. On the importance of the accident that took the life of Senator Cutting, see Nick A. Komons, *The Cutting Air Crash*, pp. 83–84.

7. For the full text of the Civil Aeronautics Act of 1938, see *United States Statutes at Large*, 75th Congress, 3rd session, 1938, pp. 985–1030.

8. *Civil Aeronautics Authority Reports*, 1: 1–4.

9. Bridden et al., *FAA Historical Fact Book*, p. 40; Davies, *Airlines of the United States since 1914*, p. 203; Smith, *Airways*, pp. 357–59. On the background and passage of the Reorganization Act of 1939, see Richard Polenberg, *Reorganizing Roosevelt's Government*, passim.

10. Dolson memorandum; Shreveport *Times*, December 23, 1939.

11. Dolson memorandum; Munson, *Airliners between the Wars*, pp. 76, 162–64.

12. Interview of Birdie Perkins Bomar by Newton, September 16, 1975; Dolson memorandum.

13. Contracts between Delta, ALMA, and ALPA, June 1 and August 1, 1940, GAF-DGO, Box C-IV (1942–43), folders bearing the names of the respective unions.

14. List of personnel, stations, and salaries, c. July 1, 1936, WF-DGO.

15. *Civil Aeronautics Authority Reports*, 1: 2; list of stockholders, 1940, folder on stock matters, MHP-DGO.

16. Prospectus, Delta Air Corporation, offering 60,000 shares of no-par value common stock, 1941, DGO (hereafter cited as "Stock Prospectus, 1941"), p. 19.

17. Interview of Richard W. Courts by Lewis and Newton, July 11, 1975.

18. Ball memorandum; Munson, *Airliners between the Wars*, pp. 77, 164–65; Miller and Sawers, *The Technical Development of Modern Aviation*, pp. 98–103.

19. *Minutes*, November 11, 1940; Ball memorandum; "Stock Prospectus, 1941," pp. 11–15, 27.

20. Courts interview; "Stock Prospectus, 1941," pp. 25–26; *Minutes*, June 12, July 19, September 9, and November 1, 1940; minutes of stockholders' meeting of September 9, 1940; memorandum, Maurer to Newton, June 16, 1975.

21. *Minutes*, November 1, 1940; "Stock Prospectus, 1941," p. 12; Dolson memorandum.

22. *Decisions of the Civil Aeronautics Board*, 2:447–502; *Minutes*, July 16, 1935, May 5, 1938, and August 21, 1939.

23. "Stock Prospectus, 1941," pp. 19, 26; Courts interview.

24. Letters to stockholders, January 7, January 28, and March 25, 1941, MHP-DGO; "Stock Prospectus, 1941," p. 26; Courts interview; CAB *Reports*, 3: 261, 279; agreement between Courts and Delta, May 12, 1941, MHP-DGO.

25. *Minutes*, 1940 and 1941, passim; Courts interview; interviews of Bernard

Biedenharn, Frances McHenry, and Mary W. McHenry Wade by Lewis and Newton, September 9 and 10, 1975. Files for both the morning and evening Monroe newspapers fail to yield any editorial or news coverage about the move. Richard Courts speculated that likely criticism stemming from natural disappointment was not forthcoming because of the influence of some of the town's leading citizens who were also members of the Delta board and/or investors; Courts interview. Various people in Monroe—Bernard Biedenharn and Esther Tarver among them—agree that the decision to move to Atlanta was not popular with the board but that in this instance, as in others, it always followed Woolman's lead in the end.

26. Bomar interview; Dolson memorandum.

CHAPTER 6 · *Wartime Interlude*

1. *Minutes*, November 25, 1940, January 27, 1941, September 22, 1941, and May 25, 1942; AR 1941, pp. 2, 9–10. There is some confusion about the disposal of the DC-2s; some Delta officials recall them as being sold to the Dutch and seeing service in the Netherlands East Indies. See for example Dolson memorandum. However, we have been unable to locate documentary evidence for this and have been forced to rely on the admittedly sketchy evidence contained in AR 1941, which makes it clear that the DC-2s were sold and that the British Purchasing Commission was the initial prospective buyer. One of the firm's Lockheed Electras was sold to Waterman Air Lines, and the rest went to the federal government after the United States entered the war.

2. See AR 1943, pp. 4–6; AR 1944, p. 4; and AR 1945, pp. 2, 16. On the mood that prevailed in the Delta organization in the closing months of the war, see also "Delta Rally Held," *DD*, May 1945.

3. For an extended account of developments in the South during World War II, including the economic growth enjoyed by the region, see George B. Tindall, *The Emergence of the New South, 1913–1945*, pp. 687–731. On Delta's role in providing cargo and passenger service that aided the Manhattan Project, see "Aids Atomic Bomb," *DD*, September 1945.

4. See for example AR 1945, p. 1. On the effect of World War II in popularizing air travel, see also William F. Ogburn, *The Social Effects of Aviation*, p. 115.

5. Delta Air Lines, Public Relations Department, "Facts and Highlights of History of the Atlanta Airport, Atlanta, Georgia," n.d., DPRF-DGO.

6. "Delta Backs Up Fighting Men with Work on Six Different Vital Army Contracts," *DD*, June 1943; AR 1945, pp. 4–6; Reginald M. Cleveland, *Air Transport at War*, p. 299; Confidential Report by Delta Air Corporation to the Chairman, Air Lines Committee for U.S. Air Policy, May 8, 1944, in GAF, Box C-V (1943–44), folder marked "Air Lines Committee for U.S. Air Policy." On the impact of the longer range which the described modifications permitted the P-51 to have, see Wesley F. Craven and James L. Cate, eds., *Men and Planes*, pp. 336–37.

7. AR 1943, p. 5; "Delta Backs Up Fighting Men," p. 7; "Two Deltas Win Bonds for Ideas," *DD*, June 1943; Confidential Report, May 8, 1944, GAF, Box C-V; Cushing to Lieutenant Thomas W. Finney, Army Air Corps, May 9, 1942, GAF, Box C-I (1941–42), folder marked "Mechanics Training for Government"; list of graduates, November 21, 1942, GAF, Box C-III (1942–43), folder marked "Contract UJ35ac30466 (8581) (Mechanics Training)."

8. On developments covered in this paragraph and the ones immediately following, see particularly "Drama in MTD," *DD*, November 1944; Confidential Report, May 8, 1944, GAF, box C-V.

9. "Drama in MTD," *DD*, November 1944; "Military Transport," *DD*, July 1944; AR 1944, p. 5; AR 1945, pp. 4–5; Col. George F. Brewer, AAC, to Woolman, June 12, 1944, GAF, Box C-V (1943–44), folder marked "Army Air Cargo Freight Service."

10. AR 1943, pp. 5–6; *Minutes*, May 31, 1943; Confidential Report, May 8, 1944, GAF, Box C-V; Woolman to Stearman, April 19, 1944, GAF, Box C-VII (1943–44), folder marked "Planes." The fact that a leading work on commercial aviation singled this aspect of Delta's wartime contributions out for special mention suggests that it was a unique service not provided by any other company in the industry. See Frederick, *Commercial Air Transportation*, pp. 27, 29. For other activities of the dusting division during the war, see especially Bill Wilkerson, "Crop Dusting," *DD*, December 1943.

11. AR 1942, p. 3; AR 1944, p. 6; *Minutes*, May 25, 1942; untitled article, *DD*, November 1944; "Parker Decorated," *DD*, March 1945; "Parker Promoted," *DD*, June 1945; Woolman to Parker, April 28, 1943, and June 27, 1945, GAF, Box C-II (1942–43) and C-X (1944–45), folders marked "Miscellaneous."

12. See Lamar Q. Ball, "College Park Pilot Helped Organize Chinese Air Force," Atlanta *Constitution*, February 22, 1942, and Doris Lockerman, "Air Ace Visiting Here Plans Woe for Tokyo," undated newspaper clipping, c. 1943, both in Woolman Scrapbook, pp. 16–18; untitled article, *DD*, September 1944; Williamson to Woolman, March 18, 1944, GAF, Box C-VIII (1943–44), folder marked "Miscellaneous"; Christmas letters, 1939–44, GAF, Box C-III (1942–43) and Box C-IX (1944–45), folders marked "Delta Air Corporation."

13. "Shealy over Tokyo," *DD*, January 1945.

14. Interviews of Dolson by Lewis and Newton, March 4, 1974, and Fritz Schwaemmle, December 18, 1973; "Drama in MTD." On Schwaemmle's wartime experiences, see also "Tipping with Eggs," *DD*, January 1945.

15. "Home Front," *DD*, April 1943; Dorothy Curtis, "Engine Overhaul," *DD*, December 1943; Celestine Sibley, "Atlanta Women Repair Airplane Motors," undated article from unidentified local newspaper, 1942 or 1943, Woolman Scrapbook, pp. 17–18.

16. Frederick, *Commercial Air Transportation*, pp. 22–25.

17. Ibid.; AR 1941, p. 4; "Drama in MTD"; *Minutes*, May 25, 1942; AR 1943, p. 5; AR 1944, p. 5; AR 1945, p. 2; Woolman to Faulk, June 27, 1944, GAF, Box C-V (1943–44), folder marked "C. E. Faulk—President."

18. AR 1945, p. 9; Harry Lee, "Delta Airlines Comes through Despite Big Equipment Cut," undated clipping from unidentified local newspaper, c. 1943, Woolman Scrapbook, p. 15.

19. Dorothy Calvert, "City Offices," *DD*, December 1943; Marguerite Steedman, "Beauty Flies the Airways," clipping from *Atlanta Journal Magazine*, May 8, 1945, in Woolman Scrapbook, p. 23; Woolman to William Y. Bell, Jr., May 19, 1944, and Bell to Woolman, June 4, 1944, GAF, Box C-IV (1943–44), folder marked "Complaints." On passenger priorities during the war, see also "Reservations," *DD*, April 1945.

20. Truman Haygood, supervisor of statistics, Delta Air Lines, "Statistical Data by Months for the Year 1958 and for Period 1934–1958," memorandum of January 15, 1959, Delta Records Collection, DGO.

21. AR 1944, p. 4.

22. Undated clipping from unidentified newspaper quoting CAB Report, early 1945, Woolman Scrapbook, p. 27; AR 1945, pp. 2–3. See also "Delta Finances Fine," *DD*, September 1945, quoting a Courts and Company memorandum based on CAB statistics to the effect that "Delta's dollar income, per ton mile, for the year 1944, was next to the lowest in the industry, *yet our profit per ton mile was third from the highest.*" The brokers' summary continued, "Delta sells its combined services at a lower cost than all except one company, but due to efficient control of expenses is able to show net profit per ton mile the third highest of these companies. The ability of a company to control expenses and to bring down to net a reasonable amount of income, reflects the success of that company. We consider the record of Delta as outstanding."

23. Woolman's activities in retrieving paper clips and other discarded items in Delta's administrative offices and repair hangars became legendary throughout the organization and have been commented upon frequently by Delta personnel with whom interviews have been conducted, among them Chairman of the Board W. T. Beebe, Vice-Chairman of the Board Richard S. Maurer, and former President and Chairman of the Board Charles Dolson. While no direct testimony has been gathered linking this sort of activity to the World War II period, it seems likely that Woolman did it then as he had earlier and would later. In any event, both the Annual Reports of the company and the files of the *Delta Digest* for the period indicate Woolman's resourcefulness in preaching the message of efficiency and productivity and his knack for dramatizing it.

24. AR 1942, pp. 6, 7; Supplemental Agreement to Government Contracts, June 25, 1943, GAF, Box C-V (1942–43), folder marked "Cargo and Training Contracts"; AR 1943, pp. 3–4, 11; AR 1944, pp. 3, 5, 9; AR 1945, pp. 1, 14–16.

25. AR 1942, pp. 2, 7; AR 1944, pp. 3–4; AR 1945, p. 3.

26. AR 1944, p. 6; AR 1945, pp. 1–2; "Sky Skippers," *DD*, April 1945.

27. In addition to the statistical breakdown in AR 1945, p. 2, see "Air Stewardesses," *DD*, April 1945, and "Trunk Line to Sunshine," undated clipping from *Trade Winds*, late 1945, Woolman Scrapbook, p. 26. For a picture of the 1944 class, giving the home towns from which the stewardesses came, see *DD*, September 1944.

28. In addition to the statistics provided in AR 1945, p. 2, see the articles entitled "Flight Control," "Field Agents," "Communications," and "Ship Maintenance" in *DD*, April 1945, and E. E. McKellar, "Flight Control," *DD*, December 1943.

29. AR 1945, p. 2; "Reservations," *DD*, April 1945; Dorothy Calvert, "City Offices," *DD*, December 1943; Ike Lasseter, "Accounting Dept.," *DD*, April 1944; "Lawyer Lasseter," *DD*, June 1943.

30. L. M. Hunt, "Plant Protection," *DD*, December 1943.

31. "The Delta Digest," news release issued by Delta Public Relations Department, 1950; "The Delta Story Unfolds in Thirty-five Years of Delta Digest Pages," *DD*, May 1977.

32. "Home Base," *DD*, September 1944; "New Annex Under Way for Expanded Delta Program," *DD*, April 1943; AR 1943, pp. 3, 6, including photograph of the Delta complex with new additions; undated clipping of article from *Southernaire* magazine, early or mid-1945, Woolman Scrapbook, p. 22.

33. "Insurance Bargain," *DD*, January 1945, and "Employees' Bank," *DD*, April 1944; *Minutes*, June 21, 1943; AR 1943, p. 6; untitled article, *DD*, June 1943; memo-

randum accompanying letter of Robert H. Wharton to Richard S. Maurer, November 16, 1976; contract with ALMA, GAF, Box C-IX (1944–45), folder marked "Air Line Mechanics Association, International."

34. On the continuity of the board throughout the war, compare AR 1941, p. 1, and AR 1945, inside back cover. On Judd's election to the board, and for brief details relative to his career, see *Minutes*, May 31, 1943, and "Director Judd," *DD*, June 1943. Judd had been elected assistant secretary in the previous year; see *Minutes*, August 31, 1942. Almost all wartime meetings of the board, conforming with previous practice, were held at the Central Savings Bank and Trust Company in Monroe, or occasionally, as on June 21, 1943, at Faulk's office in the Bernhardt Building located in the same city. Only on very rare occasions, as on October 19 and 20, 1942, did the board meet in Atlanta. Faulk's and Woolman's stock holdings fluctuated to some degree throughout the war and, of course, increased substantially when the new stock issue of early 1945 went into effect. As of December 16, 1942, Faulk held 23,291 shares and Woolman held 20,388, as the *Minutes* of that date confirm. An article in *Investor's Reader*, May 9, 1945, said of Faulk's role in Delta, "It was in those days (1930's) that a financial angel named Clarence Eugene Faulk purchased a large interest in Delta and became president. But C. E. Faulk wisely left the actual operation of the company to more experienced hands and today he is a fine old Southern gentleman in a wide brimmed hat with a lively interest in aviation." Woolman Scrapbook, p. 22.

35. AR 1941, p. 4; AR 1942, p. 3; AR 1943, p. 5; *Minutes*, August 30, 1943; "New Route Clicks," *DD*, December 1943; "Baton Rouge," *DD*, November 1944. In addition to the three airlines mentioned which had competed with Delta for the route from Shreveport to New Orleans, Eastern had sought a run from New Orleans to Dallas–Fort Worth by way of Baton Rouge and Lake Charles. Moore's role in pushing Delta's applications for new routes in Washington during this period can be traced in various letters and reports to Woolman in GAF, Box C-V (1943–44), folder marked "Ernest V. Moore."

36. "Alexandria," *DD*, September 1944.

37. "Warm Welcome," *DD*, December 1943; "New Orleans—'Air Hub of the Americas,'" *DD*, June 1945; "New Route Clicks," *DD*, December 1943.

38. *Minutes*, May 31, 1943; "Plan Department," *DD*, June 1943.

39. Woolman to Parker, April 28, 1943; "Declaration of Policy on Worldwide Aviation as Filed July 15, 1943 with the Civil Aeronautics Board by Sixteen Signatory Airlines," GAF, Box C-V (1943–44), folder marked "Airline Committee for U.S. Policy"; "Post-War Plans," *DD*, April 1944; AR 1943, p. 7.

40. AR 1944, pp. 7–8; "Post-War Plans," *DD*, April 1944.

41. AR 1944, pp. 6–7; "New Route News," *DD*, July 1944; "Kansas City–Cuba," *DD*, September 1944; "Bulletin—Delta Recommended for Caribbean Route," *DD*, January 1945; "Post-War Picture," *DD*, March 1945.

42. "Post-War Picture," *DD*, March 1945; "Kansas City Case," *DD*, March 1945; AR 1945, p. 8.

43. "Meet Paul Pate," *DD*, June 1945; "Flying Freighters," *DD*, April 1945; AR 1945, p. 10. On Pate's previous career, see also "Post-War Plans," *DD*, April 1944.

44. "Delta Sells Air Service to the Nation," AR 1945, p. 10; "Dynamic New Ads," *DD*, July 1945; "Columbus Office Opens," *DD*, March 1945; "Advertising Trends," AR 1945, p. 11.

45. "New Equipment," AR 1945, p. 11. On the history and development of the

Douglas DC-4, see particularly Miller and Sawers, *Technical Development of Modern Aviation*, pp. 22–23.

46. AR 1943, pp. 3, 10, 12; AR 1944, pp. 3, 12; AR 1945, pp. 4, 14.

47. AR 1945, pp. 4, 14. See also the three clippings from unidentified newspapers, all from early 1945, relating to this stock issue in Woolman Scrapbook, p. 22. In an accompanying clipping from *Investor's Reader*, mounted on the same page, Woolman is quoted as saying that in 1934, when Delta bid on route 24, "you couldn't get anybody to buy airmail stock. A millionaire airman was a man who could raise $5,000 cash . . . when I needed money I almost had to buy all the stock myself." By contrast, in 1945, "I have to run away from my friends because we didn't have enough shares in the recent offering . . . for everyone." The proceeds of the stock sale after broker's commissions are listed officially in AR 1945, p. 14, as $2,099,692, confirming the figure accompanying the picture of the check transmitted to Woolman. From this was debited $307,272 representing the par value credited to the stock and $10,224.71 as the expense of registering and issuing it. Thus the final amount added to the firm's capital surplus from the new issue was $1,782,196.

48. "Delta Enters Expanded Era with New Air Routes," *DD*, September 1945; AR 1945, p. 1. The new route and its importance will be discussed in greater detail in Chapter 7. It led from Chicago to Cincinnati by way of Muncie, Anderson, and New Castle, Indiana; from Cincinnati to Knoxville to Miami by way of Asheville, North Carolina, Greenville and Spartanburg, South Carolina, Augusta and Savannah, Georgia, and Jacksonville, Florida. Also awarded to Delta at the same time was an alternate route from Chicago to Charleston, South Carolina, by way of Anderson, Muncie, and New Castle, Cincinnati, Knoxville, Asheville, Spartanburg and Greenville, and Columbia, and a feeder run from Atlanta to Brunswick.

49. Clipping from *Trade Winds*, Woolman Scrapbook, p. 26; AR 1945, p. 11.

CHAPTER 7 · *New Vistas, New Planes, and New Routes*

1. *Minutes*, October 29, 1945; minutes of annual meeting of stockholders, December 17, 1945. Woolman had proposed the change of name at the board meeting of July 30, 1945, at which time it was discussed and deferred for later action. As indicated in the previous chapter, the firm apparently was already being referred to by reservations personnel as "Delta Air Lines" in telephone contacts with the public even before the change was officially proposed. See "Reservations," *DD*, April 1945.

2. *Minutes*, December 17, 1945; AR 1946, pp. 9–10.

3. "New 'Trunk Line to Sunshine' Opened," *DD*, January 1946; "'The Comet' Flashes West; Charleston–Chicago Inaugurated April," *DD*, April 1946; "Delta Begins Service into Lexington," *DD*, October 1946; "Delta Expands 2,500 Per Cent," *DD*, January 1946; AR 1946, p. 6; "New Blood for Health and Growth," *DD*, November 1945.

4. Frederick W. Gill and Gilbert L. Bates, *Airline Competition*, pp. 111–13. This study was highly critical of the way in which the postwar expansion of routes by the CAB had greatly intensified competition without in all instances rendering greatly enhanced service to the public. It is noteworthy that Gill and Bates regarded service on the Chicago-to-Cincinnati route as "an example of significant improvement of airline schedules brought about by airline competition."

5. Ibid., pp. 288–311, including detailed tables on the numbers and frequency of flights, type of equipment used, number of stops, average speeds, and numbers of passengers carried on these runs. Again, Gill and Bates argued that the entry of Delta into the service between Chicago and Miami forced Eastern to improve the quality of its schedules and equipment and thus provided an example of enhancement through competition. On previous relationships between Delta and Eastern, see particularly telegrams from Rickenbacker to Woolman, October 7, 1940, and Woolman to Rickenbacker, February 27, 1941, Travis Oliver Papers, Monroe, Louisiana.

6. The material in this and the following paragraph is based mainly on two extremely helpful memoranda, by John F. Nycum, chief engineer, and T. P. Ball, who became chief pilot in 1947, written in April or May 1975. See particularly pp. 3–4 of the Nycum memorandum and pp. 5–6 of that by Ball.

7. In addition to the Nycum and Ball memoranda, see the article "Dolson Returns" and accompanying photograph (and caption) of a yet-unreconditioned DC-4 in *DD*, January 1946.

8. Interview of Ford by Lewis, August 28, 1975; "Dallas Enthusiastic," "Jackson Greets the '4," "Triumphant Arrival: Homing from California, Delta's Regal DC-4 Drew Admiring Crowds," and "Delta's First DC-4 Delights Atlanta Passengers and Sight-seers," all in *DD*, March 1946; AR 1946, inside front cover and pp. 4–5.

9. On the seating capacity of Delta's DC-4s, see not only AR 1946, p. 4, but also C. E. Woolman, "An Answer to Airline Critics," printed statement issued c. 1946, Woolman Scrapbook, pp. 35–36, section headed "Equipment." Specifications on the speed characteristics of the DC-4 vary slightly from source to source; this account follows those given in "DC-4 Statistics," *DD*, March 1946. For a representative comparison of the DC-3 and the DC-4, see Munson, *Airliners since 1946*, pp. 19, 45, 98–99, 122–23. According to Munson (p. 123), some DC-4s still in commercial service in 1970 were laid out to accommodate as many as eighty-six passengers.

10. On the early development of the Constellation and its performance just after the war, see particularly Gill and Bates, *Airline Competition*, pp. 62–63, 73–74, 78–84, 206–19, 263, 267, et passim; John B. Rae, *Climb to Greatness*, pp. 177–78; and Munson, *Airliners since 1946*, pp. 52, 128–29. On Eastern's involvement with the plane, see Rickenbacker, *Rickenbacker*, pp. 421–24; Gill and Bates, *Airline Competition*, pp. 62, 81; and "EAL Buys Five More New-Type Connies," *Aviation Week*, August 30, 1948, p. 38.

11. Woolman to Putnam, January 30, 1947, in GAF, 1946–47, folder marked "Chicago & Southern Air Lines, Inc."; Gill and Bates, *Airline Competition*, pp. 304–7; undated memorandum from James H. Cobb to Woolman, c. late 1947, in GAF, 1947–48, folder marked "James H. Cobb, Director of Public Relations."

12. Undated article from unidentified Atlanta newspaper, Woolman Scrapbook, p. 36. The visit could not have occurred later than April 1947, for Vice-President George Cushing, who died that month in a tragic crash at Columbus, Georgia, was among those on hand to greet the plane.

13. Ball memorandum, p. 8; Nycum memorandum, pp. 4–5; interview of T. P. Ball and Arthur Ford by Lewis, August 28, 1975; "Five Douglas DC-6's Purchased by Delta," *DD*, February 1948. In a subsequent cost comparison, which reflected the rising prices of both planes in the inflationary postwar period, a leading aviation periodical pointed out that the $900,000 price of the DC-6 represented an initial investment per passenger seat of $15,000, compared to figures of $1 million and

$16,667 respectively for the Constellation, based upon an average seating capacity of 60 for each plane. See "Cost Analysis," *Aviation Week*, January 2, 1950, p. 16. As previously indicated, the seating capacity of Constellations varied and could run as high as 81. Early DC-6s were designed to accommodate up to 68 passengers, and two later models, the DC-6B and the DC-6C, could hold up to 107. See Munson, *Airliners since 1946*, pp. 123–24, 128–29. Delta's early DC-6s were designed to accommodate 56 passengers in a roomy layout; see J. F. Nycum, "DC-6 Cabin Furnishings," *DD;* April 1948.

14. On the early history of the DC-6, see Munson, *Airliners since 1946*, pp. 123–24; for the date of the first Delta commercial flight, see AR 1949, p. 1. Detailed material on the early crashes of DC-6s, the modifications required, and the losses suffered by the airlines and manufacturer in consequence is available in various issues of *Aviation Week* for 1947 and 1948. The National pilot strike will be discussed in Chapter 9.

15. On the first flight of the "Flying D," see clippings from Atlanta *Journal* and Atlanta *Constitution*, October 4, 1948, Woolman Scrapbook, and various articles in *DD*, October 1948. On the new exterior markings, see "DC-6 Contest," *DD*, March 1948, and "DC-6 Contest Ends in Composite Design," *DD*, June 1948, with accompanying illustration. For monthly statistics on the revenue miles flown by the company's DC-3s, DC-4s, and DC-6s, see *DD*, March–September 1949. On the DC-6's impact on company profits, see AR 1949, p. 1.

16. J. F. Nycum, "The Douglas DC-6," *DD*, March 1948; Ball memorandum, pp. 10–11. On Delta's stipulation that the DC-6s be designed for three-engine ferry-flight operation, see also J. F. Nycum to Nat Paschall, vice-president for domestic sales, Douglas Aircraft Company, February 20, 1948, in GAF, 1949–50, folder marked "Planes—Douglas."

17. On the development of this issue, see particularly the following articles in *Aviation Week*: "Pilots Support Flight Engineers," October 20, 1947, p. 49; "Third Crewman: Flight Engineer," April 26, 1949, pp. 38, 41; "Use of Flight Engineers Protested," July 26, 1948, p. 38; and "CAB Insists on Flight Engineers," October 18, 1948, pp. 41–42.

18. Report by Charles H. Dolson, October 10, 1947, in GAF, 1947–48, folder marked "C. H. Dolson—Operations Manager"; "CAB Insists on Flight Engineers," pp. 41–42.

19. Ball memorandum, pp. 8–9; interview of T. P. Ball by Lewis, August 28, 1975. Along with four other carriers (American, Braniff, National, and Panagra), Delta received an extension from the CAB and was given until March 31 to complete its training and qualification program. Although Delta's insistence on pilot engineers only was unique in the industry at that time, some other carriers used a mixture of pilots and mechanics in their qualification programs; one of them was American Airlines, which ran classes at Ardmore, Oklahoma. See *Aviation Week*, December 13, 1948, pp. 49–50.

20. Nycum memorandum, p. 13.

21. On the prewar history of these planes, see Munson, *Airliners between the Wars*, pp. 161–62, 167–70.

22. The development of the Martin 2-0-2 is analyzed in detail in Charles E. Anderson, "The 'Martinliner,'" *American Aviation Historical Society Journal* 7 (1962): 120–25. See also Rae, *Climb to Greatness*, pp. 184–86 et passim; and Munson, *Air-*

liners since 1946, pp. 102–3. For an example of Martin's advertising claims for the plane, see its display advertisement entitled "The Case of Airline Z," *Aviation Week*, July 5, 1948, p. 5.

23. See correspondence in GAF, 1946–47, folders marked "The Glenn L. Martin Company (Model 2-0-2)" and "The Glenn L. Martin Co., Baltimore 3, Md.," including two unexecuted copies of contract submitted by Martin to Delta on September 10, 1946; Peyton M. Magruder of Martin to Woolman, June 6, 1946, GAF, 1946–47, folder marked "Planes Miscellaneous"; "Twenty Martin 2-0-2s to Join Delta's Rapidly Growing Fleet," *DD*, July 1946; Nycum, "The Martin 2-0-2," *DD*, January 1947; and Nycum, "Seats and Buffet of Martin 2-0-2," *DD*, February 1947.

24. Cushing to John E. Soenke, business manager, Glenn L. Martin Co., January 21, 1947, in GAF, 1946–47, folder marked "The Glenn L. Martin Co., Baltimore 3, Md."; Woolman to Putnam, January 30, 1947, in GAF, folder marked "Chicago & Southern Air Lines, Inc."; report of Walter Englund to Cushing, February 12, 1947, and of Dolson to Woolman, May 26, 1947, in GAF, folder marked "The Glenn L. Martin Company (Model 2-0-2)." Several letters in the Martin files show the concern of Martin officials about Delta's failure to sign the contract for the planes. For Woolman's reluctance to abrogate his verbal commitment and the arguments that finally persuaded him to do so, the authors have drawn especially upon an interview with R. W. Courts, July 11, 1975.

25. The experience of Northwest with the Martin 2-0-2 can be followed in detail in a series of articles that appeared in *Aviation Week* as this particular drama unfolded in the period 1948–51.

26. Interview with T. P. Ball, August 28, 1975; "Douglas Decides to Build DC-9," *Aviation Week*, November 17, 1947, p. 15, and "Douglas Hints End of DC-9 Project," *Aviation Week*, May 3, 1948, p. 15; Comparative Analysis of CV 240, DC-3, Modified DC-3, and Saab Scandia 90A-2 by C. R. Dutton in GAF, 1949–50, folder marked "Planes—Douglas." On the Martin 2-0-2A and 4-0-4, see particularly Munson, *Airliners since 1946*, pp. 102–3; on the Convair series beginning with the 240, Munson, pp. 103–5. On Eastern's involvement with the Martin 4-0-4, see Rickenbacker, *Rickenbacker*, p. 424.

27. On the visit of the Douglas staff and the Super DC-3 to Atlanta on September 11–12, 1949, see "Control Tower," *DD*, October 1949, and passenger list in GAF, 1949–50, folder marked "Planes—Douglas." In addition, see "Delta's Improved DC-3 Soon Ready for Service," *DD*, April 1950; "New Features on DC-3 Popular with Passengers," *DD*, August 1950; "Modernization Planned for Entire DC-3 Fleet," *DD*, December 1950; and "Have You Noticed My New Outfit? Tell Me What You Think of It," in GAF, 1949–50, folder marked "Planes—Douglas."

28. See typescript of presentation enclosed with letter of E. V. Moore to C. E. Woolman, August 22, 1946, in GAF, 1946–47, folder marked "Ernest V. Moore, Attorney, Washington."

29. For an extended discussion of the development of the feeder concept during this period, see John H. Frederick, *Commercial Air Transportation*, pp. 195–222.

30. For the text of the CAB decision, see *Economic Decisions of the Civil Aeronautics Board, June 1946 through March 1947*, 8: 863–925. For information about the new cities added to the Delta system, see particularly "Delta's Four New Cities," *DD*, July 1947 (the reference is to four rather than five cities because the facilities at Selma were not yet ready for the inauguration of service). For other material on the

background of the case and the eventual inauguration of Delta service to the cities involved, see "Status of Cases Filed before the Board," *DD*, September 1946; "S.E. Case Decided," *DD*, April 1947; "The New Routes," *DD*, July 1947; AR 1946, p. 8; and AR 1947, p. 5.

31. For the full text of this decision, see *Economic Decisions of the Civil Aeronautics Board, January to December 1948*, 9: 38–66. On earlier maneuvering, see especially "New York–Atlanta Route Recommended," *DD*, April 1947. On the eventual award of the Atlanta–New York route to Capital, see particularly "Capital Rings Bell on N.Y.–Atlanta Run," *Aviation Week*, February 12, 1951, pp. 42–43. On the lengths to which Delta went in seeking the New York City route and on the "Main Street" concept, see AR 1946, p. 11, and AR 1947, p. 8.

32. In addition to the relevant portions of the 1948 decision, see "New Orleans–Meridian Cut-off Awarded Delta; N.Y. is Denied," *DD*, February 1948, and Circular A-10 of Schwamm and Company, Investment Securities, New York, N.Y., dated February 2, 1948, in GAF, 1947–48, folder marked "Delta Air Lines, Inc."

33. An informative running account of the infighting that took place in Washington as Delta pressed its new route applications before the CAB is provided in a series of articles published in the *Delta Digest* in 1950 by one of the company's attorneys, D. Franklin Kell, under the title "Keeping Tab on CAB." On new cities added to Delta's route structure and other rulings conferring cost-cutting or other advantages on Delta during this period, see "Richmond and Kokomo Added to Delta's Routes," *DD*, October 1947; "Gregg County Airport to Become Delta Stop," *DD*, January 1948; "Enthusiastic Crowd Sees Inaugural Flight," *DD*, March 1948; *CAB Reports*, 8: 382–83, 726–804 and 11: 18–23. For additional material on reverses suffered in attempts to expand Delta service in the Kansas City, Memphis, and Florida cases, see "Kansas City Decision Unfavorable to Delta," *DD*, August 1948, and *CAB Reports*, 11: 943–78. The unsatisfactory returns from the Kokomo-to-Richmond service and impending termination of this arrangement are discussed in Kell, "Keeping Tab on CAB," *DD*, September 1950.

34. For a particularly good discussion of the background of postwar interchange agreements in the airline industry, see Selig Altschul, "Equipment Interchange Analyzed," *Aviation Week*, August 16, 1948, p. 45.

35. *Economic Decisions of the Civil Aeronautics Board, July 1944 to May 1946*, 6: 429–70; interoffice memorandum from Kell to Woolman on negotiations between Delta and TWA, February 7, 1947, GAF, 1946–47, folder marked "D. Franklin Kell, Attorney, Atlanta"; "Delta to Interchange Equipment with TWA," *DD*, January 1948; AR 1948, p. 4.

36. In addition to Altschul, "Equipment Interchange Analyzed," p. 45, see also "Will CAB Alter Interchange Views?" in *Aviation Week*, July 17, 1950, p. 21, and "Airlines Stage California 'Gold Rush,'" *Aviation Week*, October 16, 1950, pp. 46–47.

37. Undated memorandum by Kell in GAF, 1946–47, folder marked "D. Franklin Kell"; certified copy of letter from C. R. Smith, chairman of the board, American Airlines, to Woolman, October 4, 1948, GAF, 1948–49, folder marked "American Airlines, Inc."; AR 1949, p. 6.

38. Articles entitled "Keeping Tab on CAB" by Kell in *DD*, February, April, June, and July 1949; "Delta–American Interchange Is Approved; West Coast Service Begins September 25," *DD*, September 1949; "AA–Delta Interchange Gets Temporary

OK," *Aviation Week*, September 12, 1949, p. 18; "San Diego–Dixie Air Link to Start," San Diego *Tribune-Sun*, September 20, 1949, in Woolman Scrapbook; "Smith, Woolman Review Their Air Lines' Growth," Atlanta *Constitution*, September 24, 1949, in Woolman Scrapbook; and clipping from Miami *Herald*, undated but late September 1949, in Woolman Scrapbook.

39. Clippings from Miami *Herald*, undated [late September 1949], and Atlanta *Journal*, September 26, 1949, Woolman Scrapbook.

CHAPTER 8 · *Stormy Weather and Brightening Horizons*

1. Statistics on passenger miles flown by American domestic trunk lines from 1945 through 1950 are available in *Aviation Week*, February 26, 1951, p. 109. For data on the revenue passenger miles of service provided by air, Pullman, and rail coach from 1940 through 1950, see *Aviation Week*, April 16, 1951, p. 65. The financial plight of the airlines is discussed in great detail in various issues of *Aviation Week* throughout this period. For general assessments of the postwar situation, see also *Aircraft Year Book for 1948* and "What's Wrong with the Airlines," *Fortune*, August 1946, pp. 73–79, 190–92, 195–96, 198–99, 201. Woolman responded angrily to an advance copy of the *Fortune* article, declaring in a telegram to the publishers of the magazine on July 11, 1946, that it "in nowise reflects a constructive spirit nor takes into consideration the unceasing efforts on the part of the airlines to overcome the operating problems with which they are presently confronted." A subsequent letter from Woolman to William D. Geer, the publisher of *Fortune*, on August 6, 1946, was more moderate in tone. GAF, 1946–47, folder marked "Books and Magazines."

2. AR 1946, pp. 2–3, 12–14; AR 1947, pp. 1, 3, 6–7, 10–11; AR 1948, pp. 1–2, 5, 7–8, 10–12. For a detailed analysis of Delta's problems and prospects early in this period, see also mimeographed statement issued by Securities Research Department, Courts and Company, Atlanta, Georgia, May 20, 1946, in GAF, 1946–47, folder marked "Courts & Co."

3. Woolman to Coad, December 9, 1946, and March 22, 1947, GAF, 1946–47, folder marked "B. R. Coad"; C. E. Faulk to Woolman, August 12, 1947, and September 15, 1947, GAF, folder marked "C. E. Faulk, Chairman of the Board." On Faulk's eye operation, see also telegram from Robert Faulk to Woolman, undated but sometime between September 5 and 10, 1947, and return telegram from Catherine FitzGerald to Robert Faulk, September 10, 1947, GAF, folder marked "C. E. Faulk, Chairman of the Board."

4. Woolman to C. E. Faulk, August 14, 1947, GAF, folder marked "C. E. Faulk, Chairman of the Board"; memorandum of Winship Nunnally to Woolman, May 29, 1948, GAF, 1947–48, folder marked "Winship Nunnally, Director." The beginnings of "air coach" service and Delta's part in this industry-wide movement will be discussed later in this chapter.

5. On the development of air express and air freight generally, see G. Lloyd Wilson and Leslie A. Bryan, *Air Transportation*, pp. 303–44, and, for the very early period, Roger E. Bilstein, "Technology and Commerce: Aviation in the Conduct of American Business, 1918–1929," *Technology and Culture* 10 (1969): 392–411. On postwar competition between the trunk lines and the new all-cargo lines, four of which had managed by 1949 to receive formal CAB certification over the opposition of the pas-

senger carriers, see especially "CAB Sets Up Airfreight Route Pattern," *Aviation Week*, May 9, 1949, pp. 12–14.

6. See particularly bulletin issued by James H. Cobb, director of public relations and advertising, Delta Air Lines, July 15, 1946, in GAF, 1946–47, folder marked "Bulletins—Air Cargo"; AR 1948, p. 6; AR 1949, pp. 4–5; and various articles in *DD*, 1946–50. The advertisement featuring the limerick was reprinted on the back cover of the *Delta Digest* for August 1950.

7. See "Pep Talk to Traffic," *DD*, March 1946; "Two-Day General Sales Conference in Atlanta Summons Intensified System-Wide Sales Effort," *DD*, November–December 1947; "First Sales Contest Ends as Second Period Begins," *DD*, June 1948; "Passenger of the Month Flies Western Division," *DD*, June 1948; "Second Sales Contest Rules Are Announced," *DD*, July 1948. For illustrations and captions on recognition of Anna Grace Green as Delta's two-millionth passenger, see *DD*, May 1948; "Summer Travel Tours Operated by Delta," *DD*, April 1948; "Traffic Meeting Stresses Sales Consciousness," *DD*, November 1948. For statistics on the number of passengers carried by Delta each year in the postwar period, see Truman Haygood, supervisor of statistics, Delta Air Lines, "Statistical Data by Months for the Year 1958 and for Period 1934–1958," memorandum of January 15, 1959, Delta Records Collection, DGO.

8. Docket no. 2603, CAB, brief on behalf of the carriers party to the agreements, February 15, 1947, pp. 3–6; "Report to the President by the Emergency Board," July 8, 1946, GAF, Box PW-IV. President Truman was unsuccessful in heading off the TWA strike, the first nationwide walkout in the industry; see George E. Hopkins, *The Airline Pilots*, p. 192.

9. David L. Behncke, president, ALPA, to Cushing, July 2, 1946; C. A. Hodgins, ANC, to Behncke, July 30, 1946, GAF, 1946–47, folder marked "Airline Negotiating Committee."

10. Hodgins to Behncke, October 8, 1946, and memorandum no. 4, ANC, February 25, 1947, in GAF, 1946–47, folder marked "Airline Negotiating Committee"; "Proposed Agreement between Delta Air Lines, Inc. and the Pilots in the Employ of Delta Air Lines, Inc.," GAF, folder marked "Airline Negotiating Committee, #3."

11. Memorandum, Woolman to Cushing and Dolson, September 20, 1946, and Woolman to Hodgins, July 9, 1947, GAF, 1947–48, folder marked "Airlines Negotiating Conference, #1"; Behncke to Cushing, July 2, 1946, and contract with ALPA, October 1, 1947, GAF, folder marked "Airline Pilots Association, Int'l."

12. International Association of Machinists to Woolman, February 10, 1947, and memorandum no. 11, ANC, March 25, 1947, in GAF, 1946–47, folder marked "Airline Negotiating Committee, #4"; memorandum of Robert H. Wharton accompanying his letter to R. S. Maurer, November 16, 1976. Information on the strike comes from various newspaper clippings from the Atlanta dailies, some unheaded, for May and June 1947, in Woolman Scrapbook. See, for example, Atlanta *Journal* and *Constitution* for May 9, 1947, and the *Constitution* for June 11, 1947.

13. Memorandum, Dolson to Woolman, September 5, 1947, GAF, 1947–48, folder marked "Airline Mechanics Association, Intern'l"; Wharton memorandum; broadsides against affiliation with a union issued by employees in Atlanta, Brunswick, Columbia, Chattanooga, and Jacksonville; and exchange of correspondence between Paul Chipman and Woolman, May 5 and 9, 1949, all in GAF, 1948–49, folder marked "Airline Mechanics Association, Intern'l."

14. Numerous letters and documents pertaining to this crash, including the Bolander correspondence already referred to and the official C A B *Accident Report Adopted July 31, 1947, Released August 1, 1947*, are contained in MHR-DGO, Box A-20, folder marked "Accident—Columbus, Georgia, April 22, 1947." See also "Bolander Joins Delta," *DD*, March 1946; interview of T. P. Ball by Lewis, August 28, 1975; Atlanta *Journal*, April 22, 1947; Atlanta *Constitution*, April 23, 1947.

15. Two large collections of condolence messages and correspondence relating to funeral arrangements after the Columbus accident are in GAF, 1946–47, folders marked "Accident—Columbus." For correspondence with Doolittle and Faulk, see Doolittle to Woolman, April 24, 1947, and Woolman to Doolittle, June 2, 1947, in GAF, 1946–47, unmarked folder, Box PW-IV; Faulk to Woolman, April 29, 1947, and Woolman to Faulk, April 30, 1947, GAF, 1946–47, folder marked "C. E. Faulk, Chairman of the Board." See also memorandum of James H. Cobb to all Atlanta personnel, April 22, 1947, GAF, Box A-Am; "Who Runs Delta?" *DD*, April 1946; "Charles H. Dolson Made Vice President," *DD*, November–December 1947; special executive bulletin, April 30, 1947, in GAF, 1946–47, folder marked "Bulletins—Administrative."

16. C A B *Accident Report . . . Released August 1, 1947*, passim; "Private Pilot Blamed for Delta Accident," *Aviation Week*, August 18, 1947, p. 50; AR 1947, p. 7.

17. Extensive documentation pertaining to this crash, including the C A B *Accident Investigation Report SA-167, File No. 1-0023, Adopted June 13, 1949, Released June 14, 1949*, can be found in MHR-DGO, Box A-20, folders marked "Flight 705, March 10, 1948, Chicago." For correspondence with Delta passengers and other inquirers about the accident, see GAF, 1947–48, folder marked "Accident DC-4 (NC37478, Serial #18390), Flight 705, 3/10/'48." See also "Airliner Crashes in Chicago, Killing Twelve of the Thirteen Aboard," New York *Times*, March 11, 1948, I, p. 40; "Probes Under Way in DC-4 Accidents," *Aviation Week*, March 22, 1948, p. 15.

18. See especially C A B *Accident Investigation Report SA-167 . . . Released June 14, 1949* and other documents in MHR-DGO, Box A-20, folder marked "Flight 705, March 10, 1948, Chicago." Chief Pilot Ball later speculated, after an investigation on a near-accident that had occurred to a Capital DC-4, that the Chicago crash might have been attributable to a tape that went around the edge of the horizontal stabilizer and elevators; it could have worked loose and acted as a trim tab. On the flight of the Capital DC-4 the tape came loose on the leading edge, increasing drag and forcing the elevator down, thus inducing a dive from which the Capital pilots were able to recover. Ball theorized that in the Delta crash the tape might have come loose on the bottom edge, raising the elevator and causing a steep angle of attack. Ball interview, August 28, 1975.

19. On safety awards won by Delta in 1946 and 1947, see the Annual Report for each of these years, which also contains material on the company's new facilities. For detailed correspondence and photographs recording the progress of the new facilities and the cost increases with which the company struggled, see GAF, 1946–47, files marked "The Austin Company." Delta's highly conservative executive salary policies during 1946–47, compared with those of other firms in the industry, can be seen in "Top Airline Salaries Show Increase in 1947," *Aviation Week*, April 19, 1948, p. 53. On cost increases and inventory-control efforts in 1947–48, see "Delta Supply Costs Up 25 Percent," *Aviation Week*, August 30, 1948, pp. 40–41.

20. AR 1947, pp. 4–5; Atlanta *Journal*, December 22, 1946. There is a discrepancy

between these two sources as to the precise number of institutions involved in this arrangement; we have followed the Annual Report. On the tendency of many trunk lines to resort to this method of financing, see Selig Altschul, "Bank Credits Still Aid Airlines," *Aviation Week*, August 30, 1948, p. 33. On the background of the loan obtained by Delta, see also *Minutes*, September 3, 1946, and *Minutes, Annual Meeting*, December 16, 1946.

21. On the background and execution of this stock issue, see *Minutes*, September 3, 1946; November 1, 1946; April 7, 1947; May 15, 1947; and June 11, 1947; William Hart Sibley of Alston, Foster, Sibley and Miller, Attorneys, to Woolman, May 8, 1947; R. W. Courts to Woolman, May 1 and May 13, 1947, in GAF, 1946–47, folders labeled "Alston, Foster, Sibley & Miller, Attorneys-at-Law" and "Courts & Co." For documentation on the correspondence between representatives of Delta and the SEC, see E. W. Moise of Moise, Post and Gardner, Attorneys, to Philadelphia office of Securities and Exchange Commission, April 7, 1947, and Edward H. Cashion, chief counsel, SEC, Philadelphia, to E. W. Moise, April 10, 1947, in GAF, 1946–47, folder labeled "Courts & Co." At the annual meeting on December 16, 1946, the stockholders voted to increase the authorized capital stock of the company from 500,000 to 1,000,000 shares; see *Minutes, Annual Meeting*, December 16, 1946, and photostatic copies and certificate relating to the amendment of the company's charter dated January 4 and January 21, 1947, bound with these minutes.

22. See *Minutes*, November 1, 1946, June 11, 1947, October 24, 1947, June 28, 1948; *Minutes, Annual Meeting*, December 16, 1946, and December 15, 1947; "Delta Elects Four New Directors," *DD*, July 1947; "Atlanta Leader Elected to Board of Directors," *DD*, July 1948. Reynolds had purchased 60,600 of the 99,192 shares authorized in the stock issue of 1944–45 and had subscribed another 25,000 in the issue of 1947, which made him by far the company's largest shareholder. Freeman subscribed 7,000 shares in the 1947 issue and Nunnally 10,000; various members of the Gerry family took a total of 9,000 shares. See *Minutes*, June 11, 1947.

23. AR 1948, pp. 6–7; AR 1949, p. 3; "Outlook Bright for Delta, Braniff," *Aviation Week*, September 27, 1948, pp. 40–41.

24. On the opening of the Atlanta terminal and remarks by Woolman and Rickenbacker, see clippings from Atlanta *Constitution*, May 8, 1948, and Atlanta *Journal*, May 8, 1948, in Woolman Scrapbook, as well as coverage in *DD*, June 1948. On the enhanced safety record of the airlines in 1949 and 1950, see especially "Scheduled Airlines Top Safety Record," *Aviation Week*, January 17, 1949, p. 54, and "1949 Record," *Aviation Week*, January 9, 1950, p. 44. The fatality rate per 100 million passenger miles flown by the domestic trunk lines went down from 2.7 in 1947 to 1.3 in 1948 and 1.0 in 1949; the figures for the latter two years set records for safety since the beginning of the annual compilations starting in 1930.

25. On the development of sky-coach service, see particularly the following articles in *Aviation Week*; "Skycoach Builds Traffic and Strife," April 25, 1949, pp. 46–47; "Air Coach Started on Southern Routes," October 3, 1949, p. 43; "Scheduled Lines Take Coach Leadership," November 7, 1949, pp. 12–14; and "Scheduled Lines Take Coach Lead," June 26, 1950, pp. 43–44. For representative articles among many that could be cited in the *Delta Digest* regarding constant attention to improvement of facilities and services during this period, see "Miami Invites Two Hundred to View Offices at Formal Opening of New Bldg.," April 1948; "Charleston Establishes Turn-Around Record," July 1948; "Atlanta Reservations Moves Downtown; Central Con-

trol Office Begins Operation," October 1948; and "Construction Work Heavy since First of Year," September 1950. On the background of the radio landing systems mentioned here, see "Major Radio Changes" and "Radio Efficiency," *DD*, September 1945.

26. The improving revenues and earnings of the airlines in 1949 and 1950 can be traced in various articles in *Aviation Week* from 1949 through 1952.

27. See AR 1949 and AR 1950, passim.

28. "Twentieth Anniversary Celebrated Quietly June 1," *DD*, June 1949: "Control Tower," *DD*, November 1949.

29. For Rickenbacker's own account of his proposal, made to Senator Edwin C. Johnson, chairman of the Senate commerce committee in May 1949, see *Rickenbacker*, pp. 430–31; see also Woolman to Hunter, May 27, 1949, in GAF, 1948–49, folder marked "Airlines—Other." The same folder contains other letters and documents pertaining to this episode; see also the telegram dealing with Rickenbacker's proposal sent by Wayne W. Parrish to Woolman in GAF, 1948–49, folder marked "American Aviation Publications."

30. "Twenty-fifth Anniversary," *DD*, May 1950, and collection of messages in Woolman Scrapbook, p. 59. The letters specifically quoted here are from Sidney A. Stewart and Frank T. Davis to Woolman, both dated May 3, 1950.

CHAPTER 9 · *Looking for a Partner*

1. For these and other relevant statistics, see "A Decade of Growth," AR 1952, pp. 14–15.

2. "Chairman of the Board Clarence E. Faulk Dies," *DD*, September–October 1951; "In Memory," *DD*, January 1952; "Obituary: L. B. Judd," *American Aviation*, January 7, 1952, p. 8; "Cole, Saxon Promoted in Accounting Department," *DD*, February 1952.

3. "Control Tower," *DD*, July 1951; AR 1952, p. 7; questionnaire, "Are You Interested?" in *DD*, August 1952; "Camp Cushing Dues Set; Lease Expected Shortly," *DD*, December 1952.

4. On the acquisition of the seventh DC-6 and other matters pertaining to Delta aircraft at the time, see AR 1951, pp. 7–8; on the development of the Lockheed L-1049, see Munson, *Airliners since 1946*, pp. 53, 129–31.

5. Munson, pp. 24, 103–5; articles on Convair 340 in *DD*, March 1951, December 1951, and January 1952; AR 1951, p. 7.

6. Ball memorandum; AR 1953, p. 3. The DC-4s were sold in October 1952, in order to take advantage of prevailing prices, and then temporarily leased back. It was feared that the market might be saturated with government surplus Skymasters if the company delayed the sale until the new CV-340s had actually arrived, particularly if the Korean conflict ended in the meantime. See *DD*, November 1952.

7. AR 1952, p. 5; AR 1953, p. 3; Ball memorandum; Munson, pp. 47, 124–27; "Delta's New DC-7 Planes to Seat Sixty-Nine Passengers," *DD*, May 1952.

8. AR 1951, p. 8; AR 1952, p. 4; "What to Do If the A-Bomb Should Hit Your Home Town," supplement to *DD*, May 1951; "Control Tower," *DD*, August 1950; articles and pictures in *DD*, September 1950, November 1950, January 1951, February 1951, April 1951, June 1951, September–October 1951, November 1951, January 1952, March 1952, May 1952, and June 1952.

9. Thomas K. Finletter et al., *Survival in the Air Age: A Report by the President's Air Policy Commission*, reprinted in *The Aircraft Year Book for 1948*, p. 69; Charles Adams, "Who's to Blame in Airline Crisis," *Aviation Week*, November 8, 1948, p. 45, quoting from O'Connell's speech. See also Selig Altschul, "Airline Merger Signs Increase," *Aviation Week*, August 23, 1948, p. 30.

10. GAF, 1948–49, folder marked "Delta–National Merger."

11. *Minutes*, May 17, 1948; Davies, *Airlines of the United States since 1914*, pp. 197, 290; Frederick, *Commercial Air Transportation*, pp. 148–50; E. M. Johnson, "An Analysis of the Results of a Delta–National Merger," GAF, 1948–49, folder marked "Delta–National Merger."

12. Unsigned memorandum analyzing desirability of Delta–National merger, GAF, 1948–49, folder marked "Delta–National Merger"; "NAL-ALPA Heading Toward Showdown," *Aviation Week*, March 15, 1948, pp. 11–12.

13. Johnson, "Analysis of the Results of a Delta–National Merger"; "NAL–Delta Merger to Involve PCA?" *Aviation Week*, July 5, 1948, pp. 11–12.

14. This much-condensed discussion is based on a mass of scattered documentation in Delta company files and periodicals. On the merger discussions, see correspondence among Woolman, Baker, and other officials of Delta and National in GAF, 1947–50: folders marked "Confidential," "Delta–National Merger," "Delta Air Lines, Inc.," "Management Corporation—Colonial & National Airlines," "National Airlines, Inc.," and "Airlines—Other." On the tangled history of the National pilots' strike, see various articles in *Aviation Week* for 1948 and 1949. On the course of the National Dismemberment Case, see various articles under the title "Keeping Tab on CAB" by D. Franklin Kell in *DD*, 1949 and 1950.

15. Edward H. Gerry to Woolman, June 3, 1948, GAF, 1948–49, folder marked "Directors"; "NAL–Delta Merger Still Hanging Fire," *Aviation Week*, August 2, 1948, p. 43.

16. Correspondence among Woolman, Baker, and various officials of Charles A. Rheinstrom, Inc., GAF, 1948–49, folder marked "Charles A. Rheinstrom, Inc. (Consultants)"; Woolman to George E. Gardner, January 20, 1949, GAF, 1948–49, folder marked "Airlines—Other"; AR 1949, p. 7.

17. See Kell, "Keeping Tab on CAB," *DD*, 1949 and 1950; "NAL Future Again before Board," *Aviation Week*, March 20, 1950, pp. 48–50; "NAL Moves to Drop Pan Am Stock Pact," *Aviation Week*, January 8, 1951, p. 51. On Delta's resistance to National's efforts to take part in interchange service to the west, see correspondence among Woolman, Baker, and C. R. Smith in GAF, 1949–50, folder marked "National Airlines, Inc."

18. The account of early Northeast Airlines history contained in this and the ensuing paragraphs is based largely on Robert W. Mudge, *Adventures of a Yellowbird*, pp. 15–225. See also *A Pictorial History of Northeast Airlines, 1933–1972*, passim.

19. Ernest K. Gann, *Fate Is the Hunter*, pp. 175, 200, 230, et passim.

20. "National–Northeast Merger Talk," *Aviation Week*, June 5, 1950, p. 53. On Gardner's background, see also "Northeast Airlines Founded in 1931; President Gardner Veteran Airline Official," *DD*, October 1950.

21. There is a sheaf of telegrams and letters documenting the exchanges of visits between officials of Delta and Northeast during the summer of 1950 (but largely silent about the issues discussed) in GAF, 1950–51, folder marked "Northeast Airlines, Inc." For particulars of the financial status of each line and other details on the stakes involved in the merger, see "Proposed Merger of Delta and Northeast," *In-*

vestor's Reader, December 6, 1950, p. 15, copy in GAF, 1951–52, folder marked "Merger—(Northeast–Delta Airlines)"; "NEA–Delta Merger Proposed," *Aviation Week,* October 9, 1950, p. 52; and Selig Altschul, "Will CAB Let Delta, NEA Merge?" *Aviation Week,* October 16, 1950, p. 17.

22. For a copy of the merger agreement submitted by Woolman to Gardner on September 19, 1950, see GAF, 1950–51, folder marked "Delta Air Lines." A copy of the publicity release issued on September 28, 1950, is included in GAF, 1950–51, folder marked "Northeast Airlines, Inc."; the same folder contains a copy of the *Northeast Newsletter* on November 1, 1950, with a description of the arrival in Boston of the Delta DC-6 bearing the University of Georgia football team. On the approval of the merger agreement by Delta's board of directors, see *Minutes,* September 19, 1950. For enthusiastic in-house comment see particularly the column entitled "Control Tower" in *DD,* October 1950, and the illustrations and caption pertaining to a visit to Atlanta by Northeast officials, *DD,* November 1950.

23. Kell, "Keeping Tab on CAB," *DD,* May 1952; Delta–Northeast merger agreement, GAF, 1950–51, folder marked "Delta Air Lines"; "Delta Seeks N.Y. Route through North Carolina" and Kell, "Keeping Tab on CAB," *DD,* June 1950.

24. See particularly letters of L. Welch Pogue to Woolman, September 15 and November 14, 1951, in GAF, 1951–52, folder marked "L. Welch Pogue." This folder also contains a copy of the CAB order issued after the first prehearing conference in November and a letter from Edward T. Stodola, CAB hearing examiner, announcing a further prehearing conference on November 27, 1951. For a further discussion of these matters, indicating how slowly they were progressing, see Kell, "Keeping Tab on CAB," *DD,* November 1951.

25. On the progress made by Capital during these years, see particularly various articles in *Aviation Week* for 1949 and 1950. On the attempted Capital–Northwest merger and Delta's reaction to it, see especially newspaper clippings and correspondence between Woolman and L. Welch Pogue in GAF, 1951–52, folders marked "L. Welch Pogue" and "Airlines—Other," as well as Kell, "Keeping Tab on CAB," *DD,* March 1952.

26. On the history and development of Colonial, see Davies, *Airlines of the United States,* pp. 342–43; Frederick, *Commercial Air Transportation,* pp. 140–42; and "Aviation: Colonial's Sig Janas," *Investor's Reader,* July 19, 1950, pp. 16–19. For a copy of CAB Order E-5449, June 18, 1951, as well as a CAB statement of July 3, 1951, both rehearsing the details of what Delta director Edward Gerry appropriately called "the Janas mess," see GAF, 1951–52, folder marked "L. Welch Pogue." On the attempt by the new Colonial leadership to negotiate a merger with National and the moves after this effort collapsed, see Annual Report of Colonial Airlines for 1951 and correspondence between Woolman and B. T. Dykes, president of Colonial Airlines, in GAF, 1951–52, folder marked "Airlines—Other."

27. For a mass of correspondence between Woolman and various advisers relating to this strategy, see GAF, 1951–52, folders marked "Directors—General," "L. Welch Pogue," "L. Welch Pogue . . . No. 2," "Merger—(Northeast–Delta Airlines)," "Northeast Airlines, Inc.," and "Airlines—Other." For estimates of the enhanced volume of business that would have resulted from a combination of Delta, Colonial, and Northeast, see GAF, 1950–51, folder marked "Delta Air Lines," and 1951–52, folder marked "Mergers—Delta–Colonial & Northeast Proposals."

28. For a summary of negotiations between Delta and Northeast, on one hand, and Capital and Northwest, on the other, during 1951, see draft of letter dated March

5, 1952, addressed to Northwest Airlines, Inc., and Capital Airlines, Inc., in GAF 1951–52, folder marked "Mergers—General." On the considerations affecting Capital's policies at that time, see particularly clipping from unidentified newspaper regarding Capital's problems in GAF, 1951–52, folder marked "Airlines—Other."

29. *Minutes*, September 18, 1951; telegrams between Woolman and Carmichael, early February 1952, GAF, 1951–52, folder marked "Capital Airlines, Inc."

30. This is based upon a mass of correspondence in GAF, 1951–52, pertaining to Delta's protracted efforts to purchase routes 51 and 55 from Capital. See particularly E. V. Moore to Woolman, October 3, 1951, folder marked "Ernest V. Moore—Attorney"; George Gardner to L. Welch Pogue, February 25, 1952, folder marked "Mergers (Proposed) DAL–Capital"; Pogue to Woolman, February 28, 1952, and accompanying draft of letter to be submitted to Capital and Northwest, folder marked "L. Welch Pogue"; typewritten document of March 3, 1952, "Possible Provision in Letter of Offer to Capital–Northwest," folder marked "Capital Airlines, Inc."; draft of letter of March 5, 1952, to Northwest Airlines, Inc., and Capital Airlines, Inc., folder marked "Mergers—General"; letter to Capital Airlines, Inc., and Northwest Airlines, Inc., March 6, 1952, folder marked "Merger—(Northeast–Delta Airlines)"; sheaf of telegrams to Delta directors, March 6, 1952, folder marked "Directors—General"; letters from Carmichael to Woolman, March 13 and 26, 1952, and from Woolman to Carmichael, March 18, 1952, folder marked "Capital Airlines"; and letters from Gardner to Woolman, April 28, 1952, Gardner to Irimescu, April 24, 1952, and Woolman to Pogue, March 27, 1952, folder marked "Northeast Airlines, Inc."

31. "Delta Requests CAB to Consolidate Hearing," *DD*, April 1952; memorandum from Kell to Woolman, April 8, 1952, GAF, 1951–52, folder marked "D. F. Kell, Attorney"; "Northeast, Delta Merger Seeks Link," clipping from unidentified newspaper, March 11, 1952, Woolman Scrapbook; Kell, "Keeping Tab on CAB," *DD*, June 1952; Pogue to Woolman, May 10 and May 13, 1952, in GAF, 1951–52, folder marked "L. Welch Pogue . . . No. 2."

32. Memorandum from E. M. Johnson to Woolman, May 23, 1952, in GAF, 1951–52, folder marked "Mergers (Proposals) DAL–Capital."

33. On the fortunes of Colonial and Capital in this period, see Davies, *Airlines of the United States*, pp. 342–43, 497–500. As late as the summer of 1953 Delta was still hoping that Capital might negotiate a successful merger with another carrier, such as Braniff, and sell its southern routes to Delta in the process, but this hope was as barren as previous ones. See GAF, 1953–54, folder marked "E. M. Johnson, Director, Planning & Research."

CHAPTER 10 · *The Early Years of Chicago and Southern*

1. Putnam, *High Journey*, pp. 5, 7–21, 32–140, 143.

2. Ibid., pp. 143–44, 149–59.

3. "Flight Equipment Changes and Other Historical Data," chronology of events in the histories of C&S and Delta, n.d., MHR-DGO; "Chicago and Southern Air Lines" (manuscript, dated March 25, 1935), p. 1, Erma Murray Files, DGO (hereafter cited as MF-DGO), "Through the Years," *Chicago and Southern Sky Steps* (hereafter referred to as *Sky Steps*), July 1943; Putnam, *High Journey*, pp. 159–61.

4. "Chicago and Southern Airlines," p. 1; Putnam, *High Journey*, pp. 161–62.

5. "Woman of the Month . . . Erma Murray," *Sky Steps*, October 1943; Putnam,

High Journey, p. 191; historical memorandum by William Fry, February 24, 1976; historical memorandum by L. D. Anderson, March 1, 1976; George Herrick, "Chicago and Southern History," *Air Transport* 4 (May 1946): 22; "Chicago and Southern Air Lines, Inc., Historical Chart," n.d., MF-DGO.

6. Putnam, *High Journey*, pp. 164, 172.

7. Ibid., pp. 165–67; "Chicago and Southern Air Lines," p. 1.

8. Putnam, *High Journey*, pp. 186–87; U.S. Post Office Department advertisement, March 30, 1934, MF-DGO.

9. U.S. Post Office Department advertisement, March 30, 1934; Putnam, *High Journey*, pp. 188–90; Pacific Seaboard bid, April 10, 1934, and contract for route 8, signed May 14, 1934, MF-DGO.

10. Putnam, *High Journey*, pp. 152–53, 189. Putnam credited Lord Tweedsmuir's *Pilgrim's Way* with expressing most clearly the idea that chances had shrunk for youth and that the world must provide more opportunities for its young people or all would be lost.

11. Historical memoranda by Richard S. Maurer, October 15 and 22, 1975; Herrick, "Chicago and Southern History," p. 22; Memphis *Commercial Appeal*, May 28, 1934.

12. Putnam, *High Journey*, pp. 197–99.

13. Fry memorandum, February 24, 1976; Putnam, *High Journey*, pp. 198–203.

14. Putnam, *High Journey*, pp. 204–5; analysis of Pacific Seaboard expenses and revenue for period to December 31, 1933, filed marked "Financial Statements, 1933"; analyses for January through May 1934, file marked "Financial Statements, Coast Route—1934"; analysis for period July 1 through December 1934, and monthly analyses for June through December 1934, file marked "Financial Statements, Route 8, 1934," all three files in MHR-DGO.

15. Monthly analysis of finances and operations for February 1934, file marked "Financial Statement, 1933"; monthly analysis of finances and operations for December 1934, file marked "Financial Statement, Route 8, 1934," MHR-DGO.

16. The Air Mail Act of 1934 provided for the lowering of a rate upon the ICC's investigation, but only by implication did it even hint at the possibility of raising a rate; Putnam, *High Journey*, p. 205.

17. Putnam, *High Journey*, pp. 206–12.

18. "Flight Equipment and Other Historical Data," MHR-DGO; Putnam, *High Journey*, pp. 213–15; exhibit A accompanying Pacific Seaboard affidavit, August 9, 1934; exhibit A accompanying C&S affidavit, May 20, 1935 (both documents involved in the airline's acceptance of the extensions of its mail contract in 1934 and 1935), n.d., MF-DGO; *C&S Record of Officers since December 30, 1935*, MF-DGO; "Five Year Honor Roll," *Sky Steps*, February 1943.

19. Monthly analysis of finances and operations, January through June 1935, file marked "Financial Statements, January 1–June 30, 1935," and same for July through December 1935, file marked "Financial Statements, July 1–December 31, 1935," both in MHR-DGO; exhibit B accompanying C&S affidavit, May 20, 1935; analysis of finances and operations, December 1935, file marked "Financial Statements, July 1–December 31, 1935," MHR-DGO.

20. Putnam, *High Journey*, pp. 216–24; C&S "History of Air Mail Rates," n.d., MF-DGO. According to the latter source, by an ICC order of February 11, 1935, the mail rates of airlines progressively decreased by one mill with each 1 percent increase in total mileage and increased one mill on each 1 percent decrease in total miles flown.

21. "Chicago and Southern Air Lines," p. 5; monthly analysis of finances and operations for July 1935, file marked "Financial Statements, July 1–December 31, 1935," MHR-DGO; Putnam, *High Journey*, p. 269.

22. *Air Commerce Bulletin* 7 (October 15, 1935): 93.

23. Putnam, *High Journey*, pp. 269–70; undated statement, "Options on Common Stock," folder HCS-SO; copy of charter of December 30, 1935; C&S stock prospectus, February 18, 1936, pp. 3, 6; manuscript, "Chicago and Southern Air Lines, Inc., Memphis, Tennessee, *History*," n.d., all four documents in MF-DGO.

24. "Options on Common Stock," folder HCS-SO, MF-DGO.

25. Stock prospectus, February 18, 1936, pp. 2–6; charter of December 30, 1935, pt. 4, MF-DGO; Putnam, *High Journey*, p. 271. Holders of convertible-preference stock could convert it into common stock at a certain exchange ratio. One disadvantage of holding convertible-preference stock was that it could be redeemed by the company under certain conditions, whereas common stock could not.

26. Interview of Putnam by Newton, January 22, 1976.

27. Stock prospectus, February 18, 1936, p. 5; *Record of Officers since December 30, 1935*, MF-DGO; "The Spirit of St. Louis," *Sky Steps*, November 1943.

28. Putnam, *High Journey*, pp. 272–73; monthly analysis of finances and operations, January to June 1936, file marked "Financial Statements, January 1–June 30, 1936," and July to December 1936, file marked "Financial Statements, July 1–December 31, 1936," both in MHR-DGO.

29. *Air Commerce Bulletin* 8 (November 15, 1936): 131.

30. Balance Sheet, file marked "Financial Statements, July 1–December 31, 1936," MF-DGO.

31. "The Spirit of St. Louis," pp. 6–7. On the history of Bowen Air Lines, see Davies, *Airlines of the United States since 1914*, pp. 134–36, 198–99.

32. George E. Shedd to Newton, January 19, 1976.

33. Interview of Captain William J. Spangler by Newton, December 27, 1975; monthly operations statistics, file marked "Financial Statements, January–May 1937," MHR-DGO.

34. Putnam, "The Valley Level Route," p. SM-1, and photographs, pp. SM-2, 3, 3A, and 9, *C&S Sales Manual*, September 1, 1938, MHR-DGO.

35. Information sheet of C&S schedule booklet appended to *Sales Manual*, September 1, 1938.

36. Ibid., "Traffic and Sales," p. SM-10; "Meals while Flying," p. SM-3; "Comments of Passengers," p. SM-2.

37. Ibid., "Flying Personnel," pp. 2A-2B; "Executive Staff," pp. SM-4–7.

38. Putnam, "Memorandum on Air Mail Rates under the Civil Aeronautics Act of 1938," 1947, MHR-DGO; interview of Putnam by Newton, January 22, 1974; Putnam, *High Journey*, pp. 274–75. On the "zero cents" bid submitted by Eastern for an airmail contract between Houston, San Antonio, and Brownsville, Texas, see Rickenbacker, *Rickenbacker*, pp. 258–64.

39. Section 406(b) of Act of 1938 as quoted in "Memorandum on Air Mail Rates," 1947; monthly analysis of finances and operations in files marked "Financial Statements, January–December, 1939," MHR-DGO.

40. "Chicago and Southern Air Lines, Inc., Memphis, Tennessee, *History*," n.d.; C&S Annual Report for fiscal year ending June 30, 1940, MHR-DGO.

41. Putnam, *High Journey*, pp. 275–76.

42. "Through the Years" and "These Gals Made More Than a Passing Contribu-

tion to Flying," *Sky Steps*, July 1943 and June 1944, respectively; interview of Spangler by Newton, January 19, 1976; C&S schedules, August and November 1940, in monthly analyses, file marked "Financial Statements" for these months, MHR-DGO.

43. Monthly analyses, file marked "Financial Statements," May to November, 1940, MHR-DGO; C&S Annual Reports, June 30, 1940.

44. C&S Annual Reports, June 30, 1940.

45. Monthly analyses, file marked "Financial Statements," May–July 1941, MHR-DGO; Putnam, *High Journey*, pp. 276–77.

CHAPTER 11 · *High Hopes and Rough Air*

1. Monthly analyses, file marked "Financial Statements," January 1940–February 1941, MHR-DGO.

2. C&S Annual Report for fiscal year ending June 30, 1941.

3. Ibid.

4. Maurer memorandum, October 16, 1975; Amos Culbert to Woolman, February 12, 1942, GAF, 1942–43, folder marked "Chicago and Southern Air Lines, Inc."; interview of Edward Bolton by Newton, December 17, 1975. In an official history C&S is listed, along with American, Mid-Continent, Northwest, and United, as among the first to respond to the AAF's request for modification work; see Craven and Cate, *Men and Planes*, p. 336.

5. Maurer memorandum, October 16, 1975; article by Lewis and Newton on Henderson in *Dictionary of American Biography*, supplement five.

6. Spangler interview, December 29, 1975.

7. Walker to Lt.-Colonel Robert J. Smith, May 18, 1942, GAF, 1941–42, folder marked "Chicago and Southern Air Lines, Inc."; Spangler interview, December 29, 1975.

8. C&S Annual Report, fiscal year ending June 30, 1942.

9. "These Gals Made More Than a Passing Contribution to Flying," and "Who Said It Is a Man's War?" *Sky Steps*, June 1944 and October 1943, respectively. The tribute paid to Murray by the NAA is mentioned in a memorandum on her career by Richard S. Maurer dated October 22, 1975.

10. *Sky Steps*, November 1943, May 1945, August 1944, November 1944, October 1943, September 1944.

11. Memorandum on C&S stockholders, June 21, 1943, Box A-3, MHR-DGO; Maurer memorandum, October 16, 1975; Spangler interview, December 29, 1975.

12. Maurer memorandum, October 16, 1975; Putnam, *High Journey*, p. 276; C&S stock prospectus, November 8, 1943, pp. 1, 3, 5, 6, 7, 10–18; "Financing Data," pt. 1 of typed manuscript, "Chicago and Southern Air Lines, Inc., *Historical Data*," MF-DGO. The old voting-trust agreement of 1936, amended in 1940 (at the time of the stock issue of that year) to ensure continued control by Putnam as voting trustee, was replaced by a new agreement, in October 1943, to ensure the same thing. The last shares of convertible preference stock were retired or converted to common stock by the end of 1942; "Historical Chart," MF-DGO.

13. "Historical Chart," MF-DGO; "Modification, Military Air Cargo, Continental Contracts Terminated," *Sky Steps*, July 1944; Maurer memorandum, October 16, 1975.

14. C&S Annual Report, fiscal years ending December 31, 1943, December 31, 1944, and December 31, 1945; Maurer memorandum, October 16, 1975; Putnam, "Our Two Front War in Domestic Aviation: The Challenge to Free Enterprise in the Air," from an address delivered at the annual banquet of the Houston Junior Chamber of Commerce, January 18, 1944, MHR-DGO.

15. Stephanie J. Bond, "Fly Now—Pay Later" (unpublished manuscript, April 1975, on the breaking of the Pan American monopoly), pp. 1–4; Putnam, as quoted in Maurer memorandum, October 16, 1975.

16. Letters exchanged between Putnam and Senator Pat McCarran, as quoted in *Sky Steps*, October 1944; Bond, "Fly Now—Pay Later," pp. 4–24; *Sky Steps*, February 1944; "Chicago and Southern Applies for Great Route," C&S publicity release, April 19, 1943; Maurer memorandum, October 16, 1975.

17. Maurer memorandum, October 16, 1975.

18. Ibid.

19. *Sky Steps*, October 1944, June 1945, February 1946.

20. *Sky Steps*, April 1946; Maurer memorandum, October 16, 1975.

21. C&S stock prospectus, July 17, 1946; C&S *Historical Data*, pt. 1, "Financing Data," n.d., MF-DGO.

22. Maurer memorandum, October 16, 1975; interview by Newton of Don Hettermann, December 17, 1975; interview by Newton of Thomas Miller, January 21, 1976.

23. Maurer memorandum, October 16, 1975.

24. Ibid.; Putnam, "Air Line Outlook," *Air Affairs* 2 (1949): 1.

25. C&S Annual Report, fiscal years ending December 31, 1946, and 1947; Maurer memorandum, October 16, 1975; Miller interview, January 21, 1976.

26. Memphis *Commercial Appeal*, November 28, 1946; C&S Annual Report, fiscal year ending December 31, 1946, p. 1; Maurer memorandum, October 16, 1975; C&S Annual Report, fiscal year ending December 31, 1948, p. 9.

27. Maurer memorandum, October 16, 1975; C&S Annual Report, fiscal years ending December 31, 1948, 1949, 1950, and 1951.

28. Maurer memorandum, October 16, 1975; Spangler interview, December 29, 1975; Hettermann interview, December 17, 1975.

29. Fry memorandum, February 24, 1976; folders, "Systems Board Cases," "Chambers, William B.—Grievance Case," "Stewardesses Grievances, 1947–1949," and "Bacigullupo Case," all in Box B-29, MHR-DGO; Bolton interview, December 17, 1975.

30. Maurer memorandum, October 16, 1975; C&S Annual Report, fiscal year ending December 31, 1951, pp. 4–5.

CHAPTER 12 · *Courtship, Engagement, and Marriage*

1. "Control Tower," *DD*, May 1952; testimony of Carleton Putnam in Delta–C&S Merger Case, copy in Todd Cole Papers, DGO (hereafter referred to as TCP-DGO), 1951–52, folder marked "Delta–C&S Merger."

2. R. S. Maurer to Peter T. Byrne, regional administrator, U.S. Securities and Exchange Commission, June 12, 1952, in CAB docket no. 5546, *Delta–C&S Merger Case: Joint Exhibits* (hereafter referred to as *Joint Exhibits*), vol. 1, exhibit 4, pp. 2–3; Junius H. Cooper to R. S. Maurer, May 13, 1952, in TCP-DGO, 1951–52, folder marked

"Delta–C & S, 1952"; memorandum from Dolson to Woolman, October 15, 1951, in GAF, 1951–52, folder marked "Charles H. Dolson, V.P.—Operations."

3. *Joint Exhibits*, vol. 1, exhibit 4, p. 3; Delta Air Lines, Inc., AR 1951, pp. 10–11; C & S Annual Report, fiscal year ending December 31, 1951, pp. 8–9, 12–15; unsigned memorandum, "Proposed Course of Action," October 31, 1951, in TCP-DGO, 1951–52, folder marked "Delta–C & S Merger."

4. Putnam merger testimony, copy in TCP-DGO, 1951–52, folder marked "Delta–C & S Merger"; Maurer to Byrne, June 12, 1952, in *Joint Exhibits*, vol. 1, exhibit 4, p. 3. Delta stock at this time was selling over the counter in the mid 20s; C & S stock was fluctuating between 9⅞ and 13⅜ per share. After the two firms finally announced a merger agreement in 1952, Delta stock rose by the end of that year to the high 20s and C & S stock to 18½. See *Barron's*, December 10, 1951, and December 29, 1952.

5. John R. Longmire to Woolman, November 7, 1951; Woolman to Longmire, November 12, 1951; Woolman to Longmire, November 27, 1951; Longmire to Woolman, December 1, 1951; Longmire to Woolman, December 18, 1951; Maurer to Byrne, June 12, 1952, all in *Joint Exhibits*, vol. 1, exhibit 4, pp. 3–19. Italics in the original.

6. For a succinct statement of the situation in which the new CAB policy placed C & S, see memorandum from Sidney A. Stewart to C & S employees, October 6, 1952, copy in GAF, 1952–53, folder marked "Chicago & Southern Air Lines, Inc., No. I." On the background of the mail-pay issue, which had been given protracted scrutiny by the Senate Committee on Interstate and Foreign Commerce, see correspondence between Woolman and Putnam in GAF, 1949–50, folder marked "Chicago & Southern Air Lines, Inc."; "Statement of C. E. Woolman . . . Before the Senate Interstate and Foreign Commerce Committee . . . July 20, 1951," GAF, 1951–52, folder marked "Delta Air Lines, Inc."; Selig Altschul, "Carriers' Mail Rates Due to Drop," *Aviation Week*, June 4, 1951, p. 59; and "Control Tower," DD, August 1951.

7. Longmire to Woolman, December 18, 1951, in *Joint Exhibits*, vol. 1, exhibit 4, pp. 18–19; for Putnam's views on the usefulness of Courts's convertible-debenture plan, see letter of Putnam to Newton, February 24, 1976, authors' files.

8. For accounts of this journey, see "The Grand Canyon Looks Like a Ditch . . . C & S President Host to Wayne Parrish and C. E. Woolman on Caribbean Air Jaunt," *Sky Steps*, April 1952; Wanda C. Stone, "Angel Falls," article from unidentified journal, Woolman Scrapbook. On the attractions developed by C & S in the Caribbean area and the economic potential of Venezuela as reported to Delta employees, see Wanda C. Stone, "Foreign Travel Exciting over C & S Routes" and "Venezuela . . . Land of Industry," DD, June 1952 and July 1952. For Parrish's reminiscences of the Latin American trip, see his feature page "En Route," *American Aviation*, May 12, 1952, p. 86, and May 26, 1952, p. 70.

9. Interview of Wayne Parrish by Newton, August 31, 1976.

10. Putnam to Woolman, February 13, 1952; Putnam to Woolman, February 29, 1952; Longmire to Courts, March 18, 1952; Courts to Longmire, March 19, 1952; Courts to Longmire, March 20, 1952; Longmire to Courts, March 25, 1952; Courts to Longmire, March 27, 1952; Longmire to Courts, April 12, 1952; Longmire to Courts, April 14, 1952; Putnam to Woolman, April 14, 1952, all in *Joint Exhibits*, vol. 1, exhibit 4, pp. 20–32; interview of Richard W. Courts by authors, July 11, 1975.

11. Maurer to Byrne, June 12, 1952, in *Joint Exhibits*, vol. 1, exhibit 4, p. 3; interview with Richard W. Courts, July 11, 1975; interview of L. Welch Pogue by Newton, August 30, 1976; interview of R. S. Maurer by Lewis and Newton, January 19, 1978;

Minutes, April 26, 1952; "Draft of Resolutions" and correspondence between C. E. Woolman and Carleton Putnam, April 24–26, 1952, in GAF, 1951–52, folder marked "L. Welch Pogue . . . No. 2."

12. Letter of agreement submitted by Woolman to Putnam, April 24, 1952, copy in GAF, 1951–52, folder marked "L. Welch Pogue . . . No. 2."

13. Copy of CAB document, "Bureau Counsel's Proposed Statement of Issues, Request for Evidence and Stipulation," June 9, 1952; Pogue to Woolman, May 14, 1952, enclosing copy of CAB order granting joint motion of Delta and C&S for separate hearing on merger application; Pogue to Woolman, June 12, 1952 (two letters), summarizing contents of petitions to intervene, all in GAF, 1951–52, folder marked "L. Welch Pogue . . . No. 2"; E. V. Moore to Woolman, June 10, 1952, giving hopeful analysis of CAB intentions, in GAF, 1951–52, folder marked "Ernest V. Moore,—Attorney."

14. Pogue to Woolman, May 21, 1952, enclosing copy of letter from Maurer to Pogue, May 16, 1952, GAF, 1951–52, folder marked "L. Welch Pogue . . . No. 2"; *Minutes,* July 8, 1952; reports to C&S stockholders, July 17 and 30, 1952, in GAF, 1952–53, folder marked "Chicago & Southern Air Lines, Inc., No. I"; telegram from Woolman to Moore, GAF, 1951–52, folder marked "Ernest V. Moore—Attorney." For the complete text of the agreement, see *Joint Exhibits,* vol. 1, exhibit 5a, pp. 1–44.

15. "Bureau Counsel's Proposed Statement of Issues, Request for Evidence and Stipulation," June 9, 1952, GAF, 1951–52, folder marked "L. Welch Pogue . . . No. 2"; *Joint Exhibits,* vols. 1, 2, and 3, passim.

16. See, for example, the extensive correspondence relating to these efforts in GAF, 1951–52, folder marked "Stockholders"; GAF, 1952–53, folder marked "Chicago & Southern Air Lines, Inc., No. I"; and in TCP-DGO, 1951–52, folder marked "Delta & C&S, 1952."

17. "Control Tower," *DD,* May 1952 and October 1952. See also the following articles in the same journal: "Strong Background and Able Leaders Characterize C&S," May 1952; "Control Tower," June 1952; "Keeping Tab on CAB," July 1952; "Control Tower," August 1952; "Keeping Tab on CAB," August 1952; "Control Tower," September 1952 and October 1952.

18. CAB, Delta–Chicago and Southern Merger Case, docket no. 5546, *Recommended Decision of William F. Cusick, Examiner,* November 13, 1952 (hereafter cited as Examiner's decision), copy in TCP-DGO, 1951–52, pp. 11–15; "Control Tower," *DD,* August 1952; Woolman to Delta stockholders, August 8, 1952, in GAF, 1951–52, folder marked "Stockholders." Some slight variances in the figures given in these sources have been smoothed out in our discussion. On the CAB's concern about labor-protective provisions, see Pogue to Woolman, May 2 and 5, 1952, and R. H. Wharton, Jr., to Woolman, May 5, 1952, in GAF, 1951–52, folder marked "L. Welch Pogue . . . No. 2."

19. Examiner's decision, pp. 20–22, 29–30.

20. Ibid., 17–20, 22–31; Pogue interview, August 30, 1976.

21. Pogue to Woolman, May 22 and June 3, 1952, and Pogue to Henry J. Miller, June 6 and 7, 1952, in GAF, 1951–52, folder marked "L. Welch Pogue . . . No. 2"; Woolman to Putnam, October 29, 1952, in GAF, 1952–53, folder marked "Chicago & Southern Air Lines, Inc., No. I"; *Minutes,* July 8, 1952, and October 21, 1952; AR 1953, pp. 2, 4.

22. News release, September 24, 1952, in TCP-DGO, 1951–52, folder marked "Delta—C&S, 1952."

23. Examiner's decision, passim.

24. "Combination Company Names C&S Officers," *DD*, October 1952; "Delta–C&S Consolidation Announced," *Sky Steps*, April 1953; memorandum from Maurer to Lewis and Newton, July 30, 1976.

25. Intracompany memorandum from Kell to Woolman, September 25, 1952; Maurer to Woolman, October 22, 1952; Kell to Maurer, October 28, 1952; Woolman to Maurer, October 29, 1952; and C&S news release, December 18, 1952, all in GAF, 1952–53, folder marked "Chicago & Southern Air Lines, Inc., No. I."

26. Interview with T. P. Ball, August 28, 1975; interview with William Spangler, January 20, 1976; interview with S. W. Hopkins, March 28, 1976; "Statement of Pilots of Chicago and Southern Air Lines, Inc., in Opposition to Merger," CAB docket no. 5546, copy in TCP-DGO, 1951–52, folder marked "Delta—C&S Merger"; Tommy Bridges to Roger Humphreys, October 13, 1952, and Woolman to Putnam, November 19, 1952, in GAF, 1952–53, folder marked "Chicago & Southern Air Lines, Inc., No. I."

27. Interview with Spangler and Hopkins, January 20 and March 28, 1976; Woolman to Putnam, November 19, 1952, and Putnam to Woolman, November 20, 1952, in GAF, 1952–53, folder marked "Chicago & Southern Air Lines, Inc., No. I."

28. Woolman to Putnam, November 19 and December 18, 1952; Putnam to Woolman, November 20 and December 22, 1952; Stewart to Woolman, December 31, 1952; C&S news release, December 31, 1952, all in GAF, 1952–53, folder marked "Chicago & Southern Air Lines, Inc., No. I"; "Flash: Merger Approved" and Kell, "Keeping Tab on CAB," *DD*, January 1953; *Sky Steps*, February 1953; picture of CAB members, *Delta–C&S Digest*, May–June 1953.

29. For specimen letters documenting this process from its inception, see Woolman to Stewart, October 17, 1952; Stewart to Woolman, October 21, 1952; Putnam to Woolman, October 17, 1952; and Woolman to Putnam, October 29, 1952, in GAF, 1952–53, folder marked "Chicago & Southern Air Lines, Inc., No. I"; Cooper to Cole, October 10, 1952; Cole to Cooper, December 8, 1952; and Cole to Cooper, February 23, 1953, plus memorandum from W. F. Scott to Cooper, April 22, 1953, in TCP-DGO, 1952–53, folders marked "Delta–C&S, 1952" and "Delta–C&S, 1953." For the controversy over the "one or two coupon" question, see memorandum of April 2, 1953; Cole to Cooper, April 22, 1953; and Cooper to Cole, April 24, 1953, PP-DGO, 1952–53, folder marked "C&S Merger, July 1, 1952–June 30, 1953."

30. Bulletins, PP-DGO, 1952–53, folder marked "C&S Merger, July 1, 1952–June 30, 1953"; interviews with Spangler and Hopkins, January 20 and March 28, 1976. For an example of the advance planning that went into the consolidation of maintenance functions, see memorandum from G. J. Dye, Delta superintendent of maintenance, to Dolson, June 18, 1952, copy in GAF, 1951–52, folder marked "Charles H. Dolson, V.P.—Operations." On personnel problems during this period, see for example the confidential memorandum from W. T. Beebe to C&S division heads, January 16, 1953; copy of CAB stipulations on labor-protective provisions; memorandum of Sidney Stewart on advance notice requirements and other matters, dated May 6, 1953; statement of Frank F. Rox relating to dismissal allowances dated May 8, 1953; and memorandum of R. H. Wharton to Delta department heads on moving allowances and related issues dated July 10, 1953, all in TCP-DGO, 1952–53, folder marked "Delta–C&S, 1953."

31. For lengthy correspondence pertaining to the preparation, SEC approval, and issuing of the proxy statements, dating from the first three months of 1953, see

TCP-DGO, 1952–53, file marked "Delta–C&S Merger: Proxy Statements." For a copy of the Delta proxy statement itself, which runs to eighty pages in printed form, see TCP-DGO, 1951–52, folder marked "Delta–C&S Merger"; the C&S proxy statement is in the same box in the folder marked "Delta–C&S Merger, 1952," which also contains correspondence relating to efforts to secure the conversion of remaining voting-trust certificates.

32. See correspondence and news releases relating to the opening of the new route in GAF, 1952–53, folders marked "Chicago & Southern Air Lines, Inc." and "Chicago & Southern Air Lines, Inc., No. I"; article, "New No. 6 Airline," *Forbes* magazine, February 15, 1953, copy in Woolman Scrapbook.

33. Minutes, special stockholders' meeting of April 22, 1953; Atlanta *Constitution* and Atlanta *Journal*, April 23, 1953.

34. See the voluminous correspondence on these matters in TCP-DGO, 1952–53, folders marked "Delta–C&S Bank Account Transfer," "DAL–C&S Distribution of Joint Agreements of Merger," "Final Closing," and "May 1st Board Meeting."

35. "Airline Personnel Convert to Delta–C&S," "'M' Day Brings New Name; System Converts," and "Two Pioneer Airlines Merge," illustrated articles in *Delta–C&S Digest*, May–June 1953.

36. Delta–C&S Air Lines Annual Report 1953, pp. 7, 14–15; see also Appendix 1.

CHAPTER 13 · *Shakedown Cruise*

1. "Control Tower," *Delta–C&S Digest*, October 1953. On the "model merger," see ibid., August–September 1953. For the rationale for a single corporate name and dual operating names see memo (with attachment), Woolman to all offices, August 26, 1955, MHR-DGO, Box B-31, folder marked "Miscellaneous Bulletins."

2. Woolman to Jack Kantor, October 30, 1953, GAF, Box PM-II (1952–54), folder marked "'F'—Miscellaneous."

3. Report of CAB accident-investigation team, December 3, 1953, MHR-DGO, Box A-20 (1944–54), folder marked "CAB—Accident, Flt. 318/17 May 1953, NC 28354, Marshall, Texas"; *Delta–C&S Digest*, May–June 1953.

4. Memorandum, Woolman to all department heads, August 21, 1953, GAF, Box PM-II (1953–54), folder marked "Bulletins—Executive."

5. Memoranda, R. H. Wharton, Jr., to Woolman, August 11, 1953; Wharton to all department heads, July 10, 1953; undated, unsigned memorandum describing conditions for moving from one town to another, all in GAF, Box PM-I (1953–54), folder marked "R. H. Wharton, Ass't to Pres.—Empl. Rel'ns"; interviews of Juanita Burnett Whiddon, October 17, 1974, and of George Shedd, Joseph W. Meyer, E. T. Bolton, and D. P. Hettermann, December 17, 1975, by Newton.

6. John W. Taber to Junius H. Cooper, July 20, 1953, GAF, Box PM-I, folder marked "Junius Cooper, Vice-President—Finance"; interviews of Spangler, December 29, 1975, and Hettermann, December 17, 1975, by Newton; Mrs. Charles Flesh to Woolman, September 6, 1953, GAF, Box PM-I, folder marked "Employees—General."

7. Memorandum, Woolman to Memphis-based employees, March 15, 1954, GAF, Box PM-I, folder marked "Bulletins—Executive"; AR 1954.

8. Memorandum, Wharton to Woolman, December 7, 1953, GAF, Box PM-I, folder marked "R. H. Wharton, etc."

9. Memorandum, Wharton to Woolman, December 17, 1953, ibid.

10. Memoranda, Wharton to Woolman, August 28, 1953, and Wharton to Woolman, February 11, 1954, ibid.

11. Memorandum, Cole to Woolman, November 24, 1953, GAF, Box PM-I, folder marked "Todd G. Cole, Vice-Pres.–Comptroller"; Dolson to Parker, December 4, 1953, GAF, Box PM-I, folder marked "C. H. Dolson, Vice-Pres.–Operations."

12. Interview of Hopkins by Newton, May 22, 1976; "Date of Employment and Combined Seniority List," GAF, Box PM-I, folder marked "Employees—General"; "Decision of the Delta–C&S Mediation Board, June 11, 1953," GAF, Box PM-III, folder marked "Airline Pilots Assoc., International."

13. Captain Truman R. Outland to Thomas Wrenn, August 10, 1953; Wrenn to Outland, August 12, 1953; Woolman to Wrenn, September 11, 1953; Wrenn to Woolman, September 16, 1953, in GAF, Box PM-II, folder marked "C. E. Woolman—Personal, no. 1."

14. W. T. Beebe to J. L. McFarland and James P. Harden, October 14, 1953, GAF, Box PM-III (1943–54), folder marked "Airline Mechanics Assoc.—International"; Beebe to William D. Kent, September 28, 1953, GAF, Box PM-III, folder marked "Airline Flight Engineers Assoc., Internat'l"; interview with Hopkins, May 22, 1976.

15. Memorandum, R. S. Maurer to Newton, July 3, 1978; interview of Maurer by Lewis, July 20, 1978.

16. Woolman to Tarver, March 22, 1954, GAF, Box PM-I, folder marked "Esther Tarver (Dusting Div.—Monroe)"; memorandum, James H. Cobb, Jr., to Woolman, August 19, 1953, GAF, Box PM-I, folder marked "J. H. Cobb, V.P.—Pub. Relations & Advertising"; "Preliminary Monthly Report to the Board of Directors, June 1953, GAF, Box PM-III, folder marked "Board of Directors Reports"; Allen Stutts to Woolman, October 1953, and Woolman to Stutts, October 1953, GAF, Box PM-I, folder marked "Banks—General."

17. "Report and Recommendations of the 'On-Time' Committee" to Stewart, December 1, 1953, GAF, Box PM-I, folder marked "Delta Air Lines, Inc."; reports of Asher Lane, Jr., to Woolman, September 24, 1953, with enclosure, R. H. Bonner to Woolman, October 5, 1953, and Osgood P. Willis and Dale L. Harper to Woolman, September 22, 1953, GAF, Box PM-I, folder marked "Employees General"; memorandum with attachment of Stewart to division heads, November 5, 1953, GAF, Box PM-I, folder marked "S. A. Stewart—Executive Vice-President"; memorandum of W. D. Huff to Parker, January 6, 1954, GAF, Box PM-I, folder marked "Laigh C. Parker, etc."

18. Memorandum, W. D. Huff to Parker, January 6, 1954, GAF, Box PM-I, folder marked "Laigh C. Parker, etc."

19. Unsigned memorandum dated December 7, 1953, GAF, Box PM-III, folder marked "Accounting General, no. 2." This memorandum may have been written by Stewart or Woolman but does not appear in any other file in the GAF for executives or division heads.

20. AR 1955; H. Lane Young to Woolman, February 26, 1954, and Woolman to Young, February 28, 1954, GAF, Box PM-I, folder marked "Banks—General"; "Delta Air Lines, Inc., Statements of Income, Six Months Ended December 31, 1952 and 1953, Domestic, Schedule 3-A, P-1," in "Monthly Report to the Board of Directors," GAF, Box PM-III, folder marked "Board of Directors Reports."

21. "History of the Delta/C&S Offset Mail Rate (Subsidy) Case," historical memorandum prepared by Richard H. Maurer, n.d.; AR 1955; Courts and Co., "Delta Air

Lines: A Study in Achievement," brochure published December 1955; 374 U.S. 47; Woolman to John Cecil Bessell, March 15, 1954, GAF, Box PM-III, folder marked "Brokers, Investment Agencies."

22. "Changes Announced in Supervisory Personnel," *Delta–C & S Digest*, April–May–June 1954; Putnam to Newton, February 24, 1976; historical memorandum prepared by R. H. Maurer, June 3, 1976; interviews, Lewis with Maurer and W. T. Beebe. Stewart was retained by Delta as a consultant for operational problems for some years afterward under a contract initially beginning March 11, 1954, and subsequently extended until July 31, 1960. See minutes of the board of directors, April 13, 1954, and October 19, 1955.

23. Woolman to Putnam, April 9, 1954, GAF, Box PM-I, folder marked "Carleton Putnam, Chairman of the Board"; John R. Longmire to Woolman, March 23, 1954, GAF, Box PM-I, folder marked "Directors—General."

24. O. H. Swayze to Woolman, April 16, 1954, GAF, Box PM-I, folder marked "Banks General"; AR 1954.

CHAPTER 14 · *The Big Breakthrough*

1. "Two Pioneer Airlines Merge" and "First DC-3 Leaves Fleet; Sold to Other Airline," *Delta–C & S Digest*, May–June 1953.

2. "Control Tower" and "Purchase of Ten DC-7's Announced at Rally," *Delta–C & S Digest*, July 1953.

3. AR 1953, p. 12; clippings, "Delta DC-7 Sets Mark: Sea-to-Sea in Six Hours" and "New Airliner Crosses U.S. in Six Hours" from Atlanta *Constitution* and Atlanta *Journal*, February 25, 1954, Woolman Scrapbook; *Minutes*, April 13, 1954; "Connies Now Flying for Pacific Northern," *Delta–C & S Digest*, April–May 1955.

4. Cover photo and article, "'Royal Caribe' Serves Caracas," *Delta–C & S Digest*, April–May 1955; clippings from *Daily Gleaner* and Caracas *Journal* on the flight of the Royal Caribe, Woolman Scrapbook; copy of speech before the Caracas Chamber of Commerce, April 2, 1955, GAF, Box ME-I, folder marked "Delta–C&S Air Lines, Inc.—General."

5. November monthly report from Cole to the board of directors, December 22, 1954, GAF, Box ME-I, folder marked "Directors—General"; memorandum, Maurer to Parker, April 27, 1955, folder marked "Legal Division Calendar," and letter, Louis Moravia to Miller, June 28, 1954, folder marked "Port-au-Prince," both in Box B-37, MHR-DGO.

6. *Delta–C & S Digest*, December 1954, August–September 1953, September 1954, June 1955.

7. Telegram, Woolman to Carleton Putnam, February 16, 1955, GAF, Box ME-I, folder marked "Directors—General"; *Delta–C & S Digest*, October 1954, December 1954, November 1954; *Minutes*, January 10, 1955; Putnam to Newton, February 24, 1976.

8. *Delta–C & S Digest*, June 1955.

9. Various IMU broadsides in GAF, Box ME-II, folder marked "Airline Mechanics International"; *Minutes*, January 2, 1956; Dana Jones interview, December 10, 1976.

10. Report of P. R. Crocker to Captain T. P. Ball, March 6, 1955; B. V. Hewes to superintendent of flight operations, March 7, 1955; supplemental report of Claire Randolph to inspector in charge—Atlanta Office, Bureau of Safety Investigation,

CAB, March 16, 1955; letter of commendation, Staff Sergeant Jimmy Sparkman to Woolman, March 7, 1955, all in Dolson Files, Box V-OP (1955–59), folder marked "CAB—Accident, Flight 542/5 March 1955, Atlanta Ga.," DGO.

11. *Minutes*, January 10, July 28, and September 23, 1955; memorandum, Woolman to all offices, August 26, 1955, and report of the committee of Maurer, Beebe, and Parker, n.d., Box B-31, DGO, folder marked "Miscellaneous Bulletins."

12. AR 1954; AR 1955; *Delta–C&S Digest*, October 1955; *Minutes*, October 19, 1954, and October 19, 1955.

13. Interview of T. M. Miller by Newton, November 5, 1977; copy, letter, C. R. Smith to Mrs. Travis Oliver, February 23, 1955, and letter, Smith to Woolman, May 5, 1955, GAF, Box ME-I, folder marked "American Airlines, Inc." On the career of Six, see Robert J. Serling, *Maverick*.

14. Woodall Rodgers to Woolman, October 1, 1954, Woolman to Rodgers, October 18, 1954, Edward H. Gerry to Woolman, May 4, 1955, with enclosure, and Woolman to Gerry, May 12, 1955, GAF, Box ME-I, folder marked "Woodall Rodgers, Director"; memoranda, Parker to Woolman, December 8, 1954, and Parker to Dolson, February 11, 1955, GAF, Box ME-I, folder marked "Laigh C. Parker, Vice Pres.—TRF—Sales."

15. "Big Fifth," *Time*, October 9, 1950, pp. 97–99.

16. "The Case of the South and the Southwest for Improved Air Service to New York–Philadelphia–Baltimore–Washington," extract from brief filed before the CAB on April 25, 1955, in GAF, Box ME-VI, folder marked "Routes."

17. "Control Tower," *Delta–C&S Digest*, August–September 1953; Kell, "Keeping Tab on CAB," ibid., July 1953; AR 1953; summary of Delta applications before CAB in GAF, Box ME-I, folder marked "R. S. Maurer, Vice Pres.—Legal, & Director."

18. "Control Tower," *Delta–C&S Digest*, September 1954; "The Case of the South and the Southwest."

19. Intracompany memorandum from Maurer to Woolman, September 28, 1954, in GAF, Box ME-I, folder marked "R. S. Maurer, Vice Pres.—Legal, & Director." See also Kell, "Keeping Tab on CAB," *Delta–C&S Digest*, October 1954.

20. "Control Tower," *Delta–C&S Digest*, October 1954; letter, E. V. Moore to Woolman, November 19, 1954, in GAF, Box ME-I, folder marked "Ernest V. Moore, Attorney (Washington)."

21. Kell, "Keeping Tab on CAB," *Delta–C&S Digest*, January 1955; February 1955, March 1955, April–May 1955.

22. "Control Tower," *Delta–C&S Digest*, June 1955; Kell, "Keeping Tab on CAB," ibid.

23. "Control Tower," *Delta–C&S Digest*, September 1955; Kell, "Keeping Tab on CAB," ibid.

24. Editorials in Meridian *Star*, September 25, 1955; Shreveport *Times*, October 9, 1955; and Jackson *State-Times*, August 31, 1955, copies in GAF, Box ME-VI, folder marked "Routes." The same folder contains other copies of editorials on the same issue from such newspapers as the Atlanta *Constitution* and *Journal*, the Columbus (Ga.) *Ledger*, the Jackson *Daily News*, the Macon *Telegraph*, the Montgomery *Advertiser*, and the Selma *Times-Journal*.

25. Copies of letters from James P. Furniss to CAB Chairman Ross Rizley, September 14, 1955, and from R. B. Wilby to Civil Aeronautics Board, September 20, 1955, in GAF, Box ME-VI, folder marked "Routes." The same folder contains copies of many other letters of this type.

26. Copies of letters from Woolman to N. F. Fisher, September 26, 1955, and from Hale Boggs to Rizley, October 4, 1955; editorial, Jackson *State-Times*, August 31, 1955, ibid. The same folder contains copies of letters and other evidence of support for Delta from such people as Senator Allen J. Ellender of Louisiana and Senator Walter F. George of Georgia.

27. Editorial, Selma *Times-Journal*, October 12, 1955, ibid.

28. Publicity release, Delta Air Lines, October 12, 1955; copies of editorials, "Delta Should Win in New York Bid," Atlanta *Constitution*, October 13, 1955, and "Let CAB Unlock the Gate," Atlanta *Journal*, October 13, 1955; Kell, "Keeping Tab on CAB," *DD*, October 1955.

29. Copy of letter, Woolman to John A. McDorman, October 25, 1955, in GAF, Box ME-VI, folder marked "Routes."

30. CAB release no. CAB 55-87, November 12, 1955, and Delta Air Lines Information Services release no. 112355, ibid.

31. CAB release, November 12, 1955, pp. 4–5, and copies of telegrams from S. Olive Young, Fred Glass, Mary Ann Leatherwood, and many others, ibid.

32. Telegram, Woolman to people in "the intimate circle," ibid.; "Delta Awarded New York Route" and other articles in *DD*, January 1956; "Delta Announces Purchase of Six Douglas DC-8 Jets," *DD*, February–March 1956.

CHAPTER 15 · *Into the Jet Era*

1. *DD*, February–March 1956. For additional publicity, see newspaper clippings from Atlanta *Constitution* and Atlanta *Journal*, February 1 and 2, 1956, Woolman Scrapbook.

2. *DD*, January 1956 and February–March 1956; interview by Lewis and Newton of Maurer, March 18, 1977; interview by Lewis of Charles Dolson and T. P. Ball, June 29, 1977 (hereafter cited as Dolson–Ball interview). The Constellations were eventually sold, in February 1960, after considerable effort, to American Flyers Airline Corporation; see *Minutes*, January 28 and April 28, 1960.

3. Interview by Lewis of Arthur Ford, June 30, 1977 (hereafter cited as Ford interview); E. J. Preston, "Airfreight Comes of Age," *DD*, October 1957; John Pogue, "Airfreight Soars High," *DD*, November 1958. On the background of Civil Air Transport, see *World Airline Record*, 7th ed., pp. 81–82.

4. AR 1956, pp. 5, 8; AR 1957, p. 5; AR 1959, p. 5; "Structural Overhaul Begins on DC-6 Fleet," *DD*, January 1956.

5. The following discussion of the development of jet aviation is based largely upon the analysis in Miller and Sawers, *The Technical Development of Modern Aviation*, pp. 153–210. See also Davies, *A History of the World's Airlines*, pp. 479–85; Davies, *Airlines of the United States since 1914*, pp. 508–17; Munson, *Airliners since 1946*, passim; and Rae, *Climb to Greatness*, pp. 173–92.

6. In addition to material in the sources cited in note 5, see John McDonald, "Jet Airliners: Year of Decision" and "Jet Airliners II," *Fortune*, April 1953, pp. 125–29, 242–48, and May 1953, pp. 128–31, 216–18.

7. See also the colorful evaluation of the Comet in Rickenbacker, *Rickenbacker*, pp. 441–42.

8. On the development and early history of this plane, see also Martin Caidin, *Boeing 707*.

9. On the development and early history of the DC-8, see also Richard G. Hubler, *Big Eight*.

10. On the development of turboprop aircraft, see especially Miller and Sawers, *Technical Development of Modern Aviation*, pp. 163–64, 183–84; Davies, *History of the World's Airlines*, pp. 438–50; Davies, *Airlines of the United States*, pp. 495–507; Munson, *Airliners since 1946*, passim; Rae, *Climb to Greatness*, pp. 210–11.

11. Davies, *Airlines of the United States*, pp. 500–502; Ball, historical memorandum, 1974 (hereafter cited as Ball memorandum), p. 19.

12. Dolson–Ball interview; Munson, *Airliners since 1946*, pp. 131–32, 136–37; McDonald, "Jet Airliners II," pp. 130–31, 216; Miller and Sawers, *Technical Development of Modern Aviation*, pp. 182–86. On the relative costs of the Electra and DC-8, see memorandum by Todd Cole, May 7, 1956, in GAF, Box ME-VI (1955–56), folder marked "Planes—'Golden Arrow' (Convair)."

13. J. F. Nycum, historical memorandum, 1974 (hereafter cited as Nycum memorandum), pp. 7–8; Ball memorandum, p. 19.

14. The following account of the trip to Seattle, Burbank, and Santa Monica is based on the Dolson–Ball interview; a telephone interview by Lewis of Nycum, June 30, 1977; Ball memorandum, pp. 20–21; and Nycum memorandum, p. 8.

15. According to Nycum, Lockheed offered Woolman only three Electras, partly because of Delta's reputation as a "most conservative operator" and its supposed tendency to order only a few planes at a time. On the other hand, a delivery schedule sent to Woolman shortly after the committee returned to Atlanta makes it clear that Lockheed could commit Electras only to Eastern and American until June 1959, when four of the craft would be available to other customers; see GAF, Box ME-VI (1955–56), folder marked "Planes—Other." On December 9, 1955, National did order twelve Electras, with an option for eight more, but it also agreed to late delivery. Presumably Woolman could have pressed matters with Lockheed and ordered more than three planes, but he was unwilling to settle for the late deliveries involved because of his concern about the competitive advantage that this delay would have given Eastern. On the manner in which Lockheed's contracts with Eastern and American worked to the disadvantage of other lines and the circumstances surrounding National's order, see Richard E. Caves, *Air Transport and Its Regulators*, pp. 312–15.

16. *Minutes*, January 27, 1956; news release, February 14, 1956, in GAF, Box ME-VI (1955–56), folder marked "Planes—(Douglas)." The actual contract, executed March 9, 1956, specified that Delta would purchase four planes equipped with JT-3 engines and two with JT-4s, but this order was subsequently changed, and all six of Delta's initial DC-8s were equipped with JT-3s; telephone interview by Lewis of Nycum, June 30, 1977.

17. Davies, *History of the World's Airlines*, pp. 445–47; Davies, *Airlines of the United States*, pp. 495–507.

18. Engineering Information Summary, December 2, 1955, in GAF, Box A-22 (1955–62), folder marked "*File No. 1*—DC-8 Equipment."

19. Ford interview.

20. Publicity release, "David C. Garrett, Jr., President," Delta Air Lines, Inc., April 1976; "The Atypical Alumnus: David C. Garrett, Jr.," *Georgia Tech Alumnus*, Winter 1972; interview by Lewis and Newton of Garrett, March 18, 1977. For an ex-

tended description of the methods and training department, see "Know Your Departments: Methods and Training," *DD*, December 1956 and January–February 1957.

21. John Keats, *Howard Hughes*, pp. 294–98; Munson, *Airliners since 1946*, p. 161; Nycum memorandum, p. 10; draft contract, publicity releases, photographs, and newspaper clippings in GAF, Box ME-VI (1955–56), folder marked "Planes—'Golden Arrow' (Convair)"; "Order for Ten Convair Golden Arrow Airliners Announced," *DD*, June–July 1956.

22. "Minutes of the November 14, 1956 meeting in which the Douglas Aircraft Company, Inc., and the DC-8 Conference Airline Delegates Participated," GAF, Box A-22 (1955–62), folder marked "*File No. 1*—DC-8 Equipment."

23. Memorandum on "Opening of Jet Familiarization School," March 8, 1957, with accompanying fact sheet, roster, and news release, in GAF, Box J-I (1956–57), folder marked "General Electric Company."

24. "Let's Take a Look behind the Scenes at Delta's Jet Training Program," *DD*, October 1959. In this article, however, there is the puzzling statement that Douglas did not begin its first jet-training class until September 1958. Company correspondence makes it clear that classes were already underway at Santa Monica early that year. *DD* was presumably referring to the first *maintenance* class, which started at Douglas on September 8. See memoranda and letters from C. B. Wilder to Nycum, February 13, 1958; Nycum to Ted Ledford, Douglas Aircraft Company, August 22 and 26, 1958, and February 6, 1959; Nycum to W. R. Downs, Douglas Aircraft Company, May 13, 1959, in GAF, Box A-22 (1955–62), folders marked "*File No. 2*—DC-8 Equipment" and "*File No. 3*—DC-8 Equipment."

25. Woolman to Douglas, May 6, 1957, and Douglas to Woolman, May 20 and 23, 1957, with accompanying press release of May 10 by the Long Beach Chamber of Commerce, in GAF, Box J-III (1956–57), folder marked "Planes—Douglas."

26. On the assembly of the DC-8, see illustrated progress reports and various letters between Douglas and Delta executives in GAF, Box J-V (1957–58), folder marked "Planes—Douglas." GAF, Box A-22 (1955–62) contains four massive files of technical memoranda, marked "DC-8 Equipment," covering the building of the new jetliner and modifications made after the beginning of service in 1959. For samples of the "jet aircraft planning schedules," see GAF, Box J-V (1957–58) and J-VII (1958–59), folders marked "Jet Aircraft—General."

27. See month-by-month progress reports and photographs in GAF, Box J-III (1956–57), Box J-V (1957–58), and Box J-VI (1958–59), folders marked "Planes—Convair." On the test record of the plane, see "Convair 880 Flight Test Report Summary," Box J-VI.

28. Memorandum, Dolson to Woolman, May 17, 1956, in GAF, Box J-III (1955–57), folder marked "Jets & Jet Overhaul Facilities."

29. News release and intracompany correspondence in GAF, Box J-VII (1958–59), folder marked "Jet Equipment Base—General"; undated clipping, c. 1958, Woolman Scrapbook; "Growth of a Giant (Jet Base Development in Pictures)," *DD*, July–August 1960, showing that work on the site had barely begun by December 1958 and that the framework of the main building was well along by March 1959.

30. AR 1956, pp. 1, 6–7; *Minutes*, May 30, 1956; AR 1957, p. 9; AR 1959, pp. 8–9.

31. "Jet Age Arrives at Delta," "Atlanta Turns Out to See 'The Pride of Delta,'" and "DC-8 Picture Story," *DD*, August 1959; clipping from Atlanta *Journal*, July 27, 1959, Woolman Scrapbook.

32. "New York to Atlanta in One Hour Thirty-four Minutes by Delta DC-8 Jet-liner," *DD*, October 1959; cover photo and overleaf caption of the Woolmans christening DC-8 for return flight, ibid.; miscellaneous newspaper clippings, Woolman Scrapbook; Dolson–Ball interview.

33. Nycum memorandum, p. 9; Ford interview. In fan-jet engines a ducted fan driven by the turbine gives additional thrust to the gas jet produced by the engine, thus enhancing efficiency and reducing fuel consumption. See Miller and Sawers, *Technical Development of Modern Aviation*, p. 154; "Now: Turbo Fans . . . How They Are Different," *DD*, August–September 1961. On the restrictions placed upon the Electras and the speeds attainable by the piston-driven ships Delta was using at this time, see Davies, *Airlines of the United States*, p. 505, and Munson, *Airliners since 1946*, pp. 25, 46–47.

34. Keats, *Howard Hughes*, pp. 307–12; *World Airline Record*, p. 466; Nycum memorandum, p. 10.

35. Ball memorandum, pp. 22–23; Dolson–Ball interview.

36. Nycum memorandum, p. 10; Ball memorandum, p. 23; Dolson–Ball interview; "Delta CV-880 Sets New Speed Record over Southern Transcontinental Route," *DD*, March 1960.

37. "CV-880 Highlights," *DD*, June 1960; Munson, *Airliners since 1946*, p. 161; Ford interview; correspondence and other documents in Dolson Files, Box V-OP-I (1960–61), folder marked "CV-880 Modification—Dallas (1961)," DGO; Ball memorandum, pp. 24–25.

38. "Opening Day at New Overhaul Facility" and "Jet Base Facts and Figures," *DD*, July–August 1960; "Engine Performance Prover," *DD*, May 1960; "Atlanta's Jet Age Terminal," *DD*, June 1961.

39. "End of An Era," *DD*, December 1960.

40. AR 1960, pp. 8, 17; AR 1961, p. 8. On Delta's efforts to prevent other lines from advertising turboprops as "prop-jets," see *Minutes*, April 30, 1959.

CHAPTER 16 · *On to the Coast*

1. Memorandum, Johnson to Woolman and other Delta officials, December 24, 1958, in GAF, Box J-VI (1958–59), folder marked "E. Marion Johnson, Dir'r of Plan'g & Res."; *DD*, December 1958.

2. On efforts of Delta representatives to secure support in such cities as Greensboro, High Point, Winston-Salem, and Fayetteville, N.C.; Columbia, S.C.; and Tampa and St. Petersburg, Fla., all of which were to be served by the projected artery, see memoranda by William V. Costello, D. Franklin Kell, and E. Marion Johnson in GAF, Box ME-I (1954–55), folders marked "E. M. Johnson, Dir'r, Planning & Research" and "D. Franklin Kell, Attorney." For copies of documents pertaining to the New York–Florida case, including the Wrenn decision, see GAF, Box J-III (1956–57), folder marked "Pogue and Neal," as well as the voluminous briefs and exhibits in TCP-DGO, folder marked "New York–Florida Case." For coverage in *Delta Digest*, see Kell's monthly columns, "Keeping Tab on CAB," April–October 1956.

3. Kell, "Keeping Tab on CAB," *DD*, December 1956; correspondence and documents in GAF, Box J-III (1956–57), folder marked "Pogue and Neal"; Woolman to H. T. Amon, Jr., GAF, Box J-I (1956–57), folder marked "Chambers of Commerce."

4. The progress of the Great Lakes–Southeast Service case and to some extent of

the TWA Route Transfer case, the Great Lakes Local Service proceeding, and the St. Louis–Southeast Service case, are reflected in the voluminous contents of TCP-DGO, folder marked "Great Lakes–Southeast Service Case, Docket No. 2396," including legal briefs, transcripts of testimony, statistical exhibits, and a copy of the decision of September 30, 1958. See also monthly columns by Kell and Maurer entitled "Keeping Tab on CAB," *DD*, January 1956–October 1957; "CAB Adds New Routes and Cities in Great Lakes–St. Louis Cases," *DD*, November 1958; and AR 1957 and AR 1958.

5. *CAB Reports*, 27 (1958): 342–439; interview by Lewis of Maurer, August 11, 1977 (hereafter cited as Maurer interview); AR 1958, pp. 5–6.

6. On the effort to win entry to Minneapolis–Saint Paul, see particularly correspondence in GAF, Box J-III (1956–57), folder marked "Routes," and "Northwest Loses Monopoly, Gains Route," *Aviation Week*, June 1, 1959, pp. 41–42. On the Buffalo–Toronto Case, see correspondence in GAF, Box J-XIV (1960–61), folder marked "R. S. Maurer, Vice President–Legal and Legal Department." On the failure to gain access to Sarasota and Bradenton, see AR 1960, p. 6.

7. W. V. Costello, "Behind the Scenes in the Southern Transcontinental," pt. 1, *DD*, May 1961; Reference Manual, Delta Air Lines Division of Planning and Research, Dallas-to-the-West Service case, TCP-DGO.

8. Exhibits, rebuttal exhibits, and exhibits for oral argument, Delta Air Lines, in Dallas to the West Service case, copies in TCP-DGO; initial decision of Thomas L. Wrenn, examiner, March 10, 1958, ibid. Wrenn also argued that choosing Continental would create less new route mileage because that firm already possessed operating authority from Dallas and Fort Worth to El Paso and Albuquerque.

9. See especially brief of Delta Air Lines, Inc., to Associate Chief Examiner Wrenn, October 18, 1957, TCP-DGO.

10. Reference Manual, Delta Air Lines, for Southern Transcontinental Service case (hereafter cited as Reference Manual), copy in TCP-DGO. The two other carriers directly involved, Flying Tiger Line and Universal Airlines, were cargo operators whose applications were included because the case also dealt with freight service. Ultimately they withdrew from the proceeding. Among the passenger carriers, Capital and Western were seeking limited objectives, not transcontinental routes. United was also temporarily involved in the case but voluntarily withdrew in September 1958; see memorandum from Frank F. Rox to Woolman, September 17, 1958, in GAF, Box J-VI (1958–59), folder marked "Richard S. Maurer—Vice Pres.–Legal."

11. Reference Manual, pp. 20–42. For Delta's arguments against introducing competition on the Dallas–Atlanta route, see "Atlanta–Dallas Competition" in intracompany memorandum from Maurer to Woolman et al., July 24, 1959, in GAF, Box J-XIII (1959–60), folder marked "R. S. Maurer, Vice Pres.–Legal," and *Brief of Delta Air Lines, Inc., to Examiner Edward T. Stodola*, February 18, 1960 (hereafter cited as *Brief, 1960*), copy in TCP-DGO, pp. 15–17, 36–39. The company argued that most of the traffic on this route was of a connecting nature and that the purely local market was too small to support two carriers.

12. Pogue to Woolman, September 25 and October 4, 1957, and Woolman to Pogue, October 2, 1957, in GAF, Box J-V (1957–58), folder marked "Pogue & Neal"; Maurer interview; "James W. Callison Joins Delta Legal Staff," *DD*, October 1957; Costello, "Behind the Scenes," pt. 1, p. 18. Pogue and Neal did, however, continue to represent Delta in the C&S Mail Offset case, still under litigation at this time.

13. Costello, "Behind the Scenes," pt. 1, pp. 18–19.

14. A copy of the Delta proposal could not be found in either GAF or TCP-DGO. Its contents can be inferred, however, from *Brief, 1960*, passim. Eastern and National both reestablished all-cargo divisions after the Southern Transcontinental Service case began.

15. Costello, "Behind the Scenes," pt. 1, pp. 17–18; Reference Manual, passim. According to Costello, the manual ultimately reached a length of about a hundred pages; the copy in TCP-DGO, evidently an earlier edition, is approximately sixty pages long.

16. Costello, "Behind the Scenes," pt. 1, p. 18; Maurer interview; miscellaneous correspondence, including memorandum from Rox to Maurer, January 15, 1959, in GAF, Box J-VI (1958–59), folder marked "Richard S. Maurer—Vice Pres.–Legal."

17. Costello, "Behind the Scenes," pt. 2, *DD*, June 1961. For miscellaneous correspondence reflecting the progress of the hearings, see GAF, Box J-XIII (1959–60), folder marked "R. S. Maurer, Vice Pres.—Legal, Frank F. Rox, James W. Callison."

18. Costello, "Behind the Scenes," pt. 2, p. 11; "Testimony Concluded in Southern Transcontinental," *DD*, September 1959.

19. Memorandum, Costello to Johnson, November 25, 1959, in GAF, Box J-XII (1959–60), folder marked "E. M. Johnson, Dir., Planning & Research"; "Memo Re Position of Civic Parties," February 25, 1960, in GAF, Box J-XIII (1959–60), folder marked "R. S. Maurer, Vice Pres.—Legal, Frank F. Rox, James W. Callison." The reference to the "raft" alludes to a twenty-four-day ordeal endured by Rickenbacker and the crew of a Boeing Flying Fortress, who had become lost in the Pacific on a mission to Canton Island in October 1942. See Rickenbacker, *Rickenbacker*, pp. 333–72.

20. *Brief, 1960*, passim.

21. *CAB Reports*, 33 (1961): 769–956; "Delta Air Lines Route Recommended for Southern Transcontinental Service . . . Initial Decision of Examiner Edward T. Stodola, June 20, 1960," copy in TCP-DGO, passim; Costello, "Behind the Scenes," pt. 2, p. 11; "CAB Examiner Recommends Delta for West Coast," *DD*, July–August 1960.

22. *Brief of Delta Air Lines, Inc., to the Civil Aeronautics Board . . . August 26, 1960*, copy in TCP-DGO, passim.

23. *CAB Reports*, 33 (1961): 701–69; Costello, "Behind the Scenes," pt. 2, p. 22; "Historic CAB Decision Makes Delta a . . . Transcontinental Carrier," *DD*, April 1961; New York *Times*, March 15, 1961. Among other analyses of the decision, see Robert H. Cook, "Transcontinental Routes Awarded to Strengthen Delta and National," *Aviation Week*, March 20, 1961, pp. 36–37.

24. Maurer interview.

25. "Day of Decision," *DD*, April 1961, with pictures of the celebration.

26. For a summary of the positions taken by carriers and civic parties at this stage of the proceeding, see memorandum from Robert Reed Gray to R. S. Maurer, April 27, 1961, in GAF, Box J-XIV (1960–61), folder marked "Joseph J. O'Connell—Legal."

27. *CAB Reports*, 33 (1961): 956–69.

28. See especially clipping of editorial by Robert M. Hitt, Jr., "Non-Stop Across Country: Charleston Breakfast, L.A. Lunch," Charleston *Evening Post*, June 7, 1961, and memorandum from Robert Christian to Woolman, July 5, 1961, among many other items, in GAF, Box J-XVI (1960–61), folder marked "Pre-Inaugural Flights— Transcontinental Route."

29. "Delta Launches Transcontinental Service," *DD*, July 1961; "Las Vegas Ser-

vice Begun," *DD*, August–September 1961; *Minutes*, April 27 and July 27, 1961; "Jet Links Coast to Coast," *DD*, November 1961; AR 1962, p. 3.

30. "Control Tower," *DD*, November 1961.

CHAPTER 17 · *Coping with Problems in an Age of Transition*

1. John A. Garraty, *The American Nation*, p. 823.

2. *Minutes*, January 24, 1957, p. 3; Clarence N. Sayen to Woolman, March 29, 1957, GAF, Box J-I, folder marked "Airline Pilots Association, Intern'l"; *Minutes*, April 26, 1957. Delta management, just before the sixty-day deadline, also asked for a reconsideration of the contract, except for the section dealing with the systems board of adjustment; see Dolson to Sayen, March 29, 1957, York Files, DGO, folder marked "ALPA Contract Negotiations 1957/1958 (Includes Interpretive Bulletin)." The latter folder is hereafter cited as "ALPA 1957/1958."

3. Memorandum, W. E. Stephens to Dolson, April 12, 1957, "ALPA 1957/1958." Operational duty time was the period between reporting for flight duty and release at the scheduled terminus, minus actual block-to-block time while the plane was moving under its own power from one ramp "for the purpose of flight" and stopped at another ramp for "the purpose of loading or unloading"; trip hours were defined as "all the time which passes from the time a pilot is required to report . . . at the airport of his domicile prior to proposed flight departure, to the time a pilot is released . . . for a legal rest free from all duty with the company." See contract between Delta pilots and the company, effective October 11, 1957, pp. 3–4, York Files, DGO. Because Delta was introducing C-46 aircraft for air-freight purposes, the working conditions, pay, and rules with reference to this aircraft were introduced as topics for settlement in the general negotiations. See Dolson to Sayen, May 10, 1957, and Sayen to Dolson, May 15, 1957, "ALPA 1957/1958."

4. Handwritten notes, negotiating session of August 22, 1957, York Files, DGO; letter, Beebe to C. E. Thompson, September 2, 1957, "ALPA 1957/1958."

5. Beebe to Thompson, September 2, 1957; handwritten notes of sessions of September 17 and 19, 1957, and October 11, 1957, York Files, DGO; memorandum, Dolson to Delta bases, September 20, 1957, and letter, Thompson to Beebe and Sayen, November 15, 1957, "ALPA 1957/1958."

6. Dolson to Hopkins, June 26, 1958, "ALPA 1957/1958"; minutes of meeting of the Delta MEC, April 24–25, 1958, York Files, folder marked "ALPA—Contract Negotiations—1958/1959." This folder is hereafter cited as "ALPA 1958/1959."

7. Memorandum, Beebe to Dolson, October 20, 1958, GAF, Box J-VI, folder marked "Mr. Woolman"; L. L. Doty, "Airlines Set Stage for United Labor Front," *Aviation Week*, September 29, 1958, p. 28; "Labor-Troubled Carriers Sign Mutual Aid Pact," *Aviation Week*, November 10, 1958, p. 40; "CAB Upholds Mutual Aid Pact," *Aviation Week*, May 25, 1959, p. 39; Glen Garrison, "Airline Strikes Portend Series of Battles," *Aviation Week*, December 1, 1958, pp. 36–37.

8. Freeman to Woolman, August 22, 1958, GAF, Box J-VI, folder marked "R. W. Freeman, Director & Chrm. of the Board"; Woolman to Joe Weingarten, February 16, 1959, GAF, Box J-XII, folder marked "'W'—Miscellaneous." Delta was not the only airline that had made this decision and thus largely avoided the problem. Others were Panagra, Capital, and Northeast, the latter with some exceptions. See John M. Baitsell, *Airline Industrial Relations*, p. 205.

9. Eastern Air Lines, Inc., Annual Report 1958, p. 4; Baitsell, pp. 226–77. One factor that caused Eastern to settle its 1958 strike was the fact that the walkout delayed the inauguration of Electra service on the Florida route, where its chief competitor, National, had leased two DC-8s from Pan American and put them into operation in December 1958 (Baitsell, p. 236).

10. Memorandum, Beebe to Woolman, April 29, 1959, GAF, Box J-VI, folder marked "Delta Air Lines—Directors"; Beebe to Woolman, July 17, 1959, GAF, Box J-XII, folder marked "W. T. Beebe—Vice President—Personnel."

11. Memorandum, Beebe to Woolman, February 17, 1961, GAF, Box J-XIV, folder marked "W. T. Beebe, Vice President—Personnel"; Dolson to Sayen, January 23, 1959; "Agreement between Delta . . . and [the Delta Chapter of ALPA], Effective April 10, 1959," "ALPA 1958/1959." Handwritten notes in Box OP, folder marked "Board of Directors Meetings, January, 1959," DGO, apparently made by Dolson during directors' meeting of January 22, 1959, indicate that no particular trouble was anticipated during the negotiations leading to the contract of April 10, 1959. Handwritten notes for the meeting of April 30, 1959, again seemingly by Dolson, indicate that the board was pleased by the way the negotiations had turned out.

12. "Delta Pilots Dispute Seniority Listing," *Aviation Week*, November 2, 1959, p. 41; *Minutes*, January 28, 1960.

13. Eastern Air Lines, Inc., Annual Report 1961, p. 2; Delta advertisement in Washington *Post*, March 2, 1961.

14. Bomar interview, September 16, 1975; interview of Dolson by Newton, September 8, 1977.

15. Reports, John L. Sutton to Dolson, February 19, 1951, and J. D. Gainey to T. P. Ball, February 16, 1951, Box V-OP-5, folder marked "CAB—Incidents/Drinking Passengers, 1951–1957," DGO; various reports of health crises and deaths in flight in Box V-OP-6, folder marked "In Flight Emergencies and Deaths," DGO; Bomar interview.

16. Sayen to Senator A. S. (Mike) Monroney, August 21, 1957, Box V-OP-5, folder marked "CAB—Incidents/Drinking Passengers, 1951–1957," DGO; Winship Nunnally to Woolman, June 17, 1955, GAF, Box ME-I, folder marked "Winship Nunnally, Director"; memorandum, E. H. Bishop to Sutton, December 7, 1956, and Sutton to Bishop, December 17, 1956, GAF, Box J-III, folder marked "Superintendent of Passenger Service."

17. Louis D. Newton, "This Changing World," *The Christian Index*, July 18, 1957; Woolman to Charles F. Sims, July 24, 1957; Woolman to B. L. Bridges, July 24, 1957; Woolman to W. C. Boone, August 5, 1957, GAF, Box J-V, folder marked "Liquor Service on Airplane—General." G. T. Baker of National, whose line was already serving liquor, responded bluntly to pressure from John Maguire of the Florida State Baptist Convention: "It is unfortunate you are not familiar with the subject about which you write," he said. "It is quite a shock to learn that the Executive-Treasurer of the Florida Baptist Convention advocates boycott and discrimination. I don't believe that your religion—or mine, which is Episcopal—is predicated on such unchristian principles." See copy of letter, Baker to Maguire, July 17, 1957 (copies sent to both Woolman and Rickenbacker) and Maguire's open letter to 400, 000 Florida Baptists, July 11, 1957, ibid.

18. Robert H. Bullock to Woolman, November 12, 1957; Lindsey D. Boyd to Woolman, March 29, 1957; Woolman to Boyd, May 27, 1957; and Woolman to William L. Brody, July 26, 1957, all ibid.

19. Confidential memorandum, T. M. Miller to sales managers and station managers, March 10, 1958; undated memorandum initialed by Dolson, both ibid.

20. *Christian Index*, March 6 and 12, 1958; Parker to John J. Hurt, March 24, 1958, GAF, Box J-V, folder marked "Liquor Service on Airplanes—General."

21. Memorandum, Cocke to Woolman, Parker, Dolson, Cole, Ball, Phillips, Langland, and Jones, March 11, 1958, ibid.; report of telephone interview of Lorenzer Jones by Harriette Parker, June 29, 1977.

22. Patricia Southard to Woolman, September 7, 1958, and Woolman to Southard, September 10, 1958, GAF, Box J-V, folder marked "Employees and Former Employees." The latter was actually drafted by Parker at Woolman's request and for his signature; Woolman, however, outlined the points to be made. Woolman stressed that the approach was to be "gentle." See handwritten notes by Woolman accompanying these documents.

23. Woolman to Gordon Jacobs, May 27, 1959, GAF, Box J-VIII, folder marked "Complaints #2."

24. ATA Standard Practice Agreement, June 27, 1956, signed by Parker for Delta, June 27, 1958, GAF, Box J-VII, folder marked "Liquor Service–General"; E. R. Quesada to Woolman, March 4, 1960, GAF, Box J-XIII, folder marked "Federal Aeronautics Administration"; various reports dealing with liquor-related incidents in period 1957–62 in Box V-OP-6, DGO.

25. Stuart I. Rochester, *Takeoff at Mid-Century: Federal Civil Aviation Policy in the Eisenhower Years*, passim. With the passage of the Department of Transportation Act in 1966 the function of investigating accidents was transferred to the newly established National Transportation Safety Board.

26. Woolman to Quesada, March 24, 1960, GAF, Box J-XII, folder marked "Federal Aviation Administration." Correspondence in the folder marked "Federal Aviation Administration," Box J-XII, between Quesada and Woolman began on a formal basis "Dear Mr. Woolman" and "Dear General Quesada" and progressed to "Dear C.E." and "Dear Pete." Woolman had also urged President Dwight D. Eisenhower to appoint Quesada as the first administrator of the FAA. Woolman to Eisenhower, August 19, 1958, GAF, Box J-VI, folder marked "Governmental Departments."

27. Memorandum, Beebe to Woolman, December 7, 1959, GAF, Box J-XII, folder marked "Vice-President Personnel"; Briddon, Champie, and Marraine, *FAA Historical Fact Book*, p. 96.

28. Quesada to Woolman, February 12, 1960, GAF, Box J-XII, folder marked "Federal Aeronautical Administration."

29. In a letter of December 1, 1960, to Curtis L. Kennedy, Jr., of Delta's MEC, ALPA officials J. D. Smith stated, in reference to the noise problem, that "the airline industry has been so far exposed to at least four major lawsuits without suffering defeat." GAF, Box J-XV, folder marked "Air Lines Pilots Assoc'n–Internat'l." Box J-XVI, folder marked "Lawsuits," contains documents concerning a noise abatement suit against Delta early in 1960.

30. Fritz Schwaemmle to Woolman, August 29, 1960; J. H. Gray to Dolson, August 26, 1960; and Dolson to Gray, September 9, 1960, GAF, Box J-XVI, folder marked "Noise Problem at Airport."

31. John R. Wiley to Woolman, October 4, 1960, GAF, Box J-XVI, folder marked "Noise Abatement at Airport."

32. Smith to Kennedy, December 1, 1960, ibid.; Woolman to Sidney Goldstein, November 4, 1960, GAF, Box J-XV, folder marked "Air Lines Pilots Assoc'n–Inter-

nat'l"; memorandum, Maurer to Woolman, January 16, 1961, GAF, Box XVI, folder marked "Lawsuits."

33. AR 1956 and AR 1957, inside front covers.

34. Dolson, "Engineering Objectives for Improved Passenger Service," December 3, 1957, p. 1, and Woolman, remarks introducing Donald W. Douglas at the Chicago Association of Commerce and Industry Jet Transportation Day, September 26, 1957, both in GAF, Box J-IV, folder marked "Speeches"; AR 1957, p. 3.

35. AR 1958, pp. 1–2, 4–5, and inside front cover.

36. Woolman to J. H. Green, May 26, 1958, GAF, Box J-IV, folder marked "Stockholders"; T. M. Miller to H. Hilman Smith, December 15, 1958, GAF, Box J-VII, folder marked "Travel Agents and Bureaus"; AR 1959, pp. 2–9 and inside front cover.

37. "What Is Its Meaning? The Delta Trademark," *DD*, November 1974; interview of R. S. Maurer by Lewis, July 20, 1978.

38. AR 1960, pp. 2–7 and inside front cover.

39. Woolman to Otis Kline, February 8, 1957, GAF, Box J-III, folder marked "'K'—Miscellaneous"; interview of Robert Oppenlander by Newton and Lewis, August 17, 1977.

40. Memoranda, John Delafield to Woolman, December 27, 1960, March 13, 1961, and June 27, 1961, GAF, Box J-XIV, folder marked "John Delafield, Dir'r Customer Services"; Gerald H. Rance to Woolman, January 7, 1960, GAF, Box J-XII, folder marked "Employees General." For a typical customer-service citation, see "Miami Agent Bradley Stewart Wins Customer Service Citation," *DD*, March 1959.

41. "History of the Delta/C&S Offset Mail Rate (Subsidy) Case," undated memorandum prepared by R. S. Maurer.

42. AR 1957, p. 3; transcript of United Press release, December 30, 1958, GAF, Box J-VIII, folder marked "Information Services and News Bureau"; memorandum, C. G. Sweazea, October 28, 1960, GAF, Box J-XIV, folder marked "T. M. Miller"; memorandum, T. J. Maples to Miller, September 2, 1960; memorandum, Miller to Woolman, October 4, 1960; memorandum, Cole to Woolman, December 15, 1960; note of Charlie and Tina Galan to various Delta personnel in Atlanta, February 4, 1961; Woolman to Jorge H. Miyares, January 27, 1961, the latter five documents in GAF, Box XVI, folder marked "Delta Air Lines International"; AR 1962, p. 3.

43. Woolman to Mario Lovaton, November 28, 1960, GAF, Box J-XIV, folder marked "Delta Air Lines International"; memorandum, Robert L. Griffith to Maurer, June 28, 1960, GAF, Box J-XII, folder marked "Robert L. Griffith."

44. CAB Aircraft Accident Reports SA355, File No. 1-0084, January 12, 1962, and SA349, File No. 1-0071, June 11, 1962, copies in Delta Law Library.

45. AR 1960, p. 6; notation dated March 14, 1957, of Williamson's funeral service to be held on March 15, GAF, Box J-I, folder marked "Bulletins Miscellaneous."

46. Memorandum, R. S. Maurer to Lewis, July 17, 1978.

47. Memorandum, Woolman to all Delta personnel, May 4, 1960, GAF, Box J-X, folder marked "Bulletins Miscellaneous."

CHAPTER 18 · *The Soaring Sixties*

1. AR 1961 through AR 1970; "Its Own Pace: Delta Lifted Net Less Than Most Airlines Last Year Only Because It's Done Well All Along," clipping in GAF, Box MS-1

(1964–65), folder marked "Books, Magazines, Newspapers"; Martin Rossman, "Airlines: The South Shall Rise Again," Los Angeles *Times*, June 27, 1965, ibid.; Eastern Air Lines, Annual Reports, 1961–70.

2. Rossman, "Airlines."

3. Interview of Arthur Ford and Julian May by Lewis, August 25, 1977 (hereafter cited as Ford–May interview). On many of the same points, see also Davies, *Airlines of the United States since 1914*, pp. 530–31.

4. Interview of Robert Oppenlander by Lewis and Newton, August 17, 1977; Ford–May interview. The steady drop of operating costs per mile during the decade was a frequent theme in Delta's Annual Reports during the 1960s. See for example, AR 1963, p. 2; AR 1964, p. 3; AR 1965, p. 5; AR 1966, p. 5; AR 1968, p. 5; AR 1969, p. 6; and AR 1970, p. 7.

5. AR 1967, pp. 24, 26–27. On previous stock splits, see AR 1963, p. 18.

6. Interview of Ernest R. Bennett by Lewis, September 7, 1977; "Deltamatic Sabre," *DD*, September 1964; AR 1964, pp. 10–11; AR 1965, p. 11; "Computer City" and "People in Action," *DD*, January 1969; interview of Harry Alger by Newton, March 22, 1978; interview of George Duncan by Lewis, May 30, 1978.

7. AR 1967, pp. 14–15; interview of Miller by Newton, November 4, 1977.

8. AR 1965, p. 11; AR 1970, p. 9; Ford–May interview; remarks by Miller at first Delta management conference, *DD*, November 1967. See also articles on the DC-8-61 in *DD*, January 1966; February 1966; and September 1966. On the general development of the Douglas Super Sixty series, see Munson, *Airliners since 1946*, pp. 96, 168–69. Seven of the DC-8s acquired by Delta during this period were of the DC-8-33 model, equipped with JT-4 engines and purchased for service on a transatlantic interchange route with Pan American, which will be dealt with later in this chapter.

9. Ford–May interview; telephone interview of John Nycum by Lewis, August 25, 1977; interview of C. H. Dolson and T. P. Ball by Lewis, (hereafter cited as Dolson–Ball interview), September 7, 1977. On the development of the CV-990 and Boeing 727, see Munson, pp. 79, 91, 153–54, 164–65.

10. Ford–May interview. On the BAC One-Eleven, see Munson, pp. 72–73, 146–47.

11. Ford–May interview; letter of intent by Woolman on behalf of Delta Airlines to Douglas Aircraft Company, Inc., March 13, 1963, accepted by Harry E. Hjorth, director of domestic commercial sales, April 16, 1963, Delta Air Lines file office; *Minutes*, April 25, 1963; "Delta Orders Fifteen DC-9 Jets," *DD*, May 1963. Delta also took out an option on fifteen more DC-9s at the same time.

12. "Now, the DC-9 . . . the Compact Jet," *DD*, June 1963; "DC-9 Note," *DD*, June 1963; "DC-9—On Target," *DD*, December 1963; "DC-9—Halfway Point," *DD*, October 1964; "DC-9—One Step Closer," and "Douglas Encyclopedia," *DD*, November 1964; "DC-9 News in Pictures," *DD*, December 1964; "Up Front with the DC-9," *DD*, January 1965; "The Douglas DC-9," *DD*, February 1966.

13. Interview of B. B. Barclay by Lewis, September 7, 1977; Dolson–Ball interview.

14. "Roll-Out at Long Beach," *DD*, February 1965; "Maiden Flight," *DD*, April 1965; "Testing the DC-9," *DD*, June 1965; "DC-9 News Report," *DD*, July–August 1965; "DC-9 Delivery Beats Schedule Three Months," *DD*, October 1965; "DC-9 Day," *DD*, November 1965; "Inaugural DC-9," *DD*, December 1965; "DC-9 Inaugurals," *DD*, January 1966; "1965 in Review," *DD*, January 1966; miscellaneous correspondence, GAF, Box MS-II (1964–65), folder marked "Planes—Douglas."

15. "DC-9 Option Exercised; New Jets Go on Order," *DD*, September 1965; AR 1970, p. 9; Ford–May interview.

16. AR 1968, p. 6; AR 1970, p. 9.

17. Ford–May interview; contracts GLD-263, GLD-264, and GLD-265, dated August 16, 1966, and accompanying correspondence, Delta Air Lines file office; "The L-100! Famed Lockheed Freighters Join Delta Fleet," *DD*, July 1966; "Another Delta First!" and "Twenty-six Questions about the L-100," *DD*, August 1966; "Delta's All Cargo L-100 Features New Loading System," *DD*, September 1966; Roy Vreeland, "Hercules Begins Delta Service," *DD*, October 1966. In 1968 the company's first three L-100s were "stretched" at the Lockheed plant in Marietta to yield an extra 689 cubic feet of cargo space. See *DD*, March 1968.

18. "Jet Base Expansion Announced by Delta," *DD*, March 1965; "Jet Base Addition Begins," *DD*, February 1966; "Open House at the Jet Base," *DD*, June 1968; AR 1966, p. 9; AR 1967, p. 12.

19. "New Delta Training Center," *DD*, April 1966; "The Fifty-Thousand-Foot School," *DD*, July 1966.

20. AR 1970, p. 10.

21. AR 1967, pp. 11, 24; AR 1970, p. 26. On financing earlier in the decade, see especially "Arrangements Completed for Delta's Expanded Jet Program," *DD*, January 1962.

22. AR 1961, p. 6; AR 1970, p. 12; "Peace of Mind for Delta Families" and other articles on the new plan, *DD*, July–August 1964.

23. Herbert R. Northrup, Armand J. Thieblot, Jr., and William N. Chernish, *The Negro in the Air Transport Industry*, particularly pp. 67–68, 90–92; AR 1968.

24. Northrup et al., p. 50; "Any Questions?!??" *DD*, April 1966; AR 1967, p. 12.

25. "Five Pilots, FAA Man Perish in Training Tragedy," *DD*, April 1967; "Delta Air Lines, Inc., DC-8 N802E, Kenner, Louisiana, March 30, 1967," aircraft-accident report issued by National Transportation Safety Board, Department of Transportation, Washington, D.C., January 22, 1968; Ball to Lewis, September 20, 1977, with accompanying memorandum on the accident.

26. Beebe to Charles M. Mason, November 8, 1961, York Files, box entitled "Pilots' Negotiations 1953–1964," folder entitled "ALPA Contract Negotiation 1960–1961"; "Progressive Pilot Plan," report of Council 44 study committee, signed by J. R. DeBardeleben, E. S. Coverly, and S. W. Hopkins, 1962, in file entitled "Pilot Negotiations, 1962" (blue tab); pilot contracts dated October 4, 1961, November 29, 1962, July 1, 1964, January 1, 1966, and January 1, 1968, all in York Files, DGO.

27. *CAB Reports*, 33 (February–May 1961): 307–416; *Brief for Petitioner, Delta Air Lines, Inc. In the United States Court of Appeals . . . August 4, 1961*, copy in Delta Law Library; interview of Richard S. Maurer by Lewis, September 7, 1977.

28. On the American–Eastern merger proposal in general, see CAB, *Joint Exhibits of American Airlines, Inc., and Eastern Air Lines, Inc., April 16, 1962*, vols. 1–5, copies in TCP-DGO. On the formal rationale of the merger from American's point of view, see *Testimony of C. R. Smith*, exhibit no. AE-A, 1: 1–13; for similar documentation with regard to Eastern, see *Testimony of Malcolm A. MacIntyre, President and Chief Executive Officer, Eastern Air Lines, Inc.*, exhibit AE-B, April 16, 1962, copy in TCP-DGO. Eastern's losses during this period, which totaled nearly $30 million for 1961 and 1962 alone, are spelled out in the firm's Annual Reports for 1960, 1961, and 1962. Delta's strong adversary role in the case is illustrated in the com-

pany's *Brief to Hearing Examiner Wiser . . . July 31, 1962*, copy in TCP-DGO. The same file contains copies of Delta's statistical exhibits in the case and the joint exhibits submitted by Braniff, Continental, Delta, and Northwest. For other aspects of the case from Delta's point of view, see "AAL–EAL Merger Draws Vigorous Fire," *DD*, July–August 1962; "Justice Department Hits Merger; Delta Cites Monopoly Trend," *DD*, September 1962; "CAB Examiner Recommends that Merger of EAL and AAL be Denied," *DD*, December 1962; "AAL–EAL Merger Step to Monopoly, Delta Charges in Brief to Board," *DD*, February 1963; "AAL–EAL Merger Flailed," *DD*, March 1963. See also Eastern Air Lines, Annual Report 1963, p. 8.

29. "Oral Arguments Made in Huntsville Case," *DD*, September 1963; *CAB Reports*, 39 (September 1963–February 1964): 521–55.

30. "DAL–PAA File for Europe Interchange," *DD*, June 1963; "Delta–Pan Am Interchange Argued," *DD*, November 1963; "Link to London and Paris," *DD*, June 1964.

31. "Delta Officials Testify as Hearings Begin in Pacific–Northwest Case," *DD*, October 1965; *CAB Reports*, 46 (December 1966–June 1967): 652–88.

32. "Delta Seeks to Provide Northeast–Florida Service," *DD*, July–August 1965; *CAB Reports*, 47 (July–December 1967): 112–76.

33. "On to Hawaii and the Far East," *DD*, December 1966; *CAB Reports*, 51 (June–July 1969): 161–577. The brief summary of the case provided in the present chapter does not begin to suggest its complexity, especially since it does not deal with issues affecting the northern and southern Pacific. Among other lines, Eastern was also badly disappointed by the outcome of the case, losing a series of routes to Hawaii and the South Pacific after presidential intervention reversed a preliminary CAB decision in its favor.

34. *CAB Reports*, 49 (August–December 1968): 579–621; *CAB Reports*, 51 (June–July 1969): 100–160; *CAB Reports*, 52 (August–November 1969): 1–48, 363–417.

35. *CAB Reports*, 49 (August–December 1968): 427–97. Delta served Aruba for only a ten-month period in 1961. Pan American, which had also been certificated to serve the island for a number of years, did not commence operations there until 1964 and, along with Delta, relinquished its authority there in 1968. Because of political unrest, Delta suspended service to Santo Domingo in 1959 and did not resume it. Operations to Port-au-Prince were terminated in 1962 with the introduction by Delta of four-engine jets into Caribbean service, at least partly because of the company's dissatisfaction with airport conditions there. The cessation of operations at Havana had also curtailed Delta's vacation trade to Haiti and the Dominican Republic, further reducing the company's interest in these markets.

36. *CAB Reports*, 52 (August–November 1969): 188–317; AR 1969, p. 16; "Delta Makes the Nashville Scene," *DD*, August 1969.

37. See especially CAB, Order 69-7-135, July 24, 1969, copy in Delta Law Library.

38. AR 1969, p. 17; CAB, Order 70-1-17, January 5, 1970, copy in Delta Law Library; interview of Maurer by Lewis, September 7, 1977.

39. *CAB Reports*, 51 (June–July 1969): 578–647; "In the Valley of the Sun . . . Phoenix," *DD*, October 1969.

40. CAB, Order 70-4-62, April 13, 1970, Delta Law Library; "Service to Three Carolina Points Begins June 15," *DD*, May 1970; "The Airport Codes Are GSO and RDU," *DD*, June 1970.

41. *CAB Reports*, 52 (August–December 1969): 25, 255.

CHAPTER 19 · *C. E. Woolman: End of the Route*

1. Davies, *Airlines of the United States since 1914*, pp. 532–40.

2. Interview of Barbara Woolman Preston by Newton, December 22, 1977; interview of Sue Myracle by Newton, December 23, 1977.

3. Woolman to Harry C. Walton, January 31, 1958, GAF, Box J-III, folder marked "'W'—Miscellaneous"; Woolman to Paul Chambers, May 27, 1958, GAF, Box J-IV, folder marked "C. E. Woolman—Personal #2."

4. Woolman to Reuben B. Robertson, April 29, 1958, GAF, Box J-V, folder marked "Reuben B. and Logan T. Robertson, MD"; Woolman to Paul Chambers, May 27, 1958.

5. Telegram, Laigh C. Parker to Cole, November 2, 1958, GAF, Box J-VI, folder marked "Catherine FitzGerald, Ass't Treasurer."

6. Interviews of Miller by Newton, November 4, 1977; Richard W. Freeman, Sr., December 14, 1977; and Dolson, September 8, 1977.

7. Interview of Oppenlander by Lewis and Newton, March 18, 1977; Eastern Air Lines, Annual Report 1963, p. 6; "Oppenlander Named Vice Pres.—Finance & Treas.," *DD*, February 1964.

8. Dolson interview, September 8, 1977; interview of Beebe by Newton, November 19, 1977; Freeman interview, December 14, 1977; "Delta's Woolman Is Too Busy to Look Backward," *DD*, November 1964.

9. "Death of Mrs. C. E. Woolman is Personal Loss to Delta Family," *DD*, May 1962; Dolson interview, September 8, 1977; Maurer interview, November 9, 1977.

10. "Earl D. Johnson Named Executive Vice-President," *DD*, July–August 1963; Freeman interview, December 14, 1977; interview of Helen Thones by Newton, December 21, 1977 (Thones is now executive secretary to W. T. Beebe, Delta's current chairman of the board); interview of Marjorie Langford by Newton, December 13, 1977.

11. "T. M. Miller Named an Executive V-P," *DD*, May 1964; "Top Executives Promoted," *DD*, November 1965; AR 1966, inside back cover; Freeman interview, December 14, 1977; interview of Maurer by Newton, November 19, 1977.

12. Opinions vary concerning Woolman's continual refusal to relinquish command. Richard Courts and Charles Dolson both feel that he should have retired, that his paternalistic style of managerial direction had become an anachronism. Wayne Parrish sharply disagrees, arguing that Woolman was as firmly on top of things as ever in the final years of his life. Various Delta executives also disagree, although some feel that a natural slowing down took place because of age and health problems. T. M. Miller feels, like Parrish, that he was firmly in control down to the end, and that, even had he become senile, he would still have been a stabilizing influence. W. T. Beebe states, "I never felt that anybody had the right to come into this house that he built and try to take it away from him." Woolman, Beebe emphasizes, "epitomized Delta to all of us." He does, however, think that the aging process was a limiting factor in Woolman's last years. Richard Freeman also believes that Woolman did inhibit his president, Dolson, "an engineer, a pilot, a get-done guy. . . . Woolman was a very warm, outgoing fellow . . . not a get-it-done-next-minute guy." According to Freeman, the aging process slowed Woolman a bit, but C.E. thought, like most people, that he was immortal. Freeman does not believe that Woolman's declining health prevented the growth of Delta in any appreciable way in the last years. See Courts interview, July 11, 1975; Dolson interview, September 8, 1977; Miller inter-

view, November 5, 1977; Beebe interview, October 13, 1977; Freeman interview, December 14, 1977.

13. "Thirty-fifth Anniversary: Scenes from the Past," *DD*, June 1964.

14. Photograph, *DD*, December 1964; "You Can Come Home Again; Twenty-fifth Anniversary of the Stewardesses," *DD*, May 1965. The other originals in attendance were Sybil Peacock Harmon, Bobbie Brace Nelson, LaJuan Gilmore McBride, Dorothy Kelly Poe, and Eva Parish Fitch.

15. Photograph and caption, *DD*, July–August 1965; "A Way and a Life," *DD*, February 1966.

16. Coad to Woolman, May 1, 1961, GAF, Box J-XIV, folder marked "Dr. B. R. Coad, Mgr., Agricultural Division."

17. Coad to Woolman, June 19, 1961, GAF, Box J-XIV, folder marked "Dr. B. R. Coad, Mgr., Agricultural Division"; "Dr. Bert Coad," *DD*, April 1966.

18. Untitled speech dated June 2, 1966, copy of which was supplied to the authors by Richard Maurer.

19. Dolson interview, September 8, 1977.

20. Barbara Woolman Preston interview, December 22, 1977; "Funeral Tuesday for C. E. Woolman," Atlanta *Journal*, September 12, 1966.

21. Interview of Mary Helen Payne and Mildred Crout by Newton, December 13, 1977; Dolson interview, September 8, 1977; Maurer interview, November 19, 1977.

22. Interview of Rosemary Wadewitz and Mary Johnson by Newton, December 13, 1977; interview of Diane Stanford by Newton, December 15, 1977.

23. Stanford interview, December 15, 1977; Thones interview, December 21, 1977; Wadewitz interview, December 13, 1977; interview of Captain Jack McMahan by Newton, December 22, 1977.

24. Newspaper clippings, telegrams, and letters of condolence relating to Woolman's death, September 1966, DGO; Preston interview, December 22, 1977; Jim Montgomery, "Delta Bears the Stamp of Woolman's Hand," Atlanta *Constitution*, September 14, 1966.

25. *Minutes*, September 14, 1966; Maurer interview, November 19, 1977; interview of Beebe by Lewis, December 21, 1977; AR 1967, p. 4; AR 1968, p. 28; AR 1969, list of officers facing p. 28.

26. AR 1967, p. 5.

27. AR 1967, p. 5; Beebe interview, December 21, 1977; interview of Ronald W. Allen by Lewis, December 20, 1977.

28. "The Dusters! Historic Aeroplanes Complete First Leg of Journey to Smithsonian," *DD*, December 1966; "Control Tower" and "Roll Out the Duster," *DD*, August 1967; "A Place in History," *DD*, February 1968.

CHAPTER 20 · *Acquisition and Consolidation*

1. Munson, *Airliners since 1946*, pp. 94–95, 167–68; "Delta Buys Three 747's, Plans Two More," and "Directors View 747, SST Mockups; Boeing's Cavernous Renton Facility," *DD*, June–July 1967; interview of Charles H. Dolson and T. P. Ball by Lewis, September 7, 1977; interviews of Arthur Ford by Lewis, August 25 and October 11, 1977.

2. "747 Rolls Out," *DD*, October 1968; picture, with caption, of Boeing 747 on maiden flight, *DD*, March 1969; "Our First Two Passengers on the 747," *DD*, Decem-

ber 1969; "It's Here!" and other articles featuring arrival of the 747, *DD*, October 1970; "Delta's 747's Doing Great," *DD*, December 1970; Ball memorandum, pp. 33–34. The delivery of the 747 to Atlanta was Ball's last official flight for Delta.

3. Munson, *Airliners since 1946*, pp. 155–57; interviews of Dolson, Ball, and Ford by Lewis, cited above; Ball memorandum, pp. 30–33; "Delta Signs Contract for Twenty-four Lockheed Jets," *DD*, April 1968. On the merger between Douglas and the McDonnell Aircraft Corporation, see particularly Rae, *Climb to Greatness*, pp. 213–14.

4. "First Flight," *DD*, December 1970; "DC-10, Latest of a Proud Line," *DD*, April 1971; interviews of Ford by Lewis, cited above; Munson, *Airliners since 1946*, pp. 155–56; AR 1971, pp. 8–9, 23–24; and AR 1972, pp. 8–9, 11; "This is TriStar . . . Delta's Jet of the Future," *DD*, October 1973; interview of Robert Oppenlander by Lewis, November 17, 1977.

5. On Delta's involvement in the SST venture, see AR 1967, pp. 8, 11; AR 1969, p. 6; and AR 1972, p. 30. For various perspectives on the background and fate of the American SST project, see Don Dwiggins, *The SST*, passim; T. E. Blackall, *Concorde*, pp. 96–101; John Davis, *The Concorde Affair*, passim; John Costello and Terry Hughes, *The Concorde Conspiracy*, pp. 166–90 and passim.

6. The account that follows of the history of Northeast Airlines from 1956 through 1970 is based largely upon information in Mudge, *Adventures of a Yellowbird*, pp. 285–363; Northeast Airlines, Inc., Annual Reports 1956–70; and the minutes of the board of directors, executive committee, and stockholder meetings from January 16, 1956, through June 16, 1972, in the Stockholder Relations Section of the Corporate Records Office, Delta Air Lines, Inc., Atlanta, Ga. On the acquisition of Northeast by Hughes Tool Company see also *Moody's Transportation Manual*, 1964, p. 1277; on the previous history of Storer Broadcasting and its takeover of Northeast Airlines in 1965, see *Moody's Industrial Manual*, June 1965, p. 1084, and *Moody's Transportation Manual*, September 1965, p. 1093.

7. The account of Delta's unsuccessful merger negotiations with Northeast in 1969 contained in this and succeeding paragraphs is based largely upon official exhibits and other materials including the *Deposition of George Butler Storer, Sr., April 6–7, 1970*, in Delta Law Library, docket 21819, supplemented by interviews of Maurer and Oppenlander by Lewis, November 17, 1977. The terms of the merger agreement between Northeast and Northwest are summarized in Northwest Orient Airlines, Annual Report 1969, p. 5.

8. Delta's activities in contesting the Northeast–Northwest merger plan are covered in briefs and other documents in Delta Law Library, docket 21819; see also the series of articles from the Atlanta *Journal*, *Wall Street Journal*, *Washington Star*, and other periodicals in the same file, folder marked "Newspaper Clippings."

9. On the objections raised to the Northeast–Northwest merger plan by various airlines and other parties in the dispute, see particularly CAB, *Northwest–Northeast Merger Case, Docket 21819*, Recommended Decision of Examiner Robert L. Park served December 31, 1970, pp. 4–28 and passim, copies in Delta Law Library, docket 21819, folder marked "CAB Orders."

10. *Deposition of George Butler Storer*, pp. 77–119.

11. CAB Decision served December 31, 1970; Northwest Orient Airlines, Annual Report 1970, p. 5.

12. Delta Air Lines, Inc. and Northeast Airlines, Inc., *Direct Joint Exhibits before the Civil Aeronautics Board, June 14, 1971* (hereafter cited as *Joint Exhibits*), vol. 1,

joint exhibit 103, pp. 2–3, Delta Law Library, docket 23315; Northeast Airlines, Annual Report 1971, p. 6.

13. *Joint Exhibits*, vol. 1, joint exhibit 112, pp. 1–8; *Exhibits of Eastern Airlines before the Civil Aeronautics Board, Delta Airlines, Inc.–Northeast Airlines, Inc. Merger*, copy in Delta Law Library, docket 23315, vol. 2, exhibit EA-100.

14. The following discussion of the merger negotiations between Delta and Northeast up to the signing of the definitive merger agreement in May 1971 is taken chiefly from *Joint Exhibits*, vol. 1, exhibit 102, pp. 1–13, and from interviews of Maurer and Oppenlander by Lewis, November 17, 1977. See also minutes of the Delta Finance Committee, April 23, 1971, DGO.

15. On the final approval of the definitive agreement, see Minute Books of Delta Air Lines and Northeast Airlines in the offices of the Delta Legal Department, Atlanta, Georgia, entries of May 12, 1972.

16. See copies of briefs and other documents submitted by Eastern, National, and other intervening carriers in Delta Law Library, docket 23315.

17. See particularly *Joint Brief of Delta Air Lines, Inc., Northeast Airlines, Inc. and Storer Broadcasting Co. to Examiner Arthur S. Present*, August 27, 1971, and *Brief of Delta Air Lines, Inc. to the Civil Aeronautics Board*, November 22, 1971, copies in Delta Law Library, docket 23315.

18. CAB, *Recommended Decision of Arthur S. Present, Hearing Examiner*, October 26, 1971, copy in Delta Law Library, docket 23315.

19. CAB, *Delta–Northeast Merger Case*, Decision served May 19, 1972, copy in Delta Law Library, docket 23315; "1972: A Year to Remember," *DD*, January 1973; "Merger Day, August 1," *DD*, August 1972.

20. CAB Decision in *Delta–Northeast Merger Case*, May 19, 1972, pp. 27–30; summaries of board actions and carrier responses from 1972 to 1977 in various phases of the *Miami–Los Angeles Competitive Nonstop Case* in CAB *Order on Reconsideration and Denying Stay*, June 16, 1976 and *Order Reopening Proceeding*, September 16, 1977, copies in Delta Law Library, docket 24694.

21. CAB Decision in *Delta–Northeast Merger Case*, May 12, 1972, dissenting opinions by Robert T. Murphy and G. Joseph Minetti; CAB, *New England Service Investigation*, Decision served July 17, 1974; Opinion and Order on Reconsideration served October 18, 1974; and Decision on Remand served April 30, 1976, all in Delta Law Library, docket 22973; *World Airline Record*, Data Supplements [1976], article on Delta Air Lines, pp. 86–88; interview of Maurer by Lewis, February 7, 1978.

22. Interview of Frank Rox by Lewis and Newton, January 19, 1978.

23. Interview of Maurer by Lewis, October 11, 1977; "New Guy in Town," *DD*, August 1972; interview of Cecil Brown by Lewis, February 7, 1978.

24. AR 1973, pp. 3–5 and passim.

25. National Transportation Safety Board, *Aircraft Accident Report SA-439, File No. 1-0011, Delta Air Lines, Inc. Douglas DC-9-31, N975NE, Boston, Massachusetts, July 31, 1973, Adopted March 7, 1974*; various articles, with pictures, in Boston *Evening Globe*, July 31 to August 2, 1973 and Boston *Herald American*, August 1–3, 1973; Robert Reinhold, "Eighty-eight Die, One Critically Hurt in Jet Crash in Boston Fog," New York *Times*, August 1, 1973, pp. 1, 16.

26. The ensuing account of Delta's fleet standardization program of the mid-1970s is based upon information from a variety of sources, particularly AR 1972, pp. 9–11; AR 1973, pp. 8–10; AR 1974, pp. 10–11; AR 1975, pp. 14–15; AR 1976, pp. 13–14; AR 1977, pp. 14–15; "Our Fleet," published interview with Robert Oppenlander, *DD*,

July 1974; interviews of Maurer by Lewis, October 11 and November 17, 1977; interviews of Arthur Ford by Lewis, September 7 and October 11, 1977; interview of Dolson and Ball by Lewis, September 7, 1977.

27. In addition to the sources already cited, see "Boeing 727s Would Replace Convair 880s," *DD*, April 1972; Paul W. Bennett, "The 880," *DD*, January 1974; "Number 1000 Bears Delta's Colors," *DD*, January 1974.

28. "Fleet Standardization Continues with Sale of DC-8s," *DD*, October 1974; Ford and Maurer interviews, October 11, 1977.

29. "We Transfer DC-10 Rights," *DD*, June 1972; "Welcome Aboard Delta's Magnificent DC-10," *DD*, November 1972; "DC-10's Are Delivered to United," *DD*, May 1975.

30. "Our Men at Lockheed," *DD*, August 1973; "New Navigation System Ordered for L-1011s," *DD*, December 1972; "The RB-211: The Engine That Powers the Tri-Star," *DD*, April 1974; "The Environment and Delta," *DD*, April 1975.

31. "This is TriStar . . . Delta's Jet of the Future," *DD*, October 1973; "It's a Winner," *DD*, November 1973; "Those Amazing TriStars Are Made Ready," *DD*, November 1973.

32. "TriStars Carry ¼ of Delta's Freight," *DD*, January 1975; "Last Flights," *DD*, May 1977. See also "Eighteen TriStars to Be in Service by Year's End," *DD*, March 1974, and "More TriStars for Delta," *DD*, September 1974.

33. AR 1977, pp. 2, 14.

34. See especially Joseph S. Murphy, "A Lean, Strong Management Keeps Delta Air Lines Profitable," *Airline Executive*, November 1977, p. 12; Margaret Shannon, "Flying the Money Machine," *Atlanta Journal and Constitution Magazine*, July 10, 1977, p. 14; AR 1977, p. 42–43; AR 1972, p. 32.

CHAPTER 21 · *Enduring Traditions and Changing Times*

1. See particularly statistical summaries AR 1976, pp. 42–43, and AR 1977, pp. 42–43, as well as tables in Joseph S. Murphy, "A Lean, Strong Management Keeps Delta Air Lines Profitable," *Aviation Executive*, November 1977, pp. 9, 11. In cases where discrepancies exist between these sources, we have followed the Annual Reports.

2. Margaret Shannon, "Flying the Money Machine," *Atlanta Journal and Constitution Magazine*, July 10, 1977, p. 7.

3. Interview of R. S. Maurer by Lewis, October 11, 1977.

4. "A Board Chairman and New President Are Named," *DD*, February 1970; "Delta's Board of Directors," *DD*, April 1970; "An Interview with Mr. Beebe," *DD*, January 1972; interview of W. T. Beebe by Lewis, December 21, 1977; AR 1977, p. 5.

5. Memorandum, Maurer to Lewis, July 17, 1978.

6. Murphy, "A Lean, Strong Management," pp. 9–11; interview of Maurer by Lewis, October 11, 1977; interview of Allen B. Epps and William H. Kipp by Lewis and Newton, December 15, 1976.

7. Interview of Beebe by Newton, November 19, 1977; interview of Beebe by Lewis, December 21, 1977.

8. Interview of Robert Oppenlander by Lewis, December 20, 1977; interview of Maurer by Lewis, October 11, 1977.

9. Interview of Hoyt Fincher by Lewis, December 21, 1977; memorandum, "Fuel Conservation," Delta Air Lines, Operations Division, January 8, 1976, DGO.

10. Interview of Joseph A. Cooper by Lewis, December 21, 1977; "Delta's Flying Money Machine," *Business Week*, May 9, 1977, pp. 88–89.

11. Interviews of Cooper and Beebe by Lewis, December 21, 1977; chart, "Comparison of Actual Advertising Expenditures during the July–December Period 1973–1976 vs. the Proposed for 1976," Delta Air Lines, Marketing Division, DGO.

12. Interview of Hollis Harris by Lewis, December 21, 1977; "Delta's Flying Money Machine," p. 84.

13. Interview of Ronald W. Allen by Lewis, December 20, 1977.

14. Interview of Beebe by Lewis, December 21, 1977. For an example of the pattern followed by the award banquets, see "Award Banquet—1977: 34,780 Years," *DD*, June 1977.

15. Interviews of Allen, Beebe, Cooper, Fincher, Maurer, and Oppenlander by Lewis; "Delta's Flying Money Machine," p. 88; "Flying High at Delta Air Lines," *Dun's Review*, December 1977, p. 60.

16. Interview of James A. York by Lewis, March 7, 1978; Agreement between Delta Air Lines and Office of Federal Compliance, U.S. Department of Labor, and U.S. Department of Justice, April 16, 1973, copy in DGO; Affirmative Action Program submitted by Delta Air Lines to Office of Federal Contract Compliance, U.S. Department of Labor, September 1, 1977, copy in DGO.

17. Affirmative Action Program, Chart I.

18. List, "Female Personnel in Unusual Job Classifications," prepared by Delta Air Lines, Personnel Division, December 1977, copy in DGO.

19. Interview of Sidney F. Davis, vice president–assistant general counsel, Delta Air Lines, by Lewis, January 19, 1978; for an example of the issues involved in these cases, see Delta Air Lines, Brief of Appellee, United States Court of Appeals, Fifth Circuit, docket no. 76-3961, copy in DGO.

20. For Delta's views on the issues involved, including its opposition to the Kennedy–Cannon Senate Bill and its qualified support for the Levitas House Resolution 9297, see special supplement entitled "Regulatory Reform: How It May Affect Delta, Its Personnel, and the Airline Industry," in *DD*, November 1977, and W. T. Beebe, "'Deregulation': A Statement of Position," *DD*, September 1977.

21. AR 1973, pp. 14–19; AR 1974, pp. 15–19; AR 1975, pp. 16–23; AR 1976, pp. 16–23.

22. See the numerous documents pertaining to this case in Delta Law Library, docket 20421, particularly the following: Trial Brief of Delta Air Lines Inc., May 18, 1976; Brief . . . to Associate Chief Administrative Law Judge Ross I. Newmann, July 26, 1976; Brief . . . to the Civil Aeronautics Board, December 13, 1976; and CAB Decision of April 28, 1977, all pertaining to the Oklahoma–Denver–Southeast Points Investigation; "Delta's Newest Cities," *DD*, August 1977.

23. The account that follows is based on voluminous materials in Delta Law Library, docket 25908 et al. See especially Brief of Delta Air Lines, Inc. to Associate Chief Administrative Law Judge Ross I. Newmann, September 9, 1974; Brief . . . to the Civil Aeronautics Board, March 5, 1975; Material Submitted by Delta Air Lines, Inc., for Use in Oral Argument, May 21, 1975; Recommended Decision of Ross I. Newmann, January 17, 1975; CAB Decision of July 15, 1976; CAB Supplemental Opinion and Order, January 21, 1977; CAB Decision of October 21, 1977; and Sub-

mission of Delta Air Lines, Inc. to the Executive Departments and Agencies Supporting Prompt Approval of the Atlanta–London Aspects of the Civil Aeronautics Board's
Decision of October 21, 1977, all pertaining to the Transatlantic Route Proceeding.
See also "Delta Readies for Atlanta–London Route," *Aviation Week and Space Technology*, December 5, 1977, pp. 30–32.

24. News releases, "President Carter Approves Delta's Atlanta/London Authority"
and "Delta's First Atlanta-to-Europe Application Filed More Than a Decade Ago,"
Delta Air Lines Department of Public Relations, December 21, 1977; "Delta Gets
London Route," Atlanta *Journal*, December 21, 1977, final edition.

25. See articles in *Atlanta Journal and Constitution Magazine*, July 10, 1977;
Aviation Executive, November 1977; *Business Week*, May 9, 1977; and *Dun's Re-
view*, December 1977, all previously cited; "Delta Wins ATW's Airline of the Year
Honors for 1977," *DD*, February 1978; "Delta Digest Named Best Airline Publication
of the Year," *DD*, May 1978; "Delta's Board Chairman Named Chief Executive
Officer of the Year," *DD*, April 1978; "Chief Executive Officer of the Year: Ameri-
ca's Outstanding CEO's, the Top Corporate Chiefs are Selected by Analysts and
Independent Judges," *Financial World Magazine*, March 15, 1978, pp. 17–18.

26. "Delta Posts Record Profits, Gets London Route" and "Top Execs Spark Delta's
Success," in Atlanta *Constitution*, January 27, 1978; "Delta Air Lines Sets a Record
Profit in '77" and "Garrett New CEO At Delta," Atlanta *Journal*, January 27, 1978;
interview of Maurer by Lewis and Newton, February 7, 1978.

27. "Delta is First U.S. Airline to Order Long-Range TriStar," *DD*, February 1978.

28. "Atlanta–London Flight Schedules Announced," ibid.

29. Picture of medallion and explanation of its rationale, *DD*, April 1978; "London: A City for Everyone," *DD*, May 1978.

30. The account of the inaugural flight of this and succeeding paragraphs is taken
chiefly from Joseph Parham, "New Flight to London Jolly Good," Macon (Ga.) *Telegraph and News*, May 28, 1978, and "A Delta Dream Comes True: Transatlantic
Service Becomes a Reality," *DD*, May 1978.

31. Interview of Maurer by Newton, May 30, 1978.

32. Interview of Elmer Bennett by Newton, June 5, 1978.

33. Murphy, "A Lean, Strong Management Keeps Delta Air Lines Profitable,"
p. 13.

34. Memorandum, Maurer to Lewis and Newton, February 19, 1978.

Bibliography

I. MANUSCRIPT COLLECTIONS

A. Delta Air Lines, Atlanta, Ga.

C. E. Woolman Files
Carl H. McHenry Papers
Charles H. Dolson Files
Delta Law Library Files
Delta Public Relations Files
Delta Records Collection
Erma Murray Files
General and Administrative Files
James York Files
Laigh Parker Papers
Minutes of the Board of Directors and Stockholders' Meetings, Chicago and Southern
    Air Lines, Inc., 1942–53.
Minutes of the Board of Directors and Stockholders' Meetings, Delta Air Corporation,
    Inc., 1930, 1934–45.
Minutes of the Board of Directors and Stockholders' Meetings, Delta Air Lines, Inc.,
    1946–78.
Minutes of the Executive Committee, Delta Air Lines, Inc., 1972–78.
Minutes of the Finance Committee, Delta Air Lines, Inc., 1966–78.
Minutes of the Board of Directors, Executive Committee, and Stockholders' Meet-
    ings, Northeast Airlines, Inc., 1939–72.
Miscellaneous Historical Records
Oscar Bergstrom Files
Todd Cole Papers

B. Other Manuscripts

Articles of Incorporation of Delta Air Service, filed December 3, 1928, Corporation
    Charter Book E, Ouachita Parish Courthouse, Monroe, La.
Articles of Incorporation of Delta Air Corporation, filed December 31, 1930, Corpora-
    tion Charter Book F, Ouachita Parish Courthouse, Monroe, La.
"Civil Aeronautics Board—Reply to Questionnaire of Legislative Oversight Commit-
    tee," September 1958, Box A, Accession 62-A-154, Office of Administration, Civil
    Aeronautics Board, R/G 197, Social and Industrial Section, National Archives,
    Washington, D.C.
Employment Record Card of C. E. Woolman, L.S.U. Division of Cooperative Exten-
    sion Service, Baton Rouge, La.
Flight Log No. 7 of Charles H. Dolson, in the possession of Charles H. Dolson, Atlan-
    ta, Ga.
Log Book of John Howe, in the possession of Eddie Holland, Arkansas State Division
    of Aeronautics, Little Rock, Ark.
Minutes of the Ouachita Parish Police Jury, 1931–34, Ouachita Parish Courthouse,
    Monroe, La.
Ouachita Parish Tax Records, Ouachita Parish Courthouse, Monroe, La.

Proceedings of the Parish Police Jury, vol. 3, Ouachita Parish Courthouse, Monroe, La.
Travis Oliver Papers, Monroe, La.

II. OFFICIAL CORPORATE PUBLICATIONS

Chicago and Southern Air Lines, Inc., Annual Reports, 1940–52.
Delta Air Corporation, Inc., Annual Reports, 1941–45.
Delta Air Lines, Inc., Annual Reports, 1946–78.
Eastern Air Lines, Inc., Annual Reports, 1961–70.
Northeast Air Lines, Inc., Annual Reports, 1956–72.
Northwest Orient Airlines, Inc., Annual Reports, 1969–70.

III. OFFICIAL GOVERNMENT PUBLICATIONS

Air Commerce Bulletin, vols. 2 (1930) and 7 (1935).
Biographical Directory of the American Congress, 1774–1971. Washington, D.C.: Government Printing Office, 1971.
Civil Aeronautics Authority. *Reports*. Vol. 1. Washington, D.C.: Government Printing Office, 1941.
Civil Aeronautics Board. *Accident Report Adopted July 31, 1947, Released August 1, 1947*. Washington, D.C.: Government Printing Office, 1947.
Civil Aeronautics Board. *Accident Investigation Report SA-167, File No. 1-0023, Adopted June 13, 1949, Released June 14, 1949*. Washington, D.C.: Government Printing Office, 1949.
Civil Aeronautics Board. *Civil Aeronautics Board Reports: Decisions of the Civil Aeronautics Board*. 55 vols. Washington, D.C.: Government Printing Office, 1941–70.
Civil Aeronautics Board. *Annual Reports of the Civil Aeronautics Board to the Congress*. Washington, D.C.: Government Printing Office, 1940–.
National Transportation Safety Board. *Aircraft Accident Report SA-439, File No. 1-0011, Delta Air Lines, Inc. Douglas DC-9-31, N975NE, Boston, Massachusetts, July 31, 1973, Adopted March 7, 1974*. Washington, D.C.: Government Printing Office, 1974.
U.S., Congress, Senate. *Hearings before a Special Committee on Investigation of Air Mail and Ocean Mail Contracts*. 73rd Cong., 2nd sess., 1934, pt. 4. Washington, D.C.: Government Printing Office, 1934.
U.S. *Statutes at Large*. 75th Cong., 3rd sess., 1938. Washington, D.C.: Government Printing Office, 1938.

IV. CORRESPONDENCE AND INTERVIEWS

A. Directors, Officers, and Personnel of Delta Air Lines, Inc., active and retired

Harry Alger, Ronald W. Allen, T. P. Ball, B. B. Barclay, W. T. Beebe, Elmer F. Bennett, Ernest R. Bennett, Gene Berry, Bernard W. Biedenharn, E. T. Bolton, Birdie Perkins

Bomar, Cecil D. Brown, James W. Callison, Frances Conner, Joseph A. Cooper, Richard W. Courts, Mildred Crout, Sidney F. Davis, Charles H. Dolson, George Duncan, Allen B. Epps, James L. Ewing III, Robert M. Faulk, Kathy M. Field, Hoyt Fincher, Arthur C. Ford, Richard W. Freeman, Sr., David C. Garrett, Jr., R. Marcus Godwin, Debra B. Griffeth, Hollis L. Harris, Russell H. Heil, D. P. Hettermann, S. W. Hopkins, Mary Johnson, Dana L. Jones, Lorenzer Jones, Richard E. Jones, William H. Kipp, Marjorie C. Langford, Ike Lasseter, Richard S. Maurer, C. J. May, Jack McMahan, Joe W. Meyer, T. M. Miller, Sue Myracle, Robert Oppenlander, Harriette S. Parker, Mary Helen Payne, Carleton Putnam, Jan M. Rake, Frank F. Rox, Richard M. Ryan, F. J. Schwaemmle, George E. Shedd, Linda S. Sherman, William J. Spangler, Diane Stanford, Paul T. Talbott, Esther Tarver, Helen S. Thones, Rosemary F. Wadewitz, Robert H. Wharton, Juanita Burnett Whiddon, James A. York

B. Non-Delta Personnel

W. L. Alexander, Frank Breese, Elmer Culpepper, Irene Fox, Frances French, Harold B. Grow, Harold R. Harris, Mrs. Leo Hartman, John C. Leslie, Frances McHenry, C. B. McMahan, James Noe, Wayne Parrish, Barbara Woolman Preston, Hugh D. Reagan, H. L. Rosenhein, Sidney A. Stewart, Mary McHenry Wade, T. Harry Williams

V. HISTORICAL MEMORANDA

"Facts and Highlights of History of the Atlanta Airport, Atlanta, Georgia," undated memorandum prepared by Public Relations Department, Delta Air Lines, Inc.
Historical memorandum prepared by L. D. Anderson, 1976.
Historical memorandum prepared by T. P. Ball, 1974.
Historical memorandum prepared by Charles H. Dolson, 1975.
Historical memorandum prepared by William Fry, 1976.
Historical memoranda prepared by Richard S. Maurer, 1975, 1976, 1978.
Historical memorandum prepared by John F. Nycum, 1975.
"History of the Delta/C&S Offset Mail Rate (Subsidy) Case," undated memorandum prepared by Richard S. Maurer.

VI. NEWSPAPERS

Atlanta *Constitution*, 1947, 1966, 1978.
Atlanta *Journal*, 1930, 1947, 1949, 1966, 1978.
Boston *Evening Globe*, 1973.
Boston *Herald American*, 1973.
Charleston (S.C.) *News and Courier*, 1934.
Guayaquil (Ecuador) *El Telegrafo*, 1928.
Hot Springs (Ark.) *Sentinel-Record*, 1962.
Lima (Peru) *El Comercio*, 1928.
Macon (Ga.) *Telegraph and News*, 1978.
Memphis *Commercial Appeal*, 1934, 1946.
Monroe (La.) *Morning World*, 1935.
Monroe (La.) *News-Star*, 1928–29, 1934–35.

New York *Times,* 1948, 1973.
Shreveport *Times,* 1939.
Washington *Post,* 1961.

VII. PERIODICALS

American Aviation, 1938, 1952.
Aviation Week (renamed *Aviation Week and Space Technology,* January 1960),
   1947–52, 1958–59, 1977.
Barron's, 1951–52.
Chicago and Southern Sky Steps, 1943–52.
Delta Digest (*Delta–C & S Digest* between May 1953 and August 1955), 1943–78.
Moody's Industrial Manual, 1965.
Moody's Transportation Manual, 1964–65.

VIII. BOOKS

Aircraft Year Book, 1924. New York: Aeronautical Chamber of Commerce of Amer-
   ica, 1924.
Aircraft Year Book, 1925. New York: Aeronautical Chamber of Commerce of Amer-
   ica, 1925.
Aircraft Year Book, 1926. New York: Aeronautical Chamber of Commerce of
   America, 1926.
Aircraft Yearbook for 1948. Washington, D.C.: Aircraft Industries Association of
   America, 1948.
A Pictorial History of Northeast Airlines, 1933–1972. Boston, Mass.: Northeast
   Airlines, Inc., 1972.
Baitsell, John M. *Airline Industrial Relations: Pilots and Flight Engineers.* Boston:
   Harvard University Press, 1966.
Blackall, T. E. *Concorde.* Henley-on-Thames, Oxfordshire: G. T. Foulis and Co.,
   1969.
Bridden, Arnold E.; Champie, Ellmore A.; and Morraine, Peter A. *FAA Historical
   Fact Book: A Chronology, 1926–1971.* Washington, D.C.: Department of Transpor-
   tation—Federal Aviation Administration, 1974.
Caidin, Martin. *Boeing 707.* New York: Ballantine Books, 1959.
Caves, Richard E. *Air Transport and Its Regulators: An Industry Study.* Cambridge,
   Mass.: Harvard University Press, 1962.
Cleveland, Reginald M. *Air Transport at War.* New York: Harper and Brothers, 1946.
Costello, John, and Hughes, Terry. *The Concorde Conspiracy.* New York: Charles
   Scribner's Sons, 1976.
Craven, Wesley F., and Cate, James L., eds. *Plans and Early Operations,* vol. 1 of *The
   Army Air Forces in World War II.* Chicago: University of Chicago Press, 1948.
Craven, Wesley F., and Cate, James L., eds. *Men and Planes,* vol. 6 of *The Army Air
   Forces in World War II.* Chicago: University of Chicago Press, 1955.
Davies, R.E.G. *A History of the World's Airlines.* 2d ed. London: Oxford University
   Press, 1967.
Davies, R.E.G. *Airlines of the United States since 1914.* London: Putnam, 1972.

Davis, John. *The Concorde Affair*. Chicago: Henry Regnery Co., 1970.

Dwiggins, Don. *The SST: Here It Comes Ready or Not*. Garden City, N.Y.: Doubleday, 1968.

Frederick, John H. *Commercial Air Transportation*. Rev. ed. Chicago: Richard D. Irwin, 1946.

Freudenthal, Elsbeth E. *The Aviation Business from Kitty Hawk to Wall Street*. New York: Vanguard Press, 1940.

Gann, Ernest K. *Fate Is the Hunter*. New York: Simon and Schuster, 1961.

Garraty, John A., ed. *Dictionary of American Biography*. Supplement 5. New York: Charles Scribner's Sons, 1977.

Garraty, John A. *The American Nation: A History of the United States*. New York: Harper and Row, 1966.

Gill, Frederick, and Bates, Gilbert L. *Airline Competition: A Study of the Effects of Competition on the Quality and Price of Airline Service and the Self-Sufficiency of the United States Domestic Airlines*. Boston: Division of Research, Graduate School of Business Administration, Harvard University, 1949.

Hopkins, George E. *The Airline Pilots: A Study in Elite Organization*. Cambridge, Mass.: Harvard University Press, 1971.

Hubler, Richard G. *Big Eight*. New York: Duell, Sloan and Pearce, 1960.

Kane, Robert M., and Vose, Allan D. *Air Transportation*. Dubuque, Iowa: Kendall/Hunt Publishing Co., 1969.

Keats, John. *Howard Hughes*. New York: Pyramid Books, 1970.

Komons, Nick A. *The Cutting Air Crash*. Washington, D.C.: Federal Aviation Administration—Department of Transportation, 1973.

Lindbergh, Charles A. *The Spirit of St. Louis*. New York: Ballantine Books, 1971.

Lipsner, Benjamin B. *The Airmail: Jennies to Jets*. Chicago: Wilcox and Follett, 1951.

Loening, Grover C. *Takeoff into Greatness: How American Aviation Grew So Big So Fast*. New York: Putnam, 1968.

Miller, Ronald, and Sawers, David. *The Technical Development of Modern Aviation*. London: Routledge and Kegan Paul, 1968.

Mudge, Robert E. *Adventures of a Yellowbird: The Biography of an Airline*. Boston: Branden Press, 1969.

Munson, Kenneth. *Airliners between the Wars, 1919–39*. New York: Macmillan, 1972.

Munson, Kenneth. *Airliners since 1946*. New York: Macmillan, 1972.

Newton, Wesley Phillips. *The Perilous Sky: U.S. Aviation Diplomacy and Latin America, 1919–1931*. Coral Gables, Fla.: University of Miami Press, 1978.

Northrup, Herbert R.; Thieblot, Armand J., Jr.; and Chernish, William N. *The Negro in the Air Transport Industry*. Philadelphia: University of Pennsylvania Press, 1971.

Ogburn, William F. *The Social Effects of Aviation*. Boston: Houghton Mifflin Co., 1946.

Polenberg, Richard. *Reorganizing Roosevelt's Government: The Controversy over Executive Reorganization, 1936–1939*. Cambridge, Mass.: Harvard University Press, 1966.

Puffer, Claude E. *Air Transportation*. Philadelphia: Blakiston, 1941.

Putnam, Carleton. *High Journey: A Decade in the Pilgrimage of an Air Line Pioneer*. New York: Scribner's, 1945.

Rae, John B. *Climb to Greatness: The American Aircraft Industry, 1920–1960.* Cambridge, Mass.: MIT Press, 1968.

Rickenbacker, Edward V. *Rickenbacker: His Own Story.* New York: Fawcett, 1969.

Rochester, Stuart I. *Takeoff at Mid-Century: Federal Civil Aviation Policy in the Eisenhower Years, 1953–1961.* Washington, D.C.: U.S. Department of Transportation / Federal Aviation Administration, 1976.

Serling, Robert J. *Maverick: The Story of Robert Six and Continental Airlines.* Garden City, N.Y.: Doubleday, 1974.

Simonson, G. R., ed. *The History of the American Aircraft Industry: An Anthology.* Cambridge, Mass.: MIT Press, 1968.

Smith, Henry Ladd. *Airways: The History of Commercial Aviation in the United States.* New York: Alfred A. Knopf, 1942.

Tindall, George B. *The Emergence of the New South, 1913–1945.* Baton Rouge: Louisiana State University Press, 1967.

Turpin, Edna H. L., ed. *Essays by Ralph Waldo Emerson.* New York: Charles E. Merrill Co., 1907.

Whitehouse, Arch. *The Early Birds.* New York: Modern Literary Editions, 1965.

Wilson, G. Lloyd, and Bryan, Leslie A. *Air Transportation.* New York: Prentice-Hall, 1949.

World Airline Record. 7th ed., 1972. Chicago: Roadcap and Associates, 1972.

World Airline Record. Data supplements, 1976. Chicago: Roadcap and Associates, 1976.

IX. ARTICLES

Anderson, Charles E. "The 'Martinliner,'" *American Aviation Historical Society Journal* 7 (Summer 1962): 120–25.

"Aviation: Colonial's Sig Janas," *Investor's Reader,* July 19, 1950.

Bilstein, Roger E. "Technology and Commerce: Aviation in the Conduct of American Business, 1918–29," *Technology and Culture* 10 (July 1969): 392–411.

Coad, B. R. "Killing Boll Weevils with Poison Dust," *USDA Year Book, 1920,* pp. 241–52.

Coad, B. R.; Johnson, E.; and McNeil, G. L. "Dusting Cotton from Airplanes," *USDA Bulletin* no. 1204 (January 1924), pp. 1–40.

"Delta's Flying Money Machine," *Business Week,* May 9, 1977, pp. 84–89.

Downs, Eldon W., and Lemmer, George F. "Origins of Aerial Crop Dusting," *Agricultural History* 34 (July 1965): 123–35.

"Flying High at Delta Air Lines," *Dun's Review* 110 (December 1977): 60–61.

Herrick, George. "Chicago and Southern Comfort," *Air Transport* 4 (May 1946): 22–28.

Hines, W. E., and Spencer, Herbert. "Insecticidal Control for Sugarcane Borer: A Report of Progress," *Louisiana Agricultural Experiment Bulletin* 201 (August 1927): 1–56.

McDonald, John. "Jet Airliners: Year of Decision," *Fortune* 47 (April 1953): 125–29, 242–48.

McDonald, John. "Jet Airliners II," *Fortune* 47 (May 1953): 128–31, 216–18.

Messenger, Kenneth, and Popham, W. L. "From One to Five Thousand in Thirty-four Years," *USDA Year Book, 1952,* pp. 250–51.

Murphy, Joseph S. "A Lean, Strong Management Keeps Delta Air Lines Profitable," *Airline Executive* 1 (November 1977): 9–13.

Neillie, C. R., and Houser, J. S. "Fighting Insects with Airplanes," *National Geographic Magazine* 41 (March 1922): 333–38.

Putnam, Carleton. "Air Line Outlook," *Air Affairs* 2 (Winter 1949): 491–504.

Randall, Stephen James. "Colombia, the United States, and Interamerican Aviation Rivalry, 1927–1940," *Journal of Interamerican Studies and World Affairs* 14 (August 1972): 297–324.

Riis, Roger William. "Commercial Crop Dusting," *Aviation* 18 (May 25, 1925): 573.

Rubin, Harold. "Boll Weevils Started His Air Line," *Dixie* (New Orleans *Times-Picayune* magazine), February 13, 1955.

Shannon, Margaret. "Flying the Money Machine," *Atlanta Journal and Constitution Magazine*, July 10, 1977.

Snapp, Oliver I. "Airplane Dusting of Peach Orchards," *Journal of Economic Entomology* 19 (June 1926): 450–59.

"The Atypical Alumnus: David C. Garrett, Jr.," *Georgia Tech Alumnus*, Winter 1972.

Truesdale, Julius A. "Spraying from Air," New York *Times*, January 8, 1922, VII, 4.

Van Deventer, John H., Jr., "The Story of Keystone," *Air Transportation* 6 (January 19, 1929): 54–55.

"What's Wrong with the Airlines," *Fortune* 34 (August 1946): 73–79, 190–92, 195–96, 198–99, 201.

Woolcott, George N. "The Status of Economic Entomology in Peru," *Bulletin of Entomological Research* 20 (August 1929): 225–31.

X. MISCELLANEOUS

Bond, Stephanie J. "Fly Now—Pay Later," unpublished manuscript, Auburn University, Auburn, Alabama, April 1975.

C. E. Woolman File, University of Illinois Alumni Association, Urbana, Illinois.

C. E. Woolman Scrapbook, in the possession of Barbara Woolman Preston.

Chicago and Southern Sales Manual, c. 1938, supplied by Richard S. Maurer.

L.S.U. Extension Service, *Annual Reports*, 1925 (November, Circular no. 80) and 1926 (June, Circular no. 87).

"Ouachita National Bank, Organization and Development," unpublished, undated typescript, Ouachita National Bank, Monroe, La.

"Ouachita Parish, Louisiana, 1945, Resources and Facilities," State of Louisiana Department of Public Works and Ouachita Parish Planning Board, Baton Rouge, La., 1945.

Seat pocket materials carried in Lockheed Electras, Delta Air Corporation, c. 1938, in the possession of the Reverend Vernon Broyles.

"The First Sixty Years of Central Savings Bank and Trust Company," unpublished, undated typescript, Central Savings Bank and Trust Company, Monroe, La.

Index

Index

About the Authors

W. DAVID LEWIS is Hudson Professor of History and Engineering at Auburn University. He is the author of *From Newgate to Dannemora: The Rise of the Penitentiary in New York, 1796–1848* and *Iron and Steel in America,* and coeditor of *Economic Change in the Civil War Era* and *The Southern Mystique: The Impact of Technology on Human Values in a Changing Region.*

WESLEY PHILLIPS NEWTON is professor of history at Auburn University. The author of *The Perilous Sky: U.S. Aviation Diplomacy and Latin America, 1919–1931,* he has contributed to *Air Force Combat Units of World War II* and *Militarists, Merchants, and Missionaries: United States Expansion in Middle America.*